Lecture Notes in Computer Science

Edited by G. Goos and J. Hartmanis

53

Mathematical Foundations of Computer Science 1977

Proceedings, 6th Symposium, Tatranská Lomnica
September 5–9, 1977

Edited by J. Gruska

Springer-Verlag
Berlin · Heidelberg · New York 1977

Editor
Jozef Gruska
Computing Research Centre
Dúbravská 3
885 31 Bratislava
Czechoslovakia

Library of Congress Cataloging in Publication Data
Main entry under title:

Mathematical foundations of computer science, 1977.

(Lecture notes in computer science ; 53)
Bibliography: p.
Includes index.
1. Machine theory--Congresses. 2. Formal languages
--Congresses. 3. Programming (Electronic computers)--
Congresses. I. Gruska, Jozef. II. Series.
QA267.M37 001.6'4 77-10135

AMS Subject Classifications (1970): 02B25, 02D99, 02E10, 02E15, 02F10, 02F15, 02F20, 18B20, 68A05, 68A10, 68A20, 68A25, 68A30, 68A45, 68A50, 94A20, 94A30, 94A35
CR Subject Classifications (1974): 3.61, 3.79, 4.12, 4.20, 4.33, 5.14, 5.21, 5.22, 5.23, 5.24, 5.25, 5.26, 5.27, 5.28, 5.5

ISBN 3-540-08353-7 Springer-Verlag Berlin · Heidelberg · New York
ISBN 0-387-08353-7 Springer-Verlag New York · Heidelberg · Berlin

Printing and binding: Beltz Offsetdruck, Hemsbach/Bergstr.
2145/3140-543210

MFCS'77

FOREWORD

This volume contains papers which were contributed for presentation at the 6th Symposium on Mathematical Foundations of Computer Science - MFCS´77, held at Tatranská Lomnica, Czechoslovakia, September 5-9, 1977.

The symposium was organized by the Computing Research Centre in Bratislava. The following institutions have cooperated in providing their support: The Faculty of Mathematics and Physics of the Charles University, Prague; the Faculty of Natural Sciences of the Šafárik University, Košice; the Faculty of Natural Sciences of the Komenský University, Bratislava; the Institute of Computing Technique of the Technical University, Prague; Institute of Technical Cybernetics of the Slovak Academy of Sciences; the Association of Slovak Mathematicians and Physicists and the Slovak Cybernetical Society.

The title of the symposium, "Mathematical Foundations of Computer Science" was chosen six years ago by the Polish organizers for the first meeting in the series and in 1974 it was used also for a seminar held at the International Banach Centre in Warsaw. In subsequent years it became a widely accepted designation for this new and important branch of science. It is understandable that this designation, or its close variants, will be used for other scientific events in the same areas, such as some of the recent symposia and seminars, held both in the United States and in Europe.

The present Proceedings include 15 invited papers and 46 short communications, the latter having been selected by the Program Committee from among the 117 submitted papers on the basis of, originality and relevance to the following principal areas of interest: automata and formal languages, computability theory, analysis and complexity of algorithms, theoretical aspects of programming and of programming languages, theoretical aspects of operating systems and mathematical approaches to artificial intelligence.

The papers in these Proceedings were not formally refereed. It is anticipated that most of them will appear in a more polished and complete form in scientific journals.

The organizers of the symposium are much indebted to all of the contributors to this program, especially to the authors of the papers. Thanks are also due to all the above mentioned cooperating institutions for their valuable and all round assistance and to all people who helped in the organization of the Symposium.

Special thanks are due to Professor A. Klas, director of the Computing Research Centre in Bratislava for his generous support of not only MFCS´77 but of all MFCS symposia held in Czechoslovakia.

The Program Committee of MFCS´77 consisted of the following members: I.M. Havel /chairman/, J. Bečvář, J. Gruska, J. Hořejš, I. Korec, M. Novotný, B. Rovan and J. Šturc. A number of referees helped the Program Committee evaluate the submitted papers.

The organization was done mainly by the following members of the Organizing Committee: G. Andrejková, Z. Durayová, R. Filustek, J. Gruska /Symposium Chairman/, A. Guráňová, I.M. Havel, M. Chytil, A. Jelínková, M. Markusová, P. Mikulecký, I. Prívara, B. Rovan /Organizing Secretary/, and I. Šujan.

The help of Springer-Verlag, which has published these Proceedings, is also highly appreciated.

Bratislava, May 1977 Jozef Gruska

CONTENTS

ON THE STRUCTURE AND PROPERTIES OF NP-COMPLETE PROBLEMS AND THEIR ASSOCIATED OPTIMIZATION PROBLEMS

Giorgio Ausiello
CSSCCA-CNR, Roma, Italy

SUMMARY

1. INTRODUCTION

Since the early work of Cook (1971) and Karp (1972) the research work on the properties of NP-complete problems has been intensive and widespread. The class of NP-complete problems contains all those problems which are in NP, that is which can be decided by a nondeterministic Turing machine in polynomial time, and to which all other problems in the class NP can be reduced in polynomial time. The characterization of the complexity of NP-complete problems leads to one of the most important (may be "the" most important) open questions in theoretical computer science: does there exist any Turing machine which decides any NP-complete problem in deterministic polynomial time? In that case, from the properties of the class NP, we would deduce that all NP-complete problems would be solvable within polynomial time and the two classes P and NP would coincide.

Even if it has been proved by Baker, Gill and Solovay (1975) that the question P = NP? can be positively answered in a relativized class of machines and negatively in another class of machines with different relativization and actually Hartmanis and Hopcroft (1976) have shown that there are relativized classes of machines for which the question P = NP? is independent from the axioms of set theory, the practical relevance of the issue and of its possible answers in the theory of algorithms is obvious and there is a wide belief that a solution will eventually be achieved.

Problems which have been recognized to be NP-complete problems belong to the widest variety of fields: among them we have combinatorial problems (such as the chromatic number or the node covering of a graph and the existence of hamiltonian circuits), scheduling problems, integer 0-1 programming, satisfiability of formulae of propositional calculus, solvability of quadratic Diophantine equations, inequivalence of simple programs with only one level of iteration. For any of these problems it would have important practical consequences to know whether the backtracking algorithms of polynomial depth that we should use for deterministically solving it could ever be replaced by an efficient deterministic polynomial time algorithm.

Beside the interest related to the solution of the question of whether P is equal to NP the research activities in this area of computational complexity have brought a new light on some of the most interesting properties of combinatorial problems. The results which have been obtained can very roughly be grouped into three classes. On one side (see Simon (1975), Hartmanis and Simon (1976), Hartmanis and Berman (1976,1977)),there has been a succesful attempt to strengthening the reductions among NP-complete problems in order to point out a deep similarity among these problems. The result of showing that all known NP-complete problems are isomorphic under a polynomial time mapping and the conjecture that this is the case with all infinite NP-complete problems seem to suggest that all these problems are very similar and that they actually are polynomial time permutations of the same problem.

From another point of view optimization problems related to NP-complete combinatorial problems have been considered. The literature in this field is overwhelmingly rich because this is the direction which is the most relevant for practical purposes and whose origin is certainly antecedent to the definition of NP-completeness . An extended annotated bibliography on approximate algorithms for combinatorial NP-complete problems is provided by Garey and Johnson (1976b). The general tendency in this area, analogously to what happens in concrete computational complexity , has been to consider one problem at a time and to look for the "best" approximate algorithm, that is the approximate algorithm with the best performance either from the point of view of efficiency or from the point of view of proximity to the exact solution or both.
Among those papers which have more particular interest there are also some papers with a deep methodological insight, such as those by Johnson (1974),Sahni and Gonzales (1976), Sahni (1976), Garey and Johnson (1976a); in these papers intrinsic differences among various optimization problems appear. While in some problems like knapsack and job sequencing

we can reach any desidered level of accuracy with polynomial time approximation algorithms, in some other problems, such as graph colouring, for example, any algorithm that comes too close to the optimal solution has the same complexity of the algorithms which give the optimal solution itself.

This type of results introduce a clear element of distinction among optimization problems and hence even if two NP-complete combinatorial problems are isomorphic, their isomorphism cannot be always extended to the associated optimization problems. The search for structural isomorphism among optimization problems and for classes of problems which are structurally isomorphic becomes, hence, an issue of great interest and this is the third kind of results that we want to consider in this introduction. Clearly when such a result can be proven, for those problems which are shown to be structurally isomorphic the same approximation algorithm can be used and good approximate solutions which have been found for an input in one problem can be mapped into good approximate solutions for the equivalent input in another problem. Beside these practical aspects, to be able of finding structural characterizations of classes of optimization problems and to relate their structural properties with the "degree of approximability" is certainly a relevant issue in the theory of computational complexity. Results in this direction have been achieved by Paz and Moran (1977) and Ausiello, D'Atri, Gaudiano and Protasi (1977a, 1977b).

2. ON THE ISOMORPHISM OF NP-COMPLETE COMBINATORIAL PROBLEMS

Let us first briefly review the basic terminology and notation.

Let Σ^* be the set of all words over a finite alphabet Σ. A language $L \subseteq \Sigma^*$ is said to be recognizable in time $t(n)$ by a Turing Machine (TM) M if for all $n \geq 0$, for every input x of length n M takes less then $t(n)$ steps either to accept or to reject x. If the TM is non deterministic we will consider the number of steps of the shortest accepting computation (if x is accepted) or the number of steps of the longest rejecting computation (if x is rejected).

DEFINITION 1. $NP = \{L | L$ is recognizable by a non-deterministic TM in time bounded by some polynomial $p\}$.

DEFINITION 2. A set $A \subseteq \Sigma^*$ is said to be *p-reducible to* a set $B \subseteq \Gamma^*$ (denoted $A \leq B$) if there is a mapping $f: \Sigma^* \to \Gamma^*$ which is computable in polynomial time on a deterministic TM and such that for every $x \in \Sigma^*$ $f(x) \in B$ if and only if $x \in A$.

DEFINITION 3. A set B is said to be *complete for* some class of sets C (denoted C-complete) if $B \in C$ and, for every $A \in C$, $A \leq B$.

Well known examples of NP-complete sets (problems) are:

SATISFIABILITY = {w|w is a formula of propositional calculus in CNF and there exists a truth assignment that satisfies it}.

CLIQUE = {⟨g,K⟩|g is the encoding of a graph G,K is an integer and G has a complete subgraph of K nodes}.

CHROMATIC-NUMBER = {⟨g,K⟩|g is the encoding of a graph G,K is an integer and G can be coloured with K colours with no two adjacent nodes equally coloured}.

DIOPH = {⟨a,b,c⟩|a,b,c $\geq$ 0 are integers and the quadratic diophantine equation $ax^2 + by - c = 0$ can be solved with x,y positive integers}.

SUBSET-SUM = $\{\langle a_1,\ldots,a_n,b\rangle \mid$ there is a subsequence $i_1,\ldots,i_m$ such that $\sum_{j=1}^{m} a_{i_j} = b\}$

JOB-SEQUENCING-WITH-DEADLINES = $\{\langle t_1,\ldots,t_n,d_1,\ldots,d_n,p_1,\ldots,p_n,k\rangle \mid$ there exists a permutation π such that $\sum_{j=1}^{n} (\mathit{if} \sum_{i=1}^{j} t_{\pi(i)} \leq d_j \ \mathit{then}\ p_j \ \mathit{else}\ 0) \geq k\}$.

DEFINITION 4. Two sets $A \subseteq \Sigma^*$ and $B \subseteq \Gamma^*$ are said to be *p-isomorphic* if there is a mapping $f: \Sigma^* \to \Gamma^*$ such that
- f is 1-1 and onto
- f is a p-reduction of A to B and f^{-1} is a p-reduction of B to A.

The following two theorems are both due to Hartmanis and Berman (1976) and are very important because they establish necessary conditions for two sets to be p-isomorphic; in the first case this fact can be derived from the properties of the p-reductions that hold among the two sets:

RESULT 1. Let p and q be length increasing invertible p-reductions of A to B and B to A respectively. Then A and B are p-isomorphic.

PROOF. Let us define

$$R_1 = \bigcup_{k=0}^{\infty} (q \circ p)^k \, \overline{\text{RANGE }(q)} \qquad R_2 = q(S_1)$$

$$S_1 = \bigcup_{k=0}^{\infty} (p \circ q)^k \, \overline{\text{RANGE }(p)} \qquad S_2 = p(R_1)$$

$$\varphi(z) = \begin{cases} p(z) & \text{if } z \in R_1 \\ q^{-1}(z) & \text{if } z \in R_2 \end{cases} \qquad \varphi^{-1}(z) = \begin{cases} p^{-1}(z) & \text{if } z \in S_2 \\ q(z) & \text{if } z \in S_1 \end{cases}$$

By the properties of p and q it follows that φ and φ^{-1} are inverses and:

- φ and φ^{-1} are computable in polynomial time;
- φ is 1-1 and onto and is a p-reduction of A to B. QED

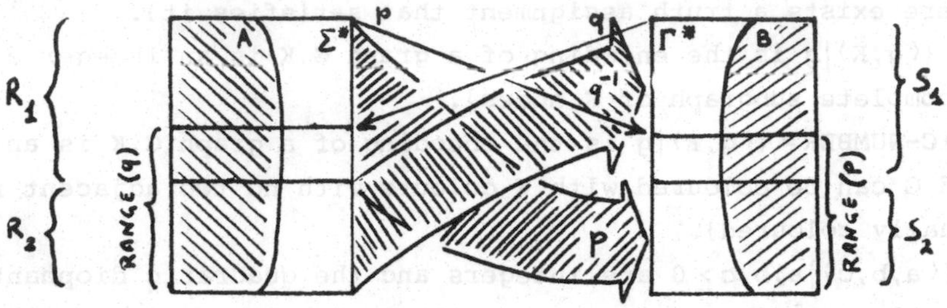

The second theorem shows instead that the existence of a p-isomorphism to SATISFIABILITY is a consequence of intrinsic properties of some NP-complete sets:

RESULT 2. An NP-complete set B is p-isomorphic to SATISFIABILITY if and only if there exists a polynomial time computable length increasing padding function S_B for B such that

- for any x and y, $S_B(x,y) \in B$ iff $x \in B$
- the padding can be obtained back by a polynomial time computable function D_B and for every x,y $D_B(S_B(x,y)) = y$.

PROOF. Let us first prove that if there is any reduction p from SATISFIABILITY to B then there is also a reduction p' which is length increasing one-one and invertible in polynomial time.

For $x \in$ SATISFIABILITY let us define

$$p'(x) = S_B(p(x),x)$$

and $t(x) = \mathit{if}\ x = S_B(p(D(x)),D(x))\ \mathit{then}\ D(x)\ \mathit{else}$ undefined.

Clearly $p'(x) = p'(y)$ implies $x = y$ and besides $t = (p')^{-1}$ and $|p'(x)| > |x|$.

In order to prove that we can also find a length increasing one-one and invertible reduction q' from B to SATISFIABILITY we only have to prove (once and forever) that also SATISFIABILITY has a padding function S and a function D with the properties stated in the theorem. Once we have proved the existence of such reductions p' and q' which are length increasing, one-one and invertible, we are in the conditions of theorem 1 to prove the p-isomorphism between B and SATISFIABILITY. QED

The intuitive meaning of theorem 2 is shown in the figure.

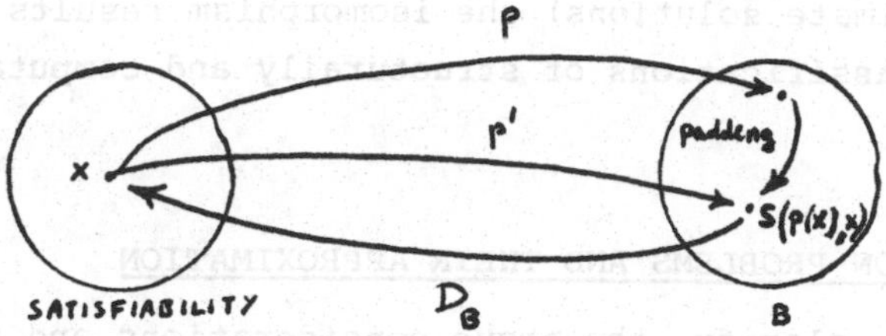

As an example of padding let us consider the case of the set CLIQUE;given the pair $\langle g,k\rangle$ where g is the description of the graph $G = \langle N,A\rangle$ and given the string y, the padding function S_{CLIQUE} outputs the pair $\langle g',k+1\rangle$ where g' is the description of the graph $G'=\langle N',A'\rangle$ and $N' = N \cup \left\{\{V_j,V_i\} \mid \text{for every } V_j \in N \text{ and } i = \begin{cases} r+2k & \text{if } y(k) = 0 \\ r+2k-1 & \text{if } y(k) = 1 \end{cases}\right.$

Suppose G is the graph 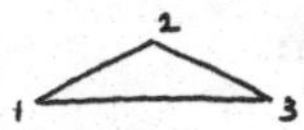 and y = 100, then G' is the graph

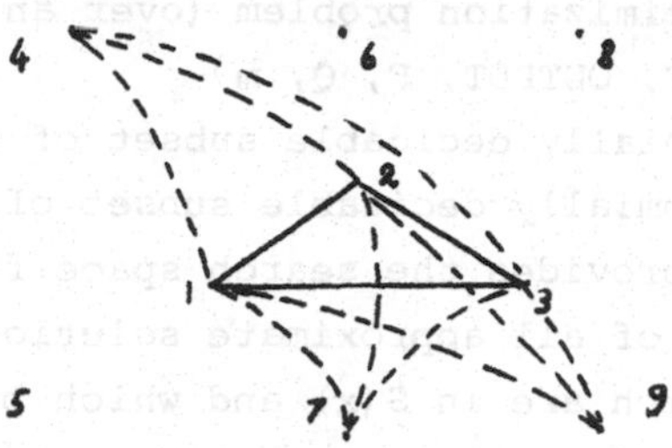

Starting from these results and from the fact that padding functions with the said properties can be easily found for all known NP-complete sets, Hartmanis and Berman prove that most of NP-complete sets which appear in the literature are indeed p-isomorphic to SATISFIABILITY and conjecture that this is true for all (infinite) NP-complete sets. In other words this would mean that all NP-complete sets are essentially the same, up to a permutation. A stronger result seems to enforce this conjecture: all the bijections f which have been exhibited between two NP-complete sets A and B can be defined in such a way that for every x the multiplicity of the solutions to the membership problem of x in A and of f(x) in B is preserved: all different "pieces" of information which show $x \in A$ $(x \notin A)$ are mapped into different "pieces" of information which show $f(x) \in B$ $(f(x) \notin B)$. This property of some reductions has been discovered first by Simon (1975) and has been called "parsimoniousness". Here the fact of having parsimonious bijections among NP-complete sets seems to suggest a deep similarity among these problems; in the next paragraphs we will see that such a similarity is the consequence of a too general approach and that if we consider the complete structure of a combinatorial problem, in terms of all of its solutions together with all solutions of all of its subproblems (approximate solutions) the isomorphism results leave the place to fine classifications of structurally and computationally different problems.

3. NP OPTIMIZATION PROBLEMS AND THEIR APPROXIMATION

In order to clarify the above considerations and to discuss results concerning various degrees of approximability of optimization problems we need a formalization of the concepts of optimization problem and of approximate solutions. Several characterizations of optimization problems have been given in the literature by Johnson (1974), Ausiello, D'Atri and Protasi (1977a), Paz and Moran (1977). According to the more general definition we have:

DEFINITION 5. An NP optimization problem (over an alphabet Σ) is the 5-tuple $\mathcal{A} = \langle$ INPUT, OUTPUT, F, Q, m $\rangle$

INPUT is a polynomially decidable subset of Σ^*

OUTPUT is a polynomially decidable subset of Σ^*

S:INPUT $\rightarrow \mathcal{P}(\Sigma^*)$ provides the search space for an input element x such that the set of all approximate solutions is given by the set of strings which are in S(x) and which belong to the output set. With the notation SOL we mean the set of approximate solutions, that is the set SOL(x) = S(x) $\cap$ OUTPUT

Q: is a totally ordered set

m: SOL(INPUT) $\rightarrow$ Q is the measure and is also polynomially computable.

For example if we consider the problem MIN-CHROMATIC-NUMBER we have:

INPUT: set of (encodings of) all undirected finite graphs;

OUTPUT: set of (encodings of) pairs $\langle G,P \rangle$ where G is a finite graph and P is a partition of the nodes of G such that (y,z) arc of G implies y and z in different classes of P

S(x): set of (encodings of all) pairs $\langle x,T \rangle$ where T is a partition of the nodes of x

Q(x): set of integers in increasing order

m : number of classes of P.

Obviously the optimal solutions of a problem $\mathcal{A}$ with input x are all y $\in$ SOL(x) such that m(y) $\geq$ m(z) (under the ordering of Q) for all z $\in$ SOL(x). We denote $m^*(x)$ the measure of the optimal solutions and $\tilde{m}(x)$ the measure of the worst solution.

The combinatorial problem associated to an optimization problem $\mathcal{A}$ is the set $\mathcal{A}^c = \{\langle x,k \rangle | m^*(x) \geq k$ under the ordering of Q$\}$. We denote NPCO problems all optimization problems associated to NP-complete combinatorial problems.For combinatorial problems associated to optimization problems we can give the following normal form result (Ausiello, D'Atri and Protasi (1976).

RESULT 3. Let $\mathcal{A}^c$ be a combinatorial problem associated to an optimization problem $\mathcal{A}$; then

$$\mathcal{A}^c=\{\langle x,k\rangle \mid (\exists z\in S_a(x))[z\in \text{OUTPUT}_a \text{ and } m_a(z)\geq k \text{ under the ordering of } Q_a]\}$$

and the Turing machine that recognizes $\mathcal{A}^c$ can be defined in the following way:

$$M_a = M_{IN} \circ M_s \circ M_{OUT} \circ M_m$$

where on input $w \in \Sigma^*$, M_{IN} rejects all the strings which are not of the form $\langle x,k\rangle$, M_s is a TM that in polynomial time nondeterministically provides $z \in S_a(x)$ and M_{OUT}, M_m are deterministic TM which in polynomial time check whether $z \in \text{OUTPUT}_a$ and $m_a(z) \geq k$. Clearly if, given a problem $\mathcal{A}^c$ there is a polynomial q such that for every $x \in \text{INPUT}_a$ $|S(x)|\leq q(|x|)$, $\mathcal{A}^c$ is in the classe P.

Another normal form result is given by Paz and Moran (1977) and is related to an interesting characterization of optimization problems. Given an optimization problem $\mathcal{A}$, for every $x \in \text{INPUT}_a$ let $F_a(x)\subseteq\text{INPUT}_a$ be a subgroup of the group of all permutations of x. Clearly $y\in F_a(x)$ implies $\text{SOL}_a(y) = \text{SOL}_a(x)$. Besides, let $\mu_a:\text{INPUT}_a \to Q_a$ be a deterministic polynomial time computable function such that, for every $x\in \text{INPUT}_a$, $\mu_a(F_a(x)) \subseteq m_a(\text{SOL}_a(x))$ and $m^*(x) \in \mu_a(F(x))$.

RESULT 4. $\mathcal{A}^c = \{\langle x,k\rangle \mid (\exists y\in F_a(x)) [\mu_a(y) \geq k \text{ under the ordering of } Q_a]\}$

and the Turing machine that recognizes $\mathcal{A}^c$ may be defined as

$$M_a = M_{IN} \circ M_F \circ M_\mu$$

where M_{IN} is as before, M_F nondeterministically provides a permutation y of x an M_μ in deterministic polynomial time computes the measure $\mu(y)$.

Now we can very generally define an approximation algorithm as a mapping that for any input provides an approximate solution:

DEFINITION 6. Given an optimization problem $\mathcal{A}$ we say that A:INPUT → → OUTPUT is an *approximation algorithm* for $\mathcal{A}$ if, for any $x\in\text{INPUT}_a$, $A(x) \in \text{SOL}(x)$.

Given an NPCO problem we are interested in approximation algorithms which run in polynomial time and, most of all, we are interested in "good" and "efficient" polynomial approximations.

For evaluating how good an approximation is, the evaluation function that is usually considered is

$$r_A(x) = \left| \frac{m^*(x) - m(A(x))}{m^*(x)} \right| .$$

Note that this function has the disadvantage that it is not invariant for linear transformations of the measure so that, surprisingly, the same algorithm may be evaluated as a good algorithm for, say, the problem MAX-CUTand as a bad algorithm for the problem MIN-CLUSTER, even if these two problems are essentially dual aspects of the same problem. For this reason the evaluation function

$$r'_A(x) = \frac{m^*(x) - m(A(x))}{m^*(x) - \tilde{m}(x)}$$

has been proposed by Aiello, Burattini, Massarotti and Ventriglia(1976). In the following we will use the more classical evaluation function r_A or the stronger version $r''_A(x) = \frac{|m^*(x) - m(A(x))|}{\min\{m^*(x), m(A(x))\}}$. Clearly in the case of a minimization problem $r''_A = r_A$ while in the case of a maximization problem $r''_A \geq r_A$.

In particular we are interested in those approximation algorithms which satisfy the following

DEFINITION 7. Given an optimization problem $\mathcal{A}$ an approximation algorithm A is said to be *ε-approximate* if, for every x, $r_A(x) \leq \varepsilon$ and $0 < \varepsilon < 1$ (maximization problem) or $\varepsilon > 0$ (minimization problem).

DEFINITION 8. An optimization problem $\mathcal{A}$ is said to be *polynomially approximable* (p-*approximable*) if for every $\varepsilon > 0$ there is an ε-approximate algorithm which runs in polynomial time(+).

DEFINITION 9. (Paz and Moran (1977)). An optimization problem $\mathcal{A}$ is said to be *fully* p-*approximable* if there exists a polynomial q(x,y) such that for every $\varepsilon > 0$ there is an ε-approximate algorithm whose running time (on input x) is bounded by $q(|x|, \frac{1}{\varepsilon})$.

(+) Is should be noted that for the purpose of characterizing p-approximability it does not matter whether we use the evaluation function r_A or the evaluation function r''_A while this is not true with the function r' in the case of minimization problems.

Examples of problems which are p-approximable (mostly variations of the knapsack problem and of scheduling problems) are given by the following results:

RESULT 5. For the following NPCO problems for every $\varepsilon > 0$ there exist polynomial ε-approximate algorithms:

i) 0-1 MAX-KNAPSACK (Sahni (1975), Ibarra and Kim (1975));

ii) MAX-SUBSET-SUM (Ibarra and Kim (1975));

iii) MAX-JOB-SEQUENCING-WITH-DEADLINES (Sahni (1976));

iv) MIN-FINISH-TIME (Sahni (1976));

v) OPTIMAL-MEAN-FLOW-TIME (Sahni (1976)).

All these problems except i) are fully p-approximable.

Unfortunately this is not the case with all NPCO problems. First of all for a large class of problems the best known accuracy achievable in polynomial time by approximation algorithms is bounded or even decreases with the size of the input. For example:

RESULT 6. (Johnson (1974)) for the following NPCO problems the best known polynomial approximation algorithm have the following worst case behaviour:

i) MAX-CLIQUE: there is a family of approximation algorithms A_j that run in time $\mathcal{O}(n^{j+2})$ such that

$$m(A_j(x)) \leq m^*(x) \cdot \frac{1}{n^{1/j+1}}$$

ii) MIN-SET-COVERING I: there exists an approximation algorithm such that

$$m(A(x)) \stackrel{\sim}{\sim} m^*(x) \cdot \ell n(n)$$

For some problems it is possible to show that efficient ε-approximate algorithms do not exist that is these problems are not fully p-approximable unless P = NP, (see Garey and Johnson (1976b)).

Finally there are problems for which it is even possible to show that no polynomial ε-approximate algorithm can exist unless the given problem is itself polynomially solvable (i.e. unless P = NP : Sahni and Gonzales (1976) call these problems "p-complete optimization problems"):

RESULT 7. If P $\neq$ NP for the following NPCO problems the following conditions hold:

i) MIN-CHROMATIC-NUMBER (Garey and Johnson (1976a)): no polynomial approximation algorithm A can give $m(A(x)) \leq r\, m^*(x) + d$ for any constant $r < 2$ and constant d. This implies that no polynomial ε-approximate algorithm can exist with $\varepsilon < 1$ (nothing is known for $\varepsilon \geq 1$);

ii) TRAVELING-SALESPERSON (under different optimization criteria: Sahni and Gonzales (1974), Papadimitriou and Steiglitz (1976)): no polynomial ε-approximate algorithm exists for every $\varepsilon > 0$;

iii) K-GENERAL-PARTITION (under the maximization of internal weights: Sahni and Gonzales (1976)): no polynomial ε-approximate algorithm exists for every $\varepsilon > 0$.

The basic idea that comes out of these results is that there are intrinsic differences among certain classes of optimization problems: some of the problems are indeed harder than others and any polynomial approximation is bound to give arbitrarily "bad" results on some inputs. This classification of NPCO problems was also considered in the survey paper by Garey and Johnson (1976b) but only more recently different methodologies have been proposed to investigate such differences and an attempt has been made to characterize optimization problems and their approximability in terms of their combinatorial structure.

4. CHARACTERIZATIONS OF CLASSES OF OPTIMIZATION PROBLEMS

Let $\mathcal{A}$ be an optimization problem. Let us consider the space INPUT × Q. Any combinatorial problem $\mathcal{A}^c$ can be seen as a set

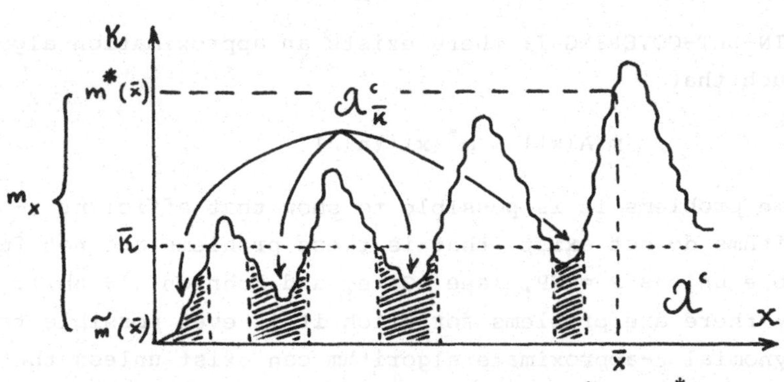

in this space. Let us denote m_x the interval $[\tilde{m}(x), m^*(x)]$ and $\mathcal{A}^c_k$ the set $\{x \in \text{INPUT} \mid m^*(x) \leq k\}$ under the ordering of Q. The basic reason why the powerful results of §2 may be used to show that two problems $\mathcal{A}^c$ and $\mathcal{B}^c$ (say CHROMATIC-NUMBER and JOB-SEQUENCING-WITH-DEADLINES) are polynomially isomorphic even if their associated optimization problems have a very different nature and are deeply different with respect to the ability of finding good and efficient approximation algorithms, is that the type of reductions that are used to prove those results neither preserve the structure that is induced on a combinatorial problem by the associated optimization problem (for example the ordering among input elements that expresses the fact that an input element is a "subproblem" of another input element) nor take into account the properties of the "projections" m_x and $\mathcal{A}^c_k$.

One way of obtaining a first refinement is to consider stronger concepts of reduction. For example, Ausiello, D'Atri, Gaudiano and Protasi (1977a, 1977b) introduce the notion of "structure" of an input element x to an optimization problem, defined in terms of the "spectrum" of SOL(x), that is the number of approximate solutions of a certain measure for any value of the measure between $\tilde{m}(x)$ and $m^*(x)$. Then the notion of "structure preserving" reduction is defined and it is shown that this type of reductions introduces a fine classification of "structurally isomorphic" problems and a partial ordering among these isomorphism classes. An extensive treatment of these concepts is developed in the said references.

Another promising way of relating the structural properties of a combinatorial problem associated to an optimization problem $\mathcal{A}$ to the approximability of $\mathcal{A}$ is to consider the properties of the sets $\mathcal{A}^c_k$ and, more generally, of the sets $\mathcal{A}^c_{f(n)}$ where f(n) is a slowly growing function. This approach has been followed by Paz and Moran (1977) and is briefly summarized here.

DEFINITION 10.

i) An optimization problem $\mathcal{A}$ is said to be *simple* if, for every k, the set $\mathcal{A}^c_k$ is in the class P ;

ii) An optimization problem $\mathcal{A}$ is said to be *rigid* if it is not simple, that is if for some k the set $\mathcal{A}^c_k$ is itself NP-complete.

Examples of simple problems are the problems MAX-CLIQUE, MAX-CUT, MAX-SUBSET-SUM, MAX-SATISFIABILITY. Examples of rigid problems are MIN-PLANAR-CHROMATIC-NUMBER ($\mathcal{A}^c_3$ is NP complete while $\mathcal{A}^c_4$ is trivially decidable by the result that says that all planar graphs are 4-colorable) and MIN-BIN-PACKING (for every k the fact that a set of integers can be divided onto k subsets, each of which sums up to less than a fixed integer, is itself an NP-complete problem).

In most cases (e.g. MAX-SATISFIABILITY, MAX-CUT) the polynomial that bounds the running time of the decision algorithm for $\mathcal{A}^c_k$ changes with k. In some cases (e.g. MAX-SUBSET-SUM, MAX-JOB-SEQUENCING-WITH-DEADLINES) all $\mathcal{A}^c_k$ can be recognized within the same polynomial bound. In order to characterize this fact the following definition is used:

DEFINITION 11. An optimization problem $\mathcal{A}$ is said to be *polynomially simple* (*p-simple*) if there exists a polynomial q(x,y) such that for every k the decision algorithm for $\mathcal{A}_k^c$ on input x takes time $\leq q(|x|, k)$.

An important property of p-simple problems is considered in the following result:

RESULT 8. Let $\mathcal{A}$ be an optimization problem: $\mathcal{A}$ p-simple implies $\mathcal{A}^c_{p_1(n)} = \{x \in \text{INPUT} | m^*(x) \leq p_1(|x|)\} \in P$

PROOF. Since there exists a q such that for every k $\mathcal{A}_k^c$ is recognizable in time $q(|x|, k)$, the set $\mathcal{A}^c_{p_1(n)}$ can be recognized within time bounded by $q(|x|, p_1(|x|))$. QED.

This result is an important tool for proving that a problem is not p-simple. For example, if $\mathcal{A}$ is MAX-SATISFIABILITY, we have that SATISFIABILITY = $\mathcal{A}_n^c = \{x | m^*(x) = \#\text{of clauses in } x\}$ and this means that $\mathcal{A}$ is not p-simple.

The interest for the study of the classes of rigid, simple and p-simple problems comes out of the following results:

RESULT 9. Let $\mathcal{A}$ be an optimization problem. A necessary condition for $\mathcal{A}$ to be p-approximable is that $\mathcal{A}$ is simple.

PROOF. Let $\mathcal{A}$ be a maximization problem. If we consider the evaluation function r" we have that if $\mathcal{A}$ is p-approximable for every $0 < \varepsilon < 1$ there exists A_ε such that for every $x \in$ INPUT

$$\frac{m^*(x) - m(A_\varepsilon(x))}{m(A_\varepsilon(x))} < \varepsilon$$

If we choose $\varepsilon = \frac{1}{k}$ we have $\frac{m^*(x)}{m(A_{1/k}(x))} - 1 < \frac{1}{k}$ and this implies that $m(A_{1/k}(x)) \leq k \Leftrightarrow m^*(x) \leq k$.

Hence $\mathcal{A}_k^c$ is decidable via the polynomial algorithm $A_{1/k}$. QED

RESULT 10. Let $\mathcal{A}$ be an optimization problem. A necessary condition for $\mathcal{A}$ to be fully p-approximable is that $\mathcal{A}$ is p-simple.

PROOF. Let q' be a polynomial such that $\mathcal{A}$ is ε-approximable in time $q'(|x|, \frac{1}{\varepsilon})$. By applying the same argument as before and by choosing $\varepsilon = 1/k$ it is possible to show that the set $\mathcal{A}_k^c$ can be decided in time $q'(|x|, k)$. QED

The following scheme gives a view of the obtained classification together with some examples of problems belonging to different classes

NPCO PROBLEMS

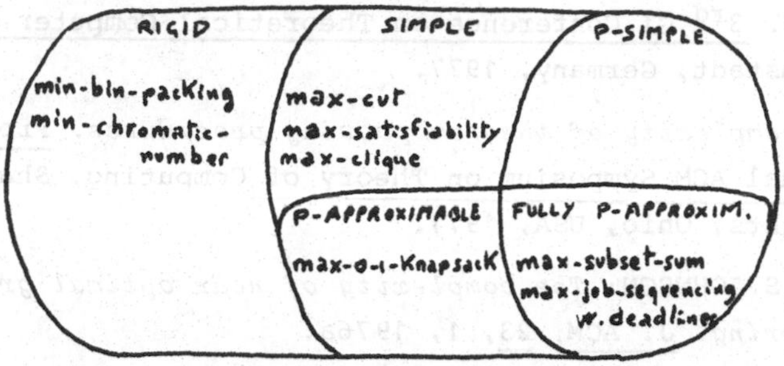

In conclusion, even if we are still far from a full characterization of NPCO problems according to their degree of approximability, we may say that both the classifications based an strong concepts of reductions (measure preserving reductions, structure preserving reductions) and the classifications based on the complexity of the projections give us some understanding of the structure and the properties of optimization problems and of their associated NP complete sets and provide us with an interesting tool for investigating an area of such a relevance both from the theoretical and practical point of view.

BIBLIOGRAPHY

1. A.AIELLO, E.BURATTINI, A.MASSAROTTI, F.VENTRIGLIA: *Toward a general principle of evaluation for approximate algorithms*. In Séminaires IRIA, Parigi, Francia, 1976.

2. G.AUSIELLO, A.D'ATRI, M.PROTASI: *A characterization of reductions among combinatorial problems*. R.76-23, Istituto di Automatica, Università di Roma, 1976.

3. G.AUSIELLO, A.D'ATRI, M.PROTASI: *On the structure of combinatorial problems and structure preserving reductions*. Proc. 4th International Colloquium on Automata, Languages and Programming, Turku, Finland, 1977a.

4. G.AUSIELLO, A.D'ATRI, M.GAUDIANO, M.PROTASI: *Classes of structurally isomorphic NP optimization problems*. These proceedings 1977b .

5. T.BAKER, J.GILL, R.SOLOVAY: *Relativizations of the P = ? NP question.* SIAM J. on Computing, 4,4, 1975.

6. L.BERMAN, J.HARTMANIS: *On polynomial time isomorphisms of complete sets.* 3rd GI Conference on Theoretical Computer Science, Darmstadt, Germany, 1977.

7. S.COOK: *The complexity of theorem proving procedures.* Proc. 3rd Annual ACM Symposium on Theory of Computing, Shaker Heights, Ohio, USA, 1971.

8. M.R.GAREY, D.S.JOHNSON: *The complexity of near optimal graph coloring.* J. ACM, 23, 1, 1976a.

9. M.R.GAREY, D.S.JOHNSON: *Approximation algorithms for combinatorial problems: an annotated bibliography.* Proc. Symposium on Algorithms and Complexity: New directions and recent results, Pittsburg, Pa, USA, 1976b.

10. J.HARTMANIS, L.BERMAN: *On isomorphism and density of NP and other complete sets.* Proc. 8th Annual ACM Symposium on Theory of Computing, Hershey, Pa., USA, 1976.

11. J.HARTMANIS, J.E.HOPCROFT: *Independence results in computer science.* TR, Department of Computer Science, Cornell University, Ithaca, N.Y., USA, 1976.

12. J.HARTMANIS, J.SIMON: *On the structure of feasible computations.* In Advances in Computers, Vol. 14, Academic Press, N.Y., 1976.

13. O.H.IBARRA, C.E.KIM: *Fast approximation algorithms for the Knapsack and sum of subsets problems.* J. ACM, 22,4,1975.

14. D.S.JOHNSON: *Approximation algorithms for combinatorial problems.* J.Computers and Systems Science, 9,3, 1974.

15. R.KARP: *Reducibilities among combinatorial problems.* In Complexity of Computer Computations, Plenum Press, 1972.

16. C.H.PAPADIMITRIOU, K.STEIGLITZ: *Some complexity results for the traveling salesman problem.* Proc. 8th Annual ACM Symposium on Theory of Computing, Hershey, Pa., USA, 1976.

17. A.PAZ, S.MORAN: *Non-deterministic polynomial optimization problems and their approximation.* Proc. 4th International Colloquium on Automata, Languages and Programming, Turku, Finland, 1977.

18. S.SAHNI: *Approximate algorithms for the 0-1 Knapsack problem.* J. ACM, 22 1, 1975.

19. S.SAHNI : *Algorithms for scheduling independent tasks.* J. ACM, 23, 1, 1976.

20. S.SAHNI, T.GONZALES: *P-complete approximation problems.* J. ACM, 23, 3, 1976.

21. J.SIMON: *On some central problems in computational complexity.* TR 75-224, Department of Computer Science, Cornell University, Ithaca, N.Y., USA, 1975.

A COMPARATIVE REVIEW OF SOME PROGRAM VERIFICATION METHODS

Andrzej Blikle
Institute of Computer Science of the Polish Academy of Sciences
P.O.Box 22, PKiN, 00-901 Warsaw, Poland

1. INTRODUCTION

This paper present a review of three program verification methods: the fixed-point approach, the inductive assertion method and the weakest precondition calculus. All the three methods are described in the framework of the algebra of binary relations. This common reference point enables the reader to see many interesting relationships and similarities between these methods.

The discussion is carried out in the abstract model of a programming language. After a short introduction to the algebra of binary relations three types of semantics of such a language are shown: operational semantics, denotational semantics and fixed-point semantics. The fixed-point semantics splits into two subcases: the well known continuation semantics, and its dual counterpart - the initiation semantics. Arguments are given to convince the reader that both are equally interesting and useful. Next, the inductive assertion method is discussed. It is pointed out that this method of proving partial correctness has a natural counterpart for proving total correctness. In the former the sets of intermediate assertions are finite, in the latter are infinite. The described method of proving total correctness implies two other methods: of well-founded sets and of weakest preconditions.

This paper is neither a tutorial nor a state-of-the-art presentation. This is simply a discussion of three well known methods written for the readers who have already some background in the field. Of course all the discussed concepts are introduced in the paper, but less care has been paid to their intuitive explanation. For the sake of transparency almost all the bibliographical remarks have been collected in the last section.

2. THE ALGEBRA OF BINARY RELATIONS

Let S be an arbitrary nonempty set called the set of states and interpreted as the set of data vector states. By $Rel(S) = \{R \mid R \subseteq S \times S\}$ we shall denote the set of all binary relations in S. For any $a,b \in S$ and $R \in Rel(S)$ we shall write aRb for $(a,b) \in R$. By $I = \{(a,a) \mid a \in S\}$ we shall denote the identity relation and by $\emptyset$ the empty relation as well as the empty set. Besides the usual set-theoretical operations we define the following four operations in Rel(S):

1) $R_1 \circ R_2 = \{(a,b) \mid (\exists c)(aR_1c \ \& \ cR_2b)\}$ 3) $R^* = \bigcup_{n=0}^{\infty} R^n$

2) $R^0 = I$; $R^{n+1} = R \circ R^n$ for $n \geqq 0$ 4) $R^+ = \bigcup_{n=1}^{\infty} R^n$

called respectively the composition, the power, the iteration and the transitive closure. It is a well known fact that the union, composition and iteration are sufficient for the description of the input-output (abbreviated I-O) relations of iterative programs. Below we list the basic properties of these operations. Everywhere in the sequel we shall omit the symbol "$\circ$" and write R_1R_2 for $R_1 \circ R_2$.

(A1) $R_1(R_2R_3) = (R_1R_2)R_3$

(A2) $R_1(R_2 \cup R_3) = R_1R_2 \cup R_1R_3$

$(R_2 \cup R_3)R_1 = R_2R_1 \cup R_3R_1$

(A3) $R(\bigcup_{i=0}^{\infty} R_i) = \bigcup_{i=0}^{\infty} RR_i$

$(\bigcup_{i=0}^{\infty} R_i)R = \bigcup_{i=0}^{\infty} R_iR$

(A4) $RI = IR = R$

(A5) $R\emptyset = \emptyset R = \emptyset$

(A6) If $R_1 \subseteq R_2$ then

$RR_1 \subseteq RR_2$ and

$R_1R \subseteq R_2R$

The operation of composition can be extended to the case where one of the arguments is a set. Let $R \in Rel(S)$ and $B \subseteq S$:

$BR = \{a \mid (\exists b)(b \in B \ \& \ bRa)\}$ $\qquad$ $RB = \{a \mid (\exists b)(aRb \ \& \ b \in B)\}$

If R is interpreted as the I-O relation of a program, then BR is exactly the set of outputs which may be reached through R from B, and RB is the set of inputs from which one can reach B through R. In particular, if the program is deterministic - i.e. if R is a function - then RS is the domain of termination and SR is the set of all possible outputs. The properties of the extended operation are very similar to (A1)-(A6). Let R and B, possibly with indices, denote relations and sets respectively. We have:

(A7) $B_1(R_2R_3) = (B_1R_2)R_3$

$R_1(R_2B_3) = (R_1R_2)B_3$

(A8) $B_1(R_2 \cup R_3) = B_1R_2 \cup B_1R_3$

$R_1(B_2 \cup B_3) = R_1B_2 \cup R_1B_3$

$(R_2 \cup R_3)B_1 = R_2B_1 \cup R_3B_1$ etc.

(A9) $BI = IB = B$ (A10) $B\emptyset = \emptyset B = \emptyset$ (A11) $R\emptyset = \emptyset R = \emptyset$

(A12) If $R_1 \subseteq R_2$ then $BR_1 \subseteq BR_2$ and $R_1B \subseteq R_2B$

(A13) If $B_1 \subseteq B_2$ then $B_1R \subseteq B_2R$ and $RB_1 \subseteq RB_2$

Of course, in (A11) $\emptyset$ denotes the empty set.

3. ABSTRACT PROGRAMS

In this section we introduce an abstract programming language which is in fact a mathematical model of a large class of programming languages. It contains all the programming constructions which we shall discuss - or need in the discussion - in the sequel. The language is represented by the set INS of instructions defined together with an auxiliary set CON of conditions. The definition is axiomatic and does not specify the sets INS and CON unambiguously (the set of axioms is not categorial). Due to this ambiguity the subsequent discussion applies to a large class of languages. We shall start with axioms describing the syntax of INS and CON.

(C1) true, false $\in$ CON

(C2) If $c_1, c_2 \in$ CON then $\sim c_1$, $(c_1 \vee c_2)$, $(c_1 \& c_2) \in$ CON

(I1) abort, skip $\in$ INS

(I2) If $c \in$ CON then istrue c eu $\in$ INS

(I3) If $c_1,\dots,c_m \in$ CON , $IN_1,\dots,IN_m \in$ INS and $\alpha_1,\dots,\alpha_n$ are appropriate characters (or strings of characters) which we call labels, then the following are also instructions in the set INS:

(I31) IN_1; IN_2

(I32) **if** c_1 **then** IN_1 **else** IN_2 **fi**

(I33) **while** c_1 **do** IN_1 **od**

(I34) **if** $c_1 \rightarrow IN_1 [\!] \dots [\!] c_m \rightarrow IN_m$ **fi**

(I35) **do** $c_1 \rightarrow IN_1 [\!] \dots [\!] c_m \rightarrow IN_m$ **od**

(I36) **begin goto** α_{i_1}

α_{i_1} : IN_1 , **goto** α_{j_1} ;

. . .

α_{i_m} : IN_m , **goto** α_{j_m} ;

$\alpha_{i_{m+1}}$: **end**

(I31)-(I35) are schemes of typical structured instructions. (I36) is a general scheme of an unstructured iterative instruction.

In order to define the semantics of INS and CON we establish the function of semantics

$$\lambda \varepsilon [\varepsilon] : \text{CON} \cup \text{INS} \longrightarrow \text{Rel}(S) \tag{3.1}$$

This function is defined by the axioms given below. For every instruction IN the corresponding relation [IN] will be called the resulting relation of IN. We start by the axioms for the set CON:

(SC1) $[\text{false}] = \emptyset$, $[\text{true}] = I$
(SC2) For any $c_1, c_2 \in \underline{CON}$, $[c_1] \subseteq I$ and $[(c_1 \vee c_2)] = [c_1] \cup [c_2]$,
$[(c_1 \& c_2)] = [c_1][c_2]$, $[c_1 \& \sim c_1] = \emptyset$

Observe that $[c_1] \cup [\sim c_1] = I$ is not an axiom, which means that our conditions correspond to partial predicates. E.g. in the computer arithmetics the predicate "x+1<1" is partial since it is undefined for all x other than reals within the bounds given by the implementation. The semantics of instructions is described by the following axioms:

(SI1) $[\text{abort}] = \emptyset$, $[\text{skip}] = I$
(SI2) If $c \in \underline{CON}$ then $[\underline{\text{istrue}}\ c\ \underline{\text{eu}}] = [c]$
(SI3) If $c_1, \ldots, c_m \in \underline{CON}$ and $IN_1, \ldots, IN_m \in \underline{INS}$ then
(SI31) $[IN_1 ; IN_2] = [IN_1][IN_2]$
(SI32) $[\underline{\text{if}}\ c_1\ \underline{\text{then}}\ IN_1\ \underline{\text{else}}\ IN_2\ \underline{\text{fi}}] = [c_1][IN_1] \cup [\sim c_1][IN_2]$
(SI33) $[\underline{\text{while}}\ c_1\ \underline{\text{do}}\ IN_1\ \underline{\text{od}}] = ([c_1][IN_1])^*[\sim c_1]$
(SI34) $[\underline{\text{if}}\ c_1 \rightarrow IN_1 [] \ldots [] c_m \rightarrow IN_m\ \underline{\text{fi}}] = [c_1][IN_1] \cup \ldots \cup [c_m][IN_m]$
(SI35) $[\underline{\text{do}}\ c_1 \rightarrow IN_1 [] \ldots [] c_m \rightarrow IN_m\ \underline{\text{od}}] =$
$= ([c_1][IN_1] \cup \ldots \cup [c_m][IN_m])^*[\sim c_1 \& \ldots \& \sim c_m]$

The semantics of the unstructured instruction (I36) has been left undefined since it cannot be described in this way. We postpone this problem to the next section.

4. OPERATIONAL SEMANTICS

The method of defining semantics of instructions by explicite formulas like these given in Sec.3 is frequently refered to as denotational semantics. An alternative method consists of providing operational descriptions of instructions. This method is called operational semantics. In order to describe it in a possibly simple way we introduce below abstract algorithms which are semantical models of (I36).

By an iterative algorithm - or shortly an algorithm - we mean a system $\mathcal{A} = (V, \alpha_1, \alpha_n, \mathcal{T})$ where $V = \{\alpha_1, \ldots, \alpha_n\}$ is an arbitrary finite set of characters called labels or control states, α_1 and α_n are distinguished elements of V called respectively the initial label and the terminal label and $\mathcal{T}$ is a finite set of triples of the form (α_i, R, α_j) where $\alpha_i, \alpha_j \in V$ and $R \in Rel(S)$. The elements of $\mathcal{T}$ will be called

<u>abstract instructions</u>.

Of course, each triple (α_i, R, α_j) is a mathematical abstraction of the expression α_i: IN , <u>goto</u> α_j where [IN] = R. The correspondence between iterative algorithms and instructions (I36) is therefore obvious. Below we define the resulting relation of $\mathcal{A}$, which by the definition, will be understood as the resulting relation of the corresponding (I36). We start from a few auxiliary notions.

By a <u>configuration</u> of $\mathcal{A}$ we mean any pair (α_i, a) where $\alpha_i \in V$ and $a \in S$. Consequently, $V \times S$ is the set of all the configurations of $\mathcal{A}$. By the <u>transition relation</u> of $\mathcal{A}$ we call the binary relation $\Longrightarrow \in Rel(V \times S)$ defined as follows: $(\alpha_i, a) \Longrightarrow (\alpha_j, b)$ <u>iff</u> there exists $(\alpha_i, R, \alpha_j) \in \mathfrak{I}$ such that aRb. According to the algebraic notation of Sec.2 $\overset{+}{\Longrightarrow}$ denotes the transitive closure of $\Longrightarrow$. For any $\alpha_i, \alpha_j \in V$ by the (α_i, α_j)-<u>resulting relation</u> of $\mathcal{A}$ we mean the relation $Res(\alpha_i, \alpha_j) \in Rel(S)$ defined as follows:

$$a \; Res(\alpha_i, \alpha_j) \; b \quad \underline{iff} \quad (\alpha_i, a) \overset{+}{\Longrightarrow} (\alpha_j, b) \tag{4.1}$$

Observe that α_i and α_j are indices of the relation $Res(\alpha_i, \alpha_j)$, rather than its arguments. To be quite formal we should probably write $Res_{\alpha_i \alpha_j}$ but this notation becomes cumbersome if $Res_{\alpha_i \alpha_j}$ is used frequentl

The relation $Res(\alpha_i, \alpha_j)$ describes the effect of the data processing in $\mathcal{A}$ between α_i and α_j. Indeed, (4.1) is equivalent to the following statement:

a $Res(\alpha_i, \alpha_j)$ b <u>iff</u> there exists a sequence of abstract instructions $(\alpha_{k_1}, R_1, \alpha_{k_2}), (\alpha_{k_2}, R_2, \alpha_{k_3}), \ldots, (\alpha_{k_p}, R_p, \alpha_{k_{p+1}})$ such that $\alpha_{k_1} = \alpha_i$, $\alpha_{k_{p+1}} = \alpha_j$ and $a \, R_1 R_2 \ldots R_p \, b$. (4.2)

The relation $Res(\alpha_1, \alpha_n)$ will be called the <u>resulting relation</u> of $\mathcal{A}$. According to the notation of Sec.3 we shall denote it by $[\mathcal{A}]$. Hence $[\mathcal{A}] = Res(\alpha_1, \alpha_n)$.

The operational semantics is more intuitive (hence easier to be accepted) than the denotational semantics, but the latter is much more convenient for program verification than the former. In the next section we deal with a mathematical technique of passing from one of these semantics to the other.

5. <u>THE FIXED-POINT SEMANTICS</u>

In this section we show two alternative approaches to the fixed--point semantics of iterative algorithms. The discussion will be carried out in the terms of the previously defined algorithms.

Let $\mathcal{A} = (V, \alpha_1, \alpha_n, \mathcal{J})$ be an iterative algorithm with $V = \{\alpha_1, \ldots, \alpha_n\}$. For the sake of technical convenience we shall assume that $\mathcal{J} = \{(\alpha_i, R_{ij}, \alpha_j) \mid 1 \leq i, j \leq n\}$ which means that for any two labels α_i, α_j there is exactly one abstract instruction (α_i, R, α_j) in $\mathcal{J}$. The unique R corresponding to α_i and α_j is denoted by R_{ij}. This assumption does not restrict the generality of investigations since any $\mathcal{A}$ can be transformed to such a form by replacing any two abstract instructions $(\alpha_i, R_1, \alpha_j)$, $(\alpha_i, R_2, \alpha_j)$ by $(\alpha_i, R_1 \cup R_2, \alpha_j)$ and by adding $(\alpha_i, \emptyset, \alpha_j)$ whenever there is no abstract instruction in $\mathcal{A}$ with α_i as the first element and α_j as the third element. The new algorithm $\mathcal{A}'$ satisfies our requirement and, of course, $[\mathcal{A}] = [\mathcal{A}']$.

With every $\alpha_i \in V$ we shall associate two relations $\mathrm{Head}(\alpha_i)$ and $\mathrm{Tail}(\alpha_i)$ defined as follows:

$\mathrm{Head}(\alpha_i) = \mathrm{Res}(\alpha_1, \alpha_i)$ for $i=1,\ldots,n$

$\mathrm{Tail}(\alpha_i) = \mathrm{Res}(\alpha_i, \alpha_n)$ for $i=1,\ldots,n$

For every execution passing through α_i, the relation $\mathrm{Head}(\alpha_i)$ describes the effect of its initial part (from α_1 to α_i), whereas the relation $\mathrm{Tail}(\alpha_i)$ describes the continuation of this initial part (from α_i to α_n). Given an algorithm $\mathcal{A}$ we have two vectors of relations: <u>Head</u> = $(\mathrm{Head}(\alpha_1), \ldots, \mathrm{Head}(\alpha_n))$ and <u>Tail</u> = $(\mathrm{Tail}(\alpha_1), \ldots, \mathrm{Tail}(\alpha_n))$. Of course, each of them contains the resulting relation of $\mathcal{A}$:

$$[\mathcal{A}] = \mathrm{Res}(\alpha_1, \alpha_n) = \mathrm{Head}(\alpha_n) = \mathrm{Tail}(\alpha_1).$$

Consequently, each of them may be used to describe this relation. The case, where we describe $[\mathcal{A}]$ as $\mathrm{Tail}(\alpha_1)$ is known in the literature as the <u>continuation semantics</u>. The case where $[\mathcal{A}]$ is described as $\mathrm{Head}(\alpha_n)$ will be called here - by the symmetry - the <u>initiation semantics</u>. Due to the theorems shown below both these semantics are also refered to as <u>fixed-point semantics</u>.

<u>THEOREM</u> 5.1 (<u>the initiation fixed-point theorem</u>) The vector of relations <u>Head</u> is the least solution of the set of equations:

$$\left\{X_i = X_1 R_{1i} \cup \ldots \cup X_n R_{ni} \cup R_{1i}\right\}_{i=1}^{n} \tag{5.1}$$

<u>THEOREM</u> 5.2 (<u>the continuation fixed-point theorem</u>) The vector of relations <u>Tail</u> is the least solution of the set of equations:

$$\left\{X_i = R_{i1} X_1 \cup \ldots \cup R_{in} X_n \cup R_{in}\right\}_{i=1}^{n} \tag{5.2}$$

The proofs of these theorems are quite simple and, of course, similar to each other. We shall concentrate on the first of them which shows some facts connected with Floyd method of inductive assertions (Sec.6). To carry out this proof we introduce an auxiliary notion.

By a <u>vector of Head-invariant relations</u> of $\mathcal{A}$ we shall mean any vector of relations $(H_1,\dots,H_n)$ which satisfies the inclusions

$$\mathrm{Head}(\alpha_i) \subseteq H_i \quad \text{for } i=1,\dots,n \tag{5.3}$$

These inclusions say that whenever the control of $\mathcal{A}$ reaches α_i the relation H_i holds between the input value and the current value of the data vector. The following lemma follows directly from (4.2):

<u>LEMMA</u> 5.1 If a vector of relations $(H_1,\dots,H_n)$ satisfies the inclusions

$$1)\ R_{1j} \subseteq H_j \quad \text{and} \quad 2)\ H_i R_{ij} \subseteq H_j \quad \text{for } i,j=1,\dots,n \tag{5.4}$$

then this is a vector of Head-invariant relations.

Of course, not all vectors of Head-invariant relations satisfy (5.4 These vectors which have this property will be called <u>consistent vectors of Head-invariant relations</u>. Since <u>Head</u> is obviously the least vector of Head-invariant relations and since it also satisfies (5.4) we have:

<u>LEMMA</u> 5.2 <u>Head</u> is the least consistent vector of Head-invariant relations.

Next simple observation is that a vector $(H_1,\dots,H_n)$ is a consistent vector of Head-invariant relations <u>iff</u> it satisfies the following set of inclusions

$$\{H_1 R_{1j} \cup \dots \cup H_n R_{nj} \subseteq H_j\}_{j=1}^{n}. \tag{5.5}$$

Therefore, by Lemma 5.2, <u>Head</u> is the least solution of (5.5). By Knaster-Tarski [29] theorem, it is therefore the least solution of (5.1).

The proof of Theorem 5.2 is quite analogous. By a <u>vector of Tail-invariant relations</u> of $\mathcal{A}$ we call any vector of relations $(T_1,\dots,T_n)$ which satisfies $\mathrm{Tail}(\alpha_i) \subseteq T_i$ for $i=1,\dots,n$. Then we formulate a lemma analogous to Lemma 5.1:

<u>LEMMA</u> 5.3 If a vector of relations $(T_1,\dots,T_n)$ satisfies the inclusions

$$1)\ R_{in} \subseteq T_i \quad \text{and} \quad 2)\ R_{ij} T_j \subseteq T_i \quad \text{for } i,j=1,\dots,n$$

then this is a vector of Tail-invariant relations.

The rest of the proof is the same as in the former case. To show how the fixed-point theorems allow us to pass from the operational to the denotational semantics, consider the following - intuitively obvious - operationally oriented description of <u>do</u>-<u>od</u> (I36):

<u>begin</u> <u>goto</u> α_1
α_1: <u>istrue</u> c_1 <u>eu</u> ; IN_1 , <u>goto</u> α_1 ;
. . .
α_1: <u>istrue</u> c_m <u>eu</u> ; IN_m , <u>goto</u> α_1 ; (5.6)
α_1: <u>istrue</u> $(\sim c_1 \& \ldots \& \sim c_m)$ <u>eu</u> , <u>goto</u> α_2 ;
α_2: <u>end</u>

The corresponding initiation equations are:

$$X_1 = X_1([c_1][IN_1] \cup \ldots \cup [c_m][IN_m]) \cup [c_1][IN_1] \cup \ldots \cup [c_m][IN_m]$$

$$X_2 = X_1[\sim c_1 \& \ldots \& \sim c_m] \cup [\sim c_1 \& \ldots \& \sim c_m]$$

Solving them in the well known way (see Blikle [6,7,8]) we get

$$X_1 = ([c_1][IN_1] \cup \ldots \cup [c_m][IN_m])^+ = \mathrm{Head}(\alpha_1)$$

$$X_2 = ([c_1][IN_1] \cup \ldots \cup [c_m][IN_m])^*[\sim c_1 \& \ldots \& \sim c_m] = \mathrm{Head}(\alpha_2)$$

which coincides with (SI35) of Sec.3.

The proofs of theorems 5.1 and 5.2 have shown many similarities between the initiation and the continuation semantics. The main differences between these semantics are listed below:

1) If $\mathcal{A}$ is deterministic (i.e. if the corresponding transition relation $\Longrightarrow$ is a function), then all Tail(α_i)'s are functions whereas Head(α_i)'s for $i \leq n-1$ are usually nonfunctional relations.

2) The continuation semantics extends very nicely to the case of parameterless recursive procedures, while the initiation semantics does not. The latter follows indirectly from the paper of de Bakker and Meertens [2].

3) The continuation semantics provide a natural way of describing the semantics of programming languages (Strachey and Wadsworth [28], Mosses [24], Milne and Strachey [22]), while the initiation semantics fits better to program verification problems (Blikle [7], Blikle and Budkowski [8], see also Sec.8).

6. <u>THE PARTIAL-CORRECTNESS SEMANTICS</u>

So far we have been dealing with the semantics where program meaning were described by relations. Here and in the next section we shall deal with another alternative, in the framework of input-output semantics, where the meanings of programs are described by pairs of predicates called <u>preconditions</u> and <u>postconditions</u>. In this section we discuss the approach known as the inductive assertions method.

Since we are working in a relational framework we shall talk about sets (subsets of S) rather than about predicates. Let IN be an arbitrary instruction and let $B, C \subseteq S$. We say that IN is <u>partially correct w.r.t. to B and C</u> if $(\forall b \in B)(\forall c)(b[IN]c \Rightarrow c \in C)$ or, in our terms, if

$$B[IN] \subseteq C \tag{6.1}$$

In the sequel B will be called a <u>partial precondition</u> of C and C will be called a <u>partial postcondition</u> of B. Now, suppose that we are facing the problem of proving the inclusion (6.1) for some B, IN and C where IN is an unstructured instruction (I36) of Sec.3. Let the semantics of IN be described - according to our new convention - by the set of inclusions $\{B_k[IN_k] \subseteq C_k\}_{k=1}^m$. The pre- and postconditions B_k and C_k are called <u>intermediate assertions</u>. It is a well known fact that if we do not choose the intermediate assertions properly, we may be unable to prove (6.1) even if it is true. The following theorem guarantees that the right intermediate assertions always exist and also show how to use them in the proof of (6.1).

<u>THEOREM</u> 6.1 (<u>inductive assertions method</u>) For any algorithm $\mathfrak{A}$ and any two sets B,C S the inclusion $B[\mathfrak{A}] \subseteq C$ is true <u>iff</u> there exists a vector of sets $(A_1, \dots, A_n)$ such that

$$1)\ B \subseteq A_1\ ,\quad 2)\ \{A_i R_{ij} \subseteq A_j\}_{i,j=1}^n\ ,\quad 3)\ A_n \subseteq C \tag{6.2}$$

<u>Proof</u>. The <u>if</u> part follows directly from (4.2). The <u>only if</u> part we prove by setting $A_1 = B(\mathrm{Head}(\alpha_1) \cup I)$ and $A_i = B\mathrm{Head}(\alpha_i)$ for i=2,...n.

Since the main problem in the application of Theorem 6.1 is the problem of finding the vector $(A_1, \dots, A_n)$ of intermediate assertions, a few remarks about the set of all such vectors are in order. Let every vector $(A_1, \dots, A_n)$ which satisfies (6.2) be called a <u>vector of inductive assertions</u> for B and C.

<u>LEMMA</u> 6.1 If $B[\mathfrak{A}] \subseteq C$ is true, then every vector $(A_1, \dots, A_n)$ of inductive assertions for B and C satisfies the inclusions

$$1)\ \{B\mathrm{Head}(\alpha_i) \subseteq A_i\}_{i=1}^n\ ,\qquad 2)\ \{A_i\mathrm{Tail}(\alpha_i) \subseteq C\}_{i=1}^n.$$

<u>Proof</u>. Immediate from Theorem 6.1 and (4.2).

The converse implication is not true (J.Leszczyłowski, personal communication). This lemma shows that we may search for inductive assertions either starting from the beginning of the program and"pushing"

B forwards or starting from the end and "pushing" C backwards (cf. Katz and Manna [13]).

In order to formulate the next lemma we shall need a new operation. For any relation R and set C let $R \rightarrow C$ denote the set defined by $a \in (R \rightarrow C)$ iff $(\forall c)(aRc \Rightarrow c \in C)$ or equivalently by $R \rightarrow C = RC \cap \overline{R\overline{C}} \cup \overline{RS}$, where the bar denotes the complementation in S. It is easy to check that for any relation R, any precondition B and any postcondition C, BR is the least (strongest) partial postcondition of B and $R \rightarrow C$ is the greatest (weakest) partial precondition of C.

LEMMA 6.2 If $B[\mathcal{A}] \subseteq C$ is true, then the set of corresponding vectors of inductive assertions is nonempty and is closed under arbitrary (componentwise) union and intersection. The least element of this set is BHead $= (B(Head(\alpha_1) \cup I), BHead(\alpha_2), \ldots, BHead(\alpha_n))$ and the greatest element is Tail→C $= (Tail(\alpha_1) \rightarrow C, \ldots, Tail(\alpha_{n-1}) \rightarrow C, , (Tail(\alpha_n) \cup I) \rightarrow C)$.

A simple proof by checking is omitted.

LEMMA 6.3 For any algorithm $\mathcal{A}$ and any set $B \subseteq S$ the vector $(BHead(\alpha_1), \ldots, BHead(\alpha_n))$ is the least solution of the set of equations:

$$\{Y_i = Y_1 R_{1i} \cup \ldots \cup Y_n R_{ni} \cup BR_{1i}\}_{i=1}^{n} \tag{6.3}$$

where Y_i's range over subsets of S.

The proof is analogous to that of Theorem 5.1. Since the operation of the extended composition (of relations and sets) is continuous in both arguments, the methods of solving (6.3) are analogous to that of solving (5.1). E.g. the least solution of $Y = YR \cup B$ is BR^*. It is an open problem if $(Tail(\alpha_1) \rightarrow C, \ldots, Tail(\alpha_n) \rightarrow C)$ has an analogous fixed-point characterization.

The general Theorem 6.1 may be used to establish theorems corresponding to the structured instructions definable in terms of (I36). We show the theorem for do-od instruction (I35) as an example.

THEOREM 6.2 For any instruction do $c_1 \rightarrow IN_1 \| \ldots \| c_m \rightarrow IN_m$ od and any sets $B, C \subseteq S$ the inclusion $B[$do $c_1 \rightarrow IN_1 \| \ldots \| c_m \rightarrow IN_m$ od$] \subseteq C$ is true iff there exists a set A such that

1) $B \subseteq A$
2) $A([c_1][IN_1] \cup \ldots \cup [c_m][IN_m]) \subseteq A$
3) $A[\sim c_1 \& \ldots \& \sim c_m] \subseteq C$

Proof. According to (5.6) let $R_{11} = [c_1][IN_1] \cup \ldots \cup [c_m][IN_m]$

$R_{12} = [\sim c_1 \& \ldots \& \sim c_m]$, $R_{21} = \emptyset$ and $R_{22} = \emptyset$. The condition of Theorem 6.1 reduces to: there exist A_1 and A_2 such that $B \subseteq A_1$, $A_1 R_{11} \subseteq A_1$, $A_1 R_{12} \subseteq A_2$, $A_2 \subseteq C$. This, in turn, is equivalent to: there exists A such that $B \subseteq A$, $AR_{11} \subseteq A$, $AR_{12} \subseteq C$.

The if part of this theorem is, of course, a Hoare-like verification rule for do-od.

7. THE TOTAL-CORRECTNESS SEMANTICS

In this section we deal with a dual counterpart of the partial--correctness semantics. Similarly as in Sec.6 the meanings of instructions are described by pairs of sets, but now the underlaying formula is $(\forall b \in B)(\exists c)(b[IN]c \ \& \ c \in C)$ or, in our notation,

$$B \subseteq [IN]C. \tag{7.1}$$

The formula (7.1) says the following: for any input of B there exists an execution of IN that terminates in C. Of course, if IN is deterministic, then this is equivalent to saying that for any input of B the (only) execution of IN terminates in C. But, if IN is nondeterministic, then - besides the execution that terminates in C - there may be another execution (for the same input) that terminates outside of C or that does not terminate at all.

By analogy to the wording of Sec.6, B in (7.1) will be called a total precondition of C and C will be called a total postcondition of B. It is evident that [IN]C is the greatest (weakest) total precondition of C and - for deterministic instructions - this is exactly the Dijkstra weakest precondition wp(IN,C). Concerning the least (strongest) total postcondition of B it exists provided $B \subseteq [IN]S$ and IN is deterministic and in that case it is equal to B[IN], hence it coincides with the least partial postcondition (Sec.6).

The problem of proving (7.1) is, in principle, similar to that of proving (6.1): one has to find a set of appropriate intermediate assertions. However, since we are dealing with termination, the problem is mathematically more complicated. Proving (7.1) usually requires either infinite sets of intermediate assertions or auxiliary functions ranging over so called well-founded sets. We shall show this on the example of do-od instructions.

THEOREM 7.1 For any instruction do $c_1 \rightarrow IN_1 [] \ldots [] c_m \rightarrow IN_m$ od and any sets $B, C \subseteq S$ the inclusion $B \subseteq [$do $c_1 \rightarrow IN_1 [] \ldots [] c_m \rightarrow IN_m$ od$]C$ is true iff there exists an infinite sequence of sets $\{A_k\}_{k=0}^{\infty}$ such that

1) $B \subseteq \bigcup_{k=0}^{\infty} A_k$

2) $\{A_k \subseteq ([c_1][IN_1] \cup \ldots \cup [c_m][IN_m])A_{k-1}\}_{k=1}^{\infty}$ (7.2)

3) $A_0 \subseteq [\sim c_1 \& \ldots \& \sim c_m]C$

Proof. The if part. Using Dijkstra's notation let DO denote the instruction do $c_1 \rightarrow IN_1 [] \ldots [] c_m \rightarrow IN_m$ od, IF denote the instruction if $c_1 \rightarrow IN_1 [] \ldots [] c_m \rightarrow IN_m$ fi and cc denote the condition $c_1 \vee \ldots \vee c_m$. Then, $[IF] = [c_1][IN_1] \cup \ldots \cup [c_m][IN_m]$, $[\sim cc] = [\sim c_1 \& \ldots \& \sim c_m]$ and, of course, $[DO] = [IF]^*[\sim cc]$. By induction, applying 2) and 3), we prove $A_k \subseteq [IF]^k[\sim cc]C$. Therefore $B \subseteq \bigcup_{k=0}^{\infty} A_k \subseteq [IF]^*[\sim cc]C = [DO]C$. The only if part: The sequence $\{A_k = [IF]^k[\sim cc]C\}_{k=0}^{\infty}$ obviously satisfies 1), 2) and 3).

The above construction of the sequence $\{A_k\}_{k=0}^{\infty}$ is very close to Dijkstra's inductive definition of wp(DO,C). Indeed, Dijkstra [10] defines: $H_0(C) = [\sim cc]C$, $\{H_k(C) = wp(IF, H_{k-1}(C) \cup H_0(C)\}_{k=1}^{\infty}$ and $wp(DO,C) = \bigcup_{k=0}^{\infty} H_k(C)$. This, in our notation, becomes: $H_0(C) = [\sim cc]C$, $\{H_k(C) = [IF]H_{k-1}(C) \cup H_0(C)\}_{k=1}^{\infty}$, which is equivalent to $\{H_k(C) = \bigcup_{i=0}^{k}[IF]^i[\sim cc]C\}_{k=0}^{\infty}$. Therefore, we have

$wp(DO,C) = \bigcup_{i=0}^{\infty}[IF]^i[\sim cc]C = [IF]^*[\sim cc]C = [DO]C$.

The following lemma is the weakest total precondition counterpart of Lemma 6.3 . The proof is analogous.

LEMMA 7.1 For any algorithm $\mathcal{A}$ and any set $C \subseteq S$ the vector $(Tail(\alpha_1)C, \ldots, Tail(\alpha_n)C)$ is the least solution of the set of equations:

$$\{Y_i = R_{i1}Y_1 \cup \ldots \cup R_{in}Y_n \cup R_{in}C\}_{i=1}^{n}$$

where Y_i's range over subsets of S.

Let us return again to the sequence of sets $\{A_k\}_{k=0}^{\infty}$ of Theorem 7.1. If the DO instruction is deterministic, i.e. if [IF] is a function, then the inclusion $A_k \subseteq [IF]^k[\sim cc]C$ says that starting from A_k one needs exactly k applications of IF in order to reach C. Mathematically this means that $A_k \cap A_j = \emptyset$ for $k \neq j$ (an easy proof is left to the reader). Now, the inclusions 2) of (7.2) guarantee that each application of IF makes the current data vector state one step "closer" to A_0. Since the "distance" from each element of $\bigcup_{k=0}^{\infty} A_k$ to A_0 is obviously finite, the execution of DO must - for any such element - terminate in a finite time. This reminds, of course, the method of well-founded sets. Indeed, this method is hidden in Theorem 7.1 in the indexing of the sequence $\{A_k\}_{k=0}^{\infty}$. The following theorem makes it explicite:

THEOREM 7.2 For any deterministic instruction $\underline{do}\ c_1 \rightarrow IN_1 [] \ldots$ $\ldots [] c_m \rightarrow IN_m\ \underline{od}$ and any sets $B, C \subseteq S$ the inclusion $B \subseteq [\underline{do}\ c_1 \rightarrow IN_1 [] \ldots$ $\ldots [] c_m \rightarrow IN_m\ \underline{od}]C$ is true iff there exists a set A and a partial function $f: S \rightarrow \underline{NAT}$ such that:

$$
\begin{aligned}
&1)\quad B \subseteq A \cap \underline{DOM}(f)\\
&2)\quad \{A \cap F_k \subseteq ([c_1][IN_1] \cup \ldots \cup [c_m][IN_m])(A \cap F_{k-1})\}_{k=1}^{\infty} \qquad (7.3)\\
&3)\quad A \cap F_0 \subseteq [\sim c_1 \& \ldots \& \sim c_m]C
\end{aligned}
$$

where NAT is the set of natural numbers, $F_k = \{s \mid f(s) = k\}$ and DOM(f) is the domain of f.

Proof. The if part. If 1), 2) and 3) are satisfies, then we set $\{A_k = A \cap F_k\}_{k=0}^{\infty}$ and apply Theorem 7.1. The only if part. Again by Theorem 7.1 we get the sequence $\{A_k\}_{k=0}^{\infty}$ which satisfies (7.2). We set $A = \bigcup_{k=0}^{\infty} A_k$. Since [IF] is a function, the sets A_k are all disjoint and, therefore, the function $f(s)=k$ iff $s \in A_k$ is well defined on A. Of course, A and f satisfy (7.3).

The function f is called by Manna and Pnueli [18] a convergence function and the if part of our theorem resembles their total-correctness rule for while instruction. Observe that in the if part of the theorem the assumption about the determinism of DO may be omitted. It remains an open question if it also can be omitted in the only if part.

8. A FEW FURTHER REMARKS ABOUT PARTIAL AND TOTAL CORRECTNESS

The idea of describing programs by pairs of unary predicates (sets of inputs and outputs) were introduced by Floyd [11] and Hoare [12] for the proofs of partial correctness and then also applied by Dijkstra [10] to the proof of total correctness. About 1973, Manna and Pnueli [18] observed that dealing with unary predicates is frequently inconvenient, E.g. if we are going to say that for each input s in B the output of IN is f(s), then this leads us to the formula with a quantifier $(\forall s \in B)(\{s\}[IN] \subseteq \{f(s)\})$ which corresponds to a (usually infinite) family of partial correctness conditions (6.1).

As a solution they suggest the description of postconditions by binary predicates which specify the relationship between inputs and outputs. In the predicate calculus this leads to the following formulas:

$$\text{partial correctness:} \quad (\forall b)(\forall c)(b \in B \;\&\; b[IN]c \Rightarrow bRc)$$
$$\text{total correctness:} \quad (\forall b)(\exists c)(b \in B \Rightarrow b[IN]c \;\&\; bRc) \tag{8.1}$$

where, of course, B is a unary precondition and R is a binary postcondition. In order to translate this into our notation let $[B] = \{(b,b) \mid b \in B\}$ for all $B \subseteq S$. We have then:

$$\text{partial correctness:} \quad [B][IN] \subseteq R \tag{8.2}$$
$$\text{total correctness for deterministic IN:} \quad B \subseteq [IN]S \;\&\; [B][IN] \subseteq R \tag{8.3}$$

Observe that for nondeterministic IN, (8.3) is stronger than (8.1). The formula that is equivalent to (8.1) for any IN is $B \subseteq ([IN] \cap R)S$, but this is hardly tractable in our approach.

If IN is an unstructured instruction (I36) of Sec.2, then (8.2) may be written as $[B]\mathrm{Head}(\alpha_n) \subseteq R$. Now, take an algorithm $\mathcal{A}$ corresponding to IN and let $\mathcal{A}_1$ results from $\mathcal{A}$ by adding new instruction $(\alpha_0,[B],\alpha_1)$ and setting α_0 to be initial. Of course $\mathrm{Head}_{\mathcal{A}_1}(\alpha_n) = [B]\mathrm{Head}_{\mathcal{A}}(\alpha_n)$. By lemmas 5.1 and 5.2 this implies immediately the following theorem:

<u>THEOREM</u> 8.1 (<u>inductive assertions method with binary postconditions</u>) For any algorithm $\mathcal{A}$, any set B and any relation R the inclusion $[B][\mathcal{A}] \subseteq R$ is true <u>iff</u> there exists a vector of relations $(H_1,\ldots,H_n)$ such that

1) $[B] \subseteq H_1$, 2) $\{H_i R_{ij} \subseteq H_j\}_{i,j=1}^{n}$, 3) $H_n \subseteq B$

This shows that the initiation semantics may be considered as the binary-postcondition counterpart of the inductive assertions method. An algebraic calculus for proving program properties in this way was described by Blikle [7] and by Blikle and Budkowski [8]. The continuation semantics does not lead to an analogue of the inductive assertions method.

Concerning the total-correctness proofs the formula (8.3) shows that in the deterministic case each such a proof may be splitted into two independent proofs: of partial correctness and of termination. In the former we may apply Theorem 8.1, in the latter - an appropriate generalization of Theorem 7.2 with C=S and A=S.

As mentioned in this and in the former section, the algebraic formulation of the total correctness is adequate only in the deterministic case. As has been observed by de Roever [26] this situation may be improved by introducing the "undefined element" $\perp$ and dealing with relations $R \subseteq (S \cup \{\perp\})^2$ that have three following properties: 1) $(\forall s \in S)(\exists \bar{s} \in S \cup \{\perp\}) sR\bar{s}$, 2) $\perp R \perp$, 3) $(\forall s \in S \cup \{\perp\})(\perp Rs \Rightarrow s = \perp)$. If [IN] denotes the resulting relation of IN in the new sense, then $s[\mathrm{IN}]\perp$ means nontermination for s (looping or blocking). The (unary) partial and total correctness have now the following formulations:

partial correctness: $(\forall b \in B)(\forall c)(b[\mathrm{IN}]c \Longrightarrow c \in C \vee c = \perp)$
total correctness: $(\forall b \in B)(\forall c)(b[\mathrm{IN}]c \Longrightarrow c \in C)$

and in our notation

partial correctness: $B[\mathrm{IN}] \subseteq C \cup \{\perp\}$
total correctness : $B[\mathrm{IN}] \subseteq C$.

Of course, these formulations are adequate for both the deterministic and the nondeterministic case. The Dijkstra weakest precondition gets also a nice formulation: $wp(\mathrm{IN}, C) = [\mathrm{IN}] \twoheadrightarrow C$ (see Sec.6).

9. BIBLIOGRAPHIC REMARKS

The calculus of binary relations in the form used in this paper were introduced and applied to program verification by Blikle [5] and then developed by Blikle and Mazurkiewicz [6-9,20,21]. The instructions fi-if and do-od are due to Dijkstra [10]. The iterative algorithms were introduced by Mazurkiewicz [9,20]. Fixed points in the description of computations appear implicitely in Kleene's [14] theory of recursion. In the context of program semantics they were used later by Scott and de Bakker [27], Bekic [4] and Park [25]. Independently Mazurkiewicz [19] introduces Tail functions with a fixed-point description. The ideas of Mazurkiewicz, combined with the similar concepts of Morris [23] and Landin [15] stimulate Strachey and Wadsworth [28] to develop their continuation semantics. A large monograph on this approach was written by Milne and Strachey [22]. A extension of the continuation semantics to the semantics of executions and to an abstract algebraic semantics was described by Blikle [6]. The fixed-point approach has also been studied extensively by the Dutch school of programming theory, for which we refer to de Bakker [1] and the references given there. Some concepts closely related to the initiation semantics appear in the Mazurkiewicz [21] paper. The initiation equations (under another name) were also used by de Bakker and Meertens [2] who also defined the $R \twoheadrightarrow C$ operation. The initiation semantics was applied to program verification by Blikle [7] and Blikle with Budkowski [8].

The idea of proving partial correctness by intermediate assertions goes back to Turing [30], but in the form known today was described by Floyd [11] and Hoare [12]. This method was studied extensively by Manna in a series of papers of which we refer to his early contribution [16] and the later monograhp [17]. Theorem 6.1 was formulated by Manna [16,17] but the first complete proof was given by de Bakker and Meertens [2] who also extended it to parameterless recursive procedures. Also in [2] BHead and Tail→C were proved to be vectors of inductive assertions. The concept of total-correctness was proposed by Manna and Pnueli [18] but the idea of well-founded sets is due to Floyd [11]. The calculus of weakest preconditions is due to Dijkstra [10]. It has also been studied by other authors, cf. de Bakker [1], Basu and Yeh [3], de Roever [26].

ACKNOWLEDGEMENT

I would like to thank my colleagues P.Dembinski, J.Leszczylowski and J. Winkowski for many stimulating discussions which contributed to the present shape of this paper.

REFERENCES

1. de Bakker, J.W. The fixed-point approach in semantics: theory and applications. In: Foundations of Comp. Sci. (J.W.de Bakker, Ed.) pp.3-53, 1975. Mathematical Centre Tracts 63, Amsterdam 1975
2. de Bakker, J.W. and Meertens, L.G.L.T. On the completeness of the inductive assertion method. J. Comp.Syst.Sci.,11(1975), 323-257
3. Basu, S.K. and Yeh, R.T. Strong verification of programs. IEEE Trans. on Software Eng., SE-1 (1975),339-345.
4. Bekić, H. Definable operations in general algebras and the theory of automata and flowcharts. unpublished manuscript, IBM Laboratory, Vienna 1969.
5. Blikle, A. Iterative systems; an algebraic approach, Bull. Acad. Polon. des Sci., Ser.sci.math.astronom. et phys., 20 (1971),51-55
6. Blikle, A. An analysis of programs by algebraic means. In: Mathematical Foundations of Comp. Sci. (A.Mazurkiewicz, Ed.), Banach Center Publications, vol.2 (1977), Polish Scientific Publishers, Warsaw 1977
7. Blikle, A. An analytic approach to the verification of iterative programs. Proc. IFIP-1977 Congress, Toronto 1977
8. Blikle, A. and Budkowski, S. Certification of microprograms by an algebraic method. Micro-9 Proc., Ninth Annual Workshop on Microprogramming, September 1976, 9-14
9. Blikle, A. and Mazurkiewicz, A. An algebraic approach to the theory of programs, algorithms, languages and recursiveness. In: Math. Found. Comp. Sci. (Proc. Warsaw-Jablonna, 1972), Warsaw 1972

10. Dijkstra, E. A Discipline of Programming. Prentice-Hall, Inc., Englewood Cliffs 1976
11. Floyd, R.W. Assigning meanings to programs. Proc. Symp. in Applied Math. 19 (1967), 19-32
12. Hoare, C.A.R. An axiomatic basis for computer programming, Communication of ACM, 12 (1969), 576-583
13. Katz, S. and Manna, Z. Logical analysis of programs. Communications of ACM, 19 (1976), 188-206
14. Kleene, S.C. Introduction to Metamathematics, North-Holland, Amsterdam 1952
15. Landin, P.J. The next 700 programming languages, Communication of ACM, 9 (1966), 157-164
16. Manna, Z. The correctness of programs. J.Comp. Syst. Sci., 3 (1969), 119-127
17. Manna, Z. Mathematical Theory of Computation. McGraw-Hill, New York 1974
18. Manna, Z. and Pnueli, A. Axiomatic approach to total correctness of programs. Acta Informatica (1974)
19. Mazurkiewicz, A. Proving algorithms by tail functions. Working paper for IFIP WG 2.2. February 1970, since published in Information and Control, 18 (1971), 220-226
20. Mazurkiewicz, A. Iteratively computable relations. Bull. Acad. Polon. Sci., Ser.sci.math.astronom. phys.,20 (1972), 793-797
21. Mazurkiewicz, A. Proving properties of processes. Algorytmy, 11 (1974), 5-22
22. Milne, R. and Strachey, Ch. A Theory of Programming Language Semantics, Chapman and Hall, London 1977
23. Morris, F.L. The next 700 programming language description, unpublished manuscript.
24. Mosses, P. The mathematical semantics of ALGOL 60. Technical Monograph PRG-12, Oxford University, 1974
25. Park, D. Fixpoint induction and proofs of program properties. In: Machine Intelligence, vol.5 (B.Meltzer and D.Michie eds.), pp.59-78. Edinburgh University Press, Edinburgh 1970
26. de Roever, W.P. Dijkstra's predicate transformer, non-determinism, recursion and termination. In: Math. Found. Comp. Sci. 1976 (Proc. Symp. Gdansk, 1976, A.Mazurkiewicz, Ed.) Lecture Note in CS, Springer, Berlin, 472-481
27. Scott, D. and de Bakker, J.W. A theory of programs, unpublished notes, IBM seminar, Vienna 1969
28. Strachey, C. and Wadsworth, C.P. Continuation, a mathematical semantics for handling full jumps. Technical Monograph PRG-11, Oxford 1974
29. Tarski, A. A lattice-theoretic fixedpoint theorem and its applications. Pacific Journal of Math., 5 (1955), 285-309
30. Turing, A.M. On checking a large routine. Report of a Conference on High Speed Automatic Calculating Machines, pp.67-69, University Mathematical Laboratory, Cambridge 1949

CLASSIFICATION OF THE CONTEXT-FREE LANGUAGES.

L. Boasson
U.E.R. de Mathématiques Université de Picardie - Amiens - F
and
"Laboratoire associé du CNRS "Informatique théorique et programmation"

The theory of Formal Languages started with a classification of the languages referred now as the Chomsky's hierarchy. Moreover, it quickly appeared that the "type 2 languages" were a very important class of languages to be studied. The first reason, and the main one in those days, was the fact it gave the best model of programming languages. This was so important they have been sometimes called "Algol-like Languages". Their classical denomination, that we shall use here, is however the Context-Free Languages. If this major aspect of this class gave raise to a lot of work, especially in the field of syntactical analysis, a lot of new reasons appeared to reenforce the interest of studying the context-free languages'family. We will briefly point out some of them.

If you consider the various areas of the Theoretical Computer Sciences, you can easily see some domains which are closely related to Formal Languages. Once more, for these domains, the context-free languages appear as fundamental. Taking, for instance, the formal power series, they appeared as a notion closely related to context free grammars [13] and various results of formal languages can be extented to power series (see [18] and especially [30]). Looking then to tree-theory, it is obvious this field can be considered (for a part) as a generalization of the languages'theory, even if this generalization is not trivial [14]. One should remark these extensions can be obtained in an easier way when working on simple subclasses of tree-grammars related to subclasses of context-free grammars.Moreover, some operations on languages can be extended to tree languages in different ways so that it gives a new point of view of these, even when considered as language operations (see [1, 17]). In these two examples, the formal languages'theory and especially the theory of context-free languages appear as a very good guide. But it turns out to be very helpful too in more recent areas. In particular, Program Schemes came up with a lot of problems about context-free languages [15]. This link is very tight for some problems like some decidability questions [19]. On the other hand, some well-known subclasses of the monadic recursive program schemes are closely related to classical subfamilies of the context-free languages [16]. Going on this way, some theory of semantics appeared rather recently. Once more the context-free languages seem to be useful. The situation here is not quite clear now, but it is undoubtful that there is some deep relation between these two areas (see for instance the algebraic semantics of [34]). In all these examples, any progress in the knowledge we have of the context-free languages may be helpful. These progresses seem to need a better insight of the family of these languages. We may hope to get it by building up a systematical and uniform way of classification of languages. When looking at this problem, the context-free languages turn out to have so many nice properties and to give raise to so many interesting questions that it seems worthwile to study them for their own sake. It is quite sure such a work will help to understand some basic problems of theoretical computer sciences.

We will describe in this paper the most powerfull ways already known to classify the languages. We will explain how they came out and point out some open questions in the field. A lot of results are not mentioned here and the bibliography is not at all complete. We arbitrarily decided to restrict our attention on the classification problem itself without looking at some other related questions.

I - The first subfamilies'definitions :

The first way which appeared to define subfamilies of the Context-Free Languages'family (abreviated here in CFL) is essentially the same one as the classical method defining the Chomsky's hierarchy : it is to add some restrictions on the grammar rules. The definition is then very clear on the grammars, but it may be difficult to prove a specific language cannot be generated by such a restricted grammar. This sort of approach started very early ; for instance, that was the original way used to define the linear languages [13] . Namely, a context-free grammar was said to be linear iff each right member of the rules contains at most one non-terminal letter. A language is then linear iff it can be generated by a linear grammar. Clearly, the first proof needed is that this family of languages, we denote here by Lin, is a proper subfamily of the CFL's. This was originally achieved by giving a counter-example, the technical details of the proof being more or less complicated. This sort of proof can be simplified or extended to various counter-examples when you can derive from the chosen restrictions a special "pumping lemma". This situation is illustrated by the linear languages case.

A very similar idea is to put restrictions on the pushdown machine recognizing the language. For instance, if you ask for the machine to be deterministic, you get the family of deterministic context-free languages, we denote by Det [21]. The situation is then the same as above : you have to prove that you define this way a proper subfamily of the CFL's, either directly or through a pumping lemma.(There is such a lemma for the family Det [35].) This way of defining subfamilies is the most natural one for defining the One-Counter Languages, Oct. You ask for the machine to use a single pushdown symbol . In this case, the first proofs, that Oct is a proper subfamily of the CFL's were rather complicated. No grammatical restrictions are known for defining this family. However, it often happens you can define the same family by both methods, each of them leading to different intuitions. This is the case, for instance for the family Lin [26] .

One of the most powerful operations on languages is the substitution. It can be extended to families of languages very easily [27] . You can then try to get new families of CFL's by such an operation applied to already known subfamilies. This construction was performed first with the linear languages. Denoting by Qr(1) the linear languages, called too the Quasi-rational languages of order 1, you define inductively the Quasi-rational languages of order n , Qr(n), by Qr(n) = Qr(n-1)σ Qr(1) where σ is the substitution of families of languages. The family Qrt of the Quasi

Rational Languages (= the "Non-Expansive Languages") is then the union over $n \geq 1$ of the Qr(n). A lot of various characterizations of these languages have been studied on grammars [33] and on machines [26]. Showing that the Qr(n) families are a proper hierarchy of families of languages and that the family Qrt is strictly included in the CFL's was done with complicated and long arguments [33, 37]. The simplification of these proofs appeared later when new techniques and results were available.

II - Rational Cones and Full AFL's :

The study of these families, as well as some others outside the CFL's showed a lot of them shared some closure properties. It led to try a uniform frame for working on families of languages. This frame came out with the AFL's theory [22]. A full AFL is defined as a family of languages closed under six operations : the three rational operations (which are the one needed to define the rational subsets of a monoïd : union, product and star) and three others : homomorphism, inverse homomorphism and intersection with regular sets. You then get two very different kinds of full AFL's : the principal ones and the non-principal ones. A full AFL $\mathcal{L}$ is said to be principal [23] iff there exists a language L_o in $\mathcal{L}$ such that any L in $\mathcal{L}$ can be obtained from L_o by using the full AFL's operations. Such a language L_o is called a full generator of the full AFL $\mathcal{L}$. For instance, the CFL's form a full AFL because of their classical closure properties [20]. It is principal because of the Chomsky-Schützenberger theorem [20]. You get from this result that $D_2'^*$, the one sided Dyck set over two pairs of parentheses, is a generator of the full AFL of the CFL's.

During the same period of time, an operation on languages was introduced [38] : it was defined by a non-deterministic finite automaton to which was added an output device. It was some sort of a non-deterministic version of the already known "generalized sequential machines" [20]. Studied in [32], these operations we call rational transductions appeared to be characterized as being the rational subsets of the product of two free monoids. Moreover, they could be described in a very useful way for formal languages' theory.

Thm 1 [32] : A subset $\hat{\tau}$ of $X^* \times Y^*$ is rational iff there exists a finite alphabet Z, a rational language R over Z and two homomorphisms ϕ and Ψ from Z^* to X^* and Y^* respectively, such that

$$\hat{\tau} = \{ (\phi h, \Psi h) \mid h \in R \}$$

(This theorem can be translated this way : whenever you map the language L_1 over X onto L_2 over Y by a rational transduction τ, you can use the R, ϕ and Ψ of the theorem and get $L_2 = \Psi(\phi^{-1} L_1 \cap R)$.)

You can then define a full AFL as a family of languages closed under the three rational operations and under rational transductions. Moreover, if you look back at our previous examples Lin and Oct, you may remark these families fail to be full AFL's because they are not closed under the rational operations. We can then naturally define.

Def : A family of languages is a rational cone iff it is closed under rational transductions.

A full AFL is a rational cone closed under the rational operations. The rela--

tions you have between cones and AFL's are then very tight.

Thm 2 [22] : The closure under the rational operations of a rational cone is a full AFL.
(This result says there is some sort of 1/2 commutativity between the rational operations and the rational transductions). We define then a principal rational cone as a cone $\mathcal{C}$ in which there exists L_o such that any L in $\mathcal{C}$ is an image of L_o under a rational transduction. As far as principality is concerned, the two notions are still related.

Thm 3 [23] : A full principal AFL is a principal rational cone.
(This result says that when dealing with a full principal AFL, you can always choose its generator in such a way you do not need the rational operations to get any language of the full AFL).

As we remarked above, we now have that Lin and Oct are two rational cones. They are both principal cones. The first one is generated by S_2 the symmetric language, that is the set of words of $D_2'^*$ which have only one "peak". The second one is generated by $D_1'^*$ the one-sided Dyck set over one pair of parentheses. From Theorem 2, we know the CFL's form a principal rational cone :

Thm 4 : The families Lin, Oct and CFL are principal rational cones.
For the CFL's, you get the principality once more through the Chomsky-Schützenberger's theorem, so that $D_2'^*$ generates the CFL's full AFL without using any rational operation. In the particular case of the CFL's, this is true for any generator (through in general, this is true only for some).

Thm 5 [10] : Any generator G of the full AFL of the CFL's is a generator of the rational cone of the CFL's.
(so that we can speak of generators of the CFL's without saying if we work with rational cones or with full AFL's).

If we look now to the Quasi-Rational languages, we get immediatly that the Qr(n) family is a principal rational cone. This follows from a general result saying the substitution of a principal cone in another principal cone gives raise to a principal cone. The fact the Qr(n) languages build up an infinite hierarchy shows the family Qrt is a non principal rational cone. Its closure under substitution shows too it is a non principal full AFL. Thus Qrt is stricly included in the CFL's. Moreover, this theory of families of languages allows a simple proof of the fact the Qr(n) are an infinite hierarchy ; the syntactic substitution of a language L_2 in a language L_1 is defined when L_1 and L_2 are on disjoint alphabets X_1, and X_2 by :

$$L_1 o L_2 = \{x_1u_1x_2u_2 \ldots x_nu_n \mid x_1x_2 \ldots x_n \in L_1,\ u_1, u_2, \ldots, u_n \in L_2,\ x_1, x_2, x_n \in X_1\}$$

We then have :

Syntactic Lemma [27] : Let $\mathcal{L}_1$ and $\mathcal{L}_2$ be two union-closed rational cones ; $L_1 o L_2 \in \mathcal{L}_1 o \mathcal{L}_2$ implies either $L_1 \in \mathcal{L}_1$ or $L_2 \in \mathcal{L}_2$.

This lemma can be used in many circumstances to prove an AFL is not principal. That is the case for instance of the family Cit of Iterated One-Counter languages defined by the substitution closure of Oct. That is the case too for the family Gre of the Greibach languages which is defined as the substitution closed full AFL generated by the linear and one-counter languages. This lemma shows also that you cannot find two proper sub-cones of the CFL's, say $\mathcal{L}_1$ and $\mathcal{L}_2$, such that $\mathcal{L}_1 \sigma \mathcal{L}_2$ = CFL which generalizes a previous result of [36] that showed this was true when the rational operations only were concerned.

This way of looking at the CFL's family leads to define naturally the largest full sub-AFL of the CFL's. It is easily shown to be exactly the family of those CFL's which are not generators of the family CFL. We denote it by Nge. The Syntactic Lemma can be used there to prove Nge is closed under substitution. It is then natural to look for an infinite hierarchy of cones the union of which would be Nge. This sort of hierarchy is not known. Moreover, it is not even known if

Conjoncture 1 [27] : Nge is a non-principal full AFL.
(The first idea [27] was that Nge was the same family than Gre. It has been proved to be false, so that Nge strictly contains Gre [7].)

III - The Rational Relations :

The classification obtained above looks like a "geography" of the CFL's. The languages are classified by the "area of the map" to which they belong. The importance of the CFL's family even in this theory appears clearly through the various properties it has. It is, in some sense, a guide to study the AFL's for themselves (See for instance, the questions dealing with AFL's closed under reversal [24] or AFL's of languages having the "semi-linear property" [25, 31].)

A closely related way of classifying languages appears when working on rational cones. The idea is very simple : it is to compare languages by comparing the rational cones they generate, with respect to inclusion (rather than to decide to which classical family they belong to). More precisely, a language L_1 dominates a language L_2 iff there exists a rational transduction mapping L_1 onto L_2 ; that is the same as saying that the rational cone generated by L_1 contains the cone generated by L_2. The languages L_1 and L_2 are rationnally equivalent iff L_1 dominates L_2 and L_2 dominates L_1, or, equivalently, iff L_1 and L_2 generate the same rational cone. Given then two languages, they may be equivalent ; if not, either one dominates the other or they are incomparable. For instance $D_2'^*$ dominates $D_1'^*$ and S_2. These two languages, S_2 and $D_1'^*$, are incomparable [9]. Obviously this approach will lead to further results if we can give some results dealing with the question "how L_1 can dominate L_2". We will show below such results can be proved. However, the idea of these came from studying the Oct family : it is by a precise looking at the way rational transductions could transform $D_1'^*$ that a special pumping lemma could be established for the One-Counter Languages [6].

Coming back to the question "how can L_1 dominante L_2", it turns out that what is generally difficult to prove is that L_1 does not dominate L_2. The first proofs that, for instance, $D_1'^*$ does not dominate S_2 were rather complicated. If you look at the way these proofs were built, you can guess there is some common method you may hope to concentrate in a methodological result. Let define an iterative pair [9] of the word f in the language L as a factorization of f in $\alpha u \beta v \phi$ such that for any integer n, $\alpha u^n \beta v^n \phi$ is in L. To such a pair, we associate two sets of integers $R_n = \{ m \mid \alpha u^n \beta v^m \phi \in L \}$ and $L_n = \{ m \mid \alpha u^m \beta v^n \phi \in L \}$. The pair is then right strict (resp. left strict) iff R_n (resp. L_n) is finite for all n . It is strict when it is left and right strict. It is very strict if it is strict and the two sets R_n and L_n have a uniformely bounded number of elements for all n . We can state now :

Thm 6 [9] : Let L_1 be a context-free language dominating L_2 . If L_2 contains a word admitting a left strict (resp. right strict, strict, very strict) iterative pair, L_1 contains a word admitting such a pair too.

This gives a formalization to the intuitive reasons why $\{ a^n b^m \mid n \geqslant m \geqslant 1 \}$ and $\{ a^m b^n \mid n \geqslant m \geqslant 1 \}$ are incomparable ; it gives too the same formalization of why the reversal operation is not a rational transduction. This result can even be sharpened [9] . Moreover, it can be generalized to simultaneous iterative pairs (see [4] for such a generalization) giving then for instance a proof which is very near the intution of why the family Lin is not closed under product. These results may be used in rather complicated situations (see for instance, the end of [9]). It may be used to give another simple proof of the fact that the Qr(n) languages family form an infinite hierarchy. It gives some ideas too of how complicated a language L has to be so that it turns out to be a generator of the CFL's. This is one of the possible ways which can be tried (but needs then some improvements !!!) to show that

Conjecture 2 [12] : Let L be a context-free language over X and a, b, c three letters not in X.
If L dominates $< L > = \{ a^n f b g c^n \mid n \geqslant 1 , f, g \in L \}$ then L is a generator of the CFL's.
(Remark that if conjecture 2 is true, then conjecture 1 is true too).

For proving a language L is a generator of the CFL's, you exhibit a rational transduction mapping L onto an already known generator G . If you look at the way this is generally achiev ed, you notice that very frequently this generator G turns out to be E_1 , the language generated by $S \to aSbSc$ and $S \to d$ over $\{a, b, c, d\}$. (The fact E_1 is a generator is proved in [36] ; see [2] for a good example of the way E_1 can be used to prove some languages are generators). This situation is not an "accident". It can be explained now because of a recent result :

Thm 7 [5] : For any generator G of the CFL's, there exists a rational language K and an homomorphism ϕ such that
$$E_1 = \phi^{-1} G \cap K.$$
The proof of theorem 7 can be used to show :

Thm 8 [5] : For any generator G of the CFL's, there exists a rational language R such that $G \cap R$ is a non-ambiguous (and even deterministic) generator.

IV - Cylinders :

The classification methods described until now appear as very powerful. The algebraic characterization of rational transduction given by theorem 1 is extensively used. However, this sort of methods will always miss any possible descriptions of families like Det. That is because whenever you allow homomorphism to be used, the properties like determinism disappear. For this reason, some techrical modifications have be proposed : let a cylinder be a family of languages closed under inverse homomorphism and intersection with regular sets. We have then that any rational cone is a cylinder. Moreover Det is a cylinder. The non-ambiguous context-free languages form a cylinder which is not a rational cone. This sort of families appears as less nice to study. However, it seems somehow interesting for some complexity questions. The already known results about cylinders are summarized by the

Thm 9 :

- The CFL's are a principal cylinder [28].
- The families Lin and Oct are non-principal cylinders [11, 3]
- The family Det is a non-principal cylinder [29]

(A cylinder $\mathcal{C}$ is principal whenever there exists L_o in $\mathcal{C}$ such that any L in $\mathcal{C}$ can be obtained from to through inverse homomorphism and intersection with regular sets.)

Remark that the fact Lin and Oct are non-principal cylinders and principal rational cones shows the relation between cones and cylinders is not so tight as between cones and AFL's. If you look back to Theorem 7, you see it essentially says that E_1 is in the cylinder generated by any generator of the CFL's rational cone.

However much more complicated to study than the rational cones and however it sometimes looks like a too much precise classification method, cylinders are very interesting for working on families which are not rational cones. In this sort of questions, one of the most interesting but difficult question is the

Conjecture 3 : The cylinder of non ambiguous languages is not principal.

Bibliography :

1. Arnold : Systemes d'Equations dans le Magmoïde. Ensembles Rationnels et Algébriques d'Arbres. Thèse de Doctorat d'Etat - Lille I (1977).

2. Autebert J.M. : Quelques générateurs des Langages algébriques. G.I. Fachtagüng (1973) - p 124-131.

3. Autebert J.M. : Non principalité du Cylindre des Langages à Compteur (à paraître dans Math. System Theory).

4. Beauquier J. : Contribution à l'étude de la complexité structurelle des langages algébriques. Thèse de Doctorat d'Etat - Paris 7 (1977).

5. Beauquier J. : Générateurs algébriques non-ambigus in Automata, Languages and Programming (Edinbourg, 1976) p 66-73.

6. Boasson L. : Two iteration theorems for some families of languages. Jour. of Computer and System Sciences, 7, n° 6 (1973), 583-596.

7. Boasson L. : The inclusion of the substitution closure of linear and one-counter languages in the largest sub-AFL of the family of context-free languages is proper. Information Processing Letters 2 (1973), 135-140.

8. Boasson L. : On the largest (full) sub-AFL of the context-free languages. Math. Foundations of Computer Sciences (1975), 194-198.

9. Boasson L. : Langages algébriques, Paires itérantes et transductions rationnelles Theoretical Computer Science, 2 (1976), 209-223.

10. Boasson L. & Nivat M. : Sur diverses familles de langages fermées par transduction rationnelle. Acta informatica, 2 (1973), 180-188.

11. Boasson L. & Nivat M. : Le cylindre des langages linéaires (à paraître dans Math. System Theory).

12. Boasson L., Crestin J.P. & Nivat M. : Familles de langages translatables et fermées par crochet. Acta Informatica, 2 (1973), 383-393.

13. Chomsky N. & Schützenberger M.P. : The algebraic theory of context-free languages. Computer Programming and Formal Systems. North Holland (1963).

14. Courcelle B. : A representation of trees by languages. Theoretical Computer Sciences

15. Courcelle B. & Nivat M. : Algebraic families of interpretations. 17^{h} annual symposium on foundations of Computer Science (1976), 137-146.

16. Cousineau G. & Rifflet J.M. : Schémas de programmes : problèmes d'équivalence et de complexité. Thèse de 3e cycle - Paris 7 (1974).

17. Dauchet M. : Transductions inversibles de foret. Thèse de 3e cycle - Université de Lille I (1975).

18. Fliess M. : Sur certaines familles de séries formelles. Thèse de doctorat d'Etat Université Paris 7 (1972).

19. Friedman E. : Simple languages and free schemes. 17th annual symposium on foundations of Computer Science (1976), 159-165.

20. Ginsburg S. : The mathematical theory of context-free languages. Mc Graw Hill (1966).

21. Ginsburg S. & Greibach S. : Deterministic context-free languages. Information and Control, 9 (1966), 620-648.

22. Ginsburg S. & Greibach S. : Studies in abstract families of languages. Memoirs of the Amer. Math. Soc., 113 (1966), 285-296.

23. Ginsburg S. & Greibach S. : Principal AFL. Journ. of Computer and System Sciences 4 (1970), 308-338.

24. Ginsburg S. & Harrison M. : On the closure of AFL under reverseal. Information and Control, 17 (1970), 385-409.

25. Ginsburg S. & Spanier E.H. : AFL with the semi-linear property. Jour. of Computer and System Sciences, 5 (1971), 365-396.

26. Greibach S. : An infinite hierarchy of context-free languages. Jour. of A.C.M., 16 (1969), 91-106.

27. Greibach S. : Chain of full AFL's. Math. System Theory, 4 (1970), 231-242.

28. Greibach S. : The hardest context-free languages. Siam. Jour. on Computing, 2 (1973), 304-310.

29. Greibach S. : Jump PDA's and hierarchies of deterministic context-free languages. Siam Jour. on Computing, 3 (1974), 111-127.

30. Jacob G. : Représentation et substitution matricielle dans la théorie algébrique des transductions. Thèse de doctorat d'Etat - Paris 7 (1975).

31. Latteux M. : Cones rationnels commutativement clos. (à paraître dans RAIRO).

32. Nivat M. : Transductions des langages de Chomsky. Annales de l'Institut Fourier, 18 (1968), 339-456.

33. Nivat M. : Transductions des langages de Chomsky (Ch. VI). Thèse de doctorat d'Etat - Paris (1967).

34. Nivat M. : On the interpretation of recursive polyadic schemes. Instituto Nazionale di Alta Matematica. Symposia mathematica. Vol. 15 (1974).

35. Ogden W. : Intercalation theorems for pushdown store and stack languages. Ph. D. Thesis - Standford (1968).

36. Schützenberger M.P. : Sur un langage équivalent au langage de Dyck. In Logic, Methodology and philisophy of science - North Holland (1973), 197-203.

37. Yntema Y.K. : Inclusion relations among families of context-free languages. Information and control, 10 (1967), 572-597.

38. Elgot C.C. & Me zei J.E. : On relations defined by generalized finite automata. IBM Jour. of Res. and Dev. 9 (1962), 47-68.

FINITE AUTOMATON FROM A FLOWCHART SCHEME POINT OF VIEW

Calvin C. Elgot

IBM Thomas J. Watson Research Center

Yorktown Heights, New York 10598

1. Introduction

The notions "finite automaton" (in the sense of Rabin and Scott, [RS]) and "finite sequential machine" (in the sense of E. F. Moore, [EM]) arose from viewing a Turing machine on the one hand and a digital computer on the other, as consisting of a "finite state control" in communication with a large, possibly infinite, memory. The digital computer -- connection is, perhaps, a bit less direct passing through various idealizations of "sequential circuit" including the nerve nets of Kleene (a further development of work initiated by McCullough and Pitts), the logical nets of Burks and Wright, [BW], and the (asynchronous) circuits of D. A. Huffman, [DH]. Since those beginnings the paths of evolution of finite automaton theory on the one hand and <u>controlled</u> <u>machine</u> <u>theory</u> on the other seldom seem to cross. While it may only be a single individual's perception, I see the "automaton path" as being most directly related to non-deterministic syntactical and the "controlled memory path" most directly connected to deterministic, semantical, considerations related to computation. This paper is intended to be one of those seemingly seldom crossings. Initially, we deal with deterministic notions.

The notions "finite automaton" and "initialized Moore machine" are very simply related. The former involves an

input set, Σ

internal state set, S

designated or final set, $D \subseteq S$

besides "an initial state" $s_0 \in S$ and the key "transition function." The <u>behavior</u> $||A||$ of the finite automaton A is a certain subset of Σ^*, the set of all finite words w which "take" s_0 into an element s_0w of D. The latter notion is obtained from the former by replacing "final set" by "output function" $S \to \mathcal{O}$, where $\mathcal{O}$ is a set (of "outputs"). The <u>behavior</u> $||M||$ of an initialized Moore machine M is a function of the form $\Sigma^* \to \mathcal{O}$. Specifically, $||M||:\Sigma^* \to \mathcal{O}$ is obtained as follows:

$||M||(w) = o \in \mathcal{O}$, where o is the result of applying the output function of M to $s_0 w$. Thus, if $\mathcal{O} = \{0,1\}$ and the output function of M is the characteristic function of D, then $||M||$ is the characteristic function of $||A||$.

Our further considerations involve the notion "Γ-flowchart scheme," briefly, "Γ-charts," as well. See [CE-SP] p. 46. Here Γ is a sequence $(\Gamma_0, \Gamma_1, \Gamma_2, \cdots)$ of pairwise disjoint sets. In that paper Γ-charts are related to "structured programming" in both narrow and broad senses. (See also a forthcoming paper with J. C. Shepherdson.)

If $f:X \to Y$ is a function and $x \in X$ we write $f(x)$ or xf for the image of x under f.

2. Γ-charts

Let $[n] = \{1,2,\cdots,n\}$, where $n \in N$ is a non-negative integer.

A two-sorted-directed graph, briefly, a digraph consists of sets V, E, (vertices, edges) together with functions $\partial_i : E \to V$, $i \in [2]$, (for source and target, respectively, of an edge). For present purposes it is sufficient to assume the digraphs are locally finite in the sense that the number of outedges of each vertex is finite. Thus such a digraph has associated with it an outdegree function $\Theta : V \to N$.

We call a locally finite digraph $(V, E, \partial_1, \partial_2)$ an outedge digraph if it satisfies

(2.1) $E = \{(v,i) \mid i \in [r]$, where $r = v\Theta\}$

(2.2) $(v, i)\partial_1 = v$.

Thus an outedge digraph is specified by (V, E, ∂_2).

We say the pair consisting of a digraph $(V, E, \partial_1, \partial_2)$ and a function $e:[p] \to V$ is a p-exit digraph if

(2.3) e is injective

(2.4) $je\Theta = 0$ for $j \in [p]$.

A digraph together with a pointing (or begin) function $b:[n] \to V$ is an n-pointed digraph. Let F be an n-pointed-p-exit outedge digraph, notation:

(2.5) $n \xrightarrow[S]{F} p$, where $S = V - \{je \mid j \in [p]\}$.

If (2.5) is further enriched by a labeling function $\lambda : S \to \bigcup\Gamma = \Gamma_0 \cup \Gamma_1 \cup \Gamma_2 \cup \cdots$, which is outdegree-compatible in the sense $s\lambda \in \Gamma_{[v\Theta]}$ for each $s \in S$, we obtain the notion Γ-chart (2.5).

The case $\Gamma_i = \emptyset$, for $i \neq 1,2$, $n = 1 = p$, is connected with structured programming in the narrow sense. The connection is suggested by calling Γ_2 a set of "predicate letters" and calling Γ_1 a set of "operation letters."

3. Theorem linking initialized Moore machines and certain Γ-charts

In [CE-SP] the notion of the strong behavior $||F||$ of a Γ-chart (2.5) is defined and related to programming semantics (see Theorem 4.7). In [EBT] it is pointed out two Γ-charts have the same strong behavior iff they "unfold" into isomorphic n-rooted, suitably labeled "trees."

Let M be an initialized Moore machine whose input set $\Sigma = [m]$ and whose internal state set is S. We correlate with M a Γ-chart, where $\Gamma_m = \mathcal{O} = \bigcup\Gamma$

$$1 \xrightarrow[S]{M\underline{\underline{c}}} 0$$

as follows. The target function of $M\underline{\underline{c}}$ is the transition function of M, the labeling function of $M\underline{\underline{c}}$ is the output function of M. The following theorem is obvious.

Theorem 3.1 The function $\underline{\underline{c}}$ described above is a bijection between $([m],\mathcal{O})$-initialized Moore machines and Γ-charts $1 \to 0$ where $\Gamma_m = \mathcal{O} = \bigcup\Gamma$. Moreover, $||M_1|| = ||M_2||$ iff $||M_1\underline{\underline{c}}|| = ||M_2\underline{\underline{c}}||$.

The significance of the theorem is that it permits us to use the methods of analysis employed for flowchart schemes to initialized Moore machines and finite automata. The result in the case of finite automata with input set $\Sigma = \{1,2,\cdots,m\}$ is a description of their behavior by means of primitive operations different from the usual ∨, •, * . These different primitives have the advantage that they honor multiplicity. They have the disadvantage that a "multi-sorted context" is necessary to make them meaningful.

In order to conveniently take multiplicity into account, we shall deal with multisubsets of Σ^*, i.e. functions $f:\Sigma^* \to N$, rather than subsets of Σ^*. If $u \in \Sigma^*$ and $uf = n$, we may say "u occurs in f with multiplicity n". (M. P. Schutzenberger [MS], seems to have been the first to consider multiplicity in connection with finite automata.) If $uf = 0$, we say f is free of u or u does not occur in f.

4. The semiring R of multisubsets of Σ^*.

Let R be the collection of all functions $f:\Sigma^* \to N$. We equip R with binary operations +,• as follows.

(4.1) $u(f_1 + f_2) = uf_1 + uf_2$, $u \in \Sigma^*$

(4.2) $w(f_1 \cdot f_2) = \Sigma\{uf_1 \cdot vf_2 \mid uv = w \in \Sigma^*\}$.

The operation defined in (4.2) makes sense because for each w there are only a finite number of pairs (u,v) such that $u \cdot v = w$. With respect to these operations R is a semiring (cf. [CE-MT]). The $1 \in R$ is the function $\Sigma^* \to N$ whose value is $1 \in N$ on the null sequence $\Lambda \in \Sigma^*$ and is $0 \in N$ elsewhere. The $0 \in R$ is the constant function $\Sigma^* \to N$ with value $0 \in N$.

By an augmented $n \times p$ matrix α over R, (also written $\alpha:n \to p$), we mean a pair $(A;a)$ where A is an $n \times p$ matrix whose entries are in R and $\underline{a}$ is an $n \times 1$ matrix whose entries are in R. Given $\beta = (B;b) : p \to q$ we define

(4.3) $\alpha \cdot \beta = (A \cdot B;\ a + A \cdot b)$

This multiplication is associative and possesses an identity for each n. The identity augmented matrix I_n consists of the $n \times n$ identity matrix 1 paired with the vector of n zeros.

We require the following definition, where $\alpha_i : n_i \to p$ is an augmented matrix $(A_i;\ a_i)$.

(4.4) The <u>source pairing</u>, or <u>row pairing</u>, (α_1, α_2) is the augmented matrix $\alpha = (A;a) : n_1 + n_2 \to p$ where

$$A = \begin{bmatrix} A_1 \\ A_2 \end{bmatrix} \quad \text{and} \quad a = \begin{bmatrix} a_1 \\ a_2 \end{bmatrix}.$$

We say a matrix A is <u>free of $w \in \Sigma^*$</u> if $wA_{ij} = 0$ for each i,j, i.e. if A_{ij} is free of w for each i,j. If $A:n \to n$ is free of $\Lambda \in \Sigma^*$ then A^{r+1} is free of all words of length $\leq r$. This observation is sufficient to show that the infinite sum

(4.5) $A^* = 1 + A + A^2 + \cdots$

is well defined if A is free of Λ.

Let $\alpha : n \to p+n$, $\alpha = (A;a)$ and suppose $A = [A_1\ A_2]$ in block matrix form where $A_1 : n \to p$, $A_2 : n \to n$ (i.e. A_1 consists of the first p columns of A and A_2 consists of the next n columns of A) and where A_2 is free of 1. Then the equation in $\xi : n \to p$

(4.6) $\xi = \alpha \cdot (I_p, \xi)$

has a unique solution among all augmented matrices over R. Indeed, if $\xi = (X;\ x)$, the solution is $X = A_2^* \cdot A_1$, $x = A_2^* \cdot a$.

We call the unique solution to (4.6) the iterate of α and represent it by $\alpha^\dagger : n \to p$.

5. <u>$n \to p$ automaton</u>

The notion (deterministic, completely defined) <u>automaton $\mathcal{A}:n \to p$ with input set [m]</u> is obtained from the notion Γ-chart where $\Gamma_m = \{0,1\}$ and $\Gamma_i = \emptyset$ for $i \neq m$, by replacing the labeling function λ of the chart by a <u>designated set</u> $D = \lambda^{-1}(0)$, i.e. the set $D \subseteq S$, for which $\lambda : S \to \{0,1\} = \cup\Gamma$ is the characteristic function. By the <u>behavior</u> $||\mathcal{A}||$ of $\mathcal{A}$ we mean the augmented $n \times p$ matrix $(A;a)$ over R (the semiring of multisubsets of Σ^* where $\Sigma = [m]$) defined as follows, where $A_{ij} : \Sigma^* \to N$, $a_i : \Sigma^* \to N$ are functions for $i \in [n]$, $j \in [p]$:

wA_{ij} is the number (necessarily finite; even in the non-deterministic case) of paths in $\mathcal{A}$ from $b(i)$ to exit j with "label" w,

wa_i is the number (necessarily finite; even in the non-deterministic case) of paths in $\mathcal{A}$ from $b(i)$ to a vertex in D with label w.

Corresponding to the three operations $\cdot$, (,), $\dagger$ on augmented matrices, there are finiteness-preserving operations (see [CCE-SP]) on automata such that

(5.1) $||\mathcal{A}\cdot\mathcal{B}|| = ||\mathcal{A}||\cdot||\mathcal{B}||$

(5.2) $||(\mathcal{A}_1,\mathcal{A}_2)|| = (||\mathcal{A}_1||, ||\mathcal{A}_2||)$

(5.3) $||\mathcal{A}^\dagger|| = ||\mathcal{A}||^\dagger$.

The $\dagger$ operation on automata (as on augmented matrices) bears a qualification. To state the qualification, let $\mathcal{A}:n \to p+n$. The qualification is this: for each $i \in [n]$, $b(i)$ is not any of the exits $p+1,p+2,\cdots,p+n$; it may, however, be exit j for some $j \in [p]$. Then $\mathcal{A}^\dagger$ is defined iff $||\mathcal{A}||$ is defined and the equality above holds.

From the definitions involved the following is obvious.

<u>Proposition 5.1</u> The behavior $||\mathcal{A}|| = (A;a)$ of a (deterministic) automaton $\mathcal{A}:n \to p$ is <u>deterministic</u> in the following sense:

the multiplicity of words in $A_{i1} + A_{i2} + \cdots + A_{ip} + a_i$ is at most one, for each $i \in [n]$.

Moreover, for each $i \in [n]$, $A_{i1} + A_{i2} + \cdots A_{ip}$ is <u>prefix-free</u> in the sense if w occurs in it (with multiplicity one) and u is a proper prefix of w, then u does not occur in it, i.e. occurs in it with multiplicity 0.

6. <u>Atomic and trivial automata</u>

Corresponding to each of the two elements in $\Gamma_m = \{0,1\}$ are two <u>atomic</u> automata γ_0, γ_1; cf. Figures 1, 2. For each $i \in \{0,1\}$ the automaton $\gamma_i:1 \to m$ consists of one non-exit vertex and m exits, $b(1)$ is the non-exit and the jth edge from $b(1)$ points to exit j for each $j \in [m]$; automaton γ_0 has $b(1)$ designated, while automaton γ_1 does not have $b(1)$ designated. Thus if $||\gamma_i|| = (C_i;c_i)$, we have for each $i \in \{0,1\}$, $C_i = [\sigma_1\sigma_2 \cdots \sigma_m] : 1 \to m$, where $\sigma_j;\Sigma^* \to N$ has the value 1 on $j \in \Sigma = [m]$ and 0 elsewhere, and $c_0 = 1 \in R$, $c_1 = 0 \in R$.

An automaton $\mathcal{A}:n \to p$ is trivial if its internal set is empty. Such an automaton is fully specified by its begin function $b:[n] \to [p]$. Thus we write $||b|| = ||\mathcal{A}||$. If $||\mathcal{A}|| = (A;a)$, then $A_{ij} = 1 \in R$ iff $b(i) = j$; if $A_{ij} \neq 1$ it is $0 \in R$; $a = 0$.

From the definitions involved the following is obvious.

Theorem 6.1 The analogue of Theorem 3.1 relating [m]-automata $n \to p$ and Γ-charts $n \to p$, with $\bigcup\Gamma = \Gamma_m = \{0,1\}$, is valid.

7. Behaviors of finite automata

An automaton or augmented matrix $n \to p$ is called scalar if $n = 1$. For scalar automata, there is a substitution operation (cf. [CE-SP], p. 52) which operates on automata $\mathcal{A}:1 \to n$, $\mathcal{B}_i:1 \to p$, $i \in [n]$, to produce an automaton $\mathcal{A}\cdot(\mathcal{B}_1, \mathcal{B}_2, \cdots, \mathcal{B}_n)$; similarly, for augmented matrices. The operation is atomic substitution if $\mathcal{A}$ is an atom.

Theorem 7.1 The collection of behaviors of finite scalar automata is the smallest class of augmented row matrices which contains $||\gamma_0||$, $||\gamma_1||$, $||b||$ for each function $b:1 \to p$ and is closed under atomic substitution and scalar iteration. (Analogue of Theorem 4.1 of [CE-SP].)

Corollary 7.2 The collection of behaviors of finite automata (i.e. the internal set is finite) is the smallest class of augmented matrices which contains $||b||$ for each function $b:[n] \to [p]$, contains $||\gamma_0||$ and $||\gamma_1||$ and is closed w.r.t. source pairing, $\cdot$ and $\dagger$ □

Explicitly, $||\gamma_0|| = ([\sigma_1\sigma_2 \cdots \sigma_m]; 1)$, $||\gamma_1|| = ([\sigma_1\sigma_2 \cdots \sigma_m]; 0)$.

Proof From Theorem 7.1, (5.1) and (5.2) □

8. The non-deterministic case

In the context of our discussion, "non-determinism" may conveniently be introduced by permitting two additional "atomic automata" as indicated in Figures 3 and 4. In contrast with Figures 1 and 2, where the edges are labelled with elements of Σ, in Figures 3 and 4, the edges are labelled with the null sequence $\Lambda \in \Sigma^*$. The heavy dot indicates a designated vertex. We restrict ourselves to well-formed (i.e. no closed path has label $\Lambda \in \Sigma^*$) non-deterministic automata. We note

$||+_0|| = ([1,1];\ 1)$

$||+_1|| = ([1,1];\ 0)$.

The analogues of Theorems 7.1 and 7.2 hold for non-deterministic automata. In 7.2 "contains $||\gamma_0||$, $||\gamma_1||$" is replaced by "contains $||\gamma_0||$, $||\gamma_1||$, $||+_0||$, $||+_1||$". Theorem 7.1 remains unchanged so long as "atomic substitution" is properly understood.

The formulas (5.1), (5.2), (5.3) remain valid for non-deterministic automata.

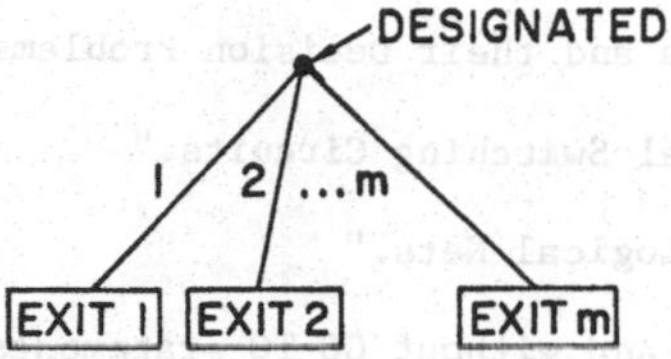

Figure 1, $\gamma_0 : 1 \to m$

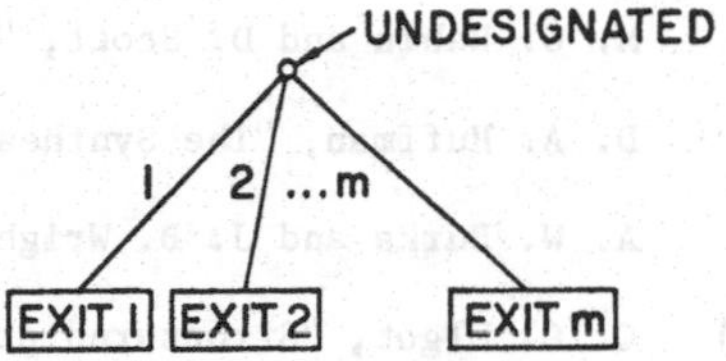

Figure 2, $\gamma_1 : 1 \to m$

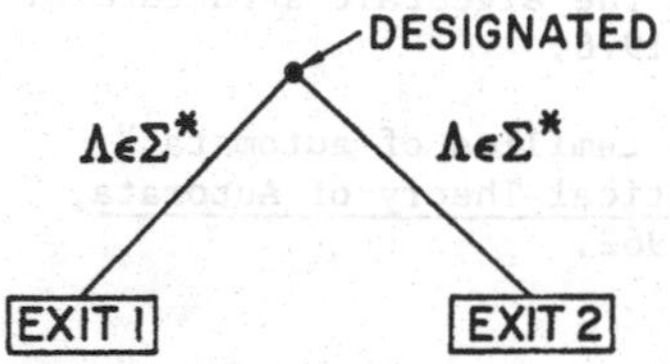

Figure 3, $+_0 : 1 \to 2$

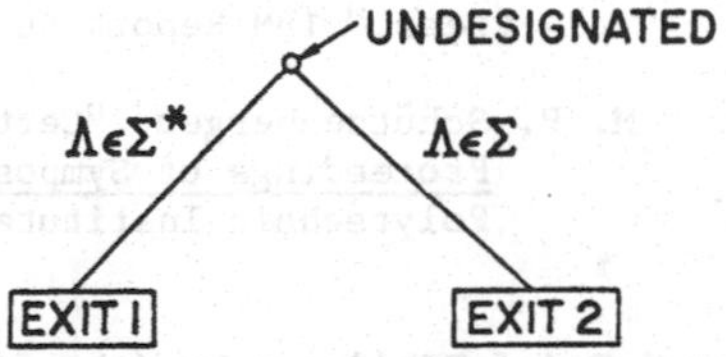

Figure 4, $+_1 : 1 \to 2$

9. Concluding Remark and Theorem

Note that the treatment of finite automata and certain aspects of "schematology" related to controlled memory machines have been entirely unified. On the other hand, at the moment, we lack a link with "tree automata".

Our discussion can be conveniently (and, perhaps, dramatically) summarized as follows.

Theorem 9.1 The family, indexed by pairs $n, p \in N$, of behaviors of finite automata $n \to p$ with input set $[m]$ is a description of the iterative theory freely generated by two morphisms $1 \to m$. (The morphisms $1 \to 0$ are the behaviors of "ordinary" finite automata.)

Proof From the first paragraph of section 3, Theorem 6.1 and Corollary 4.1.2 of [EBT].

References

The following two papers appear in Automata Studies, Annals of Mathematical Studies, No. 34, edited by C. E. Shannon and J. McCarthy, Princeton University Press 1956, where other papers of interest also appear.

[EM] E. F. Moore, "Gedanken-Experiements on Sequential Machines."

[SK] S. C. Kleene, "Representation of Events in Nerve Nets and Finite Automata."

The following three papers appear in Sequential Machines: Selected Papers, edited by E. F. Moore, Addison-Wesley 1964, other papers of interest also appear. (An extensive bibliography is also included.)

[RS] M. O. Rabin and D. Scott, "Finite Automata and their Decision Problems."

[DH] D. A. Huffman, "The Synthesis of Sequential Switching Circuits."

[BW] A. W. Burks and J. B. Wright, "Theory of Logical Nets."

[CE-SP] C. C. Elgot, "Structured programming with and without GO TO statements," IBM Research Report RC-5626, September 1975, also IEEE Trans on Software Eng. SE-2, No. 1, March 1976. Erratum and Corrigendum IEEE Trans. on Software Eng. September 1976.

[CE-MT] C. C. Elgot, "Matricial theories," IBM Research Report RC-4564, October 1973, to appear in Journal of Algebra 42, No. 2, October 1976.

[EBT] C. C. Elgot, S. L. Bloom, R. Tindell, "On the algebraic structure of rooted trees," IBM Report RC 6230, October 1976.

[MS] M. P. Schützenberger, "Certain elementary families of automata," Proceedings of Symposium on Mathematical Theory of Automata, Polytechnic Institute of Brooklyn 1962.

Additional Brief Bibliography (the first five are closely related)

[1] S. L. Bloom, C. C. Elgot, "The existence and construction of free iterative theories," IBM Research Report RC-4937, July 1974, also JCSS 12, No. 3, June 1976.

[2] S. L. Bloom, S. Ginali, J. D. Rutledge, "Scalar and vector iteration," IBM Research Report RC-5986, May 1976. (To appear in JCSS)

[3] C. C. Elgot, "Monadic computation and iterative algebraic theories," IBM Research Report RC-4564, October 1973, also in Logic Colloquium '73, Vol. 80, Studies in Logic, H. E. Rose and J. C. Shepherdson, Ed., North Holland 1975.

[4] S. Ginali, "Iterative algebraic theories, infinite trees, and program schemata," Dissertation, University of Chicago, June 1976.

[5] C. C. Elgot, "The external behavior of machines," Proceedings of Third Int'l Conf. on System Sciences (1970), also IBM Research Report RC-2740 (December 1969).

[6] E. Engeler, "Structure and meaning of elementary programs," Symposium on Semantics of Algorithmic Languages Proceedings, pp. 89-101, Springer Verlag 1971.

[7] E. G. Manes, Algebraic Theories, Academic Press, 1976.

[8] S. Eilenberg, J. B. Wright, "Automata in general algebras," Information and Control 11, pp. 452-470 (1967).

[9] J. Goguen, J. Thatcher, E. Wagner, J. Wright, "Initial algebra semantics and continuous algebras," IBM Research Report RC-5701 (1975). To appear in JACM.

[10] M. Wand, "Mathematical foundations of language theory," Dissertation. Project MAC, MIT (1973).

A NEW TYPE OF MODELS OF COMPUTATION

E. Engeler, Zurich

The present paper reports on the search of new models for computation in particular for the treatment of questions of computing with indefinite or infinite objects and operations, with non-determinism and parallelism. We pursue this search in the rather abstract framework of (type-free) Lambda calculus. This has advantages of mathematical/aesthetical nature; as for practical application, everybody now has learned to make the step to programming languages, and we shall not insist here on spelling that out.

As a dividend, our search has yielded a model construction for the pure Lambda calculus, which we shall present first in its simplest form. In the second part we make remarks, to be elaborated in the final version of this paper, about the questions mentioned above.

1. A pocket-model of the pure λβ-calculus

We presuppose a formulation of the λβ-calculus in which $X, Y, Z, \ldots$ are the variables, application is written as juxtaposition of terms, MN and abstraction by $\lambda X.M$. If M and N are terms then M_X^N is the result of substituting N for every free occurence of the variable X in M . We deal exclusively with equations between terms.

A model of the λβ-calculus consists of a set of objects on which operations of application and abstraction are defined in such a way that the well-known axioms and rules of conversion hold.

In our pocket-model the elements of the model are sets of formulas of a language L defined as follows: A is a non-empty set of atomic formulas; in the simplest case $A = \{\alpha\}$; Ξ is a set of formal variables, $\Xi = \{\xi, \eta, \zeta, \dots\}$. Formulas of L will be denoted by letters of the lower case Greek alphabet.

$A \cup \Xi \subseteq L$;
if σ and δ are in L then so are $(\sigma;\delta)$ and $(\sigma \to \delta)$;
no other words are in L.

With L_o we denote the set of formulas of L without formal variables. We say that δ is of the form $\delta(\xi/\sigma)$ if there is a formula $\delta(\xi)$ in which the formal variable ξ may or may not occur, and from which δ results by substituting σ for zero or more occurrencies of ξ.

We introduce a closure operation W^+ on sets $W \subseteq L$ by the following rules:

$W \subseteq W^+$;
(i) if σ; $(\sigma \to \delta)$ is in W^+ then so is δ;
(ii) if δ is of the form $\delta(\xi/\sigma)$ and $\rho \in L$, and
if $\delta \in W^+$, then σ; $(\rho \to \delta(\xi/\rho)) \in W^+$.

In order to construct the model we introduce a semantics function $\mathcal{S}$ which assigns to each term M of the Lambda calculus a closed set $M_{\mathcal{S}}$ of formulas of L. Such a function is determined by a map $\mathcal{S}$ from the set $\{X, Y, Z, \dots\}$ of variables with $\mathcal{S}(X) \subseteq L_o$, $\mathcal{S}(X) \neq \emptyset$. The following definition then describes $\mathcal{S}$:

$$X_{\mathcal{S}} = \mathcal{S}(X)^+ \text{ for variables } X;$$
$$(MN)_{\mathcal{S}} = \{\sigma;\delta : \sigma \in N_{\mathcal{S}},\ \delta \in M_{\mathcal{S}}\}^+;$$
$$(\lambda X.M)_{\mathcal{S}} = \{\sigma \to \alpha(\xi/\sigma) : \sigma \in L,\ \alpha(\xi) \in M_{\mathcal{S}}(X)\}^+,$$
$$\text{where } M_{\mathcal{S}}(X) = M_{\mathcal{J}},\ \mathcal{J}(X) = \{\xi\},\ \mathcal{J}(Y) = \mathcal{S}(Y) \text{ for all } Y \neq X.$$

It remains to show that under this semantics function we indeed get a model of the $\lambda\beta$-calculus, consisting of the elements $M_{\mathcal{S}}$ for closed terms M. The proof makes use of a few simple observations about $\mathcal{S}$ and the closure operation $+$.

(1) $M_{\mathcal{S}}{}^+ = M_{\mathcal{S}}$.

(2) $\quad M_{\mathfrak{g}}(X)^{+} = M_{\mathfrak{g}}(X)$.

(3) $\quad$ If $\; B = \{\alpha(\xi/\rho) : \alpha(\xi) \in M_{\mathfrak{g}}(X)\ ,\ \rho \in N_{\mathfrak{g}}\}\;$ then $\; B = B^{+}$.

<u>Proof</u>. We show that B is closed under operations (i) and (ii). - Let $\alpha(\xi/\rho)$ be of the form $\sigma(\xi/\rho);\ (\sigma(\xi/\rho) \to \delta(\xi/\rho))$. Then $\alpha(\xi) \in M_{\mathfrak{g}}(X)$ is of the form $\sigma(\xi);\ (\sigma(\xi) \to \delta(\xi))$, and $\rho \in N_{\mathfrak{g}}$. By (i) and (2), $M_{\mathfrak{g}}(X)$ contains $\delta(\xi)$, and B contains $\delta(\xi/\rho)$ by definition. - Let $\alpha(\xi/\rho)$ be of the form $\delta(\eta/\sigma, \xi/\rho)$. Then $\alpha(\xi) \in M_{\mathfrak{g}}(X)$ is of the form $\delta(\eta/\sigma, \xi)$. By (ii) and (2), $M_{\mathfrak{g}}(X)$ has an element of the form $\sigma\ ;\ (\chi \to \delta(\eta/\chi, \xi))$. Hence $\sigma\ ;(\chi \to \delta(\eta/\chi, \xi/\rho))$ is in B by definition.

(4) $\quad (M^{X}_{N})_{\mathfrak{g}} = \{\alpha(\xi/\rho) : \alpha(\xi) \in M_{\mathfrak{g}}(X)\ ,\ \rho \in N_{\mathfrak{g}}\}^{+}$.

<u>Proof</u>. By induction on the structure of M . - $(X^{X}_{N})_{\mathfrak{g}} = N_{\mathfrak{g}}$; also $\{\alpha(\xi/\rho) : \alpha(\xi) \in X_{\mathfrak{g}}(X)\ ,\ \rho \in N_{\mathfrak{g}}\}^{+} = \{\xi/\rho : \rho \in N_{\mathfrak{g}}\}^{+} = N^{+}_{\mathfrak{g}} = N_{\mathfrak{g}}$. - For application we have $((MN)^{X}_{P})_{\mathfrak{g}} = (M^{X}_{P} N^{X}_{P})_{\mathfrak{g}} = \{\sigma;\ \delta : \sigma \in N^{X}_{P}\ ,\ \delta \in M^{X}_{P}\}^{+} =$ $= \{\sigma(\xi/\rho);\ \delta(\xi/\rho) : \sigma(\xi) \in N_{\mathfrak{g}}(X)\ ,\ \delta(\xi) \in M_{\mathfrak{g}}(X)\ ,\ \rho \in P_{\mathfrak{g}}\}^{+}$ by induction assumption and (3); hence $((MN)^{X}_{P})_{\mathfrak{g}}$ equals $\{\chi(\xi/\rho) : \chi(\xi) \in (MN)_{\mathfrak{g}}(X), \rho \in P_{\mathfrak{g}}\}$. - For abstraction we may assume Y not free in N , and compute $((\lambda Y.M)^{X}_{N})_{\mathfrak{g}} = (\lambda Y.M^{X}_{N})_{\mathfrak{g}} = \{\sigma \to \alpha(\eta/\sigma) : \alpha(\eta) \in (M^{X}_{N})_{\mathfrak{g}}(Y) = (M^{X}_{N})_{\mathcal{J}}, \mathcal{J}(Y) = \{\eta\},$ $\mathcal{J}(X) = \mathcal{S}(X), \sigma \in L\}^{+} = \{\sigma \to \beta(\xi/\rho, \eta/\sigma) : \beta(\xi,\eta) \in M_{\mathcal{J}}(X) = M_{\mathfrak{g}}(X,Y), \rho \in N_{\mathfrak{g}}, \sigma \in L\}^{+}$; but also $\{\delta(\xi/\rho) : \delta(\xi) \in (\lambda Y.M)_{\mathfrak{g}}(X), \rho \in N_{\mathfrak{g}}\}^{+} =$ $= \{\delta(\xi/\rho) : \delta(\xi) = (\sigma \to \beta(\xi, \eta/\sigma)), \sigma \in L, \rho \in N_{\mathfrak{g}}, \beta(\xi,\eta) \in M_{\mathfrak{g}}(X,Y)\}^{+}$.

(5) $\quad ((\lambda X.M)N)_{\mathfrak{g}} = (M^{X}_{N})_{\mathfrak{g}}$.

<u>Proof</u>. $((\lambda X.M)N)_{\mathfrak{g}} = \{\sigma;\ \delta : \sigma \in N_{\mathfrak{g}},\ \delta \in (\lambda X.M)_{\mathfrak{g}}\}^{+} = \{\sigma; (\rho \to \alpha(\xi/\rho)) : \alpha(\xi) \in M_{\mathfrak{g}}(X),$ $\sigma \in N_{\mathfrak{g}}, \rho \in L\}^{+}$. Let the latter set be denoted by F^{+} . We claim $F^{+} = S^{+}$, where S is $\{\alpha(\xi/\sigma) : \alpha(\xi) \in M_{\mathfrak{g}}(X), \sigma \in N_{\mathfrak{g}}\}$. This would prove (5), since $S^{+} = S = (M^{X}_{N})_{\mathfrak{g}}$ by (4). - $S \subseteq F^{+}$ because $\alpha(\xi) \in M_{\mathfrak{g}}(X), \sigma \in N_{\mathfrak{g}}$ imply $\sigma\ ;\ (\sigma \to \alpha(\xi/\sigma))$ by definition of F , hence $\alpha(\xi/\sigma) \in F^{+}$ by closure operation (i). - $F \subseteq S^{+}$ since $\alpha(\xi) \in M_{\mathfrak{g}}(X), \sigma \in N_{\mathfrak{g}}$ imply $\alpha(\xi/\sigma) \in S$ by definition of S ; hence, for any $\rho \in L, (\sigma; (\rho \to \alpha(\xi/\rho))) \in S^{+}$ by closure operation (ii). Altogether we have $S^{+} \subseteq (F^{+})^{+} = F^{+}$ and $F^{+} \subseteq (S^{+})^{+} = S^{+}$, and thus $F^{+} = S^{+}$.

(6) $\quad (\lambda X.X)_{\mathfrak{g}} \neq (\lambda X.XX)_{\mathfrak{g}}$.

Proof. Observe first that the application of closure operations (ii) and (i) in this order os the identity. Hence any sequence of applications of these operations is equivalent to a sequence of (i)'s (possibly empty), followed by a sequence of (ii)'s (possibly empty). Let $a \in A$. Then $(a \to (a;a)) \in (\lambda X.XX)_{\mathbf{g}}$ for all $\mathbf{g}$. This formula is not the result of an application of (ii). Hence, if $(\lambda X.X)_{\mathbf{g}} = (\lambda X.XX)_{\mathbf{g}}$, the formula $(a \to (a;a))$ should be derived from a formula $\sigma \to \alpha(\xi/\sigma)$, where $\sigma \in L$ and $\alpha(\xi) \in X_{\mathbf{g}}(X)$, by rule (i) exclusively. But such a formula does not allow application of (i).[1]

(7) If $M = N$ is provable in the $\lambda\beta$-calculus, then $M_{\mathbf{g}} = N_{\mathbf{g}}$ for all $\mathbf{g}$.

Proof. The verifications of nontrivial axioms and rules have been made above.

2. Computing with indefinite objects and operations and other remarks

2.1. Our first example concerns a notion of type-free computability in relational structures $\underline{A} = \langle A,R,f \rangle$, where $R \subseteq A \times A$ is a binary relation, $f: A \to A$ an operation on A . Computability is relative to the set R and function f . The model is based on A as the set of atomic formulas for L , and the language of the Lambda calculus is extended by two constants, f and R . The semantics function $\mathbf{g}$ extends to these constants by:

$$f_{\mathbf{g}} = \{a \to b: f(a) = b,\ a,b \in A\}^{+} ;$$
$$R_{\mathbf{g}} = (\{a \to (b \to \alpha): \langle a,b\rangle \in R, \alpha \in K_{\mathbf{g}}\} \cup \{a \to (b \to \beta): \langle a,b\rangle \notin R, \beta \in (KI)_{\mathbf{g}}\})^{+} ,$$

where K, I are the usual combinators.

2.2. The above type of models is adequate if all objects and functions of the relational structure are finite and definite, such as is the case in $\mathbb{Z}, \mathbb{N}$ or $\mathbb{Q}$. It is less realistic in the case of $\mathbb{R}$, where

1) We thank H. Barendregt for alerting us to the need for spelling out a consistency proof.

they are infinite (decimal expansions, power series, etc.), or in the theory of geometrical constructions, where the objects may be only incompletely determined (e.g. as the result of a selection of some point outside a given line, etc.). Observe, that the objects, even if infinite or indefinite can always be satisfactorily described by a set of first-order formulas of the language of $\underline{A}$.

2.3. To make use of the last observation, let Γ be a theory in the first-order predicate calculus. Computability relative to the theory Γ is introduced as follows. - Let A be the set of all quantifier-free formulas of the language of Γ . The closure operation $+$ is modified to

$$W \cup \{\varphi \to \varphi : \varphi \in A\} \subseteq W^+ ;$$

(i) if $\sigma ; (\sigma \to \delta)$ is in W^+ , then δ is in W^+ ;
(ii) if $\delta(\xi/\sigma)$ is in W^+ , then $\sigma ; (\rho \to \delta(\xi/\rho))$ is in W^+ ;
(iii) if $\varphi \in A$ can be proved from Γ and the set of elements of W^+ which are in A , then φ is in W^+ .

Furthermore, the language of the Lambda calculus is extended by constants as follows:

Let f be a unary function symbol of Γ and let x,y be variables (of the language of Γ). We introduce the constant f^x_y into the Lambda calculus, with the interpretation

$$(f^x_y)_{\mathbf{g}} = \{\psi \to \varphi(x,y) : \psi \in \Gamma \text{ , } \varphi(x,y) \text{ provable from } \Gamma \text{ and } y = f(x)\}^+ .$$

Similarly, if R is a binary predicate symbol of Γ and x and y are variables, then Rxy is a new constant of the Lambda calculus, and its interpretation is

$$(Rxy)_{\mathbf{g}} = (\{R(x,y) \to \alpha : \alpha \in K_{\mathbf{g}}\} \cup \{\neg R(x,y) \to \beta : \beta \in (KI)_{\mathbf{g}}\})^+ .$$

2.4. To understand this model, we look at a Lambda term M as a program for the construction of a geometrical figure. During this construction we introduce and label (by different variables) all the additional points, lines, etc. that we reach. The formulas of A contained in $M_{\mathfrak{g}}$ give a description of the properties of the total labelled figure constructed by M.

The above type of models suffices to treat indefinite or infinite objects with definite operations and tests. For example, real numbers as objects can be understood as sets of formulas

$$\pi^x_{\mathfrak{g}} = \{3<x<4,\ 3.1<x<3.2,\ 3.14<x<3.15, \ldots\}^+ ;$$

and functions, such as sine, again by

$$(\sin^x_y)_{\mathfrak{g}} = \{0=0 \rightarrow x-\left|\frac{x^3}{3!}\right| < y < x+\left|\frac{x^3}{3!}\right|,\ 0=0 \rightarrow x-\frac{x^3}{3!}-\left|\frac{x^5}{5!}\right| < y < x-\frac{x^3}{3!}+\left|\frac{x^5}{5!}\right|, \ldots\}^+$$

Incidently, the following type of interpretation shows how to deal with partial functions with definable domains, such as division

$$(\mathrm{div}\ {}^{x,y}_{z})_{\mathfrak{g}} = \{y \neq 0 \rightarrow x = z \cdot y\}^+ .$$

Indefinite operations are dealt with in a similar manner, for example the squareroot function is interpreted by

$$(\mathrm{sqrt}^x_y)_{\mathfrak{g}} = \{x \geq 0 \rightarrow y^2 = x\}^+$$

2.5. We close with some remarks on actual computations in our models. The evaluation of a Lambda-term is best thought of as the output of a network of communicating indefinitely ongoing processes. - Let M and N be Lambda-terms, and let

symbolize their corresponding evaluating networks; the arrows downward indicating a pipeline where the elements of $M_{\mathfrak{g}}$, respectively $N_{\mathfrak{g}}$, continue to come through as they are produced. Then

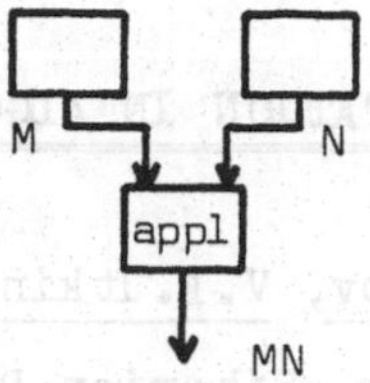

symbolizes the network for MN , the output of the box "appl" being the elements of $(MN)_g$. - Similarly for $\lambda X.M.$ -

It is clear, that the practicality of such a scheme of computation crucially depends on the sequencing of outputs of the processes. For the case of arithmetical computations with reals as infinite objects, the problem of implementation has been solved quite satisfactorily by E. Wiedmer in his Zurich thesis 1977, although in a somewhat different setting.

Computing effort may further be reduced by some prior knowledge about when sufficient formulas have passed a given pipeline in order that a desired formula be in the output. Such knowledge would have to be given by the constructor of the term (read "program"), just as is the case in a well-known approach to program-correctness.

CORRECTNESS OF MIXED COMPUTATION IN ALGOL-LIKE PROGRAMS

A.P.Ershov, V.E.Itkin

Computing Center, Siberian Division
USSR Academy of Sciences
Novosibirsk 630090

INTRODUCTION

When a program is being executed situations occure which allow "carrying out of brackets" (suspensions) some program fragments and executing them separately.

For example, if the program is a sequence of statements $A_1;\ldots;A_5$ and there is no data flow between statements A_2,A_4 and A_3,A_5 then the statements A_2,A_4 can be suspended, which means that the sequence $A_1;A_3;A_5$ will be executed first and then $A_2;A_4$.

Here is a more complicated example of a program

A_1; <u>while</u> p <u>do</u> A_2 <u>od</u>; <u>while</u> q <u>do</u> $A_3;A_4$ <u>od</u>; A_5

where there is no data flow between p,A_2,A_4 and q,A_3,A_5. Then, when executing the program, the first loop and the statement A_4 from the second loop can be suspended. Moreover, if

$$q = q(A_3) = q(A_3A_3) = 1,\ q(A_3A_3A_3) = 0,$$

then the sequence of statements

$A_1;\ A_3;\ A_3;\ A_3;\ A_5$

is executed first, and the "residual" fragment

<u>while</u> p <u>do</u> A_2 <u>od</u>; A_4; A_4; A_4

will be executed afterwards.

In contrast with conventional or *normal* computation, the above discussed two-stage computation will be called *partitioned*. The first stage of a partitioned computation consists of a *partial* computation and the formation of a *residual* program. The second stage is the execution of the residual program. The first stage as a whole will be called a *mixed* computation of the initial program.

In general, a partitioned computation contains additional actions which provide for storing information for suspended fragments. Moreover, a residual program may be modified before its execution. In particular, it may, in turn, be subjected to partitioned computation or optimization.

On the whole, mixed computation of a program can be treated as a conventional computation some parts of which are represented by not yet executed (suspended) program fragments.

The suspension of a fragment may be caused by arbitrary decisions to suspend certain fragments or may be forced by informational dependence of statements and logical conditions on previously suspended fragments (the latter is called a *forcible* suspension in contrast to an arbitrary suspension). Fragments which are situated on alternative branches of suspended logical conditions are also forcibly suspended.

The typical reason for an arbitrary suspension is undeterminedness of values of some variables in the course of mixed computation. A suspension caused by a lack of resources or slowness of the corresponding computations can also be treated as a suspension of this kind.

Mixed computation exploits the fact that some components of the informational structure of a program are separable. Partitioned computation allows separation of information components that have been intertwined by the control structure of a program. Thus, the transformation of a program in order to make informationally independent program components logically independent can be regarded as a static factorization of the program.

Mixed computation, as a general concept of algorithmic languages, has been introduced by one of the authors in [1]. It has been shown that many programming techniques, specifically, those in compilation can be naturally formulated in terms of partitioned computation [2]. The latter paper also contains references to related works.

The purpose of this preliminary publication is a formal treatment of mixed computation of algol-like programs (interpreted standard schemata) and an analysis of conditions of the functional equivalence of normal and partitioned computations.

In turns out that mixed computation can be defined differently even if the reason of arbitrary suspensions is fixed. In the general case, some definitions require preprocessing the initial program. Definitions may differ also in the depth of partial computation. We shall present and explain three definitions of mixed computation.

The first involves the smallest number of forcible suspensions but is incorrect in the general case, and so requires preprocessing the program. The other two are universally correct but require more forcible suspensions.

The study of mixed computation requires a specific proof techniques. To demonstrate these techniques, some proofs are given in detail.

PARTITIONED COMPUTATION

1°. Let $\{x\},\{c\},\{f\},\{\pi\}$ be respectively countable sets of variables with values from a countable set D, of constants from D, general recursive functions, and predicates (the last two are of various arities). Function and predicate arguments are in D, function values are in D, predicate values are in $\{1,0\}$. Constants, functions and predicates are specified as symbols with a proper interpretation.

2°. A functional term is x,c or $f^{(k)}(t_1,\ldots,t_k)$ where $k \geq 1$, and t_i is a functional term. A predicate is an expression $\pi^{(s)}(t_1,\ldots,t_s)$, where $s \geq 1$, and the t_j are functional terms. A statement is an expression x:=t where t is a functional term. Statements will be denoted by A and predicates by p.

3°. A program is an expression

$$i_1:K_1;\ldots;i_n:K_n;i_{n+1}.$$

where $n \geq 0$, the i_j are mutually distinct integers (program labels), K_j has a form either A; goto m or if p then l else s, where m, l and s are program labels. In obvious cases labels and jumps may be omitted for the sake of brevity.

When a program is graphically represented, labels become vertices of a control flow graph. The graph contains an entry (i_1) and an exit(i_{n+1}) vertex. The graph also contains operational and logical vertices with which statements and predicates, respectively, are brought into a correspondence. We will use this dual terminology in the sequel.

The notation $\Pi(R)$ indicates that Π is considered over a finite set $R \subset \{x\}$ of variables, R containing all variable occuring in Π.

4°. Let $\tau_0:R \to D$ be an initial memory state. We shall now define a (conventional) process of computation, comp(τ_0, $\Pi(R)$).

1: $\mathcal{T}:=\mathcal{T}_0$; $i:=i_1$; goto 2;
2: if i is an operational vertex then 3 else 4;
3: $\mathcal{T}:=A^i(\mathcal{T})$; i:=next(i); goto 2;
4: if i is a logical vertex then 5 else 6;
5: i:= alternative(i,p^i,$\mathcal{T}$); goto 2;
6.

Here A^i is a statement corresponding to the vertex i, and p^j is a predicate corresponding to vertex j; $A^i(\mathcal{T})$ is a memory state transition caused by the statement A^i; next(i) yields a successor of the operational vertex i; alternative(i,p^i,$\mathcal{T}$) computes the value of the predicate p^i and yields, respectively, a 1- or 0-successor of the vertex i.

A process of computation either goes infinitely or is terminated when reaching the exit vertex with some value of $\mathcal{T}$ which is denoted by $v(\mathcal{T}_0, \Pi)$ and is called by a result of the process.

5°. Let $R \subseteq R'$. $\Pi'(R')$ c o n t a i n s $\Pi(R)$ if, for each $\mathcal{T}_0'$, values $v(\mathcal{T}_0', \Pi')$ and $v(\mathcal{T}_0, \Pi)$ are either defined or not defined together and, when defined, are equal over R ($\mathcal{T}_0'$ induces $\mathcal{T}_0$).

6°. Let define for vertices i and j ($i \neq j$) in a program Π a property r(i,j): each path from i to the exit vertex contains j. In particular, j may itself be the exit vertex. Let now a predicate $r_0(i,j)$ denote that r(i,j) is true and no vertex k ($k \neq i$, $k \neq j$) belonging the set of simple (no loops) paths from i to j does not satisfy r(i,k). It will be shown that, for every i, there exists just one j which satisfies $r_0(i,j)$. This is a "closest" vertex belonging to all paths from i to the exit vertex and we shall call it a focus for i. (It is supposed, here and further, that, for each i, there exists a path from i to the exit vertex.)

Let j be the focus for i in a program Π. A vertex k ($k \neq j$) will be called i n t e r n a l for i, if k belongs to a path from i to j not containing j. In particular, i is an internal vertex for i. Let destroy in Π (in its linear representation) all segments $s{:}K_s$; for which s is not an internal vertex for i. The obtained fragment will be called a t r a i n of the vertex i and denoted by F^i. The vertices i and j are respectively called by an entry and an exit vertex for that train (j does not belong the train though the latter contains a "reference" to j).

7°. Now we shall define another computational process, a process of mixed computation $\underset{R_1}{\text{mix}}(\mathcal{T}_0, \Pi(R))$ of a program Π under a suspense of initial values $\mathcal{T}_0(x)$, where $x \in R_1 \subseteq R$.

1: $\mathcal{T} := \mathcal{T}_0$; i:=$i_1$; ssv:=$R_1$; resp:= Λ; goto 2;
2: if i is an operational vertex then 3 else 4;
3: if $\text{In}(A^i) \cap \text{ssv} = \emptyset$ then 31 else 32;
  31: $\mathcal{T} := A^i(\mathcal{T})$; ssv:=ssv/Out($A^i$);
    i:=next(i); goto 2;
  32: resp:=attach(resp, A^i, $\text{In}(A^i) \setminus \text{ssv}$, $\mathcal{T}$);
    ssv:=ssv$\cup$Out(A^i); goto 2;
4: if i is a logical vertex then 5 else 6;
5: if $\text{In}(p^i) \cap \text{ssv} = \emptyset$ then 51 else 52;
  51: i:=alternative(i, p^i, $\mathcal{T}$); goto 2;
  52: resp:=attach(resp, F^i, $\text{In}(F^i) \setminus \text{ssv}$, $\mathcal{T}$);
    ssv:=ssv$\cup$Out(F^i);
    i:=focus(i); goto 2;
6: resp:=end(resp); goto 61;
  61.

Here ssv is a set of currently suspended variables, resp is an alphanumeric variable which exit value is denoted by $\underset{R_1}{\text{rmix}}(\mathcal{T}_0, \Pi)$ and called a r e s i d u a l p r o g r a m ; the exit state of the memory $\mathcal{T}$ is denoted by $\underset{R_1}{\text{vmix}}(\mathcal{T}_0, \Pi)$; $\text{In}(F^i)$ is the union of sets of input variables of statements and predicates from F^i, $\text{Out}(F^i)$ is the union of output variables of statements from F^i.

Let

$$\text{In}(A^i) \setminus \text{ssv} = \{x_{j_1}, \ldots, x_{j_m}\};$$

then the transformation attach in the item 32 consists of the right concatenation of the fragment

$$x_{j_1} := \mathcal{T}(x_{j_1}); \ldots; x_{j_m} := \mathcal{T}(x_{j_m}); A;$$

to the current value of resp ($\mathcal{T}(x)$ are represented as constants).

Let

$$\text{In}(F^i) \setminus \text{ssv} = \{x_{j_1}, \ldots, x_{j_m}\};$$

then the transformation in the item 52 consists of the right concatenation of the fragment

$$x_{j_1} := \mathcal{T}(x_{j_1}); \ldots; x_{j_m} := \mathcal{T}(x_{j_m}); \bar{F}^i$$

to the current value of resp. Here $\bar{F}^i$ is an isomorphic image of F^i such that the exit vertex of the current value of resp is identified with the entry vertex of the concatenated fragment and the exit vertex of the latter is declared to be the exit vertex of the new value of resp. The transformation end(resp) is the right concatenation of a segment '$1.$' to the current value of resp where 1 is the exit vertex of that value.

All these transformations concatenate a current residual program by such a way that the intersection of sets of vertices of the current residual program and that of the concatenated fragment is always empty. We put end(Λ)='1.' where 1 is an arbitrary label.

8°. A process $\underset{R_1}{mix}(\mathcal{T}_0,\Pi(R))$ is c o r r e c t if the equality

$$v(\mathcal{T}_0,\Pi)=v(\underset{R_1}{vmix}(\mathcal{T}_0,\Pi),\ \underset{R_1}{rmix}(\mathcal{T}_0,\Pi))$$

does hold. Such a process is not always correct, but it is correct for some program containing $\Pi(R)$ without loosing any computation done in the process mix. We shall formulate this statement more precisely.

Let $R=\{x_1,\ldots,x_n\}$, $\widetilde{R}=\{\widetilde{x}_1,\ldots,\widetilde{x}_n,x^*\}$, $R\cap\widetilde{R}=\emptyset$, and $\widetilde{\Pi}$ be obtained from Π by substituting each occurence of each variable x_i by $\widetilde{x}_i$ $(i=1,\ldots,n)$ and then by inserting "trivial" transfers $\widetilde{x}_j:=\widetilde{x}_j$ in such a way that there will be, for each train $\widetilde{F}^k$ and for each $\widetilde{x}_i\in Out(\widetilde{F}^k)$, an assignment to x_i along all paths in $\widetilde{F}^k$ from k to its focus. Let $R'=R\cup\widetilde{R}\cup\{x^*\}$ and let Π' is obtained by concatenating the program $\widetilde{\Pi}$ to the sequence of assignments $\widetilde{x}_i:=x_i$ $(i=1,\ldots,n)$ and then by concatenating the sequence of assignments $x_i:=\widetilde{x}_i$ $(i=1,\ldots,n)$ and, finally, by the sequence $\widetilde{x}_i:=x^*$ $(i=1,\ldots,n)$.

<u>Theorem.</u> $\Pi'(R')$ contains $\Pi(R)$ and, for arbitrary $\mathcal{T}_0':R'\to D$ and $R_1\subseteq R$ the process $\underset{R_1\cup\{x^*\}}{mix}(\mathcal{T}_0',\Pi'(R'))$ is correct.

<u>CORRECTNESS</u>

9°. <u>Lemma 1.</u> If, for each vertex i of the program Π, there exists a path from i to the exit vertex then, for each i, there exists just one focus of the vertex i.

P r o o f . If i is an operational vertex then the corresponding focus is next(i). Let now i be a logical vertex. Let T(i) be the set $\{j\,|\,r(i,j)\}$. At least, the exit vertex of the program belongs to this set. Let introduce an order relation over T(i): $k<s$ $(k\neq s)$ iff all paths from k to the exit vertex contain s.

We shall prove that, for arbitrary $k,s\in T(i)$ $(k\neq s)$, either $k<s$ or $s<k$ but never $(k<s)\&(s<k)$.

Let suppose that $(k<s)\&(s<k)$. This immediately implies that there are no paths from k and s to the exit vertex (otherwise they

contained the segment k...s...k...s an infinite number of times).

Let now $\neg(k<s) \& \neg(s<k)$. Then there exist a path L_k from k to the exit vertex not containing s and a path L_s from s to the exit vertex not containing k. It is obvious that there exists either a path from i to k not containing s or a path from i to k not containing k (there exists a path from i to either k or s, since $k,s \in T(i)$; if the last statement didn't hold then each of these paths would contain an infinite path). But this implies the existence of a path from i to the exit vertex that contradicts our assumption.

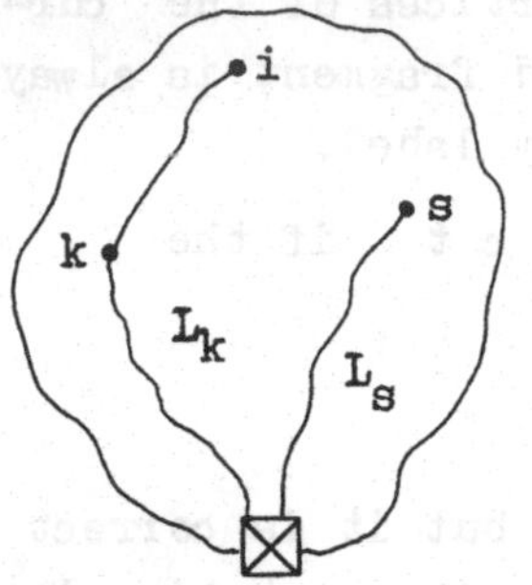

Thus, the set T(i) is completely ordered by the relation "<" and has a minimal element j. We shall show that j is the sought focus.

We shall show that no vertex $k \in T(i)$ ($k \neq i$, $k \neq j$) belongs to any simple path from i to j. Let us suppose (opposite) that there exists a simple path from i to j passing k. As we now, either $k<j$ or $j<k$. Let $j<k$. In this case the simplicity of the path i...k...j contradicts the requirement of j to be between i and k. If $k<j$ this will contradict the property of j to be minimal in T(i). QED

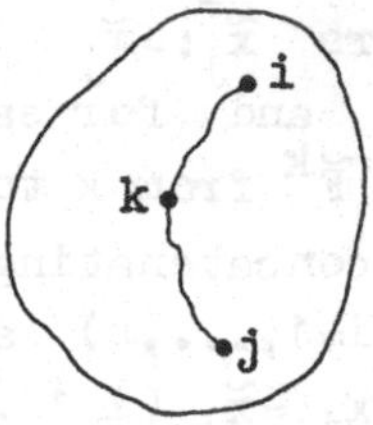

10°. A process

$$\underset{R_1}{\text{div}}(\mathcal{T}_0, \Pi(R)) \overset{\text{df}}{=} \text{comp}(\underset{R_1}{\text{vmix}}(\mathcal{T}_0,\Pi(R)), \underset{R_1}{\text{rmix}}(\mathcal{T}_0,\Pi(R)))$$

is called a p a r t i t i o n e d execution under suspension of values $\mathcal{T}_0(x)$, $x \in R_1 \subseteq R$. We also define

$$\underset{R_1}{\text{vdiv}}(\mathcal{T}_0,\Pi) \overset{\text{df}}{=} v(\underset{R_1}{\text{vmix}}(\mathcal{T}_0,\Pi), \underset{R_1}{\text{rmix}}(\mathcal{T}_0,\Pi)).$$

In these terms, the correctness of the process $\underset{R_1}{\text{mix}}(\mathcal{T}_0,\Pi)$ means that the equality

$$v(\mathcal{T}_0,\Pi) = \underset{R_1}{\text{vdiv}}(\mathcal{T}_0,\Pi)$$

does hold.

11°. Now we are approaching the direct proof of the theorem of 8°. We shall start with the assumption that both values

$$v(\mathcal{T}_0',\Pi') \quad (1)$$

and

$$\underset{R_1 \cup \{x^*\}}{\text{vdiv}} (\mathcal{T}'_0, \Pi') \tag{2}$$

exist.

Let us construct a h i s t o r y of the process

$$\underset{R_1 \cup \{x^*\}}{\text{mix}} (\mathcal{T}'_0, \Pi') \tag{3}$$

by the following way. We put into a sequence all statements occuring during the computation (both, executed and suspended) including value transfers and trains (without constant assignment prefixes). The sequence obtained has a form of

$$H = h_1 u_1 \ldots h_s u_s h_{s+1} h^*, \quad s \geqslant 0 \tag{4}$$

where each h_i ($i=1,\ldots,s+1$) is a sequence of non-suspended statements, i.e. those having executed in the process (3). The member u_m ($m=1,\ldots,s$) is a suspended (i.e. concatenated to the current value of resp) statement or train (without its prefix) and h^* is the sequence of the suspended statements $\tilde{x}_i := x^*$.

It is obvious that

$$v(\mathcal{T}'_0, \Pi') = v(\mathcal{T}'_0, H), \tag{5}$$

$$\underset{R_1 \cup \{x^*\}}{\text{vdiv}} (\mathcal{T}'_0, \Pi') = \underset{R_1 \cup \{x^*\}}{\text{vdiv}} (\mathcal{T}'_0, H). \tag{6}$$

Consequently, it is sufficient to show that

$$v(\mathcal{T}'_0, H) = \underset{R_1 \cup \{x^*\}}{\text{vdiv}} (\mathcal{T}'_0, H). \tag{7}$$

Let us denote

$$\bar{H} = h_1 \bar{u}_1 \ldots h_s \bar{u}_s h_{s+1} h^* \tag{8}$$

where $\bar{u}_m$ ($m=1,\ldots,s$) is obtained by concatenating (from the left) prefixes of constant assignment (according items 35 and 52 of the mix definition) to u_m. If a prefix is empty then $\bar{u}_m = u_m$. Let us also denote

$$\bar{H}^* = h_1 \ldots h_s h_{s+1} \bar{u}_1 \ldots \bar{u}_s h^* \,. \tag{8'}$$

It is easy to realize that (7) holds iff

$$v(\mathcal{T}'_0, H) = v(\mathcal{T}'_0, H^*) \,. \tag{9}$$

12°. We shall introduce now several auxiliary definitions. Let us represent $\bar{H}$ as

$$\bar{H} = b_1, \ldots, b_m \tag{10}$$

where b_i is a statement (possibly, a value transfer or constant assignment) or a train. More precisely, each b_i is a denotation of an occurrence of a statement or a train into the history. To this end, we may consider that $\bar{H}^*$ is obtained from $\bar{H}$ by some transposition of symbols b_i.

We will say that b_i i n f o r m s b_j by $x \in R'$ in $\bar{H}$ if

a) $i<j$,

b) $x \in Out(b_i)$ and $x \in In(b_j)$,

c) $x \notin Out(b_k)$, $k \in i+1,\dots,j-1$.

This relation will be denoted as $b_i \xrightarrow{x} b_j$.

Let $\rho(i)$ be the serial number of b_i in $\bar{H}^*$. We will say similarly that b_i i n f o r m s b_j by x in H^* if

a) $\rho(i)<\rho(j)$,

b) $x \in Out(b_i)$ and $x \in In(b_j)$,

c) between b_i and b_j in $\bar{H}^*$, i.e. in the positions $\rho(i)+1,\dots$ $\dots,\rho(j)-1$, there are only such symbols which input sets do not contain x. We will preserve the previous notation for this relation, too.

Two programs, $\bar{H}$ and $\bar{H}^*$, are called i n f o r m a t i o n a l l y s i m i l a r if, for any i,j and x ($1 \le i \le m$, $1 \le j \le m$, $x \in R'$), the relation $b_i \xrightarrow{x} b_j$ is identical in both programs.

13°. <u>Lemma 2.</u> The programs $\bar{H}$ and $\bar{H}^*$ from (8) and (8') are informationally similar.

P r o o f . (will be given from $\bar{H}$ to $\bar{H}^*$ only). Let us assume that $b_i \xrightarrow{x} b_j$ holds in $\bar{H}$. Two cases are possible:

a) b_j is a non-suspended statement in the process

$$\underset{R_1 \cup \{x^*\}}{\text{mix}} (\mathcal{T}_0', H) \ . \tag{11}$$

Then b_i is a non-suspended statement in (11) and, among $b_{i+1},\dots,b_{j-1}$, there are no statements yielding x. The segment $b_i \dots b_j$ in $\bar{H}^*$ contains a subsequence of the sequence $b_{i+1},\dots,b_{j-1}$ that implies $b_i \xrightarrow{x} b_j$ in $\bar{H}^*$.

b) b_j is a statement or train suspended in the process (11). Two subcases will be considered.

b1) x has not been suspended immediately prior to b_j in the process (11) (i.e. $x \notin ssv$). Then b_i is of the form $x{:=}c$ and belongs to the prefix of b_j. Since, when transforming $\bar{H}$ into $\bar{H}^*$, b_j is transferred together with its prefix the relation is preserved.

b2) x has been suspended immediately prior to b_j in the process (11) (i.e. $x \in ssv$). This implies that b_i must be suspended (if b_i were non-suspended then its result, x, would become non-suspended after b_i, being in such a capacity up to b_j).

In both subcases the segment $b_i \dots b_j$ in $\bar{H}^*$ contains only suspended statements or trains and their prefixes. Consequently, in both subcases, this segment contains a subsequence of the sequence $b_{i+1},\dots,b_{j-1}$ in $\bar{H}$. Thus, the relation $b_i \xrightarrow{x} b_j$ holds in $\bar{H}^*$, too. QED

Let us introduce a mapping $(1 \le i \le m)$

$$b_i \mathcal{T}: \mathrm{In}(b_i) \to D$$

which brings to $x \in \mathrm{In}(b_i)$ in a correspondence that value which x has immediately prior to the execution of b_i in the process

$$\mathrm{comp}(\mathcal{T}_0', \bar{H}). \tag{12}$$

A similar mapping $b_i \mathcal{T}^*$ is obtained by replacing $\bar{H}$ by $\bar{H}^*$ in (12).

14°. <u>Lemma 3.</u> For each i $(1 \le i \le m)$ the equality

$$b_i \mathcal{T} = b_i \tag{13}$$

holds.

P r o o f . Let

$$\bar{H} = b_1 \dots b_m \tag{14}$$

and

$$\bar{H}^* = b_{s_1} \dots b_{s_m} . \tag{15}$$

The lemma will be proved by induction: we shall prove

$$b_{s_1} \mathcal{T} = b_{s_1} \mathcal{T}^* \tag{16}$$

and

$$b_{s_1} \mathcal{T} = b_{s_1} \mathcal{T}^* \& \dots \& b_{s_k} \mathcal{T} = b_{s_k} \mathcal{T}^* \Rightarrow b_{s_{k+1}} \mathcal{T} = b_{s_{k+1}} \mathcal{T}^*. \tag{17}$$

We shall first prove (16). Let us consider the process (11). If $R_1 = R$ then $H = \bar{H} = \bar{H}^*$, thus the lemma is correct. Let now $R \setminus R_1 \ne \emptyset$. Then b_{s_1} is a transfer $\tilde{x}_i := x_i$, $x_i \in R \setminus R_i$ which implies (16).

We shall now prove (17). Let the premise from (17) hold $(1 \le k \le m)$. Let $b_{s_{k+1}}$ be a symbol b_j and $x \in \mathrm{In}(b_j)$.

a) For the case when b_j is not suspended in the process (11) we shall consider two subcases.

a1) There exists i such that $b_i \xrightarrow{x} b_j$ in $\bar{H}$. According Lemma 2, we have $b_i \xrightarrow{x} b_j$ in $\bar{H}^*$. Under the induction assumption,

$$b_i \mathcal{T} = b_i \mathcal{T}^*, \tag{18}$$

which implies that in both processes

$$\mathrm{comp}(\mathcal{T}_0', \bar{H}) \tag{19}$$

and

$$\mathrm{comp}(\mathcal{T}_0', \bar{H}^*) \tag{20}$$

b_i yields one and the same value of x, which is equal to $b_j \mathcal{T}(x)$ as well as to $b_j \mathcal{T}^*(x)$. Thus,

$$b_j \mathcal{T}(x) = b_j \mathcal{T}^*(x). \tag{21}$$

a2) There is no i such that $b_i \xrightarrow{x} b_j$ in $\bar{H}$. According Lemma 2, the same is true for $\bar{H}$* that guarantees (21).

b) Now we suppose that b_j has been suspended in the process (11) and again consider two similar subcases.

b1) There exists i such that $b_i \xrightarrow{x} b_j$ in $\bar{H}$. The proof is similar to that in the subcase a1) with only exception when b_i is a train. The matter is that even if (18) holds, in general, it does not guarantee the equality of output values of the variable x for b_i if, when executing b_i, a statement yielding x has not been occured. However, in our case, according the construction rules for the program $\Pi'(R')$, $x \in Out(b_i)$ implies that any path from the entry vertex of the train b_i to the exit one contains at least one statement yielding x. Now (18) guarantees that the paths inside the train b_i in the processes (19) and (20) coinside. Consequently, in these processes the train b_i yields one and the same value of x that implies (21).

b2) For the subcase when there is no i such that $b_i \xrightarrow{x} b_j$ in $\bar{H}$ the inference is just as in a2). QED

15°. <u>Lemma 4.</u> If values (1) and (2) are defined then they are equal.

Now it remains only to prove (9). According the construction rules for Π' it is sufficient to show that output values of each variable in the processes (19) and (20) are equal i.e.

$$v(\mathcal{T}_0',\bar{H})(x_i) = v(\mathcal{T}_0',\bar{H}^*)(x_i). \tag{22}$$

It is easy to realize, that $x_i := \tilde{x}_i$ is the only statement yielding x_i in the programs $\bar{H}$ and $\bar{H}$*. Since, in our notation, this statement is some b_j we obtain from Lemma 3 that

$$b_j \mathcal{T}(\tilde{x}_i) = b_j \mathcal{T}^*(\tilde{x}_i) \tag{23}$$

which directly implies the desirable. QED

16°. Now we are approaching to the end of the proof of the theorem. We shall prove that the values $v(\mathcal{T}_0',\Pi')$ and $vdiv(\mathcal{T}_0',\Pi')$ are defined or not defined simultaneously.

Let us consider the processes

$$comp(\mathcal{T}_0',\Pi'), \tag{A}$$

$$\underset{R_1 \cup \{x^*\}}{mix}(\mathcal{T}_0',R'), \tag{B}$$

$$\underset{R_1 \cup \{x^*\}}{div}(\mathcal{T}_0',R'), \tag{C}$$

$$comp(\mathcal{T}_0',H), \tag{D}$$

$$comp(\mathcal{T}_0',\bar{H}), \tag{E}$$

$$comp(\mathcal{T}_0',\bar{H}^*). \tag{F}$$

Let the value

$$\underset{R_1\cup\{x^*\}}{\mathrm{vdiv}}(\mathcal{C}_0',\Pi') \qquad (G)$$

be defined. It implies the finiteness of the processes (B) and (C). The finiteness of (B) implies the finiteness of the program H from (4). The finiteness of (C) ⇒ the finiteness of (F) ⇒ (Lemma 3) the finiteness of (E) ⇒ the finiteness of (D) ⇒ the finiteness of (A) ⇒ the definiteness of $v(\mathcal{C}_0',\Pi')$.

Let the value $v(\mathcal{C}_0',\Pi')$ be defined. The finiteness of (A) ⇒ the finiteness of (D) ⇒ the finiteness of (E) ⇒ (Lemma 3) the finiteness of (F) ⇒ the finiteness of (C) ⇒ the definiteness of (G). QED

17°. A process $\underset{R_1}{\mathrm{mix}}(\mathcal{C}_0,\Pi(R))$ where $R_1 \subseteq R$ is called t r i v i a l if in the cource of the process the control transfer to items 31 and 51 never happens, i.e. each current statement or predicate is to be suspended. Note, that, due to statements of the form x:=c, the suspension of all variables does not necessarily make each process $\underset{R_1}{\mathrm{mix}}(\mathcal{C}_0,\Pi(R))$ trivial.

Theorem. An arbitrary trivial process mix is finite.

P r o o f . In a trivial process a sequence

$$i_1,\ldots,i_s,\ldots \qquad (24)$$

is being formed where i_1 is the exit vertex and $i_{s+1} = \mathrm{focus}(i_s)$. Let us suppose (opposite) that (24) is infinite. Under the earlier assumption, there exists a path L from i_1 to the exit vertex. According the focus definition, each path from i_s to the exit vertex contains i_{s+1}. It implies that L contains (24) as a subsequence that contradicts the finiteness of L. QED

MIXED COMPUTATION WITH SEMISUSPENSION

18°. Let us define a process $\underset{R_1}{\overline{\overline{\mathrm{mix}}}}(\mathcal{C}_0,\Pi(R))$ of mixed computation of a program Π, where $R_1 \subseteq R$.

```
1: 𝒞:= 𝒞₀; i:=i₁; ssv:=R₁; sv:=R₁; resp:=Λ ; goto 2;
2: if i is an operational vertex then 3 else 4;
3: if In(Aⁱ) ∩ ssv=∅ & Out(Aⁱ) ∩ sv=∅ then 31 else 32;
   31: 𝒞:=Aⁱ(𝒞); i:=next(i); goto 2;
   32: resp:=attach(resp,Aⁱ); ssv:=ssv ∪ Out(Aⁱ);
       sv:=sv ∪ In(Aⁱ) ∪ Out(Aⁱ); goto 2;
4: if i is a logical vertex then 5 else 6;
```

5: <u>if</u> $\mathrm{In}(p^i) \cap ssv = \emptyset$ <u>then</u> 51 <u>else</u> 52;
  51: i:=alternative(i,p^i,$\mathcal{T}$); <u>goto</u> 2;
  52: resp:=attach(resp,F^i); ssv:=ssv $\cup$ Out(F^i);
    sv:=sv $\cup$ In(F^i) $\cup$ Out(F^i); i:=focus(i); <u>goto</u> 2;
6: resp:=end(resp); <u>goto</u> 61;
  61.

Here, sv (sv $\supseteq$ ssv) is a set which accumulates not only suspended variables but also all input variables of suspended statements and trains; "attach" has the same meaning as that for mix but without odding prefixes. The output values of the variables $\mathcal{T}$ and resp are denoted, respectively, as $\underset{R_1}{\overline{\overline{\mathrm{vmix}}}}(\mathcal{T}_0,\Pi(R))$ and $\underset{R_1}{\overline{\overline{\mathrm{rmix}}}}(\mathcal{T}_0,\Pi(R))$; we also introduce denotations

$$\underset{R_1}{\overline{\overline{\mathrm{div}}}}(\mathcal{T}_0,\Pi(R)) = \mathrm{comp}(\underset{R_1}{\overline{\overline{\mathrm{vmix}}}}(\mathcal{T}_0,\Pi(R)),\ \underset{R_1}{\overline{\overline{\mathrm{rmix}}}}(\mathcal{T}_0,\Pi(R)))$$

and

$$\underset{R_1}{\overline{\overline{\mathrm{vdiv}}}}(\mathcal{T}_0,\Pi(R)) = v(\underset{R_1}{\overline{\overline{\mathrm{vmix}}}}(\mathcal{T}_0,\Pi(R)),\ \underset{R_1}{\overline{\overline{\mathrm{rmix}}}}(\mathcal{T}_0,\Pi(R))).$$

A set of *s e m i s u s p e n d e d* variables at each moment is equal, by definition, to sv\ssv. If to assign to each variable x a "state" e_x being of one of three values 1 (non-suspended), 0 (semi-suspended), ω (suspended) then the following state transitions are possible:

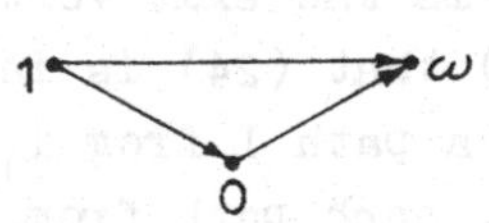

19°. <u>Theorem.</u> For arbitrary $\Pi(R)$, $R_1 \subseteq R$ and $\mathcal{T}_0$,

$$v(\mathcal{T}_0,\Pi(R)) = \underset{R_1}{\overline{\overline{\mathrm{vdiv}}}}(\mathcal{T}_0,\Pi(R)).$$

P r o o f . Let

$$H = h_1u_1 \ldots h_su_s \ldots$$

be the history of the process

$$\underset{R_1}{\overline{\overline{\mathrm{mix}}}}(\mathcal{T}_0,\Pi(R))$$

where h_s and u_s have the same meaning as that in 10° but H is allowed to be infinite. Since the process mix involves no prefix, $\overline{H}$=H. Let

$$H = b_1 \ldots b_j \ldots ,$$

where b_j is understood as in (10) of 12°. It is easy to realize that the statement of the theorem follows from the commutativity property of such pairs b_j,b_{j+1} in which b_j is suspended and b_{j+1} is not suspended in the process $\overline{\overline{mix}}$*). For that purpose it is sufficient to prove the validness of the relations

$$\mathrm{Out}(b_j) \cap \mathrm{Out}(b_{j+1}) = \emptyset \tag{1}$$
$$\mathrm{Out}(b_j) \cap \mathrm{In}(b_{j+1}) = \emptyset \tag{2}$$
$$\mathrm{In}(b_j) \cap \mathrm{Out}(b_{j+1}) = \emptyset \tag{3}$$

Note, that, since b_{j+1} is not suspended it is a statement subjected (see item 3 in the definition of $\overline{\overline{mix}}$) to the following conditions

$$\mathrm{In}(b_{j+1}) \cap ssv = \emptyset \tag{4}$$
$$\mathrm{Out}(b_{j+1}) \cap sv = \emptyset \tag{5}$$

where the values of ssv and sv are those which they have immediately prior to executing b_{j+1} in the process $\overline{\overline{mix}}$. Since b_j is suspended it is either a statement or train. When suspending b_j (according the items 32 or 52), the following transformations are performed

$$ssv := ssv \cup \mathrm{Out}(b_j) \tag{6}$$
$$sv := sv \cup \mathrm{In}(b_j) \cup \mathrm{Out}(b_j). \tag{7}$$

First, we shall prove (1). Let there exist (reductio ad absurdum) x such that

$$x \in \mathrm{Out}(b_j) \tag{8}$$

and

$$x \in \mathrm{Out}(b_{j+1}). \tag{9}$$

(8) implies (by (7)) that immediately prior to the execution of b_{j+1} in the process $\overline{\overline{mix}}$ the inclusion

$$x \in sv \tag{10}$$

takes place. But if (9) and (10) are satisfied simultaneously then this contradicts (5) that proves the desired.

Then, we shall prove (2). Let there exist x such that

$$x \in \mathrm{Out}(b_j) \tag{11}$$

and

$$x \in \mathrm{In}(b_{j+1}). \tag{12}$$

(11) implies (by (6)) that immediately prior to the execution of b_{j+1} in the process $\overline{\overline{mix}}$ the inclusion

$$x \in ssv \tag{13}$$

takes place. But if (12) and (13) are satisfied simultaneously then this contradicts (4) that proves the desired.

---

*) Here we need one more logical step: we have to show that there exist such pairs b_j, b_s that $j<s$, b_j is suspended, b_s is not suspended and b_j, b_s are commutative. But this follows from (1),(2), (3) and the monotonicity of sv and ssv.

Now, we shall prove (3). Let there exist x such that

$$x \in In(b_j) \tag{14}$$

and

$$x \in Out(b_{j+1}) \tag{15}$$

(14) implies (by (7)) that immediately prior to the execution of b_{j+1} in the process $\overline{\overline{mix}}$ the inclusion

$$x \in sv \tag{16}$$

takes place. But if (15) and (16) are satisfied simultaneously then this contradicts (5) that proves the desired. QED

20°. Observation. Relations (1),(2) and (3) suggest that in the process $\overline{\overline{vdiv}}_{R_1}$ the residual program may be executed gradually, during its formation, in parallel with the partial (mixed) execution of the initial program.

21°. Observation. A question may arise: what's the reason to introduce sv? Isn't sufficient to have (6) only? A program Π_1 clears the question.

$\Pi_1(x,y,z)$

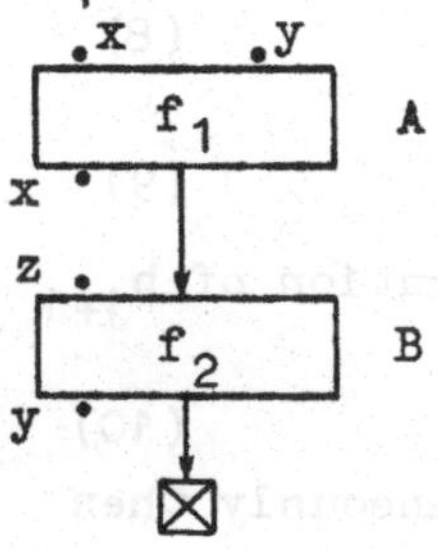

Here, $R = \{x,y,z\}$, $R_1 = \{x\}$, $\mathcal{C}_0 = (x_0,y_0,z_0)$. If in the definition of $\overline{\overline{mix}}$ in the items 32 and 52 to restrict ourself by the transformation (6) only, and to use in the conditions of the items 3 and 5 ssv instead of sv then the statement A would be suspended, ssv prior to B would equal to $\{x\}$ and B would be not suspended and having been executed in the process $\overline{\overline{mix}}$, would "spoil" the required for A value of y. We could use ssv totally instead of sv but this would reduce the degree of the partial computation of the initial program.

MEMORY FACTORIZATION THEOREM

22°. Let

$$d_1 \dots d_s \dots$$

be a sequence (finite or infinite) of statements and predicates of a program Π taken in the order of their occurrences in the process $comp(\mathcal{C}_0, \Pi(R))$. A variable $x \in R$ is called an i n p u t variable for this process if there is d_s such that

a) $x \in In(d_s)$,
b) $x \notin Out(d_k)$ $(k=1,\dots,s-1)$

Speaking differently, x is an input variable if the value $\mathcal{T}_0(x)$ is used in the process.

A feasible hypothesis arises that any variable $x \in R \setminus R_1$ is not an input variable for the process

$$\underset{R_1}{\mathrm{div}}(\mathcal{T}_0, \Pi(R)) = \mathrm{comp}(\underset{R_1}{\mathrm{vmix}}(\mathcal{T}_0, \Pi(R)),\ \underset{R_1}{\mathrm{rmix}}(\mathcal{T}_0, \Pi(R))).$$

The meaning of the hypothesis is in that the process $\underset{R_1}{\mathrm{mix}}(\mathcal{T}_0, \Pi(R))$ uses "completely" all the information on values $\mathcal{T}_0(x)$ where $x \in R \setminus R_1$. However, as the example of program $\Pi_2(R)$ shows, in the general case the hypothesis is not valid.

Indeed, let us consider the process $\underset{\{y\}}{\mathrm{mix}}(\mathcal{T}_0, \Pi_2)$. The following events will happen in this process:

$\Pi_2(R)$

$R = \{x, y, z\}$

$R_1 = \{y\}$

$\mathcal{T}_0 = (x_0, y_0, z_0)$

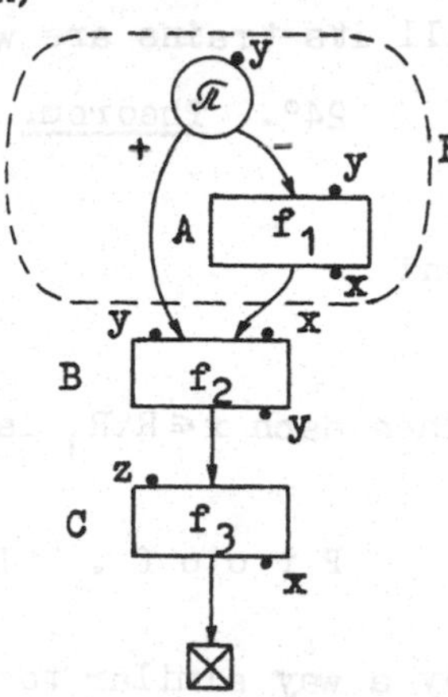

a) The train F will be suspended with

$\mathrm{In}(F) = \{y\}$

$\mathrm{Out}(F) = \{x\}$.

Since $x \notin \mathrm{In}(F)$, the prefix $x := x_0$ will not appear. However, x as an output variable of F will be further suspended.

b) The statement B="$y := f_2(y, x)$" will be suspended and, again, since both variables are suspended, no prefix will appear when attaching this statement to the residual program.

c) The statement C="$x := f_3(z)$" will be executed.

Thus,

$$\underset{\{y\}}{\mathrm{vmix}}(\mathcal{T}_0, \Pi_2(x, y)) = (f_3(z_0), y_0, z_0) = \hat{\mathcal{T}}_0,$$

$$\underset{\{y\}}{\mathrm{rmix}}(\mathcal{T}_0, (\Pi_2(x, y)) = \Bigg[$$

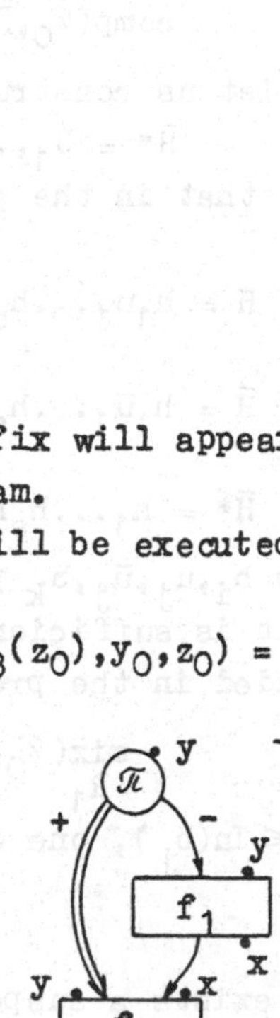

$$\Bigg] = \hat{\Pi}_2 .$$

Let us now suppose that $\mathcal{A}(y_0)=1$. Then x is an input variable for $comp(\hat{\mathcal{C}}_0,\hat{\Pi}_2)$ that contradicts the hypothesis.

The matter is that though $x \in Out(F)$ it is computed along not all paths connecting the entry and exit vertices of the train F. If we make an equivalent transformation by putting the transfer x:=x at the arc $\mathcal{A}^+$ then x will become in input variable for the train obtained and the value of x will be memorized in the train's prefix during its suspension.

23°. A train F^i is called w e l l - f o r m e d if there is an assignment to each $x \in Out(F^i)$ along any path connecting the entry and exit vertices of the train. A program Π is called well-formed if all its trains are well-formed.

24°. Theorem. Let $\Pi(R)$ be well-formed,

$$\hat{\mathcal{C}}_0 = \underset{R_1}{vmix}(\mathcal{C}_0,\Pi)$$

and

$$\hat{\Pi} = \underset{R_1}{rmix}(\mathcal{C}_0,\Pi).$$

Then each $x \in R \setminus R_1$ is not an input variable for the process

$$comp(\hat{\mathcal{C}}_0,\hat{\Pi}(R))$$

P r o o f . Let us construct a sequence

$$\bar{H}^* = b_1,..b_m$$

by a way similar to that in the proof of the theorem 8°. We construct first

$$H = h_1u_1...h_su_sh_{s+1}\ , \quad s \geq 0$$

then

$$\bar{H} = h_1\bar{u}_1...h_s\bar{u}_sh_{s+1}$$

and, finally,

$$\bar{H}^* = h_1...h_sh_{s+1}\bar{u}_1...\bar{u}_s\ ,$$

where the notations $h_i, u_j, \bar{u}_j, b_k$ preserve their meaning. In order to prove the theorem it is sufficient to show that, for an arbitrary b_j $(1 \leq j \leq m)$ suspended in the process

$$\underset{R_1}{mix}(\mathcal{C}_0,\Pi(R)) \qquad (X)$$

and an arbitrary $y \in In(b_j)$, one of the following statements (a,b,c) holds

a) $y \in R_1$,

b) there exists a suspended b_i such that $b_i \xrightarrow{y} b_j$,

c) there is an assignment to y in a prefix b_j.

Indeed, in these and only in these cases each $x \in R \setminus R_1$ is not an input variable for $comp(\hat{\mathcal{T}}_0,\hat{\Pi})$. Here, we take into account that $\hat{\Pi}$ is a sequence of suspended b_i-s and also the fact that, due to the well-formedness of the trains, the relation $b_i \xrightarrow{y} b_j$ implies that b_i contains a statement which assigns to y in the process $comp(\hat{\mathcal{T}}_0,\hat{\Pi})$.

Thus, let $y \in In(b_j)$. We shall consider the following cases.

1) y is not suspended immediately prior to b_j in the process (X). Then c) holds.

2) y is suspended immediately prior to b_j in the process (X).

2.1) There exists b_i in $\bar{H}^*$ such that $b_i \xrightarrow{y} b_j$. Then b) holds.

2.2) There is no b_i in $\bar{H}^*$ such that $b_i \xrightarrow{y} b_j$. Then a) holds. QED

A SIMPLE CASE OF MIXED COMPUTATION

25°. There exists an interesting simple and correct scheme of mixed computation which is denoted as $\underset{R_1}{\mathring{mix}}(\mathcal{T}_0,\Pi(R))$ where $R_1 \subseteq R$.

```
1: i:=i₁; 𝒯:= 𝒯₀; ssv:=R₁; resp:= Λ; goto 2;
2: if i is an operational vertex then 3 else 4;
3: if All(Aⁱ) ∩ ssv=∅ then 31 else 32;
   31: 𝒯:=Aⁱ(𝒯); i:=next(i); goto 2;
   32: resp:=attach(resp,Aⁱ); ssv:=ssv ∪ All(Aⁱ);
       i:=next(i); goto 2;
4: if i is a logical vertex then 5 else 6;
5: if In(pⁱ) ∩ ssv=∅ then 51 else 52;
   51: i:=alternative(i,pⁱ,𝒯); goto 2;
   52: resp:=attach(resp,Fⁱ); ssv:=ssv ∪ All(Fⁱ);
       i:=focus(i); goto 2;
6: resp:=end(resp); goto 61;
   61.
```

Here,

$$All(A^i) = In(A^i) \cup Out(A^i)$$
$$All(F^i) = In(F^i) \cup Out(F^i)$$

The correctness is proved similarly using the commutativity of occurrences b_j and b_s in the history H where $j<s$, b_j is suspended and b_s is not.

CONCLUSION

Three schemes of mixed computation have been defined and studied: mix, $\overline{\overline{mix}}$ and $\mathring{mix}$. For a given R_1, the following inclusions take place: $ssv(mix) \subseteq ssv(\overline{\overline{mix}}) \subseteq ssv(\mathring{mix})$. The processes $\overline{\overline{mix}}$ and $\mathring{mix}$ are correct in the general case, mix is more effective but requires a kind of memory protection.

In all three processes, suspended statements and trains are attached to the extending residual program without any modification. However, an evaluation of some functional and predicate terms is possible in a suspended statement or train that can greatly simplify the residual program.. This and some other optimizations in mixed computation are the subject of further study.

REFERENCES

1. A.P.Ershov. On the principle of partial computation. Information Processing Letters, 1977, No. 2.

2. A.P.Ershov. On the essence of compilation. IFIP Working Conference on "Formal description of programming concepts". S.Andrews, Canada, August, 1977.

ALGEBRA AND LOGIC IN THEORETICAL COMPUTER SCIENCE

Ferenc Gécseg
and
Péter E.-Tóth

Research Group on Mathematical Logic
and Automata Theory of the Hungarian
Academy of Sciences
H-6720 Szeged, Somogyi u. 7.

Introduction

The results presented in this paper were achieved in the framework of the Research Group on Mathematical Logic and Automata Theory of the Hungarian Academy of Sciences during the recent years.

The paper consists of three parts. In the first part results concerning automaton mappings and composition of automata are presented. The second part deals with tree automata as universal algebras. Moreover, in this part we shall concern with ascending tree automata (top-down tree automata in the literature), and give their canonical form. The third part is devoted to investigations of program verification.

The first two parts have the common feature that the methods used and results stated in them are algebraic in character. The methods applied in the third part are both algebraic and logical.

It should be mentioned that here we collected only results which, beside being algebraic and logical, belong to the Theoretical Computer Science. It would be worthy to mention further results grown out from practice (e.g. algebraic models for information retrieval systems etc.), but the authors regret to make this paper more heterogeneous.

1. Composition of automata, automaton mappings

The concept of simulation, generalized composition and generalized α_i-composition (shortly g. composition and g. α_i-composition) of automata was introduced by Gécseg [8]. The g. composition is that generalization of composition when we allow input words as inputs of component automata in a composition. The g. α_i-composition is a special case of the g. composition which can be interpreted in the following way. Let us order the set of component automata in a g. composition. If $j \geq i$ under this ordering and the states of the jth component are fed back to the input of the ith component then it is said that the length of this feed-back is $j-i+1$. Now in the case of g. α_i-composition there exists a well ordering on the set of all component automata of this g. composition such that the maximum of the length of the feed-backs under this well ordering is not greater than i.

The simulation is a form of homomorphic or isomorphic representation under which input words can occur as counter images of input signals.

Now let us give the terminology used in this part.

By an automaton we mean a system $\underline{A}=(X,A,\delta)$, where
(i) X is the input set,
(ii) A is the state set,
(iii) $\delta : A \times X \to A$ is the transition function.

In the sequel we assume that the automata investigated in this paper are finite, i.e., their input and state sets are finite.

For the free monoid generated by a set H we shall use the notation H^*.

Consider two automata $\underline{A}=(X,A,\delta)$ and $\underline{B}=(X',B,\delta')$. We say that $\underline{A}$ homomorphically simulates $\underline{B}$ if there exist a one-to-one mapping τ_1 of X' into X^* and a mapping τ_2 of a subset $A' (\subseteq A)$ onto B such that the equation

$$\tau_2(a\tau_1(x)) = \delta'(\tau_2(a),x)$$

holds for any $a \in A'$ and $x \in X'$. If τ_2 is also 1-1 then we speak about isomorphic simulation.

Take a system $\underline{A}_i = (X_i, A_i, \delta_i)$ $(i=1,\dots,n)$ of automata and a (nonvoid) set X. Furthermore, let

$$\varphi : A_1 \times \dots \times A_n \times X \to X_1^* \times \dots \times X_n^*$$

be a mapping. Define an automaton $\underline{A} = (X, A, \delta)$ in the following way: $A = A_1 \times \dots \times A_n$, and for arbitrary $(a_1, \dots, a_n) \in A$ and $x \in X$,

$$\delta((a_1, \dots, a_n), x) = (a_1 p_1, \dots, a_n p_n),$$

where $(p_1, \dots, p_n) = \varphi(a_1, \dots, a_n, x)$. This automaton $\underline{A}$ is called the g. composition of $\underline{A}_1, \dots, \underline{A}_n$ with respect to the set X and the mapping φ. The mapping φ is the feed-back of the g. composition. If the feed-back function φ of this g. composition can be given in the form

$$\varphi(a_1, \dots, a_n, x) = (\varphi_1(a_1, \dots, a_n, x), \dots, \varphi_n(a_1, \dots, a_n, x))$$

such that φ_j is independent of states having indices greater than or equal to $j+i$ for a fixed nonnegative integer i, then we speak about g. α_i-composition.

Obviously, if φ is of the form

$$\varphi : A_1 \times \dots \times A_n \times X \to X_1 \times \dots \times X_n$$

then we get the concept of the composition of automata, or product of automata using Gluškov's terminology (cf. [10]). Furthermore, the α_0-product is the same as loop-free composition introduced by Hartmanis [12].

Take a system M of automata. We say that M is homomorphically S-complete with respect to the g. composition (g. α_i-composition) if for each automaton $\underline{A}$ there exists a g. composition (g. α_i-composition) $\underline{B}$ of automata from M such that $\underline{B}$ homomorphically simulates $\underline{A}$. The concept of isomorphic S-completeness can be obtained by an obvious modification of the previous definition. Moreover, we speak about complete systems if in the definition above simulation is replaced by homomorphism or isomorphism.

Now we presents some results showing the interrelation between different types of compositions and representations.

Theorem 1 [8]. There exists no system of automata which is homomorphically S-complete with respect to the g. α_0-composition and minimal.

On the other hand, Dömösi [2] proved the existence of a system of automata which is homomorphically complete with respect to the α_0-product and minimal.

Theorem 2 [8]. There exists a system M of automata such that M is homomorphically S-complete with respect to the g. α_0-composition but not isomorphically S-complete with respect to the g. α_0-composition.

For g. α_1-compositions we have

Theorem 3 [8]. A system of automata is homomorphically S-complete with respect to the g. α_1-composition iff it is isomorphically S-complete with respect to the g. α_1-composition.

One can show that Theorem 1 is also valid for g. α_1-composition.

Furthermore, it is also true that homomorphic and isomorphic simulations do not coincide with respect to the g. α_1-product if the component automata are taken from an arbitrary set of automata instead of an S-complete system.

By comparing Theorems 2 and 3, we see that the g. α_1-composition is a proper generalization of the g. α_0-composition.

The next results show that for $i > 1$ the g. α_i-compositions and the g. composition are equivalent with respect to the S-completeness.

Theorem 4 [8]. A system of automata is homomorphically S-complete with respect to the g. composition iff it is isomorphically S-complete with respect to the g. α_i-composition for any $i > 1$.

From this we get the following important

Corollary. If $i > 1$ then there exists a finite system of automata which is isomorphically S-complete with respect to the g. α_i-composition.

Furthermore, a stronger version of Theorem 4 also holds. Namely, we have

Theorem 5 [8]. Let M be an arbitrary system of automata. An Automaton $\underline{A}$ can be simulated homomorphically by a g. composition of automata from M iff $\underline{A}$ can be simulated isomorphically by a g. α_2-composition of automata from M.

In the rest of this section we shall deal with representations of automaton mappings by composition of automata.

If we attach an output to an automaton then we arrive at the concept of a sequential machine. Accordingly, by a sequential machine we mean a system $\underline{A} = (X, A, Y, \delta, \lambda)$, where X, A and δ are the same as in the definition of an automaton, Y is the output set and $\lambda : A\times X \to Y$ is the output function of $\underline{A}$. One can extend λ to a mapping $\lambda' : A\times X^* \to Y^*$ in the following way: for any $a \in A$, $\lambda'(a,e)=e$, where e is the empty word, and for any $a \in A$ and $p=p'x$ $(p,p' \in X^*)$, $x \in X)$, $\lambda'(a,p) = \lambda'(a,p')\lambda(ap',x)$. Since this extension is unique, thus for λ' we use the same notation λ. Fix a state $a \in A$. Then $f_{\underline{A},a}(p) = \lambda(a,p)$ $(p \in X^*)$ is a mapping of X^* into Y^*. We say that $f_{\underline{A},a}$ is the automaton mapping induced by $\underline{A}$ in a. Furthermore, $f: X^* \to Y^*$ is an automaton mapping if there exists a sequential machine $\underline{A} = (X, A, Y, \delta, \lambda)$ and an $a \in A$ such that $f = f_{\underline{A},a}$.

We can extend the concept of product and α_i-product to sequential machines.

Take a system $\underline{A}_i = (X_i, A_i, Y_i, \delta_i, \lambda_i)$ $(i=1,\dots,n)$ of sequential machines and two nonvoid finite sets X and Y. Furthermore, let φ and ψ be mappings:

$$\varphi : A\times X \to X_1\times\dots\times X_n$$

and $(A = A_1\times\dots\times A_n)$.

$$\psi : A\times X \to Y$$

Then the sequential machine $\underline{A} = (X, A, Y, \delta, \lambda)$ for which (X, A, δ) is a product (α_i-product) of (X_i, A_i, δ_i) $(i=1,\dots,n)$ with respect to φ, and $\lambda((a_1,\dots,a_n),x) = \psi(a_1,\dots,a_n,x)$ $((a_1,\dots,a_n) \in A,\ x \in X)$ is called the product (α_i-product) of $\underline{A}_i$ $(i=1,\dots,n)$ with respect to X, Y and φ, ψ.

Let M be a system of sequential machines. M is complete with respect to the product (α_i-product) if for any automaton mapping $f: X^* \to Y^*$ there is a product (α_i-product) $\underline{A} = (X, A, Y, \delta, \lambda)$ of sequential machines from M and an $a \in A$ such that $f=f_{\underline{A},a}$.

It was shown by Gluškov [10] that there exists a finite complete system of sequential machines. Furthermore, in [6] we proved that there is no finite system of sequential machines which is complete with respect to the α_i-product with $i=0,1$. (Let us note that the above mentioned results are formulated in terms of automata instead of sequential machines. Since the output function in the composition of sequential machines is independent of the outputs of the component machines thus we can confine ourselves to automata. Therefore, both formalisms lead to the same result.)

The authors of this paper have no results concerning complete systems of sequential machines with respect to the α_i-products if $i>1$. Although if we confine ourselves to representations of automaton mappings in finite length then we can present a quite strong result.

For a word $p \in X^*$ let us denote by $|p|$ the length of p.

It is said that a machine $\underline{A} = (X, A, Y, \delta, \lambda)$ <u>induces an automaton mapping</u> $f: X^* \to Y^*$ <u>in length</u> n, where n is a natural number, if there is an $a \in A$ such that for arbitrary $p \in X^*$, $f(p) = f_{\underline{A},a}(p)$ provided $|p| \le n$.

We say that the α_i-product is <u>metrically equivalent</u> to the α_j-product if for any automaton mapping f, natural number n and system M of sequential machines, f can be induced in length n by an α_i-product of machines from M iff f can be induced in length n by an α_j-product of machines from M.

One can define metrical equivalence of any type of products in a similar way.

For metrical equivalence, we have

<u>Theorem 6</u> [7]. For any $(i=0,1,\dots)$ the α_i-product is metrically equivalent to the (general) product.

2. <u>Tree automata</u>

We assume that the reader is familiar with the basic concepts and results of the theory of universal algebras. (For a good presentation of universal algebras, see [11].)

Let $\mathfrak{A}=(A,F)$ be a universal algebra (of type F). For a given n, take a vector $\underline{a}=(a^{(1)},\dots,a^{(n)})$ $(a^{(i)}\in A;\ i=1,\dots,n)$. Moreover, let $A'\subseteq A$. Then the system $\overline{\mathfrak{A}}=(\mathfrak{A},\underline{a},A')$ is called an n-ary F-automaton, or (a tree automaton) where $\underline{a}$ is the initial vector and A' is the set of final states of $\overline{\mathfrak{A}}$ (see, [14]). In the sequel it will be assumed that $\mathfrak{A}$ is finite.

Let us denote by $T_{F,n}$ the set of all n-ary polynomial symbols of type F (or n-ary F-trees using tree automata theoretic terminology). Then the forest $T(\overline{\mathfrak{A}})$ recognized by the n-ary F-automaton $\overline{\mathfrak{A}}$ is defined by

$$T(\overline{\mathfrak{A}})=\{p\,|\,p\in T_{F,n},\ p(\underline{a})\in A'\}\ .$$

We assume that the variables of an n-ary polynomial symbol are from the set $X_n=\{x_1,\dots,x_n\}$.

Now let us recall the definition of the frontier $fr(p)$ of $p\in T_{F,n}$:

(1) if $p=x_i$ $(1\le i\le n)$ then $fr(p)=x_i$,

(2) if $p=f$ for a 0-ary operational symbol f, then $fr(p)=e$,

(3) if $p=f(p_1,\dots,p_m)$ then $fr(p)=fr(p_1)\dots fr(p_m)$.

If $T\subseteq T_{F,n}$ then $fr(T)=\{fr(p)\,|\,p\in T\}$. It is well known that for any recognizable forest T, $fr(T)$ is a context-free language, and conversely, for any context-free language L over X_n there is an and a recognizable $T\subseteq T_{F,n}$ such that $fr(T)=L$.

In [4] Ferenci presents another representation of context-free languages by tree automata. To show it, let us note that every $p\in T_{F,n}$ can be considered a word over $F\cup X_n\cup\{(,)\}=G$. Now define the homomorphism $h:G^*\to F^*$ given by

$$h(g)=\begin{cases} g & \text{if } g\in F,\\ e & \text{otherwise.}\end{cases}$$

Then the language $L(\overline{\mathfrak{A}})$ accepted by an n-ary F-automaton $\overline{\mathfrak{A}}$ is $L(\overline{\mathfrak{A}})=h(T(\overline{\mathfrak{A}}))$.

It is valid

Theorem 1 [4]. A language is context-free iff it can be accepted by a tree automaton.

Another direction in our research concerning tree automata is the investigation of how properties of the underlying universal algebras reflect in the properties of the corresponding tree automata. On this line in [9] we proved the existence of a proper equational class C of F-algebras, where F-contains a binary and a 0-ary operational symbol, having the following property: for any context-free language L over X_n there is an n-ary F-automaton $\overline{\mathfrak{A}} = (\mathfrak{A}, \underline{a}, A')$ with $\mathfrak{A} \in C$ and $fr(T(\overline{\mathfrak{A}}))=L$. Moreover, it was shown in the same paper that for any F there exists no proper equational class K of F-algebras such that for any n, recognizable $T \subseteq T_{F,n}$, T is recognized by an n-ary F-automaton whose algebra belongs to K.

Tree automata defined above investigate a tree from frontier to root. There is another type of tree automata which computes a tree from root to frontier.

Let $\mathfrak{A} = (A, F, A', \underline{a})$ be a system, where

(1) A is a nonvoid finite set, the state set of $\mathfrak{A}$,

(2) F is a set of operational symbols,

(3) $A' \subseteq A$ is the set of initial states,

(4) $\underline{a}=(a^{(1)},\dots,a^{(n)})$ $(a^{(i)} \in A;\ i=1,\dots,n)$ is the final state vector.

(5) for any m-ary $f \in F$ and $a \in A$, $a(f)_{\mathfrak{A}} \subseteq A^m$ if $m > 0$, and $(f)_{\mathfrak{A}} \subseteq A$ if $m=0$, where $(f)_{\mathfrak{A}}$ is the realization of f on $\mathfrak{A}$.

Then $\mathfrak{A}$ is called a nondeterministic n-ary ascending F-automaton. If $A'=\{a_0\}$ $(a_0 \in A)$ and $a(f)_{\mathfrak{A}} \in A^m$ if f is m-ary with $m>0$, or $(f)_{\mathfrak{A}} \in A$ if $m=0$ then $\mathfrak{A}$ is called a deterministic n-ary ascending F-automaton.

Now let us define a mapping $\alpha_{\mathfrak{A}} : T_{F,n} \to \mathcal{P}(A)$ in the following way:

(1) if $p=x_i$ then $\alpha_{\mathfrak{A}}(p)=a^{(i)}$,

(2) if p=f for some 0-ary operational symbol f, then $\alpha_{\mathfrak{A}}(p)=(f)_{\mathfrak{A}}$,

(3) if $p=f(p_1,\dots,p_m)$ then

$$a \in \alpha_{\mathfrak{A}}(p) \Leftrightarrow af \cap \alpha_{\mathfrak{A}}(p_1)\times\dots\times\alpha_{\mathfrak{A}}(p_m) \neq \emptyset .$$

Then the forest $T(\mathfrak{A})$ recognized by $\mathfrak{A}$ is defined by $T(\mathfrak{A}) = \{p \mid p \in T_{F,n},\ \alpha_{\mathfrak{A}}(p) \cap A' \neq \emptyset\}$.

It is well known that a forest can be recognized by a (deterministic) tree automaton iff it can be recognized by a nondeterministic ascending tree automaton. Moreover, the class of forests recognized by deterministic ascending tree automata is a proper subclass of the class of forests recognized by tree automata.

In the deterministic case it is useful to look for the minimal tree automata recognizing a given forest. Brainerd [1] showed that the minimal tree automaton is unique up to isomorphism, and presented a minimizing algorithm. In the literature no similar results concerning deterministic ascending tree automata are known.

Steinby and Gécseg defined a canonical form of deterministic ascending tree automata and proved that it is minimal and unique up to isomorphism. This result will be published in Acta Cybernetica, next year.

Here we present the minimizing algorithm and the idea of the proof. For sake of simplicity, we confine ourselves to the case when no 0-ary operational symbols occur. Moreover, by an ascending tree automaton we always mean a deterministic one.

If φ is a mapping of A into B, and $\underline{a} = (a_1,\dots,a_n)$ $(a_i \in A;\ i=1,\dots,n)$ is a vector then let $\varphi(\underline{a}) = (\varphi(a_1),\dots,\varphi(a_n))$.

Take two n-ary ascending F-automata $\mathfrak{A} = (A,F,a_0,\underline{a})$ and $\mathfrak{B} = (B,F,b_0,\underline{b})$. Let φ be a mapping of A onto B such that the following conditions are satisfied:

(1) $\varphi(a_0) = b_0$,

(2) for any m-ary $f \in F$ and $a \in A$, $\varphi(a)f = (\varphi(a_1),\dots,\varphi(a_m))$ if $af = (a_1,\dots,a_m)$,

(3) $\varphi(A^{(i)}) = B^{(i)}$ and $\varphi^{-1}(B^{(i)}) = A^{(i)}$, where $A^{(i)}$ and $B^{(i)}$ are respectively the ith components of $\underline{a}$ and $\underline{b}$. Then φ is a <u>homomorphism</u> of $\mathfrak{A}$ onto $\mathfrak{B}$, and $\mathfrak{B}$ is a <u>homomorphic image</u> of $\mathfrak{A}$. If φ is 1-1 then we speak about <u>isomorphism,</u> in notation, $\mathfrak{A} \cong \mathfrak{B}$.

<u>Theorem 2.</u> If $\mathfrak{B}$ is a homomorphic image of $\mathfrak{A}$ then $T(\mathfrak{A}) = T(\mathfrak{B})$.

For any equivalence relation ϱ on A and vectors $\underline{a} = (a_1,\dots,a_m)$ and $\underline{b} = (b_1,\dots,b_m)$ of elements from A let $\underline{a} \equiv \underline{b}(\varrho)$ iff $a_i \equiv b_i(\varrho)$ for all $(i=1,\dots,m)$.

Let $\mathfrak{A}$ be an n-ary ascending F-automaton and ϱ an equivalence relation on A. Then ϱ is a <u>congruence relation</u> of $\mathfrak{A}$ if the following two conditions are satisfied:

(1) for any m-ary $f \in F$ and $a,b \in A$, $a \equiv b(\varrho)$ implies

$af \equiv bf(\varrho)$,

(2) if $a \in A^{(i)}$ and $a \equiv b(\varrho)$ then $b \in A^{(i)}$ for all $i(=1,\dots,m)$.

Using congruence relations we shall define the concept of a quotient automaton of an ascending F-automaton.

Let $\mathfrak{A}$ be an n-ary ascending F-automaton and ϱ a congruence relation of $\mathfrak{A}$. Define an n-ary ascending F-automaton $\mathfrak{A}/\varrho = (A/\varrho, F, \varrho(a_0), \underline{a}/\varrho)$ in the following way: $\underline{a}/\varrho = (A^{(1)}/\varrho, \dots, A^{(m)}/\varrho)$, and for any m-ary $f \in F$ and $a \in A$, $\varrho(a)f = (\varrho(a_1), \dots, \varrho(a_m))$ if $af = (a_1, \dots, a_m)$. This $\mathfrak{A}/\varrho$ is called the <u>quotient automaton</u> of $\mathfrak{A}$ induced by ϱ.

<u>Theorem 3.</u> Let $\mathfrak{A}$ and $\mathfrak{B}$ be two n-ary ascending F-automata. If $\mathfrak{B}$ is a homomorphic image of $\mathfrak{A}$ then $\mathfrak{B}$ is isomorphic to a quotient automaton of $\mathfrak{A}$. Conversely, every quotient automaton of $\mathfrak{A}$ is a homomorphic image of $\mathfrak{A}$.

Consider an n-ary ascending F-automaton $\mathfrak{A}$, and let $a \in A$. Set

$$T_a = \{p \mid p \in T_{F,n},\ a \in \alpha_{\mathfrak{A}}(p)\} .$$

If for an $a \in A$ we have $T_a = \emptyset$ then a is called a 0-<u>state.</u> Moreover, $\mathfrak{A}$ is <u>normalized</u> if for any $f \in F$ and $a \in A$ whenever af has a component which is a 0-state then all of its components are 0-states.

Let $\mathfrak{A}$ be a normalized n-ary ascending F-automaton, and define the relation $\varrho_{\mathfrak{A}}$ on A in the following way: for two $a, b \in A$, $a \equiv b(\varrho_{\mathfrak{A}})$ iff $T_a = T_b$.

<u>Theorem 4.</u> $\varrho_{\mathfrak{A}}$ is a congruence relation of $\mathfrak{A}$.

From this result, by Theorems 2 and 3, we get the following

<u>Corollary.</u> Let $\mathfrak{A}$ be a normalized ascending tree automaton. Then $T(\mathfrak{A}) = T(\mathfrak{A}/\varrho_{\mathfrak{A}})$.

Let us note that in $\mathfrak{A}/\varrho_{\mathfrak{A}}$ if $\varrho_{\mathfrak{A}}(a) \neq \varrho_{\mathfrak{A}}(b)$ then $T_{\varrho_{\mathfrak{A}}(a)} \neq T_{\varrho_{\mathfrak{A}}(b)}$.

Consider an ascending F-automaton $\mathfrak{A}$, and let $B_1, B_2 \subseteq A$. We say that B_2 is <u>directly reachable</u> from B_1 in $\mathfrak{A}$ (in notation, $B_1 \Rightarrow_{\mathfrak{A}} B_2$) if for each $b \in B_2$ there is an $a \in B_1$ and an $f \in F$ such that b is a component of af. The reflexive, transitive closure of $\Rightarrow_{\mathfrak{A}}$ will be denoted by $\Rightarrow^*_{\mathfrak{A}}$.

We say that an ascending tree automaton $\mathfrak{A}$ is <u>connected</u> if for any $a \in A$ there is a $B \subseteq A$ such that $a \in B$ and $\{a_0\} \Rightarrow^*_{\mathfrak{A}} B$.

An ascending tree automaton $\mathfrak{A}$ is called <u>reduced</u> if $\mathfrak{A}$ is connected, normalized and $\varrho_{\mathfrak{A}}$ is the equality relation on A.

Now we are ready to formulate our main result concerning minimization of deterministic ascending tree automata.

<u>Theorem 5.</u> Let $\mathfrak{A}$ and $\mathfrak{B}$ be two connected and normalized n-ary ascending F-automata. Then $T(\mathfrak{A}) = T(\mathfrak{B})$ iff $\mathfrak{A}/\varrho_{\mathfrak{A}} \cong \mathfrak{B}/\varrho_{\mathfrak{B}}$.

<u>Corollary.</u> Let $T \subseteq T_{F,n}$ be a recognizable forest and let K_T denote the class of all connected normalized n-ary ascending F-automata recognizing $T \subseteq T_{F,n}$. Then there is a $\mathfrak{C}$ in K_T which is a homomorphic image of arbitrary $\mathfrak{A} \in K_T$. Moreover, any reduced automaton from K_T can be taken as $\mathfrak{C}$.

By the Corollary to Theorem 5, for any recognizable $T \subseteq T_{F,n}$, every reduced n-ary ascending F-automaton recognizing T is minimal among all n-ary ascending F-automata recognizing the same T. Moreover, all such reduced automata are isomorphic.

Next we present an algorithm which for any n-ary ascending F-automaton $\mathfrak{A}$ yields a reduced n-ary ascending automaton $\mathfrak{C}$ with $T(\mathfrak{A}) = T(\mathfrak{C})$.

I. For any $a \in A$ decide whether $T_a = \emptyset$. This can be done in the obvious way since $T_a \neq \emptyset$ iff there is a $p \in T_{F,n}$ with $d(p) < |A|$ such that $p \in T_a$. Thus we can determine all the 0-states of $\mathfrak{A}$. ($d(p)$ denotes the depth of p.)

II. If $\mathfrak{A}$ is not normalized then, using step I, choose an arbitrary 0-state $* \in A$, and whenever af has a component which is a 0-state then replace all its components by $*$. Denote by $\mathfrak{A}^*$ the resulting automaton. One can show that $T(\mathfrak{A}) = T(\mathfrak{A}^*)$.

III. If $\mathfrak{A}^*$ is not connected then take the subautomaton of $\mathfrak{A}^*$ whose all states are reachable from $\{a_0\}$. This subautomaton can also be determined since all its states are reachable from $\{a_0\}$ by a derivation of length shorter than $|A|$. Denote by $\mathfrak{B}$ the resulting automaton. Obviously, $\mathfrak{B}$ is connected, normalized and $T(\mathfrak{B}) = T(\mathfrak{A})$.

IV. For $\mathfrak{B}$ obtained by step III we determine $\varrho_{\mathfrak{B}}$. This can be done by defining the following system of binary relations ϱ_j $(j=0,1,\ldots)$: for any $a,b \in B$

(1) $a \equiv b(\varrho_0)$ iff $a \in B^{(i)} \Longleftrightarrow b \in B^{(i)}$ for all $i=1,\ldots,n$,

(2) $a \equiv b(\varrho_j)$ $(j>0)$ iff $a \equiv b(\varrho_{j-1})$ and $af \equiv bf(\varrho_{j-1})$ for any $f \in F$.

Since B is finite and ϱ_j is a refinement of ϱ_{j-1} $(j>0)$ thus there exists a k such that $\varrho_k = \varrho_{k+l}$ $(l=0,1,\ldots)$. One can show that $\varrho_{\mathfrak{B}} = \varrho_k$.

Finally, let $\mathfrak{C} = \mathfrak{B}/\varrho_{\mathfrak{B}}$.

3. Logical methods in program verification

Let us suppose that a programming language L_p is given and we want to prove the correctness of programs written in L_p. Then, evidently, the meaning of L_p is needed. For this we have to describe the meaning of texts (i.e., of programs) written in L_p using another language L.

The problem of finding a suitable language L for defining the semantics of L_p plays a central role in program verification. Usually three types of languages are chosen for this purpose: natural languages, computer languages and mathematical languages. At the beginning of Computer Science L was one of the natural languages or a "known" computer language. However, none of them satisfies the requirement that L should have a well defined semantics. Later formal languages over abstract machines were introduced (e.g. VDL). The fundamental disadvantage of such languages is that the semantics of L_p is defined implicitly by L. The most promising solution is to choose a mathematical, more precisely, a mathematical logical language as L. This approach receives ready results from different mathematical disciplines (e.g. mathematical logic, universal algebras, category theory, lattice theory, topology, graph theory etc.).

In this paper we assume that L is the language of classical first order logic. Here we shall only deal with results concerning deduction systems for L which is a fundamental tool in program verification.

Let $\mathcal{H} = (H;F)$ be a Herbrand universum, i.e., a word algebra generated by the empty set. Assume that the formulas of L are encoded by the elements of H. (Note that truth values are considered formulas.) Let us define the concept of a deduction system (or in other words, the concept of calculi) as follows.

A partial Turing computable function f over H is a <u>deduction system</u> (<u>calculi</u>) if the following conditions are satisfied:

(1) f is sound, i.e., φ is a tautology if $f(\varphi)$ = TRUE, and φ is unsatisfiable if $f(\varphi)$ = FALSE,

(2) f is complete for L, i.e., $f(\varphi)$ = TRUE if φ is a tautology, and $f(\varphi)$ = FALSE if φ is unsatisfiable,

(3) there are infinitely many formulas of L in the domain of f.

Then the following result was proved by E.-Tóth.

<u>Theorem 1.</u> Let $\mathcal{H}$ be a Herbrand universum and let the formulas of L be encoded by the elements of H. Then there is no "best" calculus for L under any Blum measure of computational complexity.

This result says that for any calculi there exist formulas which can be proved only in a "very" complicated way. Theorem 1 was proved by Longo and Venturini [13] in the special case when $\mathcal{H} = (H;\{f_0,f_1\})$ where H is the set of all nonnegative integers, f_0 and f_1 are 0-ary and unary, respectively; $(f_0)_{\mathcal{H}} = 0$ and $(f_1)_{\mathcal{H}}(n) = n+1$ $(n \in H)$.

With Theorem 1 in mind, one can raise the question whether there exist special types of formulas for which the best calculi exists. It has been shown that for Horn formulas the best calculi can be given.

The importance of Horn formulas is demonstrated by the observation that program verification problems can be formulated by using only Horn formulas (cf.[3]). In particular Floyd's method [5] was modified to show this fact.

References

1. Brainerd, W.S., The minimization of tree automata. Information and Control, 13(1968) 484-491.

2. Dömösi, P., On minimal R-complete systems of finite automata. Acta Cybernetica, 3(1976) 37-41.

3. Ecsedi-Tóth, P., Horn logic and its applications. Doctoral Dissertation, Rolando Eötvös University, Budapest, 1976 (in Hungarian).

4. Ferenci, F., A new representation of context-free languages by tree automata. Foundations of Control Engineering, 1(1976) 217-222.

5. Floyd, R.W., Assigning meaning to programs. In: Proc. of a Symposium in Applied Mathematics 19 (J. T. Schwartz, Ed.), pp. 19-32, 1967. Amer. Math. Soc.

6. Gécseg, F., Composition of automata. Proceedings of the 2nd Colloquium on Automata, Languages and Programming, 1974, Springer Lecture Notes in Computer Science, Vol. 14, 351-363.

7. Gécseg, F., Representation of automaton mappings in finite length. Acta Cybernetica, 2(1976) 285-289.

8. Gécseg, F., On products of abstract automata. Acta Sci. Math., 38(1976) 21-43.

9. Gécseg, F. and Horváth, Gy., On representation of trees and context-free languages by tree automata. Foundations of Control Engineering, 1(1976) 161-168.

10. Gluskov, V.M., Abstract theory of Automata.(Russian),Uspechi Matem Nauk ,16(1961) 3-62.

11. Grätzer, G., Universal Algebras, D. Van Nostrand Company, Princeton, New Yersey, 1968.

12. Hartmanis, J., Loop-free structure of sequential machines. Information and Control, 5(1962) 25-44.

13. Longo, G. and Venturini Zilli, M., Complexity of theorem proving procedures: some general properties. Rev. Francaise Automat. Informat. Recherche Operationelle Ser. Rouge 8, no. R-3.

14. Steinby, M., On algebras as tree automata. Universal Algebras, Colloquia Mathematica János Bolyai Societatis, North Holland Publishing Company, Amsterdam, 1977 (to appear).

A SURVEY OF RECENT PROBLEMS AND RESULTS

IN

ANALYTIC COMPUTATIONAL COMPLEXITY

B.Kacewicz and H.Woźniakowski
Department of Mathematics
University of Warsaw

ABSTRACT

We survey recent problems in analytic computational complexity. We deal primarily with the problem of solving nonlinear equations from complexity point of view. We summarize known results and we pose some open problems. The paper is concluded with new areas of further investigations in analytic computational complexity.

1. INTRODUCTION

Complexity measures the cost of an algorithm for solving a given problem. The costs may be defined, for example, as the number of arithmetic operations, size of storage or number of comparisons. Computational complexity deals with the complexity analysis of a class of algorithms or/and of a problem. The branch of complexity theory dealing with non-finite cost problems /e.g. nonlinear equations, approximation, differential equations/ is called analytic computational complexity. The aim of studying computational complexity is to find an optimal algorithm, i.e. an algorithm which minimizes the cost /complexity/ of solving a given problem. A detailed discussion and motivation of these concepts may be found in Traub [73, 76a, 76b].

In this paper we deal primarily with the problem of solving nonlinear equations from the computational complexity point of view. We summarize some known lower and upper bounds for complexity for a wide class of algorithms. We conclude the paper with some open problems and new areas for further investigations. Results on other problems of analytic computational complexity such as approximation, differential equations, etc may be found in Rice [76], Schultz [76] and Winograd [76].

2. COMPLEXITY OF ITERATIONS

Let

(2.1) $f : D \subset B_1 \rightarrow B_2$,

where D is an open subset of B_1, B_1 and B_2 are real or complex Banach spaces and $N = \dim(B_1) = \dim(B_2)$. We deal with a nonlinear equation

(2.2) $f(x) = 0.$

We assume α is a simple solution of (2.2), i.e., $f(\alpha) = 0$ and linear operator $f'(\alpha)^{-1}$ exists and is bounded.

Equation (2.2) is solved by an iteration $\mathcal{C}$ which generates a sequence of succesive approximations $\{x_i\}$ converging under certain assumptions to α. More precisely we assume that x_{i+1} depends on x_i and a fixed information set $\mathcal{N} = \mathcal{N}(f, x_i)$,i.e.,

(2.3) $x_{i+1} = \mathcal{C}(x_i, \mathcal{N}(f, x_i))$.

Suppose the iteration $\mathcal{C}$ terminates after k steps and the error $e_i = \|x_i - \alpha\|$ satisfies the relation

(2.4) $e_{i+1} = A_{i+1}\, e_i^{\,p}$, $i = 0,1,\ldots,k-1$,

where $p = p(\mathcal{C})$ is called the order of $\mathcal{C}$, A_{i+1} is called the error coefficient and

(2.5) $0 < \underline{A} \leq A_{i+1} \leq \bar{A} < +\infty$

for all i and all sufficiently small e_0.

We want to find x_k such that $e_k \leq \varepsilon' e_0$ for a given number $\varepsilon' \in (0,1)$. Let ε be defined by

(2.6) $e_k = \varepsilon\, e_0$ $(\varepsilon \leq \varepsilon')$.

We consider the total cost (complexity) of producing x_k by the iteration $\mathcal{C}$. Suppose that $c = c(\mathcal{C}, \mathcal{N})$ denotes the cost of one iterative step. Note that c consists of the cost of evaluating of the information set $u = u(f, \mathcal{N})$ and the cost of combining information to compute the next approximation $d = d(\mathcal{C})$.

Thus

(2.7) $c(\mathcal{C}, \mathcal{N}) = u(f, \mathcal{N}) + d(\mathcal{C})$.

Example 2.1

Let N = 1 and $\mathcal{C}$ be the Newton iteration, i.e.,

$$x_{i+1} = x_i - f'(x_i)^{-1} f(x_i) \qquad i = 0,1,\ldots,k-1 .$$

Then $\mathcal{N}(f, x_i) = [f(x_i), f'(x_i)]$. Equation (2.4) holds with p = 2 and $A_{i,1} = \left| \frac{1}{2} f''(\eta_i) / f'(x_i) \right|$, where η_i belongs to the interval spanned by α and x_i. Furthermore $u(f, \mathcal{N}) = c(f) + c(f')$, where $c(f^{(i)})$ denotes the cost of evaluating $f^{(i)}$ at a point and $d(\varphi)$ = the cost of one division and subtraction. □

The complexity of the iteration φ is defined by

(2.8) comp = k . c

We define the complexity index $z = z(f, \varphi)$ by

(2.9) $$z = \frac{c}{\log p}$$

Let

(2.10) $$\underline{w} = \left(\underline{A}^{\frac{1}{p-1}} e_o\right)^{-1}, \quad \bar{w} = \left(\bar{A}^{\frac{1}{p-1}} e_o\right)^{-1}$$

where $\underline{A}$ and $\bar{A}$ are given by (2.5). Then the following theorem holds.

Theorem 2.1 (Traub and Woźniakowski [76a])

If $2 \leqslant \underline{w} \leqslant \bar{w} \leqslant t$, $t = \lg(1/\varepsilon)$, then

(2.11) $$1 - \frac{\lg \lg t}{\lg t} \leqslant \frac{\text{comp}}{z \lg t} \leqslant 1 + \frac{\lg(1+1/t)}{\lg t} .$$

(all logarithms to base 2). □

The theorem states that complexity mostly depends on the complexity index z whenever $\underline{w}$ and $\bar{w}$ are in the interval [2, t]. Therefore we wish to find an iteration φ which for a given problem has a complexity index as small as possible. Recall that

$$z(f, \varphi) = \frac{u(f, \mathcal{N}) + d(\varphi)}{\log p(\varphi)} .$$

Let the information set $\mathfrak{N}$ be fixed and consider the class $\Phi(\mathfrak{N})$ of all iterations which use $\mathfrak{N}$. Let

(2.12) $$P_{max} = \sup_{\varphi \in \Phi(\mathfrak{N})} p(\varphi).$$

Suppose there exists an iteration $\varphi_0 \in \Phi(\mathfrak{N})$ such that $d(\varphi_0) \ll u(f, \mathfrak{N})$ and $p(\varphi_0) = p_{max}$. Then

2.13 $$\inf_{\varphi \in \Phi(\mathfrak{N})} z(f, \varphi) \cong \frac{u(f, \mathfrak{N})}{\log p_{max}}.$$

This indicates that the problem of the minimal complexity index is related to the problem of maximal order. In the next section we present a general idea on how to find the maximal order and how it depends on the information set $\mathfrak{N}$.

3. ORDER OF INFORMATION

In this section we deal with the maximal order of iterations which use a fixed information set $\mathfrak{N}$. Let $\mathcal{F}$ be a class of functions f for which we want to solve $f(x) = 0$. Let

(3.1) $$L_j : \mathcal{F} \times B_1 \longrightarrow \mathcal{F}_j, \qquad j = 1,2,\ldots,n,$$

for given spaces $\mathcal{F}_j$. We shall assume that

(3.2) $$\mathfrak{N}(f,x_i,\ldots,x_{i-m}) = [L_1(f,z_1(x_i)),\ldots,L_n(f,z_n(x_i)),\ldots,L_1(f,z_1(x_{i-m})), \ldots,L_n(f,z_n(x_{i-m}))]$$

where $z_1(x) = x$

$$z_{j+1}(x) = z_{j+1}(x,L_1(f,z_1(x)),\ldots,L_j(f,z_j(x))), \quad j = 2,3,\ldots,n,$$

and $L_j = L_j(f,x)$ is a linear operator with respect to f and continuous with respect to x. We assume that if $N = 1$ then L_j is a linear functional. Furthermore if $\mathfrak{N}_1$ and $\mathfrak{N}_2$ are information sets then we assume that $\mathfrak{N}_1(f,x_i,\ldots,x_{i-m}) = \mathfrak{N}_2(f,x_i,\ldots,x_{i-m})$ for all scalar f implies $\mathfrak{N}_1 \equiv \mathfrak{N}_2$. Note that n denotes the number of new evaluations computed at $z_1(x_i),\ldots,z_n(x_i)$ and m denotes the size of memory, i.e., the number of points of previously computed information which is reused in ith iterative step. We shall call $\mathfrak{N}$ <u>the information set with memory</u> if $m \geq 1$ and <u>the information set without memory</u> if $m = 0$.

Furthermore $\mathcal{N}$ is the <u>one-point information set</u> if $z_j(x) = x$ for $j = 1,2,\dots,n$; otherwise $\mathcal{N}$ is <u>the multipoint information set</u>.

In many cases $\mathcal{N}(f, x_i, \dots, x_{i-m})$ consists of discrete information about f and, in general, there exist infinitely many $\tilde{f} \in \mathcal{F}$ such that $\mathcal{N}(\tilde{f}, x_i, \dots, x_{i-m}) = \mathcal{N}(f, x_i, \dots, x_{i-m})$. Therefore any iteration φ can not distinquish between two problems $\tilde{f}(x) = 0$ and $f(x) = 0$ which have the same information set $\mathcal{N}(f, x_i, \dots, x_{i-m})$. The distance between two solutions $\tilde{\alpha} - \alpha$, where $\tilde{f}(\tilde{\alpha}) = 0$ and $f(\alpha) = 0$, is an inherent error of any iteration $\varphi \in \Phi(\mathcal{N})$. This error depends only on the information set $\mathcal{N}$. To formalize this idea we define the concept of equality with respect to $\mathcal{N}$. For the sake of simplicity we restrict ourselves to information sets without memory, $m = 0$. The general case with memory may be found in Woźniakowski [75].

We shall say <u>$\tilde{f}$ is equal to f with respect to $\mathcal{N}$</u> (briefly $\tilde{f} \underset{\mathcal{N}}{=} f$) iff

(i) $\tilde{f} : D \times D \to B_2$, $\tilde{f}(\cdot, x)$ and f are analytic at their simple zeros $\tilde{\alpha} = \tilde{\alpha}(x)$ and α respectively, $\lim_{x \to \alpha} \tilde{\alpha}(x) = \alpha$,

(ii) $\lim_{x \to \alpha} \tilde{f}^{(k)}(\alpha, x) = g^{(k)}(\alpha)$, $\forall k$, where g is also analytic at α which is its simple zero,

(iii) $\mathcal{N}(\tilde{f}, x) = \mathcal{N}(f, x)$.

The two first conditions mean that $\tilde{f}$ and f are sufficiently regular and the third condition states that they have the same information at x.

We are now in a position to define the order of information $\mathcal{N}$.

A number $p = p(\mathcal{N})$ is called <u>the order of information $\mathcal{N}$</u> iff

$$(3.3) \qquad p(\mathcal{N}) = \begin{cases} \sup A & \text{if } A \neq \emptyset \\ 0 & \text{if } A = \emptyset \end{cases},$$

where

$$A = \left\{ q \geq 1 : \forall \tilde{f} \underset{\mathcal{N}}{=} f, \lim_{x \to \alpha} \frac{\|\tilde{\alpha}(x) - \alpha\|}{\|x - \alpha\|^{q-\varepsilon}} = 0, \ \forall \varepsilon > 0 \right\}.$$

Thus, the order of information measures how fast $\tilde{\alpha}(x)$ tends to α as x does for the problems which coincide on the information set $\mathcal{N}(f, x)$.

Example 3.1

Let

$$\mathcal{N}(f, x) = [f(x), f'(x), \dots, f^{(n-1)}(x)].$$

This is the standard information set without memory ($m = 0$).

It is easy to verify that $\tilde{f} \underset{\mathcal{N}}{\equiv} f$ implies

$$\tilde{f}(t, x) - f(t) = O(\| t - x \|^n) \text{ and } \tilde{\alpha}(x) - \alpha = O(\|x - \alpha\|^n)$$

which yields $p(\mathcal{N}) = n$. □

Recall we want to find an iteration φ which uses the information set $\mathcal{N}$ and has order as high as possible. We shall say φ is a generalized interpolatory iteration ($\varphi \in I_{\mathcal{N}}$) iff

(3.4) $$\varphi(x, \mathcal{N}(f, x)) = \tilde{\alpha}(x),$$

where $\tilde{\alpha}(x)$ is a zero of a problem $\tilde{f}$ such that $\tilde{f} \underset{\mathcal{N}}{=} f$.

Theorem 3.1 (Woźniakowski [75]).

(i) The order of information $\mathcal{N}$ is equal to the maximal order of iterations which use $\mathcal{N}$ i.e.,

$$p(\mathcal{N}) = p_{max},$$

where $p_{max} = \sup_{\varphi \in \Phi(\mathcal{N})} p(\varphi)$, see (2.12).

(ii) The order of any generalized interpolatory iteration is equal to the order of information, i.e.,

$$p(\varphi) = p(\mathcal{N}) \quad \text{for} \quad \varphi \in I_{\mathcal{N}} \quad \square$$

The theorem states that any generalized interpolatory iteration has maximal order of convergence. Note that many classical iterations such as Newton or secant iterations are interpolatory and therefore they have maximal orders with respect to their information sets. We now present some known results and open problems concerning the order of information.

1. First consider a one-point information set without memory, i.e., $z_j(x) \equiv x$ and $m = 0$ in (3.2).

Theorem 3.2 (Traub and Woźniakowski [76c]).

For any one-point information set $\mathfrak{N}$ without memory

(i) $p(\mathfrak{N}) \leqslant n$,

(ii) $p(\mathfrak{N}) = n$, iff $\mathfrak{N}(f, x) = [f(x), f'(x), \ldots, f^{(n-1)}(x)]$. $\square$

This means that n is the upper bound of orders of one-point information sets and this bound is uniquely achievable for the standard information. Convergence and complexity of iterations which use the standard information will be discussed in the next section.

2. Consider the standard information with memory, i.e.,

$$\mathfrak{N}(f, x_i) = [f(x_i), f'(x_i), \ldots, f^{(n-1)}(x_i), \ldots, f(x_{i-m}), \ldots, f^{(n-1)}(x_{i-m})]$$

The order of this information depends on the dimension N of f.

Theorem 3.3 (Woźniakowski [74]).

If $N = 1$, i.e., f is a scalar function, then

$$p(\mathfrak{N}) = p(n, m) ,$$

where $p(n, m)$ is the unique positive zero of the polynomial $t^{m+1} - n\sum_{j=0}^{m} t^j$.

If $N \geqslant 2$, i.e., f is a vector with at least two components, then

$$p(\mathfrak{N}) = n, \quad \forall m. \quad \square$$

For the scalar problems, $N = 1$, the use of memory increases the order of information at most by one, since $p(n, 0) = n$ and $\lim_{m\to\infty} p(n, m) = n+1$.

For the multivariate and abstract cases, $N \geqslant 2$, the order of information is independent of m. This means that memory does not increase the maximal order and from this point of view is useless. However, if the successive approximations $x_i, x_{i-1}, \ldots, x_{i-m}$ are in a suitable position for any i then the use of memory increases the order of information. This leads to the so-called sets of admissible approximations, examples of which may be found in Brent [72], Jankowska [75] and Woźniakowski [75].

3. We now pass to multipoint information sets without memory. Consider the so-called <u>integral</u> <u>information set</u> defined by

$$\mathfrak{N}(f, x) = [f(x), f'(x), \ldots, f^{(n-2)}(x), \int_0^1 g(t) f(x + ty)\, dt],$$

where $n \geq 3$, $y = y(x, f(x), \ldots, f^{(n-2)}(x))$ and $g = g(t)$ is an integrable scalar function. This is a two-point information set without memory.

<u>Theorem 3.4</u> (Kacewicz [75])

(i) For any integral information set

$$p(\mathfrak{N}) \leq 2n - 3 + \delta_{N,1},$$

where $\delta_{N,1} = 1$ for $N = 1$ and $\delta_{N,1} = 0$ otherwise.

(ii) there exist a function g independent of f and a point y such that

$$p(\mathfrak{N}) = 2n - 3 + \delta_{N,1} \quad . \square$$

This theorem states that one value of integral added to the standard information increases the order of information by $n-2+\delta_{N,1}$. This is especially interesting for the multivariate case, $N < +\infty$, since the integral

$$\int_0^1 g(t) f(x + ty)\, dt$$

can be represented by one vector of size N only.

4. Consider the so-called <u>Brent</u> <u>information set</u> defined by

$$\mathfrak{N}(f, x) = [f(x), f'(x), \ldots, f^{(k)}(x), f^{(j)}(z_{k+2}), \ldots, f^{(j)}(z_n)].$$

This multipoint information set is especially interesting if the j-th derivative is easier to compute than the value of f. It was investigated by Brent [75] and Meersman [76].

<u>Theorem 3.5</u> (Meersman [76])

For the Brent information set

$$p(\mathcal{N}) \leqslant \begin{cases} 2n - k - 1 & \text{if } 0 < j \leqslant k+1, \\ k+1 & \text{if } j > k+1. \end{cases} \quad \square$$

Theorem 3.6 (Brent [75])

For $N = 1$

$$\sup_{z_i} p(\mathcal{N}) = \begin{cases} 2n - k - 1 & \text{if } 0 < j \leqslant k+1, \\ k+1 & \text{if } j > k+1. \end{cases} \quad \square$$

5. We now pass to a general case. Let $\mathcal{N}_{n, m}$ be an arbitrary information set of the form (3.2). For fixed n and m we seak an upper bound on $p(\mathcal{N}_{n,m})$. Although we do not know the solution to this problem the following conjecture is plausible.

Conjecture 3.1

$$p(\mathcal{N}_{n,m}) \leqslant \begin{cases} 2^{n-1} & \text{for } m = 0, \\ 2^n & \text{for } m > 0. \end{cases} \quad \square$$

Conjecture 3.1 is a generalization of a conjecture posed by Kung and Traub [74] and is known as the (n, m) - evaluation problem. For the scalar case Kung and Traub [74] exhibited an iteration φ which uses

$$\mathcal{N}_{n,m}(f, x_i) = [f(x_i), f(z_2(x_i)), \ldots, f(z_n(x_i)), \ldots$$

$$\ldots, f(x_{i-m}), f(z_2(x_{i-m})), \ldots, f(z_n(x_{i-m}))]$$

for a suitable chosen $z_2, \ldots, z_n$ such that $p(\varphi) = 2^{n-1}$ for $m = 0$ and $p(\varphi)$ tends to 2^n as m tends to infinity. This shows that the bounds in Conjecture 3.1 are achievable for certain information sets $\mathcal{N}_{n,m}$.

As we mentioned before the conjecture has not been proven; however many important cases have been established. For instance, suppose that

$L_j(f, z_j(x)) = f^{(i_j)}(z_j(x))$ for certain i_j and $j = 1, 2, \ldots, n$. Then

Meersman [76] proved the conjecture for $n \leqslant 3$ and $m = 0$. Woźniakowski [76] showed connections between the $(n,0)$ - evaluation problem and the Birkhoff interpolation problem and proved the conjecture for "Hermitian information". A special case of Hermitian nonstationary information with memory was considered by Brent, Winograd and Wolfe [73] who proved the conjecture for this case.

4. CONVERGENCE AND COMPLEXITY OF ONE-POINT ITERATIONS

We now deal with a one-point information set without memory of the form

$$(4.1) \qquad \mathcal{N}_n(f, x_i) = [f(x_i),\ f(x_i), \ldots, f^{(n-1)}(x_i)].$$

We mentioned in Section 3 that this standard information is uniquely optimal among all one-point information sets with respect to the order of information. We define now the interpolatory iteration I_n which has the maximal order equal to n.

Let w_i be an interpolatory polynomial of degree $\leqslant n - 1$ such that

$$w_i^{(j)}(x_i) = f^{(j)}(x_i) \quad \text{for } j = 0,1,\ldots,n-1\,.$$

The next approximation $x_{i+1} = I_n(x_i, \mathcal{N}(f, x_i))$ is defined as a zero of w_i, $w_i(x_{i+1}) = 0$, with a certain criterion of its choice (for instance, a nearest zero to x_i). The sequence $\{x_i\}$ is well-defined and converges to the simple solution α if f is sufficiently regular and a starting approximation x_0 belongs to the ball of convergence $\mathcal{J}_n = \{x: \ \|x-\alpha\| \leq \Gamma_n\}$ with a positive radius Γ_n. In many papers it is assumed that Γ_n is sufficiently small. However, a more careful analysis shows that Γ_n is an increasing function of n and may even tend to infinity with n. More precisely, let f be an entire function of the growth order ρ and the type τ, i.e.,

$$f(x) = \sum_{i=1}^{\infty} \frac{1}{i!} f^{(i)}(\alpha)(x-\alpha)^i \qquad \forall\, x \in B_1,$$

and $\displaystyle \frac{\|f^{(i)}(\alpha)\|}{i!} \leqslant M \left(\frac{\tau^i}{i!}\right)^{\frac{1}{\rho}}$

for a positive constant M and $i = 0,1,\ldots$.

Theorem 4.1 (Traub and Woźniakowski [76b])

$$\Gamma_n = (c\,n)^{1/p}\ (1 + o(1))$$

for a constant $c > 0$. □

Furthermore, if f is analytic in $D = \{x : \|x - \alpha\| \leq R\}$ then the following result holds.

Theorem 4.2 (Traub and Woźniakowski [76b])

$$\Gamma_n = \frac{R}{2}\ (1 + o(1)). \quad □$$

These theorems state a kind of global convergence of the interpolatory iterations I_n. Similar results hold for the scalar case for the standard information with memory.

$$\mathfrak{N}_{n,m}(f, x_i, x_{i-1}, \dots, x_{i-m}) = [f(x_i), \dots, f^{(n-1)}(x_i), \dots, f(x_{i-m}), \dots,$$

$$\dots, f^{(n-1)}(x_{i-m})].$$

Now the radius Γ of the ball of convergence is a function of n and m, $\Gamma = \Gamma(n, m)$ and

$$\lim_{m \to \infty} \Gamma(n, m) = +\infty \quad , \forall n \quad ,$$

for an entire function f and

$$\lim_{m \to \infty} \Gamma(n, m) = R/2 \quad , \quad \forall n$$

for a function f analytic in $D = \{x : \|x - \alpha\| \leq R\}$ (see Nowożyński and Wasilkowski [77]).

We now discuss the complexity indices of iterations which use one-point information sets of the form (4.1). Let

$$(4.2) \qquad z_n(f) = \inf_{\varphi \in \Phi(\mathfrak{N}_n)} z(\varphi) \quad ,$$

$$(4.3) \qquad z(f) = \inf_{n \geq 2} z_n(f).$$

We seek the value n^* for which $z_{n^*}(f) = z(f)$, i.e., for which the complexity index is minimized. Let the dimension N of the problem be finite and let $c(f^{(i)})$ denote the cost of evaluating $f^{(i)}$ at a point. Note that $f^{(i)}$ is represented in general by $\binom{N+i-1}{i} \cdot N$ scalar data.

Theorem 4.3 (Traub and Woźniakowski [77])

If $c(f^{(i)}) = \binom{N+i-1}{i} c(f)$ for $i = 1,2,\ldots,$ then the minimal complexity index $z(f)$ satisfies

(i) for $N = 1$

$$\frac{3}{\log 3} c(f) + \frac{3}{\log 3} \leq z(f) \leq \frac{3}{\log 3} c(f) + \frac{7}{\log 3}$$

and $n^* = 3$ whenever $c(f) \geq 23$,

(ii) for $N \geq 2$

$$(N+1)(c(f)+N) \leq z(f) \leq (N+1)(c(f) + O(N^{\beta-1}))$$

and $n^* = 2$ whenever $c(f) \geq a\,N$, where a is a positive constant and $O(N^{\beta})$ denotes the cost of solving a linear system $N \times N$, $\beta \leq 3$.

This means that the minimal complexity index is achievable for small n. This also indicates the optimality of I_3 iterations for the scalar case and I_2 (Newton iteration) for the multivariate case. However, if $c(f^{(i)}) / \binom{N+i-1}{i} \equiv \gamma$ and $c(f)$ is much higher than γ then the optimal $n^* = n^*(c(f))$ can be significantly larger.

5. ABSTRACT MODEL OF ANALYTIC COMPUTATIONAL COMPLEXITY

In the previous sections we discussed the problem of solving nonlinear equations. Many concepts and results may be generalized to a general setting which includes nonlinear equations as a special case. We give here a very brief outline of an abstract model of analytic computational complexity.

Suppose our problem is to compute an approximation to α, where

(5.1) $\alpha = H(f)$

where H: $\mathcal{F}_o \subset \mathcal{F} \longrightarrow B$ and $\mathcal{F}$ is a linear space, B is a real or complex linear and normed space. Assume that the only known information on f is given by a one-point information set without memory $\mathcal{N}_n = \mathcal{N}_n(f, x)$

$$\mathcal{N}_n(f, x) = [L_1(f, x), \ldots, L_n(f, x)],$$

where functionals L_j $(j = 1,2,\ldots, n)$ are linear with respect to f and sufficiently regular with respect to x. We pose some fundamental questions concerning the abstract problem (5.1)

(i) find an optimal iteration for solving (5.1) which uses a fixed $\mathcal{N}_n$

(ii) for a fixed n find an optimal information set $\mathcal{N}_n$, i.e., an information set $\mathcal{N}_n$ with the maximal order of information. The order of information $\mathcal{N}_n$ for the problem $\alpha = H(f)$ is defined in a similar way as (3.3).

(iii) which problems (5.1) can be solved by an iteration (with a fixed n)

(iv) find a sequence of information sets $\{\mathcal{N}_n\}$ and a sequence of methods $\{\varphi_n\}$ which use $\mathcal{N}_n$ and solve (5.1)

(v) find an optimal sequence $\{\mathcal{N}_n\}$ and optimal methods $\{\varphi_n\}$ which solve (5.1).

These and similar problems are being investigated and results will be reported in future papers of Kacewicz, Traub and Woźniakowski.

Acknowledgments

We wish to thank J.F.Traub for his valuable comments on this paper.

6. BIBLIOGRAPHY

Brent [72] Brent, R.P., "The computational complexity of iterative methods for systems of nonlinear equations", Proc.Complexity Symposium, Yorktown Heights, N.Y., Plenum Press, New York.

Brent [75] Brent, R.P., "A class of optimal-order zero-finding methods using derivative evaluations", in Analytic Computational Complexity, edited by J.F.Traub, Academic Press 1976, pp.59-73.

Brent, Winograd and Wolfe [73], Brent, R.P., Winograd, S., Wolfe, P., "Optimal iterative processes for root-finding", Numer.Math., 20, pp. 327-341.

Jankowska [75], Jankowska, J., "Multivariate secant method", Ph.D.thesis, University of Warsaw, to appear in SIAM J. on Num.Anal.

Kacewicz [75], Kacewicz, B., "Integrals with kernel in the solution of nonlinear equations in N dimensions", Computer Science Department Report, Carnegie-Mellon University, 1975.

Kung and Traub [74], Kung, K.T., Traub, J.F., "Optimal order of one-point and multipoint iterations" J.Assoc.Comput.Mach.Vol.21, No.4, 1974, pp.643-651.

Meersman [76], Meersman, R., "Optimal use of information in certain iterative processes", in Analytic Computational Complexity, Academic Press 1976, pp.109-125.

Nowożyński and Wasilkowski [77], Nowożyński, K., Wasilkowski, G., "Global convergence of interpolatory iterations in the scalar case", to appear

Traub and Woźniakowski [76a], Traub, J.F., Woźniakowski, H., "Strict lower and upper bounds on iterative computational complexity", in Analytic Computational Complexity, Academic Press 1976, pp. 15-34.

Traub and Woźniakowski [76b], "Optimal radius of convergence of interpolatory iterations for operator equations", Dept.of Computer Science Report, Carnegie-Mellon University, 1976.

Traub and Woźniakowski [76c], "Optimal linear information for the solution of nonlinear equations", Algorithms and Complexity, New Directions and Recent Results, edited by J.F.Traub, Academic Press 1976.

Traub and Woźniakowski [77], "Convergence and complexity of interpolatory - - Newton iteration in a Banach space", Computer Science Department Report, Carnegie-Mellon University, 1977.

Woźniakowski [74], Woźniakowski, H., "Maximal stationary iterative methods for the solution of operator equations", SIAM J.Numer.Anal., 11,5, pp.934-949, 1974.

Woźniakowski [75], "Generalized information and maximal order of iteration for operator equations", SIAM J.Numer.Anal., 12,1,pp. 121-135, 1975.

Woźniakowski [76], "Maximal order of multipoint iterations using n evaluations", in Analytic Computational Complexity, Academic Press 1976, pp. 75-107.

Rice [76], Rice, J.R., "On the Computational Complexity of Approximation Operators II", in Analytic Computional Complexity, Academic Press, 1976, 191-205.

Schultz [76], Schultz, M.M., "Complexity and Differential Equations", in Analytic Computational Complexity, Academic Press, 1976, 143-151.

Winograd [76], Winograd, S., "Some Remarks on Proof Techniques in Analytic Complexity", in Analytic Computational Complexity, Academic Press, 1976, 5-15.

Traub [73], Traub, J.F., "Complexity of Sequential and Parallel Numericall Algorithms", editor, Academic Press, 1973.

Traub [76a], Traub, J.F., "Analytic Computational Complexity", editor, Academic Press, 1976.

Traub [76b], Traub, J.F., "Algorithms and Complexity: Recent Results and New Directions", editor, Academic Press, 1976.

TREE-STRUCTURES FOR SET MANIPULATION PROBLEMS

H. A. Maurer
Th. Ottmann

Institut fuer Angewandte Informatik
und Formale Beschreibungsverfahren

Universitaet Karlsruhe, 75 Karlsruhe, W-Germany

Abstract

We discuss the use of tree-structures for finding efficient solutions for the well-known dictionary problem and generalizations thereof. In doing so, we present a number of known techniques together with recent developments. In particular, we mention recent results concerning trees of very small height suitable for implementing dictionaries, results concerning the non-uniform dictionary problem and new results on one-sided AVL trees.

1. Introduction and Preliminaries.

A problem occurring in many different forms in data-processing is this.

Given a set C of some elements, a sequence of so-called dictionary-operations is to be carried out. The usual dictionary operations are MEMBER(x) for searching if C contains the element x, and INSERT(x) and DELETE(x) for updating C by adding or deleting a specified element x. This kind of problem is commonly known as dictionary problem, see e.g. Aho, Hopcroft, Ullman [2]. Typical instances of this problem include the handling of a book-file in a library (we can check whether a book is present, and books can be added to and removed from the library), the handling of currently valid identifiers during the compilation of a block-structured program (we want to check whether an identifier is currently valid, and we add or delete identifiers from the list of currently valid ones as we enter or leave blocks containing their declaration), the handling of customer-accounts of a bank, etc.

It is clearly desirable to develop methods which allow to carry out each of the dictionary operations as fast as possible. The number of steps taken to carry out such an operation is usually compared with the size n of the set C involved. It is commonly accepted that provided that n is not trivially small (say less than 50) or too big to prevent the set C from being stored in internal memory, the most efficient techniques involve the use of tree-structures.

To simplify considerations to follow, and without loss of generality, we will not deal with sets of arbitrary elements or "keys", but will rather just work with sets of positive integers (i.e. assuming that each key is coded as an integer).

We now introduce the type of tree we are interested in throughout this paper.

Definition: A leaf-tree T is a binary tree in which each node has an integer value. The value of an interior node (i.e. of a non-leaf) is the maximum of the values of its sons. T is said to represent a set of numbers C iff the elements of C occur as value of the leaves of T. A leaf-tree T is called sorted if the values of the leaves read from left to right, are in ascending order.

Observe that here and in the sequel we use the terminology of Aho, Hopcroft, Ullman [2] as far as trees are concerned. We also make the following conventions. For a node k, φk will denote its father, $\sigma_1 k$, $\sigma_2 k$ its first and second son and ωk will be its value. Nodes are called brothers if they have a common father, are called neighbours if they have the same distance from the root, i.e. the same depth, and direct neighbours if they are neighbours and no node occurs between them.

Note that in a leaf-tree elements of the set C considered are stored in the leaves only, interior nodes merely being used for routing information. This fact simplifies some of our algorithms, in particular those involving the deletion of nodes. Since by e.g. Wirth [22] deletion of interior nodes can, in general, be reduced to the deletion of leaves (by replacing the node k to be deleted by the leftmost node in the right subtree of k) this is no loss of generality.

We will now briefly review how a sorted leaf-tree T can be used to solve the dictionary problem. Let T be a sorted leaf-tree with root r representing a set C of integers, and let x be an integer. The function-procedure loc(x,r) defined below always delivers a leaf k with the following property: $\omega k = x$ iff a node with value x occurs in T. If T does not contain a node with value x then k is either the leaf with the smallest value greater than x (if it exists) or the rightmost leaf of the tree (if x exceeds the values of all leaves).

<u>procedure</u> loc(x,p);
  Case 1 [p is not a leaf]:
    Case 1.1 [p has only one son σp]: <u>Return</u> (loc(x,σp));
    Case 1.2 [p has two sons]:
      Case 1.2.1 [$x \le \omega\sigma_1 p$]: <u>Return</u> (loc(x,σ_1p));
      Case 1.2.2 [$x > \omega\sigma_1 p$]: <u>Return</u> (loc(x,σ_2p));
  Case 2 [p is a leaf]: <u>Return</u> (p).

Suppose now k:=loc(x,r). To carry out MEMBER(x) it suffices to check whether $\omega k = x$ holds or not. To carry out INSERT(x), let $x' = \omega k$, add two sons to k with values x and x', put $\omega k = \max(x,x')$ and perform the procedure info(k) (to adjust the routing information) which is defined as follows.

<u>procedure</u> info(p);
  Case 1 [p is the root of the tree] : <u>Return</u>;
  Case 1 [p is not the root of the tree];
    Case 2.1 [$\omega\varphi p \ge \omega p$]: <u>Return</u>;
    Case 2.2 [$\omega\varphi p < \omega p$]: $\omega\varphi p := \omega p$;
      <u>call</u> info(φp); <u>Return</u>;

Similarly, to carry out DELETE(x), k and all its fathers with a single son are deleted and the routing information is adjusted appropriately.

2. H-trees and the dictionary problem.

Note that the number of steps to carry out either of the three dictionary operations is at most proportional to the longest path in T. Depending on the shape of the tree, such a longest path can vary in length between roughly n and $\log_2 n$. To assure good worst-case behaviour we have to assure that our sorted trees stay reasonably "bushy", technically called <u>balanced</u>, throughout. More specifically, no branch is to be longer than $c \log_2 n$, where c is a constant not much exceeding 1.

A variety of types of balanced trees have been proposed in the past, with each of which the dictionary operations can be carried out (while preserving "bushiness") in a number of steps proportional only to the longest branch in the tree, i.e. proportional to $\log_2 n$. A survey of the more important types of such trees is given in Maurer, Ottmann, Six [13] and includes a discussion of the AVL trees of Adelson, Landis [1], of the 2-3 trees of Aho, Hopcroft, Ullman [2], of the symmetric B-trees of Bayer [5], the B-trees of Bayer, McCreight [4], the H-trees of Maurer, Wood [11], the binary trees of bounded balance of Nievergelt, Reingold [16] and the HB-trees of Ottmann, Six [17].

For our purposes the conceptually particularly simple model of H-trees is most suitable.

Definition: A leaf-tree T is called an H-tree, if all leaves have the same depth and if every node with only one son has an immediate right neighbour with two sons.

Since an H-tree with n-leaves has a height of $1{,}71 \log_2 n$ according to Maurer, Ottmann, Six [13] all H-trees are balanced in the sense mentioned above. Since they are special cases of the leaf-trees considered earlier, it is clear how MEMBER(x) can be carried out. It remains to check whether INSERT(x) and DELETE(x) can be modified in such a manner that (a) the tree obtained after the operation is again an H-tree and (b) the number of steps required is still proportional to $\log_2 n$. We will consider only insertion briefly (ignoring the updating of the routing information) and refer to Maurer, Ottmann, Six [13] for details.

Let T be an H-tree with root r representing a set C of n integers. To insert into T a new node k' with value x, carry out the procedure-call insert (k',loc(x,r)).

procedure insert(k',p);
  Case 1 [p has no brother]:
   Case 1.1 [p is the root]:
      Add a new root r' with sons k' and p; Return;
   Case 1.2 [p is not the root]:
      Add k' as brother of p; Return;
  Case 2 [p has a brother p_1]:
      Arrange p, p_1, k' as q_1, q_2, q_3 such that $\omega q_1 \leq \omega q_2 \leq \omega q_3$.
   Case 2.1 [q_1 has immediate left neighbour q which has no brother];
      Add q_1 as brother of q; make q_2, q_3 the sons of $\varphi p = \varphi p_1$;
      Return;

Case 2.2 [q_1 has an immediate left neighbour q which has a brother, or q_1 has no immediate left neighbour].
Let k" be a new node with $\omega k" = \omega q_1$;
make q_1 the only son of k" and q_2, q_3 the sons of $\varphi p = \varphi p_1$; call insert(k",φp); Return;

We thus can conclude this section by noting that using H-trees, each dictionary operation can be carried out in O(log n) steps, where n is the size of C.

3. Optimal trees, HB-trees, one-sided AVL-trees and a sobering thought.

The number of steps required to carry out a MEMBER, INSERT or DELETE operation is proportional to the height of the tree involved. Note that the constant of proportionality in case of INSERT and DELETE depends on the type of leaf-tree used, but is independent of the type of leaf-tree for the MEMBER operation. Thus, if the MEMBER operation is our primary concern (for example, because searches are carried out more frequently than updates) it is important to try to keep the height of the trees used as small as possible.

Of all types of trees mentioned sofar, AVL-trees and HB-trees are optimal in the sense that the maximal height of a tree with n nodes is minimal (namely,$\sim 1.4\log_2 n$, see Knuth [8] and Ottmann, Six [17]). In Maurer, Ottmann, Six [12] this question of leaf-trees of small height suitable for the dictionary operations is examined. By using a natural generalization of the notion of an H-tree an optimal solution to the "smallest height" problem has been obtained as follows.

Definition: A leaf-tree is called a k-tree if (a) all leaves have the same depth and (b) every node m with a single son has at least one immediate right neighbour and if m has t right neighbours, then the $q = \min(t,k)$ immediately adjacent right neighbours of m all have two sons.

Note that for $k = 1$ above reduces to the definition of H-trees and that each k-tree is a leaf-tree, i.e. a binary tree.

The next theorem, taken from Maurer, Ottmann, Six [12] shows that trees for the dictionary problem can be constructed whose height is arbitrary close to the theoretical optimum of $\log_2 n$.

<u>Theorem:</u>

For every $\varepsilon > 0$ there exists a k such that

(a) each k-tree with n leaves has a height of at most $(1+\varepsilon)\log_2 n + 1$

(b) the three dictionary operations can be carried out using k-trees in time proportional to the height of the trees involved.

Returning attention to H-trees, observe that in implementing algorithms for H-trees on a computer efficiently, it must be possible to access neighbours of a given node in a straight-forward manner. While it is certainly possible to provide such access by additional "pointers" or "links" (by e.g. treating all nodes of same height as a doubly-linked list) the standard techniques of storing a binary tree in a computer, see e.g. Maurer [9], Maurer [10], provide only for direct access to the sons and possibly the father of a given node. This is one of the main reasons for the introduction of HB-trees in Ottmann, Six [17]. For the implementation of HB-trees standard techniques suffice.

<u>Definition:</u> A leaf-tree is called an <u>HB-tree</u> if (a) all leaves have the same depth and (b) every node m with a single son has a brother with two sons.

It can be shown, see Ottmann, Six [17] (and van Leeuwen [21] for a careful English exposition) that HB-trees are very well suited for dictionary (and other) operations. They also have a remarkable relationship to the AVL-trees of Adelson, Landis [1].

<u>Definition:</u> A leaf-tree is called an <u>AVL-tree</u> if (a) every node except the root has a brother and (b) for every node v the heights of left and right subtree of v differ by at most one.

The definition above differs somewhat from the original one (particularly since we consider leaf-trees) but captures the essential notion of "height-balancing". AVL-trees are historically the first type of tree providing a "logarithmic solution" for all three dictionary operations.

We will now define the notion of contracting a leaf-tree. We will then relate contracted HB-trees and AVL-trees.

<u>Definition:</u> A leaf-tree T' is the <u>contraction</u> of a leaf-tree T, if T' is obtained from T by identifying nodes k and k', where k' is the only son of k.

The following result was noted by van Leeuwen [21] and is more fully exploited in Ottmann, Six, Wood [20].

Theorem:
A leaf-tree is an AVL-tree iff it is the contraction of an HB-tree.

By virtue of above theorem many algorithms for AVL-trees can be obtained by using the corresponding algorithms for the conceptually simpler HB-trees. The relationship between AVL-trees and HB-trees remains even valid for "one-sided" versions of both kinds of trees.

Definition: An AVL-tree is called one-sided if for every node v, the right subtree of v is at most higher than the left subtree of v. An HB-tree is called a right-brother-tree if every node v with one son has a right brother with two sons.

It is an old problem to develop efficient algorithms for the deletion of nodes in a one-sided AVL-tree. (Such trees are particularly attractive from an implementor's point of view since the information of whether subtrees of a node v are of same height or whether the right subtree is higher can be stored using a single bit). Recently in Hirschberg [6] an insertion algorithm for one-sided AVL trees working in $0(\log^2 n)$ time has been presented. Ottmann, Wood [19] show that there is also a deletion procedure for this class even operating in time $0(\log n)$. The insertion algorithm of Hirschberg [6] and the deletion algorithm of Ottmann, Wood [19] are both designed for AVL trees where also interior nodes are used to store keys. That means the trees involved are AVL trees according to the original definition of Adelson, Landis [1] and not AVL leaf-trees in our sense. Surprisingly, for AVL leaf-trees insertion and deletion techniques both operating in time $0(\log n)$ are available, see Ottmann, Six, Wood [20]. These algorithms can be obtained from corresponding algorithms for right brother trees which are explained in Ottmann, Six, Wood [18] by using the notion of contraction. This raises the interesting question whether for AVL (non-leaf-)trees insertion is inherently more difficult than deletion.

It is in order to close this section with a word of caution. Using any of the described balanced types of trees, it is possible to insure that each of the dictionary operations can be carried out in $0(\log n)$ steps on a set of n elements. Since it is known, Knuth [8], that the "average" height of a sorted leaf-tree with n leaves is only roughly $1.4 \log_2 n$, average performance using balanced trees is often worse than using ordinary sorted leaf-trees, due to the "overhead" involved. Before deciding on the use of balanced trees for a particular application it is thus necessary to study whether the situation does indeed warrant their use. Typical cases in which balanced trees are recommended are e.g. real-time applications where a certain maximum response time must not be exceeded, or applications in which searches are more frequent than updates (which would tend to reduce the costs of the overhead).

4. Non uniform dictionary problems.

When implementing dictionaries using balanced trees one tacitly assumes that the relative access frequencies of all keys stored in the tree are equal. In many applications this assumption is not very realitic. Thus, for example, during the compilation of a program the relative access frequency of a reserved identifier (keyword) occurring in the directory normally exceeds the access frequency of an identifier declared by the programmer. In order to minimize the total search time in the directory the relative access frequencies should be reflected by the tree structure. Names occurring more frequently should be located nearer to the root than others.

If we associate with every leaf p_i, the relative access frequency (search probability) α_i of the key ωp_i stored in p_i, the weighted path length P of a leaf-tree T with n leaves $p_1, \ldots, p_n$ is defined by

$$P = \sum_{i=1}^{n} \text{depth}(p_i) \cdot \alpha_i \; .$$

Thus the problem is how to obtain efficiently trees which are optimal or "nearly optimal" with respect to their weighted path length. However, the choice of the appropriate data structure for representing a set of n keys depends heavily on whether the number of keys is fixed all the time or not, and whether the probability distribution of the searches is uniform or not.

Balanced trees are the appropriate data structure for the case of a varying number of keys and a uniform probability distribution. A convenient way to implement a fixed number of keys with equal access frequencies is to arrange the keys in an array in increasing order. Then storage space O(n) and search time O(log n) are enough since <u>binary search</u>, see e.g. Maurer [9], [10], becomes applicable.

In the case of a fixed number of keys but a possibly nonuniform distribution of search probabilities we further distinguish whether the probability distribution is fixed all the time (and known in advance) - called the <u>static case</u> - or not, called the <u>dynamic case</u>. Several algorithms are known for constructing optimal binary search trees in the static case. Hu and Tucker [7] proposed an algorithm operating in time

$O(n^2)$ and space $O(n)$. Knuth [8] shows how to implement this algorithm in time $O(n \log n)$. If one is satisfied with nearly optimal instead of optimal binary search trees, algorithms are available operating even in time linear in the number of nodes (see e.g. Mehlhorn [14]).

The dynamic case is treated in Mehlhorn [14]. There, trees of bounded balance Nievergelt, Reingold [16] are modified in such a way that they can be used as dynamic, "nearly optimal" binary search leaf-trees: Consider n sorted keys $k_1, \ldots, k_n$ and assume that r_i $(1 \le i \le n)$, respectively s_i $(0 \le j \le n)$ is the number of searches for key k_i, respectively for a name x in the open interval (k_j, k_{j+1}) (an "unsuccessful search") up to a given point of time.
Then $W = \Sigma r_i + \Sigma s_j$ is the total number of searches performed so far and

$$\beta_i = r_i/W, \text{ respectively } \alpha_j = s_j/W$$

are the relative access frequencies of key k_i, respectively of a name $x \in (k_j, k_{j+1})$. Then Mehlhorn's tree structure exhibits the following behaviour (see Mehlhorn [15]):

(1) The tree is always nearly optimal, i.e. a search for $x = k_i (x \in (k_j, k_{j+1}))$ can be carried out in time $O(\log 1/\beta_i)(O(\log 1/\alpha_j))$.

Note that each further search for $x = k_i$ or $x \in (k_j, k_{j+1})$ changes the relative access frequencies of all keys. Hence, to maintain property (1) a restructuring of the tree is necessary from time to time. But it is shown that the restructuring can always be restricted to the path from the root to the leaf searched for. Thus property (2) holds:

(2) Update time is proportional to searchtime.

The main idea in this construction is to associate to every leaf a "thickness" (or "weight") characterizing the total number of searches for the key performed so far and then to use a rebalancing algorithm for a balanced tree scheme to move "thicker nodes" upward. A similar idea is already contained in Baer [3] where the following heuristic strategy for "self optimizing" search trees is proposed and experimentally tested: Try to minimize locally the weighted path length on the path of insertion. This strategy is also applicable in the general case where we have a varying number of keys and a time varying, nonuniform distribution of search probabilities given by the relative access frequencies of the keys up to a given point of time. We illustrate the strategy by the following example:

One of the restructuring rules used in common rebalancing algorithms is "Rotation", i.e. a local transformation of the form:

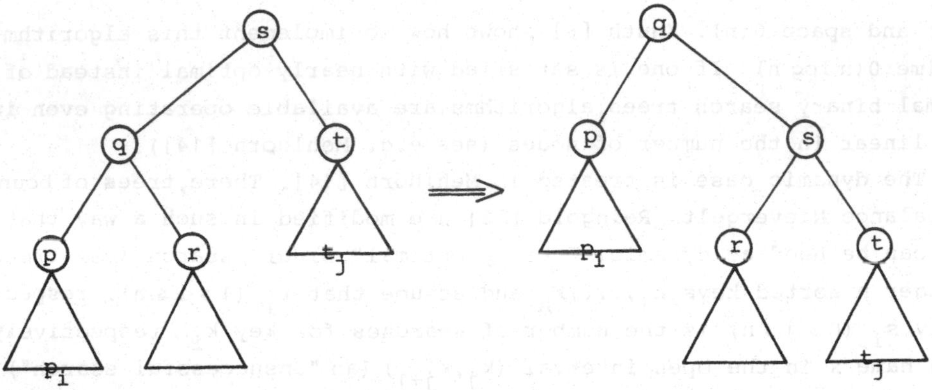

Rotation has to be performed if a certain rebalancing criterion characteristic for the underlying class of trees is true. Let us denote the distance of leaf p_i in the subtree with root p by $d(p_i,p)$. Then rotation will improve the weighted path length of the subtree with root s and new root q if we have:

$$\sum_i (d(p_i,p)+3)\cdot \text{weight}(p_i) + \sum_j (d(t_j,t)+2)\cdot \text{weight}(t_j)$$

$$> \sum_i (d(p_i,p)+2)\cdot \text{weight}(p_i) + \sum_j (d(t_j,t)+3)\cdot \text{weight}(t_j),$$

i.e. if $\sum_i \text{weight}(p_i) > \sum_j \text{weight}(t_j)$.

Thus we can store in each interior node p the total sum of weights of leaves in the subtree determined by p and restructure, if the above criterion is true. Baer [3] reports experiments demonstrating that this strategy is very efficient and he also estimates worst case behaviour. However, no general method is known to the authors at this point which has been shown to dynamically retain nearly optimal search trees and also permits the deletion and insertion of nodes in time proportional only to the depth of the leaf involved.

5. General set manipulation problem.

There are many problems involving searching and information retrieval which require operations more general than the three dictionary operations discussed sofar.

Consider, for example, a collection of job queues in a computer system and assume that each job has a unique priority. Beyond the three dictionary operations applicable for any particular queue we often want to determine and/or delete the job with the highest priority in a queue. Furthermore, due to e.g. device malfunctioning two different job-queues may have to be combined into a single one. As another example, in many graph theoretical algorithms we are faced with the problem to manipulate a collection of disjoint sets rather than a single set as in the dictionary problem. For instance, the usual algorithms to determine a minimum-cost-spanning tree involve a sequence of "union" operations for disjoint sets (of vertices) and "find" operations to determine the set which contains a given vertex. These and further examples suggest to consider the following general set manipulation problem.

Let $\mathcal{C}=\{C_1,\dots,C_t\}$ be a collection of disjoint sets of natural numbers. Then for each $i \in \{1,\dots,t\}$ the operations MEMBER(x,i), INSERT(x,i), DELETE(x,i) are the previously defined dictionary operations restricted to set C_i. MEMBER(x,i) can be considered as a special case of a more general operation FIND. FIND(x) determines that i (if it exists) for which $x \in C_i$. Then MEMBER(x,i) is true iff FIND(x) = i. MAX(i) gives the element in C_i with maximum value, MAXDELETE(i) is DELETE(MAX(i),i). Finally, if C_i and C_j are two different disjoint sets in the collection $\mathcal{C}$, then UNION(i,j,k) removes C_i and C_j from $\mathcal{C}$ and takes instead of them the set $C_k=C_i \cup C_j$ into the collection of sets (provided that indexing of sets remains unique). We will now explain how to represent the collection $\mathcal{C}$ of sets such that an arbitrary sequence of the just defined operations can be performed efficiently. The collection $\mathcal{C}=\{C_1,\dots,C_t\}$ of sets is represented by a forest $\mathcal{T}$ of trees $T_1,\dots,T_t$. Each set $C_i \in \mathcal{C}$ is represented by a (non-sorted) balanced leaf-tree. We just use H-trees for that purpose where we drop the condition used in our solution of the dictionary problem that the trees are sorted. But we assume that when encountering the root of a tree $T_i \in \mathcal{T}$ we can recognize the "name" C_i of the set represented by T_i (i.e. the index i of T_i). Observe that the restructuring algorithms for H-trees (and other balanced tree schemes) though designed for sorted trees do not depend on this fact. They are also applicable for non-sorted trees if we know the leaf where to begin the restructuring. To find out that leaf we can use a sorted H-tree T_U representing the union $\cup\mathcal{C} = C_1 \cup \dots \cup C_t$, if we assume that from each leaf of T_U there is a pointer to the leaf with same value belonging to exactly one of the trees T_i in the forest $\mathcal{T}$.

To perform FIND(x) we determine the leaf p with value x (if it exists) in T_U and use the pointer from p to enter the leaf with same value in one of the trees $T \in \mathcal{T}$, run upwards to the root of T and output its index. In the case of a DELETE(x,i) operation we first proceed similarly by determining the leaf p with value x in T_U and the leaf p' of $T_i \in \mathcal{T}$ with same value. Then we remove p from T_U and p' from T_i and use the delete procedure for H-trees to restructure T_U and T_i. If INSERT(x,i) has to be performed we proceed just conversely. We insert a new leaf with value x in T_i in an arbitrary position among the leaves of T_i and also insert a leaf with value x in T_U but preserving the ordering of the leaves of T_U. Then we use the insert procedure to restructure both T_i and T_U. Finally we put a pointer from the leaf inserted in T_U to the leaf inserted in T_i. It should be clear how to perform MAX(i) and MAXDELETE(i), since the maximum value of tree T_i is the value of the root of T_i.

Hence it remains to explain how to perform an operation UNION(i,j,k). In this case we leave the tree T_U completely unchanged (including all pointers). Let us assume that $h_i = \text{height}(T_i) \le \text{height}(T_j) = h_j$. Then we determine the leftmost (or rightmost) node p of height h_i in the tree T_j and call insert (root(T_i),p) to obtain a new H-tree T_k (with height at most $h_j + 1$). Thus the trees T_i, T_j in the forest of trees representing $\mathcal{C}$ have been replaced by one tree T_k and the forest obtained represents the new collection of sets.

We summarize our considerations in the following theorem (see also Maurer, Ottmann, Six [13]).

<u>Theorem:</u>

If $\mathcal{C} = \{C_1, \ldots, C_t\}$ is a collection of finite sets of integers and S a sequence of MEMBER, INSERT, DELETE, MAX, MAXDELETE, UNION, FIND instructions such that at each stage

(i) the total number of integers in $\mathcal{C}$ is $\le n$,

(ii) the sets in $\mathcal{C}$ are mutually disjoint,

then using H-trees each of the operations in S can be carried out in at most $O(\log n)$ steps.

In applications where no INSERT and DELETE operations are to be performed it is not necessary to use balanced trees, in particular a balanced tree T_U to represent the union of sets in collection $\mathcal{C}$. We can rather use an array a of pointers such that for any integer $x \in \cup\mathcal{C}$ a[x] points to the leaf with value x in the tree T belonging to the forest $\mathcal{T}$ of trees representing $\mathcal{C}$. In fact, we can even drop the condition that the trees $T_i \in \mathcal{T}$ are balanced and binary (e.g. H-trees). To perform UNION(i,j,k) we simply choose the root of the tree with smaller height among T_i and T_j, say T_i, and make it the son of the root of T_j. Furthermore, the performance time of a sequence of FIND operations can be improved by the following trick, called <u>path compression</u> (see Aho, Hopcroft, Ullman [2]). Whenever FIND(x) is carried out we run up the path from the leaf p with value x to the root q of a tree $T \in \mathcal{T}$ and output its index. Let $p,p_1,\ldots,p_k,q$ be the nodes on that path. Then we make each of $p,p_1,\ldots,p_k$ a son of the root q. Now it can be shown, see Aho, Hopcroft, Ullman [2] that each sequence of up to n-1 UNION and O(n) FIND operations for a collection of sets containing a total number of n integers can be carried out in time which is nearly linear in n.

References:

1. Adelson-Velskii, G.M., Landis, E.M., An algorithm for the organization of information (Russian), Doklady Akad. Nauk, SSSR 146 (1962) 263-266.

2. Aho, A.V., Hopcroft, J.E., Ullman, J.D., The design and analysis of computer algorithms, Addison-Wesley, Reading (1974)

3. Baer, J.L., Weight-balanced trees, AFIPS-Proceedings, vol.44 (1975) 467-472.

4. Bayer, R., McCreight, E., Organization and Maintenance of Large Ordered Indexes. Acta Informatica 1 (1972) 173-189.

5. Bayer, R., Symmetric B-trees, Acta Informatica 1 (1972) 29o-3o6.

6. Hirschberg, D.S., An insertion technique for one-sided height-balanced trees. Comm. ACM 19, 8 (Aug.1976) 471-473.

7. Hu, T.C., Tucker, A.C., Optimum binary search trees. SIAM J. Appl. Math., 21:4 (1971) 514-532.

8. Knuth, D.E., The art of computer programming, I, III. Addison-Wesley (1967 and 1973).

9. Maurer, H.A., Datenstrukturen und Programmierverfahren. Teubner, Stuttgart (1974).

1o. Maurer, H.A., Data structures and programming techniques. Prentice-Hall, Englewood Cliffs (1977).

11. Maurer, H.A., Wood, D., Zur Manipulation von Zahlenmengen. Angewandte Informatik 4 (1976) 143-149.

12. Maurer, H.A., Ottmann, Th., Six, H.-W., Implementing dictionaries using binary trees of very small height. Information Processing Letters 5 (1976) 11-14.

13. Maurer, H.A., Ottmann, Th., Six, H.-W., Manipulation of number sets using balanced trees. Applied Computer Science, vol.4 Carl Hanser, München (1976) 9-37.

14. Mehlhorn, K., Nearly optimal binary search trees. Acta Informatica 5 (1975) 287-295.

15. Mehlhorn, K., Dynamic binary search trees. Fourth international Colloquium on Automata, Languages and Programming, Turku (1977).

16. Nievergelt, J., Reingold, E.M., Binary trees of bounded balance. SIAM Journal of Computing 2 (1973) 33-43.

17. Ottmann, Th., Six, H.-W., Eine neue Klasse von ausgeglichenen Binärbäumen. Angewandte Informatik 8 (1976) 395-4oo.

18. Ottmann, Th., Six, H.-W., Wood, D., Right-brother-trees. Report 6O Institut fuer Angewandte Informatik und Formale Beschreibungsverfahren, Universitaet Karlsruhe, 75 Karlsruhe, W-Germany.

19. Ottmann, Th., Wood, D., Deletion in onse-sided height balanced search trees. Report: McMaster University, Hamilton, Department of Mathematics, Hamilton, Ontario, Canada (1977).

2o. Ottmann, Th., Six, H.-W., Wood, D., On the correspondence between AVL trees and brother trees. Report 61 Institut fuer Angewandte Informatik und Formale Beschreibungsverfahren, Universitaet Karlsruhe, 75 Karlsruhe, W-Germany (1977).

21. van Leeuwen, J., The complexity of data organization. Mathematical Centre Tracts 81 (1976) 37-147.

22. Wirth, N., Algorithmen und Datenstrukturen, Teubner, 7o Stuttgart, W-Germany (1975).

APPLIED ALGORITHMIC LOGIC

Andrzej Salwicki
Department of Mathematics, University of Warsaw
PKiN p.850 00-902 Warszawa POLAND

This is a survey of the last year's work of the group of algorithmic logic. Our studies have concetrated on two (not disjoint) tasks:
- design of programming language LOGLAN 77,
- studies of computational complexity.
The questions of data structures implementation and of non-sequential computing processes were the main aims of our research. The work devoted to LOGLAN language has paid back handsomely in discovering possibilities of algorithmic approach to the foundations of set theory. The survey ends with a short presentation of an early stage of research connected with P=NP problem.

§1 LOGLAN 77

Here I am going to present some intuitions and key words rather than LOGLAN language itself.

The language LOGLAN 77 is designed to be a universal programming language containing all necessary programming tools. Its closest relative is SIMULA 67 [2]. LOGLAN has: a small syntax, a precise semantics, possibility of multiprocessor execution, seven ways of transmitting parameters, unified version of assignment instruction, possibility of assigning expressions as the contents of variables, algebra of type expressions with array, class and prefix operations. Types are patterns for objects. By an object we understand a pair: ⟨valuation of attributes, list of instructions⟩. A collection of objects may constitute a configuration. Execution of a program results in the sequence of configurations forming a computation. Some examples of LOGLAN programs are given below. Here we shall discuss the relation in between objects and types. We shall say that an object o is of type T iff 1° declaration of type T contains exactly those attributes which form the domain of the valuation of the object o, 2° values of attributes are in corresponding, declared types, 3° list of instructions of o is compatible with the body of type T declaration. Let r be the relation: type T is prefixed by a type T′. Let the relation r^* be the transitive closure of r. Then the relation in is defined by the equivalence:

$$o \ \underline{in}\ T \Leftrightarrow \left(E\, T'\right)\ T\, r^* T' \wedge o\ \underline{is}\ T'$$

Examples:

Let T be a

type T : class(a:T1 , b:T2); begin variable c:T3 ; c:=a end

and o an object $\left(\begin{array}{c|c|c} a & b & c \\ \hline o1 & o2 & o3 \end{array}, I\right)$ then o is T iff

o1 in T1 and o2 in T2 and (o3=none ∧ I= c:=a or o3=o1 ∧ I=∅)

The notion of binary tree can be defined as follows:

type bintree : class(l,r : bintree);; Set of objects of bintree type contains

o: $\left(\begin{array}{c|c} l & r \\ \hline none & none \end{array}, \emptyset\right)$ $\left(\begin{array}{c|c} l & r \\ \hline none & o \end{array}, \emptyset\right)$ etc.

The first object represents a leaf, the second a two-element tree. Let elem be a type, then the notion of tree with vertices labelled by elem objects is defined as follows

type labelled bintree : bintree class(val : elem);;

An example of an object of type labelled bintree is $\left(\begin{array}{c|c|c} l & r & val \\ \hline t1 & t2 & e \end{array}, \emptyset\right)$

where t1, t2 are again in bintree and e in elem. This object is labelled bintree object and in bintree type.

The modest syntax of LOGLAN is satisfactory enough to extend the language to the desired size, data structures and functions due to the 1° prefixing, 2° allowing instructions to be parameters.

§2 DATA STRUCTURES : THEORIES AND MODELS

Let us start with a not new thesis that data structure need theories and models for them. An example will illustrate the difference between two notions. We shall indicate that formulas of first-order logic are inadequate to deal with the task of axiomatization of data structures. An axiomatic definition of a data structure like stack, queue, tree should express the finiteness of objects which is impossible within first-order language.

We shall discuss the case of dictionary theory. By a dictionary we understand any data structure which enables operations: INSERT, DELETE, MEMBER (cf Aho, Hopcroft, Ullman [1]). Here we are going to describe a formalized theory of DICTIONARIES i.e. to define its language, logic and non-logical axioms.

Language. We shall consider two sets of variables:
individual variables, denoted by e, e′ etc
set variables, denoted by S, S′ etc. (A nature of individuals will be established later, depending on application, it will turn out that the values of set variables are finite sets.)
and the following predicates and operations:
identity of individuals to be denoted by =, empty(S), member(S)
S′:=insert(e,S) , S′:=delete(e,S) , e:=amember(S)

Logic. Algorithmic logic (see Mirkowska [9], Mirkowska, Salwicki [10]) is used.

Nonlogical axioms.

[S:=insert(e,S′)](member(e,S) ∧ { e′≠e ⇒ [member(e′,S) ⇔ member(e′,S′)]})
[S:=delete(e,S′)](¬member(e,S) ∧ { e′≠e ⇒ [member(e′,S) ⇔ member(e′,S′)]})
empty(S) ⇔ amember(S) = none
amember(S) ≠ none ⇒ member(amember(S),S)
[while ¬empty(S) do S := delete(amember(S),S)] true

We are calling attention of the reader to the fact that last axiom states that every set to be considered is finite. Hence, this algorithmic formula allows us to quit from weak second-order logic. ⟨Language, logic, nonlogical axioms⟩ constitute an object called a formalized theory of DICTIONARIES. Formalized theories are studied by metamathematics. Hence, we can use metamathematical methods and study questions such as consistency, existence of models, their construction, categoricity, completeness etc.

The data structure (relational system) of queues can constitute a MODEL (first) for DICTIONARY theory.

```
type QUEUE : class begin comment QUEUE is to be conceived as a rela-
tional system with universe consisting of elem and queue objects and
functions defined below.
type elem : class begin variable next : elem end;
type queue : class begin variable front,rear : elem end;
virtual: function id : Boolean:(e,e′:elem);
```

```
function qinsert : queue : class(e : elem,S : queue);
   begin variable S1:queue ; S1 := new queue; e.next := none;
   if S==none then error else if qempty S then S1.front:=S1.rear:=e;
   else begin S1.front:= S.front; S1.rear:=S.rear.next:=e end;
   result is S1   end qinsert;
function qmember: Boolean: class(e: elem, S: queue);
   begin variable bool: Boolean, e1: elem; comment search all elements
   from front to rear; if qempty S then bool:= false else for e1:=
   S.front, e1.next while e1 ≠ S.rear do if id(e,e1)then begin bool
   := true; e1:=S.rear end; result is bool    end   qmember;
function qdelete : queue : class(e:elem,S : queue);
   comment the body of the function resembles qmember and is omitted;

function qamember : elem : class S: queue ; result is S.front;
function qempty: Boolean: class S: queue ; result is S.front =none;
hidden protected elem.next,queue.front,queue.rear; comment this dis-
ables an access to the attributes other than by functions of QUEUE;
end  QUEUE;
```

Another model of DICTIONARY may be obtained from the preceding one with the use of hash function.

```
type HASHING : QUEUE class begin
   virtual: function hash : integer(e:elem);
   type hashtable : array of queue;
   function hinsert : hashtable : class(e:elem, S: hashtable);
      begin variable i: integer,S1:hashtable; i:=hash e ; S1:=copyS;
      S1[i] := qinsert(e,S[i]); result is S1  end;
   function hmember: Boolean: class (e: elem, S: hashtable);
      begin variable i: integer; i:= hash(e); result is qmember
      (e, S[i])     end  hmember;
   function hdelete : hashtable : class(e: elem, S: hashtable);
      begin variable i: integer, S1:hashtable; i:=hash(e) ; S1 :=
      copy S; S1[i] := qdelete(e,S[i]) ; result is S1  end hdelete;
   function hamember : elem : class S: hashtable ;  ...
   function hempty : Boolean : class S: hashtable  ;  ...
end HASHING;
```

It is possible to construct other models of DICTIONARY: binary trees, balanced binary trees, 2-3 trees, etc.

A program P which makes use of terms: element, set, insert, delete, member, empty may be performed in the QUEUE environment as well as in HASHING environment. It may be done without a slightest change in the program P.

```
QUEUE begin
In-   { type element: elem class comment here the additional att-
ter-                       ributes of elements are to be defined; ...
face  { type set: queue class;;
      { function insert: set: qinsert class;;
      { ...
Pro-  { variable e1,e2: element, S,S1: set;
gram  { ...
P     { if member(e1,S1) then S := delete(e2,S1);
      { ...
      { end
```

Similarly program P can be executed in the HASHING environment.

A theory of PRIORITY QUEUES results from the theory of DICTIONARIES, simply, by adding axioms of linear order of individuals and an axiom defining MIN(S)operation. The last theory can be enlarged to a theory of MERGEABLE HEAPS. Models of PRIORITY QUEUES and of MERGEABLE HEAPS can be constructed again from stacks, queues, trees. This shows that theory of DICTIONARY and theory of PRIORITY QUEUES are incomplete.

Another approach is possible: one can build theories of queues, stacks, binary trees, 2-3 trees making use of their "geometry". A comparative study of these two families of data structure theories is very instructive.

Sometimes the discussion of data structures needed for an algorithm is harder and needs subtle tools. A hint of D.Knuth how to implement HU-TUCKER algorithm was succesfully realized by H.Oktaba, W.Ratajczak and A.Kreczmar. They consecutively refined appropriate structures for Priority Queues and Mergeable Heaps and modified them in order to obtain three different HU-TUCKER ALGORITHM DATA STRUCTURES. Every solution allows to implement the algorithm in O(nlogn) time.

Coming back to our examples: we have constructed two models QUEUES and HASHING. More strictly: the types QUEUE and HASHING define two families of data structures (relational systems)

$\langle$ elem∪Fin(elem), insert, delete, member, empty, amember $\rangle$

beeing models for DICTIONARY. A member of a family is uniquely defined by its set of elem - elements.

QUEUE may be viewed as a theory if we consider its procedures as formulas (cf Salwicki [14]). Let us observe that

qamember(S) = S.front

qempty(S) $\Leftrightarrow$ S.front = none

qdelete(e,S) = K result is S1   where K denotes a program

Obviously QUEUE is not categorical, since it possesses models of different cardinalities. It is an assumption that QUEUE is categorical in every power.

We observe that certain theories are more constructive than others, some of them can be even treated as constructions. The question: whether a consistent theory posses a construction of a model (a type) is open and of practical importance.

Let me end this section by recalling the problem stated at Jabłonna conference in 1972. The problem is of algebraic characterization of the class of constructive relational systems i.e. those systems that are costructively equivalent to the system $\langle N, 0, s \rangle$.

§3 AN ALGORITHMIC APPROACH TO SET THEORY

Notion of set does occur in programming in at least three different situations:

sp1) when one considers a collection of all objects of a given type
$T = \{o : o \ \underline{in} \ T\}$

sp2) when an object represents a finite set of other objects
examples are: stack, queue, array, tree, graph etc.

sp3) when an algorithm or a pair of algorithms (cf Heyting [5]) is considered by which one can recognize a membership of elements.

The differences are noticeable. Sets of sp1) type are collections of finite objects. However, they itself may be infinite, even uncountable if one admits an uncountable primitive type. Elements of sp2) type are not only sets, they allow an algebraic treatment of sets represented by them. Examples from the preceding section show it clearly.

It is worthwhile to observe that notions mentioned above are in correspondence with neointuitionistic concepts of Brouwer and Markov sp1) is an algorithmic counterpart of Brouwerian: species sp2) corresponds to finitary spreads and sp3) to spreads.

Continuing the examination one sees that notion of type differs from species since objects of type may be effectively constructed from urelements, moreover recursive definitions are allowed eg. definition of binary tree type. Comparison of sp3) and spreads needs more work.

On the other hand an interesting correspondence between axioms of Zermelo-Fraenkel theory and certain formulas about types, objects and in relation was observed: For every axiom of ZF (without axiom of choice) a translation of it with the help of the dictionary:

{set - type, element - object, ∈ - <u>in</u>, propositional function - algorithmic formula

results in a valid statement about types, objects and <u>in</u>-relation.

§4 PARALLEL COMPUTATIONS SYNCHRONIZED BY MONITORS

Here we shall report about an implementation of processes and monitors documented with proofs. This will be preceded by the definition of computation of nonsequential program. Observe please, that word: process used in this paper means nothing more than a sequential component of a non-sequential program .

By a snapshot we shall mean a set of objects, it is assumed that they are all objects existing at a given time. Some objects can be marked by ○ or □ depending whether the first instruction in the object is under execution marked: ○ or ready to execute marked: □ Number of marks reflects the number of processors. By a configuration we shall mean a snapshot such that at least one mark □ exists. We shall say that statements J1, J2, ..., Jk $(k > 1)$ are in conflict iff every statement Ji $(i=1,\dots,k)$ contains a common variable and at least one of Ji assigns a value to that variable.

By a tree of possible computations of a program we shall understand the tree H of configurations such that:

a) the root of the tree is a given initial configuration,

b) Let k be a vertex of tree H and let I1, I2, ... ,In are all marked statements from configuration k. Without loss of generality we can assume the first l statements I1,...,Il are marked □ i.e. ready to execute, the remaining Il+1, ...,In are marked ○ i.e. are under execution. The descendants of the vertex k are defined as follows:

b1) Vertex k has no descendants if all marks are □ and mark objects with empty list of instructions.

b2) In the other case at least one instruction marked □ is to be executed. In order to define descendants, two steps reflecting non-deterministic choice are to be executed. First, we shall consider all non-conflict subsets S1,...,Sp of the set I1,...,In which contain all instructions I1+1,...,In i.e. those under execution - they are non-conflict from the inductive assumption . Second, for every such set Si we shall consider all subsets Si and denote them Si_j $(j=1,\dots,g_i)$. Since instructions of an Si_j set are non-conflict we can consider a configuration k_i^j resulting from the configuration k by simultaneous execution of all instructions contained in Si_j. Let us remark that all these instructions are of sequential character and each of them may be viewed as a rule of "local change of a configuration". All executed instructions are deleted from their objects marked □ , all remaining instructions are marked ○ , which reflects the state of "beeing under execution". In that way we obtained a configuration k_i^j. Every such configuration is a descendant of the vertex k. This ends the definition of the tree H of possible computations.

By a computation we shall mean an arbitrary path of the tree H leading to a leaf i.e. a finite one .

T.Müldner [11] showed how to implement notions of process,monitor, entry procedure (also coroutine, swap, rotate) by introducing type PARALLEL. Declaration of PARALLEL brings tools such as mentioned above and allows every user to make use of them as prefixes.

A monitor is a data structure designed for synchronization and communication of processes (cf Brinch Hansen [4],Hoare [6]). It is protected from improper, simultaneous assignments by a logical semaphore. The only way to operate on attributes of a monitor is to call an entryprocedure of it. In order to enable scheduling each entryprocedure can use procedures: delay(Q) - process calling entryprocedure is passivated and entered into a queue Q, continue(Q) - process calling entryprocedure returns from the monitor and continues its execution and simultaneously the first process from the Q queue resumes the execution of its monitor.entryprocedure call.

A user can build his own monitors and entryprocedures around these built in PARALLEL simply by prefixing his own specifications of data structures and actions with monitor or entryprocedure.

Implementation of PARALLEL makes use of the following assumptions: Only Boolean variables may be shared by processes explicitly i.e. apart of monitors. The following tools are used: T&S operation of logical semaphore on boolean variables, a data structure of queues (which in fact is defined within PARALLEL), certain appropriate procedures to activate or passivate a process.

A diagram below should give some intuitions how the type PARALLEL is organized and places it in a larger type ALL LEVELS.

Structure of prefixes and attributes of the class ALL LEVELS (arrows indicate the prefixes, boxes contain names of attributes with some comments)

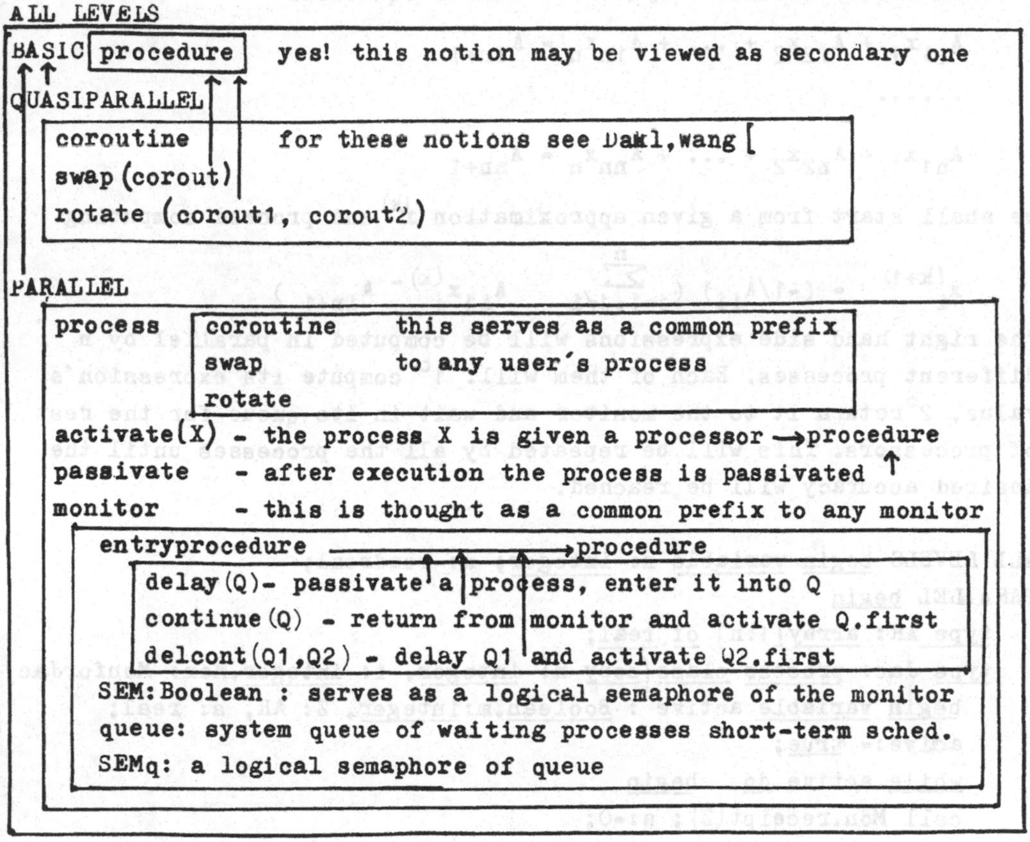

Let us assume that only one monitor object exists. Making use of semantics defined above T.Müldner [12] proved that:

a) for every configuration at most one process can execute entryprocedure (MUTUAL EXCLUSION),

b) in a final configuration the system queue of processes of the monitor is empty (DEADLOCK PREVENTED),

REMARK. It does not means that any user may not cause deadlock.

c) the sequence of executions of entry procedures by the processes which in a configuration k are delayed in the system queue is independent of the actions of the other processes which call entry-procedures in some later configurations (FAIRNESS).

REMARK. A user is, however, free to rearrange entryprocedure's calls making use of delay, continue and delcont procedures.

This may be generalized to any number of monitor objects.

As an example of processes communicating via a monitor we choose a non-trivial operating system which is connected with the parallel version of Jacobi's algorithm. Program was prepared by L Stapp.

In order to solve a system of linear equations

$$A_{11}x_1 + A_{12}x_2 + \dots + A_{1n}x_n = A_{1n+1}$$

$$\dots\dots$$

$$A_{n1}x_1 + A_{n2}x_2 + \dots + A_{nn}x_n = A_{nn+1}$$

we shall start from a given approximation $x^{(k)}$ and proceed computing

$$x_i^{(k+1)} = (-1/A_{ii}) \left(\sum_{j=1, j\neq i}^{n} A_{ij} x_j^{(k)} - A_{in+1} \right)$$

The right hand side expressions will be computed in parallel by n different processes. Each of them will: 1° compute its expression's value, 2° return it to the monitor and wait in its queue for the rest of processors. This will be repeated by all the processes until the desired accuracy will be reached.

```
ALL LEVELS begin variable n: integer; n:=readreal;
PARALLEL begin
   type AR: array[1:n] of real;
   type Jac: process class(copy n: integer, i: integer,Mon: MonforJac);
     begin variable active : Boolean,m:integer, Z: AR, s: real;
     active:= true;
     while active do   begin
     call Mon.receipt(Z); s:=0;
     for m:= 1 step 1 until i-1, i+1step 1 until n do
        s := A[i,m]× Z[m] +s;
     s:= -(s + A[i,n+1])/ A[i,i];
     call Mon.delivery(i, s, active);
                        endwhile
     end Jac;
  constant A :(array[1:n]of array[1:n+1] of real;
                begin
                variable i,j : integer;
                for i:= 1 step 1 until n do
                for j:= 1 step 1 until n+1 do
                      A[i,j] := readreal;
                end this establishes the constant A );
```

```
type MonforJac: monitor class n: integer, eps : real ;
  begin variable X,Y: AR, queue: head, k,j: integer, boo:Boolean;
  comment queue is for processes which are not the last one,
  X - preceding approvimation, Y - approximation under preparation
  k - number of processes in the queue, boo - not finish yet;
  type receipt: entryprocedure class(result copy W: AR);
              begin W := X end receipt;
  comment a copy of array X is transferred to a calling process;
  type delivery: entryprocedure class(i:integer,effect:real,
                                      result finish: boolean);
  begin  Y[i]:= effect;
  if k ≠ n-1 then comment a process is still computing;
              begin k:=k+1; call delay(queue) end
              else comment this is the last process;
               begin variable dist:real,r: integer; dist := 0;
                comment compute the distance between two con-
                secutive iterations and decide whether to finish
                boo:=false and print or to continue;
                X:=copy Y;
               end k=n-1;          finish:= boo;
   if k≠0 then begin k:= k-1; call continue(queue) end
  end delivery;
  comment now an initialisation of attributes of the monitor object;
  k:=0; boo:= true; queue:= new head; for j:= 1 step 1 until n do
   X[j] := readreal;          Y:=copyX
  end MonforJac;
  Variable MonJac: MonforJac,I:integer;
comment here the declarations end, observe that the program contains
   two instructions only;

 MonJac:= new MonforJac(n,readreal);
  comment in that way we created an object of the type monitor
  MonforJac which will be shared by all the processes;

 for i:= 1 step1 until n do call activate(new Jac(n,i,MonJac)) ;
  comment this instruction creates and activates n processes to
  compute iterations in parallel, the operating system defined
  here seems a generalize producer-consumer scheme;

 end PARALLEL
end ALL LEVELS
```

§5 PROGRAMMABILITY AND P = NP HYPOTHESIS

The P = NP problem is usually posed in the language of Turing machines. S.Radziszowski [13] indicated a way of speaking about computational complexity and nondeterminism for an arbitrary data structure i.e. relational system . This opens the possibility of application of model-theoretic tools.

A formal notion of computational complexity may be defined in an arbitrary data structure $\mathfrak{A}$ of denumerable universe. To every primitive function or relation of $\mathfrak{A}$ we associate functions of their complexity which describe the way the complexity of computation depends on length (magnitude) of arguments.

Furthermore, the notion of complexity is extended to the arbitrary algorithmic formulas $K\alpha$. This enables us to define the complexity of a problem as a smallest complexity of a formula $K\alpha$ which solves the problem.

Analogous construction of notions may be repeated for programs with non-deterministic CHOICE[K1, ... ,Kn] program - connective.

Given a relational system $\mathfrak{A}$ with associated complexity functions one can ask whether problems decidable non-deterministically in a polynomial time could be solved deterministically also in a polynomial time?

We have not an answer for a general case (to be denoted $P^{\mathfrak{A}} = NP^{\mathfrak{A}}$)

The tools used in the theories which study questions connected with complexity allow to formulate many interesting questions eg.

1 There are relational systems $\mathfrak{A}$ for which $P^{\mathfrak{A}} \subsetneq NP^{\mathfrak{A}}$ eg. $\langle N, *2, *2+1, 0 \rangle$ for the function x/2. Find other examples, find regularities.

2 Let us confine to the class K of relational sytems that allow deterministic simulation of nondeterminism. It is possible then to find conditions satisfactory for

$$P^{\mathfrak{A}} = NP^{\mathfrak{A}} \iff P = NP$$

(The conditions assert the possibility of mutual simulation of elementary actions of Turing machines and primitive functions of the system $\mathfrak{A}$ in a polynomial time).

3 Let $K' = \{\mathfrak{A} \in K : P^{\mathfrak{A}} = NP^{\mathfrak{A}} \iff P = NP\} \subseteq K$
The class K′ contains among others $\langle N, *2, /2, +0, 0 \rangle$
$\langle N, \cup, \cap, \text{shift}, = \rangle$
Is $K - K' = \emptyset$?

References

1. Aho,A.V.,Hopcroft,J.E.,Ullman,J.D., The design and analysis of computer algorithms, Addison Wesley, Reading,Mass.,1968
2. Birtwistle,G.M.,Dahl,O-J.,Mayhrhaug,B.,Nygaard,K., SIMULA begin, Studentliteratur,Lund,1973
3. Banachowski,L., An axiomatic approach to the theory of data structures, Bull.Acad.Pol.Sci.Ser.Math.Astr.Phys., 23 (1975) 315-323
4. Brinch Hansen,P., Concurrent Pascal, Information Science TR 10 Caltech,Pasadena,1976
5. Heyting,A., Intuitionism,North Holland, Amsterdam, 1956
6. Hoare,C.A.R.,Monitors: an operating system structuring concept Com.ACM,17 (1974),549-557
7. Knuth,D.E.,The art of computer programming, I,III, Addison-Wesley. Reading,Mass.,1968
8. LOGLAN 77, internal report University of Warsaw, 1977
9. Mirkowska,G.,Algorithmic logic..., to appear in Fundamenta Informaticae, see also On formalized systems of algorithmic logic, Bull.Acad.Pol.Sci.Ser.Math.Astr.Phys., 19(1971),421-428
10. Mirkowska,G.,Salwicki,A., A complete axiomatic characterization of algorithmic properties... in Proc.MFCS-76 Gdańsk, Lecture Notes in Computer Science, Springer Verlag,Berlin,1976,602-608
11. Müldner,T.,Implementation and properties of certain notions of quasi-parallel and parallel computations, to appear in Fundamenta Informaticae
12. Müldner,T., On properties of certain synchronising tool for parallel computations, Proc.FCT'77 Poznań, Lecture Notes in Computer Science, Springer Verlag, Berlin, 1977
13. Radziszowski,S., Programmability and P=NP conjecture, ibidem
14. Salwicki,A., Procedures, formal computations and models. Proc.MFCS 74 Jadwisin, Lecture Notes in Computer Science 28 Springer Verlag, Berlin 1974, 464-484
15. Salwicki,A.,An algorithmic approach to set theory, Proc FCT'77 Poznań,Lecture Notes in Compuer Science, Springer Vlg,Berlin 1977

IMPROVED LOWER BOUNDS ON THE NUMBER OF MULTIPLICATIONS/ DIVISIONS WHICH ARE NECESSARY TO EVALUATE POLYNOMIALS

C.P. Schnorr

Fachbereich Mathematik der Universität Frankfurt
6000 Frankfurt am Main, Rob. Mayer-Str.10

Abstract: We improve some lower bounds which have been obtained by Strassen and Lipton. In particular there exist polynomials of degree n with 0-1 coefficients that cannot be evaluated with less than $\sqrt{n}/(4 \log n)$ nonscalar multiplications/divisions. The evaluation of $p(x) = \sum_{\delta=0}^{n} e^{2\pi i/2^\delta} x^\delta$ requires at least $n/(12 \log n)$ multiplications/divisions and at least $\sqrt{n/(8 \log n)}$ nonscalar multiplications/divisions. We specify polynomials with algebraic coefficients that require n/2 multiplications/divisions.

1. Introduction and Notation

It is well known from the results of Belaga (1958), Motzkin (1955) and Winograd (1970) that the evaluation of a polynomial $\sum_{i=0}^{n} a_i x^i$ requires n/2 multiplications/divisions when the coefficients a_i are algebraically independent. In their model of computation arbitrary complex numbers can be used at no cost, we say complex preconditioning is allowed. The situation for polynomials with rational coefficients has been studied by Paterson, Stockmeyer (1973) and by Strassen (1974). Paterson, Stockmeyer prove the existence of rational polynomials which are hard to compute whereas Strassen's method yields lower bounds on the number of multiplications/divisions which are necessary to evaluate concrete polynomials with rational and algebraic coefficients. The results of Strassen have lateron been used by Lipton (1975) and Lipton, Stockmeyer (1976).

In this paper we improve the degree bound in Strassen's key lemma 2.4. As a consequence we can improve the lower bounds of Strassen as well as the conclusions which have been drawn by Lipton and Lipton, Stockmeyer.

Let $\mathbb{C}$ be the field of complex numbers and let Q be its prime field. A computation ß for $p(x) \in \mathbb{C}(x)$ is a sequence of computation steps S_i $i = 1,\ldots,n$ such that either

(1) $S_i \in \mathbb{C} \cup \{x\}$ or (2) $S_i = S_j \circ S_k$ with $j,k < i$ and $\circ \in \{+,-,\times,/\}$ and $S_k \not\equiv 0$ if $\circ$ is /. n is the <u>length</u> and the rational functions S_i $i = 1,\ldots,n$ are the <u>results</u> of the computation. A step $S_i = S_j \circ S_k$ is called <u>nonscalar</u> provided $\circ$ is $\times$ and both S_j and S_k are not in $\mathbb{C}$, or $\circ$ is / and S_k is not in $\mathbb{C}$.

Let ß be a computation and $\gamma \in \mathbb{C}$ such that $S_i(\gamma) \neq 0$ for all results S_i of ß, then ß is called <u>γ-admissible.</u> In this case the computation can be carried out in the ring $\mathbb{C}[[x-\gamma]]$ of formal power series in $(x-\gamma)$ and every result is a unit in $\mathbb{C}[[x-\gamma]]$. Obviously any computation is γ-admissible for all but finitely many $\gamma \in \mathbb{C}$ provided that the constant $0 \in \mathbb{C}$ is not a result of the computation.

2. Lower bounds on the number of nonscalar multiplications/divisions for specific polynomials.

In this section we revise the application of Strassen's results in Lipton (1975). As a result we prove the existence of polynomials $p(x) = \sum_{i=0}^{n} b_i x^i$ with $b_i \in \{0,1\}$ that require $\sqrt{n}/(4\log n)$ nonscalar multiplications/divisions, Lipton's lower bound is $n^{1/4}/(18\log n)$. The method can also be applied to specific polynomials with rational and algebraic coefficients. As an example we improve the $n^{1/3}$ lower bound on the number of nonscalar multiplications for $\Sigma_{i=0}^{n} \exp(2\pi i/2^j)x^j$ in Strassen, Corollary 3.7 to $\sqrt{n/8\log n}$ and in addition to Strassen we allow divisions as well as multiplications. Strassen's $n^{1/3}$ lower bound on the number of nonscalar multiplications for $\Sigma_{i=o}^{n} 2^{2^i} x_i$ can be improved as well; this is left as an exercise to the reader.

With $p(x) \in \mathbb{C}(x)$ we associate the minimal number $L(p(x))$ of nonscalar multiplications/divisions which are necessary to compute $p(x)$.

Let β be a computation for $p(x)$ with $\leq v$ nonscalar operations. Then following Paterson, Stockmeyer (1973) $p(x)$ can be computed by the following scheme with $m_{i,j}, m'_{i,j} \in \mathbb{C}$ and $m_\nu \in \{0,1\}$:

$$
2.1 \quad \left| \begin{array}{l}
P_{-3} = 1,\ P_O = x \\
P_{3r-2} = \Sigma_{j=-1}^{r-1} m_{r,j} P_{3j}\ ;\ P_{3r-1} = \Sigma_{j=-1}^{r-1} m'_{r,j} P_{3j} \\
P_{3r} = P_{3r-2}((1-m_r)P_{3r-1} + m_r/P_{3r-1}) \\
\qquad\qquad\qquad\qquad \text{for } r = 1,2,\ldots,v \\
p(x) = P_{3v+1} = \Sigma_{j=-1}^{v} m_{v+1,j} P_{3j}
\end{array} \right.
$$

Since we like to carry out this computation in a ring of formal power series we assume that β is O-admissible and this yields $P_i(O) \neq O$ for all i. Therefore

$$P_i = \Sigma_{j \geq O} Q_{i,j} x^j \text{ with}$$

$$Q_{i,j} \in \mathbb{Z}[m_{\nu,\mu}, m'_{\nu,\mu}, m_\nu \mid -1 \leq \nu,\mu \leq i/3].$$

These power series have some nonzero convergence radius. In any computation 2.1 with $P_i(O) \neq O$ for all i, we can normalize the parameters $m_{\nu,\mu}, m'_{\nu,\mu}$ such that $P_{3r-2}(O) = P_{3r-1}(O) = 1$. This can always be done by computing the rational functions $P_i/P_i(O)$ instead of P_i for $i=1,\ldots,v$ together with an appropriate change of the parameters $m_{\nu,\mu}$ and $m'_{\nu,\mu}$. Since we normalize the parameters $m_{\nu,\mu}$ and $m'_{\nu,\mu}$ as above we can assume w.r.g. that

$$Q_{3r-1,O} \equiv Q_{3r-2,O} \equiv Q_{3r,O} \equiv 1$$

This yields the following recursion scheme for the $Q_{3r,j}$ where the parameters $m_{r,-1}, m'_{r,-1}$ are eliminated:

for $r = 1,\dots,v$:

$$1 + \Sigma_{j\geq 1} Q_{3r,j} x^j =$$

$$\left[1 + \Sigma_{i=0}^{r-1} m_{r,i}\ \Sigma_{j\geq 1} Q_{3i,j} x^j\right] \times$$

2.2 $$\left[(1 - m_r) \times (1 + \Sigma_{i=0}^{r-1} m'_{r,i} \Sigma_{j\geq 1} Q_{3i,j} x^j)\right.$$

$$\left. + m_r (1 + \Sigma_{\nu=1}^{\infty} (- \Sigma_{i=0}^{r-1} m'_{r,i} \Sigma_{j\geq 1} Q_{3i,j} x^j)^{\nu})\right]$$

with $Q_{0,j} \equiv 0$ for $j > 0$.

By comparison of the coefficients of the x^j we obtain the following recursion for $\deg Q_{3r,j}$:

2.3 $$\deg Q_{3r,j} = \max \left\{ \mu + 1 + \Sigma_{\nu=1}^{\mu} \deg Q_{3i_\nu,j_\nu} \;\middle|\; \begin{array}{l} \Sigma_{\nu=1}^{\mu} j_\nu = j, \mu \geq 1 \\ 1 \leq j_\nu, 0 \leq i_\nu < r \end{array} \right\}$$

$$\deg Q_{0,j} = 0$$

(Observe that the relevant additive terms of $Q_{3r,j}$ are $m_r\ \Pi_{\nu=1}^{\mu} (-m'_{r,i}\ Q_{3i_\nu,j_\nu})$ with $\Sigma_{\nu=1}^{\mu}\ j_\nu = j, \mu \geq 1, j_\nu \geq 1, 0 \leq i_\nu < r$).

From 2.3 it can easily be seen by induction on r that

2.4 $\deg Q_{3r,1} = 2r$, $\deg Q_{3r,j} = j(2r-1) + 1$

Next we count the number of parameters in the recursion scheme 2.1 after the elimination of $m_{r,-1}$ and $m'_{r,-1}$. We have parameters $m_{r,i}$ for $i = 0,\dots,r-1$ and $r = 1,\dots,v$. This yields $\Sigma_{r=1}^{v} r = v(v+1)/2$ parameters. We have the same number of parameters $m'_{r,i}$ and in addition there are v parameters m_r and v+2 parameters $m_{3v+1,j}$ $j=-1,\dots,v$. This altogether are v^2+3v+2 parameters. Setting $Q_j = Q_{3v+1,j} = m_{v+1,j} Q_{3v,j}$ we have proved the following

<u>Theorem 2.5</u>

Let $v \in N$ then there exist polynomials $Q_j \in \mathbb{Z}[z_1,\dots,z_m]$ with

$m = v^2+3v+2, \deg Q_j = j(2v-1)+2$ such that for all $p(x) = \Sigma_{j\geq 0} a_j x^j \in \mathbb{C}[[x]]$ that can be computed with $\leq v$ nonscalar operations by some 0-admissible computation, there exist values $\gamma_i \in \mathbb{C}$ for z_i $i=1,\ldots,m$ such that $\forall j > 0 : a_j = Q_j(\gamma_1,\ldots,\gamma_m)$.

It is a basic fact from linear algebra that M linear forms in $\mathbb{Z}[B_1,\ldots,B_N]$ have a nontrivial common zero $(b_1,\ldots,b_N) \in \mathbb{Z}^N$ provided $N > M$. This yields the following

Lemma 2.6

Let $P_1,\ldots,P_q \in \mathbb{Z}[z_1,\ldots,z_m]$, $\deg P_k \leq c$. Then there exists $H \in \mathbb{Z}[y_1,\ldots,y_q]$, $H \not\equiv 0$ such that $H(P_1,\ldots,P_q) = 0, \deg H \leq g$ provided $\binom{g+q}{q} > \binom{gc+m}{m}$.

Proof: Consider the linear forms with unknowns $B_{i_1,\ldots,i_q}$ that constitute the coefficient relations with respect to

$$\sum_{i_1+i_2\ldots+i_q \leq g} B_{i_1,\ldots,i_q} P_1^{i_1} \ldots P_q^{i_q} = 0$$

Since we associate with each monomial in $z_1,\ldots,z_m$ with degree $\leq gc$ a corresponding linear form that relates all coefficients of this monomial in the above equation, we have $M = \binom{gc+m}{m}$ linear forms in total. The number N of variables $B_{i_1,\ldots,i_q}$ is the number of q-tuples $(i_1,\ldots,i_q)$ with $i_1+\ldots+i_q \leq g$, hence $N = \binom{g+q}{q}$. Therefore there is a nontrivial common zero $(B_{i_1,\ldots,i_q} | i_1,\ldots,i_q) \in \mathbb{Z}^N$ of the above linear forms provided $\binom{g+q}{q} > \binom{gc+m}{m}$. This nontrivial zero yields the asserted $H \in \mathbb{Z}[z_1,\ldots,z_m]$. ∎

Theorem 2.7 Let $q_n \leq n$, $1 \leq \delta_1 < \delta_2 \ldots < \delta q_n \leq n, \alpha_n, \varepsilon$ be such that $\alpha_n q_n \geq 1.1n$, $n/\alpha_n \to \infty$ and $\varepsilon > \sup 2.5n/(q_n\alpha_n - n)$. Then there exists n_0 such that for all $n \geq n_0$ there exists $H \in \mathbb{Z}[y_1,\ldots,y_{q_n}]$, $H \not\equiv 0$, $\deg H \leq \lceil n^{1+\varepsilon} \rceil$ such that for all

$p(x) = \Sigma_{i=0}^{\infty} a_i x^i \in \mathbb{C}(x)$ with $L(p(x)) \le \sqrt{n/\alpha_n}-2$: $H(a_{\delta_1},\ldots,a_{\delta q_n}) = 0$

Proof: Let β be a computation for $p(x)$ with $\le \sqrt{n/\alpha_n}-2$ nonscalar operations. We would like to apply theorem 2.5. β is γ-admissible for all but finitely many $\gamma \in \mathbb{C}$. Hence theorem 2.5 applies to $a_i := a_i(\gamma)$ with $p(x) = \Sigma_{i\ge 0} a_i(\gamma)(x-\gamma)^i$ for all but finitely many γ. If, however, $H(a_{\delta_1}(\gamma),\ldots,a_{\delta_{q_n}}(\gamma)) = 0$ for all but finitely many $\gamma \in \mathbb{C}$ then $H(a_{\delta_1}(0),\ldots,a_{\delta_{q_n}}(0)) = 0$ since the $a_i(\gamma)$ are continuous in γ. Therefore we can assume w.r.g. that β is 0-admissible. Then according to theorem 2.5 there exist for each n, polynomials $Q_j \in \mathbb{Z}[z_1,\ldots,z_m]$, $m=\lfloor n/\alpha_n \rfloor$ such that $\deg Q_j \le 2j\sqrt{n/\alpha_n}$ and $\forall j > 0: a_j = Q_j(\gamma_1,\ldots,\gamma_m)$ for some suitable $\gamma_1,\ldots,\gamma_m \in \mathbb{C}$.

We apply Lemma 2.6 to $P_i = Q_{\delta_i}$ $i=1,\ldots,q_n$ with $\delta_i \le n$ and $g = \lceil n^{1+\varepsilon} \rceil$. Set $c = 2n\sqrt{n/\alpha_n}$ in 2.6, then according to 2.6 there exists $H \in \mathbb{Z}[y_1,\ldots,y_{q_n}]$, $H \not\equiv 0$ such that $H(Q_{\delta_1},\ldots,Q_{\delta q_n}) = 0$ and $\deg H \le \lceil n^{1+\varepsilon} \rceil$ provided

$$(*) \qquad \binom{n^{1+\varepsilon} + q_n}{q_n} > \binom{n^{1+\varepsilon}\ 2n\sqrt{n/\alpha_n} + n/\alpha_n}{n/\alpha_n}$$

Obviously $\binom{n^{1+\varepsilon} + q_n}{q_n} \ge n^{q_n(1+\varepsilon)} / q_n^{q_n}$ and for $n \ge 3$

$$\binom{n^{1+\varepsilon}\ 2n\sqrt{n/\alpha_n} + n/\alpha_n}{n/\alpha_n} < (2.1n)^{(2.5+\varepsilon)n/\alpha_n} / (n/\alpha_n)!$$

since $\qquad n^{1+\varepsilon}\ 2n\sqrt{n/\alpha_n} + n/\alpha_n \le 2n^{2.5+\alpha} + n \le 2.1\, n^{2.5+\varepsilon}$

(observe $\alpha_n \ge 1$ because $\alpha_n q_n \ge n$ and $q_n \le n$).

From this it follows by taking logarithms to base 2 that

$$(**) \quad q_n(1+\varepsilon)\log n > q_n \log q_n + (2.5+\varepsilon)\, n/\alpha_n \log(2.1n) - n/\alpha_n \log n/\alpha_n + 2n/\alpha_n$$

implies (*). Observe that $\log(n/\alpha)! \geq n/\alpha \log n/\alpha - 2n/\alpha$.
By our assumptions there exists $b > 0$ such that for all n
$\varepsilon > 1.5n/(q_n\alpha_n - n) + b$. This implies $\varepsilon(q_n - n/\alpha_n) > 2.5n/\alpha_n + b(q_n - n/\alpha_n)$ and $q_n(1+\varepsilon) > q_n + (2.5+\varepsilon)\, n/\alpha_n + 0.1bn/\alpha_n$ since $\alpha_n q_n \geq 1.1n$. Since $n/\alpha_n \to \infty$ this yields (**) and consequently (*) for all sufficiently large n.
Therefore for some n_o and all $n \geq n_o$ there exists
$H \in \mathbb{Z}[y_1,\ldots,y_{q_n}]$, $H \not\equiv 0$ $\deg H \leq \lceil n^{1+\varepsilon} \rceil$ such that $H(Q_{\delta_1},\ldots,Q_{\delta_{q_n}}) = 0$.
Consequently $H(a_{\delta_1},\ldots,a_{\delta_{q_n}}) = 0$. ▨

Applying 2.7 to $q_n = n$, $\delta_i = i$, $\alpha_n = \alpha \geq 1.1$ yields that for any $p(x) = \Sigma_i a_i x^i$ with $L(p(x)) \leq \sqrt{n/\alpha} - 2$ there exists $H \in \mathbb{Z}[y_1,\ldots,y_n]$, $H \not\equiv 0$ such that $H(a_1,\ldots,a_n) = 0$ and $\deg H \leq \lceil n^{1+\varepsilon} \rceil$ provided $\varepsilon > 2.5/(\alpha-1)$.
On the other hand since $H \not\equiv 0$ there exist $a_1,\ldots,a_n \in \mathbb{Z}$ such that $0 \leq a_i \leq \deg H \leq \lceil n^{1+\varepsilon} \rceil$ with $H(a_1,\ldots,a_n) \not\equiv 0$. This implies

<u>Corollary 2.8</u>

Let $\alpha \geq 1.1$ and $\varepsilon > 2.5/(\alpha-1)$ and $n \geq n_o$, then there exist $a_1,\ldots,a_n \in \mathbb{Z}$ such that $1 \leq a_i \leq \lceil n^{1+\varepsilon} \rceil$ and $L(\Sigma_{i=1}^n a_i x^i) \geq \sqrt{n/\alpha} - 2$.

Since α can be chosen arbitrary near to 1, Corollary 2.8 is another version of theorem 3 in Paterson, Stockmeyer:
$\max\{L(\Sigma_{i=0}^n a_i x^i) \mid a_i \in Q) \geq \sqrt{n} - 2$ and 2.8 bounds the coefficients a_i.

Let $C_{0,1}(n) = \max\{L(\Sigma_{i=0}^n b_i x^i) \mid b_i \in \{0,1\}\}$.

Lipton (1975) proved in Lemma 2:

2.9 $\quad L(\Sigma_{i=0}^n a_i x^i) \leq C_{0,1}(n)(2 + \log \max_i a_i)$
for all $a_i \in N$. Here log is the logarithm to base 2. This yields

<u>Theorem 2.10</u>

For $n \geq n_o$ there exist $b_i \in \{0,1\}$ $i = 1,\ldots,n$ such that
$L(\Sigma_{i=0}^n b_i x^i) \geq \sqrt{n}/(4 \log n)$
2.10 improves the corresponding $n^{1/4}/(18 \log n)$ lower bounds in Lipton

(1975), theorem 5.

Proof: It follows from 2.9 and 2.8 that for $n \geq n_o$ there exist $b_i \in \{0,1\}$ for $i=1,\ldots,n$ such that

$$L(\Sigma_{i=0}^{n} b_i x^i) \geq \sqrt{n/\alpha}/[(1+\varepsilon)\log n]$$

provided $\varepsilon > 2.5/(\alpha-1)$. Here α and ε can be chosen such that $\sqrt{\alpha}(1+\varepsilon) < 4$, choose $\alpha = 4$ and $\varepsilon = 1$. This proves 2.10. ▨

Next we use theorem 2.7 in order to improve Strassen's $n^{1/3}$ lower bound on the number of nonscalar multiplications for $\Sigma_{j=0}^{n} \exp(2\pi i/2^j)x^j$ in Strassen (1974), Corollary 3.7. In addition to Strassen we allow divisions.

Corollary 2.11

$$\forall n \geq n_o : L(\Sigma_{j=0}^{n} \exp(2\pi i/2^j)x^j \geq \sqrt{n/8 \log n} - 1$$

Proof: Assume $L(\Sigma_{j=0}^{n} \exp(2\pi i/2^j)x^j) \leq \sqrt{n/8 \log n} - 2$ choose $\alpha_n, q_n, \varepsilon$ in theorem 2.7 as follows:

$$\alpha_n = 8 \log n \;,\; q_n = \lfloor (1/4)n/\log n \rfloor, \quad \varepsilon = 2.6.$$

Then $\alpha_n q_n \geq 1.1n$, $\varepsilon > 2.5n/(q_n\alpha_n - n)$, $n/\alpha_n \to \infty$.

Choose $\delta_j = 4j\lfloor \log n \rfloor$ for $j = 1,\ldots,q_n$.

Then according to theorem 2.7 there exists $H \in \mathbb{Z}[y_1,\ldots,y_{q_n}]$, $H \not\equiv 0$, $\deg H \leq n^{3.6}$ such that $H(a_{\delta_1},\ldots,a_{\delta_{q_n}}) = 0$ with $a_j = \exp(2\pi i/2^j)$.

On the other hand we have ([K:F] is the degree of K over F):

$$[\mathbb{Q}(a_{\delta_1},\ldots,a_{\delta_k}):\mathbb{Q}(a_{\delta_1},\ldots,a_{\delta_{k-1}})] \geq 2^{4\lfloor \log n \rfloor} \geq (n/2)^4.$$

Hence by Lemma 2.6, Strassen (1974) (see below) there does not exist $H \not\equiv 0$ with $\deg H < n^3$ and $H(a_{\delta_1},\ldots,a_{\delta_{q_n}}) = 0$.

This however contradicts to $n^{3.6} < (n/2)^4$. ▨

Lemma 2.6 in Strassen (1974) Let $\tau_1,\dots,\tau_q \in \mathbb{C}$ and let $\forall k:[Q(\tau_1,\dots,\tau_k):Q(\tau_1,\dots,\tau_{k-1})] > g$. Then there is no $H \in \mathbb{Z}[y_1,\dots,y_q], H \not\equiv 0$ such that $\deg H \le g$ and $H(\tau_1,\dots,\tau_q) = 0$.

Similarly Strassen's $n^{1/3}$ lower bound on the number of nonscalar multiplications for $\Sigma_{j=0}^{n} 2^{2^j} x^j$ can be improved to $c\sqrt{n/\log n}$ by taking into consideration appropriate weight bounds for the polynomials Q_j in theorem 2.3. Such weight bounds have been proved in Lemma 2.4, Strassen (1974) and they can be used to prove lower bounds on $\Sigma_{j=0}^{n} 2^{2^j} x^j$ via the pigeon hole Lemma 2.2 and Lemma 2.10, Strassen (1974).

3. Lower bounds on the total number of multiplications/divisions.

Lemma 3.1 improves the degree bound in Strassen's (1974) key Lemma 2.4. A similar statement has been proved by Sieveking (1976), prop.1. However, Sieveking proves the result for the degree of a corresponding algebraic variety.

Lemma 3.1 Let ß be a O-admissible computation with $\le v$ (scalar + nonscalar) multiplications/divisions. Then there exist $\gamma_1,\dots,\gamma_{2v} \in \mathbb{C}$ such that for each result $p(x) = \Sigma_{i\ge 0} a_i x^i \in \mathbb{C}[[x]]$ of ß there exist $P_i \in \mathbb{Z}[z_1,\dots,z_{2v}]$ such that $P_i(\gamma_1,\dots,\gamma_{2v}) = a_i$ and $\deg P_i \le 3\,vi$ for all $i \ge 1$.

Proof: We proceed by induction on the length of ß. Let $p(x)=p'(x) \circ p^*(x)$ be the computation step for $p(x)$ in ß. Let $P_i', P_i^* \in \mathbb{Z}[z_1,\dots,z_{2v'}]$ be the correponding polynomials with respect to $p'(x)$ and $p^*(x)$. Observe that by the induction hypothesis $v' = v$ if $\circ$ is $\pm$ and $v'=v-1$ if $\circ$ is $\times,/$. According to Strassen (1974) the polynomials P_i are defined as follows:

case 1: $\circ$ is $\pm$ then $P_i = P_i' \pm P_i$.

case 2: $\circ$ is $\times$ then $\gamma_{2v-1} = P'(0), \gamma_{2v} = P^*(0)$ and

$$(z_{2v-1} + \Sigma_{i\ge 1} P_i'\, x^i) \times (z_{2v} + \Sigma_{i\ge 1} P_i\, x^i) = z_{2v-1} z_{2v} + \Sigma_{i\ge 1} P_i x^i$$

case 3: o is / then $\gamma_{2v-1} = P'(0), \gamma_{2v} = 1/P^*(0)$ and

$$(z_{2v-1} + \Sigma_{i\geq 1} P_i' x^i) \times (z_{2v} * \Sigma_{\sigma\geq 0}(-z_{2v} \cdot \Sigma_{i\geq 1} P_i^* x^i)^\sigma)$$

$$= z_{2v-1} z_{2v} + \Sigma_{i\geq 1} P_i x^i$$

Observe $1/(1/\gamma_{2v} + \Sigma_{i\geq 1} P_1 x^i) = \gamma_{2v} \; \Sigma_{\sigma\geq 0}(-\gamma_{2v} \; \Sigma_{i\geq 1} P_i x^i)^\sigma$

As is shown in case 1, additions/subtractions do not increase the degree of P_i. In order to bound $\deg P_i$ let $f(i,v)$ be the maximal degree of P_i for all P_i that can be generated by the above recursion steps with at most v multiplications/divisions.

Then it follows from case 2 and case 3:

$$f(i,v) = 2 + \max \left\{ \Sigma_{\nu=1}^{\sigma} f(i_\nu, v-1) + \sigma \;\middle|\; \begin{array}{l} \Sigma_{\nu=1}^{\sigma} i_\nu = 1 \\ i_\nu \geq 1 \end{array} \right\}$$

This implies $f(1,v) = 3v$, $f(i,v) = 3(v-1)i + i + 2$.

Let $L(*|p(x))$ be the minimal number of (scalar + nonscalar) multiplications/divisions in any computation for $p(x)$.

Theorem 3.2

Suppose $L(*|p(x)) \leq v$, $p(x) = \Sigma_{i=0}^{\infty} a_i x^i \in \mathbb{C}(x)$ and let $1 \leq \delta_1 \leq \delta_2 \ldots \leq \delta_q \leq n$. Then there exists $H \in \mathbb{C}[y_1,\ldots,y_q]$, $H \not\equiv 0$ such that $H(a_{\delta_1},\ldots,a_{\delta_q}) = 0$ and $\deg H \leq g$ provided $\binom{g+q}{q} > \binom{3v(gn+1)}{2v}$

Proof: Suppose ß computes p(x) with ≤ v multiplications/divisions. As in the proof of theorem 2.7 we can assume w.r.g. that ß is 0-admissible. Therefore Lemma 3.1 can be applied. By 3.1, we set $c = 3vn, m = 2v$ in Lemma 2.6. This proves 3.2. ■

Corollary 3.3

Let $\tau_1,\ldots,\tau_n \in \mathbb{C}$ and $1 \leq \delta_1 \leq \delta_2 \ldots \leq \delta_q \leq n$ such that

$\forall k:[Q(\tau_{\delta_1},\ldots,\tau_{\delta_k}):Q(\tau_{\delta_1},\ldots,\tau_{\delta_{k-1}})] \geq (1.5nq)^q$. Then

$L(*|\Sigma_{i=0}^{n}\tau_i x^i) \geq \lceil q/2 \rceil$

<u>Proof:</u> Suppose $L(*|\Sigma_{i=0}^{n}\tau_i x^i) \leq \lceil q/2 \rceil - 1$. Then by theorem 3.2 there exists $H \in \mathbb{Z}[y_1,\ldots,y_q]$, $H \not\equiv 0$ such that $H(\tau_{\delta_1},\ldots,\tau_{\delta_q}) = 0$ and $\deg H \leq g$ provided

$$(*) \qquad \binom{g+q}{q} > \binom{1.5(q-1)(gn+1)}{q-1}$$

(Set $v = \lceil q/2 \rceil - 1$ then $2v \leq q-1$)

Since $g \geq 1$ we have $\binom{1.5(q-1)(gn+1)}{q-1} \leq \binom{1.5gqn}{q-1}$

Therefore $g^q > (1.5gqn)^{q-1}q$ implies $(*)$.

Hence $g > (1.5qn)^q/n$ implies $(*)$. It follows that there exists $H \in \mathbb{Z}[y_1,\ldots,y_n]$, $H \not\equiv 0, \deg H < (1.5qn)^q$ such that $H(\tau_{\delta_1},\ldots,\tau_{\delta_q}) = 0$. This, however, contradicts to Lemma 2.6 in Strassen (1974)(see the end of section 2) since we assumed that

$[Q(\tau_{\delta_1},\ldots,\tau_{\delta_k}):Q(\tau_{\delta_1},\ldots,\tau_{\delta_{k-1}})] \geq (1.5nq)^q$. ▨

A statement very similar to 3.3 has been proved in Sieveking (1976) prop.2 by using algebraic geometry. Using (3.2),(3.3) we improve some lower bounds of Strassen. 3.4(2) improves Corollary 2.8 and 3.4(3) improves Corollary 2.7 in Strassen (1974).

<u>Corollary 3.4</u>

(1) $L(*|\Sigma_{j=0}^{n}\exp(2\pi i/2^{f(j)})x^j) \geq \lceil n/2 \rceil$

provided $\forall j: f(j+1) \geq f(j) + 2n \log 2n$, $f(j) \in \mathbb{N}$.

(2) $L(*|\Sigma_{j=0}^{n}\exp(2\pi i/2^{j^3})x^j) \geq (n - \sqrt{n \log n})/2$

(3) $L(*|\Sigma_{j=0}^{n}\exp(2\pi i/2^{j})x^j) \geq n/(12 \log n)$.

<u>Proof:</u> (1) Set $\tau_k = \exp(2\pi i/2^{f(k)})$ then

$[Q(\tau_1,\ldots,\tau_k):Q(\tau_1,\ldots,\tau_{k-1})] = 2^{f(k)-f(k-1)} \geq 2^{2n \log 2n} \geq (2n)^{2n}$.

Set $\delta_k = k$, $q = n$ in 3.3 then (1) follows from 3.3.

(2) Set $\tau_k = \exp(2\pi i/2^{k^3})$, then for $k \geq \sqrt{(2/3)n \log n}$

$[Q(\tau_1,\ldots,\tau_{k+1}):Q(\tau_1,\ldots,\tau_k)] \geq 2^{(k+1)^3-k^3} > 2^{3k^2} \geq (2n)^{2n}$.

We apply 3.3 with $q = n - \lfloor\sqrt{n \log n}\rfloor$ and $\delta_k = n-q+k$ for $k = 1,\ldots,q$. This proves (2).

(3) We apply theorem 3.2 to $p(x) = \Sigma_{j=0}^{n} \exp(2\pi i/2^j)x^j$ and $\delta_i = 3i \lfloor \log n \rfloor$ $i = 1,\ldots,q = \lfloor n/3 \log n \rfloor$.

Suppose $p(x)$ can be computed with $v \leq q/4$ multiplications/divisions. Then by 3.2 there exists $H \in \mathbb{Z}[y_1,\ldots,y_q]$, $H \not\equiv 0$ such that $H(a_{\delta_1},\ldots,a_{\delta_q}) = 0$ and $\deg H \leq g$ provided

$$(*) \qquad \binom{g+q}{q} > \binom{q(gn+1)}{q/2}$$

Obviously $g^q > q!\,[q(gn+1)]^{q/2}/(q/2)!$ implies $(*)$ Therefore $g^{q/2} > q^q(n+1)^{q/2}$ implies $(*)$. Hence there exists H, $H \not\equiv 0$ with $\deg H \leq q^2(n+1) \leq n^3/(\log n)^2$ with $H(a_{\delta_1},\ldots,a_{\delta_q}) = 0$.

On the other hand

$$[Q(a_{\delta_1},\ldots,a_{\delta_k}) : Q(a_{\delta_1},\ldots,a_{\delta_{k-1}})] \geq 2^{3\lfloor \log n \rfloor} \geq (n/2)^3.$$

Therefore by Lemma 2.6, Strassen (1974) (see the end of section 2) there does not exist $H \not\equiv 0$ with $H(a_{\delta_1},\ldots,a_{\delta_q}) = 0$ and $\deg H < (n/2)^3$. This yields a contradiction since for $n > 8$: $n^3/(\log n)^2 < (n/2)^3$. However (3) is trivial for $n \leq 8$. Therefore $L(*\mid p(x)) > q/4 \geq n/(12 \log n) - 1$. ▨

Acknowledgement: I thank H. Bremer for reading the manuscript.

References

1. Belaga, E.G.: (1958) Some problems involved in the computation of polynomials. Dokl. Akad. Nauk 123, pp. 775-777

2. Lipton, R.: (1975) Polynomials with 0-1 coefficients that are hard to evaluate. Proceedings of 16th Annual Symp. on FCS, pp. 6-10

3. Lipton, R.J. and Stockmeyer, L.J.: (1976) Evaluation of polynomials with super-preconditioning. Proceedings of 8th Annual ACM Symp. on Theory of Computing, pp. 174-180

4. Motzkin, T.S.: (1955) Evaluation of polynomials and evaluation of rational functions. Bull. Amer. Math. Soc. 61, p. 163

5. Paterson, M.S. and Stockmeyer, L.J.: (1973) On the number of non-scalar multiplications necessary to evaluate polynomials. Siam J. Comp. 2, pp. 60-66

6. Sieveking, M.: (1976) On the number of multiplications necessary to compute rational functions. Preprint Universität Bielefeld

7. Strassen, V.: (1974) Polynomials with rational coefficients which are hard to compute. Siam J. Comp. 3, pp. 128-149

8. Winograd, S.: (1970) On the number of multiplications necessary to compute certain functions. Comm. Pure and Appl. Math. 23, pp. 165-179

FREQUENCY ALGORITHMS AND COMPUTATIONS

B.A.Trakhtenbrot

Institute of Mathematics,
Siberian Branch of the USSR Academy of Sciences,
Novosibirsk, 630090

Introduction

The investigation of many algorithmic problems encounter essential difficulties. Hence appealing to simple algorithms and computations, even if they are known to produce errors in certain cases, is justified as far as the frequency and the size of the errors do not exceed some acceptable level. In the framework of this general idea frequency algorithms and computations appear as one of the possible approaches. We give in the sequel a general characterization of this approach, a survey of some associated results and also some comments on the relation to other approaches. This paper is inspired by the IFIP-74 lecture of M.Rabin [11] , in which related topics are considered; unfortunately, I came to know Rabin's paper only recently.

As a rule, we confine ourselves with intuitive explanations and avoid formal definitions. Results and precise formulations , that are omitted in this survey,may be found in the list of references.

In reasoning about algorithmic problems, as a matter of convenience, we focus attention on value computation for arithmetic functions f, especially for predicates G (i.e. 0-1-valued functions). As to the cases when the initial or the resulting information of the problem is not numerical, straightforward numerical coding is implied. The complexity of an algorithm M upon the argument n is estimated by the number t(M,n) of computation steps it performs. By the way we don't have to choose special definitions neither for the algorithms we use (e.g. Turing machines, Markov algorithms, etc.), nor for their computation steps, because any of the generally accepted definitions will perfectly do.

§ 1. Computations with errors: probabilistic and approximative algorithms

It is well known that there exist unsolvable algorithmic problems. Moreover, among them there are many natural and important ones. On the other hand, among the algorithmic problems that are theoretically solvable, one may find very complex ones (Rabin's theorem). Let us illustrate this phenomenon by means of the fastgrowing "many-storeyed" functions hk

$$hk(n) = 2^{2^{\cdot^{\cdot^{\cdot^{2^n}}}}} \quad k \text{ - storeys}$$

though the theorem holds for arbitrary computable functions h.

For any function hk a predicate G (depending on hk) exists such that:

(i) G is computable

(ii) For any algorithm M computing G a natural n_0 exists, such that for each $n > n_0$ $t(M,n) > hk(n)$ (i.e. M needs more than hk(n) steps to answer the question "G(n) = ?").

Within recent years such concrete solvable algorithmic problems were discovered for which - despite their natural formulation and apparent simplicity - Rabin's theorem holds with a "two-storeyed" lower estimate. Besides, it is quite likely that for a lot of "vital" combinatorial problems lower exponential estimate is not removable either. Clearly, the complexity exponential explosion makes such problems practically as unaccessible as actually unsolvable ones.

The question about how to manage in such situations arise in the background of peculiar observations. The point is that even if the necessary algorithm is practically unaccessible (or it doesn't exist at all), human beings somehow manage with individual tasks they are interested in. Speculations suggested by this phenomenon vary from references to human creative ability to tautological assertions like "humans solve only such tasks that they are able to solve".

In Rabin [11] an attempt is made to project some ways how to avoid the algorithmic difficulties mentioned above. Among three ideas suggested by him on this subject, two are "semantically orientated". First of all, they concern the problem of defining appropriate measures (based on semantic contents) on the class of all the tasks that form together the algorithmic problem under consideration. Further, the idea is involved of constructing algorithms for suitable subclasses of the whole problem. Our topic is connected with another suggestion from [11] , that consists in the following. It may well be that just the persistence in searching absolutely unerronous algorithms often leads to hopeless situations, because such algorithms may not exist at all, or may be too complex. After all, humans are not so infailible: could it be that their successes are in part due especially to some lack of precision in the used procedures? Therefore, the advantage that may result from computations with errors is worth investigating.

Unfortunately, in Rabin [11] there is a lack of explanations about what concepts of computations with errors are meant (likely, probabilistic computations are implied). Hence, before attacking our main subject, i.e. frequency computations, we examine shortly the following two versions:

(i) The probability of the errors is subjected to restrictions.

(ii) The size of errors is subjected to restrictions.

In the framework of the first version let us consider probabilistic algorithms that yield for each initial information (for each argument value) the correct result with the probability exceeding a constant $p(1/2 < p < 1$; p and $1 - p$ are correspondingly the reliability and the unreliability of the algorithm). The notion of probabilistic algorithm is intuitively clear; the precise definition is already in Shannon [9]. Let us emphasize that the stochastic steps in the algorithm are operated by a Bernoulli generator that produces 0 and 1 with probability 1/2. As for the use of the words "the probabilistic algorithm M, starting with argument n, performs t(M,n) steps", various specifications are possible, e.g. the average amount may be considered, etc.; however, by any reasonable specification the following holds:

<u>Assertion A</u>. Let the probabilistic algorithm M compute the predicate G in t(M,n) steps. Then a usual (deterministic) algorithm N exists which computes the same predicate G in $t(N,n) < \mathrm{const}^{t(M,n)}$ steps.

Hence, if an algorithmic problem is unsolvable in the usual sense, this situation will not change after employing probabilistic algorithms. Moreover, if the problem is solvable in the usual sense with a "k-storeyed" lower estimation hk, then the effect of employing probabilistic algorithms can't result in lowering it more than one storey. Is there really possible such a decrease? Likely, sometimes so it is, though at the present moment the author is only aware of more modest capabilities of probabilistic algorithms (Trakhtenbrot [18], Freivald [4]). In any case, they can't liquidate the computational complexity explosion, typical of problems with many-storeyed lower estimation; but such problems, as we have mentioned above, are already in view.

The second version is correlated with approximative algorithms and computations. Of course, the substitution of the implied solution via an approximative one is widely used in mathematics. However, it should be kept in mind that here a discrete domain is dealt with, especially the set of natural numbers. Since the difference between two integers can't be less than 1, any two functions f1 and f2 such that

$$\forall n \ (|f1(n) - f2(n)| \leq 1) \qquad (*)$$

are bound to be considered as good approximations to each other. Obviously, for any given function f2, no matter how simply computable it is (e.g. for a constant function), among the f1 that satisfy (*) there exist functions of arbitrary high complexity and even non-computable ones. This evident remark may mean that there exist functions of arbitrary high complexity and even non-computable ones, that possess very simple approximative computations. The comparison suggests itself with probabilistic computations which (see Assertion A) are not able to produce such a strong effect. Nevertheless, this "advantage" of approximative computation should be treated critically, especially if we are interested in the computation of a predicate G. Clearly, for any such G, even a non-computable one, the 0-identically predicate will be a "good" (in the sense of (*)) one, and in addition, an easily computable approximation for G; but such "approximation" will hardly do. Certainly, if f2 is fast enough growing, then it might be reasonable to declare as its good approximation such a function f1, that satisfies the condition

$$\forall n\ (c1 \leqslant f1(n)\ /\ f2(n) \leqslant c2)$$

for some constants c1, c2.

Here you have an example when presumable by means of such approximation an essential simplification of an algorithmic problem is actually achieved. The problem dealt with is the following. For any given complete graph G, with edges labelled by natural numbers (the lengths of the edges), satisfying the triangle inequality, find f(G)- the length of the shortest Hamiltonian cycle. Known algorithms require a number of steps having exponential order relative to the size of the initial data, this estimate presumable being essential (conjecture P $\neq$ NP). It turns out that if approximations $\tilde{f}(g)$ are allowed such that $f(G) \leqslant \tilde{f}(G) \leqslant 2f(G)$ holds, then there exists a solving algorithm with polynomially estimated complexity(Rosenkrantz [12]). On the other hand, if complete graphs are considered with arbitrary edge lengths (i.e. the triangle inequality is not required), the computation of no function $\tilde{f}(G) = \mathcal{O}(f(G))$ can be essentially simpler than that one of f(G) (Sahni [14]).

§ 2. Frequency algorithms

Suppose that according to an algorithm A the probabilistic or the approximative computation of a function f(n) is accomplished. Clearly, at each individual application of the algorithm, the initial information it is supplied with, concerns just one argument value n. Now we are going to consider the situation when an algorithm B intended to compute (in a suitable sense) the function f, achieves this aim as follows:

Firstly, at each its individual application the algorithm B may be supplied with some sequence of non-repeating argument values. Such sequences will be named samples. Though infinite samples are in general allowed, we shall suppose them for a while to be finite (later infinite ones will be considered as well).

Secondly, being supplied with a sample

$$i1, i2, \ldots, in \qquad (1)$$

the algorithm B produces the uniquely defined by (1) sequence

$$y1, y2, \ldots, yn \qquad (2)$$

The input sample (1) is to be interpreted as a series of questions

$$f(i1) = ?, \quad f(i2) = ?, \quad \ldots f(in) = ?$$

and the sequence (2) - in which as contrasted to (1) repetitions are allowed - as the series of answers the algorithm proposes:

$$f(i1) = y1, \; f(i2) = y2, \; \ldots, f(in) = yn \qquad (3)$$

By the way, the equalities (3) need not be all true. If among them at least r are true, the algorithm B will be said to compute the function f along the sample (1) with frequency r/n. Given a set W of samples, the algorithm B is said to compute the function f on W with frequency not less than p, if this holds for each sample in W. Thus, speaking about the frequency computation of a function f, certain sample set W and guaranteed frequency p are always implied.

The following remarks are worth attention:

I. Considering an algorithm B that computes the function f on W with frequency p, one must be aware that actually other functions may also exist that are computed as well by B with the same W and p. In this sense we have an analogy with approximative computations, so far as each algorithm that produces approximative values for f(n), at the same time produces approximative values for all other functions that insignificantly differ from f. Unlike this, any probabilistic algorithm providing correct results with reliability exceeding 1/2, computes just one function.

II. On the other hand, the fact that the quality of frequency computations is specified by the frequency of correct answers, relates them somehow with probabilistic computations. Indeed, given a probabilistic algorithm M, operating with reliability p, suppose that as a result of its successive applications to the elements of the sample

(1), the sequence

$$z1, z2, \ldots, zn \qquad (2')$$

is produced. If n is large enough it is very probable that among the equalities

$$f(i1) = z1, f(i2) = z2, \ldots, f(in) = zn \qquad (3')$$

the correct ones will occur with a frequency close to p. Of course, given the sample (1) the sequence (2') may vary in different tests, as contrasted to the sequence (2) which is uniquely determined by (1). And one essential difference more: in the sequence (2) each of the answers <u>ys</u> may depend not only on the corresponding <u>is</u>, but in general on the whole sample (1). Thus, dependence is allowed on the context in which the question $f(is) \doteq ?$ appears, and the answer to this question may vary for different samples.

III. Finally, let us remark that the question about what sample set should be chosen is to be decided proceeding from the (informal) analysis of the problem under investigation; of course, also the possibility to provide for such sample set an algorithm with suitable frequency, is to be taken into account. Here it is worth noting that besides finite samples infinite ones like

$$i1, i2, \ldots, is, \ldots \qquad (4)$$

may be used as well; clearly, to each of them these corresponds an infinite output sequence

$$y1, y2, \ldots, ys, \ldots \qquad (5)$$

corresponds. Be aware that an algorithm dealing with infinite samples is actually a relative algorithm (with oracle). It may be represented, for instance, as a two-tape Turing machine M; starting with the input sample (4) on the first tape, it produces successively on the second one (which is initially empty) the elements of (5). Clearly, a precise meaning to "frequency along an infinite sample" must be given. We consider two versions, the first one being preferable:

a) <u>Strong version</u>. On all but a finite number of initial segments of the infinite sequence

$$f(i1) = y1, \ f(i2) = y2, \ \ldots, \ f(is) = ys, \ \ldots \qquad (6)$$

the rate of correct equalities is not less than p.

b) Weak version. There exists an infinite set of initial segments of the sequence (6) with the rate of correct equalities on each one not less than p.

§ 3. Is a frequency solution for some unsolvable algorithmic problems possible?

Assume that we deal with the algorithmic problem of computing the values of some predicate G. Then (see § 1) the answer to an analogous question about approximative computations, though affirmative, is vacuous; but in concern with probabilistic computations with reliability $> 1/2$ the answer is negative. As for frequency computations, it is natural to suppose that the answer will depend on what sample set and frequency p are meant. In the sequel the notation W, supplied with some suggestive indices and labels will be used for sample sets. For instance: Wn - all the samples of the length n, Wn $\geqslant$ - all the samples of the length not less than n(including all infinite ones as well), W_∞ - all the infinite samples, Wcomp - all the infinite computable samples.

Theorem 1(Trakhtenbrot [15]). Suppose the algorithm M computes the predicate G with frequency $> p \geqslant 1/2$ on some of the sample sets Wn; then the predicate G is computable in the usual sense as well.

Easy to see that in the conditions of the theorem the algorithm M is transformable into an algorithm N computing the predicate G with frequency $> p$ on a larger sample set of Wl kind, where l depends only on p and n. Therefore, the relaxation of the theorem condition could consist in only allowing infinite samples. Nevertheless, by an appropriate adaptation of the proof of Theorem 1, the following theorem is established.

Theorem 2(Kinber [7]). Suppose the algorithm M computes the predicate G with frequency $> p \geqslant 1/2$ on the set W_∞; then the predicate G is computable in the usual sense as well.

Remark. This theorem is valid even in the case when frequencies along infinite samples are implied in the weak version (see the end of § 2).

Thus, an affirmative answer to the question in the headline is only possible at the cost of further essential relaxation of the requirements to the samples or to the frequency. For instance, if good frequencies (close to 1) are not required, then the following holds.

Theorem 3(Trakhtenbrot [15]). Such an algorithm M on W2 does exist that computes with frequency 1/2 an uncountable set of predicates (including, consequently, non-computable ones as well).

On the other hand, if we confine ourselves to some countable sample set W, it is straightforward that for each $p < 1$ there exists an uncountable set of predicates G, any of which is computable on W with frequency p. Of course, since the set Wcomp is countable, this remark concerns it, too. However, in this case more interesting facts can be noted. The matter is that so far no assumptions were made about non-computable predicates for which frequency computations may exist; meanwhile this is of particular interest for the predicates which, being remarkable in some sense, may rather happen in real problems. Such is the state of affairs, for instance, concerning recursively enumerable predicates (i.e. such predicates G that the set of n for which $G(n) = 1$ is recursively enumerable).

Theorem 4(Rose, Ullian [13]). A recursively enumerable (nor recursive) predicate exists, that is computable on Wcomp for arbitrary frequency $p < 1$. On the other hand, such recursively enumerable predicate exists that is non-computable on Wcomp for any $p > 0$.

Taking into account the importance of recursively enumerable predicates it is interesting to learn in what sense some version of frequency computability is nevertheless possible for them. Theorem 2 and the remark to it show that even the giving up of the strong frequency version in favour of the weak one (see the end of § 3) won't do. A further possible relaxation may consist in giving up uniformity: instead of requiring the existence of a single algorithm M, operating with frequency p on all the samples in W_∞, one contents with the fact that for each sample in W_∞ an algorithm associated with it is to be used. It turns out that at such approach frequency computation for all recursively enumerable predicates becomes actually possible.

Theorem 5(Barzdin' [1]). Given a recursively enumerable predicate G, for arbitrary sample J in W_∞ and for arbitrary $p < 1$ an algorithm M exists that computes G along J with frequency (weak version) $> p$.

Remark. In this formulation the fact is mirrored that the computation of frequency p is provided for arbitrary large initial segments of the sample J. But actually the proof of Theorem 5 supplies additional information, and namely: a computable infinite sequence of initial segments exists, for which the frequency $> p$ is provided.

§ 4. On the complexity of frequency computations

So far attention was paid mainly to such cases when in some sense a frequency computation is possible for predicates known to be noncomputable otherwise. On the other hand, if a predicate G is known to be computable, a frequency computation may be justified if it is essentially simpler than any possible computation (in the usual sense). At the same time it is supposed that the problem under consideration does not always require correct values of G, and that rather a suitable frequency of correct values will suffice. Clearly, preliminary explanations are needed about how we intend to measure the complexity of frequency computations and to compare it with the one of common computations. Though different approaches may do, we shall only discuss here one of them, which concerns algorithms operating on samples of the set Wn(n = 2, 3, ...) with frequency p. First, among such algorithms we pick out those for which the following condition holds:

Condition (*): starting with the sample i1, i2, ..., in, the algorithm M computes the correct value G(i1), then the correct value G(i2), etc., up the correct value G(im) is computed, where m is the least number satisfying $m/n > p$; as to the rest of n-m values, they are all declared to be 0 without special computations.

The meaning of the condition (*) is straightforward: the algorithm M doesn't realize a "genuine" frequency computation, but only simulates it via usual computation of m values among all the n ones inquired. The question arises, whether a computable predicate G exists, for which the following holds: a frequency computation of G is possible, that is essentially more thrifty (the number of steps the algorithm performs is implied) than any algorithm satisfying condition (*). Avoiding further formalizations, let us only remark that if such predicate exists, the simplification accomplished by the frequency computation is due especially to the fact that there is no way to ascertain for each given sample what m answers among the n are just the correct ones. Some related results are in [5], [6], but at present we do not yet know whether there exists a predicate G, for which frequency algorithms essentially decrease the function T(s) = "max of the number of steps performed on the imput samples J = i1, i2, ..., in with i1 + i2 + ... + in = s."

Below a theorem is presented in which some natural model of real time frequency computations on Wn is considered. In this model the n elements of the sample are entered simultaneously into the computing device bit by bit, while the corresponding one-bit answers are produced as soon as the inputs are absorbed.

Theorem 6(Kinber [7]). For any computable (and fast growing!) function f and for any $n \geq 2$ a predicate G exists such that: 1) A frequency computation in real time for G is possible on Wn with frequency 1 - 1/n; 2) Given an algorithm B computing G in the usual sense, there is an infinite set of argument values such that $t(B,x) > f(x)$.

§ 5. Frequency identification algorithms

The idea of frequency computation is not exhausted by the concepts described and classified above. For instance, frequency computations of partial functions, frequency enumeration, frequency computation of functionals, frequency reduction may be considered (see Ref.).

Although their theory in details differs from what we have observed above, nevertheless, it is greatly suggested by these considerations. In this section we would like to illustrate at some real problem the eventual benefit from frequency algorithms. The identification problem for finite automata will be dealt with; however, it should be borne in mind that in this case chiefly frequency reduction algorithms will do.

The problem under consideration may be described as follows. We are given an initialized finite automaton M called a "black box", about whose internal structure (diagram) nothing is known. Input words can be applied to the input of the automaton and the corresponding words observed. The problem is to identify the automaton, i.e. to construct the diagram of an automaton which functions in the same way as M. An identification algorithm should comprise effective instructions as to what questions of the type "what is output of the black box for input x?" should be asked, and how the answers to these questions should be used to construct an automaton which presumably reproduces the functioning of the black box. Hence, as a matter of fact, an identification algorithm performs the computation of a functional with the (inessential) peculiarity that the argument ranges over word operators and the values of the functional - over descriptions of finite automata.

An algorithm of this type may be described, for example, by a computable function F(w), where w is either the finite word Λ or a finite set of word pairs; in each of these pairs $\langle x, y \rangle$, x is an input word, and y - the corresponding output, produced by the black box. Applied to a black box M the algorithm operates as follows:

Step 0(this step is degenerate and independent of M). Compute $F(\Lambda)$ There are two cases:

a) If $F(\Lambda)$ is an automaton description, the algorithm stops and the result is just this description;

b) If $F(\Lambda)$ is a set v_0 of input words, proceed to the next step.

Step i(i = 1, 2, ...). Test the black box M with the input words of the set v_{i-1} and construct the set w_{i-1} of pairs, which is the result of this and the previous tests (so that w_{i-1} is the result of testing with the words of the set $v_0, v_1, \ldots, v_{i-1}$). Then compute $F(w_{i-1})$. There are two cases:

a) If $F(w_{i-1})$ is an automaton description the algorithm stops with this result;

b) If $F(w_{i-1})$ is a set of input words, proceed to the next step.

It is easily seen that no algorithm exists which identifies all the black boxes. To investigate the possibility of frequency identification algorithms, a preliminary discussion of what samples are to be used is needed.

First, let us emphasize that by an automaton description a diagram with numbered vertices is implied; therefore, two diagrams, though isomorphic, may occur to be non-identical because of their different vertices-numerations.

Secondly, as samples finite sets S1, S2, ... will be considered, where Sn is the set of all pairwise non-identical diagrams with n vertices.

Theorem 7(Barzdin' [17]). For any $p < 1$ there is an algorithm which identifies black boxes with frequency $> p$.

Of course, in connection with this theorem, the implied sample set may be questioned. Is it really noteworthy besides its being of advantage for proving technique? This question is reminiscent of Rabin's [11] suggestions about "semantically orientated" measure on the class of tasks under consideration. But to the present it is not clear in what mathematical framework should such discussion be realized.

REFERENCES

1. Barzdin', J.M., On the frequency solution of algorithmically unsolvable mass problems, Dokl. Akad. Nauk SSSR, v. 191 (1970), № 5, 967-970.
2. Barzdin', J.M., Complexity and exactness of solving of initial segments of membership problem for recursively enumerable set, Dokl. Akad. Nauk SSSR, v. 199(1971), № 2, 262-264.
3. Freivald, R.V., On comparison of abilities of probabilistic and frequency algorithms, International symposium "Discrete systems", Riga, 1974.
4. Freivald, R.V., Speed computations by probabilistic machine, In Theory of Algorithms and Programs, II (J.M.Barzdin', ed.), Latvian State University, Riga, 1975, 201-205.
5. Ivshin, V.Ju., Complexity of the frequency computations of recursive predicates, In Third All-Union Conference on Math. Logic, Novosibirsk, 1974, 86-88.
6. Kinber, E.B., Frequency computations of the total recursive predicates and frequency enumeration of sets, Dokl. Akad. Nauk SSSR, v. 205(1972), № 1, 23-25.
7. Kinber E.B., On the frequency computations over infinite sequences,

In Theory of Algorithms and Programs, 1(J.M.Barzdin', Ed.), Latvian State University, Riga, 1974, 48-67.

8. Kinber, E.B., On the frequency computations in real time, In Theory of Algorithms and Programs, II, (J.M.Barzdin', Ed.), Latvian State University, Riga, 1975, 174-182.
9. De Leeuw, K., Moore, E., Shannon, C., Shapiro, N., Computability by probabilistic machine, Automata studies, Princeton University Press, 1956, 183-212.
10. McNaughton, R., The theory of automata, a survey, Adv. in Comput., 1961, v. 2, Acad. Press, N.-Y.-London, 379-241.
11. Rabin, M., Theoretical impediments to artificial intelligence, IFIP - 1974, 615-619.
12. Rosenkrantz, D., Stearns, R., Lewis, P., Approximate algorithms for the travelling salesperson problem, 15th Annual Switching and Automata Theory, 1974, 33-42.
13. Rose, G., Ullian, J., Approximation of functions of the integers, Pacific J. Math., 13(1963), № 2.
14. Sahni, S., Gonzales, T., P-complete approximation problems, J. of ACM, 23(1976), № 3, 555-565.
15. Trakhtenbrot, B.A., On the frequency computation of functions, Algebra and logic, 2(1963), № 1.
16. Trakhtenbrot, B.A., Frequency computations, Trudy mat. Inst. Steklov, v. 113(1973), 221-232.
17. Trakhtenbrot, B.A., Barzdin', J.M., Finite automata(behaviour and synthesis), North-Holland, 1973.
18. Trakhtenbrot, B.A., Complexity of algorithms and computations, Novosibirsk State University, Novosibirsk, 1967.
19. Trakhtenbrot, B.A., Notes on the complexity of the probabilistic machine computations, In Theory of Algorithms and Mathematical Logic, Moscow, 1974, 159-176.

GRAPH-THEORETIC ARGUMENTS IN LOW-LEVEL COMPLEXITY

Leslie G. Valiant
Computer Science Department
University of Edinburgh
Edinburgh, Scotland.

1. Introduction

A major goal of complexity theory is to offer an understanding of why some specific problems are inherently more difficult to compute than others. The pursuit of this goal has two complementary facets, the positive one of finding fast algorithms, and the negative one of proving lower bounds on the inherent complexity of problems. Finding a proof of such a lower bound is equivalent to giving a property of the class of all algorithms for the problem. Because of the sheer richness of such classes, even for relatively simple problems, very little is yet understood about them and consequently the search for lower bound proofs has met with only isolated successes.

The poverty of our current knowledge can be illustrated by stating some major current research goals for three distinct models of computation. In each case complexity is measured in terms of n, the sum of the number of inputs and outputs:
(A) Discrete problems: For some natural problem known to be computable in polynomial time on a multi-tape Turing machine (TM) prove that no TM exists that computes it in time $O(n)$. This problem is open even when TMs are restricted to be oblivious [12].
(B) Discrete finite problems: For some problem computable in polynomial time on a TM show that no combinational circuit over a complete basis exists that is of size $O(n)$.
(C) Algebraic problems: For some natural sets of multinomials of constant degree over a ring show that no straight-line program consisting of the operations $+,-$, and $\times$, exists of size $O(n)$.

Known results on lower bounds are excluded by the above specifications either because they assume other restrictions on the models, or for the following reasons: For TMs lower bounds for natural problems have only been found for those of apparent or provable exponential complexity or worse [11,6,7]. For unrestricted combinational circuits all arguments involve counting. The only problems that have been proved of nonlinear complexity are those that can encode a counting process and are of exponential complexity or more [4,20]. For algebraic problems "degree arguments" have been successfully applied to natural problems, but only when the degrees grow with n [21].

Algebraic independence arguments have been applied only to problems which we would not regard here as natural. (Various linear lower bounds do exist [9,14,19] but we are not concerned with these here).

This paper focusses on one particular approach to attempting to understand computations for the above models. The approach consists of analysing the global flow of information in an algorithm by reducing this to a combination of graph-theoretic, algebraic and combinatorial problems. We shall restrict ourselves to lower bound arguments and shall omit some related results that exploit the same approach but are better regarded as positive applications of it [7,13,24]. The hope of finding positive byproducts, in particular new surprising algorithms, remains, however, a major incentive in our pursuit of negative results.

Though organized as a survey article, the main purpose of this paper is to present some previously unpublished results. Among other things they show, apparently for the first time, that a significant computational property (the non-achievability of size $O(n)$ and depth $O(\log n)$ simultaneously) of unrestricted straight-line arithmetic programs for certain problems can be reduced to non-computational questions (see §6). The grounds on which we claim that a "meaningful reduction" has been demonstrated are perhaps the weakest that can be allowed. Nevertheless, in the absence of alternative approaches to understanding these problems, we believe that these grounds are sufficient to make the related questions raised worthy of serious investigation.

2. Preliminaries

In the main we follow [23] and [25] for definitions: A straight-line program is a sequence of assignments each of the form $x := f(y,z)$ where f belongs to a set of binary functions and x,y,z belong to a set of variables that can take values in some domain. The only restriction is that any variable x occurring on the left-hand side of some assignment cannot occur in any assignment earlier in the sequence. The variables that never occur on the left-hand side of any instruction are called input variables. The graph of a straight-line program is an acyclic directed graph that has a node, denoted by $\bar{u}$, for each variable u in the program, and directed edges $(\bar{y},\bar{x})$ and $(\bar{z},\bar{x})$ for each instruction $x := f(y,z)$.

A linear form in indeterminates $x_1,\dots,x_n$ over a field F is any expression of the form $\Sigma\lambda_i x_i$ where each $\lambda_i \varepsilon F$. A linear program over F on inputs $x_1,\dots,x_n$ is a straight-line program with $\{x_1,\dots,x_n\}$ as input variables and function set $\{f_{\lambda,\mu} \mid \lambda,\mu \;\varepsilon\; F\}$ where $f_{\lambda,\mu}(u,v) = \lambda u + \mu v$. The importance of linear programs is that, for certain fields F, for computing the values of sets of linear forms in $x_1,\dots,x_n$ with each x_i ranging over F, linear programs are optimal to within a constant factor as compared with straight-line programs in which unrestricted use of all the operations $\{+,-,*,\div\}$ is allowed [26,22,3]. Examples of such fields are the real and complex numbers. Hence the results in §6 apply to the unrestricted model in the case of arithmetic problems over these fields. (Note that there is a similar correspondence between bilinear forms and bilinear programs, and this can be exploited in the same way.)

Straight-line programs over GF(2) define just the class of combinational circuits over the complete basis <and, exclusive-or> . Also, the combinational complexity of a function bounds its oblivious TM complexity from below by a constant factor. Unfortunately the optimality of linear programs for evaluating sets of linear forms over GF(2) is at present unknown. Hence the results in §6 may be relevant only for the restricted class of circuits corresponding to linear programs.

A "graph-theoretic argument" for a lower bound on the complexity of a problem P consists of two parts:

(i) For some graph theoretic property X a proof that the graph of any program for P must have property X.

(ii) A proof that any graph with property X must be of size superlinear in n .

We note that the graph of any algorithm has indegree two, and hence the number of edges is bounded by twice the number of nodes. Conversely, isolated nodes are clearly redundant. Hence, by defining the <u>size</u> of a graph to be the number of edges, we will be measuring, to within a constant factor, both the number of nodes and the number of instructions in any corresponding algorithm. In this paper graphs will always be assumed to be <u>directed</u> and <u>acyclic</u>. The fixed indegree property will not be assumed, except where so indicated. Note that by replacing each node by a binary fanin tree a graph can be made to have fanin two without more than doubling its size or destroying any flow properties relevant here.

A <u>labelling</u> of a directed acyclic graph is a mapping of the nodes into the integers such that for each edge $(\bar{u},\bar{v})$ the label of $\bar{v}$ is strictly greater than the label of $\bar{u}$. If the total number of nodes on the longest directed path in the graph is d then d is the <u>depth</u> of the graph. It is easily verified that if each node is labelled by the total number of nodes on the longest directed path that terminates at it, then this constitutes a consistent labelling using only the integers $1,2,\ldots,d$.

3. Shifting Graphs

Connection networks are graphs in which certain sets of specified input-output connections can be realised. For simplicity we consider the canonical case of a directed acyclic graph G with n input nodes $a_0, a_1, \ldots, a_{n-1}$ and n output nodes $b_0, b_1, \ldots, b_{n-1}$. If σ is a permutation mapping of the integers $\{1,\ldots,n\}$ then G implements σ iff there are n mutually node disjoint paths joining the n pairs $\{a_i, b_{\sigma(i)} \mid 0 \leq i < n\}$. It is well-known that any graph that implements all n! different permutations has to be of size at least $n\log_2 n \approx \log_2(n!)$ simply because there are n! different sets of paths to be realised. Furthermore this order of size (in fact $6n\log_3 n + O(n)$ [2,18]) is achievable. It is perhaps remarkable that even to implement just the n distinct circular shifts $\{\sigma_i \mid \sigma_i(j) = j+i \mod n\ ;\ 0 \leq i \leq n-1\}$ a graph of size $3n\log_3 n$ is necessary. This follows from the following special case of a result proved in [18] :

Theorem 3.1 If $\sigma_1, \ldots, \sigma_s$ are any permutations such that for all $i,j,k (i \neq j)$ $\sigma_i(k) \neq \sigma_j(k)$ then any graph that implements all the s permutations has to have size at least $3n\log_3 s$. □

In fact two distinct constructions of size $3n\log_3 n + O(n)$ are known for such shifting graphs [18,23].

The above theorem has been used to prove superlinear lower bounds on the complexity of problems for various restricted models of computation. The restriction necessary is that the algorithm be conservative or be treatable as such. Conservatism as defined in [18,23] means that the input elements of the algorithm are atomic unchangeable elements that can be compared or copied in the course of the algorithm, but not used to synthesize new elements or transmuted in any way. This notion is a generic one that has to be made precise for each model of computation.

Applications of shifting graphs to proving lower bounds for various merging, shifting and pattern matching problems can be found in [18]. In each case the lower bound is closely matched by an $O(n\log n)$ upper bound and is either new or related to results proved elsewhere by more specialized arguments.

Unfortunately it appears that connection networks cannot be applied to unrestricted models (interpreted here to mean models (A), (B) and (C)). The presence of negation or subtraction allows for pairs of equivalent algorithms of the following genre:

(i) $b_1 := a_1\ ;\ b_2 := a_2\ ;$

(ii) $x := a_1 + a_2\ ;\ b_1 := x - a_2\ ;\ b_2 := x - a_1\ ;$

In the graph of the second algorithm the identity permutation is not implemented, contrary to its semantics.

4. Superconcentrators

Concentration networks are graphs in which specified sets of input nodes have to be connected to specified sets of output nodes, but it is immaterial which particular pairs of nodes in these sets are connected. Various kinds of concentration networks have been studied [16]. Superconcentrators were defined in [23] to have the most restrictive property of this kind.

Definition A directed acyclic graph with distinguished input nodes $a_1, \dots a_n$, and output nodes $b_1, \dots, b_n$ is an n-superconcentrator iff for all r $(1 \leq r \leq n)$ for all sets A of r distinct input nodes and all sets B of r distinct output nodes, there are r mutually node-disjoint paths going from nodes in A to nodes in B.

It has been shown for many computational problems that the graph of any algorithm for computing it must be a superconcentrator, or have some weaker property of a similar nature. For example for convolution a superconcentrator is necessary, for the discrete Fourier transform a hyperconcentrator, and for matrix multiplication in a ring, or for $(\wedge, \vee)$-Boolean matrix multiplication, a matrix concentrator (see [23] for definitions and proofs.) Furthermore, for at least one restricted model of computation, the BRAM [23], it can be shown that the graphs associated with these properties have to be of size $kn\log n$ and hence the algorithms must have this complexity. (A BRAM is a random access machine in which unit cost is assigned to communication between locations whose addresses differ by a power of two, and inputs are in consecutive locations.)

Contrary to expectation, however, it has been also shown [23] that superconcentrators do not account for superlinear complexity in unrestricted algorithms:

Theorem 4.1 $\exists k \, \forall n$ there is an n-superconcentrator of size kn. □

An improvement on the original construction found by Pippenger [17] has size $39n$, constant indegree and outdegree, and depth $O(\log n)$.

Although this is a negative result for lower bounds, it is also a positive result about the surprising richness of connections possible in small graphs. As hoped for, this has led to a surprising result due to V.Strassen, about the existence of new fast algorithms, and has refuted a previously plausible conjecture:

Theorem 4.2 $\exists k \, \forall n$ there is an $n \times n$ integer matrix A in which all minors of all sizes are nonsingular, but such that the n linear forms $A\underline{x}$ (where $\underline{x}$ is the column vector $(x_1, \dots, x_n)$) can be computed together in kn time.

Proof Consider an n-superconcentrator of linear size with fanin two. Give the nodes unique labels in some consistent way. Construct a linear program by identifying the n inputs with $x_1, \dots, x_n$ respectively, and defining the linear combination $f_{\lambda,\mu}(u,v)$ at each node in the order of the labels as follows: Choose λ and μ to have the property that "$\forall r$ $(1 \leq r \leq n)$, for all sets $\{w_1, \dots, w_{r-1}\}$ of functions computed at smaller labels, for all sets X of r components of $\{x_1, \dots, x_n\}$, if

$\{u,w_1,\ldots,w_{r-1}\}$ and $\{v,w_1,\ldots,w_{r-1}\}$ when restricted to X are both linearly independent then so is $\{\lambda u+\mu v, w_1,\ldots,w_{r-1}\}$ over the same set of components". Clearly for each combination of r, $\{w_1,\ldots,w_{r-1}\}$ and X at most one ratio $\lambda:\mu$ will be forbidden. Hence we can always find integral values of λ and μ at each node.

For any $r\times r$ minor B of A consider a set of r node disjoint paths from the r inputs X corresponding to the columns of B to the outputs corresponding to the rows of B. It is easily verified by induction that the $r\times r$ matrix corresponding to the restriction to X of the r linear forms computed at "parallel" nodes on the r disjoint paths as these are traced in order of their labels, is always nonsingular.□

We note that much yet remains to be understood about superconcentrators: Both of the known constructions [23,17] use as building blocks certain bipartite graphs, called "partial concentrators" in [16], for which no completely constructive construction is known [10,16]. Little is known about what restrictions have to be imposed on graphs to ensure that superconcentrators be of superlinear size. The one such restriction known is the one corresponding to BRAMs [23]. In the other direction the two restrictions considered in the next chapter (of O(log n) depth, and the "series-parallel" property), the linear construction in [17] has both. Yet another relevant restriction is the one corresponding to oblivous TM computations, called TM-graphs in [15]. W. Paul and R. Tarjan have raised the question as to whether there exist linear size TM-graphs that are superconcentrators.

5. Graphs that are Dense in Long Paths

We come to a different graph property that has been suspected of accounting for the complexity of algorithms. The first concrete evidence that it does so in at least a limited sense will be explained in the next section. The property has been studied previously by Erdos, Graham and Szemeredi [5] but only for parameters other than the ones we require. Here we shall prove the sought after nonlinear bounds for the relevant parameters for two distinct restricted classes of graphs: (i) shallow graphs (i.e. depth O(log n)), and (ii) series-parallel graphs, defined later.

Definition A directed acyclic graph G has the R(n,m) property iff whichever set of n edges are removed from G, some directed path of m edges remains in G. Let S(n,m,d) be the size of the smallest graph of depth at most d with the R(n,m) property.

The following generalizes a corresponding result in [5] and simplifies the proof. (An intermediate form was stated in [24].)

Theorem 5.1 $S(n,m,d) > (n\log_2 d)/(\log_2(d/m))$
assuming for simplicity that m and d are exact powers of 2.

Proof Consider any graph with q edges and depth d and consider a labelling of it with $\{0,1,\ldots,d-1\}$. Let X_i $(i=1,2,\ldots,\log_2 d)$ be the set of edges between pairs of labels x and y such that the most significant bit in which their binary representations differ is the ith (from the left). If X_i is removed from the graph then we can validly relabel the nodes by $0,1,\ldots,(d/2)-1$, by simply deleting the ith bits in all the old labels. Consequently if any $s \le \log_2 d$ of the X_i's are removed a graph of depth $d/2^s$ remains.

The union of the s smallest of the classes $\{X_1,\ldots,X_{\log_2 d}\}$ contains at most $qs/\log_2 d$ edges. Hence we conclude that

$$S(qs/\log_2 d \; , \; d/2^s \; , \; d) > q$$

or $$S(n,m,d) > (n\log_2 d)/\log_2(d/m). \qquad \square$$

<u>Corollary 5.2</u> For any $k > 0$ the depth of any graph with $q \le (n\log_2 d)/k$ can be reduced to $d/2^k$ by removing some set of n edges. $\square$
(Theorems 2 and 3 in [5] correspond to the cases $d \leq n\log_2 n$, $k = \log\log_2 n$ and $d = n$, k = constant.)

That Corollary 5.2 is optimal to within constant factors for all d, provided that k is a constant, follows from Theorem 1 in [5], which states that for some constants $c_1, c_2 > 0$, $S(c_1 p, c_1 p, p) \leq c_2 p\log_2 p$. Placing in parallel $n/c_2 d$ such bad graphs for $p = d$ gives the result for all d.

When k is not a constant optimality is unknown. In the extreme case of $k = \varepsilon\log_2 d$ the corollary says only that if n edges are removed from a graph of size n/ε then the depth can be reduced to at most $d^{1-\varepsilon}$.

<u>5.1 Shallow Graphs</u>

The application of Corollary 5.2 in §6 is the case $m < \log_2 n$, to which the following instance of it is applicable directly:

<u>Corollary 5.3</u> The depth of any graph with $d = c(\log_2 n)^{c'}$ can be reduced to $d/\log\log n$ by removing some set of n edges, if $q < (n\log\log n)/\log\log\log n$. $\square$
Typical applications are $d = O(\log n)$ and $d = O((\log n)\log\log\log n))$. Note that the practical significance of depth $O(\log n)$, besides its obvious optimality, is that for numerous problems the most efficient algorithms known achieve this depth (e.g. discrete Fourier transform, Strassen's matrix multiplication algorithm [1].)

<u>5.2 Series-Parallel Graphs</u>

This is roughly the class of graphs that can be constructed recursively from subgraphs placed in series or parallel. Nearly all known efficient constructions of circuits have this property, as is also the case for relevant graph constructions (e.g. superconcentrators [23,17], universal graphs [24], and graphs dense in long paths as given in [15], though not in [5].)

<u>Definition</u> A graph with designated sets of input nodes and of output nodes is an <u>sp-graph</u> iff there is a labelling of it such that all inputs have one label, all outputs another label, and for all pairs of edges (i,j) and (k,m) it is the case

that $(i-k)(m-j) \geq 0$.

Definition An sp-graph has the $R'(n,m)$ property iff whichever set of n edges are removed some directed path of at least m edges remains from an input to an output. $S_{sp}(n,m)$ is the size of the smallest sp-graph with the $R'(n,m)$ property.

Theorem 5.4 For some constant $c > 0$

$$S_{sp}(n,m) \geq cn\log\log_2 m.$$

Proof We perform "induction on edges" in the manner of [13,7]. We assume sp-graphs with designated input arcs (directed out of nodes of indegree zero and outdegree one) and output arcs (directed into nodes of indegree one and outdegree zero). Only paths that go from an input arc to an output arc will be counted. In the induction the input arcs and output arcs are not counted in the size of the graph or of the paths.

Consider a graph G with the $R'(n,m)$ property. Consider a labelling of it satisfying the sp-condition and find the smallest label i such that the following has the $R'(n/2,(m-2)/2)$ property: the graph G_1 consisting of all the nodes labelled less than i and all connections between them, with the original input arcs to this subgraph as input arcs, and all arcs directed out of these nodes to the outside as output arcs. By the choice of i if a certain set of $n/2$ arcs are removed from G_1 then no path longer than $(m-2)/2$ will remain. Clearly the complementary graph G_2 on all the nodes labelled greater than i must also have the $R'(n/2,(m-2)/2)$ property, for otherwise by removing some $n/2$ edges from each of G_1 and G_2 we would have no path longer than $(m-2)/2 + 2 + (m-2)/2 - 1 = m-1$.

The sum of the sizes of G_1 and G_2 will be the size of G minus r, the total number of edges between some node with label i and some internal node of G_1 or G_2 and between some internal node of G_1 and one of G_2. Hence

$$S_{sp}(n,m) \geq 2S_{sp}(n/2,(m-2)/2) + r . \tag{1}$$

The special property of sp-graphs that we exploit is that at least one of the following must hold in G: (i) there are no input arcs directed into nodes with label greater than i, (ii) there are no output arcs directed out of nodes with label less than i. Without loss of generality we shall assume the former. Then if the r connections are removed then no remaining input-output path in G involves any node in G_2. Hence if $r < n/4$ we have that G_1 has the $R'(3n/4,m)$ property. Since it is clear that $S_{sp}(3n/4,m) \geq S_{sp}(n/2,m) + n/4$ it follows that

$$S_{sp}(n,m) \geq 2S_{sp}(n/2,(m-2)/2) + n/4.$$

In the alternative case of $r \geq n/4$ the same inequality is immediate from (1). Solving this recurrence gives the claimed bound. □

Problem 1 Can Corollary 5.2 be improved? The particularly relevant question is to settle whether $S(n,\log_2 n,\infty)$ is linear in n or not. [N.B. We have shown that no $o(n\log\log_2 n)$ construction can be sp.]

<u>Problem 2</u> How can deep graphs, and graphs without the sp-property be exploited in algorithms and circuits to obtain substantial reductions in total complexity?

6. Grates and Rigidity

We finally discuss a pair of notions introduced in [25], which offer a proof that nontrivial complexity measures for unrestricted arithmetic programs can be related to natural non-computational properties of the function to be computed. We emphasize that the results are weak in two senses: (i) the lower bounds we prove are on the combination of size and depth achievable simultaneously by any algorithm (i.e. that simultaneous size $O(n)$ and depth $O(\log n)$ is impossible,) and (ii) while we can prove for our non-computational property that "most" sets of linear forms possess them, we have not been able to prove it for any specific natural problem. We believe, however, that further progress on both issues is possible. In particular it appears plausible to conjecture that these properties, (which are more severe than the $R(n,\log_2 n)$ property) do guarantee superlinear size.

We shall assume now that all matrices are $n \times n$ and have elements drawn from a field F.

<u>Definition</u> The <u>density</u> of a matrix A is the number of nonzero entries in A (and is denoted by $\mathrm{dens}(A)$).

<u>Definition</u> The <u>rigidity</u> of a matrix A is the function

$$R_A(r) : \{1,\ldots,n\} \to \{0,1,\ldots,n^2\}$$

defined by

$$R_A(r) = \min\{i \mid \exists B \text{ with } \mathrm{dens}(B) = i \text{ and } \mathrm{rank}(A + B) \leq r\}.$$

From elementary matrix properties it is easy to verify that for any F and any matrix A, $R_A(r) \leq (n - r)^2$ for each r. As we shall see later (Theorem 6.4) this maximal rigidity is indeed achieved by "most" matrices.

The significance of the notion of rigidity comes from the fact that it can be related intimately to the following graph-theoretic property.

<u>Definition</u> A directed acyclic graph G is an <u>$f(r)$-grate</u> iff for some subsets $\{a_1,\ldots,a_s\}$ and $\{b_1,\ldots,b_t\}$ of its nodes it has the property that "if any r nodes and adjacent edges are removed from G then for at least $f(r)$ of the st distinct pairs (a_i,b_j) there remains a directed path from a_i to b_j in G."

The function $f(r)$ will be specified on a subset of the integers and will be assumed to be zero for all other values of r. The slightly weaker restriction corresponding to specific chosen values of s and t will be called an $(f(r),s,t)$-grate.

The next theorem shows that a typical case of interest for linear forms is the $((n-r)^2,n,n)$-grate. The smallest graphs known with such properties are shifting networks which are of size $\sim 3n\log_3 n$ and are in fact $(n(n-r),n,n)$-grates

Theorem 6.1 (i) The graph of any linear program for computing a set of linear forms $A\underline{x}$ is an $R_A(r)$-grate. (ii) Conversely, if for some r $f(r) > R_A(r)$ then there exists a linear program P for computing $A\underline{x}$ whose graph is not an $f(r)$-grate (w.r.t. the natural inputs and outputs).

Proof (i) Let $s = t = n$ and identify $a_1,\dots,a_n$ with the inputs $x_1,\dots,x_n$ and $b_1,\dots,b_n$ with the nodes at which the outputs are computed. We assume for the sake of contradiction that for some r $(1 \leq r \leq n)$ if a certain set of r nodes are removed then fewer than $R_A(r)$ input-output pairs remain connected. This implies that if the multipliers λ and μ at these r nodes are changed to zero then the matrix B of the linear forms computed by the modified program has density less than $R_A(r)$. However, the rows of B differ from the corresponding ones of A only by linear combinations of the forms computed by the original program at the removed nodes. (To verify this, for each output expand the sub-program that computes it into a tree structure. Let N be the set of nodes in the tree corresponding to the (possibly repeated) occurrences of the removed nodes. Consider the contribution to the output of all the nodes in N that are not separated from the root by other nodes in N.) It follows that $A = B + X$ for some $n \times n$ matrix X of rank r and hence, by the definition of rigidity, that $R_A(r) \leq \text{dens}(B) < R_A(r)$, a contradiction.

(ii) Suppose that for some given r $f(r) > R_A(r)$. Consider a matrix C of rank r such that $\text{dens}(A-C) = R_A(r)$. Let P first compute the following $n + r$ forms in the obvious way as $n + r$ separate computations: (a) a set X of r linearly independent forms from $C\underline{x}$, and (b) $(A - C)\underline{x}$. The n outputs $A\underline{x}$ are then computed as linear combinations of the above. Clearly if the r nodes corresponding to X are removed then the remaining graph contains n disjoint trees, with the outputs as roots and with $R_A(r) < f(r)$ input-output connections. □

The above theorem motivates two complexes of problems, one to do with the size of graphs and the other with the rigidity of natural functions. Positive solutions to Problems 3 and 4 below would give the desired superlinear lower bounds on the complexity of natural sets of linear forms. An alternative result to aim for would be bilinear forms (e.g. matrix multiplication) which would require solutions to problems 3 and 5.

The main evidence we have that the above theorem does provide a reduction of a nontrivial computational property to a noncomputational problem is the conjunction of Corollary 6.3 and Theorem 6.4 below.

Proposition 6.2 $\forall\varepsilon > 0$, $\forall c > 0$, $\forall k > 0$ and for all sufficiently large n, any $f(r)$-grate of indegree two and depth $k\log_2 n$ with $f(n) > cn^{1+\varepsilon}$ has size at least $(n\log\log n)/\log\log\log n$.

Proof Assume the contrary. By corollary 5.3 some set of n nodes can be removed from any graph of size $(n\log\log n)/\log\log\log n$ and depth $k\log n$ so as to leave no path longer than $(k\log n)/\log\log n$. Hence each output will be connected to at most $n^{k/\log\log n} = o(n^{\varepsilon})$ inputs after the deletions. This implies that the graph is not an $f(r)$-grate for any sufficiently large n, which is a contradiction. □

Corollary 6.3 Let $A_1, A_2, \ldots$ be an infinite family where A_n is an $n \times n$ real matrix and for some $c, \varepsilon > 0$, $R_{A_n}(n/2) \geq cn^{1+\varepsilon}$. Then there does not exist a family of straight-line programs for the corresponding sets of linear forms that for some $c_1, c_2 > 0$, (i) achieve size $c_1 n$ and depth $c_2 \log n$ simultaneously for all n, or (ii) are series-parallel and of size $c_1 n$ for all n.

Proof (i) Immediate from Theorem 6.1(i), Proposition 6.2, and the fact that the standard translation from straight-line programs to linear programs changes both the size and depth by only a constant factor. (ii) Follows similarly from Theorem 5.4.

Theorem 6.4 (i) For F infinite, $\forall n \exists n \times n$ matrix A such that $R_A(r) = (n-r)^2$.

(ii) For F finite with c elements, $\forall n \exists n \times n$ matrix A such that for all $r < n - \surd(2n.\log_c 2 + \log_2 n)$,

$$R_A(r) \geq ((n-r)^2 - 2n \log_c 2 - \log_2 n)/(2 \log_c n + 1).$$

Proof Define a mask σ to be any subset of s pairs from the set of pairs $\{(i,j) \mid 1 \leq i,j \leq n\}$. A minor τ is any pair of subsets of $\{i \mid 1 \leq i \leq n\}$, both of size t. Define $M(\sigma,\tau)$ to be the set of all $n \times n$ matrices A with the property that "$\exists$B such that (i) all the non-zero entries of B are indexed by σ, (ii) rank $(A+B) = t$, and (iii) τ specifies one of the minors of $C = A+B$ of maximal rank t in C."

Without loss of generality we shall assume that τ is in the top left corner. We shall denote an $n \times n$ matrix X generically by

$$\begin{pmatrix} X_{11} & X_{12} \\ X_{21} & X_{22} \end{pmatrix}$$

where X_{11} is $t \times t$.

Consider the set of all matrices of rank t that have a minor of maximal rank in the top left corner. Clearly there is a fixed set $\{f_k'\}$ of $(n-t)^2$ rational functions such that for any C in this set of matrices the entries of C_{22} are given by these functions in terms of the entries of C_{11}, C_{12} and C_{21}. But each element of $M(\sigma,\tau)$ differs from some element of this class by only an additive B. It follows that there is a fixed set $\{f_k\}$ of n^2 rational functions such that the entries of any $A \in M(\sigma,\tau)$ are given by these functions in terms of $(n^2 - (n-t)^2 + s)$ arguments (i.e. the entries of C_{11}, C_{12}, C_{21} and the non-zero entries of B). Hence each element of $\{M(\sigma,\tau) \mid \sigma,\tau\}$ is the image of F^{2tn-t^2+s} under some rational mapping into F^{n^2}.

(i) Hence for any r all the matrices that can be reduced to rank r by adding a matrix of density $(n-r)^2-1$ belong to the union of the images in F^{n^2} of a finite number of rational mappings from F^{n^2-1}. But if F is infinite the result follows since for any u the finite union of the images of F^u under rational mappings into F^{u+1} is properly contained in F^{u+1}. (This last fact can be established by first showing that if $f_1,\ldots,f_{u+1}$ are rational functions of $x_1,\ldots,x_u$ then the f's are algebraically dependent. (A counting argument in the style of [3] p.442 suffices if applied to the numerators of these functions when put over a common denominator). It then follows that the points in any finite union of such images are the roots of a non-trivial polynomial, and therefore cannot fill F^{n^2}).

(ii) If F has $c < \infty$ elements then the number of elements in $M(\sigma,\tau)$ is bounded by the size of F^{2tn-t^2+s}, i.e. c^{2tn-t^2+s}. For fixed s and t the number of possible choices of σ is

$$ {}^{n^2}C_s \leq 2^{2s \log_2 n}, $$

and of τ is

$$ ({}^{n}C_t)^2 < 2^{2n}. $$

Hence for fixed s and t the number of matrices in the union of $M(\sigma,\tau)$ over all σ, τ of these sizes is bounded by

$$ c^{2tn-t^2+s+2s\log_c n+2n\log_c 2}. $$

It follows that for any $t < n - \sqrt{(2n \log_c 2 + \log_2 n)}$, if

$$ 0 \leq s < ((n-t)^2 - 2n\log_c 2 - \log_c n)/(1 + 2\log_c n) $$

then the number of such matrices is less than

$$ c^{n^2 - \log_c n} = c^{n^2}/n. $$

Hence the union of all these matrices over all values of t will not fill F^{n^2}. □

Unfortunately we do not know of any explicit characterization of matrices of high rigidity. Indeed we have the following matrix-theoretic result that there are integer matrices in which all minors of all sizes are nonsingular but whose rank can be reduced to $o(n)$ by changing a mere $o(n^{1+\varepsilon})$ elements:

<u>Proposition 6.5</u> For each n there is an $n \times n$ matrix A in which all minors of all sizes are nonsingular but

$$ R_A((n\log\log\log n)/\log\log n) \leq n^{1+O(1/\log\log n)}. $$

<u>Proof</u> Let A be the matrix of Theorem 4.2 constructed from a superconcentrator of size $O(n)$ and depth $O(\log n)$. Applying Corollary 5.3 to the graph of this algorithm in the manner of Proposition 6.2 gives that for $r = (n\log\log\log n)/\log\log n$ $f(r) \leq n^{1+O(1/\log\log n)}$. The result then follows from Theorem 6.1(i). □

We note that although grates seem more restrictive than the corresponding $R(n, O(\log n))$ graphs, Proposition 6.2 exploits them only via this weakening correspondence. There therefore remains a hope that much better bounds are provable for them.

Problem 3 Prove a lower bound superlinear in n on the size of $f(r)$-grates for appropriately "nonlinear" $f(r)$. One candidate is: $f(r) = (n-r)^2$ for $r = 1,\ldots,n$. A weaker candidate is: $f(r) = kn^2$ when $r = n$ and $f(r) = 0$ when $r \neq n$. (Alternatively prove a linear upper bound noting that no such construction can be "series-parallel" or "shallow".)

Problem 4 For some natural $n \times n$ matrix A prove that $R_A(r)$ is large. A bound of $k(n-r)^2$ is one aim. A weaker aim would be one on the value of $R_A(n/2)$ alone, of $kn^2, kn^{1+\varepsilon}$, or some other superlinear function in n. Natural candidates for A are: (i) for the integers some Vandermonde matrix (i.e. $A_{ij} = z_i^{j-1}$ for distinct $z_1, z_2, \ldots z_n$), (ii) for the complex numbers the discrete Fourier transform matrix (i.e. $A_{ij} = w^{(i-1)(j-1)}$ where w is an nth primitive root of unity), and (iii) for GF(2) the 0-1 matrix associated with a finite projective plane.

Problem 5 It is known that for computing sets of bilinear forms (e.g. matrix multiplication, convolution) bilinear programs are optimal to within a constant factor [3,26]. Prove that the graph of any bilinear program for a natural set of bilinear forms is an $f(r)$-grate for such values of $f(r)$ as in Problem 3.

7. Conclusion

We have surveyed one approach to understanding complexity issues for certain easily computable natural functions. Shifting graphs have been seen to account accurately and in a unified way for the superlinear complexity of several problems for various restricted models of computation. To attack "unrestricted" models (in the present context combinational circuits or straight-line arithmetic programs) a first attempt, through superconcentrators, fails to provide any lower bounds although it does give counter-examples to alternative approaches. The notion of rigidity, however, does offer for the first time a reduction of relevant computational questions to noncomputional properties. The "reduction" consists of the conjunction of Corollary 6.3 and Theorem 6.4 which show that "for most sets of linear forms over the reals the stated algebraic and combinatorial reasons account for the fact that they cannot be computed in linear time and depth $O(\log n)$ simultaneously." We have outlined some problem areas which our preliminary results raise, and feel that further progress on most of these is humanly feasible. We would be interested in alternative approaches also.

Problem 6 Propose reductions of relevant complexity issues to noncomputational properties, that are more promising or tractable than the ones above.

References

1. Aho, A.V., Hopcroft, J.E. and Ullman, J.D., The Design and Analysis of Computer Algorithms, Addison Wesley, 1974.

2. Beneš, V.E., Mathematical Theory of Connecting Networks and Telephone Traffic. Academic Press, New York, 1965.

3. Borodin, A.B. and Munro, I. The Complexity of Algebraic and Numeric Problems, American Elsevier, 1975.

4. Ehrenfeucht, A. Practical decidability. Report CU-CS-008-72, Univ. of Colorado (1972).

5. Erdős, P., Graham and Szemerédi, E. On sparse graphs with dense long paths. Comp. and Maths. with Appls., 1, (1975) 365-369.

6. Fischer, M.J. and Rabin, M.O. Super-exponential complexity of Presburger arithmetic. MACTR43, Project MAC,MIT,(1974).

7. Hopcroft, J.E., Paul, W.J. and Valiant, L.G. Time versus space and related problems Proc. 16th Symp. on Foundations of Computer Science, Berkeley, (1975) 57-64.

8. Hartmanis, J., Lewis, P.M. and Stearns, R.E. Classification of Computations by time and memory requirements. Proc. IFIP Congress 1965, Spartan, N.Y., 31-35.

9. Hyafil, L. and Kung, H.T. The complexity of parallel evaluation of linear recurrence. Proc. 7th ACM Symp. on Theory of Computing (1975) 12-22.

10. Margulis, G.A. Explicit constructions of Concentrators, Problemy Peredachi Informatsii, 9 :4(1973) 71-80.

11. Meyer, A.R. and Stockmeyer, L.J. The word problem for regular expressions with squaring requires exponential space. Proc. 13th IEEE Symp. on Switching and Automata Theory, (1972)125-129.

12. Paterson, M.S., Fischer, M.J. and Meyer A.R. An improved overlap argument for on-line multiplication. SIAM-AMS Proceedings Vol 7, (1974) 97-111

13. Paterson, M.S. and Valiant, L.G. Circuit size is nonlinear in depth. Theoretical Computer Science 2 (1976) 397-400.

14. Paul, W.J. A 2.5N Lower bound for the combinational complexity of boolean functions. Proc. 7th ACM Symp. on Theory of Computing, (1975) 27-36.

15. Paul, W.J., Tarjan, R.E. and Celoni, J.R. Space bounds for a game on graphs. Proc. 8th ACM Symp. on Theory of Computing, (1976) 149-160.

16. Pippenger, N. The complexity theory of switching networks. Ph.D. Thesis, Dept. of Elect. Eng., MIT, (1973).

17. Pippenger, N. Superconcentrators. RC5937. IBM Yorktown Heights (1976).

18. Pippenger, N. and Valiant, L.G. Shifting graphs and their applications. JACM 23 (1976) 423-432.

19. Schnorr, C.P. Zwei lineare Schranken fur die Komplexität Boolischer Funktionen, Computing, 13 (1974) 155-171.

20. Stockmeyer, L.J. and Meyer, A.R. Inherent computational complexity of decision problems in logic and automata theory. Lecture Notes in Computer Science (to appear), Springer

21. Strassen, V. Die Berechnungkomplexität von elementar symmetrichen Funktionen und von Interpolationskoeffizienten. Numer. Math 20 (1973) 238-251.

22. Strassen, V. Vermeidung von Divisionen, J.Reine Angew.Math., 264,(1973), 184-202.

23. Valiant, L.G. On non-linear lower bounds in computational complexity. Proc. 7th ACM Symp. on Theory of Computing, (1975) 45-53.

24. Valiant, L.G. Universal circuits. Proc. 8th ACM Symp. on Theory of Computing, (1976) 196-203.

25. Valiant, L.G. Some conjectures relating to superlinear lower bounds. TR85, Dept. of Comp. Sci., Univ. of Leeds (1976).

26. Winograd, S. On the number of multiplications necessary to compute certain functions. Comm. on Pure and App. Math. 23 (1970) 165-179.

PROPERTIES OF COMPLEXITY CLASSES
A SHORT SURVEY

Gerd Wechsung
Sektion Mathematik der Friedrich-Schiller-Universität Jena
Jena, DDR

ABSTRACT

This short survey of properties of complexity classes (CC's for short) does not pretend to be complete. We rather confine ourselves to the illustration of important features by typical examples. Simultaneously an attempt is made to find a reasonable systematization of the vast variety of papers contributing to our topic. Among the chosen examples there are four so far unpublished statements (numbered (5), (6), (19) and (35)) about the return complexity [70] and a new measure A for nondeterministic Turing machines (NDTM) which is similar to the return complexity.

1. INTRODUCTION

Let $\mathbb{P}, \mathbb{R}, \mathbb{P}_r$ denote the classes of all partial recursive, all total recursive and all primitive recursive functions. Let φ be an acceptable enumeration of $\mathbb{P}$ and Φ some complexity measure in the sense of BLUM. For $f \in \mathbb{R}$ we define

$$\Phi(f) = \left\{ A : \bigvee_{i} (c_A = \varphi_i \wedge \Phi_i \leq_{a.e.} f) \right\} ,$$

where c_A denotes the characteristic function of A. $\Phi(f)$ is the CC of the measure Φ with the resource function f. General results concerning CC's (gap, union, naming) are surveyed by HARTMANIS & HOPCROFT [25].

Sometimes we shall be interested in the class of all functions computable within Φ-bound f:

$$\widetilde{\Phi}(f) = \left\{ \varphi_i : \Phi_i \leq_{a.e.} f \right\} .$$

Furthermore, we should like to mention that ROBERTSON [57] has introduced CC's of partial recursive functions and that BARASHKO & ROIZEN [2] have proved an interesting naming theorem of such CC's.

In this paper we have in mind properties of single, special CC's and not properties of the whole entity of all CC's of a given measure, although there are known a lot of nice hierarchy results for many special measures as well as such general results like MOLL's [47] (see also ENDERTON [14]) theorem about the imbeddability of arbitrary countable partially ordered sets into $\langle\{\Phi(f): f \in \mathbb{R}\}, \subseteq\rangle$.

Our survey paper is motivated by the growing number of papers devoted to properties of CC's. This great interest in the structure of CC's has three main reasons:

-) All important and hard problems of contemporary complexity theory (determinism versus nondeterminism, time versus space) are questions about CC's. That is why a profound knowledge of the structure of CC's can be (and in fact is) helpful for solving these problems.
-) The computational power of complexity bounded machines can be better understood. To which extent CC's grow if larger resource functions are chosen becomes more transparent if the corresponding CC's are characterized in terms of AFA, AFL or grammars instead of quantitative differences of their resource functions.
-) The study of AFA- or AFL-theoretic properties of CC's leads to a closer relationship between complexity theory and AFL theory (see [17] for all AFL and AFA notions).

We classify the results according to the following aspects.

Complexity theoretic properties. Relations to CC's of other measures.

Algebraic-recursion theoretic properties. Algebraic generation of CC's using operations from the theory of recursive functions.

Algebraic-language theoretic properties. Algebraic closure properties, especially AFL-properties of CC's.

Grammatical properties. Characterization of CC's by grammars.

Subrecursive properties. Characterization of CC's by AFA.

Reducibility properties.

Although stated seperately, these aspects are closely interdependently connected. Nevertheless, for the sake of clarity we shall maintain this frame.

2. NOTATIONS

It is convenient to have short and clear notations for families of languages, measures and CC's.

Families of languages. REG, CF, CS denote the classes of the regular, context-free and contextsensitive languages, respectively. FA, CA, PDA, SA denote the classes of languages accepted by finite automata, counter automata, pushdown automata and stack automata , resp. Further specifications of these types of automata are expressed by prefixes such as N (nondeterministic), NE (nonerasing), W (writing). For Turing machines the following prefixes are added: 1 or 2 (one-way or two-way read only input tape), aP (auxiliary pushdown tape), aS (auxiliary stack tape), k-tape or k-head (the machine has k tapes resp. k input heads).

Measures. The following measures, if used without further specification, correspond to deterministic Turing machines with one tape and one head without special input tape (TM): T (time), S (storage, tape), R (reversal), C (crossing measure), V (return), A (returns within the active phase). V and A are defined as follows: Let $\mathfrak{M}$ be a TM with input w. V(w) is the maximal number of visits of a tape square after the first altering of its initial content, where the maximum is to be taken over all squares necessary for the computation performed by $\mathfrak{M}$ on input w. A(w) is likewise the maximal number of visits of a tape square between the first and last altering of its content.

Complexity classes. When we consider CC's for other types of machines than TM, we can make use of the above mentioned prefixes. Thus, for instance Nk-tape T(f) means the class of all languages acceptable by nondeterministic k tape TM within time f, NaPS(f) means the class of all languages acceptable by nondeterministic TM with auxiliary pushdown tape within storage f and unrestricted pushdown tape etc. Differing from this systematic notation we adopt the following commonly used abbreviations $P = \bigcup_k T(n^k)$, $NP = \bigcup_k NT(n^k)$, $PSPACE = \bigcup_k S(n^k)$, $NPSPACE = \bigcup_k NS(n^k)$, $EXPTIME = \bigcup_k T(2^{kn})$, $NEXPTIME = \bigcup_k NT(2^{kn})$.

3. COMPLEXITY THEORETIC PROPERTIES

To this area belong mainly relationships betwen CC's of different measures.

1) Equalities

A typical result of this kind has been proved by CHYTIL [8] :

(1) $NS(f) = NC(f) = NR(f)$, provided $f \geq id$.

There are several important relations between time and tape. For random access machines with built-in multiplication (MRAM) we have the remarkable fact (HARTMANIS, SIMON [27]):

(2) $P_{MRAM} = NP_{MRAM} = PSPACE$.

COOK [12] has proved

(3) $\bigcup_k T(2^{kf(n)}) = aPS(f) = NaPS(f)$, provided $f(n) \geq \log n$,

and IBARRA [33] has found for $f(n) \geq \log n$.

(4) $aSS(f) = NaSS(f) = \bigcup_k aPS(2^{kf(n)}) = (\bigcup_k T(2^{2^{kf(n)}}))$.

We can relate time and aPS to the return measure:

(5) NV(f) = NaPS(f), provided $f(n) \geq \log n$.

The proof is similar to the proof of the main result in [70] .
As a consequence, some AFL's connected with several types of stack automata (see sect. 7) can be described in terms of return complexity. Because of (3), CHYTIL's [9] question, whether CS = NV(id), becomes the known open question whether CS = NaPS(id). However, introducing a new measure, called oscillation, (which is not a Blum measure) allows the finding of a characterization of CS in terms of V. If the length of the pushdown tape of a TM with auxiliary pushdown tape during a computation on input w is treated as a function F of the time, we can define a "derivative" of F by connecting any two minima with adjacent abscissae by a straight line in a graphical representation of F. Repeating this construction we get derivatives of higher order. The number of different derivatives is the oscillation O(w). Let BONaPS(f) be the class of all languages acceptable by nondeterministic TM with auxiliary pushdown tape within storage f and bounded oscillation. In a similar way we can define BONV(f), because it is possible to transfer the notion of oscillation to TM. Then we have

(6) NS(f) = BONaPS(f) = BONV(f), provided $f \geq id$, and especially
CS = BONaPS(id)= BONV(id).

2) Inclusions

Some of the most interesting known inclusions are

(7) $NS(f) \subseteq S(f^2)$ (SAVITCH [60])

(8) $NT(f) \subseteq S(\sqrt{f})$ for $f(n) \geq n^2$ (PATERSON [54]) .

3) Inequalities

BOOK [5] and [3] has shown for instance: If $\Phi \in \{S,NS\}$ and $A \in \{P,NP\}$ then there is no pair (r,s) of real numbers $1 \leq r \leq s$, such that

$$\Phi(n^r) \subseteq A \subseteq \Phi(n^s).$$

As a consequence we have

(9) P ≠ CS, P ≠ DCS, NP ≠ DCS, NP ≠ CS.

A further result is NP ≠ EXPTIME. These and other results of this kind have been derived using reducibility notions (see section 8).

4) Relations between equalities

(10) $NS(\log n) = S(\log n) \longleftrightarrow \bigwedge_{f(n) \geq \log n} (NS(f) = S(f)).$ [60]

(11) NEXPTIME = EXPTIME $\longleftrightarrow$ P = NP for tally languages (i.e. single letter alphabet languages) BOOK [4] .

(12) k-tape T(id) = 2-tapeT(id) $\longleftrightarrow$ k-tapeT(f) = 2-tapeT(f), if f is a running time (HARTMANIS [24]).

LEWIS [40] investigates so called pyramids similar to ENDERTON's complexity degrees [14]. The pyramid with its peak at f is the class of all functions g, such that

$$\bigwedge_{\varphi_i = f} \bigvee_{\varphi_j = g} \bigvee_{k} \bigwedge_{n} (S_j(n) \leq k S_i(n)).$$

He then finds a necessary and sufficient condition for a set of functions to be a tape complexity class $\tilde{S}(f)$.

4. RECURSION THEORETIC PROPERTIES

Each of the aspects mentioned in the introduction has two sides. One can start from a given CC and find some other description for it, and one can find that a class with certain properties turns out to be a CC.

An example for the latter is a result due to COBHAM [10] and McCREIGHT [44] which is extended by WEIHRAUCH [71] to the case of word functions.

(13) The GRZEGORCZYK classes $\mathcal{E}^n$ $(n \geq 2)$ and $\mathcal{P}r$ are time complexity classes for DTM.

The remaining examples of this section illustrate the first problem. COBHAM [10], CONSTABLE [11] and LIND [42] have found recursion theoretic definitions of $\tilde{P}$ (the class of all functions computable within polynomial time by DTM). As an example we present CONSTABLE's version. Γ_{Ω} means the closure operator with respect to the operations of Ω. Define $(\Sigma', f)(y,x) = \sum_{i=0}^{|y|} f(i,x)$, where $|y|$ = length of y in binary notation. Π' is defined likewise. Then we have

(14) $\tilde{P} = \Gamma_{\{SUB, \Sigma', \Pi'\}}(+, \dot{-}, \cdot, \div)$.

LIND has found such a characterization for $\tilde{S}(\log n)$. A further result of this kind is MONIEN's [51] description of EXPTIME. He says that f is defined from g and h by bounded recursion iff $f(x,o) = g(x)$, $f(x,y+1) = h(x,y,f(x,y),f(x,l(x,y)))$, $l(x,y) \leq y$ and proves

(15) $A \in \text{EXPTIME} \leftrightarrow c_A \in \Gamma_{\{\text{substitution, bounded recursion}\}}(\mathcal{E}^2)$,

$\mathcal{E}^2$ being the second GRZEGORCZYK class.

MONIEN [48] in a similar way characterizes time CC's of RAM with primitive recursive resource functions.

Let 2,2-tape $[T,S](f,g)$ denote the class of all languages acceptable by two-tape DTM with 2-way input tape working within time f and simultaneously within space g. For such double complexity classes NEPOMNYASHCHI [52] has proved

(16) For every integer $a,b > 1$ the class 2,2-tape $[T,S](n^a, n^{1-1/b})$ contains only rudimentary sets in the sense of SMULLYAN.

5. LANGUAGE THEORETIC PROPERTIES

The results of this section belong to either of three types: To state closure properties of several kinds for CC's, to characterize CC's in terms of AFL or to establish general relationships between AFL- and complexity theory.

Typical results of the first kind are the well known closure properties of the class of all realtime languages for multitape TM resp. counter automata due to ROSENBERG [58] resp. FISCHER, MEYER and ROSENBERG [15] . A mainly negative result has been proved by PECKEL [55]

(17) $\bigcup_{k=1}^{\infty} V(k)$ is closed under complement, but not under intersection, union, iteration and homomorphisms.

HOŘEJŠ [31] has investigated closure properties for a certain class of time bounded computable functions.

The most general results about CC's which are AFL's are obtained by BOOK, GREIBACH, IBARRA and WEGBREIT [6], [7] and GINSBURG and ROSE [18]. In [6], [7] sufficient conditions for time and tape CC's of TM to be AFL's are given. In [18] sufficient conditions are given for AFL's generated by tape CC's of TM and aPTM to be principal. In particular they prove once more WEGBREIT's result that CS is principal, and likewise aPS(id) is principal.

6. GRAMMATICAL PROPERTIES

Our first example of a grammatical characterization of a CC is EXPTIME (see also (15) and section 3), for which we know even two different grammatical descriptions. ROUNDS [59] characterizes EXPTIME by means of certain restricted transformational grammars, and MONIEN [51] by context-sensitive grammars with context-free control sets. By the way, EXPTIME is known to be the set of all spectra of first order logic with equality [35].

KAMEDA [36] uses the notion of k-unfolded regular languages in order to characterize 1NR(k) for natural k. Consider regular grammars with k-tuples as nonterminals. Define

$$\begin{pmatrix} a_1 \\ \vdots \\ a_k \end{pmatrix} \begin{pmatrix} b_1 \\ \vdots \\ b_k \end{pmatrix} \cdots \begin{pmatrix} c_1 \\ \vdots \\ c_k \end{pmatrix} = \begin{pmatrix} a_1 b_1 \cdots c_1 \\ \vdots \\ a_k b_k \cdots c_k \end{pmatrix} \text{ and } \mu\begin{pmatrix} w_1 \\ \vdots \\ w_k \end{pmatrix} = w_1 w_2^{-1} w_3 w_4^{-1} \cdots w_k^{\varepsilon_k}, \varepsilon_k = (-1)^{k+1}.$$

Then A is called a k-unfolded regular language over X if there exists a regular language B over X^{k+1} such that $A = \{\mu(\xi) : \xi \in B\}$. Let kUREG be the class of all k-unfolded regular languages. KAMEDA has proved

(18) $1NR(k) = kUREG.$

In an analogous manner we can define k-unfolded context-free languages. The set kUCF of all k-unfolded context-free languages can be characterized by conditions with respect to two measures, namely reversal R and return V. Let $\langle R,V\rangle(f,g)$ be the class of all languages acceptable by 1NTM which work on inputs of length n with no more than f(n) reversals up to the moment of receiving the last input symbol and afterwards with no more than g(n) returns. Then we have

(19) $kUCF = \langle R,V\rangle(k,1) = \bigcup_{i=1}^{\infty} \langle R,V\rangle(k,i).$

The proof uses a combination of KAMEDA's result and (26) (see below).

7. SUBRECURSIVE PROPERTIES

The first characterizations of CC's by AFA are

(20) $CS = S(id)$

due to LANDWEBER (1963) and KURODA (1964) and

(21) $REG = C(1) = \bigcup_{k=1}^{\infty} C(k)$

due to TRACHTENBROT [69] , HENNIE [28] and HARTMANIS [23]. The last result may be stated in a more general form

(22) If $\lim_{n\to\infty} \frac{f(n)}{\log n} = 0$, then $C(f) = REG.$

From (21) it easily follows SHEPHERDSON's result 2FA = REG.
For REG exist representations as time complexity classes [69] and [23] and as tape complexity classes [66]. For CF only inclusion results have been known so far:

(23) $CF \subseteq 2S((\log n)^2)$ (LEWIS, STEARNS, HARTMANIS [41])

(24) $CF \subseteq 3\text{-tape}T(n^3)$ (YOUNGER [73]).

Using the fast simulation of TM by RAM's due to HOPCROFT, PAUL and VALIANT [29] , from YOUNGER's result it follows

(25) $CF \subseteq RAMT(\frac{n^3}{\log n})$

which is exactly the result of GRAHAM, HARRISON and RUZZO [21]. A characterization of CF is possible in terms of the return complexity V. We have a complete analogon to the result (21) of TRACHTENBROT, HENNIE and HARTMANIS, namely [70]

(26) $CF = NV(1) = \bigcup_{k=1}^{\infty} NV(k).$

(In [70] we had only CF = NV(4) = NV(5) = ... The completion and correction (26) has been found together with A. BRANDSTÄDT.)

Examples (27) - (31) show how AFA characterizations of CC's make possible transparent comparisons of different CC's. COOK [12] proved

(27)
$$2SA = aPS(n\log n) = \bigcup_{k=1}^{\infty} T(n^{kn}),$$
$$N2SA = aPS(n^2) = \bigcup_{k=1}^{\infty} T(2^{kn^2})$$

and HOPCROFT, ULLMAN proved [30]

$$(28)\quad \begin{aligned} NE2SA &= S(n\log n) \\ NEN2SA &= NS(n^2). \end{aligned}$$

The result (27) has been extended by IBARRA [33] :

$$(29)\quad \begin{aligned} k\text{-head2SA} &= aPS(n^k \log n) \\ k\text{-headN2SA} &= aPS(n^{2k}). \end{aligned}$$

The question whether similar results hold for pushdown devices as (27) and (29) is answered by COOK [13] :

$$(30)\quad k\text{-head2PDA} = \bigcup_{c=1}^{\infty} RAMT(cn^k).$$

From (30) follows

$$(31)\quad \text{multihead2PDA} = aPS(\log n) = P.$$

A similar work has been done by MONIEN [49] . Further restriction leads to the class of multihead 2-way finite automata which has been considered by HARTMANIS [24]

$$(32)\quad \begin{aligned} \text{multihead2FA} &= S(\log n), \\ \text{multiheadN2FA} &= NS(\log n). \end{aligned}$$

According to SPRINGSTEEL [65] S(logn) represents exactly the computational power of so called marking automata.

An extension of (27) and (28) to the case of writing stack automata investigated by GIULIANO [19] shows that there is no difference between the deterministic and the nondeterministic versions:

$$(33)\quad \begin{aligned} WSA = NWSA &= \bigcup_{k=1}^{\infty} aPS(2^{kn}), \\ NEWSA = NENWSA &= \bigcup_{k=1}^{\infty} S(2^{kn}). \end{aligned}$$

The device of a writing stack automaton is a generalization of MAGER's [43] writing pushdown automata. For the special case of writing counter automata MAGER has proved:

$$(34)\quad \begin{aligned} NWCA &= CS \\ WCA &= DCS. \end{aligned}$$

Very different types of automata have been brought together with CC's. SMITH III [63] uses bounded cellular spaces to characterize CS and GLEBSKI, KOGAN [20] find a description of the real-time counter languages of FISCHER, MEYER, ROSENBERG [15] by means of special additive control systems.

To finish this section we describe a new result about the measure A introduced in section 2. Define a generalized stack automaton to be a (nondeterministic) device with a 1-way read only input tape and a storage tape with one read-write head which may reprint a nonblank symbol (or more general, a bounded number of such symbols) only if the input head receives an input symbol. Furthermore, it may erase only from the top (like a pushdown head) or from the bottom of the storage (like a buffer head). A word is accepted if and only if its complete reception leads to an empty storage and an accepting state. Let GSA be the class of all languages accepted by generalized stack automata. Then we have

(35) $$\mathrm{GSA} = \bigcup_{k=1}^{\infty} A(k) \subseteq \mathrm{CS}.$$

8. REDUCIBILITY PROPERTIES

In recent years a growing number of papers have been devoted to this topic, and the complexity bounded reducibilities thus have become themselves objects of mathematical investigations (see [38], [39], [45]). Although all reducibility notions known in the recursion theory may be modified we shall be mainly concerned with complexity bounded versions of m-reducibility which in a general setting looks like follows: Let $\mathcal{C}$ be a class of functions and A,B sets. $A \leq_{\mathcal{C}} B$ is defined by $\bigvee_{f\in\mathcal{C}} \bigwedge_{x} (x \in A \longleftrightarrow f(x) \in B)$. The most important applications thus far are $\mathcal{C} = \tilde{P}$ and $\mathcal{C} = 2\tilde{S}(\log n)$ introduced by KARP resp. MEYER, STOCKMEYER [46] and JONES [34] and designated $\leq_p$ and $\leq_{\ell g}$, resp. We shall refer to them as p-reducibility and logspace-reducibility.

For a class $\mathcal{L}$ of sets we define:

$\mathcal{L}$ is closed under $\mathcal{C}$-reducibility $\longleftrightarrow \bigwedge_{A} \bigwedge_{B\in\mathcal{L}} (A \leq_{\mathcal{C}} B \rightarrow A \in \mathcal{L})$.

L is $\mathcal{C}$-complete in $\mathcal{L} \longleftrightarrow L \in \mathcal{L} \wedge \bigwedge_{B\in\mathcal{L}} (B \leq_{\mathcal{C}} L)$.

These concepts provide a useful tool for investigations in complexity theory. Complete problems of a class are the hardest problems of this class because all other problems of this class can be efficiently encoded into them. Most questions about classes can be transformed to questions about their complete problems (see the lemmas below). Thus, it is sufficient to study complete problems.

Some facts stated as lemmas in BOOK [5] are reformulated as follows.

Lemma 1: If L is $\mathcal{C}$-complete in B and A is closed under $\mathcal{C}$-reducibility then $B \subseteq A$ if and only if $L \in A$.

Lemma 2: If $A = \bigcup_{i\in I} A_i$ and $\bigwedge_{i\in I} (A \neq A_i)$ and all A_i are closed under $\mathcal{C}$-reducibility then A cannot be closed under $\mathcal{C}$-reducibility.

In spite of the simplicity of these facts there are a lot of very interesting applications which give a rather deep insight into the very hard problems of time-space trade-offs and determinism versus nondeterminism. We illustrate this by some examples.

1) In KARP [37] a large amount of practically highly important p-complete problems in NP is given. As P is closed under p-reducibility the question whether all NP problems are feasible (i.e. belong to P)

is reduced by means of lemma 1 to the question whether some special p-complete problems belong to P. It is interesting to note that there are p-complete problems in NP which may be accepted by a very weak version of stack automata, namely 1-way nondeterministic checking stack automata [62] . The set of known NP-complete problems is too numerous to be listed here. We mention only the papers GREIBACH [22] and HUNT III [32] because of interesting equivalent formulations of the P = NP problem and the books [64] and [1]. As to the importance of the P = NP problem for the complexity theory see HARTMANIS, SIMON [27].

2) Hardest problems with respect to the logspace reducibility have been found in CS, and DCS is closed under logspace reducibility. (MEYER, STOCKMEYER [46] , see also [26]). Thus, by lemma 1 the LBA problem is reduced to the question whether such a hard problem (among them the equivalence problem for regular expressions in $\cup, \cdot, *$) belongs to DCS.

3) SAVITCH [60] pointed out that for $f(n) \geq \log n$, NS(f) = S(f) if and only if NS(logn) = S(logn). In fact he found a logspace complete set (codes of threadable mazes) in NS(logn).

4) A further example is given by SUDBOROUGH [68] and NEPOMNYASHCHI [53] . They constructed a context-free logspace-complete problem in NS(logn). From this follows that an affirmative solution of the LBA problem is equivalent to $CF \subseteq 2S(\log n)$. The best known result concerning the space complexity of context-free languages on 2DTM is formulated as statement (23), section 7.

5) logspace-complete problems in PSPACE are exhibited by MEYER, STOCKMEYER [46] , HUNT III [32], SCHAEFER [61] and others. MEYER and STOCKMEYER reveal a surprising relationship between their polynomial time hierarchy and PSPACE. As to the polynomial time hierarchy see also [67] and [72].

6) The close relationship between the CC's in the chain

$$S(\log n) \subseteq NS(\log n) \subseteq P \subseteq NP \subseteq PSPACE$$

is emphasized by a nice result by GALIL [16] , who found some of the so called hierarchies of complete problems in graph theory, automata theory, theorem proving and game theory. A hierarchy of complete problems is a quintuple $(A_1, \ldots, A_5)$ such that A_1 is logspace-complete in S(logn),...,A_5 is logspace-complete in PSPACE and every A_i is a special case of A_{i+1}, i.e. A_i is obtained from A_{i+1} by adding some restrictions to A_{i+1}.

7) Lemma 2 is applied by BOOK [5] to establish inequalities for CC's

some of which are listed in section 3.

I would like to thank Dr. Klaus Wagner for many helpful suggestions.

1. Aho, A. V., Hopcroft, J. E., Ullman, J. D., The Design and Analysis of Computer Algorithms. Addison-Wesley, Reading, Mass., 1974.
2. Barashko, A. S., Roizen, S. I., Kernels of partial recursive functions naming complexity classes. Kibernetika (Kiev) 5 (1976) 10-15.
3. Book, R. V., On languages accepted in polynomial time. SIAM J. Comp. 1,4 (1972) 281-287.
4. Book, R. V., Tally languages and complexity classes. Inf. and Contr. 26 (1974) 186-193.
5. Book, R. V., Translational lemmas, polynomial time and $(\log n)^j$-space. TCS 1 (1976) 215-226.
6. Book, R. V., Greibach, S. A., Ibarra, O, H., Wegbreit, B., Tape bounded Turing acceptors and principal AFL. JCSS 4 (1970) 622-625.
7. Book, R. V., Greibach, S. A., Wegbreit, B., Time and tape bounded Turing acceptors and AFLs. JCSS 4 (1970) 606-621.
8. Chytil, M. P., Crossing-bounded computations and their relation to LBA-problem. Kybernetika 12 (1976) 76-85.
9. Chytil, M. P., Analysis of the non-context-free component of formal languages. LNCS 45 (1976) 230-236.
10. Cobham, A., The intrinsic computational difficulty of functions. Proc. Int. Congr. Logic, Methodology a. Philosophie of Science 1964, North Holland, Amsterdam 1965, 24-30.
11. Constable, R. L., Type two computational complexity. Proc. 5th Ann. ACM Symp. Theory of Comput. (1973) 108-121.
12. Cook, S. A., Characterizations of pushdown machines in terms of time bounded computers. JACM 18,1 (1971) 4-18.
13. Cook, S. A., Linear time simulation of deterministic two-way pushdown automata. In: Information processing 71 (Proc. IFIP Congress Ljubljana 1971), Vol. 1, pp. 75-80. Amsterdam 1972.
14. Enderton, H., Degrees of computational complexity. JCSS 6 (1972) 389-396.

15. Fischer, P. C., Meyer, A. R., Rosenberg, A. L., Counter machines and counter languages. MST 2,3 (1968) 265-283.

16. Galil, Z., Hierarchies of complete problems. Acta Inf. 6 (1976) 77-88.

17. Ginsburg, S., Algebraic and Automata-Theoretic Properties of Formal Languages. North-Holland Amsterdam, 1975.

18. Ginsburg, S., Rose, G., On the existence of generators for certain AFL. Inform. Sci. 2(1970) 431-446.

19. Giuliano, J. A., Writing stack acceptors. JCSS 6 (1972) 168-204.

20. Glebski, Ju. V., Kogan, D. I., Additive control systems and languages,some algorithmic problems. Kibernetika (Kiev) 4 (1971) 25-29.

21. Graham, S. L., Harrison, M. A., Ruzzo, W. L., On line context-free language recognition in less than cubic time. Proc. 8th Ann. ACM Symp. Theory of Comput., Hershey 1976, 112-120.

22. Greibach, S. A., The hardest context-free language. SIAM J. Comp. 2 (1973) 304-310.

23. Hartmanis, J., Computational complexity of one-tape Turing machine computations. JACM 15,2 (1968) 325-339.

24. Hartmanis, J., On non-determinacy in simple computing devices. Acta Inf. 1(1972) 336-344.

25. Hartmanis, J., Hopcroft, J. E., An overview of the theory of computational complexity. JACM 18 (1971) 444-475.

26. Hartmanis, J., Hunt III, H. B., The LBA problem and its importance in the theory of computing. SIAM-AMS proceedings, vol. 7 (1974) 1-26.

27. Hartmanis, J., Simon, J., On the structure of feasible computations. In: Advances in Computers, vol. 14, pp. 1-43. Academic Press, New York, 1976.

28. Hennie, F. C., One-tape off-line Turing machine computations. Information and Control 8,6 (1965) 553-578.

29. Hopcroft, J., Paul, W., Valiant, L.,On time versus space and related problems. 16th Ann. Symp. on Found. of Comp. Sc. 1975, 57-64.

30. Hopcroft, J. E., Ullman, J. D., Nonerasing stack automata. JCSS 1,2 (1967) 166-186.

31. Hořejš, J., Recursive functions computable within Cflogf. Kibernetika 5,5 (1969) 384-398.

32. Hunt III, H. B., On the time and tape complexity of languages I. Proc. 5th Ann. A CM Symp. Theory of Comput. 1973, 10-19.

33. Ibarra, O. H., Characterizations of some tape and time complexity classes of Turing machines in terms of multihead and auxiliary stack automata. JCSS 5 (1971) 88-117.

34. Jones, N. D., Reducibility among combinatorial problems in log n space. Proc. 7th Ann. Princeton Conf. on Information Sciences and Systems 1973, 547-551.

35. Jones, N.D., Selman, A. L., Turing machines and the spectra of first-order formulas. JSL 39, 1 (1974) 139-150.

36. Kameda, T., Constant-tape-reversal bounded Turing machine computations. Proc. Intern. Computing Symposium 1970, Bonn, 649-654.

37. Karp, R. M., On the computational complexity of combinatorial problems. Networks 5 (1975) 45-68.

38. Ladner, R. E., Polynomial time reducibility. Proc. 5th Ann. ACM Symp. Theory of Comput. 1973, 122-129.

39. Ladner, R. E., Lynch,N. A., Selman, A. L., A comparison of polynomial time reducibilities. TCS 1 (1975) 103-123.

40. Lewis, F. D., On computational reducibility. JCSS 12,1 (1976) 122-131.

41. Lewis II, P. M., Stearns, R. E., Hartmanis, J., Memory bounds for recognition of context-free and contextsensitive languages. IEEE Conf. Rec. Switch. Circuit Theory and Logig Design pp. 191-202, New York, 1965.

42. Lind, J. C., Computing in logarithmic space. MAC MEM 52, MIT, 1974.

43. Mager, G., Writing pushdown acceptors, JCSS 3 (1969) 276-318.

44. Mc Creight, E. M., Classes of computable functions defined by bounds on computation. Diss., Carnegie-Mellon University, Pittsburgh, Pennsylvania, 1969.

45. Mehlhorn, K., Polynomial and abstract subrecursive classes. JCSS 12,2 (1976) 147-178.

46. Meyer, A. R., Stockmeyer, L. J., Word problems requiring expo-

nential time. Proc. 5th Ann. ACM Symp. Theory of Computing 1973) 1-9.

47. Moll, R., An operator imbedding theorem for complexity classes of recursive functions. TCS 1 (1976) 193-198.

48. Monien, B., Characterization oftime bounded computations by limited primitive recursion. LNCS 14 (1974) 280-293.

49. Monien, B., Relationships between pushdown automata with counters and complexity classes. MST 9 (1975) 248-264.

50. Monien, B., About the simulation of nondeterministic log n-tape bounded Turing machines. LNCS 33 (1975) 118-126.

51. Monien, B., A recursive and grammatical characterization of the exponential time languages. TCS 3 (1977) 61-74.

52. Nepomnyashchi, V. A., A rudimentary interpretation of two-tape Turing computations. Kibernetika (Kiev) 2 (1970) 29-35.

53. Nepomnyashchi, V. A., On tape complexity for recognition of context-free languages. Kibernetika (Kiev) 5 (1975) 64-68.

54. Paterson, M. S., Tape bounds for time bounded Turing machines. JCSS 6 (1972) 116-124.

55. Peckel, J., On a deterministic subclass of context-free languages. This volume.

56. Ritchie, R., Springsteel, F. N., Language recognition by marking automata. Inf. and Contr. 20 (1972) 313-330.

57. Robertson, E. L., Complexity classes of partial recursive functions. JCSS 9 (1974) 69-87.

58. Rosenberg, A. L., Real-time definable langugages. JACM 14,4 (1967) 645-662.

59. Rounds, W. C., A grammatical characterization of exponential time languages. 16th Ann. Symp. on Found. of Computer Sc. (1975) 135-143.

60. Savitch, W. J., Relationship between nondeterministic and deterministic tape complexities. JCSS 4 (1970) 177-192.

61. Schaefer, T. J., Complexity of decision problems based on finite two-person perfect-information games. 8th. Ann. ACM Symp. Theory of Computing (1976) 41-49.

62. Shamir, E., Beeri, C., Checking stacks and context-free programmed grammars accept p-complete languages. LNCS 14 (1974) 27-33.

63. Smith III, A.R., Cellular automata complexity trade-offs. Inf. and Control 18 (1971) 466-482.

64. Specker, E., Strassen, V., Komplexität von Entscheidungsproblemen. LNCS 43, Springer Verlag 1976.

65. Springsteel, F. N., On the pre-AFL of logn space and related families of languages. TCS 2 (1976) 295-304.

66. Stearns, R. E., Hartmanis, J., Lewis II, P. M., Hierarchies of memory limited computations. IEEE Conf. Rec. Switch. Circuit Theory and Logic. Design, New York 1965, 179-190.

67. Stockmeyer, L. J., The polynomial-time hierarchy. TCS 3 (1977) 1-22.

68. Sudborough, I. H., On tape-bounded complexity classes and multihead finite automata. JCSS 10 (1975) 62-76.

69. Trachtenbrot, B. A., Turing computations with logarithmic delay. Algebra i Logika 3,4 (1964) 33-48.

70. Wechsung, G., Kompliziertheitstheoretische Charakterisierung der kontextfreien und linearen Sprachen. EIK 12 (1976) 289-300.

71. Weihrauch, K., Teilklassen primitiv-rekursiver Wortfunktionen. Ges. f. Mathematik und Datenverarbeitung, Bonn 1974, Nr. 91.

72. Wrathall, C., Complete sets and the polynomial-time hierarchy. TCS 3 (1977) 23-33.

73. Younger, D. H., Recognition and parsing of context-free languages in time n^3. Inf. and Contr. 10,2 (1967) 189-208.

A UNIFORM APPROACH TO INDUCTIVE POSETS AND INDUCTIVE CLOSURE

J. B. Wright

E. G. Wagner

J. W. Thatcher

Mathematical Sciences Department

IBM Thomas J. Watson Research Center

Yorktown Heights, New York 10598

Introduction

The definition schema, "A poset P is Z-inductive if it has a subposet B of Z-compact elements such that for every element p of P there is a Z-set S in B such that $p = \bigsqcup S$," becomes meaningful when we replace the symbol Z by such adjectives as "directed", "chain", "pairwise compatible", "singleton", etc. Furthermore, several theorems have been proved that seem to differ only in their instantiations of Z. A similar phenomena occurs when we consider concepts such as Z-completeness or Z-continuity. This suggests that in all these different cases we are really talking about Z same thing. In this paper we show that this is indeed the case by abstracting out the essential common properties of the different instantiations of Z and proving common theorems within the resulting abstract framework.

The results in this paper are presented as pure mathematics, that is, without applications. However the underlying motivation comes from the application of posets with Z-set structure to problems in computer science and, in particular, to fixed-point semantics for programming languages. See, for example ADJ(1975)†, where, in fact, we use the term "Z-set" but primarily as a notational device.

The investigations here on Z-inductive posets were initiated by the need to answer questions that arose in the process of formalizing the introduction of higher type variables into recursion equations. The actual construction employed ordered algebraic theories and required showing that the resulting ordered algebraic theory was Z-complete for some suitable choice of Z. The work of Courcelle and Nivat(1976) suggested that the desired results could be obtained by restricting our attention to Z-complete Z-inductive algebraic theories‡. However Nivat's paper dealt only with the case Z = "directed", and we were interested in other cases as well. In the process of looking at other choices of Z we realized that the desired results could be proved in a abstract framework and it was therefore not necessary to treat each case individually. The present paper sums up our results on Z-inductive posets; we hope to present results on other topics, such as Z-continuity, in future papers.

† Papers referred to by the letters ADJ have grown out of collaboration amongst the authors and J. A. Goguen, UCLA, Computer Science Department, Los Angeles, Ca. 90024.

‡ Birkhoff(1967) and many following, including Scott(1972) and Courcelle and Nivat(1976), use the adjective "algebraic" rather than the combination of "inductive, complete." We use "inductive" in order to avoid barbarisms such as "algebraic algebras" and worse, "algebraic algebraic theories" in our applications of these results.

As noted above, many of the results and ideas used here have previously appeared for particular instances of Z. In addition to Courcelle and Nivat(1976) we have found much of use in Markowsky and Rosen(1976), Birkhoff(1967), and Bloom(1976).

In the next section the basic concepts such as poset, monotonic function, etc. are reviewed. The abstract concept of a subset system on posets is defined. Some elementary results are proved and we give a number of important and familiar examples of subset systems on the category of posets.

In Section 2 a Z-inductive poset is defined to be a poset P which has a Z-basis consisting of a subposet B of Z-compact elements such that for each $p \in P$ there exists a Z-set in B with $p = \bigsqcup S$. Elementary properties of Z-inductive posets are investigated. Necessary and sufficient conditions are given for a Z-inductive poset to be Z-complete. "Extension theorems" are given for extending a monotonic function $f: B \to P'$, defined on the Z-basis of P, to a function $\bar{f}: P \to P'$.

The third section considers completions. We show how, given a suitable poset P, to construct a new poset $\bar{P}$ of Z-ideals which is Z-inductive with, in effect, P as its Z-basis. Necessary and sufficient conditions for the construction are given, as well as necessary and sufficient condition for $\bar{P}$ to be Z-complete.

The results of the preceeding sections are combined and restated within a categorical framework in Section 4. We present three different contexts within which the construction of the inductive closure $\bar{P}$ of a poset P corresponds to an adjoint functor.

We conclude in Section 5 with a discussion of what we consider to be some natural and interesting questions that would extend this work in important directions.

1. Posets with a Subset System

A <u>poset</u> is a set P equipped with a partial order $\sqsubseteq$ on P. Let $S \subseteq P$; then $u \in P$ is a <u>upper bound</u> for S if $p \sqsubseteq u$ for every $p \in S$; u is a <u>least upper bound</u> for S if u is an upper bound for S and $u \sqsubseteq v$ for every upper bound v of S. We write $\bigsqcup S$ for the least upper bound of S if it exists.

Let P and P' be posets; then a mapping $f:P \to P'$ is said to be <u>monotonic</u> if it preserves the ordering, i.e. for all $p,p' \in P$, $p \sqsubseteq p'$ implies $pf \sqsubseteq p'f$. (Note that we usually write the argument to the left of the function.) The collection of all posets together with the monotonic mappings forms a category **Po**, called the <u>category of posets</u>†.

We say that an element $\perp$ of a poset P is the <u>bottom</u> element of P if it is minimum in P, i.e. if $\perp \sqsubseteq p$ for all $p \in P$. We say a poset is <u>strict</u> if it has a bottom element; we say a monotone mapping $f:P \to P'$ between strict posets is <u>strict</u> if $\perp f = \perp$. The strict posets together with the strict monotonic mappings

† Basic definitions from category theory are in ADJ(1973,1976) with computer science examples. An excellent comprehensive reference is Mac Lane(1971).

between them form a category $Po_{\perp}$ called the category of strict posets.

Let Po be the category of posets with monotonic functions as morphisms. A subset system on Po is a function Z which assigns to each poset P, a set Z[P] of subsets of P such that:

(1) there exists a poset P such that Z[P] contains some non-empty set; and,

(2) if $f:P \to P'$ in Po and $S \in Z[P]$ then $Sf = \{sf \mid s \in S\} \in Z[P']$.

We call the elements of Z[P], the Z-sets of P, and say "S is a Z-set in P", when $S \in Z[P]$.

A subset I of a poset P is an ideal iff it is downward closed: $p \in I$ and $p' \sqsubseteq p$ implies $p' \in I$. Let S be an arbitrary subset of P; then the ideal generated by S is

$$\hat{S} = \{p \mid p \sqsubseteq p' \text{ for some } p' \in S\}.$$

An ideal in P is a Z-ideal iff it is generated by some Z-set in P. Z-ideals form the basis for the Z-inductive closure construction of Section 3.

Given a subset system Z on Po, we say that a poset P is Z-complete iff every Z-set of P has a least upper bound in P. A morphism $f:P \to P'$ is Z-continuous iff for every Z-set S in P such that $\bigsqcup S$ exists, we have

$$(\bigsqcup S)f = \bigsqcup \{sf \mid s \in S\}.$$

So Z-continuous functions preserve least upper bounds of Z-sets that exist in their source.

We first used the term "Z-set" in ADJ(1975) as a notational device, without an abstract definition of a "subset system on Po." We were interested in a few specific instances of Z's which we enumerated and which are included in the list below. The property we used is now the principal part of the definition, i.e., that the image, under a monotonic map, of a Z-set is a Z-set. We didn't realize this simple abstraction and relied on the reader checking that the proofs worked for each of our Z's.

One of the principal uses of subset systems in ADJ(1975) was to pick out subcategories of Po consisting of the Z-complete posets with Z'-continuous (possibly different Z') morphisms. For now we are going to write Po[Z,Z'] for this category, we already have an example; if for each P, Z[P] is the set of subsets of cardinality less than or equal to 1 (singletons or empty) then Po[Z,Z] is $Po_{\perp}$. Z-completeness in this case just requires $\bigsqcup \emptyset$ exist (since $\bigsqcup \{p\} = p$) and this must be $\perp$; Z-continuity of f just means f is strict. Observe that for any Z, if there exists P with $\emptyset \in Z[P]$, then preservation of Z-sets (condition (2) above) insures $\emptyset \in Z[P]$ for all P so we will say Z is strict if $\emptyset \in Z[P]$ for any (all) P and observe that Po[Z,Z] is always a subcategory of $Po_{\perp}$ when Z is strict.

Let P be a poset; we define (non-strict) subset systems on Po with each of the following definitions of what it means for a subset S of P to be a Z-set in P.

S is a $\bigsqcup$-set	iff	S is non-empty
S is an n-set	iff	S is non-empty with cardinality less than or equal to n.
S is a PC-set	iff	S is non-empty and every pair from S has an upper bound in P

		(a pairwise compatible subset).[†]
S is a C-set	iff	S is non-empty and every finite subset of S has an upper bound in P (a compatible subset).
S is a $\dot{\bigsqcup}$-set	iff	S is non-empty and bounded in P (bounded subsets).
S is a Δ-set	iff	S is non-empty and every pair from S has an upper bound in S (iff every non-empty finite subset of S has an upper bound in S) (a directed subset).
S is an ℓ-set	iff	S is non-empty and linearly ordered (a chain)
S is a wo-set	iff	S is a non-empty well-ordered chain.[‡]
S is an ω-set	iff	S is a chain of order type ω.
S is a $\sqcup$-set	iff	S is a finite $\bigsqcup$-set.
S is a pc-set	iff	S is a finite PC-set.
S is a c-set	iff	S is a finite C-set.
S is a $\dot{\sqcup}$-set	iff	S is a finite $\dot{\bigsqcup}$-set (iff S is a c-set).

We write $\Delta \subseteq C$ to mean $\Delta[P] \subseteq C[P]$ for every poset P, i.e., every directed subset of a poset is a compatible subset. It is easy to check that

$$\omega \subseteq \text{wo} \subseteq \ell \subseteq \Delta \subseteq C \subseteq PC \subseteq \bigsqcup.$$

1-sets are singletons, 2-sets are doubletons and n-sets are defined for any cardinal n. Similarly, we could have defined α-set for any order type α just as we did for ω.

Each of the Z's in our list is non-strict and it is convenient to speak of their strict counterparts. For notation we can use $Z_\perp$ to mean $Z_\perp[P] = Z[P] \cup \{\emptyset\}$ but generally we will just use the qualifier "strict" and also, by example, write $\mathbf{Po}_\perp[\Delta]$ instead of $\mathbf{Po}[\Delta_\perp]$ or $\mathbf{Po}[\Delta_\perp, \Delta_\perp]$

From the proof of the following proposition one sees that singletons are always Z-sets for subset systems on **Po**.

Proposition 1.1. Let Z be a subset system on **Po**. Then for each poset P and each $p \in P$ there exists a Z-set $S \in Z[P]$ such that $\bigsqcup S = p$.

Proof: Let P be a poset and $p \in P$. By the definition of subset system there exists a poset Q with $\emptyset \neq S \in Z[Q]$. Now define $f:Q \to P$ by $qf = p$ for all $q \in Q$. Clearly f is monotonic, $Sf = \{p\}$ and $\bigsqcup \{p\} = p$. □

Corollary 1.2. For any subset system Z and poset P, if $p \in P$ then $\{p\} \in Z[P]$. □

† The term "pairwise compatible" is from Markowsky and Rosen(1976) although the concept is to be found in Egli and Constable(1976).

‡ The wo-sets were added to our list when we found that Tiuryn(1976) used the notions wo-complete and wo-continuous.

Let P and Q be posets with respective partial orders $\sqsubseteq_P$ and $\sqsubseteq_Q$. We say P is a <u>subposet</u> of Q if $P \subseteq Q$ (as sets) and if for all $p, p' \in P$, $p \sqsubseteq_P p'$ iff $p \sqsubseteq_Q p'$.

<u>Fact 1.3</u>. Let P be a subposet of Q. Then for every $S \subseteq P$, if S is a Z-set in P then S is a Z-set in Q (but S can be a Z-set in Q without being one in P).

<u>Proof</u>. Clearly the inclusion morphism $\iota: P \to Q$ ($p\iota = p$) is monotonic and takes any Z-set S to itself. That the converse fails is easily seen by considering $\dot{\bigsqcup}$-sets. Clearly we can choose a poset Q a bounded-set ($\dot{\bigsqcup}$-set) $S \subseteq Q$ and a subposet P of Q which contains S but no upper bound for S. □

In light of the above it is important for the reader to remember that when P is a subposet of Q and we say "S is a Z-set in P" this means $S \in Z[P]$, and it is not equivalent to saying "$S \in Z[Q]$ such that $S \subseteq P$". Failure to remember this distinction will cause confusion in reading the remainder of the paper.

2. Z-inductive Posets

Let Z be a subset system on **Po** and P a poset. An element $p \in P$ is <u>Z-compact</u> in P if for each Z-set D in P such that $\bigsqcup D$ exists, if $p \sqsubseteq \bigsqcup D$ then $p \sqsubseteq d$ for some $d \in D$.

We call the set of Z-compact elements of P the <u>Z-core</u> of P and sometimes denote it Core[P]. Because of analogy with the posets of partial functions (which is $PC_\perp$-complete) and of relations ($\bigsqcup_\perp$-complete), the Z-compact (actually Δ-compact) elements are sometimes called "finite", but note that any non-limit ordinal less than a given ordinal α is ℓ-compact (or Δ-compact) in the poset of all ordinals less than α, so the use of "finite" can be misleading. On the other hand the poset of cofinite subsets of any set of S is $\bigsqcup$-complete with empty core (is a sense, the strongest possible completeness condition and the weakest compactness condition). Throwing the empty set in with the cofinite sets gives a complete lattice ($\bigsqcup_\perp$-complete) with $\emptyset$ the only compact element.

Another observation (that may confound the intuition) is that if Z is strict ($\emptyset \in Z[P]$ for all P) then $\perp$ is never Z-compact because $\perp \sqsubseteq \bigsqcup \emptyset$ and $\perp \sqsubseteq d \in \emptyset$ is impossible. On the other hand, if Z is non-strict ($\emptyset \notin Z[P]$ for all P) then $\perp$ is always Z-compact.

The following fact says that compact elements are only trivially obtained as least upper bounds.

<u>Fact 2.1.</u> For any Z-set $D \subseteq \text{Core}[P]$, $\bigsqcup D$ exists in Core[P] iff $\bigsqcup D \in D$.

<u>Proof</u>: If $\bigsqcup D \in \text{Core}[P]$ then its compactness ($\bigsqcup D \sqsubseteq \bigsqcup D$) says $\bigsqcup D \sqsubseteq d'$ for some $d' \in D$. But $d' \sqsubseteq \bigsqcup D$ so $\bigsqcup D = d' \in D$. The converse is immediate. □

Defining a condition weaker than Z-completeness, we say a poset P is <u>Z-core complete</u> iff every Z-set in Core[P] has a least upper bound in P Let $\mathbf{Po}_{\text{Z-core}}$ be the subcategory of **Po** with objects which are

Z-core complete and morphisms which are Z-continuous and preserve compactness, i.e., $f:P \to P'$ and $p \in \mathrm{Core}[P]$ then $pf \in \mathrm{Core}[P']$.

A poset P is Z-inductive iff every $p \in P$ is the least upper bound of some Z-set in Core[P]. Let $\mathbf{Po}_{Z\text{-ind}}$ be the subcategory of **Po** with objects which are Z-inductive and, morphisms which are both Z-continuous and preserve compactness.

Let P be a poset and $p \in P$. In contexts to follow it is reasonable to call the set of all compact elements less than or equal to p, the support of p, written $\sigma[P]$; generalizing slightly, we define the support of a subset S of P by,

$$\sigma[S] = \{b \mid b \in \mathrm{Core}[P] \text{ and } b \sqsubseteq s \text{ for some } s \in S\}.$$

Of course, $\sigma[S] = \bigcup\{\sigma[s] \mid s \in S\}$.

We say P has Z-closed support iff for every Z-set S in P there exists a Z-set D in Core[P] such that $\sigma[D] = \sigma[S]$. Equivalently, because the support is always an ideal in Core[P], P has Z-closed support iff for every Z-set S in P, $\sigma[S]$ is a Z-ideal.

The support function is a monotonic function to the poset of subsets of Core[P]; if P is Z-inductive then $\sigma[p] \subseteq \sigma[q]$ implies $p \sqsubseteq q$:

Fact 2.2. Let P be a Z-inductive poset with $p,q \in P$. Then $p \sqsubseteq q$ iff $\sigma[p] \subseteq \sigma[q]$.

Proof. $p \sqsubseteq q$ implies $\sigma[p] \subseteq \sigma[q]$ by transitivity.

Assume $\sigma[p] \subseteq \sigma[q]$. Let D_p be a Z-set in Core[P] such that $\bigsqcup D_p = p$. Now $d \in D_p$ implies $d \sqsubseteq p$, $D_p \subseteq \sigma[p] \subseteq \sigma[q]$ so if $d \in D_p$ then $d \sqsubseteq q$. Thus q is an upper bound for D_p and thus $p = \bigsqcup D_p \sqsubseteq q$. □

We will be connecting together and applying the various concepts introduced above. The proofs manipulate subsets of a poset and their least upper bounds. Some confusing quantifiers are eliminated from those proofs if we make careful use of the cofinality relation on subsets. Let P be a poset and S, S' subsets of P. S' is cofinal in S (written $S \lesssim S'$) iff for every $s \in S$ there exists $s' \in S'$ with $s \sqsubseteq s'$. S and S' are mutually cofinal (written $S \sim S'$) iff $S \lesssim S'$ and $S' \lesssim S$. An important use of cofinality is that it is preserved under monotonic maps and mutually cofinal sets have identical least upper bounds (if they exist). The following lemma collects together these and some other useful facts.

Lemma 2.3. Let P and P' be posets, $f:P \to P'$ monotonic, S, S' arbitrary subsets of P and D a subset of Core[P].

(a) $S \subseteq S'$ implies $S \lesssim S'$

(b) $S \lesssim S'$ implies $Sf \lesssim S'f$

(c) $S \sim S'$ implies $Sf \sim S'f$

(d) If $\bigsqcup S$ exists, u' is an upper bound for S' and $S \sqsubseteq\!\!\!\sqsupseteq S'$ then $\bigsqcup S \sqsubseteq u'$. In particular if $\bigsqcup S'$ exists, $\bigsqcup S \sqsubseteq \bigsqcup S'$.

(e) If $\bigsqcup S$ exists and $S \sim S'$ then $\bigsqcup S = \bigsqcup S'$.

(f) $\sigma[S] \sqsubseteq\!\!\!\sqsupseteq S$

(g) $\sigma[D] \sim D$

(h) If $\bigsqcup D$ exists then $D \sim \sigma[\bigsqcup D]$

(i) If $\bigsqcup D$ exists then $\bigsqcup D = \bigsqcup \sigma[\bigsqcup D]$.

Proof: We check only the least obvious.

(d) Every $s \in S$ has some $s' \in S'$ with $s \sqsubseteq s' \sqsubseteq u'$ so that u' is also an upper bound for S, i.e., $\bigsqcup S \sqsubseteq u'$.

(g) From (f) $\sigma[D] \sqsubseteq\!\!\!\sqsupseteq D$, but $D \subseteq \sigma[D]$, because D consists of compact elements so, by (a), $D \sqsubseteq\!\!\!\sqsupseteq \sigma[D]$.

(h) Again we have $D \sqsubseteq\!\!\!\sqsupseteq \sigma[\bigsqcup D]$ because $D \subseteq [P]$. For the other direction, if $d' \in \sigma[\bigsqcup D]$, i.e., d' compact and $d' \sqsubseteq \bigsqcup D$ then $d' \sqsubseteq d \in D$, i.e., $\sigma[\bigsqcup D] \sqsubseteq\!\!\!\sqsupseteq D$.

(i) This follows from (h) and (d). □

Proposition 2.4 Let P be a Z-inductive poset and let S be a Z-set in P. If $\bigsqcup S$ exists then $\sigma[S] = \sigma[\bigsqcup S]$. Conversely, if there exists $p \in P$ with $\sigma[p] = \sigma[S]$ then $p = \bigsqcup S$.

Proof: By transitivity, $\sigma[S] \subseteq \sigma[\bigsqcup S]$. Now assume $d \in \sigma[\bigsqcup S]$, i.e., $d \in$ Core[P] and $d \sqsubseteq \bigsqcup S$. Since d is compact, $d \sqsubseteq s$ for some $s \in S$, i.e., $d \in \sigma[S]$.

For the converse consider any $s \in S$. Since P is Z-inductive, there exists a Z-set $D_s \subseteq$ Core[P] with $s = \bigsqcup D_s$. Thus $D_s \subseteq \sigma[S] = \sigma[P]$ so that $s \sqsubseteq p$ and p is an upper bound for S. If u is any upper bound for S, then $\sigma[p] \subseteq \sigma[u]$ because $\sigma[p] = \sigma[S]$ (hypothesis) and $d \sqsubseteq s \in S$ implies $d \sqsubseteq u$ for compact d. Thus (Proposition 2.2) $p \sqsubseteq u$. □

Z-inductive posets were defined existentially, i.e., for every $p \in P$ there exists a Z-set in Core[P] with p as its least upper bound. We can use Proposition 2.4 to get an alternative characterization without that existential quantifier.

Proposition 2.5. P is Z-inductive iff for every $p \in P$, $\sigma[P]$ is a Z-ideal and $p = \bigsqcup \sigma[P]$.

Proof: If P is Z-inductive and $p \in P$ then $p = \bigsqcup D$ for some Z-set D in Core[P]. Proposition 2.4 says $\sigma[p] = \sigma[D]$, but σ is a Z-ideal and $\sigma[D] \sim D$ (Lemma 2.3(g)) so $\bigsqcup \sigma[p] = \bigsqcup \sigma[D] = \bigsqcup D = p$ (Lemma 2.3(e)). The converse is immediate from the definition and Lemma 2.3 (e,g). □

We move now to consider conditions under which a Z-inductive poset is also Z-complete.

Proposition 2.6. Let P be a Z-inductive. Then P is Z-complete iff P is Z-core complete and has Z-closed support.

Proof: Assume P is Z-complete. Then P is clearly Z-core complete since every Z-set in Core[P] is a Z-set in P (Fact 1.3). Now assume $S \subseteq P$ is a Z-set in P and $\bigsqcup S = p$. Then since P is inductive there exists a Z-set $D \subseteq \mathrm{Core}[P]$ such that $p = \bigsqcup D$. By Proposition 2.4, $\sigma[D] = \sigma[p] = \sigma[S]$ as required to show that P has Z-closed support.

Now assume P is Z-core complete and has Z-closed support. Then given a Z-set S in P let D be a Z-set in Core[P] such that $\sigma[D] = \sigma[S]$ (such exists since P has Z-closed support). Since P is Z-core complete there exists $p \in P$ such that $p = \bigsqcup D$. That $p = \bigsqcup S$ then follows immediately from Proposition 2.4. □

Fact 2.7. Among Z-inductive posets, the properties of Z-closed support and Z-core completeness are independent.

Proof. Let $P = \{a,b,c,x,y,z\}$ with order as indicated in Figure 2.1 Let $Z = 2$ (Z-sets are doubletons or singletons).

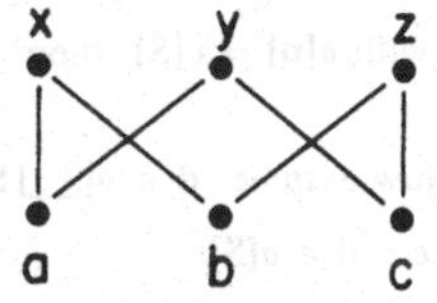

Figure 2.1

Then $\mathrm{Core}[P] = \{a,b,c\}$, P is inductive and Z-core complete but P does not have Z-closed support (e.g. $\{x,y\}$ is a Z-set in P but $\sigma(\{x,y\}) = \{a,b,c\}$ is not a Z-set in Core[P].)

Let $Q = \{a,b,c\}$ with $\sqsubseteq$ the equality relation, and again $Z = 2$. Then $\mathrm{Core}[Q] = Q$; Q is inductive and Q (trivially) has Z-closed support but Q is not Z-core complete. □

The following is the principal theorem of this section (a slight variant follows). This extension theorem says that monotonic maps defined on the core of a Z-inductive poset extend uniquely to monotonic Z-continuous maps on the whole poset provided there is sufficient completeness in the target.

Theorem 2.8. Let P and Q be posets with P, Z-inductive, and Q, Z-core complete. Let $f:\mathrm{Core}[P] \to \mathrm{Core}[Q]$ be monotonic. Then there exists a unique monotonic Z-continuous $\bar{f}:P \to Q$ which extends f.

Proof: Given $p \in P$ we know there exists a Z-set $D \subseteq \mathrm{Core}[P]$ with $p = \bigsqcup D$. Since f is monotonic, Df is a Z-set in Core[Q] and since Q is Z-core complete, $\bigsqcup(Df)$ exists in Q. Now for $\bar{f}$ to extend f and be Z-continuous we must have $p\bar{f} = \bigsqcup(Df)$. We need to show that $\bar{f}$ defined this way is indeed well-defined, monotonic, and Z-continuous.

Note that $\bar{f}$ does extend f because for $p \in$ Core[P], {p} is a Z-set (Corollary 1.2) and $p\bar{f} = \bigsqcup\{pf\} = pf$. With $p = \bigsqcup D$ and $D \subseteq$ Core[P], Lemma 2.3(h) $D \sim \sigma[p]$ so by Lemma 2.3(e), $\bigsqcup Df = \bigsqcup \sigma[p]f$. Thus no matter what Z-set D we choose with $\bigsqcup D = p$, we have

$$(*) \quad p\bar{f} = \bigsqcup Df = \bigsqcup(\sigma[p])f$$

and this tells us $\bar{f}$ is well defined.

If $p \sqsubseteq p'$ then (Fact 2.2) $\sigma[p] \subseteq \sigma[p']$ so $p\bar{f} = \bigsqcup(\sigma[p])f \sqsubseteq \bigsqcup(\sigma[p'])f = p'\bar{f}'$ by Lemma 2.3(a,b,d), and we see $\bar{f}$ is monotonic.

Finally, for continuity, let S be a Z-set in P with $a = \bigsqcup S$. $a\bar{f}$ is an upper bound for $S\bar{f}$ because $s \sqsubseteq a$ and $\bar{f}$ monotonic implies $s\bar{f} \sqsubseteq a\bar{f}$. Let u be any upper bound for Sf. We know $\sigma[a] = \sigma[S] \precsim S$ by Proposition 2.4 and Lemma 2.3(f). With (*) above, Proposition 2.4, and Lemma 2.3(d) we get $a\bar{f} = \bigsqcup \sigma[a]f = \bigsqcup \sigma[S]f \sqsubseteq u$ so $a\bar{f} = \bigsqcup S\bar{f}$. □

If P and Q are both Z-inductive and Z-core complete and if f:Core[P] → Core[Q] is an isomorphism then Theorem 2.8 immediately yields $\bar{f}$:P → Q is an isomorphism.

<u>Corollary</u> <u>2.9.</u> If P and Q are Z-inductive and Z-core complete and if Core[P] ≅ Core[Q] then P ≅ Q. □

One can check the proof of the previous theorem to see that compactness of elements of the target of f was not used; we needed only that $\bigsqcup Df$ exist for Z-sets D in Core[P]. Therefore the same proof yields:

<u>Theorem</u> <u>2.10.</u> Let P and Q be posets with P, Z-inductive, and Q, Z-complete. Let f:Core[P] → Q be monotonic. Then there exists a unique monotonic Z-continuous $\bar{f}$:P → Q which extends f. □

Inductive posets are intimately related to the "extension basis" for posets discussed in Markowsky and Rosen(1976). A subset B of a Z-complete poset P is an Z-<u>extension</u> <u>basis</u> iff, for every Z-complete poset Q and monotonic map f:B → Q, there exists a unique monotonic Z-continuous $\bar{f}$:P → Q that extends f. This is an exact generalization of Markowsky and Rosen's definition with Z replacing "chain", i.e., taking $Z = \ell$ gives their definition. We see immediately from Theorem 2.10.

<u>Corollary</u> <u>2.11.</u> If a Z-complete poset P is Z-inductive then Core[P] is a Z-extension basis for P. □

There is a converse to Corollary 2.11 which we will consider at the end of the next section.

3. Z-inductive Closure

In this section we show how, given a suitable poset P, to construct from it a Z-inductive poset I[P] with, in effect, P as its core. We present two approaches, both of which give the same result. In the first approach I[P] consists of suitably defined equivalence classes of Z-sets of P (the equivalence relation is mutual cofinality); in the second approach we use the Z-ideals of P as the elements of I[P]. Because of the equivalence of the two approaches (each equivalence class is uniquely representable by a Z-ideal) we prove all the theorems in terms of Z-ideals.

Recall from the last section that S' is cofinal in S ($S \precsim S'$) iff for every $s \in S$ there exists $s' \in S'$ with $s \sqsubseteq s'$. S and S' are mutually cofinal ($S \sim S'$) iff $S \precsim S'$ and $S' \precsim S$.

Fact 3.1. $\precsim$ is a quasi-order (i.e., a reflexive, transitive relation) on Z[P], and $\sim$ is an equivalence relation on Z[P]. □

Given $P \sqsubseteq$, $\precsim$ and $\sim$ as above, then for each $S \in Z[P]$ let [S] denote its $\sim$-equivalence class. Given $[S], [S'] \in Z[P]/\sim$ we write $[S] \sqsubseteq [S']$ if $S \precsim S'$.

Fact 3.2. $Z[P]/\sim$ equipped with the above ordering is a poset. □

Recall that a Z-ideal in P is an ideal generated by a Z-set in P. Let I[P] denote the poset of Z-ideals ordered by set inclusion.† An ideal is principal if it is generated by a singleton; let C[P] be the poset of principal ideals. Since every singleton set is a Z-set (Corollary 1.2) we know $C[P] \subseteq I[P]$. Let $\iota_P: P \to I[P]$ be the monotonic map sending each $p \in P$ to the principal ideal generated by {p}.

Fact 3.3. $\iota_P: P \to I[P]$ is an injection and its target restriction to C[P], $\iota_P: P \to C[P]$, is an isomorphism. □

In what follows we abuse notation slightly, using ι_P to denote both the function to I[P] and the restriction to C[P]; context will, we hope, eliminate any confusion.

In the beginning of this section we mentioned that equivalence classes modulo mutual cofinality and ideals were alternative (equivalent) approaches to the inductive closure construction. The following proposition captures that equivalence.

---

† Note that we really should write $I_Z[P]$ but the additional notation seems to be unnecessary.

Proposition 3.4. For any poset P, $I[P] \simeq Z[P]/\sim$ (as posets).

Proof: Define $\wedge : Z[P]/\sim \to I[P]$ by $[S]\wedge = \hat{S}$, the ideal generated by S. We need $S \sim S'$ implies $\hat{S} = \hat{S}'$. $\wedge$ is obviously a monotonic function from Z[P] to I[P] so by Lemma 2.3(c) $S \sim S'$ implies $\hat{S} \sim \hat{S}'$. But two ideals are mutually cofinal just in case they are equal: if $\hat{S} \precsim \hat{S}'$ and $s \in \hat{S}$ then there exists $s' \in S'$ with $s \sqsubseteq s'$ so that $s \in \hat{S}'$; because $\hat{S}'$ is downward closed. Thus $\hat{S} \subseteq \hat{S}'$ and similarly $\hat{S}' \subseteq \hat{S}$. Besides showing that $\wedge$ is a well defined function this also shows that it is monotonic because $[S] \sqsubseteq [S']$ iff $S \precsim S'$, which implies $\hat{S} \subseteq \hat{S}'$. $\wedge$ is clearly surjective (I[P] consists exactly of Z-ideals). To see that it is injective (and thus an isomorphism), assume $\hat{S} = \hat{S}'$. Then each $s \in S$ is also in S' and can only be there by virtue of there being some $s' \in S'$ with $s \sqsubseteq s'$, i.e., $S \precsim S'$. Similarly $S' \precsim S$, so $S \sim S'$ and $[S] = [S']$. □

At this point we leave $Z[P]/\sim$ and consider the isomorphic poset I[P] of Z-ideals.

We now introduce conditions on subset systems that ensure that the construction $P \to I[P]$ has desirable properties. The first, and weaker of the two, is necessary for I[P] to be Z-inductive; the second is necessary for, in addition, I[P] to be Z-complete.

We say a subset system Z is unionized iff for every poset P, if S is a Z-set in I[P] and $\bigsqcup S$ exists then $\bigsqcup S = \cup S$. Z is union-complete iff I[P] is Z-complete and for any Z-set $S \in Z[I[P]]$, $\bigsqcup S = \cup S$.

We acknowledge that the notions of Z being unionized or union-complete are somewhat obscure if not mystifying. All the more so because we know of no Z (no subset system) which is unionized but not union complete. With the exception of the finite cardinals greater than one (n-sets for n finite and greater than 1, e.g., doubletons) all the examples listed in Sectons 1 are union-complete. For Z any finite cardinal greater than one, on the other hand, we can always construct a poset P to show that Z is not unionized. Looking at the most trivial case, take Z = 2 (singleton and doubleton sets) and consider the poset P = {a,b,c,d} with the $a \sqsubseteq d$, $b \sqsubseteq d$ and $c \sqsubseteq d$ (Figure 3.1).

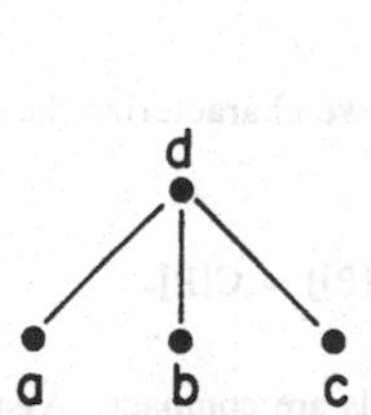

Figure 3.1

The doubleton of 2-sets, {{a,b}, {c}} has a least upper bound {a,b,c,d} in I[P] but it is not the union of {a,b} and {c}. Thus Z = 2 is not unionized.

Although we know of no subset system that is unionized but not union-complete it is possible to see a difference between the two concepts if we look at a single poset rather than at all posets as required by the definition. Let $Q = \{a,b,c\}$ be the (discrete) poset ordered by equality (the second example in Fact 2.7) and take $Z = 2$. Then I[Q] (Figure 3.2) is ordered as in the first example of Fact 2.7,

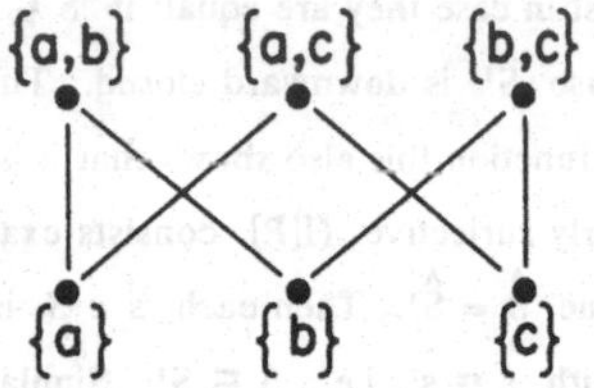

Figure 3.2

In effect, I[P] is "unionized" because if the least upper bound of a doubleton of ideals exists then it is the set union of those ideals. However I[P] is not 2-complete.

Despite these diffculties, the two theorems to follow (3.8, 3.9) seem to indicate the importance of the properties, unionized and union-complete, because the first is necessary for I[P] to be Z-inductive and Z-core complete while the second is necessary for I[P] to be Z-inductive and Z-complete.

The problem being confronted with the properties of unionized and union-complete is that we have no guarantee that the (set-) union of Z-ideals is a Z-ideal. The following facts further delineate this situation; they are immediate because set inclusion is the ordering on I[P].

Fact 3.5. Let P be a poset. If S is a set of ideals such that $\cup S \in I[P]$ ($\cup S$ is a Z-ideal) then $\cup S = \bigsqcup S$ in I[P]. □

Corollary 3.6. If u is a Z-set in a poset P and $\hat{u}$ is the ideal generated by u. Then $\hat{u} = \bigsqcup (u\iota)$ in I[P]. □

Under the assumption that Z is unionized we characterize the compact elements of I[P].

Proposition 3.7. Z is unionized iff Core[I[P]] = C[P].

Proof: We first show that the principal ideals are compact. Assume S is a Z-set in I[P] and $p\iota \subseteq \bigsqcup S$, for $p \in P$. Since Z is unionized, $p\iota \subseteq \cup S$ so that p is in some $s \in S$ which gives us $p\iota \subseteq s$ by transitivity and the fact that both $p\iota$ and s are ideals. So $p\iota \subseteq \bigsqcup S$ implies $p\iota \subseteq s$ for some $s \in S$, i.e., the principal ideals are compact. We need to know that every compact element of I[P] is principal. Let u be a Z-set in P and $\hat{u} \in I[P]$ its ideal which we assume to be compact. From Corollary 3.6 we have $\hat{u} \subseteq \bigsqcup (u\iota)$ and compactness says $\hat{u} \subseteq p\iota$ for some $p \in u$. But we also have $p\iota \subseteq \hat{u}$ so $\hat{u} = p\iota$ and $\hat{u}$ is the principal ideal generated by p.

For the converse assume Core[I[P]] = C[P] and that $\bigsqcup S$ exists for a Z-set S in I[P]. If $p \in$

$\bigsqcup S$ then $p\iota \sqsubseteq \bigsqcup S$ which gives us $p\iota \sqsubseteq s$ for some $s \in S$ since $p\iota$ is compact. Therefore $p\iota \sqsubseteq US$ and trivially $p \in US$. Thus we have $\bigsqcup S \sqsubseteq US$. Conversely $p \in US$ means $p \in s \in S$ and $s \sqsubseteq \bigsqcup S$ so $p \in \bigsqcup S$. This gives $US \sqsubseteq \bigsqcup S$ and we have $\bigsqcup S = US$ as required. □

Theorem 3.8. If Z is unionized then for each poset P, I[P] is Z-inductive and Z-core complete.

Proof: From Proposition 3.7, we know the compact members of I[P] are the principal ideals. But each element of I[P] is the ideal $\hat{u}$ generated by some u in Z[P] and $\hat{u} = \bigsqcup(u\iota)$ by Corollary 3.6. Thus I[P] is Z-inductive. Let S be a Z-set of principal ideals and $u \subseteq P$ the set of generators of those ideals. u is also a Z-set since ι^{-1}:C[P] → P is monotonic. Thus the ideal $\hat{u}$ generated by u is in I[P]; with Corollary 3.6 again, $\hat{u} = \bigsqcup(u\iota) = \bigsqcup S$. Thus I[P] is Z-core complete. □

We know (Proposition 3.7) Core[P] ≅ Core[I[Core[P]]]. If Z is unionized then I[P] is both Z-inductive and Z-core complete; if P is also Z-inductive and Z-core complete then that isomorphism extends to P ≅ I[Core[P]] by Corollary 2.9.

Corollary 3.9. If Z is unionized and P is Z-inductive and Z-core complete then P ≅ I[Core[P]]. □

Theorem 3.10. If Z is union-complete then for each poset P, I[P] is Z-inductive and Z-complete.

Proof. If Z is union-complete then it is unionized and thus I[P] is Z-inductive (Theorem 3.8). But Z being union-complete means $US \in$ I[P] for every $S \in$ Z[I[P]] and US is $\bigsqcup S$ by Fact 3.5. □

We promised to return to finish explaining the relationship between Z-inductive, Z-complete posets and posets with extension bases. The following lemma will be helpful.

Lemma 3.11. If P and Q are posets and h:P → Q is a Z-continuous isomorphism then for all $p \in P$, p is Z-compact in P iff ph is Z-compact in Q.

Proof. Let g:Q → P be the (Z-continuous) inverse of h. Assume p is Z-compact and $ph \sqsubseteq \bigsqcup D$ for some Z-set in Q. Then $p = phg \sqsubseteq \bigsqcup(Dg)$ by continuity of g. Since p is Z-compact in P, $p \sqsubseteq dg$ for some $d \in D$, and when we apply h we have $ph \sqsubseteq dgh = d$ as needed. So ph is Z-compact. The converse works the same way. □

Now we can state the converse to Corollary 2.11.

Proposition 3.12. Assume Z is union-complete. If B is an Z-extension basis for a Z-complete poset P then P is Z-inductive and B = Core[P].

Proof:† Let $h:P \to I[B]$ be the unique extension of $\iota:B \to I[B]$ ($b\iota$ = principal ideal generated by b) given to us by the definition of Z-extension basis. Let $g:I[B] \to P$ be the unique extension of $\iota^{-1}:C[B] \to B$ (taking a principal ideal to its generator) given to us by Theorem 3.10. Now $hg:P \to P$ is Z-continuous and extends the inclusion map $B \subseteq P$ and by uniqueness for extension bases must be 1_P, while $gh:I[P] \to I[P]$ must be $1_{I[P]}$ by uniqueness in Theorem 3.10. Since h is a Z-continuous isomorphism and I[P] is Z-inductive it follows that P is Z-inductive. Proposition 3.7 together with Lemma 2.11 give us Core[P] = B. □

4. Z-inductive Closure as an Adjunction

In this section we combine and restate the results of the preceeding sections to show how, in four different contexts, the construction of the Z-inductive closure I[P] of a poset P corresponds to an adjoint functor. If we accept "Doctrine 4" of ADJ(1973) then these results show that inductive closure is (in these contexts) a "natural construction". More significantly, it is these results, especially Theorem 4.4, which are the key to our above mentioned application to recursion equations with higher order variables.

For review now, **Po** is the category of all posets with monotonic maps between them. $\mathbf{Po}_{Z\text{-core}}$ is the subcategory of **Po** with objects which are Z-core complete and morphisms which are Z-continuous and preserve Z-compactness. $\mathbf{Po}_{Z\text{-ind}}$ is the subcategoy of **Po** with the Z-inductive posets as objects and with morphisms which again are Z-continuous and preserve compactness. We will prove there is an equivalence between **Po** and the intersection of these two ($\mathbf{Po}_{Z\text{-core}} \cap \mathbf{Po}_{Z\text{-ind}}$). Finally, using the notation of Section 1, **Po** [Z] is the category of Z-complete posets with Z-continuous monotonic morphisms.

The construction "I", which yields the poset of ideals from a poset P actually gives rise to several functions (and functors) depending on its target; for example there is the target restriction of $I:\mathbf{Po} \to \mathbf{Po}$ to $I':\mathbf{Po} \to \mathbf{Po}_{Z\text{-core}}$ when Z is unionized. But we are not going to burden the reader with additional notation for these rather trivial modifications and instead consistently refer to the source and target of the functions or functors involved. Thus $I:\mathbf{Po} \to \mathbf{Po}\,[Z]$ is the target restriction of the construction (defined when Z is union-complete (Theorem 3.9)) and using the same convention, $\mathrm{Core}:\mathbf{Po}_{Z\text{-core}} \to \mathbf{Po}$ is the source restriction of $\mathrm{Core}:\mathbf{Po} \to \mathbf{Po}$, the latter being the functor that picks out the poset of compact elements from any poset.

There are many equivalent formulations of "adjunction" or "adjoint situation" (c.f. Mac Lane(1972), page 81, Theorem 2). We use the following definition (and its dual) for our presentation.‡

Let **A** and **X** be categories, U a functor from **A** to **X**, |F| an object, map, $|F|:|\mathbf{X}| \to |\mathbf{A}|$, and $\langle \eta_X\ X \to X|F|U \rangle$ a family of morphisms in **X** induced by objects in $|\mathbf{X}|$. Then we say U is a

† This is essentially the same as the proof in Markowsky and Rosen(1976) (where $Z = \ell$) that the basis must coincide with the core.

‡ We use this form because we believe it is likely to be most familiar to the reader; for example U is the underlying set functor from monoids to sets, $X|F|$ gives the free monoid generated by a set X and $\eta_x:X \to X|F|U$ is the injection of X into the underlying set of the free monoid generated by X. The universal condition given below says that any mapping of the generators to the underlying set of a monoid M extends uniquely to a monoid homomorphism from $X|F|$ to M .

right adjoint functor with respect to $<|F|, \eta>$ whenever the following universal condition is satisfied.‡

(*) For every object A of **A** and morphism $h:X \to AU$ of **X** there exists a unique morphism $h^{\#}:X|F| \to A$ such that

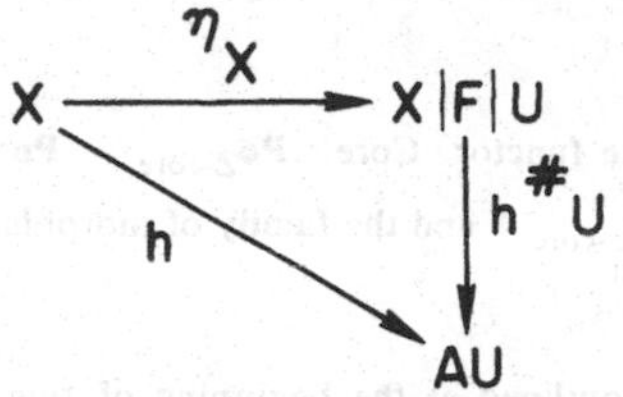

commutes, i.e., $\eta_x (h^{\#}U) = h$.

The data $<U,|F|,\eta>$ determine a functor F (with object part $|F|$) which is (left-) adjoint to U: let $g:X \to X'$ be a morphism in **X**. Then $g\eta_{X'}:X \to X'|F|U$ and $gF = (g\eta_X)^{\#}:X|F| \to X'|F|$. Now η is a natural transformation from 1_X to FU and is the unit of the adjunction.

The dual formulation is as follows: let **A** and **X** be categories, $F:X \to A$, $|U|:|A| \to |X|$ and $\varepsilon_A:A|U|F \to A$, a family of morphisms in **A**. Then F is a left adjoint functor with respect to $<|U|, \varepsilon>$ whenever the following universal condition holds.

(**) For every object X of **X** and morphism $g:XF \to A$ of **A** there exists a unique morphism $g^{\#}:X \to A|U|$ such that

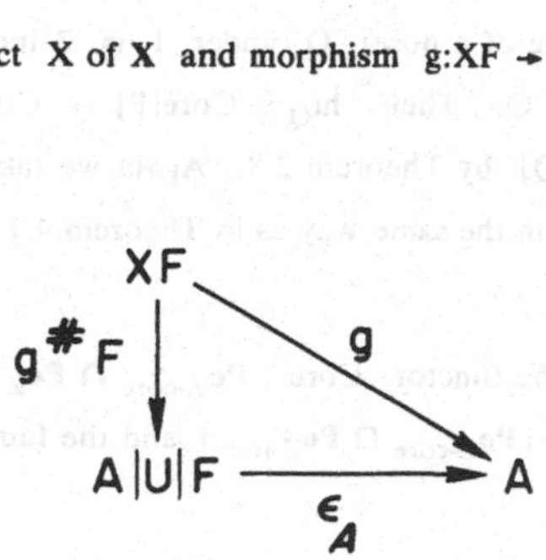

commutes.†.

The extension of $|U|$ to a functor is given for $h:A \to A'$ by $hU = (\varepsilon_A h^{\#}:A|F| \to A'|F|)$. F is adjoint to U and $\varepsilon:UF \to 1_A$ is the counit of the adjunction.

An equivalence between categories is usually defined "existentially," i.e., a functor $S:A \to C$ for which there exists a functor $T:C \to A$ and natural isomorphisms $TS \cong 1_C$ and $ST \cong 1_A$ (see Mac Lane(1971),

‡ The proof that this determines an adjunction is obtained from the proof of part (ii), Theorem 2, page 81 of Mac Lane(1971). "Each η is a universal arrow from x to U" in Mac Lane's terminology.

† The paraphrase of this universal condition in the context of free monoids is that any homomorphism defined on the free monoid is uniquely determined by its (set-) restriction to the generators.

page 91). We believe the situation is clearer if we use the same format as that for adjunctions.

Let **A** and **C** be categories, S a functor from **A** to **C**, |T| an object map, $|T|:|C| \to |A|$, and $<\eta_C:C \to C|T|S>$ a family of morphisms in C indexed by |C|. Then we say S is an equivalence with respect to $<|T|, \eta>$ iff S is full and faithful and each η_C is an isomorphism.†

Theorem 4.1. When Z is unionized, the functor Core : $\mathbf{Po}_{Z\text{-core}} \to \mathbf{Po}$ is a right adjoint functor with respect to the object map I: | **Po** | → | $\mathbf{Po}_{Z\text{-core}}$ | and the family of morphisms η_p: P → Core[I[P]].

Proof: Following the scheme of things outlined at the beginning of this section, let P be a Z-core complete poset, Q on arbitrary poset, and h:P → Core[Q]. Under the hypothesis that Z is unionized, I[P] is Z-inductive, Z-core complete and Core[I[P]] = C[P] (Proposition 3.7 and Theorem 3.8). Thus h determines the monotonic map $\iota^{-1}h$:Core[I[P]] → Core[Q] which has, by Theorem 2.8, a unique monotonic Z-continuous extension $\overline{\iota^{-1}h}$:I[P] → Q. This is the required $h^{\#}$ since ι Core[$h^{\#}$] = ι (Core[I[P]] ↿ $\overline{\iota^{-1}h}$ ↾ Core[Q]) = $\iota\,\iota^{-1}h$ = h and if ι (Core[I[P]] |g| Core[Q]) = h then multiplying by ι^{-1} tells us that g is a monotonic Z-continuous extension of $\iota^{-1}h$. The uniqueness part of Theorem 2.8 gives g = $\overline{\iota^{-1}h}$. □

Theorem 4.2. When Z is unionized the functor Core : $\mathbf{Po}_{Z\text{-ind}} \to \mathbf{Po}$ is a left adjoint functor with respect to the object map I: | **Po** | → | $\mathbf{Po}_{Z\text{-ind}}$ | and the Family of morphisms ι_p^{-1}: Core[I[P]] → P.

Proof: Again, since Z is unionized, the image of a poset Q under I is Z-inductive. Now let P be Z-inductive, Q arbitrary, and h : Core[P] → Q. Then $h\iota_Q$: Core[P] → Core[I[Q]] has a unique monotonic Z-continuous extension $\overline{h\iota_Q}$: P → I[Q] by Theorem 2.8. Again we take $h^{\#}$: P → I[Q] to be $h\iota_Q$ and Core[$h^{\#}$] ι_Q^{-1} = h. Uniqueness follows in the same way as in Theorem 4.1. □

Proposition 4.3. Assume Z is unionized. The functor Core : $\mathbf{Po}_{Z\text{-core}} \cap \mathbf{Po}_{Z\text{-ind}} \to \mathbf{Po}$ is an equivalence with respect to the object map I : |**Po**| → |$\mathbf{Po}_{Z\text{-core}} \cap \mathbf{Po}_{Z\text{-ind}}$ | and the family of morphisms ι_p : P → Core[I[P]].

Proof: The extension theorem (2.8) tells us that Core is full and faithful because for every g: Core[P] → Core[P'] there exists (full) a unique (faithful) monotonic Z-continuous extension $\bar{g}$: P → P'; but extension just means Core[$\bar{g}$] = g. We already know that the injections ι_p : P → Core[I[P]] are isomorphisms so we have an equivalence. □

Theorem 4.4. When Z is union-complete, the inclusion functor from **Po**[Z] to **Po** is a right adjoint functor with respect to the object map I : |**Po**| → |**Po**[Z]|, and the family of morphisms ι_p: P → I[P].

Proof: Theorem 3.10 says that when Z is union-complete, I[P] is Z-complete, so the object map is well-defined. Now let Q be Z-complete, P arbitrary and h: P → Q in **Po**; we need a unique Z-

† That this captures the notion of equivalence is essentially Mac Lane's Theorem 1, page 91.

continuous $h^{\#}$: I[P] → Q such that $\iota_p h^{\#} = h$. The monotonic map $\iota_p^{-1}h$: Core[I[P]] → Q has a unique monotonic Z-continuous extension $\overline{\iota_p^{-1}h}$: I[P] → Q by Theorem 2.10 since Q is Z-complete and I[P] is Z-inductive. Indeed we again take $h^{\#}$ to be $\overline{\iota_p^{-1}h}$ and $\iota_p h^{\#} = h$ as required; uniqueness of $h^{\#}$ rests, as before, on uniqueness of it extending $\iota_p^{-1}h$. □

Each of the adjunctions (Theorems 4.1, 4.2 and 4.4) and the equivalence (Theorem 4.3) involve the inductive closure construction I only as an object map. Now we want to look at it as a functor. As we indicated at the beginning of this section, each adjunction determines the extension of I to morphisms (to a functor) but we first describe it directly as a functor (which we expect any construction to be, "Doctrine 2," ADJ(1973)) from **Po** to **Po** and check that, under the conditions for the adjunctions, I : **Po** → **Po** agrees on morphisms with the target restriction determined in each case.

Let P and Q be posets and f: P → Q monotonic. Then I[f] : I[P] → I[Q] sends $\hat{S} \in$ I[P] to $(Sf)^\wedge \in$ I[Q], where S is a Z-set in P and $\hat{S}$ its ideal. We know that if $\hat{S} = \hat{S}'$ then $S \sim S'$ (Proposition 3.4) and $S \sim S'$ gives $Sf \sim S'f$ (Lemma 2.3(c)), so $(Sf)^\wedge = (S'f)^\wedge$ by Proposition 3.4 again. Thus I[f] is well defined. Functorality of I is immediate with this definition: $(\hat{S})$ I[f] I[g] = $(Sf)^\wedge$ I[g] = $(Sfg)^\wedge = \hat{S}$ I[fg].

Now we compare this functor I with the one determined by the first adjunction (Theorem 4.1, I : **Po** → $\mathbf{Po}_{Z\text{-core}}$ adjoint to Core). There I must be defined on morphisms to be $(f\iota_Q)^{\#}$ for f: P → Q in **Po**. But from the proof of Theorem 4.1 $(f\iota_Q)^{\#} = \overline{\iota_p^{-1}f\iota_Q}$ which is the unique extension of $\iota_p^{-1} f \iota_Q$ to a monotonic Z-continuous function form I[P] to I[Q] guaranteed by Theorem 2.8. Now our I[f] extends the composite

$$\text{Core [I[P]]} \xrightarrow{\iota_p^{-1}} P \xrightarrow{f} Q \xrightarrow{\iota_p} \text{Core [I[Q]]}$$

because it also sends $\hat{p}$ to $(pf)^\wedge$; unfortunately we can't conclude $\overline{\iota_p^{-1}f\iota_Q}$ = I[f] by uniqueness of extension because I[f] will not in general (without the unionized condition) be Z-continuous. So we have to look at how the extension is actually defined in the proof of Theorem 2.8. Given a Z-set S in P, $\hat{S} = \cup\{\hat{s} \mid s \in S\}$ and all $\hat{s}$ (principal ideals) are in Core [I[P]]; the extension given to us in Theorem 2.8 takes $\hat{S}$ to $\cup(sf)^\wedge = (Sf)^\wedge$ as needed. Thus we know $(f\iota_Q)^{\#}$ = I[f].

For the second adjunction, the extension of the object map takes a morphisims f: P → Q to $(\iota_p^{-1}f)^{\#}$ which is $\overline{\iota_p^{-1}f\iota_p}$ again, and we have just agreed that this gives the same value on morphisms as on I: **Po** → **Po**.

In the same way one can check that, with appropriate target restriction, I is the same as the other functor obtained from the inclusion. (**Po**[Z] ⊆ **Po**) being a right adjoint functor with respect to <I, ι_p>. In this case, since I : **Po** → **Po**[Z] is adjoint to the inclusion, it is a reflector and thus the category of Z-complete posets with Z-continuous morphisms is reflective subcategory of the category of posets.

By a slight change in the definition of I we get a (correspondingly slight) strengthening of the first two adjunctions. In particular if we take I'[P] to be P together with all ideals generated by Z-sets of

cardinality greater than one, then $\iota_P : P \to I'[P]$ is an inclusion and $I: \mathbf{Po} \to \mathbf{Po}_{Z\text{-core}}$ is left-adjoint-left-inverse to Core : $\mathbf{Po}_{Z\text{-core}} \to \mathbf{Po}$ from the first adjunction and $I : \mathbf{Po} \to \mathbf{Po}_{Z\text{-ind}}$ is right-adjoint-left-inverse to Core : $\mathbf{Po}_{Z\text{-ind}} \to \mathbf{Po}$ from the second adjunction (see Mac Lane(1971) page 91).†

We might also try to improve things in the union-complete case, since for each poset P, I[P] is Z-inductive as well as being Z-complete but still we only have that this category of Z-complete, Z-inductive posets with Z-continuous morphisms is a reflective subcategory of Po; we have no inverse for I or equivalence of categories because I is not full (I(f) is always core-preserving).‡ The only further refinement possible takes us to $I : \mathbf{Po} \to \mathbf{Po}[Z] \cap \mathbf{Po}_{Z\text{-ind}}$ (now morphisms on core preserving) but we find nothing new; indeed I is an equivalence, but it is the same one as obtained from Theorem 4.3 because of the following.

<u>Fact 4.5.</u> If Z is union-complete and P is Z-inductive and Z-core complete then P is Z-complete.

<u>Proof:</u> Union-complete implies unionized so Corollary 3.9 says P ≅ I[Core[P]]. But with Z being union-complete I[Core[P]] is Z-complete (Theorem 3.10) and the isomorphism tells us P is also Z-complete. □

Thus under the assumption that Z is union-complete $\mathbf{Po}_{Z\text{-core}} \cap \mathbf{Po}_{Z\text{-ind}}$ and $\mathbf{Po}.\ [Z] \cap \mathbf{Po}_{Z\text{-ind}}$ are the same.

5. Problems and Further Considerations

In Section 3 we left an embarrassing problem: does there exist a subset system Z on Po such that Z is unionized but not union-complete. Since the many examples listed in Section 1 were of no help in this regard we have considered methods of constructing (possibly pathological) subset systems in an effort to bridge this unfortunate gap. For example, take any poset P and let Z[P] be a set of subsets (including some non empty subset) of P closed under monotonic maps from P to P. Now for any poset Q, let Z[Q] be all sets which are obtained as images of sets in Z[P] under monotonic maps $f : P \to Q$. The result is a subset system because if $S \in Z[Q]$ and $f : Q \to Q'$, then Sf is in Z[Q'] because S was obtained as S'h for some $h : P \to Q$ and $S' \in Z[P]$, and Sf = S'hf which is in Z[Q'] by construction.

† **Note that I' would have to be carefully defined as a disjoint union with P, e.g., $P \cup \{<P,\hat{S}> \mid S \text{ is a Z-set in } P \text{ of cardinality greater than one}\}$, and then the ordering is further complicated by this bothersome technicality.**

‡ **This category, with Z-complete, Z-inductive posets and Z-continuous, monotonic morphisms (for which we haven't introduced notation) should probably be called the category of Z-algebraic posets if it weren't for our aversion to the use of "algebraic" in this context (see the second footnote in the introduction). The closest thing to the category of Z-algebraic posets that we look at in detail here is $\mathbf{Po}_{Z\text{-ind}} \cap \mathbf{Po}[Z]$, but note that morphisms here, besides being Z-continuous, also preserve compactness which is a condition we have not seen in the literature.**

Another method is to have an arbitrary function Z' assigning subsets $Z'[P]$ to each P (some $Z'[P]$ having a non-empty set) and then define $Z[P]$ to be the images Sf for all posets Q, monotonic maps $f : Q \to P$ and sets $S \in Z[Q]$. The resulting Z is a subset system.

Neither construction, however, has led us to a subset system which is unionized and not union-complete.

We have considered other conditions on subset systems which seem interesting but for which we have found no application. The following two seem particularly intriguing.

(A) A subset system is <u>strong union complete</u> iff each $Z[P]$ is Z-complete. Most of our examples are strong union complete but now, besides including the finite cardinals, which are not even unionized, the ordinals are not strong union complete. For example it is possible to construct an ω-chain of ω-chains in the rationals whose union is all of the rationals and thus is not an ω-chain.

(B) A subset system is <u>downward consistent</u> iff for each poset P and subposet $P' \subseteq P$ if $S \in Z[P]$ and $S \subseteq P'$ then $S \in Z[P']$. Many of the standard subset systems are downward consistent (e.g., ω, wo, ℓ, Δ, $\bigsqcup$, $\sqcup$) but those requiring bounds outside S are not: C, PC and $\dot{\bigsqcup}$ are not downward consistent.

Our focus in this paper has been entirely on the order-theoretic aspects of inductive posets and inductive closure. As indicated in the beginning our motivation is to carry these ideas over to algebras and algebraic theories. In investigating the problems there, we have found (not surprisingly) that additional conditions are needed on a subset system Z in order for the construction to carry over to the algebraic framework. Previewing that work, and adding a couple of conditions on subset systems that we know are applicable, we say Z is <u>crossed-up</u> if for all posets P_1 and P_2 and Z-sets $S_i \in Z[P_i]$, there exists $S \in Z[P_1 \times P_2]$, such that S and $S_1 \times S_2$ an mutually cofinal. Z is <u>crossed-down</u> if for each $S \in Z[P_1 \times P_2]$, S and $S\pi_1 \times S\pi_2$ are mutually cofinal where $S\pi_i$ is the projection of S in P_i.

The source category for the completion construction is **Po** where the morphisms are only monotonic, in particular the injection $\iota_p : P \to I[P]$ is monotonic but need not be Z-continuous, even for nice Z. All the questions of this paper can be asked again when the source category has Z'-continuous (possibly a $Z' \neq Z$) morphisms; then the Z-completion construction would be required to preserve those least upper bounds of Z'-sets that exist in the source. Indicative of this process, Birkhoff(1967, p. 126) gives a construction which takes a poset to a complete lattice while preserving both upper and lower bounds of finite sets.

A subset system Z will be called <u>topological</u> iff for every $D \in Z[P]$ and $A \subseteq D$ either $D \cap A \in Z[P]$ and $D \cap A \sim D$ or $D \cap (P-A) \in Z[P]$ and $D \cap (P-A) \sim D$. It is the fact that Δ is topological that permits the definition of a topology on a complete lattice as in Scott(1972). The Δ-compact elements in a complete lattice are sometimes (for topological reasons) called "isolated." As Scott(1972) points out, the isolated points "might well be called <u>finite</u>" although this is a "very generalized notion of finite and is only an analogy." (This is something we have alluded to above.) The important point here is the idea of compactness which is key to this paper, has a relativized version which Scott(1972) calls "relatively finite" and the generalization for subset systems is immediate: in a poset P, an element x is said to be relatively Z-compact with respect to $y \in P$ (in symbols $x \prec y$), iff whenever $S \in Z[P]$ and $y \sqsubseteq \bigsqcup S$ then $x \sqsubseteq z$ for some $z \in S$. Then Scott's continuous lattices (1971,1972) have a generalized counterpart in the notion of a

Z-complete poset P in which every element y is the least upper bound of the elements relatively Z-compact to it; $y = \bigsqcup \{x \mid x \prec y\}$. It may be only a curiosity, but we think it would be interesting to investigate this generalized concept: It might lead to a better understanding of the role of "continuity" as used in "continuous lattice."

As a final problem area, we feel that it is important to clearly delineate the conditions under which passage to function spaces preserves completeness, compactness, inductiveness, and the like. We hope that the concept of subset system will facilitate this investigation.

Bibliography

ADJ (Authors: J. A. Goguen, J. W. Thatcher, E. G. Wagner, and J. B. Wright)

(1973) (JAG, JWT, EGW, JBW) "A junction between computer science and category theory: I, Basic definitions and examples," Part 1, IBM Research Report RC 5426, September 1973.

(1975) (JAG, JWT, EGW, JBW) "Initial algebra semantics and continuous algebras," IBM Research Report RC 5701, November 3, 1975. JACM 24 (1977) 68-95.

(1976) (JAG, JWT, EGW, JBW) "A junction between computer science and category theory: I, Basic definitions and examples," Part 2, IBM Research Report RC 5908, March, 1976.

Birkhoff, G.

(1967) Lattice Theory, Amer. Math. Soc. Colloy. Pub. 25, New York (1948). Revised edition (1967).

Bloom, Stephen L.

(1976) "Varieties of ordered algebras," J. Comp. Sys. Sci. 13 (1976) 200-212.

Courcelle, Bruno and Nivat, Maurice

(1976) "Algebraic families of interpretations," Proceedings 17th Annual IEEE Symposium on Foundations of Computing, Houston, Texas, October, 1976, pp. 137-146.

Egli, H. and Constable, R. L.

(1976) "Computability concepts for programming language semantics," Theoretical Computer Science 2 (1976) 133-145.

Mac Lane, S.

(1971) Category Theory for the Working Mathematician, Springer-Verlag, New York (1971).

Markowsky, George

(1974) "Categories of chain-complete posets," IBM Research Report RC 5100, October, 1974.

Markowsky, G. and Rosen, B. K.

(1976) "Bases for chain complete posets," IBM J. Res. Dev. 20 (1976) 138-147.

Scott, D.

(1970) "Outline of a mathematical theory of computation," Proceedings, 4th Ann. Princeton Conference on Information Sciences and Systems (1970) 169-176.

(1971) "Continuous lattices," Oxford University Computing Laboratory Technical Monograph PRG 7. Also, Lecture Notes in Mathematics 274, Springer-Verlag, Berlin (1971) 97-136.

(1972) "Data types as lattices", Unpublished notes, Amsterdam (1972).

Tiuryn, Jerzy

(1976) "Regular Algebras", (Extended Abstract). Manuscript, Warsaw University (1976).

GENERALIZED PROBABILISTIC GRAMMARS

V.N.Agafonov
Institute of Mathematics, Novosibirsk 90, USSR

1. Motivation.

Three different notions of a probabilistic context-free grammar are known in the literature. The most popular and early definition (see [3] - [6]) has a natural probabilistic interpretation but only very specific nonprobabilistic grammars can be obtained from probabilistic grammars defined in such a way if all probabilities included in the definition are equal to 1. Our main goal is to formulate a generalization of this notion which meets the following requirements:

(1) it is a generalization of conventional context-free grammars in the same sense as probabilistic automaton is a generalization of deterministic automaton;

(2) it may be probabilistically interpreted, i.e. it specifies one or several stochastic processes.

Moreover, we want our notion to allow new natural probabilistic interpretations (for example, a random choice of syntactical constructions).

The first attempt to give appropriate formulation was made by the author in [1]. All the previously known definitions are not satisfactory from our point of view. The notion introduced by Salomaa [7] does not satisfy both (1) and (2). The notion introduced by Santos [8] satisfies (1) but in general Santos grammar is not really probabilistic (and so (2) fails). It is a kind of weighted grammar with weights from the segment [0,1] (like Salomaa grammars). "A random language" is defined by Santos as an arbitrary function f from strings to [0,1]. It is clear that some additional assumptions about f are to be made for f really to be random.

In [4] and [8] an equivalence between probabilistic automata and probabilistic grammars of some types was stated. But we feel that these results are not relevant since in them grammars corresponding to probabilistic automata are not in fact probabilistic. The point is that a probabilistic automaton specifies a family of random processes (one process for each input string), whereas grammars just mentioned do not take this into account. Given a probabilistic pushdown automaton we shall construct the generalized probabilistic grammar G and the family of "strategies" F (strategies $f \in F$ are in one-to-one correspondence with input strings) such that the pair (G,f) specifies a random process which corresponds to random process generated in the automaton by the input string corresponding to f.

2. Definitions and examples.

A generalized probabilistic (GP) grammar is a pair $G = (G', P)$, where

(1) $G' = (N, \Sigma, R, S)$ is a context-free (CF) grammar (we use the notations from [2], but the set of production rules is denoted by R);

(2) $P = \{P_A \mid A \in N\}$ is a family of probability distributions such that the domain of P_A is a partition $\Pi_A = \{\Pi_A^1, \dots, \Pi_A^{I(A)}\}$ of the set of A-productions $A \to \alpha_1 | \alpha_2 | \dots | \alpha_{n(A)}$ and the range of P_A is the segment $(0,1]$ (so $\sum_{1 \le i \le I(A)} P_A(\Pi_A^i) = 1$).

A GP grammar G is canonical if for every $A \in N$ either $I(A) = 1$ or each Π_A^i consists of one production. In the latter case the nonterminal A is called probabilistic and the set of probabilistic nonterminals is denoted by N_P ($N_P \subseteq N$). If $N = N_P$ in a canonical grammar G, then it is strict probabilistic (in this case G is the grammar of the first type mentioned in section 1).

To describe how GP grammars work we begin with canonical grammars and then extend our approach to noncanonical ones. First, some preliminary definitions and notations are necessary. Let δ be a derivation tree in a CF grammar G'. The leader of δ is the leftmost nonterminal node of the frontier of δ (if it exists). If the leader of δ is substituted by a tree τ we denote the resulting tree by $\delta(\tau)$. If the frontier of δ is the string $\varphi_0 X_1 \varphi_1 X_2 \dots \varphi_{n-1} X_n \varphi_n$, where $X_i \in N_P$ and $\varphi_i \in (\Sigma \cup (N - N_P))^*$, then the string $\rho = X_1 X_2 \dots X_n$ is called the characteristic of δ .

A derivation tree δ with the root labelled by nonprobabilistic nonterminal is called completed if its frontier contains only terminals and probabilistic nonterminals and all intermediate nodes are labelled only by nonprobabilistic nonterminals.

A canonical grammar G is <u>single-processed</u> if for each $A \in N - N_P$ all completed trees with the root A have the same characteristic.

A single-processed grammar G specifies a single random process. Each step of this process transforms a class Δ of derivation trees with the same characteristic ρ into another class Δ'. There are steps of two types: probabilistic and nonprobabilistic.

On <u>a probabilistic step</u> each tree $\delta \in \Delta$ has the same probabilistic leader A. If τ is the tree corresponding to a production r = $A \rightarrow \alpha$, then we say that Δ is transformed into $\Delta' = \{\delta(\tau) \mid \delta \in \Delta\}$ with probability $P_A(r)$ by means of the production r and we write $\Delta \models_r \Delta'$.

On <u>a nonprobabilistic step</u> each tree $\delta \in \Delta$ has the same nonprobabilistic leader A. We say that Δ is transformed into $\Delta' = \{\delta(\tau) \mid \delta \in \Delta$ and r is a completed tree with the root A$\}$ with probability 1 (i.e. deterministically) and we write $\Delta \models_d \Delta'$.

If $\Delta = \Delta_0 \models_{x_1} \Delta_1 \models_{x_2} \dots \models_{x_n} \Delta_n = \Delta'$, where each x_i is either a production or d, then the sequence $t = x_1 x_2 \dots x_n$ is called <u>the trajectory</u> from Δ to Δ', we write $\Delta \overset{+}{\models}_t \Delta'$, and the number p(t) = $p(x_1)p(x_2)\dots p(x_n)$, where $p(d) = 1$ and $p(A \rightarrow \alpha) = P_A(A \rightarrow \alpha)$, is the probability of the trajectory t.

Further we define $L(\Delta) = \{\varphi \in (N \cup \Sigma)^* \mid \varphi$ is the frontier of $\delta \in \Delta\}$ and $T(\Delta) = \{t \mid S \overset{+}{\models}_t \Delta\}$.

Finally a single-processed grammar G = (G',P) specifies <u>a generalized language</u> $\mathcal{L}(G) = (\mathcal{L}, p)$, where

$$\mathcal{L} = \{L \subseteq \Sigma^* \mid L = L(\Delta) \text{ for some } \Delta \text{ and } t \text{ such that } \{S\} \overset{+}{\models}_t \Delta\}$$

and p is a measure defined on $\mathcal{L}$ by

$$p(L) = \sum_{L = L(\Delta)} \; \sum_{t \in T(\Delta)} p(t)$$

Note that $\sum_{L \in \mathcal{L}} p(L) \leq 1$. If $\sum_{L \in \mathcal{L}} p(L) = 1$, then G is called <u>proper</u>.

<u>Example 1.</u> Let us consider the single-processed grammar $G_o = (G_o', P_o)$ which specifies statements of a simple programming language together with probabilities of types of the statements. The GP grammar G_o is not strict probabilistic and may be intuitively interpreted as a model of a random choice of syntactic constructions (or categories). The CF grammar G_o' consists of productions

$$\langle st\rangle \to \langle \text{assignment st}\rangle \mid \langle \text{if st}\rangle \mid \langle \text{while st}\rangle$$

numbered by 1,2,3 and subgrammars G_1', G_2', and G_3' which define statements of the first, second and third type respectively. Let $\Pi_{\langle st\rangle} = \{\{1\}, \{2\}, \{3\}\}$, $P_{\langle st\rangle}(1) = 1/2$, $P_{\langle st\rangle}(2) = 1/3$, $P_{\langle st\rangle}(3) = 1/6$ and for each other nonterminal A the set of all A-productions constitutes a single class Π_A^1 of the partition Π_A. Then $\mathcal{L}(G_o) = (\mathcal{L}_o, P_o)$, where $\mathcal{L}_o = \{L(G_1), L(G_1), L(G_3)\}$ and $p_oL(G_1) = 1/2$, $p_oL(G_2) = 1/3$, $p_oL(G_3) = 1/6$.

<u>Example 2.</u> The GP grammar $G_1 = (G_1', P_1)$ defines arithmetical expressions with the probability distribution which does not distinguish + from −, and * from /. To make the definition visual we indicate the classes of the partitions by underlines and write below them the corresponding probabilities:

$$E \to \underset{0.313}{\underline{A}} \mid \underset{0.687}{\underline{T}} \qquad A \to \underset{1}{\underline{E+T \mid E-T}} \qquad T \to \underset{0.187}{\underline{M}} \mid \underset{0.813}{\underline{F}}$$

$$M \to \underset{1}{\underline{T*F \mid T/F}} \qquad F \to \underset{0.072}{\underline{(E)}} \mid \underset{0.928}{\underline{a}}$$

Obviously, $L = \{a+a,\ a-a\} \in \mathcal{L}_1$ and $pL = 0.313 \cdot 0.813 \cdot 0.928$.

Let us proceed to a canonical grammar G which is not single-processed. Since there is $A \in N - N_P$ and completed trees δ and δ' with the root A and different characteristics ρ and ρ' we can not perform non-probabilistic step as before. In the new situation we must choose a characteristic and so the class of completed trees with this characteristic. For this purpose we introduce a notion of a strategy.

<u>The core</u> of a derivation tree δ is the sequence of productions corresponding to the path in δ from the root to the leader. <u>A strategy</u> f is a function from the set R^+ of all positive cores to the set N_P^* of all possible characteristics.

Given a strategy f a nonsingle-processed grammar G specifies a random process corresponding to f and thus generalized language $\mathcal{L}(G,f) = (\mathcal{L}_f, p_f)$ in the following manner. Probabilistic steps and the relation $\Delta \models_r \Delta'$ are defined as before. On a nonprobabilistic step Δ' is undefined if there are δ_1 and δ_2 in Δ such that $f(\delta_1) \neq f(\delta_2)$. Otherwise, if ρ is the core of $\delta \in \Delta$, then $\Delta' = \{\delta(\tau) \mid \delta \in \Delta$ and τ is a completed tree with the root A and the characteristic $f(\rho)$ and we write $\Delta \models_f \Delta'$ instead of $\Delta \models_d \Delta'$. The rest is the same as before except we write $p(f) = 1$ instead of $p(d) = 1$.

If a set F of strategies is given then G specifies the family $\mathcal{L}(G,F) = \{(\mathcal{L}_f, p_f) \mid f \in F\}$.

Example 3. Let $M = (\{q_0, q_1\}, \{a,b\}, \{P_M(a), P_M(b)\}, q_0, \{q_1\})$ be the probabilistic finite automaton, where $\{a,b\}$ is the input alphabet, q_1 is the final state,

$$P_M(a) = \begin{pmatrix} 0.1 & 0.9 \\ 0.3 & 0.7 \end{pmatrix}, \quad P_M(b) = \begin{pmatrix} 0.2 & 0.8 \\ 0 & 1 \end{pmatrix}$$

are the matrices of transition probabilities. Let $p_M(\varphi)$ be the probability of transition from q_0 to q_1 for the input string φ. Then we construct the GP grammar G_M and the family of strategies $F_M = \{f_\varphi \mid \varphi \in \{a,b\}^*\}$ which define the family $\{(\mathcal{L}_{f_\varphi}, p_{f_\varphi}) \mid f_\varphi \in F_M\}$ such that $\mathcal{L}_{f_\varphi} = \{\{\varphi\}\}$ and $p_{f_\varphi}(\varphi) = p_M(\varphi)$. The grammar G_M with the family F_M naturally corresponds to the automaton M and may be considered equivalent to M.

G_M is defined as follows:

$$q_0 \to \frac{q_0^a \mid q_0^b}{1} \qquad q_1 \to \frac{q_1^a \mid q_1^b \mid \varepsilon}{1}$$

$$q_0^a \to \frac{aq_0 \mid aq_1}{0.1 \quad 0.9} \qquad q_1^a \to \frac{aq_0 \mid aq_1}{0.3 \quad 0.7}$$

$$q_0^b \to \frac{bq_0 \mid bq_1}{0.2 \quad 0.8} \qquad q_1^b \to \frac{bq_1}{1}$$

For an input string $c_1 \ldots c_n$ (each $c_i \in \{a,b\}$) we define the corresponding strategy $f_{c_1 \dots c_n}$ as follows. Let $r_1 \dots r_k$ be the core of a derivation tree δ such that the part of the frontier from the leftmost symbol up to the leader forms the string $c_1 \dots c_n q_i$. Then

$$f_{c_1 \dots c_n}(r_1 \dots r_k) = \begin{cases} q_i^{c_{l+1}}, & \text{if } l < n \\ \varepsilon, & \text{if } l = n \text{ and } i = 1 \\ \text{undefined otherwise.} & \end{cases}$$

If $r_1 \dots r_k$ does not satisfy the above conditions then $f_{c_1 \dots c_n}(r_1 \dots r_k)$ is undefined.

If a GP grammar G is noncanonical, we transform it into <u>the corresponding canonical grammar</u> G^c and suppose $\mathcal{L}(G) = \mathcal{L}(G^c)$. If there is $\Pi_A^i = A \rightarrow \alpha_{j_1} | \dots | \alpha_{j_k}$ with $k > 1$ and $P_A(\Pi_A^i) < 1$ then instead of $A \rightarrow \alpha_1 | \dots | \alpha_{n(A)}$ we include in G^c the new nonterminals $X_1, \dots, X_{I(A)}$ and the new productions $A \rightarrow X_1 | \dots | X_{I(A)}$ and $X_i \rightarrow \alpha_{j_1} | \dots | \alpha_{j_k}$ for each $1 \leq i \leq I(A)$. Further, $P_A^c(A \rightarrow X_i) = P_A(\Pi_A^i)$ and $P_{X_i}^c(X_i \rightarrow \alpha_{j_1} | \dots | \alpha_{j_k}) = 1$.

3. <u>Observations.</u>

First we observe that the notion of GP grammar satisfies the requirements (1) and (2) from section 1. The random process corresponding to a GP grammar $G = (G', P)$ was described in the definition and if all probabilities in P are equal to 1 then $\mathcal{L}(G) = (\mathcal{L}, p)$, where $\mathcal{L} = \{L(G)\}$ and $pL(G) = 1$, that is the corresponding process gives $L(G)$ deterministically.

Let us consider the connection between GP grammars and probabilistic pushdown automata defined in the natural manner (like in [4]).

<u>Theorem 1.</u> If M is a probabilistic pushdown automaton which defines the function P_M such that $P_M(\varphi)$ is the probability of the event "M accepts the input string φ" then a GP grammar G

and a family of strategies $F = \{f_\varphi \mid \varphi$ is an input string$\}$ can be constructed such that $\mathcal{L}(G) = \{(\mathcal{L}_{f_\varphi}, p_{f_\varphi}) \mid f_\varphi \in F\}$, where $\mathcal{L}_{f_\varphi} = \{\{\varphi\}\}$ and $p_{f_\varphi}(\{\varphi\}) = P_M(\varphi)$.

The construction is natural enough and for the more simple case of finite automata was illustrated by Example 3.

In fact we can state the equivalence between GP grammars (with strategies corresponding to input strings) and generalized probabilistic pushdown automata which are related to nondeterministic pushdown automata as well as GP grammars are to CF grammars.

Much attention was given in the literature to conditions under which a strict probabilistic grammar is proper (see [6], [3], [5]). The criteria formulated by Booth [3] and Hutchins [5] can be extended to single processed GP grammars.

Let $G = (G', P)$ be a single-processed grammar with $N_P = \{B_1, \dots B_s\}$ and $B_i \to \beta_{i1} \mid \dots \mid \beta_{in(i)}$ be the set of all B_i-productions ($1 \leq i \leq s$). If $\beta_{ij} = \varphi_0 X_1 \varphi_1 X_2 \dots X_t \varphi_t$, where $X_l \notin N - N_P$ and each $\varphi_l \in (N_P \cup \Sigma)^*$, and ρ_l is the characteristic of the completed trees with the root X_l then let be the number of the occurences of $B_k (1 \leq k \leq s)$ in the string $\varphi_0 \rho_1 \varphi_1 \dots \rho_t \varphi_t$ and

$$m_{ik} = \sum_{1 \leq j \leq n(i)} m_{ijk} P_{B_i} (B \to \beta_{ij})$$

The following theorem is formulated in terms of the characteristic roots of the matrix $M = \{m_{ik}\}$ and the maximum value of their moduli denoted by μ.

<u>Theorem 2</u>. A single-processed GP grammar G is proper if $\mu \leq 1$ and it is not proper if $\mu > 1$.

The important problem is connected with the approximation of a probabilistic language with a small probability of a failure.

Let $G = (G', P)$ be a proper single-processed GP grammar which defines $\mathcal{L}(G) = (\mathcal{L}, p)$ with $\sum_{L \in \mathcal{L}} pL = 1$. Given $\varepsilon > 0$ we say that a (nonprobabilistic) language L_0 <u>ε-approximates</u> a generalized language $(\mathcal{L}, p)$ if $L_0 \subseteq \bigcup_{L \in \mathcal{L}} L$ and $\sum_{L \subseteq L_0} pL \geq 1 - \varepsilon$.

A similar but different definition for strict probabilistic languages was given by Booth [3] and from his results it follows that every $(\mathcal{L},p)$ can be ε-approximated (for each $\varepsilon > 0$) by a finite language. But we feel that an "intuitively justified" approximation problem consists in finding a CF grammar G_0 such that $L(G_0)$ ε-approximates $(\mathcal{L},p)$ for sufficiently small $\varepsilon > 0$ and the following conditions hold:

(1) G_0 is better in some sense than G'(i.e. it has the smaller size or it is simpler parsable, and so on);

(2) G_0 is related to G' closely enough (i.e. derivation trees in G_0 are similar in some sense to the corresponding trees in G').

Booth's result seems not to solve the approximation problem in the above sense. We conjecture that there are a strict probabilistic grammar G = (G',P) and $\varepsilon > 0$ such that if a finite-state grammar G_0 ε-approximates G (i.e. $L(G_0)$ ε-approximates $\mathcal{L}(G)$), then"the size" of G_0 is considerably larger than the size of G'. In fact we mean some asymptotic dependence of the size on ε and G and instead of finite-state grammars other "restricted" classes of grammars may be chosen.

Now we can present only a preliminary result concerning the approximation problem. Given GP grammar G = (G',P) we construct an approximating grammar G_0 simply by removing from G' some "superfluous" productions. If these productions cause conflicts in a parser of some type(precedence conflicts, LL(1) and so on) then G_0 may turn out to be effectively parsable whereas G' is not.

If G_0 is obtained from G' by a deletion of production rules $r_1,\ldots,r_k$ such that $\sum_{r_j \in \Pi_A^i} P_A(\Pi_A^i) \leq \delta$ we say that G_0 is δ-<u>similar</u> to G'.

<u>Theorem 3.</u> If in a single-processed GP grammar G = (G',P) the index of the CF grammar G' is bounded by n, G_0 is δ-similar to G' and there is $t \geq 1$ such that $(1-\delta)^{nt} \geq 1 - \varepsilon/2$ then $L(G_0)$ ε-approximates $\mathcal{L}(G)$.

REFERENCES

1. Agafonov, V.N. On the notion of probabilistic grammar. 2-nd All-

Union Symposium on Probabilistic Automata. Tbilisi, 1976, 3-5(in Russian).

2. Aho, A.V., Ullman, J.D. The theory of parsing, translation and compiling, vol. 1, Prentice-Hall, Inc., Englewood Cliffs, N.Y., 1972.
3. Booth, T.L. Probability representation of formal languages. 10-th Annual IEEE Symposium on Switching and Automata Theory, 1969.
4. Huang, T., Fu, K.S. On stochastic context-free languages. Information Sciences, 3 (1971), № 3.
5. Hutchins, S.E. Data compression in context-free languages. Information Processing 71 (IFIP Congress), vol. 1, 104-109.
6. Khertz, M.M. Entropy of languages generated by unambiguous finite-state or context-free grammars. Naučno-tehničeskaja informazija, (1968) NI, 29-34(in Russian).
7. Salomaa, A. Probabilistic and weighted grammars. Information and Control, 15 (1969), № 6, 529-544.
8. Santos, E.S. Probabilistic grammars and automata. Information and Control 21 (1972), № 1, 27-47.

CLASSES OF STRUCTURALLY ISOMORPHIC NP-OPTIMIZATION PROBLEMS

Giorgio Ausiello, CSSCCA-CNR, Via Eudossiana 18, 00184, Roma, Italy
Alessandro D'Atri, Istituto di Automatica dell'Università di Roma
Marco Gaudiano, Istituto di Automatica dell'Università di Roma
Marco Protasi, Istituto di Matematica dell'Università di Roma

INTRODUCTION

The motivation for studying the structural properties of optimization problems related to NP-complete sets [4] is extensively considered in [2] (in this volume). In particular from the point of view of the theory of computational complexity it is interesting to deepen the knowledge about the class of NP-complete sets and to introduce new concepts which allow to classify such sets in terms of their combinatorial structure. On the other side these problems have a large practical interest and, for their intrinsic difficulty, it is very important to find under what conditions they admit "good" approximation algorithms, and how these conditions are related to the structural properties (see, for example [5]).

In this paper, following the approach introduced in [3] the concept of structure of the input to an optimization problem is formally defined in terms of the "spectrum" of approximate solutions of different measure and then structure preserving reductions among optimization problems are defined such that the same mapping that maps input element x of problem $\mathcal{A}$ into input element y of problem $\mathcal{B}$ also maps all approximate solutions of x into approximate solutions of y.
On the base of the existence of structure preserving reductions we can establish the structural isomorphism of some optimization problems and the partial ordering among such isomorphism classes.

BASIC DEFINITIONS

Let us first give the following basic definitions.

DEFINITION 1 i) An *optimization problem* $\mathcal{A}$ is a 5-tuple
$\mathcal{A} \equiv \langle$ INPUT, OUTPUT, SOL, Q, m $\rangle$ where:
INPUT, OUTPUT are countable domains,

SOL: INPUT → {A | A is a finite subset of OUTPUT}
is a recursive mapping that provides approximate solutions for any given element of INPUT

Q: is the set of rational numbers under increasing or decreasing order

m: OUTPUT → Q is the measure

ii) The *optimal value* $m^*(x)$ of an input x of $\mathcal{A}$ is
$m^*(x) = \text{best } \{m(y) \mid y \in SOL(x)\}$ under the ordering of Q

iii) The *trivial value* $\tilde{m}(x)$ of an input x of $\mathcal{A}$ is
$\tilde{m}(x) = \text{worst } \{m(y) \mid y \in SOL(x)\}$ under the ordering of Q(*)

DEFINITION 2. An optimization problem is said to be *convex* if m(OUTPUT) is the set of non-negative integers and for every $x \in$ INPUT, for every integer n between $\tilde{m}(x)$ and $m^*(x)$ there is at least one approximate solution of x whose measure is equal to n.

DEFINITION 3. Let y be an element of SOL(x). The *normalized measure* $\bar{m}_x$ of y is

$$\bar{m}_x(y) = \frac{m(y) - \tilde{m}(x)}{m^*(x) - \tilde{m}(x)}$$

Besides we denote $\bar{M}(x)$ the set $\{q \mid q = \bar{m}_x(y) \text{ and } y \in SOL(x)\}$.

Obviously, for every x and every $y \in SOL(x)$, $0 \leq \bar{m}_x(y) \leq 1$.

Note that the concept of normalized measure is more suitable to express how good an approximate solution is with respect to the range of all possible solutions and, in fact, it can be conveniently used in the definition of an evaluation function of approximation algorithms [1]. For the same reason we have:

FACT. The normalized measure is invariant for linear transformations of the measure m.

Among all optimization problems which are characterized by the very general definition 1, we restrict our attention to those optimization problems which are related to NP-complete sets.

DEFINITION 4. Let $\mathcal{A}$ be an optimization problem, let the set OUTPUT of $\mathcal{A}$ be polynomially recognizable, and let $\mathcal{A}^c = \{\langle x,k \rangle \mid k \leq m^*(x)$ under the ordering of Q$\}$; we say that $\mathcal{A}$ is an *NP optimization problem associated to an NP-complete set* (briefly NPCO problem) if and only if $\mathcal{A}^c$ is an NP-complete set.

(*) In the problems we will consider the worst solution is unique and coincides with the trivial solution.

Given an NPCO problem $\mathcal{A}$ we say that such a problem has a polynomial approximation if there is a polynomially computable function that for every x provides at least one element of SOL(x).

Now, let $\mathcal{A}$ be an NPCO problem; in the following definition we introduce the concept of structure of an element of INPUT, which is a fundamental concept in the development of our work.

DEFINITION 5. Let $x \in$ INPUT; we define *structure* of *x* the list $\ell_x = \langle a_0, \ldots, a_c \rangle$ where c is the least common denominator of the values in $\overline{M}(x)$ and $a_i = |\{y | y \in \mathrm{SOL}(x) \text{ and } \overline{m}_x(y) \cdot c = i\}|$

The concept of structure, which provides a representation of the number of approximate solutions at different levels of the measure, contains enough information to capture the combinatorial properties of the input to an optimization problem, and, as we will see, allows us to introduce an ordering over all input elements that, as it is remarked in [3], expresses the concept of "subproblem".

EXAMPLES 1) Let $\mathcal{A}$ be the problem MIN-SET-COVERING; let x be the family of sets

$$S_1 = \{1,2,3,4\} \quad S_2 = \{1,2,5\} \quad S_3 = \{3,4,6\} \quad S_4 = \{5,6,7\}$$

$$S_5 = \{1,2,3,4,5,6,7\}$$

$$\tilde{m}(x) = 5 \quad m^*(x) = 1 \quad \ell_x = \langle 1,5,9,5,1 \rangle$$

2) Let $\mathcal{A}$ be the problem MAX-SUBSET-SUM; let x be the input $\langle [3,5,2,7];\ 11 \rangle$

$$\tilde{m}(x) = 0 \quad m^*(x) = 10$$

$$\mathrm{SOL}(x) = \Big\{\{\},\{3\},\{5\},\{2\},\{7\},\{3,5\},\{3,2\},\{3,7\},\{5,2\},\{2,7\},\{3,5,2\}\Big\}$$

$$\overline{M}(x) = \Big\{0,\ \frac{1}{5},\ \frac{3}{10},\ \frac{1}{2},\ \frac{7}{10},\ \frac{4}{5},\ \frac{9}{10},\ 1\Big\}$$

$$\ell_x = \langle 1,\ 0,\ 1,\ 1,\ 0,\ 2,\ 0,\ 2,\ 1,\ 1,\ 2 \rangle$$

If we now consider the second example and we make a change on the input element such as eliminating one of the elements in the multiset or lowering the value of the constraint, what we have is essentially a "subproblem" of the given problem: say

$$y = \langle [3,\ 2,\ 7];\ 9 \rangle \qquad \ell_y = \langle 1,\ 0,\ 1,\ 1,\ 0,\ 1,\ 0,\ 1,\ 0,\ 1 \rangle$$

where ℓ_y is a "sublist" of ℓ_x according to the following definitions which are a formalization of the concept of "subproblem".

DEFINITION 6. Let x and y be two input elements to a problem $\mathfrak{A}$ and let $\ell_x = \langle a_0, \dots, a_c \rangle$, $\ell_y = \langle b_0, \dots, b_d \rangle$.
We say that

i) $x \equiv y$ if ℓ_x coincides with ℓ_y,

ii) $[x]$ is the equivalence class of x,

iii) $[x] \leq [y]$ if for all $0 \leq i \leq \min\{c,d\}$ $a_i \leq b_i$

Note that the definitions of structure of an element of INPUT and of ordering over INPUT/$_\equiv$ are a modification of the corresponding definitions given in [3]. While in the case of convex problems the two definitions of structure coincide, the definition given in this paper seems to be more meaningful in the case of non convex problems. At the same time the new definitions characterize as a lattice the ordered set of all possible structures and this makes possible to consider the introduction of a topology over the input set of an optimization problem. Anyway all the results given in [3] still hold true under the present formulation.

DEFINITION 7. Given two NPCO problems $\mathfrak{A}$ and $\mathfrak{B}$ we say that $\mathfrak{A}$ *is polynomially reducible to* $\mathfrak{B}$ if there are two recursive polynomial time computable functions $f_1: \mathrm{INPUT}_{\mathfrak{A}} \to \mathrm{INPUT}_{\mathfrak{B}}$, $f_2: \mathrm{INPUT}_{\mathfrak{A}} \times Q_{\mathfrak{A}} \to Q_{\mathfrak{B}}$ such that for every x and k

$$k \in m_{\mathfrak{A}}(\mathrm{SOL}_{\mathfrak{A}}(x)) \text{ iff } f_2(x,k) \in m_{\mathfrak{B}}(\mathrm{SOL}_{\mathfrak{B}}(f_1(x))).$$

Clearly if $\langle f_1, f_2 \rangle$ is a reduction between two optimization problems $\mathfrak{A}$ and $\mathfrak{B}$, we have $\langle x,k \rangle \in \mathfrak{A}^c$ iff $\langle f_1(x), f_2(x,k) \rangle \in \mathfrak{B}^c$ and hence there exists a reduction between the corresponding combinatorial problems.

DEFINITION 8. A reduction $\langle f_1, f_2 \rangle$ from $\mathfrak{A}$ to $\mathfrak{B}$ is said to be

i) *order preserving* if, given $x,y \in \mathrm{INPUT}_{\mathfrak{A}}$, $[x] \leq [y]$ implies $[f_1(x)] \leq [f_1(y)]$

ii) *structure preserving* if for every $x \in \mathrm{INPUT}_{\mathfrak{A}}$ $\ell_x = \ell_{f_1(x)}$.

In the next paragraph we will introduce a partial ordering over the set of all NPCO problems based on the existence of polynomial reductions among them. Results concerning such reductions and the corresponding ordering among classes of problems will be shown.

MAIN RESULTS

Let us consider the class of all NPCO problems; an ordering over the class can be introduced according to the following.

DEFINITION 9. Given two NPCO problems $\mathfrak{A}$ and $\mathfrak{B}$ we say that

i) $\mathfrak{A} \underset{sp}{\leq} \mathfrak{B}$ if there exists a polynomial structure preserving reduction from $\mathfrak{A}$ to $\mathfrak{B}$;

ii) $\mathfrak{A} \underset{sp}{\equiv} \mathfrak{B}$ if $\mathfrak{A} \underset{sp}{\leq} \mathfrak{B}$ and $\mathfrak{B} \underset{sp}{\leq} \mathfrak{A}$; in this case we say that $\mathfrak{A}$ and $\mathfrak{B}$ are *structurally isomorphic*;

iii) $\mathfrak{A} \underset{sp}{\nleq} \mathfrak{B}$ if no structure preserving reduction is possible from $\mathfrak{A}$ to $\mathfrak{B}$;

iv) $\mathfrak{A} \underset{sp}{|<} \mathfrak{B}$ if $\mathfrak{A} \underset{sp}{\leq} \mathfrak{B}$ and $\mathfrak{B} \underset{sp}{\nleq} \mathfrak{A}$

v) $\mathfrak{A} \underset{sp}{*} \mathfrak{B}$ if $\mathfrak{A} \underset{sp}{\nleq} \mathfrak{B}$ and $\mathfrak{B} \underset{sp}{\nleq} \mathfrak{A}$

The above definitions characterize the fact that given two optimization problems it may be i) that one of them is at mast as rich as the other one with respect to the combinatorial structure and we have a polynomial reduction among them, ii) that they have exactly the same combinatorial structure and polynomial mappings in both directions can be exhibited, iii) that some structures that are present in the second one cannot be found in the first one, iv) that one of them is strictly richer than the other one, v) that their combinatorial structures are incomparable.

FACT. Definitions 9 i) and ii) induce a partial order among isomorphism classes of NPCO problems.

Note that results such as MAX-SIMPLE-CUT $\underset{sp}{*}$ MIN-PARTITION-INTO-EQUAL-SIZE-SUBSETS [3], show that the ordering is not a total one.

Because of the given definitions we have the following

FACT. No structure preserving reduction can exist from non convex problems to convex problems.

<u>THEOREM 1</u>. MAX-CLIQUE $\underset{sp}{\equiv}$ MIN-NODE-COVER $\underset{sp}{\equiv}$ MAX-SET-PACKING

PROOF. The results MAX-CLIQUE $\underset{sp}{\leq}$ MIN-NODE-COVER and MAX-CLIQUE $\underset{sp}{\leq}$ MAX-SET-PACKING are proved [2]. The fact that MIN-NODE-COVER $\underset{sp}{\leq}$ MAX-CLIQUE can be easily verified by considering the inverse reduction of [4]. Finally we can give a reduction from MAX-SET-PACKING to MAX-CLIQUE in which $f_1(x)$ is a graph where the nodes correspond to the sets in x and the arcs correspond to pairs of disjoint sets, and $f_2(x,k) = k$; clearly this reduction satisfies the lemma to theorem 2 in [3]. QED

<u>THEOREM 2</u>. MIN-SET-COVERING $\equiv_{sp}$ MIN-HITTING-SET

PROOF $\leq_{sp}$) is proved in [3].

$\geq_{sp}$) can be proved by inverting the same reduction. QED

<u>THEOREM 3</u>. i) MIN-NODE-COVER $|\!<_{sp}$ MIN-SET-COVERING

ii) MIN-NODE-COVER $|\!<_{sp}$ MIN-FEEDBACK-NODE-SET

PROOF i) $\leq_{sp}$ is proved in [3]

$\not\geq_{sp}$ let us consider the family of sets $x = \{S_1, \ldots, S_n\}$ where $S_i = A - a_i$ and $A = \{a_1, \ldots, a_n\}$ with $n \geq 3$. In this case $\ell_x = \langle 1, \binom{n}{n-1}, \binom{n}{n-2}, \ldots, \binom{n}{2}\rangle$ and such a list does not exist in the problem MAX-CLIQUE because if $\ell_x = \langle 1, \binom{n}{n-1}, \binom{n}{n-2}, \ldots\rangle$ x must be an n-clique and hence its list must be $\langle 1, \binom{n}{n-1}, \binom{n}{n-2}, \ldots, \binom{n}{2}, n, 1\rangle$ and hence the same list ℓ_x does not exist in the problem MIN-NODE-COVER.

ii) $\leq_{sp}$) is proved in [3]

$\not\geq_{sp}$) let us consider the family of graphs

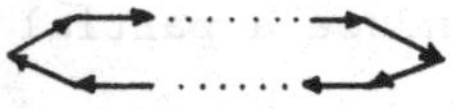

formed by just one cycle on n nodes. For such a graph the list in MIN-FEEDBACK-NODE-SET would be

$$\langle 1, \binom{n}{n-1}, \binom{n}{n-2}, \ldots, \binom{n}{2}, n\rangle$$

and such a list does not exist in MIN-NODE-COVER for the same reason as in part i). QED

<u>THEOREM 4</u>. MIN-FEEDBACK-ARC-SET $|\!<_{sp}$ MIN-FEEDBACK-NODE-SET

PROOF. $\leq_{sp}$) Let $G = \langle V, E\rangle$ be a diagraph. Let us consider the digraph $G' = \langle V', E'\rangle$ where $V' = E$ and $E' = \{\langle e, e'\rangle \mid (\exists x, y, v \in V)[e = \langle x, v\rangle,\ e' = \langle v, y\rangle]\}$. In the case that G has no selfloop we have a 1-1 correspondence between all cycles in G and all cycles in G' so that to any distinct feedback arc cover in G there is a corresponding distinct feedback node cover in G'. In the case that G has selfloops the correspondence between cycles drops but the correspondence between coverings is still preserved.

$\not\geq_{sp}$) Let us consider the family of complete digraphs of n nodes without selfloops. These digraphs have the list $\langle 1, n\rangle$ in MIN-FEEDBACK-NODE-SET. For $n \geq 3$ this list cannot be found in MIN-FEEDBACK-ARC-SET because this would imply that any pair of arcs is itself a loop and this is obviously impossible. QED

THEOREM 5. MIN-CHROMATIC-NUMBER $\equiv_{sp}$ MIN-EXACT-CLIQUE-COVER

PROOF. $\le_{sp}$) is proved in [3];

$\ge_{sp}$) the inverse reduction can be easily proved to be a structure preserving reduction. QED

Note that in some cases we might prove that the structures that can be found in one NPCO problem are also present in another NPCO problem, that is for any $x \in$ INPUT$_{\mathcal{B}}$ there is $y \in$ INPUT$_{\mathcal{A}}$ such that $\ell_x = \ell_y$, even if we are unable of exhibiting a structure preserving reduction from $\mathcal{B}$ to $\mathcal{A}$ that given x computes such a y in polynomial time. In this case we will write $\mathcal{B} \subseteq \mathcal{A}$. For example we have

THEOREM 6. MIN-FEEDBACK-NODE-SET $\subseteq$ MIN-SET-COVERING.

PROOF. Let us first introduce the NPCO problem MIN-MSC (minimum multisetcovering: minimum covering obtained with sets chosen out of a multiset of sets). We can prove the following

LEMMA. MIN-MSC $\equiv_{sp}$ MIN-SET-COVERING.

$\ge_{sp}$) Obvious.

$\le_{sp}$) Let $x = [A_1, \ldots, A_n]$ be a multiset of sets. If for no i and j, $A_i = A_j$ clearly the problem becomes a set covering problem. Otherwise, let us suppose to have $m \ge 1$ families of equal sets. Let $[A_1, \ldots, A_k]$ be such a family, that is $A_1 = \ldots = A_k$ and $A_{k+1}, \ldots, A_n \ne A_1$. We will show that there is another element y of MSC which has exactly m-1 families of equal sets and $\ell_x = \ell_y$.

Such an element of MSC is $y = [B_1, \ldots, B_k, C_{k+1}, \ldots, C_n, D_{n+1}]$

where $B_i = A_i \cup \{z_i\}$ $\quad 1 \le i \le k$

$C_i = A_i \cup \{z_1, \ldots, z_k\}$ $\quad k+1 \le i \le n$

$D_{n+1} = \{z_1, \ldots, z_k, z_{k+1}\}$

where $z_1, \ldots, z_{k+1}$ are new elements not in $\cup A_i$.

By induction the lemma is proved. QED.

In order to prove theorem 6 we still have to prove that MIN-FEEDBACK-NODE-SET $\subseteq$ MIN-MSC. Let $G = \langle V, E\rangle$ be a digraph. We may define the following multiset of sets $[A_1, \ldots, A_n]$ where n is the number of vertices in V, $\cup A_i = \{u_1, \ldots, u_m$| where m is the number of cycles in G} and for every i and j $u_j \in A_i$ if and only if the i-th node is in the j-th cycle. Note that since the number of cycles in a digraph can grow exponentially with the number of nodes this construction cannot be used as a polynomial reduction from MIN-FEEDBACK-NODE-SET to MIN-SET-COVERING-I, but it is sufficient to show that every structure present in the first problem can be found in the second problem. QED.

As far as non-convex problems are concerned besides the results already shown in [3] we can prove:

THEOREM 7. i) MIN-PARTITION $\equiv_{sp}$ MIN-FINISH-TIME-ON-2-PROCESSORS

ii) MIN-PARTITION $|\!<_{sp}$ MIN-FINISH-TIME-ON-K-PROCESSORS

PROOF. i) Obvious.

ii) In a general problem of scheduling n jobs on K processors the number of possible approximate solutions is $\sum_{i=1}^{k} \bar{s}(n,i)$, where $\bar{s}(n,i)$ are the Stirling numbers of second kind, while in the problem of partitioning a set of n elements in two subsets of minimal distance the number of approximate solutions is always 2^{n-1}. QED.

THEOREM 8. MAX-CUT $\equiv_{sp}$ MIN-CLUSTER.

PROOF. Let G be a graph whose set of arcs is $A = \{a_i\}$ and the weight of arc a_i is w_i. The following reduction works in both ways: $f_1(G) = G$,

$$f_2(G,k) = \sum_{a_i \in A} w_i - k$$ QED.

BIBLIOGRAPHY

[1] A.AIELLO, E.BURATTINI, A.MASSAROTTI, F.VENTRIGLIA: *Towards a general principle of evaluation for approximate algorithms.* Seminaries IRIA, 1976.

[2] G.AUSIELLO: *On the structure and properties of NP-complete problems and their associated optimization problems.* This volume.

[3] G.AUSIELLO, A.D'ATRI, M.PROTASI: *On the structure of combinatorial problems and structure preserving reductions.* 4th ICALP, Turku, Finland, 1977.

[4] R.M.KARP: *Reducibility among combinatorial problems, in "Complexity of computer computations".* R.E.Miller and J.W.Thatcher Eds., Plenum Press, New York, 1972.

[5] S.MORAN, A.PAZ: *NP optimization problems and their approximation.* 4th ICALP, Turku, Finland, 1977.

PUSHDOWN-AUTOMATA AND FAMILIES OF LANGUAGES GENERATING CYLINDERS

Jean-Michel Autebert
Laboratoire associé du C.N.R.S.:
Informatique Théorique et Programmation
Institut de Programmation, 4 place Jussieu,
75230 - PARIS CEDEX 05

INTRODUCTION

A family of languages closed under inverse homorphism and intersection with regular set is called a cylinder. Most of the classical families of context-free languages are cylinders: the family Alg of context-free languages is a principal cylinder (i.e. the cylinder generated by one C.F. language only: the nondeterministic version of the Dyck set given by S. Greibach *[5]*). Det, the family of deterministic languages is a non-principal cylinder (S. Greibach *[6]*). L. Boasson and M. Nivat have proved *[3]* that the cylinder Lin of linear languages is non-principal; we show that the cylinder Ocl of one-counter languages is not principal either *[1]*. The family of unambiguous C.F. languages is also a cylinder, but it is not known whether it is principal or not.

On the other hand, a lot of families of languages are characterised or even defined as the family of the languages recognized by push-down automata of some kind, that is to say, recognized by p.d.a. with some particular restrictions. In particular, this is true for Alg, Det, Ocl and also for the families of simple deterministic languages and realtime languages.

We propose here a general construction that yields for a special class of push-down automata, a family of languages generating the cylinder of languages recognized by push-down automata of that special class. This construction points out the role of prime importance played by the theorem of E. Shamir *[7]* for the context-free languages and it was inspired by the construction that S. Greibach used for her hardest C.F. language *[5]*, introducing in addition an equivalent of the state control notion.

The construction can be used for all classes of push-down automata which do not allow the use of ε-moves (it is the case with C.F. real-time languages) or with such classes of push-down automata that the family of languages remains the same when ε-moves are not used (it is the case with Alg and also with the family of simple deterministic languages). The construction can be generalized for some other families of languages recognized by automata with ε-moves (as for the family of onecounter languages).

In all the studied cases, the construction yields families of languages that are recognized by push-down automata of the corresponding kind. So, in each case we get a subfamily of representatives that may be sufficient to study instead of the whole cylinder (from the point of view of complexity for instance). Moreover, owing to the way they are constructed, they consist of series of elements (elements subscripted with integers). This enables us either to prove the generated cylinder to be principal or non-principal, this being done by the following classical argument: the cylinder is described as the infinite union of (strictly or not strictly) nested principal cylinders.

Thus we repeat or establish the proof of the principality or the non-principality of the cylinder in a lot of cases: For Alg we get the non-deterministic Dyck-sets, leading to the hardest C.F. language. For the families Lin and Ocl, the subfamilies obtained enable us to conclude that they are not principal cylinders. If applied to the families of simple deterministic languages and of realtime languages, it enables us to exhibit a simple deterministic language which is the generator of the whole cylinder of realtime languages [2].

PRELIMINARIES

We will use the classical notations and definitions of the theory of languages. We recall some of the most important ones.

Dyck-set:

The Dyck-set (denoted D_n^*) over the alphabet $Z_n = \{z_i, \bar{z}_i \mid i = 1,\dots,n\}$ with 2n letters is the set of all words that can be reduced to the empty word ε by a succession of deletions of sequences $z_i \bar{z}_i$.

Push-down automaton: we will use the following general definition. A push-down automaton is a septuplet $A = \langle X, Q, Z, q_1, z_1, Q_T, \lambda \rangle$ where

X is the input alphabet
Q is the set of states
q_1 is the initial state
$Q_T \subseteq Q$ is the set of final states
Z is the stack-symbol alphabet
z_1 is the initial stack symbol and
λ is a mapping from $(X \cup \{\varepsilon\}) \times Q \times Z$ in $2^{Q \times Z^*}$

A triple (ε,q,z) for which $\lambda(\varepsilon,q,z) \neq \emptyset$ is called an ε-rule.

A push-down automaton is said to be deterministi if λ is a partial mapping of $(X \cup \{\varepsilon\}) \times Q \times Z$ into $Q \times Z^*$ such that for every $(q,z) \in Q \times Z$ either $\lambda(\varepsilon,q,z)$ is not defined or $\lambda(\varepsilon, q, z)$ is defined and for every $x \in X$, $\lambda(x, q, z)$ is not defined.

A deterministic p.d.a. is said to be realtime if it has no ε-rule.

A deterministic p.d.a. is said to be simple if it has only one state.

A language L is deterministic (realtime, simple) if there is a deterministic (realtime, simple) push-down automaton which recognizes L.

Cylinder:

A cylinder is a family of languages closed under inverse homomorphism and intersection with regular sets.

A cylinder C is principal if there exists a language L, called generator in C, such that every element of C can be obtained from L by means of the two cylindrical operations.
One easily proves the following lemma:

Lemma: C is a principal cylinder $\Longleftrightarrow \exists L_o \in C$ such that $\forall L \in C$, $\exists$ homomorphism φ, $\exists$ regular set K such that $L = \varphi^{-1}(L_o) \cap K$

MAIN CONSTRUCTION

a/ Definition of some particular families of languages

We define here the most general form of the languages we will use later on in each particular case, with particular restrictions.

Let $Z_n = \{z_i, \bar{z}_i \mid i \in [n]\}$ be a Dyck alphabet, (composed of $\Sigma_n = \{z_i \mid i \in [n]\}$ and of $\bar{\Sigma}_n = \{\bar{z}_i \mid i \in [n]\}$) , and a, c, d be three symbols not in Z_n. Call $Y_n = Z_n \cup \{a,c,d\}$ and θ the homomorphism from Y_n^* to Z_n^* deleting only these three symbols and leaving all others unchanged.

For each $p \in N$, we will call S_p the regular set over Y_n^* such that:

$S_p = \{f \in Y_n^* \mid$ f has never more than p consecutive letters a as a factor and f has never more than p consecutive letters c as a factor$\}$

For each p and n in N, we defined the regular set

$$R_{n,p} = ((a^+ \bar{\Sigma}_n \Sigma_n^* c^+)^+ d)^* \cap S_p$$

For a word f in $R_{n,p}$ a factor of the form $a^i \bar{z}_j g\, c^k$ with $g \in \Sigma_n^*$ will be called an elementary factor; such elementary factors are concatenated into blocks, each block being followed by an occurence of the letter d.

A path in a word f in $R_{n,p}$ is the choice of exactly one elementary factor in each block: $h_1, h_2, \ldots h_k$ such that $|h_i|_c = |h_{i+1}|_a$.

The word $p(f) = h_1 h_2 \ldots h_k$, obtained by the concatenation of all choosen factors, will also be called a path in f.

b/ Construction

Now we go back to push-down automata, and consider p.d.a. with no ε-rules:

$A = \langle X, Q, Z, q_1, z_1, Q_T, \lambda \rangle$

Let v be an enumeration of the states of the automaton. $v : Q \to [p]$ where p is the number of states of the automaton.

Denote $z_1, z_2, \ldots, z_n$ the n stack symbols.

With each rule $x, q, z_i \to q', z_{i_1} z_{i_2} \ldots z_{i_k}$ we associate the word

$a^{v(q)} \bar{z}_i z_{i_1} z_{i_2} \ldots z_{i_k} c^{v(q')}$ which has exactly the form of an elementary factor as defined above.

With each letter x of the input alphabet X, we associate a block, which is defined as a concatenation of all elementary factors associated with the transition rules for the letter x.

Finally, we introduce an homomorphism $\varphi : X^* \rightarrow Y_n^*$ defined by: $\varphi(x)$ is the block just described, followed by a single letter d.

Remarks:

1. To give φ is just another way of giving λ.
2. A path in a word $\varphi(h)$ is exactly what corresponds to a computation of the automaton A when reading h, legal in respect to the state control.
3. We can allways suppose that $v(q_1)=1$.for the initial state q_1 of the automaton A. Let $I = v(Q_T)$ denote the set of the numbers associated with the final states. The fact that a computation in A begins in the intitial state, and ends in a final state can be now exactly described by saying that the corresponding path begins with a number of letters a equaling $1 = v(q_1)$ and ends with a number of letters c equalling $i \in I = v(Q_T)$.

In the following we will implicitly assume that these two conditions (of rational type) are satisfied. The next remark is important enough to be stated as a propisition:

Proposition 1

A word $f \in X^*$ is recognized by the automaton A if and only if there exists a path p in $\varphi(f)$ such that $\theta(p) \in \bar{z}_1 D_n^*$ (where z_1 is the initial stack symbol).

So if we call $L_{n,p}$ the language

$$L_{n,p} = \{ h \in R_{n,p} \mid \exists \text{ a path } p(h) \text{ in } h \text{ such that } \theta(p(h)) \in \bar{z}_1 D_n^* \}$$

we get:

Proposition 2

The family of languages $L = \{ L_{n,p} \mid n \in N, p \in N \}$ generates (in the sense of cylinders) the family of languages recognized by push-down automata with no ε-rule.

If L is a language recognized by such an automaton A with p states and n stack symbols, and φ is the homomorphism obtained from A by our construction, then $L = \varphi^{-1}(L_{n,p})$.

The family L is a description of the behaviour of push-down automata without ε-rules, and a specific automaton of this type is given by n, p and φ.

If we now add restrictions on these automata and are able to translate these restrictions in terms of new conditions for the words of $L_{n,p}$ such as belonging to some regular set, we get in each case a new family of languages describing the behaviour of some special kind of push-down automata and generating, always with the same homomorphisms, the family of all the languages recognized by push-down automata of that special kind.

c/ Extension of the construction

Before going through examples we give an extention of the construction. So far we have supposed that there is no ε-rule.

If we now suppose that after each transition involving the reading of one letter on the input tape, there may be at most a fixed number of ε-moves, we can do the same construction and add, for each sequence (necessarily finite) of rules:

$$x,\ q_o,\ z_o \rightarrow q_1,\ z_{1,1}\ z_{1,2} \dots z_{1,i_1}$$

$$\varepsilon,\ q_1,\ z_1 \rightarrow q_2,\ z_{2,1}\ z_{2,2} \dots z_{2,i_2}$$

$$\varepsilon,\ q_3,\ z_2 \rightarrow q_3,\ z_{3,1}\ z \dots\dots z_{3,i_3}$$

$$\dots\dots\dots\dots\dots\dots\dots\dots\dots$$

$$\varepsilon,\ q_{r-1},\ z_{r-1} \rightarrow q_r,\ z_{r,1} \dots\dots z_{r,i_r}$$

where $z_j = z_{j,i_j}$, the following elementary factors in $\varphi(x)$:

$a^{v(q_o)} \bar{z}_o\ z_{1,1} \dots z_{1,i_1}\ c^{v(q_1)}$, $a^{v(q_o)} \bar{z}_o\ z_{1,1} \dots z_{1,i_1-1}\ z_{2,1} \dots$

$z_{2,i_2}\ c^{v(q_2)}, \dots,\ a^{v(q_o)}\ \bar{z}_o\ z_{1,1} \dots z_{1,i_1-1}\ z_{2,1} \dots z_{2,i_2-1}\ z_{3,1} \dots$

$z_{r,i_r}\ c^{v(q_r)}$

APPLICATIONS

a/ Context free languages

The context-free languages form a cylinder and are recognized by push-down automata with one state and no ε-rules. So if we impose $p = 1$ and call $D_n = L_{n,1}$ we get a family of languages which is the same, but for the notation, as the family of the nondeterministic Dyck sets of S. Greibach *[5]*.

The languages D_n are context-free languages and in order to show that the cylinder of context-free languages is principal one only has to verify that for all n there exists an homomorphism φ such that $D_n = \varphi^{-1}(D_2)$.

b/ One-counter languages

The family of one-counter languages is a cylinder. One counter languages are recognized by push-down automata with only one stack symbol, and it has been proved by S. Ginsburg, J. Goldstine and S. Greibach *[4]* that the number of consecutive ε-transitions can be bounded. So if we impose $n = 1$ and call $C_p = L_{1,p}$ we get a new family of languages. We have proved *[1]* that the languages C_p are one-counter languages and generate an infinite hierarchy of cylinders.

c/ Linear languages

The family of linear languages is a cylinder. These languages can be described as one-peak languages. This means that if $p(f)$ is a path in a word f, $\theta(p(f))$ must belong to $\bar{z}_1 (\Sigma_n^+ \bar{\Sigma}_n)^* \bar{\Sigma}_n$ instead of $\bar{z}_1 D_n^*$. Addition of this new condition induces a new family of languages. Then one can either simulate states with new stack symbols, with a bounded number of ε-rules, or encode stack symbols with only two stack symbols by adding new states. This leads to two families of languages. The former has been studied by L. Boasson and M. Nivat *[3]* who have proved it to be a family of linear languages and to generate an infinite hierarchy of cylinders of linear languages.

d/ Realtime languages

The family of realtime languages is a cylinder of the languages recognized by deterministic push-down automata without ε-rules.

Extend the partial mapping λ to a (total) mapping from $X \times Q \times Z$ into $Q \times Z^*$ (by adding a new stack symbol that is never removed).

Then in each block there are exactly np elementary factors, n elementary factors for each of the p states. Suppose now that we order these elementary factors by writting first the elementary factors corresponding to the first state, then to the second state and so on, and for each state we order the elementary factors according to the natural order over the letters $\bar{z}_1, \bar{z}_2, \ldots, \bar{z}_n$. Then, from the rank of an elementary factor in a block one can deduce the number of the states corresponding to that elementary factor. Moreover, the number of consecutives letters a in an elementary factor is useless, so we set it equal to 1 everywhere.

These restrictions can be expressed by introducing new regular sets, say $K_{n,p}$ instead of $R_{n,p}$, where

$$K_{n,p} = ((a\,\bar{z}_1\,\Sigma_n^*\,c^+\;a\,\bar{z}_2\,\Sigma_n^*\,c^+ \ldots a\,\bar{z}_n\,\Sigma_n^*\,c^+)^p\,d)^* \cap S_p$$

This leads to a new family of languages $PS_{n,p}$.
The realtime languages cylinder is generated by the family of languages $PS_{n,p}$ and every simple deterministic language can be generated from the languages $PS_{n,1}$. We have proved [2] that every $PS_{n,p}$ language is a realtime language and that every $PS_{n,1}$ language is a simple deterministic language. We have proved, too, using these languages, that the smallest cylinder containing all simple deterministic languages is a cylinder of realtime languages and that the latter is a principal cylinder.

CONCLUSION

In our sense, our construction is an application of the theorem of E. Shamir [7], the novelty being here the treatment of the states of push-down automata. The introduction of these states does not give rise to more complicated things as one could think, but on the contrary it can help us to distinguish more families of languages.

Second, the notion of cylinder comes out here naturally. We can remark that the operation of intersection with regular sets does not play a great role in the generation of cylinders. We cojecture that, every time a family of languages is both a cylinder and an A. F. D. L., both the cylinder and the A. F. D. L. are principal or both are not principal.

REFERENCES

1. Autebert, J.-M., Non-principalité du cylindre des langages a computeur. To appear in Mathematical Systems Theory.

2. Autebert, J.-M., Cylindres de langages simples et pseudo-simples. In: Lecture Notes in Computer Science, 48 Springer-Verlag. (1977) 149-153.

3. Boasson, L. and Nivat, M., Le cylindre des langages linéaires. To appear in M.S.T.

4. Ginsburg, S., Golstine J., and Greibach, S., Some uniformely erasable families of languages. Theoretical Computer Science, 2, (1976) 29-44.

5. Greibach, S., The hardest C. F. language. SIAM Journal, 2 (1973) 304-310.

6. Greibach, S., Jump PDA´s and hierarchies of deterministic C. F. languages. SIAM Journal, 3 (1974) 111-127.

7. Shamir, E., A representation theorem for algebraic and C. F. power series in non-commutating variables. Information and Control, 11 (1967) 239-254.

SEMANTICS OF INFINITE PROCESSES USING GENERALIZED TREES

J.W. de Bakker
Mathematisch Centrum
Amsterdam

1. INTRODUCTION

In this paper, we give a preliminary account of an attempt we have made at using generalized trees for the definition of the semantics of infinite processes. Often, e.g. in the study of operating systems or of various forms of concurrent processes in general, one considers processes which continue indefinitely as normal rather than undesirable objects. A language construct which gives a first impression of the problems involved is, e.g., do $S_1 \cup S_2$ od. The operational semantics of this construct is fairly clear: (*) Choose, nondeterministically, between S_1 and S_2, execute the selected statement, and repeat (*). I.e., an infinite sequence of statements $S^{(1)}, S^{(2)}, \ldots$, is performed, where each $S^{(i)}$ is either S_1 or S_2. However, it is less clear what meaning to attribute to such a statement in the framework of denotational semantics. There, it is customary to view the meaning of statements as functions from states to states, with the convention that for an input state for which the computation specified by the statement does not terminate, as output state some special undefined state, often denoted by "$\perp$", is delivered. Thus, all infinite computations become indistinguishable, and any analysis of their structure is virtually impossible. As a remedy we propose to attribute meaning to statements not as functions from states to states, but from (generalized) trees to trees. More specifically, each tree t (with states labelling its nodes) is transformed by (the function describing the meaning of) statement S into a tree t' which is an extension of t in that t' results from t by replacing its leaves by subtrees. E.g., the process do A od (with A some elementary action) transforms

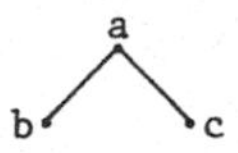

into

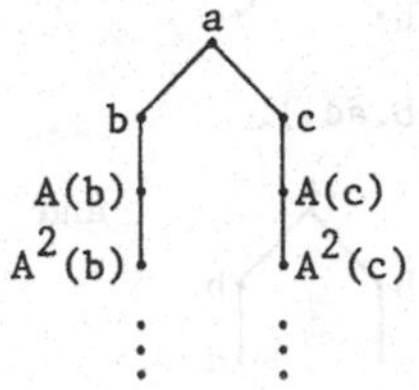

To some extent, it may seem that this idea amounts to nothing but the incorporation of infinite computation sequences determined by statement S (or, rather, trees instead of sequences because of the presence of nondeterminacy) into the framework of denotational semantics. And, indeed, this is one way of viewing our proposal. There is more to it, however. In order to deal with recursion, it is necessary to introduce some ordering on the various tree-transforming functions involved, which ordering is in its turn determined by an ordering on the trees. So we have to define this ordering, which has in addition to serve the following purpose: We want to be able to distinguish between two interpretations of a tree as indicated here, viz. as specifying on the one hand the set of all paths aa, aaa, ... (i.e. aa^+), and on the other hand this same set *together* with the infinite sequence a^ω (i.e., $aa^+ \cup \{a^\omega\}$). Fixed points methods are used for this set, and the difference just mentioned is obtained through the distinction between least and greatest solutions of equations between (sets of paths associated with) trees. The following is an example of this: Let, in general, $t = \langle a, \{t_1, \dots, t_n\} \rangle$ be a tree with root a and subtrees $t_1, \dots, t_n$, $n \geq 0$. Consider the equation $t = \langle a, \{t, \langle a, \emptyset \rangle\} \rangle$. Its least solution has as associated set of paths aa^+, whereas its greatest solution has as associated set of paths $aa^+ \cup \{a^\omega\}$. Corresponding to this distinction at the level of trees, we have a distinction in the semantics of the language construct of recursion. Consider - in a notation to be used only in this introduction - a recursive procedure P, the body of which consists of a choice between either some elementary action A, or A followed by a recursive call of P. Formally, $P \Leftarrow A;P \cup A$, say. For input state a we can choose between two possibilities for the set of output states:

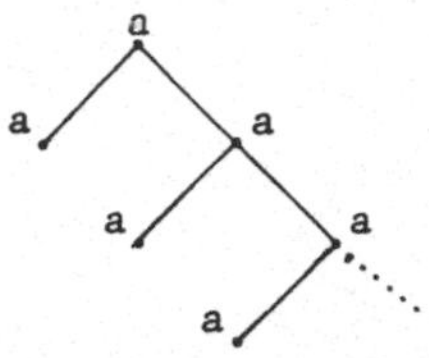

- $\{A(a), A^2(a), \dots, \perp\}$
- $\{A(a), A^2(a), \dots, A^\omega(a)\}$.

Clearly, the second choice, which preserves more information, may be preferable in certain situations, and requires a formalism which refines the method of simply delivering $\perp$ whenever an infinite computation is encountered.

Our system of generalized trees is a candidate for such a formalism. Why do we call them generalized? As suggested already, we view trees as specifying sets of paths, and identify trees which have identical such sets. Therefore we identify, e.g.,

1. Trees such as 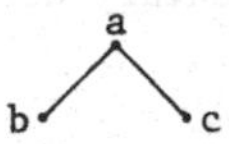 and 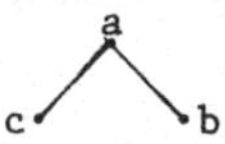

   (both specify {ab,ac}).

2. Trees such as 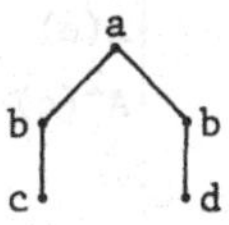 and 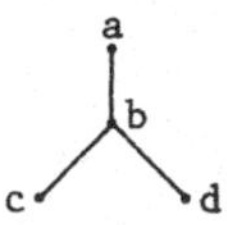

   (both specify {abc, abd}).

Section 2 of the paper describes the syntax and semantics of our tree constructs, section 3 the programming language (with elementary actions, sequential composition, nondeterministic choice, (normal) recursion and infinite recursion (cf. the second interpretation above)) to which meaning is attributed using fixed point techniques in the domain of operators on functions from trees to trees.

Greatest fixed points (but without our generalized trees) have been used by Hitchcock & Park [1], Mazurkiewicz [2], and De Roever [3]. For the framework of denotational semantics in general see, e.g., Scott & Strachey [4] or Milne & Strachey [5].

2. SYNTAX AND SEMANTICS OF GENERALIZED TREES

We first present the syntax. Let V be a set of *tree variables*, with typical elements x,y,... and let T be the set of trees, with typical elements t,... . Before giving the definition proper, we discuss a preliminary version which, for reasons to be mentioned in a moment, turns out to be insufficient. We use as syntactic formalism a variant of BNF which should be self-explanatory.

DEFINITION 2.0 (to be rejected).

$$t ::= 0 \mid x \mid \langle a,\tau\rangle \mid \mu x[t] \mid \nu x[t]$$

where $\tau = \{t_1,\ldots,t_n\}$ is a finite (possible empty) set of trees

END 2.0

This definition tells us that a tree is one of

a) the tree constant 0 (which stands for the undefined tree, and has the empty set of paths as its meaning);

b) a tree variable x;

c) a tree with root a and subtrees $t_1,\ldots,t_n$;

d) the *least* solution of the equation (in t_0) $t_0 = t[t_0/x]$;

e) the *greatest* solution of the equation $t_0 = t[t_0/x]$.

(In clause d and e, $t[t_0/x]$ denotes the result of substituting t_0 for x in t.)
The problem with definition 2.0 is that, e.g., the equation $t_0 = t_0$ does have a least solution but not a greatest solution. In fact, as least solution (denoted by $\mu x[x]$) we have the tree (also denoted by 0) with associated set of paths $\emptyset$, whereas for the greatest solution ($\nu x[x]$) we need a tree such that the associated set of paths is both a tree-set (in the sense of definition 2.3 below) and greatest within the collection of all tree-sets. No such set exists, which explains why we impose a syntactic restriction on the use of the $\nu x[t]$ formation in that t has no free occurrences of x, unless these occurrences are shielded by some intermediate use of the $\langle a,\tau\rangle$ formation rule. E.g., we do not allow $\nu x[x]$, nor $\nu x[\mu y[x]]$, but we do allow $\nu x[\langle a,\{x\}\rangle]$, or $\nu x[\langle a,\{\mu y[\langle b,\{x,y\}\rangle]\}\rangle]$.

DEFINITION 2.1. Let Σ be the set of *states*, with typical elements $a,b,\ldots,a_1,\ldots,a',\ldots$.

For each $W \subseteq V$ we define a tree t_W (where W records the tree variables which do not allow ν-formation).

$$t_W ::= \ 0 \ |x| \ <a,\tau> \ |\mu x[t_W]| \nu x[t_{W \cup \{x\}}]$$

- provided that $x \notin W$
- where $\tau = \{t_\emptyset^1, \ldots, t_\emptyset^n\}$ is a finite (possibly empty) set of trees with respect to $\emptyset$

END 2.1.

Below, we simply write t for $t_\emptyset$.

EXAMPLES. Possible trees are: 0, x, $<a, \{<b, \emptyset>, <c, \{<d, \emptyset>\}>\}>$, $\mu x[<a,\{x\}>]$, $\nu x[<a, \{x\}>]$, $\mu x[<a, \{x,<a, \emptyset>\}>]$, $\nu x[<a, \{x, <a, \emptyset>\}>]$, $\nu x[<a, \{\mu y[<b, \{x, y\}>]\}>]$.

We now define a way of assigning meaning to these constructs. As indicated already, we use sets of (finite or infinite) paths over Σ as meaning of $t \in T$. More specifically, we introduce

- Σ, the set of states, as before
- Σ^*, the set of all finite sequences of elements in Σ (with ε denoting the empty sequence)
- Σ^ω, the set of all infinite sequences of elements in Σ,
- s,... denote typical elements of $\Sigma^* \cup \Sigma^\omega$
- *S*, with typical elements σ,σ', the set of all *subsets* of $\Sigma^* \cup \Sigma^\omega$.

The meaning $T(t)$ of $t \in T$ is given as an element $\sigma \in S$, but for the complication that we need an environment function mapping tree variables in V to elements in *S*, in order to cope with the presence of free tree variables in t.

DEFINITION 2.2. Let $\Theta = V \to S$, with typical elements θ,... . Let, for $\sigma_1,\sigma_2 \in S$, $\sigma_1 \sqsubseteq \sigma_2$ whenever $\sigma_1 \subseteq \sigma_2$ (where the second ordering is the customary set-theoretic inclusion). Let, for $\Phi_1, \Phi_2 \in S \to S$, $\Phi_1 \sqsubseteq \Phi_2$ whenever $\Phi_1(\sigma) \sqsubseteq \Phi_2(\sigma)$ for all $\sigma \in S$. Let, for Φ a monotonic function, (i.e., $\sigma_1 \sqsubseteq \sigma_2 \Rightarrow \Phi(\sigma_1) \sqsubseteq \Phi(\sigma_2)$) from *S* to *S*, μΦ denote its least fixed point and νΦ its greatest fixed point. (Both exist because of the Knaster-Tarski theorem.) Let, for each $\theta \in \Theta$, $x \in V$ and $\sigma \in S$, $\theta\{\sigma/x\}$ be an element of Θ which is defined by: $\theta\{\sigma/x\}(x) = \sigma$, $\theta\{\sigma/x\}(y) = \theta(y)$ for $x \not\equiv y$. Let, for each θ,x and t, $\lambda\sigma.\ T(t)(\theta\{\sigma/x\})$ be that function from *S* to *S* which, when applied to $\sigma_0 \in S$, yields $T(t)(\theta\{\sigma_0/x\}) \in S$ (i.e., λσ•... embodies the customary λ-notation). We put, for each $\theta \in \Theta$:

a) $T(0)(\theta) = \emptyset$ (the empty subset of $\Sigma^* \cup \Sigma^\omega$)

b) $T(x)(\theta) = \theta(x)$

c) $T(<a,\tau>)(\theta) = aT(\tau)(\theta)$

d) $T(\mu x[t])(\theta) = \mu[\lambda\sigma \cdot T(t)(\theta\{\sigma/x\})]$

e) $\mathcal{T}(\nu x[t])(\theta) = \nu[\lambda\sigma.\mathcal{T}(t)(\theta\{\sigma/x\})]$

where, in clause c, $\mathcal{T}(\tau)(\theta)$ is defined as $\mathcal{T}(\tau)(\theta) = \bigcup_{t\in\tau} \mathcal{T}(t)(\theta)$ $(\tau\neq\emptyset)$, and $\mathcal{T}(\emptyset)(\theta) = \{\varepsilon\}$. Moreover, we have, as usual, that $a\sigma = \{as \mid s\in\sigma\}$.

END 2.2.

EXAMPLES. Choose any θ. $\mathcal{T}(0)(\theta) = \emptyset$, $\mathcal{T}(x)(\theta) = \theta(x)$, $\mathcal{T}(\langle a,\{\langle b,\emptyset\rangle,\langle c,\{\langle d,\emptyset\rangle\}\rangle\}\rangle)(\theta) = \{ab,acd\}$, $\mathcal{T}(\mu x[\langle a,\{x\}\rangle])(\theta) = \emptyset$, $\mathcal{T}(\nu x[\langle a,\{x\}\rangle])(\theta) = \{a^{\omega}\}$, $\mathcal{T}(\mu x[\langle a,\{x,\langle a,\emptyset\rangle\}\rangle])(\theta) = \{aa,aaa,\ldots\}$, $\mathcal{T}(\nu x[\langle a,\{x,\langle a,\emptyset\rangle\}\rangle])(\theta) = \{aa,aaa,\ldots,a^{\omega}\}$, $\mathcal{T}(\nu x[\langle a,\{\mu y[\langle b,\{x,y\}\rangle]\}\rangle])(\theta) = (ab^{+})^{\omega}$.

DEFINITION 2.3. A set of sequences $\sigma \in S$ is called a tree-set whenever the following two conditions are satisfied:

a) Each pair $s_1,s_2 \in \sigma$ has a finite non-empty sequence s as common prefix.

b) For each finite non-empty sequence s, the set of all sequences in σ which have s as maximal common prefix is finite.

END 2.3.

EXAMPLES. The set {a,b} is not a tree-set, because it violates condition a, and the set $\{aa_1,aa_2,\ldots\}$ is not a tree-set, because it violates condition b.

The following proposition is stated here without proof:

PROPOSITION 2.4. *For each* $t \in T$ *and each* $\theta \in \Theta$ *such that* $\theta(x)$ *is a tree-set for all* $x \in V$, *we have that* $\mathcal{T}(t)(\theta)$ *is a tree-set.*

END 2.4.

3. SYNTAX AND SEMANTICS OF INFINITE PROCESSES

Let $\mathcal{A}$ be a set of elementary actions, with typical elements $A,A_1,\ldots$, and $\mathcal{X}$ a set of statement variables, with typical elements $X,X_1,\ldots$. We define the class of statements *Stat*, with typical elements S,... , in

DEFINITION 3.1.

$$S ::= A \mid X \mid S_1;S_2 \mid S_1 \cup S_2 \mid \mu X[S] \mid \nu X[S]$$

END 3.1.

Here, $S_1 \cup S_2$ indicates a nondeterministic choice between S_1 and S_2. Also, $\mu X[S]$ corresponds to a parameterless recursive procedure declared in an ALGOL 60-like language by proc P;S[P/X]. Moreover, $\nu X[S]$ extends $\mu X[S]$ in that possible infinite computations are also taken into account. E.g., the two procedures mentioned in the introduction are written in this syntax as $\mu X[A;X \cup A]$ and $\nu X[A;X \cup A]$.

Now let $M = T \to T$, with, for $\phi_1, \phi_2 \in M$, $\phi_1 \sqsubseteq \phi_2$ iff $\phi_1(t) \sqsubseteq \phi_2(t)$ for all $t \in T$ (where $t_1 \sqsubseteq t_2$ iff $T(t_1)(\theta) \sqsubseteq T(t_2)(\theta)$ for all $\theta \in \Theta$). Let, moreover, Λ be the set of all *finite* subsets of Σ, and let $\Gamma = (X \to M) \cup (A \to (\Sigma \to \Lambda))$. (The first part of each $\gamma \in \Gamma$ gives some (arbitrary) meaning to statement variables, the second part tells us how elementary actions $A \in A$ transform $a \in \Sigma$ to $\{a_1,\dots,a_n\}(n \geq 0) \in \Lambda$. I.e., elementary actions are of bounded nondeterminacy.) We now give the definition of the meaning of a statement.

<u>DEFINITION</u> 3.2. M: *Stat* $\to (\Gamma \to M)$ is given by

a) For each t which is not of the form $<a,\emptyset>$:
$M(S)(\gamma)(0) = 0$, $M(S)(\gamma)(x) = x$, $M(S)(\gamma)(<a,\tau>) = <a, M(S)(\gamma)(\tau)>$ $(\tau \neq \emptyset)$,
$M(S)(\gamma)(\mu x[t]) = \mu x[M(S)(\gamma)(t)]$, $M(S)(\gamma)(\nu x[t]) = \nu x[M(S)(\gamma)(t)]$.
(Here, $M(S)(\gamma)(\tau) = \bigcup_{t\in\tau} M(S)(\gamma)(t)$.)

b) For $t = <a,\emptyset>$ we use induction on the structure of S:

1. $M(A)(\gamma)(\ a,\emptyset\ ) = \begin{cases} <a,\{<a_i,\emptyset> \mid a_i \in \gamma(A)(a)\}>, & \text{if } \gamma(A)(a) \neq \emptyset \\ <a,\{0\}>, \text{ otherwise} & \end{cases}$

2. $M(X)(\gamma)(<a,\emptyset>) = \gamma(X)(<a,\emptyset>)$
3. $M(S_1;S_2)(\gamma)(<a,\emptyset>) = M(S_2)(\gamma)(M(S_1)(\gamma)(<a,\emptyset>))$
4. $M(S_1 \cup S_2)(\gamma)(<a,\emptyset>) = <a,\{M(S_1)(\gamma)(<a,\emptyset>), M(S_2)(\gamma)(<a,\emptyset>)\}>$
5. $M(\mu X[S])(\gamma)(<a,\emptyset>) = \mu[\lambda\phi.M(S)(\gamma\{\phi/X\})](<a,\emptyset>)$
6. $M(\nu X[S])(\gamma)(<a,\emptyset>) = \nu[\lambda\phi.M(S)(\gamma\{\phi/X\})](<a,\emptyset>)$

END 3.2.

<u>EXAMPLES</u>. Let $\gamma(A)(a) = \{a',a''\}$, $\gamma(A_1)(a) = \{a_1\}$, $\gamma(A_2)(a) = \{a_2\}$.

1. $M(A)(\gamma)(\mu x[<a,\{x,<a,\emptyset>\}>]) = \mu x[M(A)(\gamma)(<a,\{x,<a,\emptyset>\}>)] =$
$\mu x[<a,\{M(A)(\gamma)(x), M(A)(\gamma)(<a,\emptyset>)\}>] = \mu x[<a,\{x,<a,\{<a',\emptyset>,<a'',\emptyset>\}>\}>]$.
Thus,

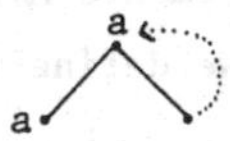

is transformed into
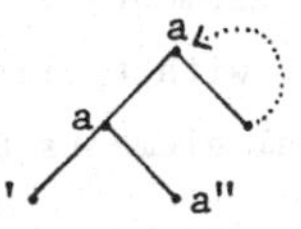

2. $M(\mu X[A_1;X \cup A_2])(\gamma)(<a,\emptyset>)$ and $M(\nu X[A_1;X \cup A_2])(\gamma)(<a,\emptyset>)$

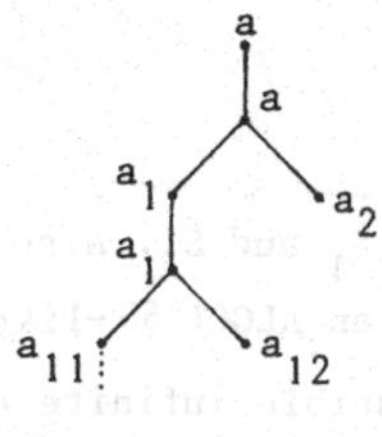

yield this tree with the infinite path $a\ a\ a_1\ a_1\ a_{11}\ a_{11}\ \dots$ excluded in the μ-case and included in the ν-case.

REFERENCES

1. Hitchcock, P. and D.M.R. Park, Induction rules and proofs of termination, Proc. 1st ICALP (M. Nivat, ed.), pp. 225-251, 1973, North-Holland, Amsterdam.

2. Mazurkiewicz, A., Proving properties of processes, CC PAS reports 134, Warsaw, 1973.

3. De Roever, W.P., Maximal fixed points solve some of the problems with Scott induction, Proc. 4th ICALP, to appear.

4. Scott, D. and C. Strachey, Towards a mathematical semantics for computer languages, Proc. Symp. Computers and Automata (J. Fox, ed.), pp. 19-46, 1971, Polytechnic Institute of Brooklyn.

5. Milne, R. and C. Strachey, A Theory of Programming Language Semantics, Chapman & Hall, 1976.

CHARACTERIZATION OF RECOGNIZABLE FAMILIES BY MEANS OF REGULAR LANGUAGES

Václav Benda
Research Institute for Mathematical Machines
150 00 Prague 5 - Jinonice, Stodůlecká

and

Kamila Bendová
Mathematical Institute ČSAV
115 67 Prague 1, Žitná 25
Czechoslovakia

Various results concerning finite branching automata were reported several times at previous MFCS conferences [1], [2], [3], [4] (cf. also [5], [6], [7]). In our earlier paper we focused on those properties of finite branching automata (resp. of families recognizable by them) which have no analogy in classical automata theory (the problem of cardinalities, well-recognizable families, etc.).

Here we approach the subject from another direction: our aim is to present a characterization of recognizable families (that means recognizable by finite branching automata) with the help of regular languages of the classical automata theory.

We use the following notation and terminology. Σ is a finite alphabet, Σ^* the free monoid of strings over Σ (including the empty string Λ). We denote $\Sigma_\Lambda = \Sigma \cup \{\Lambda\}$. For $u \in \Sigma^*$, $lg(u)$ denotes the length of u. Arbitrary subset $L \subseteq \Sigma^*$ is called a language. $\mathcal{L}(\Sigma)$ is the class of all non-empty languages and any subset $X \subseteq \mathcal{L}(\Sigma)$ is called a family of languages. Pref L is the set of all prefixes of L ; we define the set of first letters: $\mathrm{Fst}\, L = \mathrm{Pref}\, L \cap \Sigma$ and $\mathrm{Fst}_\Lambda L = (\mathrm{Pref}\, L \cap \Sigma) \cup (L \cap \{\Lambda\})$. $\partial_u L = \{v;\ uv \in L\}$ is the derivative of L with respect to $u \in \Sigma^*$;

$$\partial_u X = \{\partial_u L ;\ L \in X\} \setminus \{\emptyset\}$$

is the derivative of a family X with respect to $u \in \Sigma^*$, the family

$$C(X) = \{L;\ (\forall u \in \Sigma^*)(\exists L_u \in X)[\mathrm{Fst}_\Lambda \partial_u L = \mathrm{Fst}_\Lambda \partial_u L_u]\}$$

is the <u>C-closure of a family</u> X.

We say that a family X is <u>finitely derivable</u> if the set $D(X) = \{\partial_u X\ ;\ u \in \Sigma^*\}$ is finite. X is <u>self-compatible</u> if $C(X) = X$.

In vieu of the original definition of a recognizable family of languages based on the concept of a finite branching automaton we use the following characterization (Theorem 4.4 from [5])

<u>Definition 1</u>. A family of languages is recognizable iff it is finitely derivable and self-compatible.

<u>Notation</u>. Throughout the present paper we shall often use the family $Z = \{L;\ \emptyset \neq L \subseteq \Sigma_\Lambda^*\}$. Elements of Z are denoted by Γ. Further, $\mathcal{R}$ is the power set of the relation $\Sigma^* \times Z = \{\langle u,\Gamma\rangle;\ u \in \Sigma^* \ \&\ \Gamma \in Z\}$, i.e. $\mathcal{R} = 2^{\Sigma^* \times Z}$. Elements of $\mathcal{R}$ are denoted by R.

<u>Definition 2</u>. We say that $R \in \mathcal{R}$ is a <u>regular graph</u> if for any $\Gamma \in Z$ the language $L_\Gamma = \{u;\ \langle u,\Gamma\rangle \in R\}$ is regular (in the sense of classical automata theory).

<u>Definition 3</u>. We define a pair of functions $G: 2^{\mathcal{L}(\Sigma)} \rightarrow \mathcal{R}$ and $\widetilde{G}: \mathcal{R} \rightarrow 2^{\mathcal{L}(\Sigma)}$ as follows. For $X \subseteq \mathcal{L}(\Sigma)$

$$G(X) = \{\langle u,\Gamma\rangle;\ (\exists L \in X)[\mathrm{Fst}_\Lambda \partial_u L = \Gamma \ \&\ \Gamma \in Z]\}$$ and for $R \in \mathcal{R}$

$$\widetilde{G}(R) = \{L;\ L \in \mathcal{L}(\Sigma)\ \&\ (\forall u \in \mathrm{Pref}L)[\langle u, \mathrm{Fst}_\Lambda \partial_u L\rangle \in R]\}.$$

The two functions G and $\widetilde{G}$ enable to obtain the following characterization of recognizable families, based solely on the concept of regularity.

<u>Theorem 1</u>. Let X be an arbitrary family of languages (thus $X \subseteq \mathcal{L}(\Sigma)$), G, $\widetilde{G}$ the functions just defined. Then the following conditions are equivalent:

1) X is recognizable.

2) $\tilde{G}(G(X)) = X$ and $G(X)$ is a regular graph.

3) There exists $R \in \mathcal{R}$ such that $X = \tilde{G}(R)$ and $G(X)$ is a regular graph.

<u>Outline of the proof</u>. First we prove the equivalence of the following conditions:

1') X is self-compatible.

2') $\tilde{G}(G(X)) = X$.

3') There exists $R \in \mathcal{R}$ such that $X = \tilde{G}(R)$.

Clearly, 2') implies 3'). Furthermore, 3') implies 1') because $\tilde{G}(R)$ is self-compatible for any R (cf. the definition of the C-closure and of the function $\tilde{G}$).

It is easy to show that for every family X, $X \subseteq \tilde{G}(G(X)) \subseteq C(X)$. Thus also 1') implies 2').

Now it remains to show that a self-compatible family X is finitely derivable iff G(X) is a regular graph. Let $G(X) = \{\langle u,\Gamma\rangle ;\ u \in L_\Gamma \ \& \ \Gamma \in Z\}$. It is easy to show that $G(\partial_v X) = \{\langle u,\Gamma\rangle ;\ u \in \partial_v L_\Gamma \ \& \ \Gamma \in Z\}$. Since the derivative preserves the self-compatibility of families (Theorem 5.5 from [5]) and since by the condition 2') the function

$$G \restriction \{X;\ C(X) = X\}$$

is injective we have for self-compatible family X, $v,w \in \Sigma^*$ and corresponding L_Γ of G(X):

$\partial_v X = \partial_w X$ iff $G(\partial_v X) = G(\partial_w X)$ iff $(\forall \Gamma \in Z)(\partial_v L_\Gamma = \partial_w L_\Gamma)$.

Z is a finite family, thus self-compatible family X is finitely derivable iff all the corresponding L_Γ are regular languages. This concludes the proof. Q.e.d.

In the remaining part of the paper we shall give the sufficient conditions for a regular graph to determine a recognizable family.

<u>Notation</u>. For $R \in \mathcal{R}$ we denote $L_R = \{u;\ (\exists \Gamma \in Z)\ \langle u,\Gamma\rangle \in R\}$.

Theorem 2. For any $R \in \mathcal{R}$, the equation $G(\tilde{G}(R)) = R$ holds iff the following two conditions are fulfilled:

(1) $(\forall u \in \mathrm{Pref}\, L_R)\ [\mathrm{Fst}_\Lambda \partial_u L_R = \bigcup\{\Gamma;\ \langle u,\Gamma\rangle \in R\} \cup \{\Lambda\}]$

(2) $L_R = \bigcup_{\Lambda \in \Gamma} \mathrm{Pref}\, L_\Gamma$.

Thus if R is a regular graph satisfying the conditions of Theorem 2 the family $X = \tilde{G}(R)$ is recognizable.

Outline of the proof. It is easy to see that for any family X (and thus, in particular, for $\tilde{G}(R)$) $G(X)$ satisfies both conditions.

Now suppose that a graph R satisfies both conditions. We have to show that for any $\langle u,\Gamma\rangle \in R$ there is $L_{\langle u,\Gamma\rangle} \in \tilde{G}(R)$ such that $\mathrm{Fst}_\Lambda \partial_u L_{\langle u,\Gamma\rangle} = \Gamma$ since then clearly $G(\tilde{G}(R)) = R$. Let $\langle u,\Gamma\rangle$ be an arbitrary element of R. We shall construct $L_{\langle u,\Gamma\rangle}$ by the following process:

$L_0 = \{\Lambda\}$;

let L_n be the language constructed in the n-th step, then for every $v \in L_n$ we choose $\Gamma_v \in Z$ such that

a) $\langle v, \Gamma_v\rangle \in R$;

b) if $vaw = u$ then $a \in \Gamma_v$;

c) if $v = u$ then $\Gamma_v = \Gamma$;

d) if v is not a prefix of u then either $\Lambda \in \Gamma_v$ or there exists $a \in \Gamma_v$ for which

$\min\{\lg(w);\ w \in \partial_{va} \bigcup_{\Lambda\in\Gamma} L_\Gamma\} < \min\{\lg(w);\ w \in \partial_v \bigcup_{\Lambda\in\Gamma} L_\Gamma\}$

and we define

$$L_{n+1} = \bigcup\{v \cdot \Gamma_v;\ v \in L_n\} \setminus L_n .$$

Now we put $L = \bigcup_{n=0}^{\infty} L_n$ and finaly

$$L_{\langle u,\Gamma\rangle} = \{v;\ v \in L\ \&\ \Lambda \in \Gamma_v\}.$$

I. First we show by induction on n that the above construction is feasible.

Base. If $u = \Lambda$ then Γ is the corresponding Γ_Λ.

Let $u = aw$. By the assumption, $u \in L_R$ thus $\Lambda \in \mathrm{Pref}\, L_R$. By the condition (1), $\mathrm{Fst}_\Lambda \partial_\Lambda L_R = \bigcup\{\Gamma;\ \langle \Lambda, \Gamma\rangle \in R\} \cup \{\Lambda\}$, and since $a \in \mathrm{Fst}_\Lambda \partial_\Lambda L_R$ there exists Γ_Λ such that $a \in \Gamma_\Lambda$ and $\langle \Lambda, \Gamma_\Lambda\rangle \in R$.

Induction step. If $v \in L_n$ then $v = wa$ where $w \in L_{n-1}$, $a \in \Gamma_w$ and $\langle w, \Gamma_w\rangle \in R$. By the condition (1) of the theorem, $a \in \mathrm{Fst}_\Lambda \partial_w L_R$, i.e. $v \in L_R$. The conditions (1) and (2) guarantee the existence of the set Γ_v satisfying conditions a),b),c),d) required in the above construction.

II. Next we shall prove that the language $L_{\langle u,\Gamma\rangle}$ obtained by the construction has the required properties. The languages L_n are mutually disjoint and contain only strings of length n which are prolongations of strings from L_m, $m < n$. Thus for any $v \in L$, $\lg(v) = n$ we have

$$\mathrm{Fst}\, \partial_v L = \mathrm{Fst}\, \partial_v L_{n+1} = \Gamma_v \setminus \{\Lambda\} .$$

Due to d), $\mathrm{Pref}\, L_{\langle u,\Gamma\rangle} = L$ and thus by the preceding

$$\mathrm{Fst}_\Lambda \partial_v L_{\langle u,\Gamma\rangle} = \mathrm{Fst}\, \partial_v L = \Gamma_v \quad \text{iff} \quad \Lambda \notin \Gamma_v ,$$

$$\mathrm{Fst}_\Lambda \partial_v L_{\langle u,\Gamma\rangle} = \mathrm{Fst}\, \partial_v L \cup \{\Lambda\} = \Gamma_v \quad \text{iff} \quad \Lambda \in \Gamma_v$$

for any $v \in L$.

Therefore, according to the conditions on the choice of Γ_v, $L_{\langle u,\Gamma\rangle} \in \tilde{G}(R)$ and, in particular, $\mathrm{Fst}_\Lambda \partial_u L_{\langle u,\Gamma\rangle} = \Gamma$.

Q.e.d.

REFERENCES

1. Havel, I.M., Nondeterministically recognizable sets of languages. In: Mathematical Foundations of Computer Science 1975 (J.Bečvář, Ed Lecture Notes in Computer Science 32, Springer-Verlag, Berlin 1975 pp. 252-257.

2. Karpiński,M., Decision algorithms for Havel's branching automata. In: Mathematical Foundations of Computer Science 1975 (J.Bečvář,Ed.) Lecture Notes in Computer Science 32, Springer-Verlag, Berlin 1975, pp. 273-280.

3. Havel,I.M., On the branching structure of languages. In: Mathematical Foundations of Computer Science 1976 (A.Mazurkiewicz,Ed.) Lecture Notes in Computer Science 45, Springer-Verlag, Berlin 1976, pp. 81-99.

4. Benda,V.and Bendová,K., On specific features of recognizable families of languages. In: Mathematical Foundations of Computer Science 1976 (A.Mazurkiewicz,Ed.) Lecture Notes of Computer Science 45, Springer-Verlag, Berlin 1976, pp. 187-194.

5. Havel, I.M., Finite branching automata. Kybernetika 10 (1974), pp. 281-302.

6. Benda, V. and Bendová, K., Recognizable filters and ideals. Commentationes Math.Univ.Carolinae 17,2 (1976), pp. 251-259.

7. Benda, V. and Bendová, K., On families recognizable by finite branching automata (submitted for publication).

AN ALGEBRAIC APPROACH TO PROBLEM SOLUTION AND PROBLEM SEMANTICS

A. Bertoni, G. Mauri, M. Torelli

Università di Milano - Istituto di Cibernetica

Via Viotti n. 5 - 20133 Milano (Italy)

Abstract

The usual approach to the synthesis of algorithms for the solution of problems in combinatorial mathematics consists of two steps.

1 - Description: the problem is embedded in a general structure which is rich enough to permit a mathematical modelling of the problem.

2 - Solution: the problem is solved by means of techniques "as simple as possible", with respect to some given notion of complexity.

We give a formalization of this approach in the framework of category theory, which is general enough to get rid of unessential details.
In particular such a framework will be provided by the category of ordered complete Σ-algebras, and we will describe the relation between description and solution by means of a variant of so called "Mezei-Wright like results" [10], relating the concept of least fixed point to that of a suitable natural transformation between functors.

1. Introduction

Many problems are set on a given structure, but can be solved on a structure having "less information". As an example, we consider the following problems:

1 - To count the number of strings, in a language $\mathcal{L} \subseteq \{a,b\}^*$, containing a given number of a's and b's.

2 - To count the number of strings, in a language $\mathcal{L} \subseteq \{a,b\}^*$, containing a given number of a's.

3 - To count the number of strings, in a language $\mathcal{L} \subseteq \{a,b\}^*$, having given lenght.

More precisely, we call these "problem schemata", since each of these resumes a class of concrete problems, abstracting from the particular language assigned.

If we consider the structures $R^{\{a,b\}^*}$ of formal power series with non commutative variables $\{a,b\}$, and $R^{\{x,y\}^c}$, $R^{\{t\}^c}$ of formal power series with commutative variables $\{x,y\}$ and $\{t\}$ respectively, and assign the language by assigning the formal power series $r = \sum \chi(w)\, w$ $(w \in \{a,b\}^*)$, it is possible to solve problem (1) making the substitutions $a \longrightarrow x$ and $b \longrightarrow y$ thus obtaining the generating function of the required number of strings. In this way we have solved the problem, assigned on the structure $R^{\{a,b\}^*}$ on $R^{\{x,y\}^c}$. Likewise, the solution to problem (2) is found by means of the substitutions $a \longrightarrow t$, $b \longrightarrow 1$, and to problem (3) by $a \longrightarrow t$, $b \longrightarrow t$.

These substitutions define homomorphisms Ψ_1, Ψ_2, Ψ_3 between formal power series semirings. We thus have the general scheme:

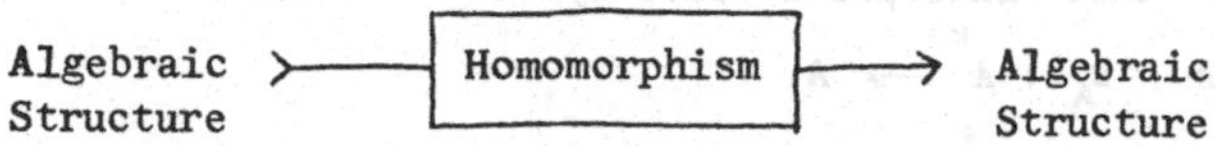

as an abstraction of the scheme:

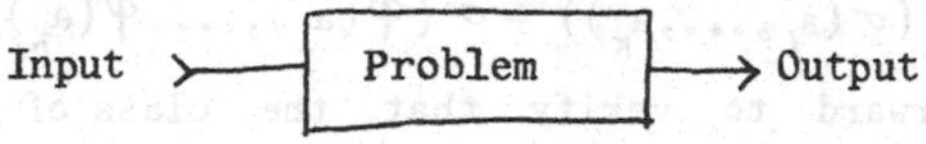

Finally, we note that, intuitively, for every solution of (1) there exists a (unique) solution of (2) and a solution of (3), but not conversely, while (2) and (3) are not related. This fact is correlated to the existence of two morphisms φ_2, φ_3 that, composed with the morphism Ψ_1 which solves (1), produce the morphisms for (2) and (3), respectively.

The notions of problem schemata, problem solution, problem hierarchy etc., that we have introduced on the basis of combinatoric motivations, can be formalized in the frame of category theory [2,3], whose expressive power permits to treat these questions in a simple manner.

2. Preliminary definitions

Def. 2.1 - A category is a pair $\mathcal{C} = \langle O_{\mathcal{C}}, M \rangle$ where $O_{\mathcal{C}}$ is a set of objects and M a class containing for every ordered pair (a,b) of objects, a set $\mathcal{C}(a,b)$ of morphisms from a to b, with the properties:

a) A partial associative composition law is defined that associates with every pair (f,g) of morphisms with $f \in \mathcal{C}(a,b)$ and $g \in \mathcal{C}(b,c)$ a morphisms g.f of $\mathcal{C}(a,c)$.

b) For every object a morphism $1_a \in \mathcal{C}(a,a)$, called identity morphism, exists, such that, for every $f \in \mathcal{C}(a,b)$ $(g \in \mathcal{C}(b,a))$, we have $f \cdot 1_a = f$ $(1_a \cdot g = g)$.

In the following, we will use the notation $f : a \longrightarrow b$ or $a \xrightarrow{f} b$ for $f \in \mathcal{C}(a,b)$.

Def. 2.2 - An ordered complete Σ-algebra or CΣ-algebra, is a quadruple $\langle \Sigma, \nu, A, i \rangle$ where: Σ is a finite set of symbols, called alphabet; $\nu : \Sigma \longrightarrow N$ is the arity function; A is a complete poset with g.l.b. $\perp$; i is a map that interprets each symbol $\sigma \in \Sigma$ with arity k as a continuous function $\sigma_A : A^k \longrightarrow A$.

Def.2.3 - A morphism $\varphi : \langle \Sigma, \nu, A, i \rangle \longrightarrow \langle \Sigma, \nu, A', i' \rangle$ between two CΣ-algebras is a continuous function $\varphi : A \longrightarrow A'$ such that

$$\varphi(\sigma(a_1, \ldots, a_k)) = \sigma(\varphi(a_1), \ldots, \varphi(a_k)) \qquad \varphi(\perp) = \perp'$$

It is straightforward to verify that the class of CΣ-algebras together with their morphisms equipped with the usual morphism composition is a category which we shall denote by CΣ-ALG.

Def.2.4 - An object a in a category $\mathcal{C}$ is called initial if, for every object $b \in \mathcal{C}$, there is an unique morphism $f : a \longrightarrow b$.

Def. 2.5 - A functor between two categories $\mathcal{A}$ and $\mathcal{B}$ is an application $F : \mathcal{A} \rightarrow \mathcal{B}$ that associates with every object of $\mathcal{A}$ an object of $\mathcal{B}$ and with every morphism of $\mathcal{A}$ a morphism of $\mathcal{B}$, in such a way that:

a) $F(a \xrightarrow{f} b) = F(a) \xrightarrow{Ff} F(b)$

b) $F(1_a) = 1_{Fa}$

c) If f and g are composable morphisms in $\mathcal{A}$, then $F(f.g) = F(f).F(g)$.

We can now construct an important category, CAT, assuming categories as objects and functors as morphisms; the definitions of identity functors and functor composition are obvious.

Def. 2.6 - A natural transformation between two functors F,G: $\mathcal{A} \rightarrow \mathcal{B}$ is a function τ, if exists, that associates to every object a of $\mathcal{A}$ a morphism τ_a in $\mathcal{B}$ in such a way that, for every pair (a,b) of objects and for every morphism $a \xrightarrow{f} b$, the diagram

$$\begin{array}{ccc} Fa & \xrightarrow{\tau_a} & Ga \\ {\scriptstyle Ff}\downarrow & & \downarrow{\scriptstyle Gf} \\ Fb & \xrightarrow{\tau_b} & Gb \end{array}$$

commutes.

Def. 2.7 - A functor F: $\mathcal{B} \rightarrow \mathcal{A}$ is called left adjoint of G: $\mathcal{A} \rightarrow \mathcal{B}$ if, for every $B \in O_{\mathcal{B}}$, there is a morphism $B \xrightarrow{\eta_B} GFB$ such that, for every f: B $\longrightarrow$ GA, there exists one and only one morphism φ:FB $\longrightarrow$ A such that the following diagram commutes:

$$\begin{array}{ccc} B & \xrightarrow{\eta_B} & GFB \\ & {\scriptstyle f}\searrow & \downarrow{\scriptstyle G\varphi} \\ & & GA \end{array}$$

The pair $\langle B, \eta B\rangle$ that satisfies this property is said to be a free object on B with respect to G.

3. The category of problem schemata generated by a CΣ-Algebra

In this section, we introduce the notion of "problem schema" and show that a suitable interpretation of the theory of quotient algebras permits to determine simple relations within the class of problem schemata.

Def. 3.1 - Let $A \in C\Sigma$-ALG. The subcategory S(A) of CΣ-ALG containing only objects B such that there is a surjective morphism φ :A $\longrightarrow$ B is said to be the category of structures subordinated to A. Its objects are isomorphic to the quotient structure A/φ (Birkhoff [1]), hence containing less information than A.

Def. 3.2 - A problem schema generated by A is a pair $\langle \varphi, B\rangle$ where φ : A $\longrightarrow$ B is in S(A).

Def.3.3 - The category P(A) of problem schemata generated by A has problem schemata as objects, and morphisms $\varphi : \langle \varphi', B\rangle \longrightarrow \langle \varphi'', B'\rangle$ such that the diagram:

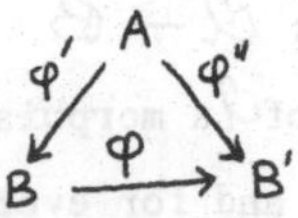

commutes in S(A). The product of morphisms is their product in S(A).

The first important result is the following:

Th.3.1 - A) Two problem schemata $\langle e_1, B\rangle$, $\langle e_2, C\rangle$ in P(A) are connected by a unique morphism $\varphi : \langle e_1, B\rangle \longrightarrow \langle e_2, C\rangle$, or by an isomorphism, or are not related.

B) The problem schema $\langle 1_A, A\rangle$ is initial in $\mathcal{S}$(A).

Point A) formalizes the intuitive concept of problem hierarchy, which we drew from the example in section 1, introducing in P(A) an ordering relation in an obvious way, while point B) warrants the existence of an initial object that can be considered a "semantics" for every problem schema generated by A, in the sense that for every problem schema $\langle \varphi, B\rangle$ in P(A) there is a unique surjective morphism $\langle 1_A, A\rangle \rightarrow \langle \varphi, B\rangle$ (interpretation). Obviously, if D is a subset (diagram of problem schemata in P(A)), $\langle 1_A, A\rangle$ is not the only possible semantics for D; in particular the limit of D, if it exists, is a semantics for D, and it is minimal in the set of all possible semantics. The existence of this semantics is warranted by the theorem: [5]

Th.3.2 - If there exist products in CΣ-ALG, then there exist products in P(A).

The proof of this theorem gives a constructive method to find the minimal semantics, via canonical factorization of morphisms. We give an example of this construction.

From the example in section 1, we obtaine the commutative diagram:

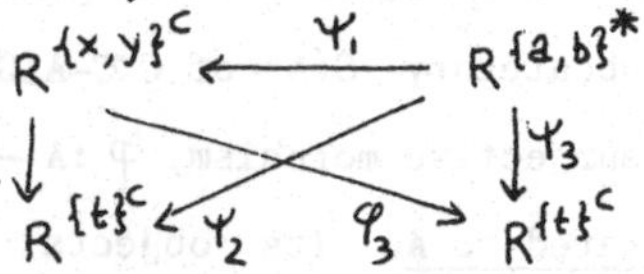

The diagram

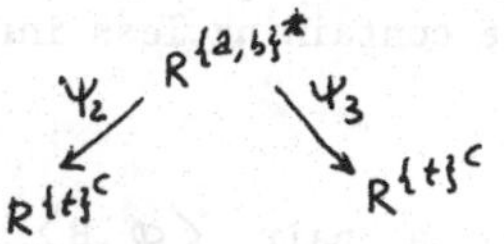

has $\langle \psi_1, R^{\{x,y\}^c}\rangle$ as its semantics, but this, although "less general" than $R^{\{a,b\}^*}$, is not the minimal semantics. We construct minimal semantics following TH.2, by steps:

A) We determine the product $R^{\{t\}^c} \times R^{\{t\}^c} \simeq (R \times R)^{\{t\}^c}$ in CΣ-ALG

B) We determine the canonical factorization

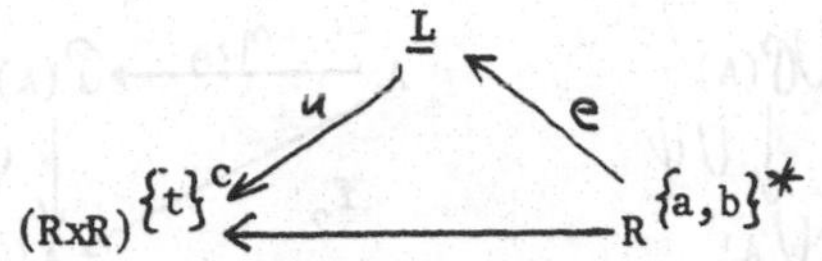

The minimal semantics is $\langle e, \underline{L} \rangle$, where $\underline{L}$ is the set of formal power series of form $\sum_K \langle r_k, s_k \rangle t^k$, and the pairs of reals $\langle r_k, s_k \rangle$ are defined by an infinite array (m_{hi}) of non negative reals such that:

$$1)\ r_k = \sum_{i=0}^{\infty} m_{ik} \quad ; \quad 2)\ s_k = \sum_{h+i=k} m_{hi} \ .$$

4. Problems, their solutions, fixed points and natural transformations

So far, we have been concerned with problem schemata. A problem is obtained from a problem schema by specifying the initial data.

Def.4.1 - A problem on A is a pair (r, φ) where $r \in A$ and $\varphi : A \longrightarrow B$. The solution of a problem (r, φ) on A is the object $\varphi(r) \in B$.

Now, we observe that the datum r is often assigned implicitly, i.e. as the least fixed point of a transformation t on A: in the example in section 1, a language $\mathcal{L}$ can be assigned as the least fixed point of a system of equation on the formal power series semiring [6].

In this case, we have an "implicit problem" on A, defined by the pair (t, φ) and the solution is reached by finding the least fixed point of t in A, and then interpreting it in B trough φ. This way, although immediate, is not generally the simplest way with regard to complexity, in actual computations, so that it is preferable, if possible, to look for the solution $\varphi(r)$ directly as the least fixed point of a transformation $t' : B \longrightarrow B$.

To prove the equivalence of these alternative procedures, we define "via universals" the notion of $C\Sigma$-algebra of polynomials in a variable x over a $C\Sigma$-algebra A.

Def.4.2 - Let $A \in C\Sigma ALG$. The $C\Sigma$-algebra of formal polynomials in a variable x over $\underline{A}$ is a $C\Sigma$-algebra $\mathcal{P}(A)$ together with the pair of morphisms

$$\eta_{1A} : \{x\} \longrightarrow U\mathcal{P}(A) \quad , \quad \eta_{2A} : A \longrightarrow \mathcal{P}(A)$$

such that for every $C\Sigma$-Algebra A' the two morphisms $f_1 : \{x\} \rightarrow A'$ and $f_2 : A \rightarrow A'$ admit a unique morphism $\psi : \mathcal{P}(A) \longrightarrow A'$ such that the two following diagrams commute:

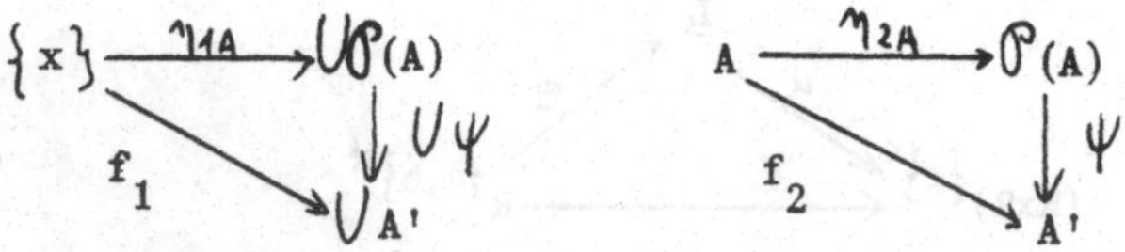

We sketch the construction of $\mathcal{P}(A)$, which is similar to many other constructions [5, 9].

Let M be the set of trees defined by:

1) $x \in M$; if $a \in A$ then $a \in M$

2) If σ is a k-ary operation symbol of Σ and $T_1,\dots,T_k$ are elements of $\mathcal{P}(A)$, at least one of which contains x, then $\sigma(T_1 \dots T_k)$ (the tree with root σ and subtrees $T_1 \dots T_k$) is an element of $\mathcal{P}(A)$.

We introduce in M the following partial order:

1) $\perp \leq x$; $a' \leq a''$ iff $a' \leq a''$ in A;

2) $\sigma(T_1 \dots T_k) \leq \sigma(T'_1 \dots T'_k)$ iff $T_1 \leq T'_1 \dots T_k \leq T'_k$

σ can be interpreted as usual as a <u>monotonic</u> application $\sigma : M^K \longrightarrow M$.

Let M^∞ be the completion of M, and σ^∞ the continuous extension of σ ; $\langle \Sigma, M^\infty \rangle$ is the $C\Sigma$-Algebra $\mathcal{P}(A)$.

Every element p of M^∞ can be interpreted as a continuous function $p: A \longrightarrow A$.

Given a morphism $f : A \to A'$, we shall denote by $\mathcal{P}(f)$ the <u>unique</u> morphism wich makes the following diagrams commutative ones:

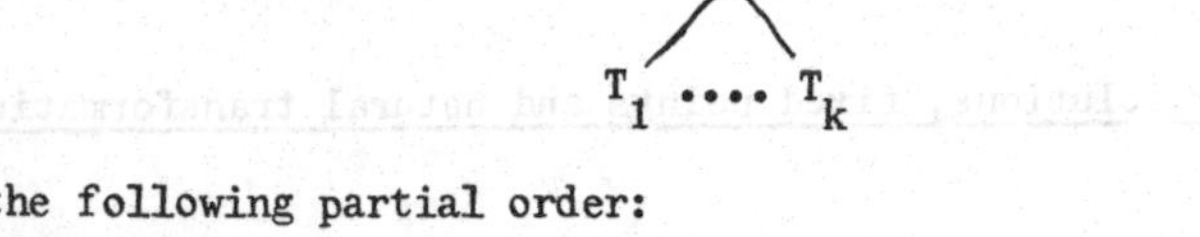

Th. 4.1 - $\mathcal{P} : C\Sigma\text{-ALG} \longrightarrow C\Sigma\text{-ALG}$ is a functor. In fact it can be easily verified that $(1_A) = 1_{\mathcal{P}A}$, $\mathcal{P}(f.g) = \mathcal{P}(f).\mathcal{P}(g)$.

We have seen that every element p of $\mathcal{P}(A)$ may be interpreted as a continuous function $p : A \to A$, in which we forget the algebraic structure of A, but <u>not</u> its ordering. Such a transformation p admits a unique least fixed point $\mu(p) = \lim_{n\to\infty} p^n(\perp)$.

μ is then an application of $U\mathcal{P}(A)$ into UA.

Th. 4.2 - $\mu : U\mathcal{P} \to U$ is a natural transformation.

In fact, $f\mu(p_A(x)) = f \lim_{n\to\infty} p_A^n(\perp) = \lim_{n\to\infty} fP_A^n(\perp)$, since f is continuous; and $\lim_{n\to\infty} fP_A^n(\perp) = \lim_{n\to\infty} P_{A'}^n(f(\perp))$ since f is a morphism. Finally, we have:

$\lim_{n\to\infty} P_{A'}^n(f(\perp)) = \lim_{n\to\infty} P_{A'}^n(\perp') = \mu(P_{A'}(x)) = \mu\mathcal{P}f(P_A(x))$.

This means that the following diagram commutes:

$$\begin{array}{ccc} U\wp(A) & \xrightarrow{\mu_A} & U_A \\ {\scriptstyle U\wp(f)}\downarrow & & \downarrow{\scriptstyle U_f} \\ U\wp(A') & \xrightarrow{\mu_{A'}} & U_{A'} \end{array}$$

that is that $\mu : U\wp \rightarrow U$ is a natural transformation, q.e.d..

As an example of use of the concepts that we have exposed, we consider the following problem schema:

Ex.: Given a context free grammar G, determine the number of derivations (not necessarily leftmost) in G of length n.

Supposing $G = \langle Q,P, q_1 \rangle$ in Chomsky normal form, with labelled productions $r_k : q_s \longrightarrow x$, we codify the derivations in G in the following way:

If $r_k \in P$ and $n_k \in N = \{0,1,\dots\}$, we set:

1) $(r_k,n_k): y \longrightarrow z$ iff $y = aq_s b$, $l(a) = n_k$, $r_k : q_s \longrightarrow x$, $z = axb$.

2) $(r_1,n_1)\dots(r_k,n_k) : q_1 \longrightarrow z$ iff $\begin{cases} \text{a) } k=1, (r_1,n_1): q_1 \longrightarrow z \\ \text{b) } k\neq 1, (r_1,n_1)\dots(r_{k-1},n_{k-1}): q_1 \longrightarrow z_{k-1} \\ \qquad (r_k,n_k) : z_{k-1} \longrightarrow z \end{cases}$

We call the list $(r_1,n_1)\dots(r_k,n_k)$ <u>derivation of z from q_1</u>, and the string $r_1 r_2 \dots r_k$ <u>code</u> of this derivation.

We set the problem Ex. on the structure $S = \langle \{N^{P^*}\}^{\Sigma^*}, +,\cdot,\otimes \rangle$ where:

$\otimes$ is the Cauchy product on the semiring $E' = \langle N^{P^*}, +, \circ \rangle$, where $\circ$ is the Hurwitz product $(\sum_x \varphi(x)\cdot x) \circ (\sum_y \varphi(y)\cdot y) = \sum_{x,y} \varphi(x)\cdot \varphi(y) x \circ y$, recursively defined by 1) $xr_k \circ yr_j = (x \circ yr_j)r_k + (xr_k \circ y)r_j$; 2) $x \circ 1 = 1 \circ x = x$.

$\cdot$ is the Cauchy product on the semiring $E'' = \langle N^{P^*}, +, \cdot \rangle$, where $\cdot$ is the usual Cauchy product of formal power series;

$+$ is the sum of formal power series on both semirings E',E".

In this structure, we can define an ordering relation [4] and construct an operator t whose least fixed point p have the following meaning:

To every string $w \in \Sigma^*$ is associated $\sum n(d)\cdot d$, where d is the code of a derivation of w from q, and n(d) the number of distinct derivations having such a code.

To fix ideas, we apply the method to a concrete example; the generalization is straightforward.

For the grammar $G = \langle \{q\}, \{r_1 : q \longrightarrow qq,\ r_2 : q \longrightarrow a\}, q \rangle$ on terminal set $\{a\}$, the desired fixed-point system is:

$$p = r_1(p \otimes p) + r_2 \cdot a$$

The problem schema Ex. is then solved by the morphism φ defined by:

$$a \longrightarrow 1 \ , \ r_1 \longrightarrow t \ , \ r_2 \longrightarrow t$$

We obtain a formal power series $g(t)$ that is the generating function of the number of derivations (not necessarily leftmost) of lenght n. We have thus, from the example,

$$g = t(g \otimes g) + t$$

or, equivalently:

$$g(0) = 0 \quad , \quad \frac{1}{t} g = g \otimes g + 1$$

Since the isomorphism from ordinary to exponential generating functions I [7] maps the $\otimes$ operation in the usual function product and the operator 1/t in the usual derivation operator d/dt, we have, setting e(t) for the exponential generating function corresponding to g(t):

$$\begin{cases} d/dt\ e(t) = e^2(t) + 1 \\ e(0) = 0 \end{cases}$$

Hence, from this system, the exponential generating function for the number D of derivations of lenght n is the trigonometric function tg t, and we have:

$$D_{2n} = 0$$

$$D_{2n-1} = \frac{4^n(4^n-1)}{2n} \cdot B_n$$

where B_n are the Bernoulli numbers [8].

If G is the structure of usual generating functions, and E the structure of exponential generating functions, the proposed method is synthesized by choosing the way

$$U\mathcal{P}S \xrightarrow{U\mathcal{P}\varphi} U\mathcal{P}G \xrightarrow{U\mathcal{P}I} U\mathcal{P}E \xrightarrow{\mu} UE$$

in the commutative diagram

$$\begin{array}{ccc} U\mathcal{P}S & \xrightarrow{\mu} & US \\ {\scriptstyle U\mathcal{P}\varphi}\downarrow & & \downarrow{\scriptstyle U\varphi} \\ U\mathcal{P}G & \xrightarrow{\mu} & UG \\ {\scriptstyle U\mathcal{P}I}\downarrow & & \downarrow{\scriptstyle UI} \\ U\mathcal{P}E & \xrightarrow{\mu} & UE \end{array}$$

REFERENCES

1. Birkhoff,G.,Lattice theory, Am.Math. Soc. Coll. pub.25 ,New York

2. Arbib,M.A.,Manes,E.G., Basic concepts of category theory applicable to computation and control, Proc. First Internat. Symp., San Francisco (1974)

3. MacLane,S., Categories for the working mathematician, Springer Verlag, New York-Berlin (1971)

4. Bertoni,A., Equations of formal power series over non commutative semirings, Proc. MFCS Symp., High Tatras (1973)

5. Goguen, J.A., Thatcher,J.W., Wagner,E.G., Wright,J.B., Factorizations, congruences, decomposition of automata and systems, IBM Research Report RC 4934 (1974)

6. Chomsky,N.,Schuetzenberger,M.P., The algebraic theory of context free languages, Computation, Programming and Formal Systems, North Holland, Amsterdam (1963)

7. Riordan,J., An introduction to combinatorial analysis, Wiley and Sons, New York-Toronto (1958)

8. Boole,G., Finite differences, Dover Publications, New York (1960)

9. Nivat,M., On the interpretation of recursive polyadic program schemata, Ist. di Alta Matematica, Symposia Matematica Vol XV, Bologna (1975)

10. Mezei,J., Wright,J.B., Algebraic automata and context free sets, Information and Control,11 (1967), 3-29

ACKNOWLEDGEMENT

This research has been developped in the frame of the C.P. Project of Università di Milano and Honeywell Information Systems Italia.

COMPLEXITY AND MINIMALITY OF CONTEXT-FREE GRAMMARS AND LANGUAGES

A. Černý

Department of Theoretical Cybernetics
Comenius University
Mlynská dolina, 816 31 Bratislava, Czechoslovakia

1. Introduction

In the paper by Gruska [2] basic algorithmic problems for descriptional complexity measures of context-free grammars and languages have been formulated: to determine complexity of a given language, to construct a minimal equivalent grammar, to decide minimality of a given grammar and so on. All those problems have been shown to be undecidable for several basic naturally defined complexity measures (Gruska [2], [3], [4]). These are negative results. One would like to have such measures for which at least some of these problems are decidable. Are there such (naturally defined) measures? What are their properties? These are the problems we are going to deal with in this paper.

We start the investigation of these problems by considering several "simpler" complexity measures of the same type in Section 3. In spite of their apparent simplicity, the typical undecidability results are obtained again. After this (unsuccessful) attempt to find measures with more rational properties we switch to investigate, in general, dependence relations among basic algorithmic problems in Section 4, where also several properties of complexity measures are shown which can be derived from decidability or undecidability of basic problems. Nonexistence of relations is shown in Section 5 where the examples of complexity measures are presented, for which the particular combination of decidability and undecidability of basic algorithmic problems holds. In this way all but one cases are solved, the remaining one being open problem.

2. Preliminaries

The basic notions and notations of context-free language theory to be used here are those of Ginsburg [1]. A context-free grammar is a quadruple $G=(V,\Sigma,P,S)$ where V is a finite alphabet, $\Sigma \subset V$ a set of terminals, P a set of productions and S a start symbol. Denote by L(G) the language generated by a grammar G and by $L_n(G)$ the set of all words of L(G), the lenght of which is less than $n+1$. The empty word is denoted by ε.

A survey of descriptional complexity theory of context-free languages is given in Gruska [5]. A (descriptional) complexity measure is defined to be an arbitrary mapping $K: \mathcal{G} \longrightarrow N$ where $\mathcal{G}$ is the class of context-free grammars and N the set of nonnegative integers. An extension of K to the class $\mathcal{L}$ of context-free languages is defined for $L \in \mathcal{L}$ by

$$K(L) = \min \{K(G); L(G) = L,\ G \in \mathcal{G}\}$$

and is said to be a complexity measure of context-free languages (K-complexity).

With every complexity measure $K: \mathcal{G} \longrightarrow N$ we associate the following algorithmic problems:

P1 : to determine K(G) for a given grammar G

P2 : to determine K(L(G)) for a given grammar G

P3 : to decide, whether K(G) = K(L(G)) for a given grammar G

P4 : to construct a grammar G' equivalent to a given grammar G and minimal with respect to K (i.e. $K(G')=\min\{K(G''), L(G'')=L(G)\}$)

$P5_n$: to decide, whether K(G)=n for an arbitrary context-free grammar G and a fixed integer n

$P6_n$: to decide, whether K(L(G))=n for an arbitrary context-free grammar G and a fixed integer n

The problems P_i, i {1,2,3,4,5n,6n} are said to be decidable, iff there is an algorithm that solves P_i. Let us make the following conventions which will simplify the presentation. We shall say that the problem P5 (P6) is decidable, iff for every integer $n \in N$ the problem $P5_n$ ($P6_n$) is decidable. We shall say that the problem P5 (P6) is undecidable, iff it is not decidable.

For any $n \geq 0$ the class of context-free grammars of K-complexity n is defined by

$$\mathcal{G}_K^n = \{G \in \mathcal{G} \mid K(G) = n\}$$

Finaly let

$$\mathcal{G}_K^{min} = \{G \in \mathcal{G} \mid K(G) = K(L(G))\}$$

denote the class of context-free grammars minimal with respect to the measure K.

3. Productions counting complexity measures

The complexity measures defined in this section seem to be simpler than those of Gruska [2], [3], [4] from two points of view:

- they induce only a finite hierarchy of languages over a fixed alphabet
- to express the complexity of a grammar, only a part of productions of this grammar is to be taken into account.

However, as we shall see in the following, in spite of their apparent simplicity the basic algorithmic problems remain to be undecidable for these measures.

Definition 3.1: Let $G=(V,\Sigma,P,S)$ be a context-free grammar. Then PT(G)= = the number of productions in P, the right-hand side of which contains a terminal.

The basic properties of the measure PT are summarized in the following theorem:

Theorem 3.1: (i) Let Σ be a finite alphabet, and $L \subset \Sigma^*$ a context-free language. Then $PT(L) \leq |\Sigma|$ (the number of symbols in Σ).

(ii) The problems P1, P5 are decidable and the problems P2, P3, P4, P6 undecidable for the measure PT.

Remark: The undecidability of the problem P6 for PT can be proved in a stronger form. For the measure PT the problem $P6_n$ is undecidable for every integer $n \geq 1$.

The property (i) follows easily from the definition of PT and (ii) can be shown by reduction of problems P_i to the Post correspondence problem using Ginsburg's language $L_{x,y}$ (Ginsburg [1]).

The measure PT has been defined according to the following schema:

Let $k(G,p) \in \{0,1\}$ be an integer associated with every context-free grammar $G=(V,\Sigma,P,S)$ and every $p \in P$. A complexity measure K of context-free grammars induced by k can now be defined by

$$K(G) = \sum_{p \in P} k(G,p) \qquad (1)$$

In this way some other complexity measures can be defined. Let us denote by PT_ε, EP, PTB (PTE) [PTBE] the measures induced by the following mappings k:

$k(G,p)= 1$ iff
- p is an ε-production or the right-hand side of p contains a terminal - the measure PT_ε
- the right-hand side of p contains only terminals - the measure EP
- the right-hand side of p begins (ends) [begins and ends] with a terminal - the measure PTB (PTE) [PTBE]

For all these measures a theorem similar to Theorem 3.1 holds.

If a complexity measure K is defined by a schema (1), then we can define in a natural way a "complementary" complexity measure CK as follows:

$$CK = \sum_{p \in P}(1 - k(G,p))$$

<u>Theorem 3.2:</u> (i) The problems P1, P5 are decidable, the problems P2-P4 and P6 are undecidable for the measure CEP.

(ii) For the measures CK, $K \in \{PT, PT_\varepsilon, PTB, PTE, PTBE\}$, all the problems P1-P6 are decidable.

4. Reducibility of complexity problems and properties of complexity measures

As far as the decidability of algorithmic problems P1-P6 is concerned, the properties of complexity measures from Gruska [2], [3], [4] and of complexity measures from the previous section are identical. This gives an arise to a natural question, which other combinations of decidability results for algorithmic problems P1-P6 are possible and what are the properties of the corresponding complexity measures.

At first we show dependence relations among problems P1-P6.

Lemma 4.1: (i) Decidability of P1 (P2) implies decidability of P5 (P6).

(ii) Decidability of P1 and P2 implies decidability of P3, P5 and P6.

(iii) Decidability of P1 and P4 implies decidability of P2, P3, P5 and P6

The following properties of complexity measures can be derived from decidability and undecidability of problems P1-P6:

Lemma 4.2: (i) Let P1(P2) be undecidable and P5 (P6) be decidable for a measure K. Then K defines an infinite hierarchy of context-free grammars (languages).

(ii) Let P1 and P3 be decidable and P2 undecidable for a complexity measure K. Then either there is an integer $n \geq 0$ such that the class $\mathcal{G}_K^n$ is infinite, or all the classes $\mathcal{G}_K^i, i \geq 0$ are finite and the function $f: N \longrightarrow N$, $f(i) = |\mathcal{G}_K^i|$, is not recursive.

(iii) Let $\mathcal{E}$ be a class of context-free grammars such that there is an algorithm that decides for arbitrary two grammars $G \in \mathcal{G}$, $G' \in \mathcal{E}$, whether $L(G) = L(G')$. Let for a measure K the class $\mathcal{G}_K^{min}$ be recursively enumerable. Then P4 is decidable for K on $\mathcal{E}$.

(iv) Let K_1, K_2 be complexity measures with the following property: There is a strictly increasing recursive function such that for every context-free grammar G $K_2(G) = f(K_1(G))$. Then

a) P_i, $i \in \{1,2,3,4\}$ is decidable for K_1 iff it is decidable for K_2

b) $P5_n$ $(P6_n)$ is decidable for K_1 iff $P5_{f(n)}$ $(P6_{f(n)})$ is decidable for K_2.

Remark: For example the following classes of context-free grammars satisfy the property (iii): the class of grammars generating bounded context-free languages (Ginsburg [1]) and the class of grammars generating parentheses languages (Knuth [7]).

5. Complexity measures with special properties

In Lemma 4.1 four dependence relations among algorithmic problems

P1-P6 have been shown. The aim of this section is to show that other dependence relations do not exist in general. To achieve this aim, to every other combination of decidability results for problems P1-P6 we shall construct a complexity measure with the corresponding decidability results for P1-P6.

First of all let us turn our attention to the problems P1-P4. We start with defining four measures on which the definition of other measures will be based.

Definition 5.1: Let G be a context-free grammar. Let us define

(i) C(G) = 0 iff G is a grammar in Chomsky normal form
= 1 otherwise

(ii) S(G) = 0 iff L(G) is a language in at most three-letter alphabet
= 1 otherwise

(iii) R(G) = 0 iff the language L(G) is regular
= 1 otherwise

Proposition 5.1: (i) Problems P1-P4 are decidable for C and S
(ii) Problems P1, P2 are undecidable and problems P3, P4 decidable for R.

In the following definition of the measure P we assume that G_1, G_2,... is a fixed effective enumeration of the class $\mathcal{G}$ of all context-free grammars. Further, let us denote by G_o the grammar

$$S \rightarrow aS \mid bS \mid cS \mid \varepsilon$$

(We assume $G_o \in \mathcal{G}$ -if necessary the symbols can be renamed.)

Definition 5.2: The measure P is defined as follows

$P(G_n) = 0$ iff $G_n = G_o$
$= 1$ iff $L_n(G_n) \neq L_n(G_o)$
$= 2$ otherwise

Proposition 5.2: Problems P1, P3 are decidable and problems P2, P4 undecidable for P.

The proof of this proposition is also based on the reduction to the Post correspondence problem.

Now we can proceed to the construction of other complexity measures. In the following definition eight new complexity measures are defined and in parentheses the decidability (+) or undecidability (-)

of the problems P1-P4 for these measures is shown.

Definition 5.3 Let G be a context-free grammar. Let us define

(i) $P'(G) = \lfloor P(G)/2 \rfloor$ (+ + + -)

(ii) $CR(G) = C(G).R(G)$ (- + - +)

(iii) $CRC(G) = C(G) + CR(G)$ (- + + +)

(iv) $RCR(G) = R(G) + CR(G)$ (- - - +)

(v) $RC(G) = |C(G) - R(G)|$ (- + - -)

(vi) $RP'(G) = 2\,P'(G) + R(G)[1 - P'(G)]$ (- - + -)

(vii) $RSRC(G) = R(G) + S(G)[RC(G) - R(G)]$ (- - - -)

(viii) $P'SCRC(G) = P'(G) + S(G)[CRC(G) - P'(G)]$ (- + + -)

There are 16 potential combinations of decidability and undecidability of the problems P1-P4. Eleven other combinations have been illustrated on the measures from Definitions 5.1, 5.2 and 5.3. The last one is typical for "natural" complexity measures, e.g. the measure PT from Definition 3.1. These results are summarized in the following theorem.

Theoreem 5.1: The only dependence relations among the problems P1-P4 are those described in Lemma 4.1.

Finaly the dependence relations among all the problems P1-P6 are investigated. The crucial problem is to find a measure M (M′) such that P6 (P5) is decidable but P2 (P1) is undecidable. According to (i) of Lemma 4.2

P6 (P5) is decidable iff P2 (P1) is decidable

holds true for all complexity measures of Section 5. Obviously the measure M (M′) has to imply the existence of an infinite hierarchy of complexity classes $\mathcal{G}_M^n$ ($\mathcal{G}_{M'}^n$).

At first the measure A is introduced:

Definition 5.4: Let $G=(V,\Sigma,P,S)$ be a context-free grammar. Let us define $A(G) = |\Sigma|$ (the number of elements in Σ)

Proposition 5.4: All the problems P1-P6 are decidable for A.

The definition of the measure M is based on the following results by Hopcroft [6]:

A sequence $G_1', G_2', \ldots$ of context-free grammars with the following two properties can be effectively generated:

a) for each $i \geq 1$ there is an algorithm to decide for an arbitrary context-free grammar G, whether $L(G) \subset L(G_i')$

b) there is no effective procedure for the construction of all algorithms from a).

Now let $G_1, G_2, \ldots$ be a fixed effective enumeration of all context-free grammars.

<u>Definition 5.5</u>: The measure M is defined as follows

$$\begin{aligned} M(G_n) &= A(G_n) \quad \text{iff } A(G_n) \leq 3 \\ &= A(G_n)-3 \text{ iff } A(G_n) > 3 \text{ and } L_n(G_n) \not\subset L_n(G_i'), \text{ where } \\ &\qquad\qquad i = A(G_n) - 3 \\ &= A(G_n)-2 \text{ otherwise} \end{aligned}$$

<u>Proposition 5.5</u>: The problems P1,P5,P6 are decidable, the problems P2,P3,P4 are undecidable for M.

The measures A, M, together with C, S, R, P form the base for a construction of complexity measures with suitable decidability properties (the decidability/undecidability of P1-P6, respectively, is shown in parentheses):

<u>Definition 5.6</u>: Let G be a context-free grammar. Then we define the following complexity measures:

(i) $M'(G) = M(L(G))$ (- - + + + +)

(ii) $CM'(G) = C(G).M'(G)$ (- + + + + +)

(iii) $MCM'(G) = M'(G) + C(G)[M(G) - M'(G) - 1]$ (- - - - + +)

(iv) $CAM'(G) = A(G) + C(G)[M'(G) + 3 - A(G)]$ (- + - + + +)

(v) $M'CAM'(G) = M'(G) + CAM'(G)$ (- - - + + +)

(vi) $M'CRC(G) = M'(G) + CRC(G)$ (- - + + - +)

(vii) $PSMCM'(G) = P(G) + S(G)[MCM'(G) - P(G)]$ (- - - - + -)

(viii) $P'SM'CRC(G)=P'(G) + S(G)[M'CRC(G) - P'(G)]$ (- - + - - +)

(ix) $CRSM'(G) = CR(G) + S(G)[M'(G) - CR(G)]$ (- - - + - +)

(x) $PSM'(G) = P(G) + S(G)[M'(G) - P(G)]$ (- - + - + -)

(xi) $P'SCAM'(G)= P'(G)+S(G)[CAM'(G) - P'(G)]$ (- + - - + +)

(xii) $P'SM'(G) = P'(G) + S(G)[M'(G) - P'(G)]$ (- - + - + +)

(xiii) $P'SCM'(G) = P'(G) + S(G)[CM'(G) - P'(G)]$ (- + + - + +)

(xiv) $RCSM(G) = RC(G) + S(G)[M(G) - RC(G)]$ (- - - - - +)

In order to be able to show a theorem similar to Theorem 5.1 in which all dependence relations among problems P1-P6 would be listed one has to solve the following problem.

<u>Open problem:</u> Is there a complexity measure, for which the problems P1, P3, P5, P6 are decidable and P2, P4 undecidable?

However, the following theorem holds.

<u>Theorem 5.2:</u> With the possible exception of the relation described as an open problem, the only dependence relations among the problems P1-P6 are those described in Lemma 4.1.

References

1. Ginsburg, S., <u>The Mathematical Theory of Context-Free Languages</u>, McGraw-Hill, New York 1966
2. Gruska, J., Some Classifications of Context-Free Languages, <u>Information and Control</u>, <u>14</u> (1969) 152-179
3. Gruska, J., On a Classification of Context-Free Languages, <u>Kybernetika</u> <u>3</u> (1967) 22-29
4. Gruska, J., Complexity and Unambiguity of Context-Free Grammars and Languages, <u>Information and Control</u> <u>18</u> (1971) 502-519
5. Gruska, J., Descriptional Complexity of Context-Free Languages, <u>Proc. MFCS'73</u>, High Tatras, 71-83
6. Hopcroft, J. E., On the Equivalence and Containment Problems for Context-Free Languages, <u>Math. Syst. Theory</u> <u>3</u> (1969) 119-124
7. Knuth, D. E., A Characterization of Parenthesis Languages, <u>Information and Control</u> <u>11</u> (1967) 269-289

COMPARISON OF THE ACTIVE VISITING AND THE CROSSING COMPLEXITIES

Michal P. Chytil

Charles University
Malostranské nám. 25
118 00 Praha 1 - M. Strana
Czechoslovakia

Introduction

The complexity measure of active visits (or "return" complexity) introduced by Wechsung in [9] has proved to have many interesting properties. For example, the constant bounds imposed on this complexity yield exactly the class of context-free languages as demonstrated by Wechsung in [10] . For supralinear bounds, on the other hand, the complexity of active visits can be used to separate two components of formal languages which could be intuitively characterized as a "context-free" and a "context-sensitive" component (cf. [3] and [4]). In both cases, the nondeterministic one-tape, one-head model of Turing machine was considered. The complexity measure of active visits for other models of Turing machine has been studied e.g. by Brandstädt and Saalfeld [2] and by Peckel [7] .

The active visiting complexity of a computation of one-tape, one-head Turing machine is determined by the maximal number of so called active visits payed to a tape square by the head during the computation. The measure is therefore related to the measure determined by the maximal number of all visits payed to a square. This measure is (up to the multiplicative constant 2) equal to the well-known crossing complexity given by the maximal length of crossing sequences (cf. e.g. Trachtenbrot [8]). In this paper, we study the relation of the crossing complexity and the complexity of active visits.

Deterministic machines

By Turing machine (TM) we shall mean the one-tape, one-head model throughout this paper. We consider only deterministic ones in this paragraph.

By function we mean arithmetic function.

DC(f) will denote the class of languages recognized by deterministic Turing machines with the crossing complexity bounded by f, i.e.

$L \in DC(f) \iff$ there is a deterministic TM M such that

1) for every $w \in L$ there is a computation of M accepting w and not crossing any bound between tape squares more than $f(|w|)$-times,
2) for $w \notin L$ there is no accepting computation of M.

By active visit of a tape square we mean every visit payed by the head to the square after the first rewriting of the content of the square.

The measure of active visits of a computation is given by the maximal number of active visits payed to a square during the computation. Then analogously to DC(f),

DV(f) denotes the class of languages recognized by deterministic TM with the measure of active visits bounded by f.

For any function f, $\Theta(f)$ will denote the class of functions $\hat{f}$ for which constants $c_1, c_2 > 0$ exist such that $c_1 . f(n) \leq \hat{f}(n) \leq c_2 f(n)$ for all n. Then define

$$DC(\Theta(f)) =_{df} \bigcup_{\hat{f} \in \Theta(f)} DC(\hat{f}) \quad \text{and}$$

$$DV(\Theta(f)) =_{df} \bigcup_{\hat{f} \in \Theta(f)} DV(\hat{f}) \quad .$$

Lemma. $DC(\Theta(f)) \subseteq DV(\Theta(f))$ for all f.

The lemma follows immediately from the definitions.

Theorem 1. Let f be a function such that $(\forall n)(f(n) \geq n)$. Then $DC(\Theta(f)) = DV(\Theta(f))$.

Proof. $DC(\Theta(f)) \subseteq DV(\Theta(f))$ by the lemma. Let $L \in DV(\Theta(f))$. Then there is an $\hat{f} \in \Theta(f)$ and a Turing machine M recognizing L with DV-complexity $\hat{f}$. Moreover, M can be chosen so that there is a constant $c \geq 0$ such that for every accepting computation of M there are sequences $s_1,\dots,s_m$ and $r_1,\dots,r_n$ of tape squares with the following properties:

i) $s_1,\dots,s_m$ are situated on the right of the tape segment which contained initially the input word w (let us call it w-segment);

ii) s_{i+1} is on the right of s_i $(1 \leq i < m)$ and s_i and s_{i+1} are separated by at most c tape squares. The square s_1 is placed at most c squares to the right of the w-segment;

iii) $s_1,\dots,s_m$ are all the tape squares (on the right of the w-segment) which are rewrited during the first visit of the head.

The squares $r_1,\dots,r_n$ are chosen analogously from the part of tape on the left of the w-segment. (Cf. Fig. 1.)

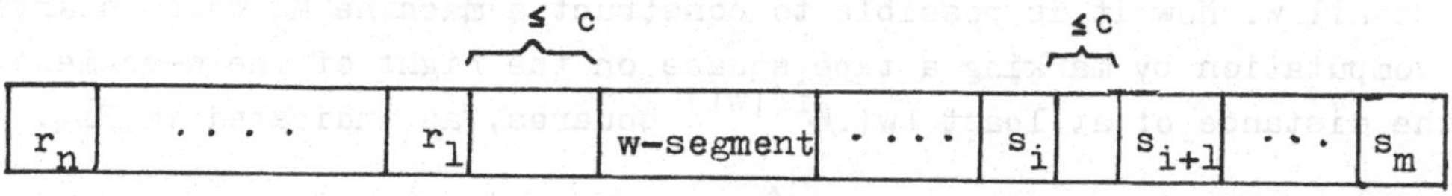

Fig. 1

By (iii) and the assumption about complexity, every s_i and r_j is visited at most $\hat{f}(|w|)+1$-times during the computation. By (ii), there is a constant $d > 0$ (depending on M only) such that M cannot spend continuously more then d steps between s_i and s_{i+1} $(1 \leq i < m)$ or r_j and r_{j+1} $(1 \leq j < n)$. It would enter an infinite cycle, otherwise.

The working alphabet of the machine can therefore be extended so that all the information between s_i and s_{i+1} (including s_{i+1}, excluding s_i) can be encoded in a single symbol and every part of computation spent continuously between s_i and s_{i+1} can be reduced to a single step. Analogously for the left part of the tape. Such a machine M_1 also accepts w and every square out of the w-segment is visited at most $\hat{f}(|w|)+1$-times. Cf. Fig. 2.

It is easy to see that there is a constant k such that M_1 cannot spend more than $k^{|w|}$ steps within the w-segment continuously. But by assumption, it leaves the w-segment maximally $2.\hat{f}(|w|)$-times. That

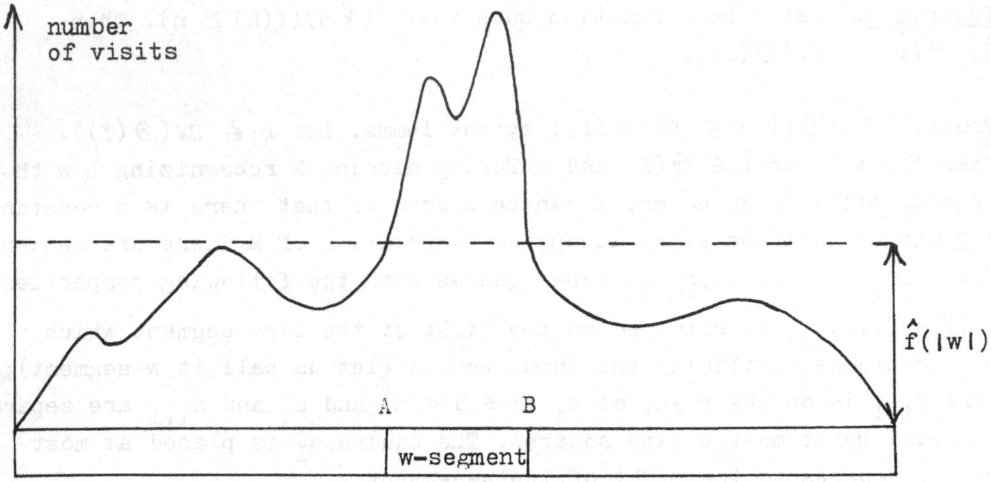

Fig. 2

is why it cannot spend more than $2.\hat{f}(|w|).k^{|w|}$ steps altogether on the w-segment.

Let us chose a constant ℓ such that $2.\hat{f}(|w|).k^{|w|} \leq \ell^{\hat{f}(|w|)}$ for almost all w. Now it is possible to construct a machine M_2 which starts its computation by marking a tape square on the right of the w-segment in the distance of at least $|w|.\ell^{\hat{f}(|w|)}$ squares, as indicated in Fig. 3.

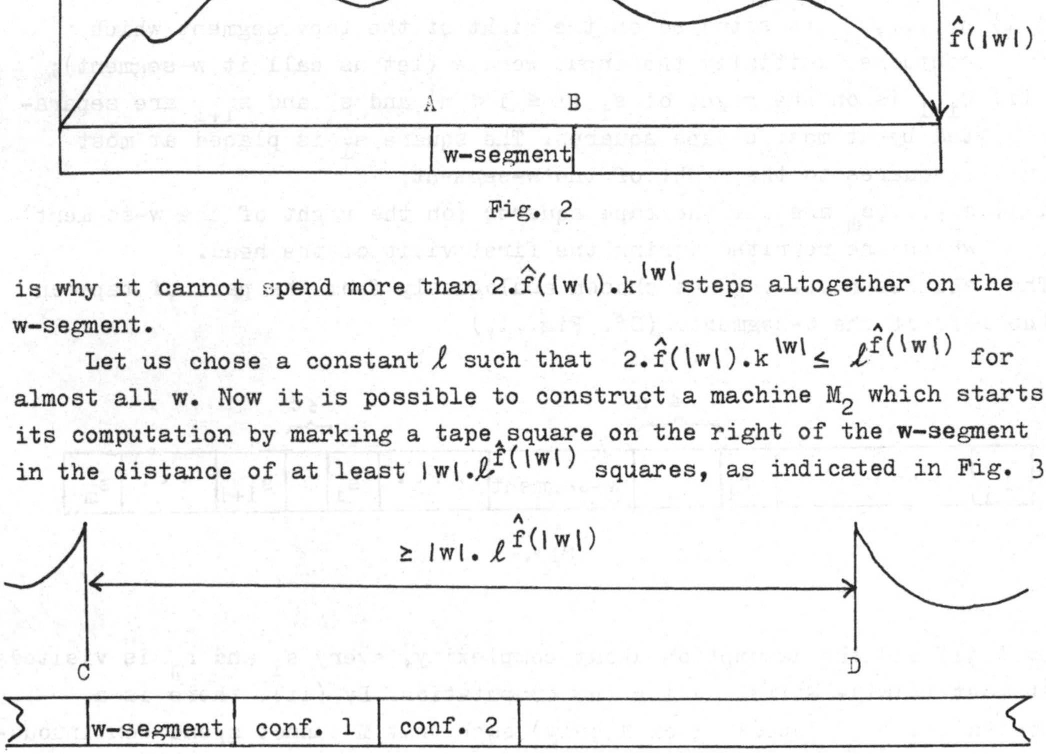

Fig. 3

The computation of M_2 will be on the left of the point C (on the right of the point D) the same as the computation of M_1 on the left of the point A (on the right of the point B) - cf. Fig. 2 and Fig. 3.

The steps of the computation of M_1, in which the head is between A and B are successively simulated by M_2 in the area between C and D. It is done so that the configurations of M_1 in these steps, restricted to the w-segment, are in their turn printed in the free space between C and D, each configuration to the right of the preceding one (cf. Fig 3) If M_2 reaches a situation when M_1 leaves the left (or right) end of the w-segment, it moves the head to the point C (or D) and performs the same computation as M_1 behind it. If M_1 reenters the w-segment, M_2

finds the recently written configuration between C and D and continues the simulation. M_2 obviously recognizes the same language as M_1 and it is not difficult to prove that it recognizes the language with the crossing complexity a.f(n) for some constant a. □

Theorem 2. Let f be a function such that $\underline{\lim}\ \frac{f(n)}{n} = 0$ and $f(n) \geq 1$ for infinitely many n. Then

$$DC(\Theta(f)) \subsetneqq DV(\Theta(f)).$$

Proof. Denote $L = \{wcw^R; w \in \{a,b\}^*\}$. For the functions of the assumed properties, $L \notin DC(\Theta(f))$, by a result of Barzdin [1]. On the other hand, $L \in DV(1)$ as can easily be demonstrated by the analysis of the DV-complexity for the machine which recognizes L by comparing the first symbol of the input word with the last one, the last but one with the second and so on. □

Nondeterministic machines

C(f) and V(f) will denote, respectively, the class of languages recognizable by nondeterministic Turing machines with the crossing and active visiting complexity bounded by f. In other words, we get the definition of C(f) and V(f) if we replace "deterministic TM" by "nondeterministic TM" in the definition of DC(f) and DV(f), respectively.

Theorem 3. Let f be a function such that $\underline{\lim}\ \frac{f(n)}{n} = 0$ and $f(n) \geq 1$ for infinitely many n. Then

$$C(f) \subsetneqq V(f).$$

The proof of the theorem is quite analogous to the proof of Theorem 2.

Theorem 4. Let f be a tape constructable function such that $(\forall n)(f(n) \geq n)$. Then

$$C(f) \cup \text{complements of } C(f) \subseteq V(f).$$

The theorem is an immediate consequence of the Theorem 3 in [3] and Theorem 14 from [5].

In the following paragraph we give an alternative version of the proof of Theorem 4 based on a characterization of active visiting measure in terms of auxiliary pushdown machines introduced by Cook [6] .

CTX-measure and auxiliary pushdown machines

Let us recall the measure of context-sensitivity CTX defined in [3]. Let X_1, X_2 be disjoint alphabets, $w \in X_1^*$, $L_o \subseteq (X_1 \cup X_2)^*$. We say that a word $\hat{w} \in (X_1 \cup X_2)^*$ is an L_o-valorization of w iff $\hat{w} \in L_o$ and w can be obtained from $\hat{w}$ by omitting all symbols from X_2.

We say that a language L is recognizable with the measure of context-sensitivity f (denote $L \in CTX(f)$) iff there is a deterministic TM M and a context-free language L_o such that for any w

$w \in L \iff$ there is an L_o-valorization of w which is accepted by M and no bound between two tape squares is crossed more than $f(|w|)$-times during the accepting computation.

Informally, the CTX-measure is derived from the DC-measure by adding the possibility to insert an auxiliary "context-free" information. The CTX-measure is studied in [3] and [4]. Here, we give a characterization of this measure in terms of one-way auxiliary pushdown machines.

By 1-way auxiliary pushdown machine (abbrev. 1PDM) we mean a nondeterministic device including a finite control unit attached to
1) an input tape by a one-way read only head,
2) a work tape by a two-way read-write head and to
3) a pushdown store.

The only essential feature which distinguishes our model from the auxiliary pushdown machines introduced by Cook [6] is the one-way input head.

By 1 PDM(f) we denote the class of languages recognized by 1PDMs with the work tape complexity bounded by f.

Theorem 5. $1PDM(f) = CTX(f)$, for every function f.

Proof. Let $L \subseteq X_1^*$ and $L \in 1PDM(f)$. Let M be a 1PDM accepting L with work tape complexity f. Every resultative computation of M can be encoded by a word α of the form

$\alpha = w_0 ¢ a_1 w_1 ¢ a_2 w_2 \dots w_{n-1} ¢ a_n w_n$, where

1) each w_i describes the situation of M in the i-th step of computation, i.e. it is of the form
$w_i = u_i(c_i, q_i, x_i, \tau_i)v_i$, where $u_i x_i v_i$ is the content of the work tape, x_i indicates the symbol scanned by the head, q_i is the state of the control unit, c_i is the symbol scanned by the input head and τ_i is the symbol on the top of the pushdown store;

2) $$a_i = \begin{cases} c_i & \text{if } i = 1 \text{ or the input head move rightwards in the i-1 th step of the computation} \\ \text{empty word} & \text{otherwise} \end{cases}$$

It is easy to see that $a_1 \dots a_n$ equals the input word w, by 2).

The language consisting of the words α of the above properties can be recognized jointly by a nondeterministic pushdown automaton M_0 and a deterministic TM M_1 which operates as follows.

M_0 checks whether the part of the information contained in α describing the actions on the input tape, in the pushdown store and in the control unit corresponds with a computation of M. Meanwhile, M_0 "takes for granted" the part of information concerning the work tape.

The machine M_1, on the other hand, relies upon the information concerning the input tape and the pushdown store and checks whether $w_0, w_1, \dots, w_n$ could be consecutive configurations of the work tape during a computation. This can be achieved deterministically with the crossing complexity bounded by max $\{|w_i| ; 0 \le i \le n\}$, i.e. bounded by $f(|w|)$, provided α is the encoding of a f-bounded computation of M accepting w.

Since the language recognized by M_0 is context-free, $L \in CTX(f)$ by the definition of the CTX-measure. This encloses the first part of the proof.

To prove the converse inclusion, assume that $L \in CTX(f)$, $L \subseteq X_1^*$. Then there is a context-free language $L_0 \subseteq (X_1 \cup X_2)^*, (X_1 \cap X_2 = \emptyset)$, and a deterministic machine M_0 such that $w \in L$ iff there is an L_0-valorization of w , which is accepted by M_0 with the crossing complexity $f(|w|)$.

We describe a 1PDM M, now, which recognizes L with the work tape complexity f.

The finite control unit of M contains a nondeterministic generator of symbols from the alphabet $X_1 \cup X_2$. The generator produces sequentially (symbol by symbol) a word $\hat{w}$, during each computation of M with an input word w. In the meantime,

1) M checks whether $\hat{w}$ is an L_o-valorization of w.
   To accomplish it, M uses the input tape and the pushdown store. At the same time,
2) M checks whether $\hat{w}$ is accepted by M_o.
   This is achieved by consecutive guessing all crossing sequences ocurring in the computation of M_o, beginning with the leftmost one. The guessed sequence σ_i is printed on the (two tracks) work tape. Then σ_i is compared with the recently guessed sequence σ_{i-1}, still stored on the work tape. If σ_i could appear as the right neighbour of σ_{i-1}, provided the square between σ_{i-1} and σ_i contains the i-1 th symbol produced by the generator, then M erases σ_{i-1} and proceeds to the next crossing sequence. (A more detailed treatment of this technique can be found e.g. in [5].)

M apparently uses a segment of the work tape as long as the longest of the guessed crossing sequences. It follows that $L \in 1PDM(f)$. □

Theorem 5 immediately implies the following corollary which was proved by Wechsung [11] by a straightforward argument.

By 2PDM(f) we denote the class of languages recognizable by 2-way auxiliary pushdown machines using at most f(n) work tape squares in some accepting computation, for every accepted input word of length n. Our 2DPM is simply PDM of Cook [6].

<u>Corollary</u>. (Wechsung) Let f be a function such that $(\forall n)(f(n) \geq n)$. Then

$V(f) = 2PDM(f)$.

Proof. 1PDM(f) = 2PDM(f) for every function of the assumed property. For the same class of functions, V(f) = CTX(f) (cf. [3] and [4]). The result follows by Theorem 5. □

<u>Corollary</u>. Let f be such that $\lim \frac{f(n)}{n} = 0$. Then

$1PDM(f) \subsetneq 2PDM(f)$.

Proof. Let $L = \{wcw;\ w \in \{a,b\}^*\}$. Then $L \notin CTX(f)$ as demonstrated in [4], for any function f of the assumed property. But it is easy to see that $L \in 2PDM(0)$. The corollary follows from Theorem 5. □

Corollary. Let f be such that $\overline{\lim}\ \frac{f(n)}{\log\log n} = 0$. Then

1PDM(f) = CFL (the class of context-free languages).

Proof. By a result of Trachtenbrot [8], DC(f) coincides with the class of regular languages for any f of the above property. Then CTX(f) = CFL, by the definition of the CTX-measure and the fact that CFL is closed under intersection with regular sets. Therefore, 1PDM(f) = CFL, by Theorem 5. □

Finally, Theorem 4 is also a simple consequence of Theorem 5 and of some results proved by Cook [6]:

1PDM(f) = 2PDM(f) for functions of the property assumed in Theorem 4. Then 2PDM(f) equals the class of languages recognizable by deterministic Turing machines with the time bounded by $2^{c.f(n)}$, for some constant c (cf. [6]). This class is closed under complements, provided f is tape constructable. And Theorem 4 follows from the fact that $C(f) \subseteq V(f)$.

References

1. Barzdin J., Complexity of recognition of symmetry by Turing machines (in Russian). In Problemy kibernetiki, vol. 15 (1965), 245-248.

2. Brandstädt A. and Saalfeld D., Eine Hierarchie beschränkter Rückkehrberechnungen auf on-line Turingmachinen, preprint.

3. Chytil M. P., Analysis of the non-context-free component of formal languages. In Proceedings of MFCS 1976, Lecture Notes in Computer Science 45, 230-236.

4. Chytil M. P., Separation of the context-free component from formal languages, paper in preparation.

5. Chytil M. P., Crossing-bounded computations and their relation to the LBA-problem, Kybernetika 12 (1976), 2, 76-85.

6. Cook S. A., Characterizations of pushdown machines in terms of time-bounded computers, JACM, 18, 1 (1971), 4-18.

7. Peckel J., this volume.

8. Trachtenbrot B. A., Turing computations with logarithmic delay (in Russian), Algebra i logika, III, 4 (1964), 33-48.

9. Wechsung G., Characterization of some classes of context-free languages in terms of complexity classes. In Proceedings of MFCS 1975, Lecture Notes in Computer Science 32, 457-461.

10. Wechsung G., Kompliziertheitstheoretische Characterisierung der kontext-freien und linearen Sprachen, Elektronische Informationsverarbeitung und Kybernetik 12 (1976), 6, 289-300.

11. Wechsung G., private communication.

ARITHMETICAL COMPLEXITY OF SOME PROBLEMS IN COMPUTER SCIENCE

P. Hájek

Mathematical Institute, CSAV, 115 67 Prague

Abstract

We show that the set of all (indices of) Turing machines running in time n^2 is a complete Π_1^0 set and that the set of all (indices of Turing machines computing characteristic functions of) recursive sets A such that $P^A \neq NP^A$ is a complete Π_2^0 set. As corollaries we obtain results saying that some assertions concerning running time of Turing machines and some instances of the relativized P = NP problem are independent of set theory (or of another theory containing arithmetic).

Introduction

In spite of a considerable amount of effort paid to the investigation of the P = NP problem, this problem remains unsolved and various results seem to show that its solution will be hard or perhaps impossible. Let us recall some definitions. For a set A, let P^A be the class of languages accepted in polynomial time by deterministic Turing machines with the oracle set A and let NP^A be the corresponding class of languages accepted in polynomial time by non-deterministic Turing machines with the oracle set A. If φ_i (the i-th partial recursive function) is total and if $A = \{n;\ \varphi_i(n) = 0\}$ then we also write P^{φ_i} and NP^{φ_i} instead of P^A and NP^A. Baker, Gill and Solovay [BGS] construct two recursive sets A, B such that $P^A = NP^A$ and $P^B \neq NP^B$. This shows that the P = NP problem cannot be solved by any uniform (easily relativizable) method. Various closely related results were obtained by Dekhtyar [D]. Hartmanis and Hopcroft [HH] point out that the P = NP problem may well be independent of the axioms of set theory. They show that there are instances of various important problems of computer science that are independent of set theory. In particular, they exhibit besides other things (1) a Turing machine running in time n^2 but such that there is no proof in set theory that this machine runs in time n^2, and (2) a Turing machine with index i such that φ_i is total and the assertion "$P^{\varphi_i} = NP^{\varphi_i}$" is independent of set theory. (Set theory can be replaced by any similar formal system containing arithmetic.) The aim of the present note is to elucidate the nature of the corresponding problems (i.g. the running time problem and the relativized $P = NP$ problem) in terms of the arithmetical hierarchy. We prove the following two theorems:

__Theorem 1__. The set $\{i;\ \varphi_i \text{ runs in time } n^2\}$ is a complete Π_1^0 set of integers.

__Theorem 2__. The set $\{i;\ \varphi_i \text{ is total and } P^{\varphi_i} \neq NP^{\varphi_i}\}$ is a complete Π_2^0 set of integers.

Of course, φ_i is the function computed by the Turing machine with index i. Assertions (1) and (2) are then obtained as corollaries.

__Proof of Theorem 1__. Put $X = \{i;\ \varphi_i \text{ runs in time } n^2\}$. Then X is a Π_1^0 set: $i \in X$ iff $(\forall n)(\exists y < bo(i, n))$ (y is a halting computation with $\leq n^2$ steps on φ_i with the input n), where $bo(i, n)$ is a primitive recursive function giving an upper bound of codes of all computations with $\leq n^2$ steps on φ_i with the input $k \leq n$. The inside clause is primitive recursive and the existential quantifier is bounded.

Let us prove that X is complete. For each i, let $\varphi_{\sigma(i)}$ be the Turing machine which for input n simulates $\varphi_i(i)$ for n steps and if $\varphi_i(i)$ has not halted in n steps $\varphi_{\sigma(i)}(n)$ halts in n^2 steps; if $\varphi_i(i)$ does halt in n steps then $\varphi_{\sigma(i)}(n)$ halts in exactly 2^n steps. (Cf. [HH] p. 21.) Evidently, $\varphi_{\sigma(i)}$ runs in time n^2 iff $\varphi_i(i)$ does not halt. Thus the function σ reduces the complete Σ_1^0 set $\{K = i;\ \varphi_i(i) \text{ converges}\}$ to the complement of X (cf. [Rog]) and so X is a complete Π_1^0 set.

__Remarks__. (1) Put $X_o = \{i;$ it is provable in set theory that φ_i runs in time $n^2\}$. Evidently, X_o is Σ_1^0 (recursively enumerable) and $X_o \subseteq X$ (intuitive soundness of set theory assumed). By Theorem 1, X_o must be a proper subset of X, thus we have $X - X_o \neq \emptyset$. (This is Assertion (1).)

(2) Note that whenever i is such that the assertion "φ_i runs in time n^2" is independent of set theory (or a similar system), then φ_i does run in time n^2 since the assertion in question is a Π^0_1 assertion; if its negation were true it were provable. (Cf. [Fe] 3.10.) Note by passing a mistaken remark in [HH] p. 16:
The authors claim that there exist diophantine equations for which there exist (integer) solutions but that their existence is independent from the axioms of set theory. This is false: if a diophantine equation has a solution then this fact is provable (by [Fe] 3.10). But there are diophantine equations having no solution but such that this fact is independent of set theory).

Proof of Theorem 2. Put $Y = \{e;\ \varphi_e$ total and $P^{\varphi_e} \neq NP^{\varphi_e}\}$. We first show that Y is Π^0_2. Indeed, $e \in Y$ iff

$$\underbrace{\varphi_e \text{ is total}}_{\Pi^0_2} \text{ and } (\forall i,n)(\exists w)(w \in K(\varphi_e) \not\equiv (\exists z < bd(w,i,n))$$
$$(z \text{ is a halting computation on } \varphi_i \text{ with an oracle for } \varphi_e \text{ having at most } |w|^n \text{ steps})$$

Here $K(\varphi_e)$ is the Karp-complete language for NP^{φ_e} as constructed in [BGS]; $bd(w,i,n)$ is a primitive recursive upper bound. Observe that if φ_e is total then

"z is a computation on φ_i with an oracle for φ_e"

is Δ^0_1. Thus the formula in the scope of the quantifier $(\exists z < bd(w))$ is also Δ^0_1 and the whole condition is Π^0_2.

We are going to prove that Y is Π^0_2-complete. Let A be a recursive set such that $P^A = NP^A$ (cf. [BGS]). We modify the construction of a set B such that $P^B \neq NP^B$ from [BGS] as follows: With each index e we effectively associate a recursive function $\varphi_{\tau(e)}$ such that $P^{\varphi_{\tau(e)}} \neq NP^{\varphi_{\tau(e)}}$ iff W_e is infinite. Since $\{e;\ W_e$ is infinite$\}$ is a complete Π^0_2 set ([Rog]

Theorem 13-VIII) our set Y is also a complete Π_2^0 set.

Let P_i^x be the enumeration of deterministic Turing machines working in polynomial time as described in [BGS]; P_i^x uses an oracle for φ_α and works in time $p_i(n) = i + n^i$. Put $n_0 = 0$; given n_i, let $\bar{n}_i = \min_n(n > n_i$ and $p_i(n) < 2^n)$ and put $n_{i+1} = 2^{\bar{n}_i}$. Given an index e , we construct a set B_e with the characteristic function $\varphi_{\tau(e)}$ in countably many steps. Put $B_e(0) = \emptyset$; given $B_e(s)$ we construct $B_e(s + 1)$.

Case 1. For no k , there is a halting computation z of $\varphi_e(k)$ such that $n_s \leq z < n_{s+1}$. In this case put

$A(s) = \{w \in A;\ n_s \leq |w| < n_{s+1}\}$ and $B_e(s + 1) = B_e(s) \cup A(s)$.

Case 2. There is a k and a halting computation z of $\varphi_e(k)$ such that $n_s \leq z < n_{s+1}$. Suppose that s is the i-th step for which Case 2 occurs. We investigate the behaviour of $P_i^{B_e(s)}$ for the input $0^{\bar{n}_s}$. If $P_i^{B_e(s)}$ accepts $0^{\bar{n}_s}$ (in $p_i(\bar{n}_s)$ steps) then we set $B_e(s + 1) = B_e(s)$ (nothing added); otherwise we set $B_e(s + 1) = B_e(s) \cup \{w\}$ where w is a word of length $\bar{n}_s$ not used by the oracle during the computation of $P_i^{B_e(s)}(0^{\bar{n}_s})$. Evidently, $p_i(\bar{n}_s) < 2^{\bar{n}_s}$ and w exists.

The set $B_e = \bigcup_s B_e(s)$ is recursive and an index $\tau(e)$ of its characteristic function is primitively recursively computable from e . If W_e is finite then B_e differs at most finitely from A and consequently $P^{B_e} = NP^{B_e}$. On the other hand, if W_e is infinite then each machine P_i is eventually used during the construction of B_e; thus we can prove $L(B_e) \notin P^{B_e}$ exactly as in [BGS]. (Recall that $L(X) = \{w;$ for some x such that $|x| = |w|$ we have $x \in X\}$. We use the fact that $P_i^{B_e(s)}(0^{\bar{n}_s}) \cong P_i^{B_e}(0^{\bar{n}_s})$.) Thus $P^{B_e} \neq NP^{B_e}$ which concludes the proof.

Say "φ_e is provably total" if the assertion "the e-th Turing machine computes a total function" is provable in set theory. Similarly for "P^{φ_e} provably $= NP^{\varphi_e}$" etc. Observe that our construction of the set B_e is such that the corresponding characteristic function $\varphi_{\tau(e)}$ is provably total. Thus we can prove the following lemma:

Lemma. (1) The set $\{e;\ W_e \text{ is infinite}\}$ is recursively reducible to the set $Y' = \{e;\ \varphi_e \text{ provably total and } P^{\varphi_e} \neq NP^{\varphi_e}\}$.

(2) The set $\{e;\ W_e \text{ is finite}\}$ is recursively reducible to the set $Z' = \{e;\ \varphi_e \text{ provably total and } P^{\varphi_e} = NP^{\varphi_e}\}$.

Remark. Y' is a Π^0_2 set and hence a complete Π^0_2 set; since "φ_e is provably total" is a Σ^0_1 condition one can show that Z' is a Σ^0_2 set and hence a complete Σ^0_2 set. Put

$Y_o = \{e;\ \varphi_e$ provably total and P^{φ_e} provably $\neq NP^{\varphi_e}\}$ and
$Z_o = \{e;\ \varphi_e$ provably total and P^{φ_e} provably $= NP^{\varphi_e}\}$.

Then both Y_o and Z_o are Σ^0_1; hence $Y' - Y_o \neq \emptyset$ and $Z' - Z_o \neq \emptyset$.

Corollary. We have (1) a Turing machine φ_e computing a total function such that $P^{\varphi_e} \neq NP^{\varphi_e}$ but the assertion "$P^{\varphi_e} = NP^{\varphi_e}$" is independent of set theory and (2) a Turing machine φ_f computing a total function such that $P^{\varphi_f} = NP^{\varphi_f}$ but the assertion "$P^{\varphi_f} = NP^{\varphi_f}$" is independent of set theory.

Remark. The preceding result differs from [HH] where one has an e such that "$P^{\varphi_e} = NP^{\varphi_e}$" is independent from set theory and its truth value is unknown and equal to the truth value of "$P = NP$".

References.

[BGS] Baker, T., Gill, J. and Solovay, R., Relativizations of the P = ? NP question, SIAM J. on Comp. 4 (1975), 431-442.

[D] Dekhtyar, M.I., On the relation of deterministic and non-deterministic complexity classes, Mathematical Foundations of Computer Science 1976 (A. Mazurkiewicz, ed.), Lecture Notes in Computer Science vol. 45, p. 255-259, Springer-Verlag 1976.

[Fe] Feferman, S., Arithmetization of metamathematics in a general setting, Fundamenta Mathematicae 49 (1960), 35-92.

[HH] Hartmanis, J. and Hopcroft, J.E., Independence results in computer science, SIGACT News 8, Number 4 (Oct.-Dec. 1976), 13-21.

[Rog] Rogers, H., Jr., Theory of recursive functions and effective computability, McGrow-Hill, New York, 1967.

FORMAL TRANSFORMATIONS AND THE DEVELOPMENT OF PROGRAMS

Friedrich W. von Henke

Gesellschaft für Mathematik und Datenverarbeitung Bonn

D-5205 St.Augustin 1, Germany

Introduction

In recent years an approach to the development of programs has emerged that is based on transformations on programs (cf., e.g. [1,6,7]). This approach may be characterized roughly as follows. We start with specifications that are precise and clear so that it can easily be checked whether they are adequate, i.e. correspond to the programmer's intentions. The specifications may be actual programs written in a high level language, or non-procedural statements, possibly expressed within a logical calculus. In general such specifications are not acceptable as programs because they tend to be rather inefficient if executed or compiled directly. Therefore, transformations are applied to them to generate programs which are, in a certain sense, more efficient than the original ones, but usually also less comprehensible as regards their structure. The transformations are required to preserve meanings; the resulting programs can then be considered 'correct' in that they meet the specifications from which they were derived.

It is obvious that this approach is related to the much popularized 'structured programming' and 'programming by stepwise refinement' techniques. In contrast to the latter, however, where an executable program is developed stepwise from an informal description, which is replaced by specific details as the development proceeds, the transformational approach presupposes complete and formal specifications to which transformations can be applied. Furthermore, if program validation is to become an integrated part of program development - as it is an ultimate goal of this kind of work - it is necessary to employ for specifications a sort of language that is amenable to formal reasoning.

In this paper we are mainly concerned with transformations that arise naturally when recursive data abstractions are used in specifications. Such data structures are typical of structure manipulating programs such as translators, theorem provers, verification systems etc. We adopt a logical framework which allows us to specify data structures, programs and transformations in a formal manner and to prove, for example, that a transformation is meaning-preserving under certain conditions.

Preliminaries

The formal basis of this paper is the Logic for Computable Functions (LCF) [8,9], an equational calculus which is particularly suited for expressing and proving facts about recursively defined objects. The terms of LCF are those of the λ-calculus, augmented by conditional expressions 'p ⇒ r,s' and fixed points 'μF.t(F)' (the least fixed point of λF.t(F)). A formula of LCF is, for the purposes of this paper, an equivalence 'r = s' between such terms. Furthermore, we have constants TT, FF and UU denoting the truth values true, false and undefined respectively; the logical connectives are expressed as <u>not</u> = λx y.x⇒FF,TT, <u>and</u> = λx y.x⇒y,FF and <u>or</u> = λx y.x⇒TT,y. In the following, <u>or</u> and <u>and</u> will mostly be used as infix operators. For the sake of greater readability we adopt here, in contrast to earlier papers, the following conventions: (a) a recursive definition f = t(f) is always meant to define the least fixed point, i.e. to abbreviate f = μF.t(F); (b) to denote conditional expressions we employ the more familiar notation 'if p then r else s' in place of 'p⇒r,s'.

Data structures are defined in the style of McCarthy's abstract syntax. We shall use the following examples:

```
llist := nil | comp(hd:atom, tl:llist)

bintree := abt(aof:atom) | cons(fir:bintree, sec:bintree)
```

which define the structures of linear lists and binary trees of atoms. The meaning of such definitions is partly expressed by a recursive identity function which is a mere transcription of the definition; for example,

```
llist = λx. if is-nil(x) then nil
            else comp(atom(hd(x)), llist(tl(x))).
```

(The structure is characterized further by axioms describing properties of the primitives.) Those functions that correspond closest to the data structure are representable by means of a functional which derives from the identity. The functional corresponding to llist, for instance, is

```
LLhom = λf c op. μF. λx. if is-nil(x) then c
                          else  op(f(hd(x)), F(tl(x)));
```

similarly,

```
BThom = λf op. μF. λx.  if is-abt(x) then f(aof(x))
                        else  op(F(fir(x)), F(sec(x))).
```

is the functional associated with the structure bintree. (Examples of the use of these functionals will be given below.) The functionals are called "hom-functionals" since functions defined by means of them may be interpreted as homomorphisms in an algebraic sense. For a detailed discussion of the logical and algebraic framework, including the axiomatization and algebraic interpretation of data structures and the derivation and use of hom-functionals, see [3,4,5]. In what follows we will call a function defined by means of a hom-functional a 'hom'. The following properties of hom's are stated without proof.

Prop. 1: (i) A hom is uniquely determined by the parameters of the hom-functional.
(ii) If all parameters of a hom-functional are total (i.e. yield defined results for defined arguments) then the resulting function (hom) is total on (the defined elements of) the data structure.

Program Specification and Hom's

As examples of the use of hom's we give definitions for the common set-theoretic operations. Assuming that sets are represented by linear lists of non-repeating elements, we define

```
member    = λx y. LLhom((λz.z=x), FF, or)(y)

app(end)  = λx y. LLhom(id, y, comp)(x)      (id = identity)

union     = λx y. LLhom(fu(y), y, app)(x)
intersect = λx y. LLhom(fi(y), nil, app)(x)
```

where

```
fu = λu v. if member(v,u) then nil else comp(v,nil)
fi = λu v. if member(v,u) then comp(v,nil) else nil.
```

In the following we will use the more readable notation with infix operators $\in$, $\cup$ and $\cap$. Quantification over finite sets is similarly representable: Let

all $= \lambda P\ S.\ \text{LLhom}(P, TT, \underline{\text{and}})(S)$

exist $= \lambda P\ S.\ \text{LLhom}(P, FF, \underline{\text{or}})(S)$

Then

$\forall x \in S.\ P(x) := \text{all}(P,S)$

$\exists x \in S.\ P(x) := \text{exist}(P,S)$

Obviously, all these functions may be helpful in specifying function meanings. Note that every LCF expression (like the functions defined above) is not only a term of the logic, but also carries a 'computational meaning'. LCF terms can be interpreted (and evaluated) as programs very much like ordinary expressions of the λ-calculus or programs written in Pure LISP. We will therefore not distinguish between recursively defined functions and (abstract) programs. It is helpful to regard a hom as mapping a structure onto an expression denoting a <u>computation</u> ("computation tree"); for example, BThom(f,op) maps the binary tree

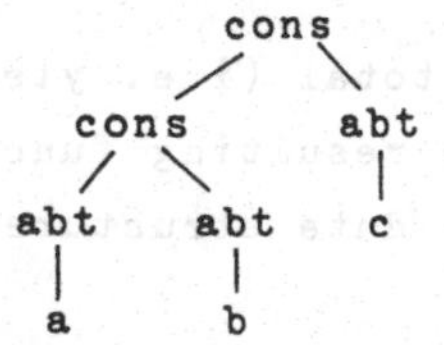

onto the isomorphic computation tree

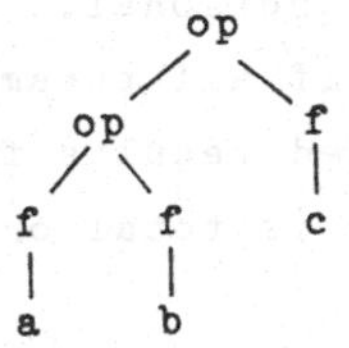

In the remainder of the paper we discuss aspects of transformations that are associated with the use of hom's in specifications. We concentrate of two types of transformations: (a) merging of recursions and (b) recursion removal. We take for granted the presence of other kinds like algebraic simplifications; these are already provided by the LCF system and not specific to the problem area.

<u>Merging of Recursions</u>

Consider the composition of two hom's H_1 and H_2. If $H_1 \circ H_2$ is applied to an argument x and executed as a program an intermediate structure y is being built up as the result of $H_2(x)$ before H_1 is evaluated. In other words, two recursions are necessary to evaluate $H_1 \circ H_2$. We may attempt to merge them into one recursion, which always leads to an increase in efficiency. For instance, with the definitions of $\in$ and $\cap$ as given above the expression $a \in x \cap y$ corresponds to the composition (member(a) $\circ$ intersect)(x,y) of two hom's on linear lists. For such compositions we have the following (cf. [4,5])

<u>Prop. 2</u>: $L_1 \circ L_2$ = LLhom(f,c,op) if and only if

(a) $(L_1 \circ L_2)$(nil) = c and

(b) $(L_1 \circ L_2)$(comp(x,y)) = op(f(x), $(L_1 \circ L_2)$(y)).

For a restricted class of hom's the transformation is immediately available.

<u>Prop. 3</u>: Let L_1 = LLhom(f_1,c_1,op_1) and L_2 = LLhom(f_2,c_2,comp). Then

$$L_1 \circ L_2 = \text{LLhom}(f_1 \circ f_2,\ L_1(c_2),\ op_1).$$

(Similar propositions hold for other data structures.) As an example, consider concatenation of three linear lists, which, if defined as λx y z. app(app(x,y),z), is

λx y z. (LLhom(id,z,comp) $\circ$ LLhom(id,y,comp)) (x)

This is transformed by prop. 3 into

λx y z. LLhom(id, LLhom(id,z,comp)(y), comp) (x)

which is just λx y z. app(x,app(y,z)). An application of prop. 3 to simplifying a form of function iteration is given in [5].

In the general case we have to construct f, c and op by attempting to solve the equivalences (a) and (b) of prop. 2. For the example mentioned above we find

$a \in x \cap y$ = LLhom(id, FF, op(a,y)) (x)

with

op(a,y) = λu v. if u=a then $a \in y$ else v.

(The right-hand side is just another way of writing 'if $a \in x$ then $a \in y$ else FF'.)

As another example, consider the function

F = λx. $\forall a \in$ leaves(x). P(a)

which tests whether property P holds for all leaves of a binary tree x. Here leaves is a 'set-valued' function defined by leaves = norep $\circ$ front with

front = BThom(λa.comp(a,nil), app)

norep = LLhom(id,nil,compr)

```
compr = λx y. if member(x,y) then y else comp(x,y)
```

(norep removes repeating elements from a linear list.) F is a composition of three hom's; we can simplify it by constructing f and op such that F = BThom(f,op). By some formulae manipulation we find f = P and op = <u>and</u>.

Recursion Removal

A recursive function (program) is <u>in iterative form</u> if the identifiers indicating recursive calls occur only as the outermost symbols of applicative terms. Such forms correspond to iterative programs; for example,

```
f = λx y. if p(x) then g(y) else f(h(x),k(x,y))
```

is transcribed to

```
begin while not(p(x)) do
            y := k(x,y);  x:= h(x)  endwhile
      return g(y)
end
```

In this section we discuss to what extent transformation of programs from recursive to iterative form depends on the data structure. Specifically, we show, by way of analysing well-known examples, that the following holds:

<u>Assertion</u>: Replacing recursion by iteration is possible only if a linear structure is (explicitly or implicitly) present.

As the first example (cf. [6]), consider an arbitrary hom fun_1 = BThom(f,op) from binary trees into some domain D. Compare fun_1 with fun_2 = λx.fun'(x,u) where

```
fun' = λx y. if is-abt(x) then op(f(x),y)
                else  fun'(fir(x), fun'(sec(x),y))
```

(In fun' the first occurrence of fun' in the else-part is an 'iterative' call.) The computation trees generated by fun_1 and fun_2 for an argument x = cons(cons(a,b),c) are

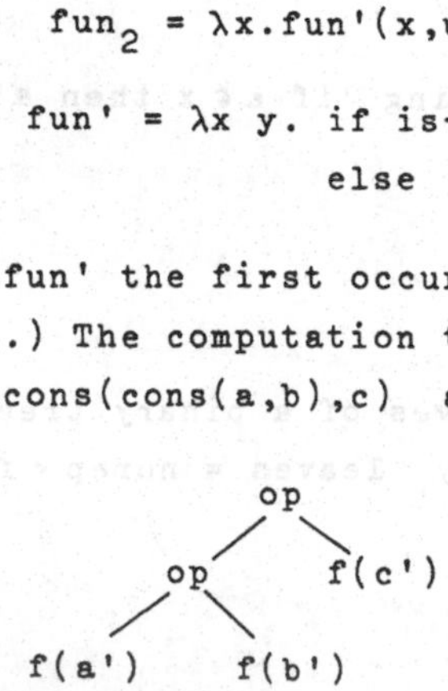

and

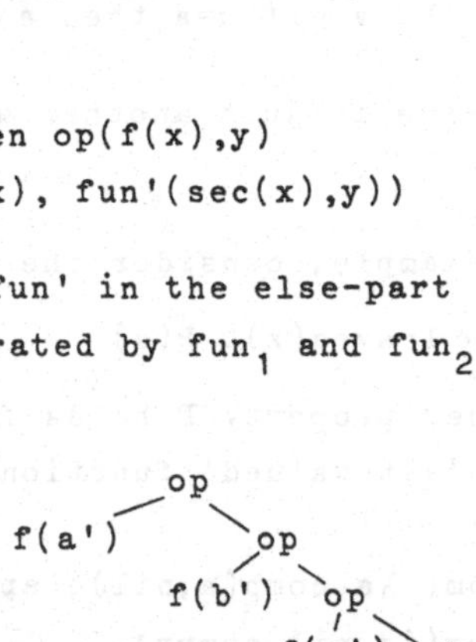

This suggests that $fun_1 = fun_2$ if the two computations are equivalent.

<u>Theorem 4</u>: $fun_1 = fun_2$ if and only if the following hold:

(a) op is associative on the range of fun_1.

(b) u is a right identity of op.

Conditions (a) and (b) essentially mean that the computation tree can be linearized. This can also be interpreted in a different way. If $fun_1 = fun_2$ then the result does not depend on the particular structure of the argument but only on the 'front' (the sequence of leaves, see above). This means that fun_1 can be factorized through llist.

<u>Corollary 5</u>: $fun_1 = fun_2$ iff the diagram

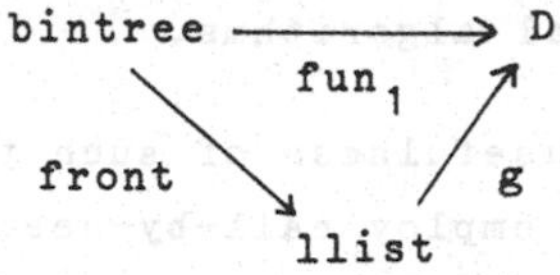

with g = LLhom(f,u,op) commutes.

The corollary demonstrates that the linear structure that is required by the assertion is hidden in the computation even in those cases where it is not manifest in the structure of the domain D.

The recursive call remaining in fun' can be removed by introducing an explicit stack, i.e. a linear list of trees. Let

fun_3 = λx. fun"(x,nil,u)

where

```
fun" = λx y z. if is-abt(x) then
                   (if is-nil(y) then op(f(x),z)
                     else  fun"(hd(y), tl(y), op(f(x),z)) )
                 else  fun"(sec(x), comp(fir(x),y), z).
```

<u>Prop. 6</u>: $fun_3 = fun_2$

This transformation does not change the actual computation tree, thus it can always be applied.

As a second example, we consider a function that changes only the leaves of a tree, i.e. a hom F = BThom(f,cons). In this case we can again replace one of the recursive calls by an auxiliary structure. Let n be a 'new' atom which does not occur in any binary tree, and

$$G = \lambda x\ y.\ \text{if is-abt}(x)\ \text{then}\ (\text{if}\ x{=}n\ \text{then}\ y\ \text{else}\ G(y,f(x)))\ \text{else}\ G(\text{fir}(x), \text{cons}(\text{sec}(x),y)).$$

Prop. 7: F = G

The second argument of G is used first to keep the right subtrees; after the leftmost atom has been encountered it becomes the current (partial) result. Of course, there is again a hidden linear structure. The trick here is that the stack that keeps the subtrees still to be processed is simulated within the tree structure (the new atom n corresponds to nil). The transformation from F to G is particularly attractive because G can be implemented by very simple pointer manipulations; it is at the heart of many tree traversal algorithms.

It is necessary to comment on the usefulness of such transformations. Recent work on interpreters that employ call-by-need evaluation of expressions (e.g. [2]) indicates that a similar gain in efficiency can be obtained by changing the interpreter rather than the individual programs. The exact relationship needs to be studied further. However, if a program is to be compiled any optimizing tranformation will also result in improved object code.

Transformations and Program Verification

As demonstrated in the preceding sections, transformations are related to proofs of program equivalence. Generally speaking, a transformation that has been proved to be meaning-preserving may be considered a verification scheme or abstract correctness proof in the sense that for every proper instantiation the result program is correct relative to the specification because of equivalence. This includes termination, too, if we start with compositions of hom's as specifications, which are total by prop. 1 (ii).

The transformational approach is obviously more economical than verifying each instance separately. Apart from that, the standard verification technique based on inductive assertions cannot do away with the induction proofs underlying some of the transformations. Moreover, a purely functional language is more amenable to formal proofs than programs involving assignments etc.; the transformation into such programs should therefore be postponed as long as possible.

The regular structure of hom's facilitates application of transformations in that complex pattern matching is replaced by 'structured definitions'. Furthermore, as indicated above, certain forms of specification directly indicate the possibility - and need - of improvement as regards efficiency. It remains to be seen how useful these techniques will prove in practice.

References

1. R.M. Burstall and J. Darlington: A transformation system for developing recursive programs. Journal of the ACM 24 (1977), 44-67.
2. D.P. Friedman and D.S. Wise: Output driven interpretation of recursive programs, or writing creates and destroys data structures. Information Processing Letters 5 (1976), 155-160.
3. F.W. v. Henke: On the representation of data structures in LCF. Memo AIM-267, Stanford University, 1975.
4. F.W. v.Henke: Recursive data types and program structures. Internal report, GMD Bonn, 1976.
5. F.W. v. Henke: An algebraic approach to data types, program verification, and program synthesis. Proc. MFCS'76, Springer Lecture Notes in Computer Science No. 45, 1976.
6. D.E. Knuth: Structured programming with go to statements. Computing Surveys 6 (1974), 261-301.
7. D.B. Loveman: Program improvement by source-to-source transformation. Journal of the ACM 24 (1977), 121-145.
8. R. Milner: Implementation and applications of Scott's logic for computable functions. Proc. ACM Conf. on Proving Assertions about Programs, Las Cruces, 1972.
9. R. Milner: Logic for Computable Functions - description of an implementation. Memo AIM-169, Stanford University, 1972.

OPTIMAL RASP PROGRAMS FOR ARBITRARILY COMPLEX 0-1 VALUED FUNCTIONS

Sándor Horváth
Eötvös Loránd University
Department of Computer Mathematics
H-1445 Budapest 8, Pf.323, Hungary

1. Introduction

The notion of a RASP as a general abstract model of a random access stored program machine was introduced by Elgot and Robinson [1]. After the appearance of Blum's work [2] on generalized algorithmic complexity theory, Cook [3, 4] investigated the computational complexity of a simpler machine model, called RAM. Later Hartmanis [5], motivated by [2-4], returned to Elgot and Robinson's model and studied the computation speed of some specific RASP's. His most important results were presented in Engeler's book [7] too. Recently, the research of Cook and Hartmanis has been continued by Sudborough and Zalcberg [8]. They obtained several new results, but still leaving open a considerable part of the problems raised in [5] . Our purpose is to make further steps toward the full solution of these problems.

We consider the following four machine models: RASP1 and $RASP1^x$ of [5], and RASP3' and RASP3, where RASP3' is a RASP3 of [8] without base register, and both machines output the result, instead of HALT-0 and HALT-1, through the accumulator (like RASP1 and $RASP1^x$). Both the accumulator and its content will be denoted by AC, while the r-th register as well as its content by $\langle r \rangle$. 'RASP' may denote any of these four machines. Here they will compute functions from P_1 only. In our complexity measure $\{\varphi, \Phi\}$, $\Phi_i(n)$ is the number of **instructions executed** during the computation of $\varphi_i(n)$. We introduce various concepts of optimality of a RASP program i (for simplicity we can identify the i-th program with i) . 'i.o.' and 'a.e.' stand as usual for "infinitely often" and "almost everywhere", respectively.

Definition. RASP program i is said to be

(1) linearly i.o./a.e. ε-optimal for a given $0<\varepsilon<1$ iff
$$(\forall j,\ \varphi_j = \varphi_i)\left[(1-\varepsilon)\,\Phi_i(n)<\Phi_j(n) \text{ i.o./a.e.}\right];$$
(2) linearly i.o./a.e. optimal iff
$$(\forall j,\ \varphi_j = \varphi_i)(\forall \varepsilon,\ 0<\varepsilon<1)\left[(1-\varepsilon)\Phi_i(n)<\Phi_j(n) \text{ i.o./a.e.}\right];$$
(3) logarithmically i.o./a.e. optimal iff
$$(\forall j,\ \varphi_j = \varphi_i)(\forall \varepsilon,\ 0<\varepsilon<1)\left[\Phi_i(n)^{1-\varepsilon}<\Phi_j(n) \text{ i.o./a.e.}\right].$$

In [5] it is proved for RASP1, by calculating the maximal growth rate of AC, that there exist arbitrarily complex functions having linearly a.e. optimal programs. Optimality questions of 0-1-output RASP programs are first considered in [8], in connection with RASP3. The authors prove firstly, by a diagonal argument, the existence of i.o. arbitrarily complex 0-1 valued total functions having for any $0<\varepsilon<1$ linearly i.o. ε-optimal programs. Secondly, they construct a 0-1 valued partial function which is i.o. arbitrarily complex, and which has a linearly i.o. optimal program.

In section 2 we generalize the first result of [8] to the other three RASP models, further, we prove a general existence result concerning logarithmic a.e. optimality. In section 3 we improve the second result of [8] , by constructing i.o. arbitrarily complex 0-1 valued total functions with linearly i.o. optimal programs.

2. Linearly ε-optimal and logarithmically optimal 0-1-output programs

The first result of [8] is based on a numerical encoding of RASP3 programs such that program reconstruction from code number can be done in linear time. By means of a simpler sequence encoding

$$G : (x_1, \dots, x_k) \mapsto 2^{x_1} + 2^{1+x_1+x_2} + \dots + 2^{k-1+x_1+\dots+x_k} = x$$
$$G : \Lambda \mapsto 0$$

(which turns out to be, in a sense, the simplest possible one, see [9]) we can do the same in time $\mathcal{O}(\log_2 x)$ (because we can construct the sequence $1, 2, \dots, 2^{k-1+x_1+\dots+x_k}$ from x in $\mathcal{O}(\log_2 x)$ steps, even on RASP1). Further, linear-time program simulation is clearly possible on all four RASP models, so,

Theorem 1. For all four RASP models, for any $0 < \varepsilon < 1$ there exist i.o. arbitrarily complex 0-1 valued total functions having linearly i.o. ε-optimal programs.

To get logarithmically a.e. optimal programs, we use on one hand the easy fact that for all four RASP models there exist arbitrarily large, linear-time computable functions T for which

$$(1\cdot T(1) + \ldots + (n-1)T(n-1))/(1+n\cdot T(n)) = \mathcal{O}(1),$$

on the other the following version of Blum's algorithm ([2], [6]) for constructing a.e. arbitrarily complex functions:

$$s(n) := \min\left(\{n\} \cup \{x \mid x < n \wedge \Phi_x(n) \leq T(n) \wedge (\forall m,\ x < m < n)[s(m) \neq x]\}\right);$$

$$f(n) := 1 \dot{-} \varphi_{s(n)}(n) \text{ if } s(n) < n,\ 0 \text{ otherwise.}$$

It is easy to see that f(n) can be computed in time $\mathcal{O}(n\cdot T(n))$, from which, again for sufficiently large T, we have

Theorem 2. For all four RASP models there exist a.e. arbitrarily complex 0-1 valued functions with logarithmically a.e. optimal programs.

3. Linearly i.o. optimal programs for 0-1 valued total functions

In this section we deal with computations on $RASP1^{sb}$, a new RASP model which we define by adding to RASP1 ([5], [7]) a base register BR (see [8]), a one-bit remainder register RR, and four new instructions: STB, LDR, SFR and SFL. STB and LDR mean BR := AC and AC := RR, respectively, and the effect of SFR is $AC := \lfloor AC/2 \rfloor$ and $RR := AC - 2\lfloor AC/2 \rfloor$ simultaneously, while that of SFR is $AC := 2\cdot AC$ (i.e. SFR and SFL means shifting AC by one binary position to the right and to the left, respectively, hence the 's' in our notation, while the 'b' comes from 'base register') A further important feature of $RASP1^{sb}$ is that the operation and addressing type code part and the operand part of an instruction are always placed in two consecutive registers, in order to have relatively simple arithmetical structure of occurring register contents. (So the instruction counter IC is normally incremented by 2.) Of course, if an instruction has no operand other than AC and/or some special register(s), then the operand part is 0; and the HALT instruction is represented by two consecutive 0's. We also suppose that at any moment of computation all but a finite number of registers contain 0, and that the starting value of BR is 0.

We mention that of course, Theorems 1 and 2 are valid for $RASP1^{sb}$ too. Our optimality result concerning 0-1-output $RASP1^{sb}$ programs will be based on a refined growth rate argument. The following Lemma seems fairly plausible, but its rigorous proof is not quite trivial.

Lemma. For any (fixed or self-modifying) $RASP1^{sb}$ program i of

$$f(n) := 1 \text{ if } n=2^k \text{ for some } k\in N, \text{ 0 otherwise}$$

we have $\Phi_i(n) \geqslant \log_2 n - c$ i.o., namely, $\Phi_i(2^k) \geqslant k-c$ a.e., where c depends only on i.

Proof. Clearly the quickest possible way of increasing/decreasing AC is executing SFL/SFR instructions, respectively. Suppose now indirectly that for any c we have $\Phi_i(2^k) < k-c$ i.o. Let the number a, depending on the initial values of $\langle 1\rangle, \langle 2\rangle, \ldots$ under i, be such that starting with AC = 0, after executing any number z of $RASP1^{sb}$ instructions,

$$\max \{AC, \langle 1\rangle, \langle 2\rangle, \ldots\} \leqslant 2^{z+a}$$

will hold (such an a clearly exists). Now, if i takes, for input 2^k (=AC), $x \leqslant k-a$ steps, then AC and $\langle 1\rangle, \langle 2\rangle$, ... will all be of the form

$$u\cdot 2^k + v \qquad (*)$$

where $u=r\cdot 2^{-x_1}$ for some $r\in N$ (of course, $r\cdot 2^k \in N$ too), $|v| \leqslant 2^{x_2+a}$, and x_1 and x_2 are the numbers of executed SFR's and SFL's, respectively (so $x_1+x_2 \leqslant x$). If here even $x\leqslant k-a-2$ then for any two expressions of the form (*) we have

$$u\cdot 2^k + v \geqslant \bar{u}\cdot 2^k + \bar{v} \implies u \geqslant \bar{u}. \qquad (**)$$

(By a simple calculation we get $\bar{u}-u \leqslant 2^{-x_1-1}$, from which (**) already follows, because both u and $\bar{u}$ are of the form $r\cdot 2^{-x_1}$.) If $c \geq a+2$ is sufficiently large (but fixed), and i computes $f(2^k)$ in $x < k-c$ steps then from (**) it follows that for any integer $m > 1$, the computation of $f(m\cdot 2^k)$ is "isomorphic" to that of $f(2^k)$, namely, both consists of the same number of steps, and at any stage, the executed instructions are one by one of the same kind, and every address (taking here into account the effect of BR too) or operand in the latter may be obtained simply by substituting $m\cdot 2^k$ for 2^k in the corresponding expression of the form (*) in the former, and in case of test instructions, either computation takes always the same "yes" or "no" branch. This means that we have $f(m\cdot 2^k) = f(2^k)$ which is impossible for m odd, contradiction.

Now we are ready to prove the following

<u>Theorem 3.</u> For $RASP1^{sb}$ there exist i.o. arbitrarily complex 0-1 valued total functions with linearly i.o. optimal programs.

<u>Proof.</u> First we easily observe that there exists a recursively enumerable sequence $i_1, i_2, \ldots$ of $RASP1^{sb}$ programs for f (in the Lemma) such that i_j works in time $(1+\varepsilon_j)\log_2 n$ a.e. where $\varepsilon_i \to 0$ if $j \to \infty$. Further, let i_0 be a program of some 0-1 valued total function such that $(\forall k, \varphi_k = \varphi_{i_0})[\Phi_k(n) \geq g(n)$ i.o.$]$ for some $g \in R_1$. Then there exists a $t \in R_1$ such that $(\forall j \in N)[t(j) = i_j]$. We define the function $h := \varphi(t \times I)\sigma^{-1}$ where $\sigma : (j, x) \mapsto 2^j(2x+1)-1$ is a pairing function, and $I : x \mapsto x$ is the identity function of one variable. Clearly h is 0-1 valued and $h \in R_1$. From now on, following roughly the line of the proof of the second result in [8] , we can prove that h is i.o. arbitrarily complex if g is large enough, and, by using our Lemma (namely that f cannot be computed in time $(1-\varepsilon)\log_2 n$), that h has a linearly i.o. optimal $RASP1^{sb}$ program.

<u>Problem.</u> For what RASP models is Theorem 3 valid with 'a.e.' in place of 'i.o.'?

References

1. Elgot, C. C. and Robinson, A., Random-access stored program machines, an approach to programming languages, <u>JACM, 9</u> (1964), 365-399.

2. Blum, M., A machine-independent theory of the complexity of recursive functions, JACM, 14 (1967), 322-336.

3. Cook, S. A., Computational complexity using random access machines, Course Notes, University of California, Berkeley, 1970.

4. Cook, S. A., Linear-time simulation of deterministic two-way pushdown automata, Proc. IFIP congr. 71, Foundations of Information Processing, North-Holl., 1972.

5. Hartmanis, J., Computational complexity of random access stored program machines, Math. Syst. Theory, 5 (1971), 232-245.

6. Hartmanis, J. and Hopcroft, J. E., An overview of the theory of computational complexity, JACM, 18, (1971), 444-475.

7. Engeler, E., Introduction to the Theory of Computing, Acad. Press, 1973, pp. 172-189.

8. Sudborough, I. H. and Zalcberg, A., On families of languages defined by time-bounded random access machines - the second part of this paper which has three versions: 1st ver.: TR, Dept. Comp. Sciences, The Techn. Inst., Northwest. Univ., Evanston, Illin., USA, 1973.; 2nd ver.: 2nd MFCS Symp., High Tatr., CSSR, 1973.; 3rd ver.: SIAM J. Comp., 5 (1976), 217-230, sect. 3 (223-230).

9. Horváth, S., Complexity of sequence encodings, to be presented at the int.-l conf. Fundamentals of Computation Theory, Poznań-Kórnik, Poland, September 19-23, 1977; the proc. of the conf. will appear as a volume of Springer Lect. Notes Comp. Sci., 1977.

THE EXPRESSIVE POWER OF INTENSIONAL LOGIC IN THE SEMANTICS OF PROGRAMMING LANGUAGES

T.M.V. Janssen,
Mathematical Centre, 2e Boerhaavestr. 49, Amsterdam
&
P. van Emde Boas,
Inst. Appl. Math./VPW, Univ. of Amsterdam, Roetersstr. 15, Amsterdam

1. INTRODUCTION

The purpose of the theory of semantics of programming languages is to describe in a computer independent way those aspects of the processes taking place during execution of a program which are considered as mathematically relevant. Depending on whether the computations themselves or the results of the computations are the subject of the description one obtains operational or denotational semantics. In the latter case the result is often expressed using predicate transformers, which tell how a description of the state of the computer before execution of the program is transformed into a description of the state afterwards (forward semantics) or conversely, given a "goal"-state the transformer yields a description of a state from which the goal-state is obtained by execution of the program (backward semantics). In this approach one always aims at the forward transformation yielding as much information as possible (a strongest postcondition) or the backwards transformer yielding the least restrictive description (a weakest precondition).

For several elementary programming constructs forward and backward transformers have been described. We will consider in particular those for the assignment statement: the forward one of Floyd (1967) and the backward one of Hoare (1969). These rules are given below; with $[z/x]\phi$ is denoted the expression obtained from ϕ by replacing all occurrences of x by z.

(1) $\{\phi\}$ x:=t $\{\exists z[[z/x]\phi \wedge x = [z/x]t]\}$ (Floyd),

(2) $\{[t/x]\psi\}$ x:=t $\{\psi\}$ (Hoare).

Gries (1976) consideres for Hoare's rule the case

(3) $\{1{=}a[j]\}$ a[i]:=1 $\{a[i]{=}a[j]\}$.

The weakest precondition in fact should be $1 = a[j] \vee i{=}j$.

De Bakker (1976) considers for Floyd's rule the case

(4) $\{a[1]{=}2 \wedge a[2]{=}2\}$ a[a[2]]:=1

$\{\exists z[[z/a[a[2]]](a[1]{=}2 \wedge a[2]{=}2) \wedge a[a[2]] = [z/a[a[2]]]1]\}$.

The postcondition reduces to $a[1]{=}2 \wedge a[2]{=}2 \wedge a[a[2]]{=}1$ which is a contradiction. In fact afterwards $a[a[2]]\neq 1$. He also considers Hoare's rule for this assignment

(5) $\{[1/a[a[2]]](a[a[2]]{=}1)\}$ a[a[2]]:=1 $\{a[a[2]]{=}1\}$.

The precondition reduces to 1=1 and this is not restrictive enough as we conclude from (4). Clearly the same problems arise if we consider arrays of higher dimension, e.g.

(6) q[q[2][2]][2]:=1.

Another source for problems is the use of pointers. Consider for Hoare's rule the program p:=x; x:=x+1 (in this p is a pointer):

(7) {x=x+1} p:=x; {p=x+1} x:=x+1 {p=x}.

It is impossible to satisfy the weakest precondition; while we only required that finally the value of p should be x. Floyd's rule also causes problems with pointers

(8) $\{x=4\}$ p:=x; $\{x=4 \wedge p=x\}$ x:=3 $\{\exists z[z=4 \wedge p=z] \wedge x=3\}$.

In the final state, however, the integer value related with p is 3 and not 4! The integer value related with p is modified by x:=3 although this is hardly visible from the program text!

De Bakker (1976) gives a solution to the problems illustrated in (3), (4) and (5). Gries (1976) does so for the backward transformation only. Another solution is implicitely present in Pratt (1976). No one of them treats (6), (7) or (8).

The approach in this paper is based on work of the logician R. Montague, treating the semantics of English. A motivation for doing so was the observation concerning the role of identifiers in assignment statements.

Assume that both x and y have the value 7. Then in the assignment x := y+1 we can replace y by x or by 7 without changing the result; after execution x has the value 8. If we replace however x by y the effect is modified. So sometimes an identifier may be replaced by an expression with the same value, and sometimes not. It is striking that the same phenomenon can be observed in English. Assume that Ghica and John are married. Then "John's wife has blue eyes" is true just in case "Ghica has blue eyes". So in this context we may replace "John's wife" by "Ghica". Next consider (*) "Peter believes that Ghica has blue eyes". In this sentence we cannot freely replace "Ghica" by "John's wife", since it is not clear that Peter knows that John and Ghica are married; it is possible that Peter affirms (*) and at the same time denies "John's wife has blue eyes" since he thinks John to be married to the black-eyed Selma.

Problems concerning such expressions constitute an intriguing part of language philosophy. Many linguists, philosophers and logicians worked on attempts to deal with them. The investigations culminated in the work of R. Montague. In *The proper treatment of quantification in ordinary English* (1973) he presents the syntax and semantics of a fragment of English in which such problems are treated. References to the earlier works in this direction can be found in the introductory article of Partee (1975). We will refer in the sequel to Montague's article by "PTQ".

In the sequel of this paper we shall illustrate how Montague's framework can be used to obtain satisfactory and correct forward and backward transformers for all assignment types mentioned above. The solutions involve higher order modal logic. By using the concept of intension the problems with pointers are solved, whereas the problems with array identifiers are dealt by treating them as functions. Finally using the necessity operator from modal logic we obtained a relation between forward and backward predicate transformers enabling us to transform the two in each other. The present paper is a sequel to Janssen & Van Emde Boas (1977) *On the proper treatment of referencing, dereferencing and assignment* (fromnow on "PTR"). In that paper forward predicate transformers are considered, while in this we focus on the backward one and the relation between both.

2. MONTAGUE's APPROACH

The basic idea in Montague's treatment of semantics is the distinction extension/ intension. The extension of an expression is its value in the current world; the intension is the function yielding this value in any possible world. Consider the sentence "John walks". Its extension is a truth-value; in order to decide which one, we have to investigate the current world and find out whether John is walking or not. Its intension is the boolean function which tells us for each possible world whether John is walking or not

The same concepts can be applied in the semantics of programming languages. The extension of an integer identifier x is the integer value of x in the present situation. Its intension is the function which for any possible world (situation) yields the corresponding integer value. In the context of programs and computers, these possible worlds may of course be considered as possible states of a computer.

The idea to distinguish between two values related to an identifier is not a new one. In denotational semantics one connects with an integer identifier an L-value (playing the role of a computer address) and an R-value (being the content of such an address). So extension corresponds with R-value, and intension has some correspondence with L-value. We wish, however, to point out that the concepts intension and extension are more general since they are defined in a model without appeal to some "address-content" structure. Therefore, intension and extension are defined (in contrast with L- and R-value) for all kinds of expressions: pointers, array identifiers as well as boolean expressions.

The mathematical language used by Montague to describe the semantics of natural language is called intensional logic (IL). This is a kind of modal logic which provides the tools for working with intensions and extensions. In PTR we have presented a formal definition of syntax and model-theory for an extension of IL which we use for describing the semantics of the assignment statement. We shall not repeat this complete definition, but present instead an informal model-theoretic exposé, illustrating the features which will be used in the sequel.

For each expression δ in the programming language we will have a corresponding expression δ'; this is called the translation of δ. For each identifier used in the programs we introduce a corresponding logical constant in IL; e.g. identifier x corresponds with constant x, so x' = x (notice the different type face used). These constants will be interpreted as intensions of the corresponding type. The set of possible computer states is denoted S. For each expression ϕ in IL we denote its valuation (interpretation) in state $s \in S$ by $V_s(\phi)$.

(9) PROPERTY. If x is an simple integer identifier then $V_s(x) \in \mathbb{N}^S$. This property ex-

presses that intensions of integers are functions from states to integers. Similar properties hold for pointers and arrays.

(10) PROPERTY. If p is a pointer then $\mathcal{V}_s(p) \in (\mathbb{N}^S)^S$.

(11) PROPERTY. If a is an array identifier then $\mathcal{V}_s(a) \in (\mathbb{N}^{\mathbb{N}})^S$.

It is a crucial aspect of a variable that its identity remains the same while its value is changed. This is expressed by the requirement

(12) PROPERTY. If χ is some identifier, then for all states s and t: $\mathcal{V}_s(\chi') = \mathcal{V}_t(\chi')$.

The extension corresponding with x is denoted as $^{\vee}x$, so

(13) DEFINITION. $\mathcal{V}_s(^{\vee}\phi) = (\mathcal{V}(\phi))(s)$.

Consequently the assertion that (the value of) x equals 7 is denoted by $^{\vee}(x)=7$. So

(14) EXAMPLE. $\quad \mathcal{V}_s(^{\vee}(x)=7) \in \{T,F\}$.

The intension corresponding with an IL expression ϕ is denoted as $^{\wedge}\phi$. So

(15) DEFINITION. $\mathcal{V}_s(^{\wedge}\phi) = \lambda t[\mathcal{V}_t(\phi)]$.

(16) EXAMPLE. $\quad \mathcal{V}_s(^{\wedge}(^{\vee}x=7)) \in \{T,F\}^S$.

(17) LEMMA. $\quad \mathcal{V}_s(^{\vee}{}^{\wedge}\phi) = \mathcal{V}_s(\phi)$.

PROOF. $\quad \mathcal{V}_s(^{\vee}{}^{\wedge}\phi) = \mathcal{V}_s(^{\wedge}\phi)(s) = \lambda t[\mathcal{V}_t(\phi)](s) = \mathcal{V}_s(\phi)$.

(18) REMARK. In general it is not true that $\mathcal{V}_s(^{\wedge\vee}\phi) = \mathcal{V}_s(\phi)$. For a counterexample see Janssen (1976).

(19) DEFINITION. The translation of a[n] in IL is $^{\wedge}((^{\vee}(a))(n))$.

The naive approach to states as demonstrated above does not yet provide a workable framework for treating semantics of programming languages since computer states have certain properties which have to be reflected in the model. Clearly a state s $\in$ S determines the values of all identifiers but is not guaranteed that two states where all identifiers have equal values are equal. More important the crucial effect of an assignment is that it modifies the value of a single identifier, and in order to model this assignment we have to require that the resulting state always exists. These problems have been dealt with extensively in PTR.

(20) DEFINITION. $<\chi \leftarrow \mathcal{V}_s\delta>s$ denotes the (unique) state in which all constants except χ have the same value as in state s, and in which the value of χ equals the value of the expression δ in state s.

The essential extension to IL introduced for describing assignment is the *state switcher* $\{\delta/^{\vee}\chi\}$ whose meaning is described semantically by

(21) DEFINITION. $\mathcal{V}_s(\{\delta/^{\vee}\chi\}\phi) = \mathcal{V}_{<\chi\leftarrow\mathcal{V}_s(\delta)>s}(\phi)$.

The needed properties of this substitution operator are expressed by

(22) SUBSTITUTION THEOREM. *The syntactic behaviour of the semantically defined operator* $\{\delta/^{\vee}\chi\}$ *is described as follows*:

1. $\{\delta/^{\vee}\chi\}[\phi \wedge \psi] = \{\delta/^{\vee}\chi\}\phi \wedge \{\delta/^{\vee}\chi\}\psi$ *and also for the other connectives.*
2. $\{\delta/^{\vee}\chi\}\exists v[\phi] = \exists v[\{\delta/^{\vee}\chi\}\phi]$ *provided that v does not occur in* δ *(otherwise we take an alphabetical variant). Analoguously for* $\exists z$, $\forall z$, λz.
3. $\{\delta/^{\vee}\chi\}\phi(\psi) = \{\delta/^{\vee}\chi\}\phi(\{\delta/^{\vee}\chi\}\psi)$.
4. $\{\delta/^{\vee}\chi\}^{\wedge}\phi = {}^{\wedge}\phi$.
5. $\{\delta/^{\vee}\chi\}\{\gamma/^{\vee}\chi\}\phi = \{\{\delta/^{\vee}\chi\}\gamma/^{\vee}\chi\}\phi$.

6. $\{\delta/{}^\ulcorner\chi\}c = c$ *for any constant c, including* $c \equiv \chi$.
7. $\{\delta/{}^\ulcorner\chi\}^\vee\chi = \delta$; $\{\delta/{}^\ulcorner\chi\}^\vee c = {}^\vee c$ *for any constant* $c \not\equiv \chi$.
Note that in other cases $\{\delta/{}^\ulcorner\chi\}^\vee\phi$ *does not reduce any further.*

(23) CONSEQUENCE. The state switcher has almost the same properties as the ordinary substitution operator.

It must be mentioned that in IL the rule of λ-conversion is no longer valid in all circumstances. Instead one has the following weaker rule:

(24) THEOREM. *Let* $[\alpha/z]\phi$ *denote the expression obtained from* ϕ *by substituting* α *for each free occurrence of z. If* (I) *no free occurrence of a variable in* α *becomes bound by substitution of* α *for z in* ϕ *and* (II) *for all states* s *and* t: $V_s(\alpha) = V_t(\alpha)$ *then we have for each state* s: $V_s\lambda z[\phi](\alpha) = V_s[\alpha/z]\phi$.

As a consequence we see that λ-conversion is allowed for arguments which are intensions like the constants corresponding to program identifiers, or state predicates (i.e., elements from $\{T,F\}^S$). For arguments not satisfying (II) wrong results may be obtained.

3. ASSIGNMENT STATEMENTS

The semantics of assignment statements is dealt with by translating them into predicate transformers. State predicates being intensions of truth values, i.e., elements of $\{T,F\}^S$ are denoted in the format $^\wedge\phi$ where ϕ is a truth value expression. Then predicate transformers become functions from $\{T,F\}^S$ to $\{T,F\}^S$, and they will be denoted in the format $\lambda P^\wedge\phi$. As seen in (24) above λ-conversion for P is allowed.

The backward predicate transformer corresponding to a simple assignment is easy to describe. Since the assignment changes the value of a single identifier the resulting state is described using a state switcher. For instance if the assignment is x:=10 the corresponding state switcher is $\{10/{}^\ulcorner x\}$. If in the resulting state ψ has to hold then in the starting state $\{10/{}^\ulcorner x\}\psi$ has to hold. Therefore, we introduce the following

(25) DEFINITION. Let χ be an identifier and δ some expression with translations χ' and δ' respectively. Then the *backward predicate transformer* corresponding to the assignment $\chi{:=}\delta$ is defined by $\lambda P^\wedge[\{\delta'/{}^\ulcorner\chi'\}^\vee P]$.

Note that except for the use of extension and intension this rule is a functional variant of Hoare's original rule. Rule (25), however, can be used for pointers and arrays as well.

(26) EXAMPLE. x := x+1. The corresponding backward predicate transformer reads $\lambda P^\wedge[\{(x+1)'/{}^\ulcorner(x)'\}^\vee P]$. Taking for P the assertion $^\wedge({}^\vee(x) > 1)$ we obtain $^\wedge[\{(x+1)'/{}^\ulcorner(x)'\}^\vee{}^\wedge({}^\vee(x) > 1)] = {}^\wedge(\{{}^\vee x+1/{}^\ulcorner x\}({}^\vee x > 1)) = {}^\wedge(x+1 > 1) = {}^\wedge({}^\vee x > 0)$.

Programs consisting of more than one assignment are dealt with by

(27) DEFINITION. Let π_1 and π_2 be (sequences of) assignment statements translated by backward predicate transformers π_1', π_2' respectively. Then the backward predicate transformer corresponding to the program $\pi_1;\pi_2$ is defined as $\lambda P[\pi_1'(\pi_2'(P))]$.

(28) EXAMPLE. p:=x; x := x+1. Taking for P the assertion $^\wedge({}^\vee p{=}x)$ as the argument of the backward transformation corresponding with x := x+1 we obtain: $^\wedge(\{{}^\vee x+1/{}^\ulcorner x\}[{}^\vee p{=}x]) = {}^\wedge(p{=}x)$

(since $^\vee x$ does not occur in P). Applying the backward transformation corresponding to p:=x we obtain $^\wedge(\{x/^\vee p\}^\vee {}^\wedge(^\vee p{=}x)) = {}^\wedge(\{x/^\vee p\}(^\vee p{=}x)) = {}^\wedge(x{=}x) = {}^\wedge\underline{true}$. We have thus obtained, in contrast with Hoare's rule, the correct weakest precondition.

It turns out that the forward predicate transformer for the assignment $\{\chi:=\delta\}$ reads $\lambda P[^\wedge\exists z[\{z/^\vee\chi'\}^\vee P \wedge {}^\vee\chi'=\{z/^\vee\chi'\}\delta']]$. Except for the use of intension and extension this rule is a functional variant of Floyd's rule. For details see PTR.

In the case where the left-hand side of an assignment is a subscripted variable the new state is obtained from the old one by changing the value of a single identifier, provided we take for this identifier the corresponding array identifier. Since we treat arrays as functions this means that a new function is assigned to the array. IL contains the needed λ-expressions to denote this assignment by a state switcher.

(29) DEFINITION. The predicate transformers (forward as well as backward) corresponding to the assignment $\alpha[\mu]:=\delta$ are the same as those corresponding to

$$\alpha := \lambda n\ \underline{if}\ n = \mu\ \underline{then}\ \delta\ \underline{else}\ \alpha[n]\ \underline{fi}.$$

(30) REMARKS. The idea of considering arrays as functions appears not to be new. Gries (1976b) dues this remark to Hoare. They do not mention, however, the above reduction to simple variable assignments. Repeated application of the above definition deals with assignments to higher dimensional array elements.

(31) EXAMPLE. The predicate transformers corresponding to a[i]:=1 and a := λn[if n=i then 1 else a[n] fi] are equal. Consequently transforming the assertion $^\wedge(^\vee a(i){=}^\vee a(j))$ backwards we obtain $^\wedge(\lambda n[\underline{if}\ n{=}i\ \underline{then}\ 1\ \underline{else}\ {}^\vee a(n)\ \underline{fi}])(i) = {}^\wedge(\lambda n[\underline{if}\ n{=}i\ \underline{then}\ 1\ \underline{else}\ {}^\vee a(n)\ \underline{fi}](j)$, which reduces to $^\wedge(1 = \underline{if}\ j{=}i\ \underline{then}\ 1\ \underline{else}\ {}^\vee a(j)\ \underline{fi}) = {}^\wedge(j{=}i \vee {}^\vee a(j){=}1)$. Thus we have treated Gries' problem correctly.

(32) EXAMPLE. The predicate transformers corresponding to a[a[z]]:=1 and a := λn[if n = a[z] then 1 else a[n] fi] are equal. If we transform the assertion $^\wedge(^\vee a(^\vee a(2)){=}1)$ backwards, we obtain after some calculations $^\wedge[\lambda n[\underline{if}\ n{=}^\vee a(2)\ \underline{then}\ 1\ \underline{else}\ {}^\vee a(n)\ \underline{fi}](\underline{if}\ 2{=}^\vee a(2)\ \underline{then}\ 1\ \underline{else}\ {}^\vee a(2)\ \underline{fi}) = 1]$, which reduces to $^\wedge((2{=}^\vee a(2) \wedge {}^\vee a(1) = 1) \vee (2 \neq {}^\vee a(2)))$. Thus we have treated de Bakker's problem correctly.

Examples concerning the forward predicate transformer can be found in PTR.

4. STRONGEST AND WEAKEST

Predicate transformers should be well behaved. We desire that the forward transformer yields the strongest possible postcondition, and that the backward one yields the weakest possible precondition. In order to define these requirements formally, we need a second kind of semantics: an operational one.

(33) DEFINITION. An *operational semantics* " is a mapping which for each program π yields a function π"; this function gives for each starting state the corresponding final state (intuitively: the state obtained by executing the program).

(35) DEFINITION. $s \models \phi$ means $\underset{s}{V}(\phi) = T$. $\models \phi$ means that for all s: $s \models \phi$.

(36) DEFINITION. The state predicate $sp(\pi,\phi)$ is called the *strongest postcondition* with respect to program π, predicate φ and operational semantics " if the following two conditions are satisfied: (I) if $s \models {}^\vee\phi$ then $\pi''(s) \models {}^\vee sp(\pi,\phi)$, (II) if for all s holds that

$s \models {}^{\vee}\phi$ implies $\pi''(s) \models {}^{\vee}\eta$, then $\models {}^{\vee}sp(\pi,\phi) \rightarrow {}^{\vee}\eta$.

(36) DEFINITION. The state predicate $wp(\pi,\psi)$ is called the *weakest precondition* with respect to program π, predicate ϕ and operational semantics " if the following two conditions are satisfied: (I) if $s \models {}^{\vee}wp(\pi,\psi)$ then $\pi''(s) \models {}^{\vee}\psi$, (II) if for all s holds that $s \models {}^{\vee}\eta$ implies $\pi''(s) \models {}^{\vee}\psi$, then $\models {}^{\vee}\eta \rightarrow {}^{\vee}wp(\pi,\psi)$.

(37) REMARK. There are of course several syntactic formulations of state predicates satisfying the above definitions, but they all denote the same semantic function from states to truth values. Therefore, we feel free to speak about *the* strongest postcondition (weakest precondition). We adopt here the convention to denote this semantic function in IL by the expression $sp(\pi,\phi)$ (respectively $wp(\pi,\phi)$). We assume " fixed.

If a program can be characterized by its forward as well as by its backward transformer, there must be some relation between these characterizations. This relation is given in the next theorem. In them P and Q are variables over state predicates and $\Box$ is the necessity operator from modal logic.

(38) DEFINITION. $V_s(\Box\phi) = T$ iff $\forall t\, V_t(\phi) = T$.

(39) THEOREM. (α) $\models wp(\pi,\phi) = {}^{\wedge}\exists Q[{}^{\vee}Q \wedge \Box[{}^{\vee}sp(\pi,Q) \rightarrow {}^{\vee}\phi]]$,

(β) $\models sp(\pi,\phi) = {}^{\wedge}\forall Q[\Box[{}^{\vee}\phi \rightarrow {}^{\vee}wp(\pi,Q)] \rightarrow {}^{\vee}Q]$.

PROOF. We show that the right-hand sides satisfy cond. I and II, of the corresponding definitions (35) and (36).

(α)(cond.I): suppose $s \models \exists Q[{}^{\vee}Q \wedge \Box[{}^{\vee}sp(\pi,Q) \rightarrow {}^{\vee}\phi]]$. Then for some ψ $s \models {}^{\vee}\psi$ and $s \models \Box[{}^{\vee}sp(\pi,\psi) \rightarrow {}^{\vee}\phi]$. By definition (35) we conclude $\pi''(s) \models {}^{\vee}sp(\pi,\psi)$ and by definition of $\Box$ one has $\pi''(s) \models {}^{\vee}sp(\pi,\psi) \rightarrow {}^{\vee}\phi$. Therefore, $\pi''(s) \models {}^{\vee}\phi$.

(α)(cond. II): suppose for all s we have $s \models {}^{\vee}\eta$ implies $\pi''(s) \models {}^{\vee}\phi$. Then by definition (35) $\models {}^{\vee}sp(\pi,\eta) \rightarrow {}^{\vee}\phi$ and consequently $s \models \Box[{}^{\vee}sp(\pi,\eta) \rightarrow {}^{\vee}\phi]$. Taking $Q = \eta$ we conclude that $s \models {}^{\vee}\eta \rightarrow \exists Q[{}^{\vee}Q \wedge \Box[{}^{\vee}sp(\pi,Q) \rightarrow {}^{\vee}\phi]]$; since s was arbitrary, this proves (cond. II

(β)(cond. I): suppose $s \models {}^{\vee}\phi$ and let ψ be some arbitrary predicate for which $\pi''(s) \models \Box({}^{\vee}\phi \rightarrow wp(\pi,\eta))$. Then $s \models {}^{\vee}\phi$ implies $s \models {}^{\vee}wp(\pi,\eta)$ and by definition (36) this implies $\pi''(s) \models {}^{\vee}\eta$. This shows $\pi''(s) \models {}^{\wedge}\forall Q[\Box[{}^{\vee}\phi \rightarrow {}^{\vee}wp(\pi,Q)] \rightarrow {}^{\vee}Q]$.

(β)(cond. II): suppose for all s $s \models {}^{\vee}\phi$ implies $\pi''(s) \models {}^{\vee}\eta$. Then by definition (37) $\models {}^{\vee}\phi \rightarrow {}^{\vee}wp(\pi,\eta)$. If $t \models \forall Q[\Box[{}^{\vee}\phi \rightarrow {}^{\vee}wp(\pi,Q)] \rightarrow {}^{\vee}Q]$ we derive by taking $Q = \eta$ that $t \models {}^{\vee}\eta$. Since t was arbitrary this proves (cond. II).

(40) COROLLARY. *If for arbitrary* ϕ *either* $wp(\pi,\phi)$ *or* $sp(\pi,\phi)$ *can be syntactically described by predicate transformers in IL, then so can both.*

Clearly it is unlikely that formulas with quantification over predicates are the expressions for wp or sp one likes to handle. The importance of (39) is that it enables to prove theoretically that some expression describes $wp(\pi,\phi)$, given a method to obtain $sp(\pi,\phi)$ or conversely. For example in PTR we have shown for some particular operational semantics " that the strongest postcondition for the program $\chi := \delta$ is obtained by $sp(\chi:=\delta,\phi) = {}^{\vee}\exists z[\{z/{}^{\vee}\chi'\}^{\vee}\phi \wedge {}^{\vee}\chi' = \{z/{}^{\vee}\chi'\}\delta']$.

(41) THEOREM. α) $\models sp(\chi:=\delta,\phi) = {}^{\wedge}\exists z[\{z/{}^{\vee}\chi'\}^{\vee}\phi \wedge {}^{\vee}\chi'=\{z/{}^{\vee}\chi'\}\delta']$ *is equivalent with*

β) $\models wp(\chi:=\delta,\phi) = {}^{\wedge}\{\delta'/{}^{\vee}\chi'\}^{\vee}\phi$.

PROOF. α) ⇒ β). We have to show for arbitrary s and ψ

(I) $s \models \{\delta'/{}^{\vee}\chi'\}^{\vee}\psi$ <u>iff</u>

(II) $s \models \exists Q[{}^{\vee}Q \wedge \Box[\exists z[\{z/{}^{\vee}\chi'\}^{\vee}Q \wedge {}^{\vee}\chi' = \{z/{}^{\vee}\chi'\}\delta'] \rightarrow {}^{\vee}\psi]]$.

(I) $\Rightarrow$ (II). Take $Q = {}^{\wedge}\{\delta'/{}^{\vee}\chi\}^{\vee}\psi$, then $s \models {}^{\vee}Q$. Remains to show that for t arbitrary

(*) $t \models \exists z[\{z/{}^{\vee}\chi'\}\{\delta'/{}^{\vee}\chi'\}^{\vee}\psi \wedge {}^{\vee}\chi' = \{z/{}^{\vee}\chi'\}\delta']$ implies $t \models {}^{\vee}\psi$. If (*) holds for $z = z_0$, then $t \models \{\{z_0/{}^{\vee}\chi'\}\delta/{}^{\vee}\chi'\}^{\vee}\phi \wedge {}^{\vee}\chi' = \{z_0/{}^{\vee}\chi'\}\delta'$, so $t \models \{{}^{\vee}\chi'/{}^{\vee}\chi'\}^{\vee}\psi$ and hence $t \models {}^{\vee}\psi$. Q.E.D.

(II) $\Rightarrow$ (I). Assume (II) holds for $Q = \phi$. Then $S \models {}^{\vee}\phi$ and $s \models \Box[\exists z[\{z/{}^{\vee}\chi'\}^{\vee}\phi \wedge {}^{\vee}\chi' = \{z/{}^{\vee}\chi'\}\delta] \rightarrow {}^{\vee}\psi]$. Taking $z = z_0$ such that for arbitrary t $V_t(z_0) = V_s({}^{\vee}\chi')$ we infer $\langle\chi' \leftarrow V_s(\delta')\rangle s \models \{z_0/{}^{\vee}\chi'\}^{\vee}\phi$ and also $\langle\chi' \leftarrow V_s(\delta')\rangle s \models {}^{\vee}\chi = \{z_0/{}^{\vee}\chi'\}\delta$. So $\langle\chi' \leftarrow V_s(\delta')\rangle s \models {}^{\vee}\psi$, i.e., $s \models \{\delta'/{}^{\vee}\chi'\}^{\vee}\psi$. Q.E.D.

$\beta) \Rightarrow \alpha)$. We have to show that for arbitrary s and ψ

(III) $s \models \forall Q[\Box[{}^{\vee}\phi \rightarrow \{\delta'/{}^{\vee}\chi'\}^{\vee}Q] \rightarrow {}^{\vee}Q]$ <u>iff</u>

(IV) $s \models \exists z[\{z/{}^{\vee}\chi'\}^{\vee}\phi \wedge {}^{\vee}\chi' = \{z/{}^{\vee}\chi'\}\delta']$.

(III) $\Rightarrow$ (IV). Take for Q in (III) the assertion from IV. We prove now that the antecedens of III holds; then (IV) follows immediately. So suppose $t \models {}^{\vee}\phi$. We have to prove that $t \models \exists z[\{\delta'/{}^{\vee}\chi'\}\{z/{}^{\vee}\chi'\}^{\vee}\phi \wedge \{\delta'/{}^{\vee}\chi'\}[{}^{\vee}\chi' = \{z/{}^{\vee}\chi'\}\delta']]$ or, equivalently $t \models \exists z[\{z/{}^{\vee}\chi'\}^{\vee}\phi \wedge \delta' = \{z/{}^{\vee}\chi'\}\delta']$. This becomes true if we choose z equal to ${}^{\vee}\chi'$.

(IV) $\Rightarrow$ (III). Let η be some state predicate and suppose that the antecedens of (III) holds, so (V): $\models {}^{\vee}\phi \rightarrow \{\delta'/{}^{\vee}\chi'\}^{\vee}\eta$. We have to prove that $s \models {}^{\vee}\eta$.

From (IV) follows that for some z_0 holds $\langle\chi' \leftarrow V_s(z_0)\rangle s \models {}^{\vee}\phi$, so $\langle\chi' \leftarrow V_s(z_0)\rangle s \models \{\delta'/{}^{\vee}\chi'\}^{\vee}\eta$, consequently $s \models \{\{z_0/{}^{\vee}\chi'\}\delta'/{}^{\vee}\chi'\}^{\vee}\eta$.

Moreover, from (IV) follows $s \models {}^{\vee}\chi' = \{z_0/{}^{\vee}\chi'\}\delta'$, consequently $s \models {}^{\vee}\eta$. Q.E.D.

(42) <u>COROLLARY</u>. *The weakest precondition for* $\chi := \delta$ *is* ${}^{\wedge}\{\delta'/{}^{\vee}\chi'\}^{\vee}\phi$.

<u>REFERENCES</u>.

De Bakker, J.W. (1976), *Correctness proofs for assignment statements*, Report IW 55/76, Mathematical Centre, Amsterdam.

Floyd, R.W. (1967), *Assigning meanings to programs*, <u>in</u>: <u>Proc. Symp. in Appl. Math. 19</u> (J.T. Schwartz ed.), *Math. aspects of computer sciences*, AMS. pp.19-32.

Gries, D. (1976), *The assignment statement*, unpublished manuscript, Cornell University/ Technical University Munich.

Gries, D. (1976b), *A note on multiple assignment to subscripted variables*, unpublished manuscript, Cornell University.

Hoare, C.A.R. (1969), *An axiomatic base for computer programming*, <u>Comm. ACM</u>, <u>12</u>, pp.576-580.

Janssen, T.M.V. (1976), *A computer program for Montague grammar: theoretical aspects and proofs for the reduction rules*, <u>in</u>: Amsterdam papers in formal grammar <u>1</u>, (J. Groenendijk & M. Stokhof eds.), <u>*Proceedings of the Amsterdam colloquium on Montague grammar and related topics*</u>, pp.154-176 Centrale Interfaculteit, University of Amsterdam.

Janssen, T.M.V. & P. van Emde Boas (1977), *On the proper treatment of referencing, dereferencing and assignment*, Proc. 4th ICALP Conf. (Turku), Lecture Notes in Comp. Sci., Springer Verlag, Berlin, to appear.

Montague, R. (1973), *The proper treatment of quantification in ordinary English*, in: *Approaches to natural language* (J. Hintikka, J. Moravcsik & P. Suppes eds. reprinted in R.H. Thomason (1974), *Formal philosophy, selected papers of Richard Montague*, Yale University press, New Haven and London, pp. 247-270.

Partee, B. (1975), *Montague grammar and transformational grammar*, Linguistic Inquiry 6, pp.203-300.

Pratt, V.R. (1976), *Semantical considerations on Floyd-Hoare logic*, in: Proc. 17th IEEE Symp. on Foundations of Computer Science, Houston, pp.109-122.

ON THE COMPLEXITY OF EQUIVALENT TRANSFORMATIONS IN PROGRAMMING LANGUAGES

Max I. Kanovič

Kalinin State University

Kalinin, USSR

Let PL be a programming language (e.g., ALGOL-60, FORTRAN, PL/1, etc.). An approach to the problem of minimizing the program size is based on the search for a suitable system of equivalent transformations. One can try to simplify programs (in PL) by consecutive equivalent transformations from this system.

An equivalent transformation is an algorithm (e.g., Markov algorithm, Turing machine, etc.) transforming any program (in PL) into an equivalent one. The length of the description of an algorithm is called its complexity; by the complexity of a system of equivalent transformations $A_1, A_2, \ldots, A_k$ we mean the sum of complexities of all the algorithms $A_1, A_2, \ldots, A_k$.

A program P is a word of a certain kind in the (finite) alphabet of the language PL and hence the size of P is defined as the length of the word P.

A system S of equivalent transformations is said to be complete with respect to a program P iff P can be transformed into the shortest (or an almost shortest) equivalent program Q by consecutive application of transformations from S. (Repetitions of the same transformation are permissible.)

Note that there is no transformation system S which is complete with respect to every program.

We shall consider now the following <u>bounded problem:</u> construction of a system of equivalent transformations which is complete with respect to every program of a finite class. A system of equivalent transformations will be called <u>n-complete</u> iff it is complete with respect to every program of the size not exceeding the integer n.

We prove a lower bound of the form $\underline{\exp(C_1 n)}$ for the complexity of n-complete systems of equivalent transformations. An upper bound of the form $\underline{\exp(C_2 n)}$ is evident for the complexity of some n-complete system.

If we consider programs only on inputs of a bounded length (the "equivalence" is replaced by the correspondent "slight equivalence"), then both the lower and upper bounds for this <u>doubly bounded</u> (with respcet to the size of programs and inputs) <u>problem</u> can be reduced to bounds which are <u>linear.</u>

Let us add one more restriction. A system S of slight equivalent transformations is said to be <u>(n,t)-complete,</u> where t is a total recursive function, iff every program P of the size not exceeding the integer n can be transformed into the shortest (or an almost shortest) slight equivalent program Q by such a sequence of transformations from S that both the number of elements of this sequence and the processing time of its every element are bounded by t(n).

For any total recursive function t both the lower and upper bounds for the complexity of (n,t)-complete systems of slight equivalent transformations are proved to be <u>exponential</u> as above.

References

1. Gluškov, V. M., Ceĭtlin, G. E. and Juščenko, E. L., Algebra, languages,programming. Kiev, 1974.
2. Markov, A. A., The theory of algorithms. Trudy Mat. Inst. Steklov, 42 (1954).
3. Markov, A. A., Normal algorithms connected with the computation of Boolean functions. Math. USSR Izv. 1 (1967) pp. 151-198.
4. Kanovič, M. I., On the complexity of enumeration and decision of predicates. Soviet Math. Dokl. 11 (1970) pp. 17-20.
5. Kanovič, M. I., The complexity of complete systems of equivalent transformations in programming languages. Soviet Math. Dokl. 18 (1977).

SCHEMATOLOGY IN A MULTI-LANGUAGE OPTIMIZER

V.N.Kasyanov
S.B.Pokrovsky
Computing Center of the Siberian Division
of the USSR Acad. Sci., Novosibirsk 630090

1. Introduction

With the progress of computer programming the problem emerges of integrating the many branches of this discipline. One approach to it is being tried in Novosibirsk in the framework of the BETA Project (Ershov [3]). In this paper we consider the experience gained in developing a uniform semantic basis which could be used both as a standard interface of a multi-language multi-computer compiler (an internal language as described by Pokrovsky [6]) and as a set of program schemata convenient for analysis and transformations (see Kasyanov and Trakhtenbrot [5], Pottosin [13], Sabelfeld [7]). This work combines the traditional search for better semantic primitives for schematological studies with more recent research in structured programming and uniform description of source languages and target computers (for both TWS and machine-oriented optimization).

Now, before discussing the chosen semantic basis (in Section 3) let us briefly review the external commitments of the optimization phase in the BETA System, and establish the definition of correctness of a program transformation.

2. An Overview of the BETA System

The BETA System is designed as an optimizing coordinated implementation of the major "general purpose programming languages" (Pascal, Simula 67, ALGOL 68, PL/1). The system is based on a unique Internal Language (IL) and consists of five phases: -

(a) the Parse Phase
(b) the IL-Program Generation Phase
(c) the Data and Control Flow Analysis Phase

(d) the Optimization Phase

(e) the Target Program Generation Phase.

There are two notable points in this scheme.

First, the algorithms of the Analysis and Optimization Phases are expressed in terms of IL constructs and thus do not depend on any source language.

Secondly, the output of (c) and (d) being again an IL program, it is possible to disable some optimizations or repeat them; here we take advantage of the fact that once the processed program is expressed in a sufficiently flexible language, the optimization need not change the language level.

2.2. Optimizing Transformations and Related Schemata

Optimizing transformations are best expressed in terms of program schemata (the subsequent classification follows Ershov [4]). Most transformations (code motion, elimination of useless statements and redundant computations; equivalencing static variables) are formulated in terms of Lavrov schemata, which only reflect the information and control relations between statements.

In the standard schemata the interpretation of assignments and the termal structure of statements make them suitable for description of constant propagation and common subexpression elimination.

The procedure schemata (Constable and Gries [2]) formalize inline procedure substitution and "factorization" of non-recursive parts.

The optimizations which involve indirect access (static dereferencing, change of procedure parameter,passing mode etc.) can be described in terms of the schemata introduced by Kasyanov [9].

In fact more practical optimization algorithms use some extentions of these schemata, e.g. in the Lavrov schemata we distinguish between total and partial results, and in the standard schemata we mark associative and/or commutative operators.

2.3. Definition of Correctness

One reason why the naive requirement of functional equality is insufficient is the possibility of an incomplete definition of the program semantic by the language description. There are two sources of such underdefinition.

First, in order to improve program's readability and efficiency semantic description leaves undefined the order of some evaluations. Note that (in contrast to theoretical studies of non-determinism) there is no need for all variants to be feasible - cf. "collateral elaborations" in ALGOL 68 (van Wijngaarden et al. [8]).

Secondly, the source programs may be meaningful only for some inputs (and terminate abnormally - e.g. diverge - for the others). Ascribing an output (i.e. normal termination) to some illegal inputs is also considered permissible in the optimizing processor design.

Definition. A program transformation T is correct if for any program P and any of its inputs I the transformed program Q=T(B) satisfies the following property: if no execution of A over I leads to an abnormal termination, then B also terminates normally, and in this case B(I) ⊆ A(I).

As an example consider the transformation of the following ALGOL 68 program (Pokrovsky [12]):

```
begin int beta, sergei := 0, victor := 0;
  par((beta := sergei + victor; print(sergei); print(sergei+victor)),
     (victor := 10; sergei := 1)) end
```

This program prints a pair of integers, and if the first of them is 1, the second is bound to be 11. - Now, a straightforward elimination of common subexpressions in the first process

(beta := sergei + victor; print(sergei); print(beta)),

is incorrect: a new output (1,0) becomes possible, while the original program always terminates normally. A correct transformation could produce

```
begin int beta, sergei :=0, victor := 0;
  (beta := sergei + victor; print(sergei); print(beta));
  (victor := 10; sergei := 1) end
```

Apart from the correctness issue, the transformation we are interested in should also meet the quality criterion: they must improve run-time properties of the program.

3. A Scheme-Oriented Language

To meet the objectives outlined in Section 2 we need a unique semantic basis to represent the program being optimized. Its development is one of most interesting theoretical issues in the BETA Project.

3.1. The Internal Language

The Internal Language is not human-oriented, and this enables us to use fairly complicated graphs to represent IL programs (rather than linear texts which are not convenient for the Analysis and transformations).

The multiplicity of functions of IL leads to an unusual stratification of its description, which is an interesting semiotic phenomenon. Actually we have: -

- a syntactic definition (in the form of a data base)
- a schematological definition which describes the semantics of data and control flows
- a machine-independent definition
- a set of environment enquiries (full interpretation).

In this paper we deal only with the first two layers of IL specification, which provide only minimal interpretation. For reader's convenience we use an ad hoc "extended ALGOL 68" to represent the sample IL programs.

As usual, an IL program specifies actions to be performed over values. The actions are denoted by statements, the values - by names (variables) and literal constants. Both statements (actions) and variables (values) may be atomic or structured.

The structure of a variable is determined by its mode. There are atomic and structured modes. Values of atomic modes are always computed "totally" (this does not prevent them from being declared, non-standard modes). All structured values and variables have declared modes.

Atomic actions are specified by instructions, structured actions are expressed by program fragments.

Any instruction is given a set of operands, which are subdivided into arguments and results. These are names of declared variables, or names of statements which evaluate (resp. use) the operand in question. As to the arithmetic and Boolean instructions, their interpretation at the schematological level is irrelevant, and at that level they do not differ from the "black boxes" (pseudoinstructions which represent various run-time library routines, and whose specification is not given even at the level of machine-independent specification).

There is a specifically schematological instruction "forget", introduced earlier by Martynyuk [11] for another purpose.

Some other interpreted instructions use constructs of the control graph. This graph is a hierarchy of fragments which denote control structures. At the lowest level of the hierarchy we have basic blocks represented as linear lists of consecutively executed instructions. The header of this list represents a label (name); similar names are given to larger fragments, which are composed of subfragments (rather then of instructions).

The last instruction of a basic block must be a transfer of control to an explicit or computable fragment name, in form of a jump, procedure activation, swap with a co-routine, or initiation of a parallel process.

More complex structures give schematological expression of most of "constructs for the structured programming". The most frequent one is the "closed subgraph" (like those introduced by Martynyuk [10]), which represents a set of basic blocks that are dominated by a specific entry instruction. ALGOL 68 case and if clauses are naturally expressed in IL as closed subgraphs.

Most of other control structures are particular cases of closed subgraphs, e.g. begin-blocks, procedure calls, procedure blocks, regular for statements (like in ALGOL 68).

Of great importance are hammocks (closed subgraphs with a single external successor).

A strongly connected region (Allen [1]) is not, in general, a closed graph, although we always try to make it into a single-entry region (this structure naturally corresponds to non-regular for-statements of ALGOL 60).

For some fragments, a linearization of their subfragments is considered, which is analogous to the arrangement of instructions in basic blocks. Such subfragment aglignments are called linear components with respect to their superfragments.

The importance of hammocks and linear components is due to the possibility to move them (like instructions).

3.2. The Expressive Power

The results of many optimizing transformations can be expressed in conventional programming languages (cf. the use of ALGOL 68 for illustration of procedure optimizations by Sabelfeld [7]). Here we consider only original IL features.

First, for some actions to be optimized they must be stated explicitly. The explicit formulation of component access in IL enables the use of common subexpression elimination techniques to optimize index expressions.

Secondly, some machine-dependent optimizations are expressed with attributes which govern casing at the Object Program Generation Phase.

A new feature is introduced in IL, which ensures a correct application of very powerful optimizations. This is the possibility to associate with some fragments a prologue or an epilogue.

The use of prologues is illustrated by the transformation of the for-statement

```
    for i to n do a[i]:=(y:=1/sin(x)) ↑ i od
```

which becomes

```
    for i to n prolog y:=1/sin(x) golorp do a[i]:=y↑k od
```

Here is an example of recursion optimization which uses the epilogue feature. The original procedure

```
    proc f = void : begin S1;SR;S2 end
```

in which SR is the recursive part, may be transformed into

```
proc f:=ff;
proc ff = void : begin f:=fr;S1;SR;S2;epilog f:=ff golipe end;
proc fr = void : begin SR end;
```

3.3. Correctness

As we have mentioned earlier, most of program transformations are expressed in terms of standard (or even Lavrov) schemata. Now let us consider how these relatively poor schemata are made to express real (much more complex) dependencies.

The control graph is split into parts each of which may be taken as a Lavrov scheme, i.e. every procedure body is considered separately with call instructions inheriting all the properties of procedure bodies it could invoke. For computable jumps their possible successors are also indicated. The statements standing higher in the hierarchy are also given attributes of an "operator".

Separately is established a graph of procedure calls.

To express the data flow any statement (an instruction or a fragment) is given a list of arguments and results. The difficulty here lies in the operand concept.

The naive semantics of arguments and results in which they are taken as atomic explicitely named variables is replaced by classes of object denotations with a set of special relations defined over them. The latter include identity (i.e. two object denotations refer to the same object), intersection (for overlayed objects), membership (for components of structured objects), and referencing.

The notion of object denotation is very close to the ALGOL 68 "external object" concept: it is a part of the program, i.e. an occurence of declared variable, or a statement which evaluates an object name (such statements are specially marked in IL).

Another amendment is differentiation of results. These are generally considered as partial (which means that the corresponding object may be redefined partially or/and only in some execution of the statement), and as a very important particular case we consider total results which only were possible in conventional Lavrov schemata. This approach was firstly considered by Pottosin [14].

To alleviate the restrictions on optimizing transformations which ensue from the presence of parallelism (cf. example in Section 2.3) we put special marks on objects used in process communications, and include critical sections as a special fragment kind.

3.4. Transformation-Oriented Language

In this section we consider the influence of IL on the effectiveness of a given set of optimizing transformations. The actual catalogue of optimizations and their ordering have been considered by Pottosin [13].

The hierarchical structure of the Control Graph enables a uniform treatment of structured and atomic actions. The "hierarchical" application of the same transformation at various levels may produce an effect which could not be achieved by iteration of that transformation at the lowest level. For instance, in the for-statement

```
for i to n do int x:=b(i); if x ≥ 0 then L fi; x:=x↑2;
                  L : if p[i] then print(x) od
```

a hammock may be moved only entirely:

```
for i to n do int x;
                  if p[i] then x:=b(i); if x ≥ 0 then pr fi;
                               x:=x↑2; pr : print(x) fi od
```

4. Conclusion

The relative stabilization in language design and schematology, which succeeded to their rapid growth in 1960s, puts forward the problem of practical synthesis of their achievements. We have reviewed the experience gained in a practical design of this kind. Of special interest here are the amendments to the conventional definition of transformation correctness and the development of a common semantic basis for a very important family of programming languages, which is oriented to flow analysis and optimization.

This orientation suggests new facilities, like prologues and epilogues mentioned in Section 3.2. On the other hand, the work with real-life languages requires a more flexible concept of object.

Among the most important features which are taken into account for correctness reasons, but are not optimized we have arithmetic interrupts, parallelism and optimal choice of internal representation for structured data.

References

1. Allen, F.E. Program optimization. "Annual Review in Automatic Programming", Vol. 5, Pergamon Press, N.Y. 1969.
2. Constable, R.L., Gries, D. On classes of program schemata. "SIAM Journal of Computing", Vol. 1, No. 1 (1972).
3. Ershov, A.P. A multilanguage programming system oriented to language description and universal optimization algorithms. In: "ALGOL 68 Implementation", J.R.L.Peck ed., North-Holland Publ. Co. 1971.
4. Ershov, A.P. Theory of program schemata. "Proceed. IFIP Congress '71" (Invited Papers), North-Holland Publ. Co. Amsterdam 1971.
5. Kasyanov, V.N., Trakhtenbrot, M.B. Program structure analysis in global optimization. "Lecture Notes in Computer Science", 47, Springer-Verlag 1977.
6. Pokrovsky, S.B. Semantic unification in a multi-language compiler. Ibid.
7. Sabelfeld, V.K. Procedure implementation in the multi-language translator. Ibid.
8. Van Wijngaarden, A. et al. Revised report on the algorithmic language ALGOL 68. "Acta Informatica", Vol. 3, Fasc. 1-3 (1975).
9. Касьянов, В.Н. О нахождении аргументов и результатов операторов в схемах с косвенной адресацией. "Программирование", № I, 1976.
10. Мартынюк, В.В. Об анализе графа переходов для операторной схемы. "Журнал вычислительной математики и математической физики", т. 5, № 2 (1965), стр. 298-310.

II. Мартынюк, В.В. Об изменении порядка выполнения операторов в операторной схеме. В сб. "Цифровая вычислительная техника и программирование", вып. 2, М., Сов. радио, 1967.

I2. Покровский, С.Б. Асинхронность и локальные оптимизации. "Системное и теоретическое программирование" (Труды Всесоюзной конференции), т. I, КГУ, Кишинев, 1974.

I3. Поттосин, И.В. Глобальная оптимизация: практический подход. "Труды симпозиума по методам реализации новых алгоритмических языков", т. I, Новосибирск, 1975.

I4. Поттосин, И.В. К задаче чистки циклов. В сб. "Цифровая вычислительная техника и программирование", вып. 4, Сов. радио, М., 1968.

Translation of Russian references

9. Kasayanov, V. N., On finding arguments and results of operators in schemas with indirect addressation. Programmirovanie 1 (1976)

10. Martinyuk, V. V., On analysis of transition graphs for an operator schema. Ž. Vyčisl. Mat. i Mat. Fiz., (1965) 298-310

11. Martinyuk, V. V., On changing the order of the execution of operators in an operator schema. In Digital computers and programming, 2, Soviet Radio, 1967

12. Pokrovsky, S. B., Asynchrony and local optimization. In System and theoretic programming. (Proceedings of ALL-union Conference), 1, Kishinev, 1974

13. Pottosin, I. V., Global optimization: a practical approach. Proceedings of Symposium on the methods of implementation of new algorithmic languages, 1, Novosibirsk, 1975

14. Pottosin, I. V., On the loop cleaning problem. In Digital computers and programming, 4, Soviet Radio, 1968.

DECIDABILITY (UNDECIDABILITY) OF EQUIVALENCE OF MINSKY MACHINES WITH COMPONENTS CONSISTING OF AT MOST SEVEN (EIGHT) INSTRUCTIONS

Ivan Korec
Department of Algebra, Faculty of Sciences of Comenius University
816 31 Bratislava, Czechoslovakia

1. Introduction.

S. Ginsburg and H. Spanier [1] investigated semilinear sets, i. e. the sets which are first order definable in the monoid (N, +) of non-negative integers. The relation of semilinear /partial/ functions defined below to the semilinear sets is analogous to the relation of /partial/ recursive functions to the recursive sets. Semilinear /partial/ functions will be characterized by the so called semilinear Minsky machines. We shall find a rather large recursive class of these machines and its very simple subclasses sufficient for computing of all semilinear /partial/ functions. Minsky machines are sets of instructions but we shall also consider them as oriented graphs; roughly speaking, an arc from A to B means that the instruction B can immediately follow the instruction A in a computation. Hence machines can be partitioned into (strongly connected) components. We shall show that all machines with components consisting of at most seven instructions are semilinear; then we shall prove their equivalence is decidable. On the other hand, Minsky machines with components consisting of at most eight instructions compute all polynomials with integer coefficients. We shall reduce the undecidable problem of solvability of Diophantine equations to the equivalence problem of these machines. In this way we shall show that the last problem is undecidable. It is interesting that the halting problem for these machines can be shown to be decidable.

Our notations are widely used or introduced in [2] and [3]. We only mention that $x_1, \ldots, x_n$ is abbreviated by X_n and 0, ..., 0 (n times) by O_n. Some other notations will be explained later. All /partial/ functions are mappings of /subsets of/ N^n into N.

2. Semilinear /partial/ functions and semilinear sets

This section contains basic definitions and some theorems concerning their relations. Results concerning semilinear sets and Presburger formulas are mostly contained in [1] and their modifications are inessential.

A set M of /partial/ functions is said to be a system of /partial/ functions if M contains all the projections $I^n_m(X_n) = x_m$ $(1 \leqq m \leqq n)$ and M is closed under the composition of partial functions, i. e. if $g(X_m), f_1(X_n), \dots, f_m(X_n) \in M$ then $h(X_n) = g(f_1(X_n), \dots, f_m(X_n)) \in M$. If M is a set of partial functions then let SPF(M) denote the system of partial functions generated by M, i.e. the least system of partial functions containing M. (If M is a set of functions then SPF(M) is a system of functions.) An example of a system of /partial/ functions is the set of /partial/ recursive functions. Let $x \dot{-} y = x - \min(x, y)$ and $\mathrm{cond}(x, y) = x$ if $y = 0$, $\mathrm{cond}(x, y) = 0$ if $y \neq 0$. Elements of the system

$$\mathrm{Islf} = \mathrm{SPF}(\{x + y, x \dot{-} y, \mathrm{cond}(x, y), 1\})$$

will be called integer semilinear functions. Elements of the systems

$$\mathrm{Slf} = \mathrm{SPF}(\mathrm{Islf} \cup \{[x/k] ; k \in N\})$$

$$\mathrm{Islpf} = \mathrm{SPF}(\mathrm{Islf} \cup \{x - y\})$$

$$\mathrm{Slpf} = \mathrm{SPF}(\mathrm{Slf} \cup \{x - y\})$$

will be called semilinear functions, integer semilinear partial functions and semilinear partial functions, respectively. The functions $\min(X_n)$, $\max(X_n)$, $|x - y|$, $\mathrm{sg}(x)$, $\overline{\mathrm{sg}}(x)$ and linear functions (with coefficients in N) are integer semilinear. If $f(X_n)$, $g(X_n)$ are integer semilinear functions and one of them is bounded then $f(X_n).g(X_n)$ is an integer semilinear function.

2.1. Theorem. a) Let $f(X_n)$ be a partial function, $g(X_n)$ be a function and let $f(X_n) = g(X_n) - 1$ for all X_n. Then $f(X_n)$ is an /integer/ semilinear partial function if and only if $g(X_n)$ is an /integer/ semilinear function.

b) A (total) function $f(X_n)$ is an /integer/ semilinear partial function if and only if it is an /integer/ semilinear function.

In what follows capitals with two indices denote matrices consisting of nonnegative integers; indices will denote the number of their rows and columns (in this order). If the first index is 1 it will be sometimes omitted and the matrix will be considered as a vector. We shall use basic matrix operations. Linear dependence will be considered over the field of rational numbers.

2.2. Definition. a) For every matrix $P_{k,n}$ and every vector C_n denote

(2.2.1) $$L(C_n, P_{k,n}) = \{C_n + T_k.P_{k,n} ; T_k \in N^k\}$$

b) A set $M \subseteq N^n$ is said to be linear if there are C_n, $P_{k,n}$ satisfying $M = L(C_n, P_{k,n})$. $P_{k,n}$ will be called a matrix of periods of M and its rows will be called periods.

c) A set $M \subseteq N^n$ is said to be semilinear if

(2.2.2) $$M = \bigcup_{i=1}^{r} L(C_n^{(i)}, P_{k(i),n}^{(i)})$$

for some vectors $C_n^{(i)}$ and some matrices $P_{k(i),n}^{(i)}$ $(i = 1, \ldots, r)$.

A Presburger formula is a formula of the first order language with the only predicate symbol $=$, two binary functional symbols $+$, $\dot{-}$ and one constant 1. We shall always interprete Presburger formulas in the standard way and use them also instead of the corresponding predicates. A predicate $P(X_n)$ is said to be semilinear if it is equivalent with a Presburger formula. A set $M \subseteq N^n$ is said to be a Presburger set if there is a Presburger formula $A(X_n)$ such that

(2.2.3) $$M = \{X_n \in N^n; A(X_n)\}$$

2.3. Theorem. A set M is semilinear if and only if it is Presburger. Moreover, there are algorithms transforming (2.2.2) into (2.2.3) and conversely.

2.4. Corollary. It is recursively solvable whether arbitrary Presburger sentence is true.

A set $M \subseteq N^n$ is said to be an independent linear set if M consists of one element or $M = L(C_n, P_{k,n})$ for some vector C_n and some matrix $P_{k,n}$ with linearly independent rows.

2.5. Lemma. a) Every semilinear set is a finite union of independent linear sets.

b) The characteristic function of every independent linear set is semilinear. If the graph G of a partial function $f(X_n)$ is an independent linear set then $f(X_n)$ is semilinear.

2.6. Theorem. a) A partial function is semilinear if and only if its graph is a semilinear set.

b) A set $M \subseteq N^n$ is semilinear if and only if its characteristic function is semilinear.

Now it is natural to call a set $M \subseteq N^n$ /or a predicate $P(X_n)$/ an integer semilinear set /integer semilinear predicate, respectively/ if its characteristic function is integer semilinear.

2.7. Theorem. A predicate $P(X_n)$ is integer semilinear if and only if it is equivalent with an open Presburger formula.

3. Machine characterization of semilinear /partial/ functions

We briefly mention some definitions from [2] and [3] concerning Minsky machines; "Minsky" will be often abbreviated by "M" or omitted. Minsky instructions are quadruples

(3.0.1) $(q_iS_jq_mq_n)$, $(q_iS_jPq_k)$, $(q_iS_jM\,q_k)$

where $i, j, k, m, n \in N$. A Minsky machine is a finite set of Minsky instructions which do not contain any two different quadruples with the same first elements. The counters $S_0, S_1, S_2, \ldots$ contain nonnegative integers; $q_0, q_1, q_2, \ldots$ are states of finite control units of Minsky machines. The first instruction in (3.0.1) will be called conditional; the states q_m, q_n correspond to positive content of S_j and to zero in S_j, respectively. The second and the third instruction in (3.0.1) denote addition of 1 and subtraction of 1 (in the sense $\dot{-}\,1$), respectively. An M-configuration is a pair $(q_i; A_\omega)$ where q_i is a state and A_ω is a sequence of nonnegative integers containing only finitely many positive members; we shall usually write only an initial segment of A_ω comtaining all of them. Now it is clear how to define the computation of a machine from a configuration as a (finite or infinite) sequence of configurations. If a machine Z do not use any counter except $S_0, S_1, \ldots, S_{n-1}$ we shall write

$$\text{(3.0.2)} \qquad \mathrm{Comp}_Z^n(i, X_n, j, Y_n)$$

if the computation of Z from $(q_i; X_n)$ halts in $(q_j; Y_n)$. A machine Z is said to compute the k-ary partial function Φ_Z^k defined by

$$\text{(3.0.3)} \qquad y = \Phi_Z^k(X_k) \leftrightarrow \exists U_n \ \mathrm{Comp}_Z^{n+1}(1, 0, X_k, 0_{n-k}, 0, y, U_n)$$

The time of the corresponding computation will be denoted by $\mathcal{T}_Z^k(X_k)$. The predicates Comp_Z^n are defined only for sufficiently large n; we shall always assume n being suitable. The partial functions Φ_Z^k, $\mathcal{T}_Z^k$ are defined for all $k \in N$, and they do not depend on the choice of n in (3.0.3).

Every machine Z will be also considered as a directed arc-labelled graph. Denote <u>$St_i(Z)$</u> the set of states occuring at the i-th places of the instructions of a machine Z and <u>$St_{34}(Z)$</u> $= St_3(Z) \cup St_4(Z)$. An arc from $A \in Z$ to $B \in Z$ exists (and we write <u>$A \succ B$</u>) if the first element q_k of B belongs to $St_{34}(\{A\})$. The arc is labelled S_jP, S_jM, S_jn or S_jz if there are $i, j, r \in N$ such that

$A = (q_iS_jPq_k)$, $A = (q_iS_jMq_k)$, $A = (q_iS_jq_kq_r)$, or $A = (q_iS_jq_rq_k)$,

respectively. (If $r = k$ two arcs from A to B exist.) The label or its parts shall be written over the symbol $\succ$. We shall denote $Lab(Z)$ the set of all labels of arcs of Z. We shall write <u>$A \gg B\ (Z)$</u> if there are $A_0, A_1, \ldots, A_n \in Z$ such that $A = A_0 \succ A_1 \succ \ldots \succ A_n = B$. A subset $X \neq \emptyset$ of a machine Z is said to be a <u>block</u> of Z if for every $A, B \in X$, $A \gg C\ (Z) \wedge C \gg B\ (Z)$ implies $C \in X$. Minimal blocks will be called <u>components</u>. A <u>branching</u> of a machine Z is a conditional $A \in Z$ satisfying $St_{34}(\{A\}) \subseteq St_1(Z)$. Let <u>$Br(Z)$</u>, <u>$Cn(Z)$</u> denote the number of branchings of Z and the number of conditionals of Z, respectively. A machine M is said to be <u>simpler</u> than Z if

$$Lab(M) \subseteq Lab(Z) \wedge (Br(M) < Br(Z) \vee (Br(M) = Br(Z) \wedge Cn(M) < Cn(Z)))$$

Let Q be a subset of N. Machines M, Z are said to be <u>Q- equivalent</u> if

$$(\forall i, j \in Q) \forall X_n \forall Y_n \ (\mathrm{Comp}_M^n(i, X_n, j, Y_n) \leftrightarrow \mathrm{Comp}_Z^n(i, X_n, j, Y_n))$$

__3.1. Lemma.__ Let Q be a finite subset of N, let a machine Z contain a conditional using a counter S_j and let one of the following condition hold:

(i) $S_jM \notin Lab(Z)$ and $\{S_jn, S_jz\} \cap Lab(Z) \neq \emptyset$;

(ii) $S_jP \notin Lab(Z)$ and $S_jz \in Lab(Z)$;

(iii) all branchings of Z use the same counter.

Then a machine Z' Q-equivalent with Z can be constructed such that every component of Z' is simpler than the machine Z.

A machine Z is said to be __a semilinear machine__ if the predicate $Comp_Z^n(i, X_n, j, Y_n)$ is semilinear. A recursive class $\mathcal{M}$ of machines is said to be an __effectively semilinear class__ if there is an algorithm constructing a Presburger formula equivalent with $Comp_Z^n(i, X_n, j, Y_n)$ to every $Z \in \mathcal{M}$ (and suitable $n \in N$).

__3.2. Lemma.__ If every component of a machine Z is semilinear then the machine Z is also semilinear.

__3.3. Lemma.__ The class of all machines satisfying the condition (iii) of 3.1 is effectively semilinear.

If u, v are unary functions and Z is a machine then let $Z_{u,v}$ be the set obtained from Z if we replace all q_i and S_j in the instructions of Z by $q_{u(i)}$, $S_{v(j)}$, respectively. Machines Z, M are said to be isomorphic if there are bijective unary functions u, v satisfying $M = Z_{u,v}$. If $\mathcal{M}$ is a class of machines then __ISOM($\mathcal{M}$)__ will be the class of machines isomorphic to elements of $\mathcal{M}$ and __BLOCK($\mathcal{M}$)__ the class of machines which can be partitioned into blocks belonging to ISOM($\mathcal{M}$). We shall write ISOM(Z) instead of ISOM($\{Z\}$).

__3.4. Theorem.__ For every effectively semilinear class $\mathcal{M}$, the class BLOCK($\mathcal{M}$) is effectively semilinear.

Combining 3.3 and 3.4 we can obtain a rather large effectively semilinear class which can be used for a machine characterization of the semilinear partial functions. Now we shall find a smaller class for this purpose. At the same time we shall characterize some subsystems of Islpf. Let __$BLOCK_{1,0}(\mathcal{M})$__ be the class of all machines $Z \in$ BLOCK($\mathcal{M}$) containing an instruction A with the first element q_1

and satisfying the conditions $q_0 \in St_{34}(Z) - St_1(Z)$ and $A \succ B\,(Z)$ for all $B \in Z$.

<u>3.5. Definition.</u> Let P be the set of primes and $k > 1$. Denote:

$$Copy = ISOM(\{(q_1S_1q_2q_0),\ (q_2S_1Mq_3),\ (q_3S_0Pq_4),\ (q_4S_2Pq_1)\})$$

$$Subt = ISOM(\{(q_1S_1q_2q_0),\ (q_2S_1Mq_3),\ (q_3S_0Mq_1)\})$$

$$Cond = ISOM(\{(q_1S_1q_2q_0),\ (q_2S_1Mq_3),\ (q_3S_2q_1q_4),\ (q_4S_0Pq_1)\})$$

$$Diff = ISOM(\{(q_1S_1q_2q_0),\ (q_2S_1Mq_3),\ (q_3S_0q_4q_3),\ (q_4S_0Mq_1)\})$$

$$Div_k = ISOM(\{(q_1S_1Mq_2),\ (q_2S_1Mq_3),\ \ldots,\ (q_{k-1}S_1Mq_k),\ (q_kS_1q_{k+1}q_0),\ (q_{k+1}S_1Mq_{k+2}),\ (q_{k+2}S_0Pq_1)\})$$

$$Pdiv = \bigcup_{k \in P} Div_k$$

$$Islm = Copy \cup Subt \cup Cond$$

<u>3.6. Theorem.</u> Let $f(X_n)$ be a partial function. Then

a) $f(X_n)$ is an integer semilinear function if and only if there is a machine $Z \in BLOCK_{1,0}(Islm)$ computing $f(X_n)$.

b) $f(X_n)$ is an integer semilinear partial function if and only if there is a machine $Z \in BLOCK_{1,0}(Islm \cup Diff)$ computing $f(X_n)$.

c) $f(X_n)$ is a semilinear function if and only if there is a machine $Z \in BLOCK_{1,0}(Islm \cup Pdiv)$ computing $f(X_n)$.

d) $f(X_n)$ is a semilinear partial function if and only if there is a machine $Z \in BLOCK_{1,0}(Islm \cup Pdiv \cup Diff)$ computing $f(X_n)$.

4. The equivalence problem

We shall consider the following variant of the equivalence problem for a class M of machines: For given $k \in N$ and given $Z_1, Z_2 \in M$ determine whether Z_1, Z_2 compute the same k-ary partial function, i.e. whether $\phi^k_{Z_1} = \phi^k_{Z_2}$. However, the results below hold also for other natural variants of the equivalence problem, e.g. if k is fixed.

<u>4.1. Theorem.</u> If M is an effectively semilinear class of machines then the equivalence problem for M and the halting problem for M are recursively solvable.

Proof. For every $k \in N$ and every $Z_1, Z_2 \in M$ we can find Presburger formulas $A(X_n, y)$, $B(X_n, y)$ equivalent with $y = \phi^n_{Z_1}(X_n)$ $y = \phi^n_{Z_2}(X_n)$, respectively. Then $\phi^n_{Z_1} = \phi^n_{Z_2}$ if and only if the Presburger sentence $\forall X_n \forall y\ (A(X_n, y) \leftrightarrow B(X_n, y))$ is true, what is decidable. The proof for halting problem is similar.

Denote M_n the class of machines consisting of at most n instructions and $\text{Block}_n = \text{BLOCK}(M_n)$.

4.2. Theorem. a) The equivalence problem for the class Block_7 is recursively solvable.

b) The equivalence problem for the class Block_8 is recursively unsolvable.

Proof. a) It suffices to show that the class Block_7 is effectively semilinear. Since M_7 contains only finitely many pairwise non-isomorphic machines it suffices to prove that every machine $Z \in M_7$ is semilinear. Let $Z \in M_7$ and Z is not semilinear. We may assume that Z is strongly connected and it satisfies neither (i) nor (ii) of 3.1 (otherwise Z' mentioned in 3.1 belongs to Block, and we may consider a component of Z' instead of Z). Lemma 3.3 implies that Z contains two branchings using different counters, say S_0, S_1. Then Z must also contain instructions with S_0P, S_0M, S_1P and S_1M at the second and the third place. Z must also contain a conditional which is not branching; the conditional must use one of the counters S_0, S_1, say S_1. It can be shown that Z must contain two disjoint simple circuits, one with the arcs labelled S_1n, S_1M, S_0P and the other with the arcs labelled S_0n, S_0M, S_1P; otherwise Z is semilinear. We can achieve (by a process similar to reductions in 3.1) that the third conditional of Z does not belong to any of two circuits mentioned above. Furthemore, we may assume that the arc from it is labelled S_1n. Now it is easy to verify that either all computations of Z consisting of at least three configurations are infinite or they all have the same last member. In both cases Z is semilinear, q.e.d. (Notice that despite of this fact $\mathcal{T}^1_Z$ need not be semilinear in the last case.)

b) The partial functions computed by machines from Block_8 form a system F of partial functions; obviously $\text{Islpf} \subseteq F$. Since the machine

$$\{(q_1S_1q_2q_4),\ (q_2S_1Mq_3),\ (q_3S_2Pq_8),\ (q_4S_2q_5q_0),\ (q_5S_2Mq_6),\ (q_6S_2q_7q_8),\ (q_7S_1Pq_5),\ (q_8S_0Pq_1)\}$$

computes the function $c(x, y) = [(x + y).(x + y + 1)/2] + x$ and

$$x.y = c(0, x + y) - c(0, x) - c(0, y)$$

all polynomials (with coefficients in N) belong to F. A Diophantine equation $f(X_n) = g(X_n)$ where f, g are polynomials has a solution (in N^n) if and only if $sg|f(X_n) - g(X_n)| = 0$ for some $X_n \in N^n$. To every Diophantine equation $f(X_n) = g(X_n)$ we can construct a machine Z computing the function $sg|f(X_n) - g(X_n)|$, $Z \in Block_8$. Then the equation has a solution in N^n if and only if the machines Z and $\{(q_1S_0Pq_0)\}$ compute different n-ary functions. Since the problem whether a Diophantine equation has a solution is recursively unsolvable (see [4]), the equivalence problem for $Block_8$ is also recursively unsolvable, q.e.d. (The class $Block_8$ in 4.2b can be replaced by $BLOCK_{1,0}(Islm \cup \{Z\})$ where Z is the machine computing c(x, y).)

References

1. **S. Ginsburg and E. Spanier: Semigroups. Presburger Formulas and Languages. Pacific Journal of Math., Vol. 16, No. 2, 285-296.**

2. **I. Korec: A Complexity valuation of the partial recursive functions following the expectation of the time ... Acta F. R. N. Univ. Comen. - Mathematica XXIII 1969, 53-112.**

3. **I. Korec: Computational Complexity Based on Expectation of the Time of Computations on Minsky Machines. Proceedings of MFCS 73, High Tatras, September 1973, 247-250.**

4. **J. V. Matijasewitch: Diophantine Representation of Recursively Enumerable Predicates. Contributions of Soviet Mathematicians at the International Mathematical Congress in Nice, 1970 (in Russian), Moscow 1972, 203-206.**

A TOP-DOWN NO BACKTRACK PARSING OF GENERAL CONTEXT-FREE LANGUAGES

Jaroslav Král

ÚVT ČVUT, Horská 3, Prague 2, Czechoslovakia

Summary

A new parsing algorithm is presented. The algorithm works in a top-down manner and it is easily implementable. The algorithm works for all non left-recursive ε-free context-free grammars. For LR(1) left-recursion-free grammars works like an LR(1) push-down acceptor. The time bounds are $O(n^3)$ for all context-free grammars, $O(n^2)$ for a superset of unambiguous grammars and $O(n)$ for a superset of LR grammars (see Graham, Harrison [1]). It is hoped that the ideas used in the algorithm can help to find an accepting algorithm working in time $O(n^2)$. The method has promising properties for error recovery in compilers and produces all the possible parses in a string encoding. In any case, the ideas presented in the paper can contribute to the understanding of the parsing problem of general context-free languages.

Preliminaries, introduction

$\{a_1,\dots,a_n\}$ denotes the set of elements $a_1,\dots,a_n$. If no confusion can arise $\{a\}$ will be often written as a. $\emptyset$ is the empty set, $\{x|P(x)\}$ is the set of all x satisfying P. We shall always assume that the sets under discussion are totally ordered in some way. If A is a set then A_i is the i-th element of A in the assumed ordering. $\otimes$ denotes the cartesian product. Card (A) is the number of elements in A. 2^A is the set of all subsets of A.

Alphabet A is a finite set of symbols, A^* is the set of all words over A, ε is the empty word, $|x|$ is the length of the word x. $|\varepsilon| = 0$. $A^+ = A^* - \{\varepsilon\}$. For two words $x = x_1 \dots x_s$, $y = y_1 \dots y_t$ from A^* $xy = x_1 \dots x_s y_1 \dots y_t$ is the concatenation of x and y. For $B,C \subseteq A$ $BC = \{xy | x \text{ in } B, y \text{ in } C\}$. A transformation h transforming A^* into B^*

where A,B are alphabets is a homomorphism if $h(xy)=h(x)h(y)$ for every x,y in A^*.

A grammar G is the quadruple G = (N,T,P,S). N,T are disjoint alphabets of nonterminal and terminal symbols respectively. N is the nonterminal alphabet, T is the terminal alphabet, S is a nonterminal called the initial symbol. $P \subset N \otimes (N \cup T)^*$ is a finite set of productions. If (A,x) is in P we write $A \to x$. In our notation P_i is the i-th production in P. The symbol p_i corresponds to P_i. For x,y in $(N \cup T)^*$ $x \Rightarrow y$ ($x \Rightarrow_L y$, $x \Rightarrow_R y$) if $x = x_1Ax_2$, $y = x_1ux_2$ and $A \to u$ (for $\Rightarrow_L$ x_1 in T^*, for $\Rightarrow_R$ x_2 is in T^*). If R is a relation then R^* is its reflexive and transitive closure. A sequence of words $W = w_1,\dots,w_s$ is a derivation (left-most derivation, right-most derivation) if for i=1,2, ...,s-1 $w_i \Rightarrow w_{i+1}$ ($w_i \Rightarrow_L w_{i+1}$, $w_i \Rightarrow_R w_{i+1}$ respectively). The set L(G) = $\{x | x \text{ in } T^*, S \Rightarrow^* x\}$ is the language generated by G. A grammar G is unambiguous if for each x in L(G) there is just one left-most derivation $S, w_0, \dots, w_{m-1}, x$ (see Aho, Ullman [4]).

Let G = (N,T,P,S) be a grammar. Then the grammar TD(G) = $(N, T \cup D, P_{TD}, S)$ is the <u>top-down grammar</u> for G if $P_{TD} = \{ A \to [_i x_1 \uparrow_{i.1} \dots \uparrow_{i.t-1} x_t]_i \mid P_i = A \to x_1 x_2 \dots x_t$ is a production of G, x_j in $N \cup T$ for $j=1,2,\dots,t\}$. D are all the symbols occuring in P_{TD} but not in $N \cup T$. td is a homomorphism on $(T \cup D)^*$ for which $td(d) = \varepsilon$ for d in D, td(a) = a otherwise. A <u>top-down parse</u> of an x in L(G) is any y in L(TD(G)) such that td(y) = x. Note that if G is unambiguous then each x in L(G) has just one top-down parse (see Král [3],[2]). For w in T^*, $^{(k)}w = w$ if $|w| \le k$; $^{(k)}w = x$, $|x| = k$, $w = xu$ otherwise.

For w in $(N \cup T)^*$ $\mathrm{FIRST}_k(w) = \{ ^{(k)}w_1 \mid w_1 \text{ in } T^*, w \Rightarrow^* w_1\}$. For A in N $\mathrm{FOLLOW}_k(A) = \{ ^{(k)}u \mid S \Rightarrow^* xAx_2, x_2 \Rightarrow^* u, u \text{ in } T^*\}$. The j-th configuration of the production $P_i = A \to y$ is the pair $c = (i,j)$, $0 \le j \le |y|$. The configuration x will be often written in an equivalent notation $c = A \to x_1 \dots x_j . x_{j+1} \dots x_{|y|}$. <u>Analysis picture</u> is any nonempty set of configurations. <u>Analysis state</u> $\mathbb{A} = (\mathbb{A}_0, \dots, \mathbb{A}_q)$ is any nonempty sequence of analysis pictures. $\mathbb{A}_q$ is called the highest picture in $\mathbb{A}$. Note that $\mathbb{A}_{ij}$ is the j-th configuration in $\mathbb{A}_i$. A <u>pointer</u> (in $\mathbb{A}$) is the pair p= (k,m) where $0 \le k \le q$, $1 \le m \le \mathrm{card}(\mathbb{A}_k)$. We say that p points the configuration $\mathbb{A}_{km}$. A linked configuration (<u>l-configuration</u> for short) is the pair $c_I = (c, I)$ where c is a configuration and I a finite set of pointers.

Write $(i,j) \prec (k,m)$ if $i < k$ or $i=k$ and $j < m$. We shall assume that the elements of pointer sets are numbered according to $\prec$. c_I will be often written $A_I \to x.y$. <u>l-picture</u> is any finite set of l-configurations. <u>l-state</u> is any finite sequence $\mathbb{A}_0, \dots, \mathbb{A}_q$ of l-pictures. The pointer (j,k) points the l-configuration A_{jk}. The l-configurations

$c_I = A_I \to x.y$, $c_J = A_J \to x.y$ in an l-picture P_c are united if (i) c_I, c_J are deleted from P_c, (ii) $c_{I\cup J} = A_{I\cup J} \to x.y$ is added to P_c.

The grammars in examples will be given by giving their productions. Each production will be prefixed by its number followed by a collon (e.g. $3{:}A \to x$). $i{:}A \to x$, $j{:}A \to y$ will be abbreviated to $i.j{:}A \to x|y$. S will always be the initial symbol.

In the sequel we shall assume that each grammar is in the parsable form, i.e. it is

(1) reduced (for each A in N there are x,y in $(N\cup T)^*$, u in T^* such that $S \Rightarrow^* xAy$, $A \Rightarrow^* u$)

(2) $\mathcal{E}$-free (if $A \to x$ is a production then $|x| > 0$),

(3) left-recursion-free ($A \Rightarrow y \Rightarrow^* Aw$ for no A,y,w) and

(4) the initial symbol S and the markers $\vdash \dashv$ occur only in the production $S \to \vdash S' \dashv$.

The assumption (1) causes no loss of generality. For (2),(3) note that any grammar can be transformed into a left recursion free and $\mathcal{E}$-free grammar G′ such that $L(G') = L - \{\mathcal{E}\}$. It is not difficult to modify the our algorithm to treat the case $\mathcal{E}$ in L. (4) can be cancelled if we modify our algorithm in an obvious way. (4) simplifies the explanation.

The algorithm

We shall assume that the grammar $G = (N,T,P,S)$ is in a parsable form. Our algorithm is described in terms of abstract automata. It will be clear that all the below transformations are RASP (Aho, Hopcroft [6]) realizable. The situation $\mathcal{S}$ is the quadruple $\mathcal{S} = (w_1, w_2, \mathbb{A}, d)$ where w_1 is the read part of the input string, w_2 the part of the input string to be read, w_1w_2 in T^*, $\mathbb{A}$ is an l-state, d an output, d in $(T\cup 2^{D^*})^*$. For the meaning of D see the definition of TD(G).

Our algorithm transforms situations into situations by moves. For situations Q_1, Q_2 write $Q_1 \models Q_2$ if there is a move transforming Q_1 into Q_2. $\models^*$ is the reflexive transitive closure of $\models$. ACCEPT($\vdash w \dashv$) = $(\vdash w \dashv, \mathcal{E}, \mathbb{A}, d)$, where $\mathbb{A} = (\mathbb{A}_1, \ldots, \mathbb{A}_{q-1}, \{S_\emptyset \to \vdash S' \dashv .\})$. INIT($\vdash w \dashv$) = $(\vdash, w\dashv, \{(S \to \vdash .S' \dashv)\}, [_0 \vdash \uparrow_{0.1})$ provided that FIRST(S′) $\supseteq$ FIRST(w), INIT is not defined otherwise. We write FIRST instead FIRST_1, FOLLOW instead FOLLOW_1.

There are three types of moves.

(A) Reduce move. It is defined only if $\mathbb{A} = (\mathbb{A}_0, \ldots, \mathbb{A}_q)$ and $\mathbb{A}_q$ contains an l-configuration $c_I = (B_I \to x.)$. We say that c_I is prepared for reduction. Each l-configuration $c_I = B_I \to x. = ((i,s),I)$ prepared for reduction is deleted from $\mathbb{A}_q$, the configurations $((h,j+1),K) = H_K \to y_1B.y_2$, a pointer from I points $((h,j),K)$, are added with the associated output $M]_i$, M is the output associated with c_I. Unitable configurations in $\mathbb{A}_q$ are united.

(B) The develop move. This move can be performed if no reduce move is applicable. A nonterminal A is dominated by a nonterminal B, written $B \vdash A$, if $B \overset{*}{\Rightarrow} Ax$ for some x. As we excluded the left recursion $\vdash$ is a partial ordering of N. An 1-configuration $c_I = A_I \to x_1.Bx_2$, B in N, is called developable. The develop move is applicable on the situation $\mathcal{S} = (w_1,w_2,(\mathbb{A}_0,\dots,\mathbb{A}_q),d)$ only if $\mathbb{A}_q$ contains a developable configuration. Let $\mathcal{C} = \{c_1,\dots,c_s\}$ be the set of the configurations in $\mathbb{A}_q$ of the form $c_I = A_I \to x_1.Bx_2$, there is no 1-configuration c' in $\mathbb{A}_q$, $c' = H_J \to x_1'.Dx_2$ such that $D \vdash B$. The develop move transforms $\mathcal{S}$ into $\mathcal{S}_1 = (w_1,w_2,(\mathbb{A}_0,\dots,\mathbb{A}_q,\mathbb{A}_{q+1}),d)$ where $\mathbb{A}_{q+1} = A_{q,1} \cup A_{q,2}$, $A_{q,1} = \{c \mid c \text{ in } A_q - \mathcal{C}\}$, $A_{q,2} = \{A_I \to x \mid \text{there is } c = H_k \to x_1.Ax_2 \text{ in } \mathcal{C}$ such that $FIRST(w_2) \subseteq FIRST(x)$, the pointers in I point just all such c' in $\mathcal{C}\}$. The output associated with $A_I \to .x = ((h,0),I)$ in $A_{q,2}$ is $M\{[_h\}$, M is the union of the outputs associated with the configurations pointed by I. The outputs associated with the configurations in $A_{q,1}$ are the same as in $A_q - \mathcal{C}$.

(C) Read move. The move can be used if no reduce, and/or develop move can be applied. It transforms $\mathcal{S} = (w_1,aw_2,(\mathbb{A}_0,\dots,\mathbb{A}_q),d)$ into $(w_1a,w_2,(\mathbb{A}_0,\dots,\mathbb{A}_{q-1},\mathbb{A}_q'),dMa)$. $\mathbb{A}_q' = \{A_I \to x_1a.x_2 \mid A_I \to x_i.ax_2 \text{ in } \mathbb{A}_q$, $FIRST(x_2) \supseteq FIRST(w_2)\}$. $M = \bigcup_i M_i$, M_i is the output associated with the configuration c_i in $\mathbb{A}_q$. The output associated with $A_I \to x_1a.x_2 = ((h,j),I)$ is $\{\uparrow_{i,j}\}$.

The output associated with $S \to \vdash.S'\dashv$ is empty. A word w is accepted iff $INIT(w) \models^* ACCEPT(w)$. It is easily seen that the algorithm is deterministic and it must reach in at most $K(w+2)$ moves the state for which no move is possible.

Note: If all pointers in A_q have the form (k,m), where $k \le n < q$ then the 1-state $(\mathbb{A}_0,\dots,\mathbb{A}_n,\dots,\mathbb{A}_q)$ can be replaced by $(\mathbb{A}_1,\dots,\mathbb{A}_n,\mathbb{A}_q)$.

Example

Let us have the grammar G: $0.S \to \vdash S'\dashv$, $1.2{:}S' \to AS' \mid A$, $3.4.5.6{:}$ $A \to aAa \mid aa \mid bAb \mid bb$. Obviously $INIT(\vdash baabbaab \dashv) = (\vdash, baabbaab\dashv, (\{S_\emptyset \to \vdash.S'\dashv\}), [_0 \uparrow_{01})$. The output associated with $S_\emptyset \to \vdash.S'\dashv$ is empty. Let RE = read, RD = reduce, A = accept, D = develop. The algorithm works as follows (in obvious notations, we write $A_{1-6,2-7}$ instead of $A_{\{(1,6),(2,7)\}}$).

Move	to be read	pointer	highest picture	associated output	performed output
	baabbaab$\dashv$	0-1	$S_\emptyset \to \vdash .S'\dashv$	$\emptyset$	$[_0 \vdash \uparrow_{0.1}$

Here 0-1 denotes the pointer (0,1) pointing the $S_\emptyset \to \vdash .S'\dashv$

D	baabbaab$\dashv$	1-1	$S'_{0-1} \to .AS'$	$\{[_1\}$	
		1-2	S'_{0-1} .A	$\{[_2\}$	

Note that develop move remains the "old" pictures A_0, A_1 unchanged. Below we often write a instead of $\{a\}$. Note that incomming symbol is b.

D	baabbaab$\dashv$	2-1	$A_{1-1} \to .bAb$	$[_1[_5$	
		2-2	$A_{1-1} \to .bb$	$[_1[_6$	
		2-3	$A_{1-2} \to .bAb$	$[_2[_5$	
		2-4	$A_{1-2} \to .bb$	$[_2[_6$	

This gives after the uniting

	baabbaab$\dashv$	2-1	$A_{1-1,1-2} \to .bAb$	$\{[_1,[_2\}[_5$	
		2-2	$A_{1-1,1-2} \to .bb$	$\{[_1,[_2\}[_6$	
RE	aabbaab	2-1	$A_{1-1,1-2} \to b.Ab$	$\uparrow_{5.1}$	$\{[_1,[_2\}[_5 b$
		2-2	$A_{1-1,1-2} \to b.b$	x	

The crossed configuration is excluded as the comming symbol a is not in FIRST(b).

D	aabbaab$\dashv$	3-1	$A_{2-1} \to .aAa$	$\uparrow_{5.1}[_3$	
		3-2	$A_{2-1} \to .aa$	$\uparrow_{5.1}[_4$	
RE	abbaab$\dashv$	3-1	$A_{2-1} \to a.Aa$	$\uparrow_{3.1}$	$\uparrow_{5.1}\{[_3,[_4\}a$
		3-2	$A_{2-1} \to a.a$	$\uparrow_{4.1}$	
RE,D	bbaab$\dashv$	4-1	$A_{3-1} \to a.Aa$	$\uparrow_{3.1}$	
		4-2	$A_{3-1} \to a.a$	x	
		4-3	$A_{2-1} \to aa.$	$\emptyset$	$\{\uparrow_{4.1},\uparrow_{3.1}[_3\}a$

Note that in the reduce move (4-3) points (2-1).

RD	bbaab$\dashv$	4-1	$A_{3-1} \to a.Aa$	$\uparrow_{3.1}$	
		4-2	$A_{1-1,1-2} \to bA.b$	$]_4\uparrow_{5.2}$	

RE,D	baab$\dashv$	5-1	$A_{4-1} \to b.Ab$	$\uparrow_{5.1}$	
		5-2	$A_{4-1} \to b.b$	$\uparrow_{6.1}$	$\{\uparrow_{3.1}\{[_5,[_6\},]_4\uparrow_{5.2}\}b$
		5-3	$A_{1-1,1-2} \to bAb.$	$\emptyset$	
RD,RD	baab$\dashv$	5-1	$A_{4-1} \to b.Ab$	$\uparrow_{5.1}$	
		5-2	$A_{4-1} \to b.b$	$\uparrow_{6.1}$	
		5-3	$S'_{0-1} \to A.S'$	$]_5\uparrow_{1.1}$	
		5-4	$S_\emptyset \to \vdash S'.\dashv$	x	

Further moves are D,D,RE,D,RE,RD,D,RE,RD,D,RE,RD,RD,RD,RE with the ACCEPT situation

$$(10\text{-}1)\ S_\emptyset \to \vdash S'\dashv. \qquad]_5\{]_2,]_2]_1\}\uparrow_{0.2}\dashv]_0$$

and the output is

$$[_0\vdash\uparrow_{0.1}\{[_2,[_1\}[_5\ b\uparrow_{5.1}\{[_3,[_4\}a\{\uparrow_{4.1},\uparrow_{3.1}[_3\}a\{\uparrow_{3.1}\{[_5,[_6\},]_4\uparrow_{5.2}\}b$$
$$\{\uparrow_{5.1},]_5\uparrow_{1.1}\}[_1,[_2\}[_5,\uparrow_{6.1}\}b\{\uparrow_{5.1}\{[_3,[_4\},]_6\uparrow_{5.2}\}a\{\uparrow_{3.1}\{[_3,[_4\},\uparrow_{4.1},$$
$$]_3\uparrow_{3.2}\}a\{]_3,]_4\}\uparrow_{5.2}\ b]_5\{]_2,]_2]_1\}\uparrow_{0.2}\dashv]_0 .$$

The output codes in an obvious form two possible parses for the input string.

Results

A sequence of 1-configurations $c_1,\dots,c_s$ (c-sequence for short) is <u>contained in a situation</u> $\varphi=(w_1,w_2,(\mathbb{A}_0,\dots,\mathbb{A}_q)$ if c_s is in $\mathbb{A}_q$ and for $j=0,2,\dots,s-1$ c_{j+1} points c_j. A sequence of 1-configurations $c_0 = S_\emptyset \to x_{01}.A^{(1)}x_{02}$, $c_2 = A_I^{(1)} \to x_{21}.A^{(2)}x_{22},\dots,c_s = A_K^{(s)} \to x_{s1}.x_{s2}$ is admissible for (w_1,w_2) if $x_{01}\dots x_{s1} \Rightarrow^* w_1$, $\mathrm{FIRST}(w_2) \subseteq \mathrm{FIRST}(x_{s2},\dots x_{02})$. It is not difficult to prove that if $\mathrm{INIT}(\vdash w\dashv) \models^* \varphi = (\vdash w_1, w_2\dashv, \mathbb{A}, d)$ then φ contains just all the c-sequences admissible for $(\vdash w_1, w_2\dashv)$. It follows

<u>Theorem 1.</u> $\mathrm{INIT}(\vdash w\dashv) \models^* \mathrm{ACCEPT}(\vdash w\dashv)$ iff $\vdash w\dashv \in L(G)$.

<u>Theorem 2.</u> The algorithm performs at most $K_G|w|$ moves before it reaches ACCEPT or a situation for which no move is possible. K_G depends on the grammar.

So the time complexity of the algorithm is the $O(n\,s(n))$ where $s(n)$ is the time complexity of the move. It is easily seen that $s(n)$ is determined by the complexity of the set union. If we use no information on the pointer set $s(n)$ is $O(n^2)$ (we form the union of $O(n)$

sets of O(n) elements). This gives the time bounds $O(n^3)$ on usual RASP machine. If we assume that the bit string operations are of finite complexity for strings of arbitrary length the algorithm works in time $O(n^2)$.

We can now take the following strategy. For a pointer set I denote max(I) the maximal element in I. For two pointer sets write $A \prec B$ if $\max(A) \prec \max(B)$ and if $\max(A) = \max(B)$ then $\operatorname{card}(A) \leq \operatorname{card}(B)$. For A,B, $A \succ B$, write $C = A \cup^t B$ if C contains all the elements of A and all the elements B_k of B having the property, that there are no $j \geq k$ such that $B_j, B_{j+1}, \ldots, B_{j+t-1}$ are in A. C contains also the least t elements of A as well as of B.

The operation $\bigcup_i^{k,t} A_i$, where $\operatorname{card}(A_i) \leq n$, $k \leq Hn$ can be performed in O(n) RASP operations. Let $\models_t$ denotes the move defined as above but with the $\cup$ replaced by $\cup^t$. t-parser is our algorithm modified in such a way.

<u>Theorem 3.</u> For $t > 0$ write $ACC_t(G) = \{ \vdash x \dashv \mid INIT(\vdash x \dashv) \models_t^* ACCEPT(\vdash x \dashv)$. $ACC_t(G) \subseteq L(G)$. If the grammar G is unambiguous then $ACC_t(G) = L(G)$. The modified parsing algorithm reject or accepts any x in T^* in time $O(|x|^2)$.

<u>Theorem 4.</u> t-parse for $t \geq 1$ accepts in time O(n) a superset of LR-grammars. There are unambiguous grammars G which are LR(k) for no k for which t-parser accepts L(G) in time O(n)(for example $0{:}S \to \vdash S' \dashv$, $1.2{:}S' \to A|B$, $3.4{:}A \to aA|a$, $5.6{:}B \to aB|a$).

It is an open problem whether for each grammar G there is a t such that t-parser accepts L(G) or whether (using the properties of pointer sets) $\cup^t$ can be modified in order to obtain a parse algorithm enabling to parse (for each grammar G in parsable form) L(G) in time $O(n^2)$.

Error recovery

Our method follows in parallel all the parses admissible for the part of the input read up to now. This property is very suitable for error recovery in compilers. In fact if an error is detected (i.e. our algorithm is blocked) we must apply some hypothesis about the reasons of the error (like "missing symbol, redundant symbol, wrong symbol" etc), modify the parser situation and continue. Our algorithm allows to take several hypothesis into account (similar idea appeared in Irons [7] as it was pointed out by Sklenář [9]). Moreover we are able to continue the parsing (without recovering) to the right of the occurence of the error similary to Graham, Rhodes [8] .

Without giving rather cumbersome technical details we shall show the possibilities on an example.

Let us have the grammar 0:S →⊢S′⊣ ,1:S′→ begin B end,2.3:B→D;Bl| Bl , 4.5:D→real i;D|real i,6.7:Bl→i|i;Bl. Let the input be begin i; real i end. This string drives the parser into the blocked situation.

(0-1) S →⊢.S′⊣
(1-1) S'_{0-1} → begin.B end
(2-1) B_{1-1} → .D;Bl   x
(2-2) B_{1-1} →.Bl
(3-1) Bl_{2-2} → i;.Bl   x
(3-2) Bl_{2-2} → i.   x

An error is detected, so we must find a new situation. We replace the highest picture by the picture containing

(a) The 1-configurations from the highest picture and the configurations with the point moved one place to the left

(b) The configurations prepared for reduction are reduced; the obtained configurations are marked by "skip one symbol"

(c) All the configurations having the comming symbol in the left set of their left hand side are added and marked as "ERROR"

(d) The copies of the configurations from (a) - (c) are added with the mark 'skip one symbol'. This leads to

(3-1) Bl_{2-2} → i.;Bl   x
(3-2) Bl_{2-2} → i.;Bl skip(1)
(3-3) Bl_{2-2} → .i   x
(3-4) Bl_{2-2} → .i skip(1)
(3-5) D_{ERR} → .real i
(3-6) D_{ERR} → .real i skip(1)
(3-7) Bl_{2-2} → i;.Bl
(3-8) Bl_{2-2} → i;.Bl skip(1)
(3-9) B_{1-1} → begin B.end   x
(3-10) S'_{0-1} → begin B.end skip(1)

The crossed configurations are excluded. Incomming symbol (real) is read, the point in configurations with skip(1) is not moved, the skip marker is excluded. This leads to

(3-1) Bl_{2-2} → i.;Bl   x
(3-2) Bl_{2-2} → .i
(3-3) D_{ERR} → real.i
(3-4) D_{ERR} → .real i   x
(3-5) Bl_{2-2} → i;.Bl
(3-9) S'_{0-1} → begin B.end   x

Now we must go on in usual way. We obtain after the develop and read moves

(4-1) Bl_{2-2} → i.

(4-2) D_{ERR} → real i. x

(4-3) Bl_{3-5} → i.;Bl x

(4-4) Bl_{3-5} → i.

And after reducing we obtain (except (4-2))

(3-1) S'_{0-1} → begin B.end

Note, however, that in the case of a more complex declaration (Algol 68, SIMULA) the algorithm would be again blocked in (4-1) D_{ERR} → real i.. In this case we have to compare the read parts of configurations (here begin i;) and the required continuation (here Bl) with the really detected (i.e. D) and to replace D by Bl.

Our (incompletely given) procedure reflect the hypothesis one symbol missing/redundant/wrong quite well. It can be modified in various ways.

References

1. Graham,S.L., Harrison,M.A., Parsing of General Context-Free Languages, Advances in Computers 14,(1976), pp. 77-185.
2. Král,J., Bottom-up Versus Top Down Syntax Analysis Revised, Report of Institute of Comp. Technique, 10/74, Prague, Dec. 1974.
3. Král,J., Semitop-Down Transition Diagrams Driven Syntax Analysis, Report of the Institute of Computation Technique, Dec. 1974.
4. Aho,A.V., Ullman,J.D., The Theory of Parsing, Translation and Compiling, Vol.1,2, Prentice Hall, Englewood Cliffs, 1972, 1973.
5. Král,J., Demner,J., Parsing as a Subtask of Compiling, Mathematical Foundations of Computer Science 1975, Lecture Notes in Computer Science 32, Springer V., Berlin (1975), pp. 61-74
6. Aho,A.V., Hopcroft,J.E. and Ullman,J.D., The Design and Analysis of Computer Algorithms, Addison-Wesley, Reading, Mass., 1974.
7. Irons,T., An Error Correcting Parse Algorithm, Comm. ACM 6, (1963), pp. 669 - 673.
8. Graham,S.L., Rhodes,S.P., Practical Syntactic Error Recovery, Comm. ACM 18, (1975), 639 - 649.
9. Sklenář,I., Private Communication.
10. Tseitin,G.S., ALGOL 68, the implementation methods (in Russian), Leningr. Univ. Press, Leningrad 1976.

A PROBABILISTIC RESTRICTION OF BRANCHING PLANS

Ivan Kramosil

Institute of Information Theory and Automation

Czechoslovak Academy of Sciences

Pod vodárenskou věží 4, 180 76 Prague 8

1. Introduction

The idea of branching plan introduced to artificial intelligence and robotics some years ago and studied in a more detail by Štěpánková and Havel [3] can be considered, at least from the theoretical point of view, as an adequate tool to overcome the problems arising in automated problem solving because of the nondeterministic character of more complex environments. Any branching reflects the necessity to take into a simultaneous consideration two or more possible successors of the operator just performed, this necessity being forced by the unability to decide a priori which operator will be applicable in this intermediate stage of plan execution. E.g., let us admit the possibility that an operator may fail; in such a case we must consider two branches following any application of this operator, one corresponding to the successful execution, the other to the admitted possibility of a failure. An analogous situation occurs in connection with automatic synthesis of computer programs. The intuitive difference resides in the fact that in the current deterministic conception of the computer the source of uncertainty of the "environment" (which in this case is represented by the memory space and input data) is reduced just to the uncertainty of input data. In fact, almost all the ideas given in the present paper can be immediately or after a straightforward reformulation applied also to automatic program synthesis. However, this particular paper is based on the motivation and terminology from the area of robot problem solving in which this research actually originated. In particular, we use the terms "plan" and "operator" where others would use "program" and "instruction".

In real cases when the complexity of problems and operators is high enough and when the nondeterministic character of the environment makes an a priori assurance of an operator application very difficult and doubtful, the number of necessary branches (i.e. paths from the root to a terminal node) in any branching plan solving such a problem causes the extent and complexity of such plans to be too high from the point of view of a practical application. Hence, the idea immediately occurs to consider, instead of a branching plan as a whole, some its restricted or reduced forms which would be able, in a sense, to supply for the plan in question.

In this paper, a way of restricting branching plans is investigated, based on the following two principles. First, no matter how complex a branching plan may be, any execution of this plan follows just one branch. Second, the environment (or input data) is (are) supposed to be of stochastic character and for any branch a probability is defined with which just this branch will be followed when the plan in question is executed. In this way to any node i.e. operator occurence of this plan the probability of its actual achieving may be ascribed and the plan can be restricted in such a way that the nodes with probability values not exceeding a given treshold value (Piper [2] says "pruning level") are omitted.

As far as the author knows there are two papers, Fikes et al. [1] and Piper [2], originating from 1972 and independently dealing with probabilistically evaluated branching plans. Fikes et al. [1] just suggest this idea and mention briefly some consequences, Piper [2] goes into more details, however, his argumentation is based rather on some empirical and programming practice oriented facts. Piper suggests a program looking for the best way in an evaluated branching plan. Here we try to give a theoretical justification for this way of reasoning. It is worth to note, by passing, that any admissible probability distribution on the input data, say natural numbers, would automatically underrate data of high complexity e.g. large numbers, which is a challenging idea to the common interpretation of results in current complexity theory.

2. Branching Plans and Their Characteristics

Our formal structure for representing the environment is based on the concept of the image space, see Štěpánková and Havel [3] . Mathematically, an <u>image space</u> I is a collection of formal theories with a common first-order langugage $\mathcal{L}$ and a common subset of axioms T_I (called the core theory of I) representing the unchangeable facts about the environment (thus an "image" can be treated as an extension $T_I[A]$ of T_I by a "specific" axiom $A \in \mathcal{L}$) . In addition, a set Σ of operators is given, each $\varphi \in \Sigma$ presented by a pair $\langle C_\varphi, R_\varphi \rangle \in \mathcal{L} \times \mathcal{L}$ (the condition and result of φ, respectively). An operator φ is applicable in $T_I[A]$ iff $T_I[A] \vdash C_\varphi$,the outcome of such application is then $T_I[R_\varphi]$. A problem in I is just a pair of formulas $\langle X, Y \rangle \in \mathcal{L} \times \mathcal{L}$ (the initial and the goal formulas, respectively).

For limited space we shall not describe details of the intuition leading to the notion of branching plan (see Štěpánková and Havel [3]). A formal definition reads:

Definition 1. Let I be an image space with a language $\mathcal{L}$, core theory T_I and operators Σ . Denote, for any $\Gamma \in \Sigma^*$, by $\mathrm{Fst}(\Gamma)$ the set of first symbols of the words from Γ, by $\partial_\gamma \Gamma = \{\vartheta : \gamma\vartheta \in \Sigma\}, \gamma \in \Sigma$, the derivative of Γ with respect to γ . Denote, for any $\gamma \in \Sigma^*$, $\Gamma \subset \Sigma^*$, $Y \in \mathcal{L}$, $\bar{Y}(\gamma, \Gamma) = Y$, if $\gamma \in \Gamma$, $\bar{Y} = Y \wedge$ non Y (i.e. "false"), if $\gamma \in \Sigma^* - \Gamma$, denote by $\Lambda \in \Sigma^*$ the empty word. Let $\langle X, Y \rangle \in \mathcal{L} \times \mathcal{L}$ be a problem. A finite non-empty subset* $\Gamma \subset \Sigma^*$ is called a branching plan for the problem $\langle X, Y \rangle$ in I, if

(i) $T_I[X] \vdash (\bigvee_{\varphi \in \mathrm{Fst}(\Gamma)} C\varphi) \vee \bar{Y}(\Lambda, \Gamma)$,

(ii) for any $\gamma = \gamma_1 \varphi_1 \in \mathrm{Pref}(\Gamma), \varphi_1 \in \Sigma$
$T_I[R_{\varphi_1}] \vdash (\bigvee_{\varphi \in \mathrm{Fst}(\partial_\gamma \Gamma)} C\varphi) \vee \bar{Y}(\gamma, \Gamma)$.

Any branching plan can be seen either as a set of words over Σ or as a finite tree with labels from Σ . When Γ is considered as a tree, we denote by $|\Gamma|$ its support, by s_0 its root, by $\mathrm{Fr}(\Gamma)$ the set of terminal nodes, by $S(x)$ the set of all immediate successors of a node x, by $\leq$ the corresponding partial ordering, by $\mathrm{Int}(\Gamma) = \Gamma - \mathrm{Fr}(\Gamma)$ the interior of Γ .

Definition 2. Let Γ be a branching plan, let $x \in \Gamma$ be a branch (i.e. a path from the root to a terminal node in Γ) , denote by $\ell(x)$ the length of x . Then the value $\max\{\ell(x) : x \in \Gamma\}$ is called the length of Γ and denoted by $\ell(\Gamma)$, the sum of $\ell(x)$ over all the branches in Γ which are not prefixes of another branches in Γ is called the extent of Γ and denoted by $e(\Gamma)$.

By the extent we shall measure the complexity of a plan. Consider a branching plan Γ in which every branch is of the length $\ell(\Gamma)$ and any node from $\mathrm{Int}(\Gamma)$ has just K immediate successors. Then the extent of Γ is maximal among all the plans with the same length and with card $S(x) \leq K$, $x \in \mathrm{Int}(\Gamma)$, hence,

$$e(\Gamma) \leq \ell(\Gamma) \cdot K^{\ell[\Gamma]}$$

and no better upper bound for this class of plans can be given. The exponential character of this estimation is the source of practical difficulties connected with using branching plans as a whole. To avoid this undesirable size of dependence between $e(\Gamma)$ and $\ell(\Gamma)$ is the intention of our idea of restricted branching plans.

3. Probabilistic Restriction of Branching Plans

Definition 3. Probabilistically evaluated branching plan (PEBP) is a pair $\langle \Gamma, P \rangle$, where Γ is a branching plan and P is a mapping from $|\Gamma|$ into $\langle 0,1 \rangle$ such that (i) for all $x \in \mathrm{Int}(\Gamma)$ holds $P(x) = \sum_{y \in S(x)} P(y)$ and (ii) $\sum_{x \in Fr(\Gamma)} P(x) = 1$.

Suppose there is, for any $x \in \mathrm{Int}(\Gamma)$, a probability distribution $p(x,.)$ on the set $S(x)$. If the random events consisting in following particular y's from $S(x)$ are supposed to be statistically independent (as will be the case in the rest of this chapter), then the system $\{p(x,.) : x \in \mathrm{Int}(\Gamma)\}$ of distributions defines uniquely a probabilistic evaluation P on Γ, on the other hand, any such P on Γ defines uniquely a system $\{p(x,.) : x \in \mathrm{Int}(\Gamma)\}$. Suppose, on the other hand, that we know a probability distribution P_Γ on the set $Fr(\Gamma)$ of terminal nodes of Γ, then the demand (ii) of Definition 3 enables to define immediately and uniquely the probabilistic evaluation on Γ ascribing to any node the sum of probabilities of branches on which it lies.

Definition 4. Let $\langle \Gamma, P \rangle$ be a PEBP, let $\varepsilon > 0$ be a real, denote $|\Gamma_\varepsilon| = \{x : x \in |\Gamma|, P(x) > \varepsilon\}$, $\Gamma_\varepsilon = \langle |\Gamma_\varepsilon|, \leq \upharpoonright |\Gamma_\varepsilon|, s_0 \rangle$, $P_\varepsilon = P \upharpoonright |\Gamma_\varepsilon|$. Then the pair $\langle \Gamma_\varepsilon, P_\varepsilon \rangle$, denoted also by $R(\Gamma, P, \varepsilon)$, will be called the ε-restriction of the PEBP Γ.

Clearly, $R(\Gamma, P, \varepsilon)$ is uniquely defined by Γ, P and ε.

Theorem 1. Let $\langle \Gamma, P \rangle$ be a PEBP, let $\varepsilon > 0$ be a real, let $\varepsilon \leq p(x,y) \leq 1-\varepsilon$ for any $x, y \in |\Gamma|$, $y \in S(x)$. Then $e(R(\Gamma, P, \varepsilon)) < (1/\varepsilon) \cdot \log_2 (1/\varepsilon)$.

Proof. It follows immediately that card $S(x) \geq 2$ for any $x \in \mathrm{Int}(\Gamma)$. A more general assertion can be proved, according to which the extent of the sub-plan rooted by a node $x \in |\Gamma|$ is majorized by $(P(x)/\varepsilon) \cdot \log_2(P(x)/\varepsilon)$. This assertion can be proved by induction on the length of a shortest path from x to $Fr(\Gamma)$.

Theorem 1 follows when $x = s_0$.

Theorem 2. Let $\langle \Gamma, P \rangle$ be a PEBP, let $\varepsilon > 0$ be a real. Then

$$e(R(\Gamma, P, \varepsilon)) \leq (1/\varepsilon)\,\ell(\Gamma)$$

Proof. No branch in Γ and no one in $R(\Gamma, P, \varepsilon)$ can be longer than $\ell(\Gamma)$. $R(\Gamma, P, \varepsilon)$ contains at most $1/\varepsilon$ branches which are not prefixes of another ones from $R(\Gamma, P, \varepsilon)$, as the random events consisting in achieving particular terminal modes of $R(\Gamma, P, \varepsilon)$ are mutually disjoint and the probability of any of them exceeds ε.

Thus the extent (or structural complexity) of restricted branching plans grows at most linearly in dependence on their length- a very favourable fact if compared with the inequality in Section 2. The terminal nodes of $R(\Gamma, P, \varepsilon)$, which are not terminal nodes of Γ can be understood as formal counterparts to those situations, when the restricted plan or program stops because of its incompleteness and the planning (or program synthesis) must be applied again to obtain the rest of the desired plan or program (hierarchical planning or programming).

4. Experience - Based Transformations of Restricted Branching Plans

This chapter will be devoted to the problem how to obtain, in an actual case, a probabilistic evaluation P of a branching plan Γ. The intuition connected with PEBP's was that for any $x \in |\Gamma|$ the value P (x) should correspond to the probability with which x will be actually achieved when Γ executed. Hence, an immediate idea is to replace P (x) by the relative frequency of the actual achieving of x in a "large enough" collection of executions of Γ. In the terms of automatic program synthesis: it is easier to "remember" the frequencies of applications of certain instructions than to define the actual probability distribution on input data.

Definition 5. Statistically evaluated branching plan (SEBP) is a pair $\langle \Gamma, S \rangle$, where Γ is a branching plan and S is a mapping of $|\Gamma|$ into the set of all pairs of naturals (we denote $S(x) = \langle S_1(x), S_2(x) \rangle$) such that (i) $S_1(x) \leq S_2(x)$, $S_2(x) = S_2(y) > 0$, $x, y \in |\Gamma|$, i.e. $S_2(x)$ corresponds rather to Γ that to x and denotes the number of executions of Γ, (ii) denoting by $P(S)$ the mapping of $|\Gamma|$ into $\langle 0,1 \rangle$ defined, for any $x \in |\Gamma|$, as $P(S)(x) = S_1(x)/S_2(x)$, then $\langle \Gamma, P(S) \rangle$ is a PEBP.

Definition 6. Let $\langle \Gamma, S\rangle$ be a SEBP, let α be a branch of Γ. Consider the set of all mappings from $|\Gamma|$ to the pairs of integers and define a transformation of this set into itself, defined only if $\langle\Gamma,S\rangle$ is SEBP:

(i) if $x \in |\Gamma|$, $x \notin \alpha$, then $(f\alpha\, S)(x) = \langle S_1(x),\ S_2(x) + 1\rangle$,

(ii) if $x \in |\Gamma|$, $x \in \alpha$, then $(f\alpha\, S)(x) = \langle S_1(x) + 1,\ S_2(x) + 1\rangle$.

Clearly, $\langle \Gamma, f\alpha\, S\rangle$ is also SEBP. $f\alpha$ describes the changes involved in a statistical evaluation S by the fact that Γ has been executed once more and this execution has followed the branch α. Let us write f_α^n, if f_α applied n-times. In general, $R(\Gamma, P(S), \varepsilon) \neq R(\Gamma, P(f_\alpha\ S), \varepsilon)$, the possible difference can be seen as the result of an experience-based self-learning process.

The following definition contains terms "environment" and "execution" which have not been formalized in this paper. Such a formalization can be given and actually has been by Kramosil[4], however, it necessitates to develop a complex semantics for some notions studied here. The limited extent does not allow to reproduce it and it is why we ask the reader to understand the mentioned notions on their intuitive level.

Definition 7. The environment is called stochastically stabile (w.r.t. a probler $\langle X,Y\rangle$, operator set Σ and branching plan Γ), if for any $x \in Fr(\Gamma)$ and any two executions of Γ the probabilities for both executions to terminate in x are the same. If, moreover, $P(x_o) = 1$ for an $x \in Fr(\Gamma)$, the environment is called deterministic (w.r.t. $\langle X,Y\rangle, \Sigma, \Gamma$). The environment is called statistically independent if the probability with which an execution of Γ terminates in an $x \in Fr(\Gamma)$ does not depend on the terminal node (s), where foregoing execution (s) terminate(s).

First we treat the deterministic environment.

Theorem 3. Let $\Sigma, \langle X,Y\rangle$ and Γ have the same sense as in Definition 7. Consider a sequence of n executions of Γ such that all executions starting from certain, say, $n_o + 1$-st, take place in a deterministic environment. Denote by α the branch of Γ to which the probability one is ascribed. Then, for any ε real, $1/2 \geq \varepsilon \geq 0$, and any statistical evaluation S of Γ the following holds:

if $n \geq \max\{(\varepsilon S_2(x) + n_o)/(1-\varepsilon),\ (S_2(x) + n_o - \varepsilon S_2(x))/\varepsilon\}$, then

$R(\Gamma, P(f_\alpha^{n-n_o}\ f_{\beta_{n_o}} \cdots f_{\beta_1}\ S), \varepsilon) = \langle\{\alpha\}, P(f_\alpha^{n-n_o}\ f_{\beta_{n_o}} \cdots f_{\beta_1}\ S)\rangle$, where $\beta_1, \beta_2, \beta_3, \ldots, \beta_{n_o}$ are the branches of Γ followed during the first n_o executions. The right side tends to $\langle \{\alpha\}, I_\alpha \upharpoonright \{\alpha\} \rangle$, if $n \to \infty$, I_α ascribes 1 to any $x \in \alpha$, 0 to any $x \in |\Gamma| - \{\alpha\}$.

Proof. All the realizations since $n_o + 1$-st follow the branch α. $n/n+k \to 1, n \to \infty$, k fixed, so $P(f_\alpha^{n-n_0} f_{\beta n_0} \cdots f_{\beta_1} S)(x) \to 1$ for any $x \in \alpha$, hence, this evaluation tends to 0 for any $x \in |\Gamma| - \{\alpha\}$. An easy calculation gives that for any

$$n \geq \max\{(\varepsilon S_2(x) + n_o) / (1-\varepsilon), (S_2(x) + n_o - \varepsilon S_2(x)) / \varepsilon\}$$

and any $x \in |\Gamma|$ this evaluation is below ε, if $x \notin \alpha$, and it is above ε, if $x \in \alpha$. Hence, just $\{\alpha\}$ rests when restriction applied to Γ.

The branch α is a linear plan solving $\langle X, Y \rangle$ in the considered deterministic environment. Not being able to derive immediately this linear plan because of the lack of sufficient and specific information about the environment, robot can find this linear plan empirically after a certain number of experiments. Theorem 3 is of special importance for robotics, as for the practical and technical reasons linear plans are much favorized to branching plan, this difference not being for so important in program synthesis. The following theorem shows in which sense and under which conditions the process of experience-based restriction of branching plans tends to a limit even in a stochastic environment.

Theorem 4. Let Σ, $\langle X, Y \rangle$ and Γ have the same sense as in Definition 7. Let S be a statistical evaluation of Γ, let P_Γ be a probability distribution on $Fr(\Gamma)$, let $\tilde{P}_\Gamma$ be the probabilistic evaluation of Γ uniquely determined by P_Γ, let $\varepsilon \geq 0$ be given. Suppose $\tilde{P}_\Gamma(x) \neq \varepsilon$ for any $x \in |\Gamma|$. Consider a sequence of executions of Γ in a stochastically stabile and statistically independent environment corresponding to the distribution P_Γ on $Fr(\Gamma)$. Denote by $\alpha(n)$ the branch followed during the n-th execution, then with the probability one the following holds: there exists an index n_o such that for all $n \geq n_0$,

$$R(\Gamma, P(f_{\alpha(n)} f_{\alpha(n-1)} \cdots f_{\alpha(1)} S), \varepsilon) = R(\Gamma, \tilde{P}_\Gamma, \varepsilon).$$

Formally written, $\alpha(n)$ is a random variable defined on a probability space $\langle \Omega, \mathcal{S}, \mu \rangle$ and taking its values in Γ (taken as the set of branches). The assertion then sounds:

$$\mu\left(\bigcap_{n=n_0}^{\infty} \{\omega : \omega \in \Omega, R(\Gamma, P(f_{\alpha(n,\omega)} \cdots f_{\alpha(1,\omega)} S), \varepsilon) = R(\Gamma, \tilde{P}_\Gamma, \varepsilon)\}\right) = 1.$$

Proof. The actual application of an operator occurence $x \in |\Gamma|$ is a random event with the same probability in any of the statistically independent experiments. The strong law of large numbers gives that with the probability one the relative frequency of the actual achieving of x tends to $\tilde{P}_\Gamma(x)$. Hence, starting from an index, this frequency is continually above ε, so $x \in R(\Gamma, P(f_{\alpha(n)} \cdots f_{\alpha(1)} S), \varepsilon)$ or it is continually below ε, so $x \notin R(\Gamma, P(f_{\alpha(n)} \cdots f_{\alpha(1)} S), \varepsilon)$. Taking the maximum of these indices for all $x \in |\Gamma|$ we prove the stability of $R(\Gamma, P(f_{\alpha(n)} \cdots f_{\alpha(1)} S), \varepsilon)$. If $\tilde{P}_\Gamma(x) = \varepsilon$ for an $x \in |\Gamma|$ the theorem fails as in this case x will be infinitely many times in $R(\Gamma, P(f_{\alpha(n)} \cdots f_{\alpha(1)} S), \varepsilon)$ but for infinitely many times x will be outside this restriction.

Combining Theorems 1 and 2 with Theorems 3 and 4 we can easily see that experimenting and experience using enable to reduce the necessary extent of branching plan to a degree rather significant and important from the practical point of view.

The author thanks to I.M.Havel for his valuable remarks and comments which have helped to improve this paper.

References

1. Fikes, R.E., Hart, P.E. and Nilsson, N.J., Some New Directions in Robot Problem Solving. In: Machine Intelligence 7 B.Meltzer and D.Michie, Eds., pp. 405-430, 1972. Edinburgh Univ. Press.

2. Piper, J., Integrated Planning and Acting in a Stochastic Environment. Research Rep., School of Artificial Intelligence, University of Edinburgh, 1972.

3. Štěpánková, O. and Havel, I.M., A Logical Theory of Robot Problem Solving. Artificial Intelligence, 7 1976, pp. 129-161.

4. Kramosil, I., Probabilistic Restriction of Branching Plans for Goal-Oriented Automaton Behaviour. Research Rep., Institute of Information Theory and Automation, 1977. In Czech.

REDUCING OPERATORS FOR NORMED GENERAL FORMAL SYSTEMS

Manfred Kudlek
Institut für Informatik, Universität Hamburg
Schlüterstraße 70 , D-2000 Hamburg 13, FRG
Miroslav Novotný
Československá Akademie Věd, Matematický Ústav
Janáčkovo Nám. 2a, 66295 Brno, ČSSR

1. Introduction

By Novotný I1I reducing operators have been introduced which reduce type 0 grammars generating sentential form languages. Using similar methods such operators could be defined also for OL-systems (Novotný I2I) and for Combinatorial systems (Kudlek, Novotný I3I).
By inspecting the definitions and theorems it could be seen that they could be generalized to arbitrary General Formal Systems in a more or less straightforward way. This is the content of the present article. Where proofs are not given they may be found in Kudlek I4I.
In section 2 Normed General Formal Systems generating sentential form languages are introduced, together with the definition of norms for derivations. Some relations on Normed General Formal Systems are defined.
In section 3 reducing operators are defined which reduce the alphabet, the set of axioms, and the set of rules. The properties of these operators are investigated, and it is shown that there exist only 10 relevant ones by combination. Furthermore, order relations are defined for these operators.
In section 4 the problem is considered whether a reducing operator gives a finite Normed Formal System. The main theorem states that if there exists such an operator at all, then it may be also achieved by the special operator $\mu\zeta\beta$.
Finally, in section 5, the problem is considered whether a given language may be generated by a finite Normed Formal System.
All the theorems also hold for all subclasses of Normed General Formal Systems which are closed under an order relation defined in section 2.
It should be mentioned, however, that many of the methods are not constructive.

2. Normed General Formal Systems (NGFS)

D 2.1 Normed General Formal System

An ordered quadruple $G = (V,S,R,n)$ is called a NGFS, if V is a set (the alphabet), $S \subset V^*$ (the set of axioms), R a set of relations on V^* (the rules), and $n : R \to \underline{N}$ a function defining the norm of $r \in R$, $\underline{N}$ denoting the set of integers. To each $r \in R$ there is associated another integer $k(r) \geq 2$, its arity. Threrefore $r \subset (V^*)^{k(r)}$. It is assumed that $\emptyset \notin R$.
If each of the sets V, S, R is finite, $F = (V,S,R,n)$ is simply called a Normed Formal System (NFS). Finally, let NGFS and NFS denote the set of all NGFSs or NFSs.

D 2.2 Derivation

If $A \subset V^*$ is an arbitrary set, $x \in V^*$, then write $A \Rightarrow x\ (R)$ iff there exists a rule $r \in R$ and strings $a_i \in A$ with $1 \leq i < k(r)$ such that $(a_1,\ldots,a_{k(r)-1},x) \in r$. Write $A \overset{*}{\Rightarrow} x\ (R)$ iff either $x \in A$ or there exists an integer $p \geq 1$ and strings $s_i \in V^*$ such that $x = s_p$ and $A_{i-1} \Rightarrow s_i\ (R)$ with $A_0 = A$ and $A_i = A_{i-1} \cup \{s_i\}$ ($1 \leq i \leq p$).
$d(A,x,R,\underline{s})$ with $\underline{s} = \{s_1,\ldots,s_p\}$ will denote a derivation of x from A by R, and $D(A,x,R)$ the set of all derivations of x from A by R. As usually, the sentential form language generated by G is defined by $L(G) = \{x \in V^* \mid S \overset{*}{\Rightarrow} x\ (R)\}$.

D 2.3 Derivation norm

Using the norm of a NGFS there may be defined a norm for derivations.
If $A \Rightarrow x\ (R)$ define $n_0(A,x,R) = \min_{r \in R} \{n(r) \mid A \Rightarrow x\ (\{r\})\}$. If $A \overset{*}{\Rightarrow} x\ (R)$ and $d(A,x,R,\underline{s}) \in D(A,x,R)$ then define

$$n(d(A,x,R,\underline{s})) = \begin{cases} 0 & \text{if } p = 0 \\ \max\limits_{1 \leq i \leq p} n_0(A_{i-1},s_i,R) & \text{if } p > 0 \end{cases}$$

Since this norm is defined for special derivations only, define

$$n(A,x,R) = \min_{d \in D(A,x,R)} n(d(A,x,R,\underline{s})) .$$

The following lemmata are trivial consequences from the definitions.

L 2.1 If $A \overset{*}{\Rightarrow} x\ (R)$ then $n(A,x,R)$ is the least integer $N \geq 0$ such that there exists a subset $R' \subset R$ satisfying the conditions :
$A \overset{*}{\Rightarrow} x\ (R')$ and $\max_{r \in R'} n(r) \leq N$ for all $r \in R'$.

L 2.2 If $B \subset V^*$ is finite, $A \stackrel{*}{\Rightarrow} x\ (R)$ for all $x \in B$, and $B \stackrel{*}{\Rightarrow} y\ (R)$ then $A \stackrel{*}{\Rightarrow} y\ (R)$ and $n(A,y,R)\quad \max(\max_{x \in B} n(A,x,R), n(B,y,R))$.

L 2.3 Let $R_1 \subset R_2$. If $A \stackrel{*}{\Rightarrow} x\ (R_1)$ then $A \stackrel{*}{\Rightarrow} x\ (R_2)$ and $n(A,x,R_2) \leqslant n(A,x,R_1)$.

L 2.4 If $G_i = (V,S_i,R,n) \subset$ NGFS with $i=1,2$ and $S_1 \subset S_2$, then $L(G_1) \subset L(G_2)$ and $n(S_2,z,R) \leqslant n(S_1,z,R)$ for each $z \in L(G_1)$.

By the following definitions NGFSs may be compared.

D 2.4 Rule restriction

Let $G = (V,S,R,n) \in$ NGFS and $V' \subset V$. Then define the restriction of $r \in R$ onto R' by $r/V' = r \cap (V'^*)^{k(r)}$ and the restriction of R onto V' by $R/V' = \{r/V' \mid r \subset R\} - \{\emptyset\}$. The norm of a restricted rule will be defined by $n(r/V') = \min\{n(r') \mid r' \in R,\ r'/V' = r/V'\}$.

D 2.5 Relations on NGFS

If $G_i = (V_i,S_i,R_i,n_i) \in$ NGFS with $i=1,2$, then define $G_1 \equiv G_2$ iff $L(G_1) = L(G_2)$. Define $G_1 \leqslant G_2$ iff $V_1 \subset V_2$, $S_1 \subset S_2$, $R_1 \subset R_2/V_1$, and $n(r'/V_1) = n_1(r)$ if $r'/V_1 = r \in R_1$.

L 2.5 The relation $\equiv$ is an equivalence relation, and $\leqslant$ is an order relation on NGFS. This is a trivial cosequence from the definitions.

D 2.6 Subclasses of NGFSs

A subclass NC $\subset$ NGFS is called closed under $\leqslant$ iff $G \in$ NC , $G' \in$ NGFS , and $G' \leqslant G$ imply $G' \in$ NC .

3. Operators on NGFSs

In this section several operators on NGFS will be introduced. They have the property to be idempotent, to reduce NGFSs, and that all subclasses of NGFS which are closed under $\leqslant$ are also closed under them.

D 3.1 Set norm

For any set $A \subset V^*$ define its norm $\lVert A \rVert$ by $\lVert \emptyset \rVert = 0$ and $\lVert A \rVert = \max_{x \in A} |x|$ where $|x|$ denotes the length of x.

D 3.2 Operator μ

If $G = (V,S,R,n) \in \underline{NC} \subset \underline{NGFS}$, define $\mu G = (V(\mu G),S,R(\mu G),n(\mu G))$ by $V(\mu G) = \{x \in V \mid \text{there exists } (u,v) \in (V^*)^2 \text{ such that } uxv \in L(G)\}$, $R(\mu G) = R/V(\mu G)$, and $n(\mu G)(r/V(\mu G)) = n(r/V(\mu G))$.
Clearly, $\mu G \leqslant G$ and $\mu G \in \underline{NC}$ if $\underline{NC}$ is closed under $\leqslant$.

The following lemmata are trivial consequences again.

L 3.1 If $A \subset S$, then $A \overset{*}{\Rightarrow} z\ (R(\mu G))$ is equivalent to $A \overset{*}{\Rightarrow} z\ (R)$. Furthermore, $L(\mu G) = L(G)$ and $n(\mu G)(S,z,R(\mu G)) = n(S,z,R)$ for all $z \in L(G)$.

L 3.2 For $G \in \underline{NGFS}$: $V(\mu\mu G) = V(\mu G)$, $R(\mu\mu G) = R(\mu G)$, and $n(\mu\mu G) = n(\mu G)$. Hence $\mu\mu G = \mu G$.

D 3.3 Operator β

If $G = (V,S,R,n) \in \underline{NC} \subset \underline{NGFS}$, define $\beta G = (V,S(\beta G),R,n)$ by $S(\beta G) = \{s \in S \mid A \subset S \text{ finite and } A \overset{*}{\Rightarrow} s\ (R) \text{ imply } \|A\| \geqslant |s|\}$.
Clearly, $\beta G \leqslant G$ and $\beta G \in \underline{NC}$ if $\underline{NC}$ is closed under $\leqslant$.

L 3.3 If $z \in L(G)$, then there exists a finite $A \subset S(\beta G)$ such that $A \overset{*}{\Rightarrow} z\ (R)$. A proof of this lemma may be found in |4|.

The following lemmata again are easy to prove.

L 3.4 $L(\beta G) = L(G)$, $S(\beta\beta G) = S(\beta G)$ and $\beta\beta G = \beta G$.

L 3.5 If $G_1 = (V,S,R_1,n)$, $G_2 = (V,S,R_2,n)$ (the same n), $R_1 \subset R_2$ then $S(\beta G_2) \subset S(\beta G_1)$.

L 3.6 For $G \in \underline{NGFS}$: $V(\mu\beta G) = V(\mu G)$, $R(\mu\beta G) = R(\mu G)$, $n(\mu\beta G) = n(\mu G)$ and $S(\beta\mu G) = S(\beta G)$, hence also $\mu\beta G = \beta\mu G$.

D 3.4 Operator ζ

If $G = (V,S,R,n) \in \underline{NC} \subset \underline{NGFS}$, define $\zeta G = (V,S,R(\zeta G),n)$ by $R(\zeta G) = \{r \in R \mid \text{there exists a } z \in L(G) \text{ such that } n(r) \leqslant n(S,z,R)\}$.
Clearly, $\zeta G \leqslant G$ and $\zeta G \in \underline{NC}$ if $\underline{NC}$ is closed under $\leqslant$.

Again, it is easy to prove the following lemmata.

<u>L 3.7</u> If $z \in L(G)$, $A \subset S$, $d(A,z,R,\underline{s}) \in D(A,z,R)$ with $n(d(A,z,R,\underline{s})) = n(A,z,R) = n(S,z,R)$ then $d(A,z,R,\underline{s})$ is a derivation of z from A by $R(\zeta G)$ and $n(d(A,z,R(\zeta G),\underline{s})) \leq n(d(A,z,R,\underline{s}))$.

<u>L 3.8</u> $L(\zeta G) = L(G)$, $n(S,z,R(\zeta G)) = n(S,z,R)$, $R(\zeta\zeta G) = R(\zeta G)$ and $\zeta\zeta G = \zeta G$.

<u>L 3.9</u> If $G_1 = (V,S_1,R,n)$, $G_2 = (V,S_2,R,n) \in \underline{NGFS}$, $S_1 \subset S_2$, and $L(G_1) = L(G_2)$ then $R(\zeta G_2) \subset R(\zeta G_1)$.

<u>L 3.10</u> For $G \in \underline{NGFS}$: $V(\mu\zeta G) = V(\mu G)$, $R(\zeta\mu G) = R(\mu\zeta G)$, and $\mu\zeta G = \zeta\mu G$.

<u>L 3.11</u> For $G \in \underline{NGFS}$: $\beta\zeta\beta G = \zeta\beta G$ and $\zeta\beta\zeta G = \beta\zeta G$.

The following example shows that all operators ι (identity), β, ζ, $\beta\zeta$, $\zeta\beta$, μ, $\mu\beta$, $\mu\zeta$, $\mu\beta\zeta$, and $\mu\zeta\beta$ are different.

<u>E 3.1</u> Consider $G = (V,S,R,n)$ with $V = \{a,b,c\}$, $S = T \cup U$, $T = \{a^{2m} \mid 1 \leq m \leq K_1\}$, $U = \{x \in \{c\}^+ \mid |x| \leq K_2\}$, $3 < K_1,K_2,K_3$, $R = \{r_{kl} \mid 1 \leq k < l \leq K_3\} \cup$ $(\{r_{xy} \mid (x,y) \in (\{c\}^+)^2, |x|,|y| \leq K_2\} - \{r_{c,c}, r_{c,cc}, r_{cc,c}, r_{cc,cc}\})$,

$r_{kl} = \{(ua^k v, ua^l v) \in (V^*)^2 \mid (u,v) \in (V^*)^2\} \cup \{(ub^k v, ub^l v) \in (V^*)^2 \mid (u,v) c (V^*)^2\}$,

$r_{xy} = \{(uxv, uyv) \in (V^*)^2 \mid (u,v) \in (V^*)^2\}$, $n(r_{kl}) = \max(k,l)$, $n(r_{xy}) = \max(|x|,|y|)$.

Then $L(G) = \{a^m \mid m \geq 2\} \cup \{c\}^+$, and

$G = (V,S,R,n)$, $\beta G = (V,\{a^2,c\},R,n)$, $\zeta G = (V,S,\{r_{12}\},n)$, $\beta\zeta G = (V,\{a^2\} \cup U,\{r_{12}\},n)$

$\zeta\beta G = (V,\{a^2,c\},\{r_{12},r_{13},r_{23},r_{c,ccc},r_{cc,ccc},r_{ccc,c},r_{ccc,cc},r_{ccc,ccc}\},n)$,

$\mu G = (V',S,R',n')$, $\mu\beta G = (V',\{a^2,c\},R',n')$, $\mu\zeta G = (V',S,\{r'_{12}\},n')$,

$\mu\beta\zeta G = (V',\{a^2\} \cup U,\{r'_{12}\},n')$,

$\mu\zeta\beta G = (V',\{a^2,c\},\{r'_{12},r'_{13},r'_{23},r'_{c,ccc},r'_{cc,ccc},r'_{ccc,c},r'_{ccc,cc},r'_{ccc,ccc}\},n')$

with $V' = \{a,c\}$, $R' = \{r'_{kl} \mid 1 \leq k < l \leq K_3\} \cup (\{r'_{xy} \mid (x,y) \in (\{c\}^+)^2, |x|,|y| \leq K_2\} - \{r'_{c,c}, r'_{c,cc}, r'_{cc,c}, r'_{cc,cc}\})$, $r'_{kl} = \{(ua^k v, ua^l v) \in (V'^*)^2 \mid (u,v) \in (V'^*)^2\}$,

$r'_{xy} = \{(uxv, uyv) \in (V'^*)^2 \mid (u,v) \in (V'^*)^2\}$, $n'(r'_{kl}) = \max(k,l)$, and $n'(r'_{xy}) = \max(|x|,|y|)$.

<u>D 3.5</u> Let Γ denote the free monoid of all operators on <u>NGFS</u> generated by μ,β,ζ with the binary operation of composition and identity ι.

<u>L 3.12</u> Γ consists of precisely 10 elements given above.

For all $\xi \in \Gamma$ and $G \in \underline{NGFS}$: $\xi\xi = \xi$, $\xi G \equiv G$, and $\xi G \leq G$.

This is an easy consequence from the preceding lemmata.

D 3.6 Reducing operator

Let $\underline{NC} \subset \underline{NGFS}$ be closed under $\leqslant$. If ξ is an operator on $\underline{NC}$ such that $\xi G \equiv G$ and $\xi G \leqslant G$ for all $G \in \underline{NC}$, then ξ is called a reducing operator on $\underline{NC}$. Let $\Delta(\underline{NC})$ denote the set of all reducing operators on $\underline{NC}$.

Clearly, if $\xi, \eta \in \Delta(\underline{NC})$, then $\xi\eta \in \Delta(\underline{NC})$. Trivially, $\Gamma \subset \Delta(\underline{NC})$ for all $\underline{NC} \in \underline{NGFS}$ closed under $\leqslant$.

Define $\xi \leqslant_{\underline{NC}} \eta$ iff $\xi G \equiv \eta G$ and $\xi G \leqslant \eta G$ for all $G \in \underline{NC}$.

L 3.13 $\leqslant_{\underline{NC}}$ is an order relation on $\Delta(\underline{NC})$, and the following order diagram of $\leqslant_{\underline{NGFS}}$ holds for Γ :

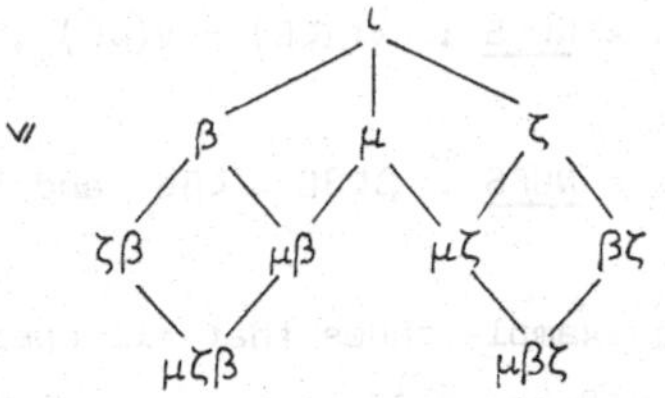

4. Well reducible NGFSs

D 4.1 Well-reducibility

Let $\underline{NC} \subset \underline{NGFS}$ be closed under $\leqslant$. $G \in \underline{NC}$ is called well reducible by $\xi \in \Delta(\underline{NC})$ iff $\xi G \in \underline{NFS}$. $G \in \underline{NC}$ is called well reducible iff there exists a $\xi \in \Delta(\underline{NC})$ such that $\xi G \in \underline{NFS}$. For $\xi, \eta \in \Delta(\underline{NC})$ define $\xi \vdash_{\underline{NC}} \eta$ iff each $G \in \underline{NC}$ is well reducible by η if it is well reducible by ξ.

The following lemmata are easy to prove.

L 4.1 $G \in \underline{NC}$ is well reducible iff there exists a $F \in \underline{NFS}$ such that $F \equiv G$ and $F \leqslant G$.

L 4.2 $\vdash_{\underline{NC}}$ is reflexive and transitive, and $\xi \leqslant_{\underline{NC}} \eta$ implies $\eta \vdash_{\underline{NC}} \xi$.

The following example shows that the well-reducibility depends on the norm chosen.

E 4.1 Consider $G = (V,S,R,n)$ with $V = \{a\}$, $S = \{a^{2m} \mid m \geq 1\}$, $R = \{r_{kl} \mid 1 \leq k \leq l\}$ $r_{kl} = \{(ua^k v, ua^l v) \in (V^*)^2 \mid (u,v) \in (V^*)^2\}$, but $n(r) = 1$ for all $r \in R$.

Then $R(\mu\zeta\beta G) = R$ and therefore G is not well reducible by $\mu\zeta\beta$.

On the contrary, if $n'(r_{kl}) = \max(k,l)$, then $\mu\zeta\beta G' = (V,\{a^2\},\{r_{12}\},n')$ and thus G' is well reducible by $\mu\zeta\beta$.

D 4.2 Let $\widetilde{NGFS} \subset NGFS$ denote the subclass of all NGFSs with the following property : for each integer $K \geq 0$ there exists only a finite number of rules with $n(r) \leq K$.

With this definition the main theorem may be formulated.

T 4.1 If $G \in NC \cap \widetilde{NGFS}$ is well reducible then it is well reducible by $\mu\zeta\beta$.

Proof : 1. If $G = (V,S,R,n) \in NC \cap \widetilde{NGFS}$ is well reducible, then there exists $F' = (V',S',R',n') \in NFS$ such that $F' \equiv G$ and $F' \leq G$. Since V' is finite and $L(F') = L(G) \subset V'^{*}$, it follows that $V(\mu G) \subset V'$ is finite too.

2. If $G' = (V',S,R/V',n")$ with n" defined by n as in D 2.4, then $S(\beta G') = S(\beta G)$. This is obvious by D 3.3 and L 3.1 . Furthermore, $L(G') = L(G)$.

3. If $z \in S$, $|z| > \|S'\|$, then $z \in L(G') = L(G) = L(F')$ and there exists a finite $A \subset S'$ such that $A \overset{*}{\Rightarrow} z\ (R')$. Therefore $\|A\| \leq \|S'\| < |z|$, $A \subset S$, and $A \overset{*}{\Rightarrow} z\ (R/V')$ because of $S' \subset S$ and $R' \subset R/V'$. Thus $z \notin S(\beta G') = S(\beta G)$. Hence $z \in S(\beta G)$ implies $|z| \leq \|S'\|$, and therefore $S(\beta G)$ is finite because of V' being finite.

4. Since R' is finite there exists an integer $N \geq 0$ such that $n(S',z,R') \leq N$ for all $z \in L(F')$. Define $P = 0$ if $S' = \emptyset$ and $P = \max_{t \in S'} n(S(\ G),t,R)$ if $S' \neq \emptyset$.

Since S' is finite, P is well defined. Define $Q = \max(N,P)$.

5. For each $z \in L(G) = L(F')$ there exists a finite $A \subset S'$ such that $A \overset{*}{\Rightarrow} z\ (R')$ and $n(A,z,R') \leq N$. By L 2.3 $A \overset{*}{\Rightarrow} z\ (R)$ and $n(A,z,R/V') \leq n(A,z,R') \leq N$.

Since $A \subset S' \subset S \subset L(G)$, by L 3.3 for any $t \in A$ there exists a finite $D_t \subset S(\beta G)$ such that $D_t \overset{*}{\Rightarrow} t\ (R)$ with $n(D_t,t,R) = n(S(\beta G),t,R) \leq P$.

Define $D = \bigcup_{t \in A} D_t$. Then $D \overset{*}{\Rightarrow} t\ (R)$ and $n(D,t,R) \leq P$ for all $t \in A$.

Therefore, by L 2.2 $D \overset{*}{\Rightarrow} z\ (R)$ and $n(D,z,R) \leq \max(\max_{t \in A} n(D,t,R), n(A,z,R)) \leq Q$.

Since $D \subset S(\beta G)$ it follows that $n(S(\beta G),z,R) \leq n(D,z,R) \leq Q$.

6. If $r \in R(\zeta\beta G)$ then there exists a $z \in L(\beta G) = L(G)$ such that $n(r) \leq n(S(\beta G),z,R) \leq Q$. Therefore $R(\zeta\beta G)$ is finite because of $G \subset \widetilde{NGFS}$. Thus, $R(\zeta\beta G)/V(\mu G)$ is finite too. Hence $\mu\zeta\beta G = (V(\mu G),S(\beta G),R(\zeta\beta G)/V(\mu G),n")\ \in NFS$ where n" is defined by n as in D 2.4 .

By E 4.1 it has been shown that T 4.1 does not hold if $\widetilde{NGFS}$ is replaced by NGFS . The following lemmata are easy consequences.

L 4.3 $G \in \widetilde{NGFS}$ is well reducible iff it is well reducible by $\mu\zeta\beta$.

L 4.4 If $G = (V,S,R,n) \in \widetilde{NGFS}$ with V finite is well reducible, then it is well reducible by $\zeta\beta$.

E 4.2 Consider $G = (V,S,R,n) \in$ NGFS with $V = \{c\}$, $S \subset \{c\}^+$, $R = \{r_{xy} \mid (x,y) \in (\{c\}^+)^2, |x|,|y| \leq 3\}$, $r_{xy} = \{(uxv,uyv) \in (V^*)^2 \mid (u,v) \in (V^*)^2\}$, and $n(r_{xy}) = \max(|x|,|y|)$. Then $L(G) = \{c\}^+$, $\beta G = (V,V,R,n)$, $\zeta G = (V,S,\emptyset,n)$, $\beta\zeta G = (V,S,\emptyset,n)$, $\zeta\beta G = (V,V,\{r_{c,c}, r_{c,cc}, r_{cc,c}, r_{cc,cc}\},n)$.
Therefore $\beta \nvdash_{NGFS} \beta\zeta$ and $\zeta\beta \nvdash_{NGFS} \beta\zeta$.

L 4.5 $\xi \vdash_{NC} \mu\zeta\beta$ for all $\xi \in \Gamma$ and all NC closed under $\leq$. The following order diagram of $\vdash_{NC}$ holds on NC $\subset$ NGFS :

T

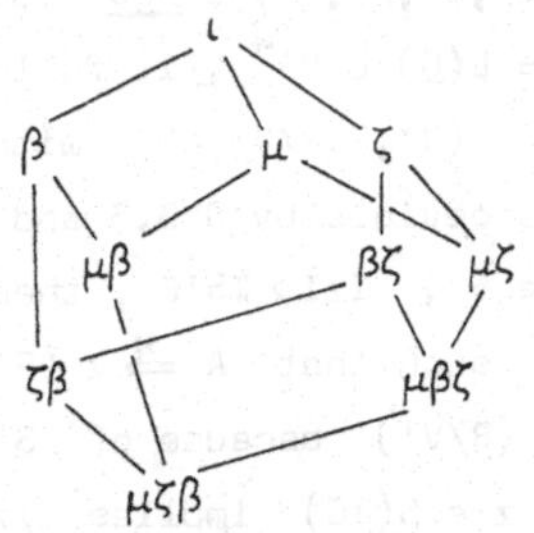

L 4.6 If $\xi \in \Gamma$ and $\mu\zeta\beta \vdash_{NC} \xi$ on NC $\subset$ NGFS, then $\xi = \mu\zeta\beta$.

L 4.7 If $\xi \vdash_{NC} \mu\zeta\beta$ then $\mu\zeta\beta \leq_{NC} \xi$ does not hold for all $\xi \in \Delta$(NC) on NC $\cap$ NFS. This may be shown by E 3.1 where $\mu\beta\zeta \vdash_{NFS} \mu\zeta\beta$, but $\mu\zeta\beta \nleq \mu\beta\zeta$.

5. Formalizable languages

D 5.1 For NC $\subset$ NGFS define $\underline{R}$(NC) $= \{ r \mid$ there exists a $G = (V,S,R,n) \in$ NC with reF
If $\underline{R} \subset \underline{R}$(NGFS) define NC($\underline{R}$) $= \{ G \in$ NGFS $\mid G = (V,S,R,n)$ and $R \subset \underline{R} \}$.

D 5.2 Let $L \subset V^*$ be a language. Then define
$>_{\underline{R}}(L) = \{ r \in \underline{R} \mid (x_1,\ldots,x_{k(r)-1}) \in L^{k(r)-1}$ and $(x_1,\ldots,x_{k(r)-1},x) \in r$ imply $x \in L$.
Clearly, $(V,L,>_{\underline{R}}(L),n) \in$ NC($\underline{R}$) for all n.

L 5.1 If $L \subset V^*$ is a language, n an arbitrary norm, and $R \subset >_{\underline{R}}(L)$, then $L((V,L,R,n)) = L((V,L,>_{\underline{R}}(L),n)) = L$.

L 5.2 If $G = (V,S,R,n) \in$ NGFS with $R \subset \underline{R}$ generates $L \subset V^*$, then $S \subset L$ and $R \subset >_{\underline{R}}(L)$.

These two lemmata are trivial consequences.

D 5.3 Formalizability

A language $L \subset V^*$ is called formalizable by $\underline{R}$ if there exists a $F = (V',S,R,n) \in \underline{NFS}$ with $R \subset \underline{R}$ and $L(F) = L$.
With this definition the following theorem may be stated.

T 5.1 Let $\underline{NC}(\underline{R})$ be closed under $\leqslant$. A language $L \subset V^*$ is formalizable by $\underline{R}$ iff there exists a norm with $G = (V,L,>_{\underline{R}}(L),n) \in \widetilde{\underline{NGFS}}$ and $\mu\zeta\beta G \in \underline{NFS}$.
This is a consequence from T 4.1.

The following examples show some classes of rules of NGFSs.

E 5.1 General Post Canonical System (GPCS)
Let k, p, q be functions from $\underline{N}$ into $\underline{N}$, e a function from $\underline{N}^2 \times \underline{N}^2$ into $\{0,1\}$, and $s,t \in \underline{N}$. Then write $H = H(s,k,t) = \{a_{ij},b_l\} \subset V^*$ with $1 \leq i \leq s$, $0 \leq j \leq k(i)$, $0 \leq l \leq t$. Define $r_H = \{(a_{10}x_{11}a_{11}\ldots x_{1k(1)}a_{1k(1)},\ldots,a_{s0}x_{s1}a_{s1}\ldots x_{sk(s)}a_{sk(s)},$
$b_0x'_1b_1\ldots x'_tb_t) \in (V^*)^{s+1} \mid \{x_{11},\ldots,x_{sk(s)},x'_1,\ldots,x'_t\} \subset V^*$ with $x_{ij} = x_{i'j'}$ iff $e((i,j),(i',j')) = 1$ and $x'_m = x_{p(m)q(m)} \in \{x_{ij}\}\}$.
Define $n(r_H) = \max |a_{ij}|,|b_j|$.

E 5.2 OL-System
Let $H = \{(x_i,a_i) \mid 1 \leq i \leq l\}$ with fixed $x_i \in V$, $a_i \in V^*$, and $\bigcup_{1 \leq i \leq l} \{x_i\} = V$.
If $\underline{P}(H)$ denotes the power set of H, then for each $D \in \underline{P}(H)$ define a rule $r_D = \{(y,z) \in (V^*)^2 \mid y = y_1\ldots y_m,\ z = z_1\ldots z_m$ with $y_i \in V$, $z_i \in V^*$, and $(y_i,z_i) \in D$, $\bigcup_{1 \leq i \leq m} \{(y_i,z_i)\} = D$. Define $n(r_D) = \max_{a_i \in D} (1,|a_i|)$.

6. References

|1| Miroslav Novotný, On some operators reducing generalized grammars. IC 26, pp. 225-235, 1974.

|2| Miroslav Novotný, Operators reducing generalized OL-systems. LNCS 14, pp. 481-494, 1974.

|3| Manfred Kudlek, Miroslav Novotný, On a reducing operator for combinatorial systems. Submitted for publication.

|4| Manfred Kudlek, Reducing Operators for General Formal Systems. Institut für Informatik, Universität Hamburg, Bericht 19, 1975.

INVARIANT PROPERTIES OF INFORMATIONAL BULKS

L.A. Levin, V.V.V'jugin

U.S.S.R.

1. Introduction

Many properties of informational bulks are not preserved under recodings (for example, from the binary system to a ternary one) and thus they are not properties of the informational bulk itself, but, rather, they characterize the text which is the bearer of this information. Different texts may contain approximately the same information.

Contrary to such properties, our report dwells on invariant properties of informational bulks, i. e. the properties preserved under recodings of the information bearers. For simplicity of mathematical formulation, infinite sequences of natural numbers will be considered as the information bearers (though only finite ones are of practical importance). The recodings are carried out by computable operators: sequences α and β are equivalent, if $\alpha = F(\beta)$ and $\beta = G(\alpha)$ for some computable operators F and G. Such α and β contain approximately the same information up to the finite description of F and G.

Using methods of the theory of algorithms it is possible to prove the existence of sequences which possess quite exotic properties. For example (see [1], § 13.5), there exist sequences containing "indivisible" information: such α is incomputable and for any incomputable β, if $\beta = F(\alpha)$ for some computable operator F, then β is equivalent to α, i. e. the information in α is infinite and equivalent - up to the (finite) description of the recoding algorithm - to any infinite part of it. It is dubious whether sequences with such properties may exist in reality. And in fact, as it was pointed out in [1], in any combination of computable and random processes (in the sense specified below) the probability of obtaining "indivisible" sequences equals 0. The specificness of the present paper is that we eliminate such properties by means of the notion of an "ignorable" set. A set of sequences A is unattainable, if for any computable operator F and any $\omega \notin A$ it holds $F(\omega) \notin A$. A set of sequences B is called ignorable, if it is contained in an unattainable set of the Lebesgue measure 0. Any other computable measure of such a set B equals 0, so the probability of obtaining a sequence from B in any random process with "simple" distribution of probability equals 0. No $\omega\varepsilon B$ can be obtained as $\varepsilon=F(\omega')$, where $\omega'\notin B$. So we may claim that no sequence of an ignorable set can be obtained by a physical process, reducible to a combination of algorithmic and random processes. In part 3 of this paper invariant properties are considered "up to the ignorable ones", a Boolean algebra L being introduced for this purpose.

2. Some notions of algorithmic theory of information

Let Ω be a set of all infinite sequences of natural numbers. Concatenating finite sequences α and β, the sequence $\alpha\beta$ can be constructed; $\alpha\subset\beta$, if $\beta=\alpha\delta$ for some δ. ω_i is the i-th member of ω, $(\omega)_i=\omega_1\omega_2\ldots\omega_i$. $l(\omega)$ is the length of ω. A semimeasure is a function P, defined on the set of all finite sequences, acquiring nonnegative real values and satisfying the condition $P(\Lambda)=1$, $\sum_k P(xk)\leq P(x)$ for all x. A semimeasure P is called a measure, if $\sum_k P(xk)=P(x)$. If P is a measure, then we can define $P\{\omega\varepsilon\Omega|x\subset\omega\}=P(x)$. Now P may be extended to all measurable subsets of Ω. The Lebesgue measure is a measure L, such that $L(x)=2^{-l(x)}$, if x contains only zeros and ones, and $L(x)=0$ in the opposite case. Semimeasure P is called recursively enumerable (further r.e.) if $\{(\tau,x)|\ \tau<P(x),\ \tau$ is a rational number$\}$ is a r.e. set. If P is a r.e. measure, then $\{(\tau,x)|\ \tau>P(x)\}$ is also a r.e. set, so P(x) can be calculated with any degree of accuracy (r.e. measure is also called computable).

Proposition. There exists a r.e. semimeasure M such that for any r.e. semimeasure P a constant C can be found, such that $C.M(x)\geqslant P(x)$ for all x (abbreviated $M(x)\succcurlyeq P(x)$).

Semimeasure M is called universal. With every semimeasure P a maximal measure $\overline{P}$ not exceeding P and satisfying the condition

$$\overline{P}(x)=\inf_n \sum_{x\subset y,\ l(y)=n} P(y)$$

is naturally associated. $\overline{M}$ is called a universal measure. Note that $\overline{M}$ is not a r.e. measure. A computable operator is a r.e. set F consisting of pairs of finite sequences such that if $(x,y)\varepsilon F$, $(x',y')\varepsilon F$ and $x\subset x'$, then $y\subset y'$.

If $(x,y)\varepsilon F$, we write $y=F(x)$. For $\omega\varepsilon\Omega$, $F(\omega)$ is the union of all sequences $y\subset F((\omega)_n)$. The value of F is defined on $\omega\varepsilon\Omega$ if $F(\omega)\varepsilon\Omega$. It can be shown that any r.e. semimeasure may be presented as $P(x)=L\{\omega|x\subset F(\omega)\}$ for some computable operator F. Thus $\overline{P}(x)=L\{\omega|x\subset F(\omega),F(\omega)\varepsilon\Omega\}$.

According to the definition, $A\subseteq\Omega$ is ignorable if and only if $L(F^{-1}(A))=0$ for any computable operator F, i. e. $\overline{P}(A)=0$ for any r.e. semimeasure P. It follows from the above proposition that this is equivalent to the condition $\overline{M}(A)=0$.

If $l(x)=l(y)$, the pair of sequences (x,y) is encoded by the sequence, which we denote as (x,y), such that $(x,y)_i=x_i+\frac{1}{2}(x_i+y_i)\ (x_i+y_i+1)$. On the basis of that we may identify any semimeasure on Ω with the corresponding semimeasure on the set of all pairs of infinite sequences. Let $d(\omega/Q)=\log_2\frac{dM}{dQ}(\omega)$ be deficiency of randomness of ω with respect to Q, where

$$\frac{dP}{dQ}(\omega)=\lim_n\frac{P((\omega)_n)}{Q((\omega)_n)}$$

is the Radon-Nicodim derivative of semimeasure P by a semimeasure Q. $P\otimes Q$ is a product of semimeasures P and Q. Let us define the quantity of information in the sequence α about the sequence β as the deficiency of indenpendence of α and β:
$I(\alpha:\beta)=d((\alpha,\beta)/M\otimes M)$.

The following theorem characterizes the class of all ignorable sets in terms of quantity of information.

<u>Theorem 1.</u> A set $A\subseteq\Omega$ is ignorable if and only if there exists $\alpha\varepsilon\Omega$ such that $I(\omega:\alpha)=\infty$ for any $\omega\varepsilon A$.

The value $|\log_2 M(x)|$ characterizes the full quantity of information in the finite sequence x (the complexity of x). Unfortunately it is incomputable. We shall single out the class of sequences not having this defect. The sequence $\omega\varepsilon\Omega$ is called <u>complete</u>, if $M((\omega)_n)\asymp P((\omega)_n)$ for some r.e. <u>measure</u> P.($\Phi\asymp F$ means $\Phi\preccurlyeq F$ and $F\preccurlyeq\Phi$). Such ω contains all information necessary for the computation of its complexity by means of P. It can be shown that for any r.e. measure P, $M((\omega)_n)\asymp P((\omega)_n)$ if and only if ω is random with respect to the measure P in the sense of Martin Löf *[2]*.

<u>Theorem 2</u>. Any r.e. measure of the set of all complete sequences equals 1 and any everywhere defined computable operator transforms it into itself.

This theorem shows that only complete sequences can be obtained in any combination of random processes with "simple" distribution of probability and everywhere defined algorithmic processes.

3. Algebra L and its natural elements

The set $A \subseteq \Omega$ is invariant, if with each sequence it contains all equivalent sequences. Let K be the class of all invariant subsets Ω measurable by the universal measure $\overline{M}$ (specifically, K contains all invariant Borel subsets of Ω). K is the Boolean algebra with the usual set-theoretic operations. Let us define the equivalence relation on K : $A \approx B$, if $(A \setminus B) \cup (B \setminus A)$ is ignorable. Taking the quotient of K modulo this equivalence relation we obtain a Boolean algebra L. The meaning of these notions can be clarified in the following way. Each invariant property of informational bulks defines the invariant set of sequences. If two such properties define the sets, which differ from each other on an ignorable set, then, according to the introduction of this paper, we can claim that they define the same set of natural informational bulks (i. e. a set that can be obtained in some combinations of algorithmic and random natural processes). Such elements of L correspond to the properties of real informational bulks. Each specific mathematical property of sequences can be defined by the formula of a strictly determined language. The requirement of measurability by measure $\overline{M}$ is much weaker; L may contain elements undeterminable by any mathematical properties. But all elements of L constructed further will be defined by some formulae of the arithmetical language.

The simplest elements of L : 0 is defined to be the class of all ignorable sets, 1 is defined to be the class containing Ω. These are the minimal and the maximal elements of L.

Let us consider the elements formed by complete sequences, and sequences equivalent to them. The information contained in a complete sequence can be encoded with "maximal density". One should be aware of the fact that any information in the densest codification becomes indistinguishable by its properties from random noise and, therefore, the only invariant characteristic of such information is its quantity (finite or infinite). This fact is illustrated by Theorem 3. Each computable sequence is complete. Let C be the set of all computable sequences, $c \in L$ be such that $C \in c$. R is the set of all incomputable complete sequences, and sequences equivalent to them, $\mathfrak{r} \in L$ is such that $R \in \mathfrak{r}$ It is evident that c is an atom of L, i. e. $c \neq 0$ and it cannot be represented as $c=a\cup b$ where $a\cap b=0$, $a\neq 0$, $b\neq 0$.

Theorem 3. τ is an atom of L and, thus, any element of L, formed by complete sequences (and by those equivalent to them), coincides with 0, c, τ or $c\cup\tau$.

In [3] these results are applied to the problems of intuitionism. It is shown below that in a commom case the situation is more complex since not all sequences allow optimal encoding.

4. Elements of L, formed by sequences not equivalent to complete ones

The main result of this part is that the set $\Omega\setminus(C\cup R)$ is not ignorable (see [4] for proof), moreover, sequences of this set form an infinite number of various elements of L. The information contained in any sequence from $\Omega\setminus(C\cup R)$ does not allow optimal encoding. $p=1\setminus(c\cup\tau)$.

Theorem 4. The set of all atoms of L is countable.

For each atom x distinct from c and τ, $x\subseteq p$ i. e. x is formed by sequences from $\Omega\setminus(C\cup R)$.

Sequences of the atom-forming set are not distinguishable by any invariant property. However among the sequences from $\Omega\setminus(C\cup R)$ there are ones possessing infinitely divisible properties. Let $d_0, d_1, \dots d_n, \dots$ be all atoms of L.

Theorem 5. $d=1\setminus\bigcup_{i=0}^{\infty} d_i\neq 0$.

The element d has the property that for any $x\subseteq d$, x is not an atom.

We shall point out in conclusion, that it follows from Theorem 2, that algorithmic processes which are not universally defined are essentia for the obtaining of sequences which are non-equivalent to complete ones.

The main results of Sections 2 and 3 are due to L. Levin, the results of Section 4 are due to V.V. V´jugin.

BIBLIOGRAPHY

1. Rogers, H., Theory of recursive functions and effective computability, McGraw-Hill, New York, 1967.

2. Martin-Löf, P., Definition of random sequences, Information and Control, 9, (1966) N6, 602-619.

3. Levin, L.A., On the principle of conservation of information in intuitionistic mathematics, Dokl. Akad. Nauk SSSR, 227 (1976) N6, 1293-1296.

4. V'jugin, V.V., On Turing invariant sets, Dokl. Akad. Nauk SSSR, 229, (1976) N4, 790-793.

TWO DECIDABILITY RESULTS FOR DETERMINISTIC PUSHDOWN AUTOMATA

Matti Linna

Department of Mathematics, University of Turku,
20500 Turku 50, Finland

Introduction

One of the most important open questions in formal language theory is the equivalence problem for deterministic pushdown automata (dpda). The decidability of this problem for some subclasses of dpda´s is already known (see [3,4,9,10,11,12,13]). Valiant [11] proved the decidability of the equivalence for non-singular dpda´s using a new effective method, so called alternate stacking method. Later on this result was generalized by Taniguchi and Kasami [10] to the case where only one of the given dpda´s is non-singular whereas the other is an arbitrary dpda. Another important question is the inclusion problem. Friedman [1] has shown that even in the class of simple dpda´s (a proper subclass of non-singular dpda´s) the inclusion problem is undecidable.

In this paper, we consider so called stack uniform dpda´s which form a subclass of real-time dpda´s. These machines have no λ-rules and for each input letter a, every a-rule has the same effect on the length of the pushdown stack, i.e., if $(s_1,A) \overset{a}{\rightarrow} (s_2,w)$ and $(s_1',A') \overset{a}{\rightarrow} (s_2',w')$ are two a-rules, then the lengths of w and w' are equal. This paper contains two results: (1) The inclusion problem for stack uniform dpda´s with empty store acceptance is decidable, and (2) the equivalence problem for stack uniform dpda´s is decidable. The proofs are based on Valiant´s alternate stacking method. As a corollary of the first result we get that the inclusion problem for left Szilard languages (or left derivation languages for context-free grammars [7,8]) is decidable. We mention here that the inclusion problem for Szilard languages (the fitting problem [5]) is also decidable, and moreover, it is decidable whether a given left Szilard language is in the family of Szilard languages (the left fitting problem [6]).

As for a context-free grammar, one can define a derivation language for a pushdown automaton by labelling each rule by a symbol such that different rules are labelled by different symbols. A sequence of labels is accepted iff the corresponding derivation leads to an accepting mode. Since there is exactly one rule corresponding to each label, it immediately follows that the derivation languages associated with pushdown automata are (properly) contained in the family of stack uniform languages. Hence, their equivalence problem is decidable by the second result.

1. Preliminaries

For deterministic pushdown automata we use the same notation as [10] and [11]. Let $M = (\Sigma,\Gamma,Q,F,\Delta,c_s)$ be a deterministic pushdown automaton, where Σ, Γ and Q are finite sets of input symbols, stack symbols and states, respectively, $F \subseteq Q\times(\{\Omega\}\cup\Gamma)$ is the set of accepting modes (here Ω is a special empty stack symbol), Δ is a finite set of transition rules and $c_s = (s_0,Z_0) \in Q \times \Gamma$ is the initial configuration. In general, a configuration $c = (s,w)$ is an element of $Q \times (\{\Omega\} \cup \Gamma^+)$ and describes the state and stack content of the machine at some instant, and the mode mode(c) of a configuration c is an element of $Q \times (\{\Omega\} \cup \Gamma)$ and describes the state and top stack symbol of c. The dpda M makes the move $(s,wA) \overset{a}{\to} (s',ww')$, for $a \in \Sigma \cup \{\lambda\}$, iff Δ contains the rule $(s,A) \overset{a}{\to} (s',w')$. A derivation $c \overset{\alpha}{\to} c'$ is a sequence of successive moves where α is the concatenation of the input symbols read by these moves. The length of a word w is denoted by $|w|$, and the height of a configuration c, i.e. the length of its stack is denoted by $|c|$. The language L(c) accepted from a configuration c is defined by

$$L(c) = \{\alpha \in \Sigma^* \mid c \overset{\alpha}{\to} c',\ \text{mode}(c') \in F\},$$

and $L(M) = L(c_s)$ is the language accepted by M. If X is a subclass of dpda's, we will abbreviate $\{L(M) \mid M \in X\}$ to $L(X)$. An input string $\alpha \in \Sigma^*$ is said to be live for a dpda M iff it is a proper prefix of some accepted string, and a configuration c is said to be live iff $L(c) \neq \phi$. The derivation $c \overset{\alpha}{\to} c'$ is written as $c\uparrow(\alpha)c'$ if $|c| \leq |c'|$ and every intermediate configuration in the derivation has height greater than or equal to $|c|$. Now we define the class U of stack uniform dpda's.

Definition. A dpda M is stack uniform iff (i) it has no λ-rules, and (ii) for any $s_1,s_2,s_1',s_2' \in Q$, $A,A' \in \Gamma$, $a \in \Sigma$ and $w,w' \in \Gamma^*$, if $(s_1,A) \overset{a}{\to} (s_2,w)$ and $(s_1',A') \overset{a}{\to} (s_2',w')$ are in Δ, then it holds that $|w| = |w'|$.

Moreover, we denote by U_0 the class of stack uniform dpda's with empty store acceptance. The main property of the stack uniform dpda's is characterized by the following trivial lemma.

Lemma 1. Let $M \in U$. Then for any $\alpha \in \Sigma^*$ and configurations c_1, c_2, c_1', c_2', if $c_1 \overset{\alpha}{\to} c_2$ and $c_1' \overset{\alpha}{\to} c_2'$, then it holds that $|c_1| - |c_2| = |c_1'| - |c_2'|$.

The inclusion relations between stack uniform languages and some other known language families are illustrated by the following diagram.

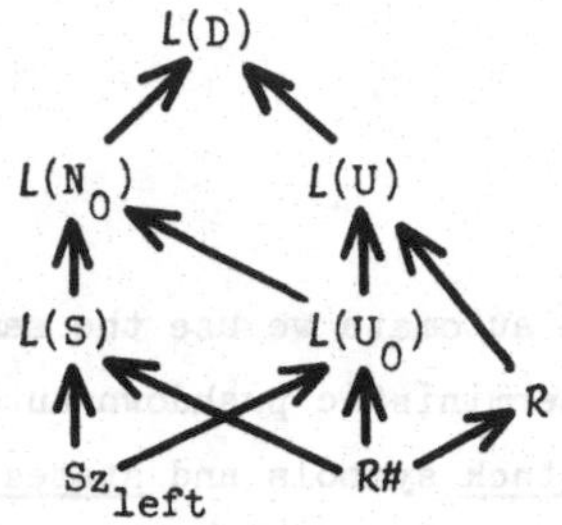

An arrow means a proper inclusion and two families are incomparable unless they are connected by a directed path. Here R, $R\#$, Sz_{left}, $L(S)$, $L(N_0)$ and $L(D)$ are the families of regular languages, regular languages with endmakers, left Szilard languages, simple languages ([4]), non-singular languages ([11]) and deterministic context-free languages, respectively. All of the inclusion relations follow easily from the definitions except the relation $L(U_0) \nsubseteq L(S)$. This holds true, because the language $L_n = \{a^m b^k c^m d^{k-1} e \mid m \geqq 1, 1 \leqq k \leqq n\}$, $n \geqq 2$, is in $L(U_0)$ but not in $L(S)$. That L_n is not in $L(S)$ can be proved as Lemma 4.1 in [2]. We further note that the families $L(N_0)$ and $L(U)\#$ ($L(U)$ with endmakers) are incomparable, since for example the language $\{a^n b^m \mid m \leqq n\}\#$ is in $L(U)\#$ but not in $L(N_0)$ as is easily verified.

2. The inclusion problem

For a dpda $M \in U$, let d_M be the cardinality of the set $Q \times \Gamma$ and

$$h_M = \max\{|w| \mid M \text{ has a rule } (s,A) \overset{a}{\to} (s',w) \text{ for some } s,s' \in Q,\ A \in \Gamma \text{ and } a \in \Sigma\} - 1.$$

Definition. A derivation of the form

(1) $$c_1 \overset{a_1}{\to} c_2 \overset{a_2}{\to} \cdots \overset{a_{n-1}}{\to} c_n \quad (a_i \in \Sigma)$$

is of type 1 iff there exist integers i and j such that $1 \leqq i < j \leqq n$,

$c_i\uparrow(a_i\ldots a_{j-1})c_j$, $|c_i| = |c_j|$ and $\mathrm{mode}(c_i) = \mathrm{mode}(c_j)$. A derivation of the form (1) is of type 2 iff there exist integers i,j,h,k such that $1 \leq i < j < h < k \leq n$,

$$c_i\uparrow(a_i\ldots a_{j-1})c_j\uparrow(a_j\ldots a_{h-1})c_h \overset{a_h\ldots a_{k-1}}{\rightarrow} c_k,$$

$|c_i| = |c_k| < |c_j| = |c_h|$, $c_i\uparrow(a_i\ldots a_{k-1})c_k$, $\mathrm{mode}(c_i) = \mathrm{mode}(c_j)$ and $\mathrm{mode}(c_h) = \mathrm{mode}(c_k)$.

The following lemma is intuitively obvious.

Lemma 2. Let D be a derivation of the form (1) and m_1,m_2 non-negative integers such that $|c_n| \leq |c_1| + m_1$ and $|c_i| \geq |c_1| - m_2$ for $i = 1,\ldots,n$. Then there exists an integer $l(m_1,m_2)$ such that if D is neither of type 1 nor 2, then $n \leq l(m_1,m_2)$.

It can be shown that for example the constant $l(m_1,m_2) = (m_1+2m_2+1)(d_M+1)^{h_M d_M^2}$ satisfies the requirement of Lemma 2.

In the following we shall assume that $M,\bar{M} \in U_0$ and that $L(M) \subseteq L(\bar{M})$. Further, we shall denote by $\min(L(c))$ the length of the shortest word in L(c).

Lemma 3. For any live $\alpha_1\alpha_2$ for M, if $c_s \overset{\alpha_1}{\rightarrow} c_1\uparrow(\alpha_2)c_2$ in M, $|c_1| = |c_2|$, $\mathrm{mode}(c_1) = \mathrm{mode}(c_2)$ and $\bar{c}_s \overset{\alpha_1}{\rightarrow} \bar{c}_1 \overset{\alpha_2}{\rightarrow} \bar{c}_2$ in $\bar{M}$, then $|\bar{c}_1| = |\bar{c}_2|$.

Proof. Assume first that $|\bar{c}_1| > |\bar{c}_2|$ and $|\bar{c}_1| = m$. Consider the derivation $c_s \overset{\alpha_1}{\rightarrow} c_1(\alpha_2^{m+1})c_2$. Then $\alpha_1\alpha_2^{m+1}$ is live for M but, by Lemma 1, it is not live for $\bar{M}$, a contradiction. Assume in the second place that $|\bar{c}_1| < |\bar{c}_2|$. Let n be an integer such that $n > \min(L(c_2))$. Then

$$c_s \overset{\alpha_1}{\rightarrow} c_1\uparrow(\alpha_2^n)c_2 \text{ and } \bar{c}_s \overset{\alpha_1\alpha_2^n}{\rightarrow} \bar{c}$$

for some $\bar{c}$ (if defined) with $|\bar{c}| > n$. So L(M) contains a word which is not in $L(\bar{M})$, a contradiction.

The proof of the following lemma is similar to that of lemma 3.

Lemma 4. For any live $\alpha_1\alpha_2\alpha_3\alpha_4$ for M, if $c_s \overset{\alpha_1}{\rightarrow} c_1\uparrow(\alpha_2)c_2\uparrow(\alpha_3)c_3 \overset{\alpha_4}{\rightarrow} c_4$, $|c_1| = |c_4| < |c_2| = |c_3|$, $\mathrm{mode}(c_1) = \mathrm{mode}(c_2)$, $\mathrm{mode}(c_3) = \mathrm{mode}(c_4)$, $c_1\uparrow(\alpha_2\alpha_3\alpha_4)c_4$ and $\bar{c}_s \overset{\alpha_1}{\rightarrow} \bar{c}_1 \overset{\alpha_2}{\rightarrow} \bar{c}_2 \overset{\alpha_3}{\rightarrow} \bar{c}_3 \overset{\alpha_4}{\rightarrow} \bar{c}_4$ in $\bar{M}$, then it holds that

(i) $|\bar{c}_2| - |\bar{c}_1| = |\bar{c}_3| - |\bar{c}_4|$, and

(ii) $|\bar{c}_2| \geq |\bar{c}_1|$.

Now we introduce the main lemmas.

Lemma 5. For $M,\bar{M} \in U_0$, assume that $L(M) \subseteq L(\bar{M})$. Then for any non-negative integers m_1,m_2 and any live $\alpha_1\alpha_2$ for M, if $c_s \overset{\alpha_1}{\rightarrow} c_1 \overset{\alpha_2}{\rightarrow} c_2$ in M, $|c_2| \leq |c_1| + m_1$, any intermediate configuration of $c_1 \overset{\alpha_2}{\Rightarrow} c_2$ has height greater than or equal to $|c_1| - m_2$ and $\bar{c}_s \overset{\alpha_1}{\rightarrow} \bar{c}_1 \overset{\alpha_2}{\Rightarrow} \bar{c}_2$ in $\bar{M}$, then it holds that $|\bar{c}_2| < |\bar{c}_1| + h_{\bar{M}}\, l(m_1,m_2)$.

<u>Proof</u>. By Lemmas 2, 3 and 4(i) we may assume that $|\alpha_2| < l(m_1,m_2)$. Since $\bar{M}$ is a real-time dpda, we have $|\bar{c}_2| < |\bar{c}_1| + h_{\bar{M}} \cdot l(m_1,m_2)$.

<u>Lemma 6</u>. For $M,\bar{M} \in U_0$, assume that $L(M) \subseteq L(\bar{M})$. Then for any non-negative integer m and any live $\alpha_1\alpha_2$ for M, if $c_s \overset{\alpha_1}{\rightarrow} c_1 \overset{\alpha_2}{\Rightarrow} c_2$ in M, any configuration in the derivation $c_1 \overset{\alpha_2}{\Rightarrow} c_2$ has height greater than or equal to $|c_1| - m$ and $\bar{c}_s \overset{\alpha_1}{\rightarrow} \bar{c}_1 \overset{\alpha_2}{\Rightarrow} \bar{c}_2$ in $\bar{M}$, then it holds that $|\bar{c}_2| > |\bar{c}_1| - [l(0,m) + l(h_M d_M^2-1,0)]$.

<u>Proof</u>. By Lemmas 2, 3 and 4 we may assume that $|\alpha_2| < l(0,m) + l(h_M d_M^2-1,0)$ (the details of the proof of this fact are omitted here), and so the claim follows by the real-time property of $\bar{M}$.

We shall use Lemmas 5 and 6 only in the cases, where $m_1 = m_2 = m = h_M-1$. Define $l_1 = h_{\bar{M}} \cdot l(h_M-1,h_M-1)$, $l_2 = l(0,h_M-1) + l(h_M d_M^2-1,0)$ and $l = l_1 + l_2$. The following construction of a single stack machine M' is closely related to that in [10].

The machine M' has the stack alphabet $\Gamma \cup \bar{\Gamma}$ and state set $Q \times \bar{Q}$. A typical configuration of M' is described by

$$c_1' = ([s_1,\bar{s}_1], w_0\bar{w}_0 w_1\bar{w}_1 \ldots w_n\bar{w}_n),$$

where the configurations of M and $\bar{M}$ at that time are $c_1 = (s_1, w_0w_1\ldots w_n)$ and $\bar{c}_1 = (\bar{s}_1, \bar{w}_0\bar{w}_1\ldots\bar{w}_n)$, respectively. The initial configuration of M' is $([s_0,\bar{s}_0], Z_0\bar{Z}_0)$. The segmentation of the stack is determined as follows. Let c_1' be as above and $w_n = \xi A$, $\xi \in \Gamma^*$, $A \in \Gamma$, $\bar{w}_n = \bar{\xi}\bar{A}$, $\bar{\xi} \in \bar{\Gamma}^*$, $\bar{A} \in \bar{\Gamma}$. If for some $a \in \Sigma$, $(s_1,A) \overset{a}{\rightarrow} (s_2,\eta)$ and $(\bar{s}_1,\bar{A}) \overset{a}{\rightarrow} (\bar{s}_2, \bar{\eta})$ are rules of M and $\bar{M}$, respectively, then the next configuration of M' is defined as follows:

1) The case $|\eta| > 1$, i.e. $\eta = B\eta'$ for some $B \in \Gamma$ and $\eta' \in \Gamma^+$.
   - 1a) If $|\bar{\xi}\bar{\eta}| \leqq l_2$, then $w_n\bar{w}_n$ is replaced by $\xi\eta\bar{\xi}\bar{\eta}$.
   - 1b) If $|\bar{\xi}\bar{\eta}| > l_2$, i.e. $\bar{\xi}\bar{\eta} = \bar{\xi}_1\bar{\xi}_2$ with $|\bar{\xi}_2| = l_2$, then $w_n\bar{w}_n$ is replaced by $\xi B\bar{\xi}_1\eta'\bar{\xi}_2$.

2) The case $|\eta| = 1$, i.e. $\eta = B$ for some $B \in \Gamma$. Then $w_n\bar{w}_n$ is replaced by $\xi\eta\bar{\xi}\bar{\eta}$.

3) The case $\eta = \lambda$.
   - 3a) If $|\xi| \geqq 1$, then $w_n\bar{w}_n$ is replaced by $\xi\bar{\xi}\bar{\eta}$.
   - 3b) If $\xi = \lambda$, then $\bar{w}_{n-1}w_n\bar{w}_n$ is replaced by $\bar{w}_{n-1}\bar{\xi}\bar{\eta}$.

By the following lemma, the proof of which is based on Lemmas 5 and 6, the simulating machine M' can be converted into a pushdown automaton.

<u>Lemma 7</u>. For each live α for M, if $c_s' \overset{\alpha}{\rightarrow} c' = ([s,\bar{s}], w_0\bar{w}_0 \ldots w_n\bar{w}_n)$ in M', then $1 \leqq |\bar{w}_n| \leqq l$.

<u>Theorem 1</u>. The inclusion problem for the family $\mathcal{L}(U_0)$ is decidable.

<u>Proof</u>. The proof is essentially the same as that of [11, Theorem 3.3] and [10, Theorem 2] except that now we need no partial decision procedure as in the case of non-singular dpda's, where the non-singular constant is not known. We construct a non-deterministic pda M" with the property that $L(M") = \phi$ iff $L(M) \subseteq L(\bar{M})$. The pda M" simulates the machine M' by encoding the top segment $\bar{w}_n$ in its finite state control. As long as $\bar{w}_n$ never gets λ or larger than l M" simulates M and $\bar{M}$, and M" accepts the input iff M accepts but $\bar{M}$ not. In the case where a transition is defined for M but not for $\bar{M}$, M" continues the simulation of M and accepts if it does. When the length of $\bar{w}_n$ is 0 or exceeds the bound l, M" continues the simulation of M and accepts if it does. It is easy to verify that $L(M") = \phi$ iff $L(M) \subseteq L(\bar{M})$.

<u>Corollary</u>. The inclusion problem for left Szilard languages is decidable.

3. <u>The equivalence problem</u>

Let $l(m_1,m_2)$ be the constant defined for M as in the preceding section and let $\bar{l}(m_1,m_2)$ be the corresponding constant for $\bar{M}$. Define $l_3 = l(2h_M d_M^2-1,0)$, $\bar{l}_3 = \bar{l}(2h_{\bar{M}} d_{\bar{M}}^2-1,0)$ and $l' = l_3\bar{l}_3 + \max(h_M,h_{\bar{M}},2)$.

Assume that M, $\bar{M} \in U$ and $L(M) = L(\bar{M})$. The following three lemmas are analogous to Lemmas 3,4 and 6 in the preceding section. Moreover, they are symmetric with respect to M and $\bar{M}$.

<u>Lemma 3'</u>. (i) For any live $\alpha_1\alpha_2$, if $c_s \overset{\alpha_1}{\rightarrow} c_1\uparrow(\alpha_2)c_2$ in M, $|c_1| = |c_2|$, mode(c_1) = mode(c_2) and $\bar{c}_s \overset{\alpha_1}{\rightarrow} \bar{c}_1 \overset{\alpha_2}{\rightarrow} \bar{c}_2$ in $\bar{M}$, then $|\bar{c}_1| \leq |\bar{c}_2|$.

(ii) For any word $\alpha_1\alpha_2\alpha_3 \in L(M)$, if $c_s \overset{\alpha_1}{\rightarrow} c_1\uparrow(\alpha_2)c_2\uparrow(\alpha_3)c_3$ in M, mode(c_1) = mode(c_2) and $\bar{c}_s \overset{\alpha_1}{\rightarrow} \bar{c}_1 \overset{\alpha_2}{\rightarrow} \bar{c}_2 \overset{\alpha_3}{\rightarrow} \bar{c}_3$ in $\bar{M}$, then $|\bar{c}_1| \leq |\bar{c}_2|$.

<u>Lemma 4'</u>. For any live $\alpha_1\alpha_2\alpha_3\alpha_4$, if $c_s \overset{\alpha_1}{\rightarrow} c_1\uparrow(\alpha_2)c_2\uparrow(\alpha_3)c_3 \overset{\alpha_4}{\rightarrow} c_4$ in M, $|c_1| = |c_4| < |c_2| = |c_3|$, mode$(c_1)$ = mode(c_2), mode(c_3) = mode(c_4), $c_1\uparrow(\alpha_2\alpha_3\alpha_4)c_4$ and $\bar{c}_s \overset{\alpha_1}{\rightarrow} \bar{c}_1 \overset{\alpha_2}{\rightarrow} \bar{c}_2 \overset{\alpha_3}{\rightarrow} \bar{c}_3 \overset{\alpha_4}{\rightarrow} \bar{c}_4$ in $\bar{M}$, then

(i) $|\bar{c}_2| - |\bar{c}_1| \geq |\bar{c}_3| - |\bar{c}_4|$ and

(ii) $|\bar{c}_2| \geq |\bar{c}_1|$.

<u>Lemma 6'</u>. For any live $\alpha_1\alpha_2$, if $c_s \overset{\alpha_1}{\rightarrow} c_1\uparrow(\alpha_2)c_2$ in M and $\bar{c}_s \overset{\alpha_1}{\rightarrow} \bar{c}_1 \overset{\alpha_2}{\rightarrow} \bar{c}_2$ in $\bar{M}$, then $|\bar{c}_2| > |\bar{c}_1| - l_3$.

The following lemma together with Lemma 6' assures that the alternate stacking succeeds. The proof is based on Lemmas 3' and 4'.

Lemma 8. For any live $\alpha_1\alpha_2$, if $c_s \overset{\alpha_1}{\to} c_1 \uparrow(\alpha_2)c_2$ in M, $|c_2| \geq |c_1| + l_3\bar{l}_3$ and $\bar{c}_s \overset{\alpha_1}{\to} \bar{c}_1 \overset{\alpha_2}{\to} \bar{c}_2$ in $\bar{M}$, then either
(i) $|\bar{c}_2| > |\bar{c}_1|$ or
(ii) for each live $\alpha_1\alpha_2\alpha_3$, if $c_2 \overset{\alpha_3}{\to} c_3$, then $|c_3| > |c_2| - l_3\bar{l}_3$.

Now we shall construct a single stack machine M' simulating the dpda's M and $\bar{M}$. The set of stack symbols of M' is $\Gamma_1 = \Gamma \cup \Gamma^\# \cup \bar{\Gamma} \cup \bar{\Gamma}^\#$, where $\Gamma^\# = \{A^\# \mid A \in \Gamma\}$ and $\bar{\Gamma}^\# = \{\bar{A}^\# \mid \bar{A} \in \bar{\Gamma}\}$. The initial configuration is $c'_s = ([s_0,\bar{s}_0],Z_0\bar{Z}_0)$. A typical configuration of M' is of the form

$$c'_1 = ([s_1,\bar{s}_1],w_1),$$

where $w_1 \in \Gamma_1^+$. Define $v = w_1$ if $|w_1| \leq l'$ and otherwise v is the suffix of w_1 of length l'. The transition $c'_1 \overset{a}{\to} c'_2$ is defined as follows.

1) The case $v = \xi A\bar{\xi}\bar{A}$, where $\xi \in \Gamma_1^*$, $A \in \Gamma$, $\bar{\xi} \in (\bar{\Gamma} \cup \bar{\Gamma}^\#)^*$ and $\bar{A} \in \bar{\Gamma}$. Assume that $(s_1,A) \overset{a}{\to} (s_2,B\eta)$ and $(\bar{s}_1,\bar{A}) \overset{a}{\to} (\bar{s}_2,\bar{B}\bar{\eta})$ (where $B \in \Gamma$ if $\eta \neq \lambda$ and $B \in \Gamma \cup \{\lambda\}$ otherwise and similarly for $\bar{B}$). Then for the input a in M', the segment $\xi A\bar{\xi}\bar{A}$ will change to $\xi B\bar{\xi}\bar{B}\eta\bar{\eta}$ and the state from $[s_1,\bar{s}_1]$ to $[s_2,\bar{s}_2]$. The case $v = \xi'\bar{A}\xi A$, where $\xi' \in \Gamma_1^*$, $\bar{A} \in \bar{\Gamma}$, $\xi \in (\Gamma \cup \Gamma^\#)^*$ and $A \in \Gamma$, is handled symmetrically.

In the following cases 2) and 3) M' makes a λ-transition while the state of M' remains unchanged.

2) If $v = A_1A_2\ldots A_{l'}$, where $A_i \in \Gamma$ for each $i = 1,\ldots,l'$, then v is replaced by $A_1A_2^\#A_3\ldots A_{l'}$. The case $v = \bar{A}_1\bar{A}_2\ldots\bar{A}_{l'} \in \bar{\Gamma}^*$ is handled symmetrically.

3) If $v = A_1A_2\ldots A_{|v|}$ and for some i, $1 \leq i \leq |v| - 2$, $A_i \in \Gamma \cup \Gamma^\#$, $A_{i+1} \in \Gamma^\#$ and $A_j \in \Gamma$ for all $j = i+2,\ldots,|v|$ (or symmetrically, $A_i \in \bar{\Gamma} \cup \bar{\Gamma}^\#$, $A_{i+1} \in \bar{\Gamma}^\#$ and $A_j \in \bar{\Gamma}$ for all $j = i+2,\ldots,|v|$), then v is replaced by $A_1\ldots A_{i-1}A_{i+1}\ldots A_{|v|}$, i.e. the ith letter of v is removed.

If $L(M) = L(\bar{M})$, the rule 3) assures that in each accepting derivation after a finite number of λ-moves, the rule 1) becomes applicable. This together with the following lemma implies that M' is able to simulate every accepting derivation of M and $\bar{M}$.

Lemma 9. Assume that $L(M) = L(\bar{M})$. Then for each $\alpha \in \Sigma^*$, if $c'_s \overset{\alpha}{\to} c' = ([s,\bar{s}],w)$ in M', where w is of the form $w = w_1A^\#w_2$, $w_1 \in \Gamma_1^*$, $A \in \Gamma$ and $w_2 \in (\bar{\Gamma} \cup \bar{\Gamma}^\#)^*$ (or symmetrically, $w = w_1\bar{A}^\#w_2$, $w_1 \in \Gamma_1^*$, $\bar{A} \in \bar{\Gamma}$ and $w_2 \in (\Gamma \cup \Gamma^\#)^*$), it follows that α is not live.

For a given dpda M one can test for each $s,s' \in Q$ and $A \in \Gamma$ whether or not the languages $L((s,A))$ and $L = \{\alpha \in \Sigma^* | (s,A) \overset{\alpha}{\to} (s',\lambda)\}$ are empty. Using this fact one can construct, for a given stack uniform dpda M, a stack uniform dpda M_1 which simulates M and during each derivation associates to every stack letter subsets of states as follows. If $(s_1, A_1A_2...A_n)$ is a configuration derivable from the initial configuration of M, then the corresponding configuration in M_1 is $(s_1,(A_1,Q_1)(A_2,Q_2,Q_1)...(A_n,Q_n,Q_{n-1}))$, where for each i, $1 \leq i \leq n$, $Q_i = \{s \in Q | L(s,A_1A_2...A_i) \neq \phi\}$. In the following we assume that M and $\bar{M}$ already are in this form, i.e. the state and top stack letter indicate whether or not a configuration is live.

Theorem 2. The equivalence problem for stack uniform dpda´s is decidable.

Proof. Assume that stack uniform dpda´s M and $\bar{M}$ with the property explained above are given. Construct a non-deterministic pda M" such that $L(M") = \phi$ iff $L(M) = L(\bar{M})$. M" simulates the machine M' by encoding the top segment of length l' in its finite state control. As long as the situation of Lemma 9 does not occur M" simulates M and $\bar{M}$, and M" accepts the input iff exactly one of M and $\bar{M}$ accepts. In the case where a transition is defined for one of M and $\bar{M}$, but no transition is defined for the other, M" accepts if the first dpda is in a live configuration. If the situation of Lemma 9 occurs, M" accepts iff M or $\bar{M}$ is in a live configuration. It is easy to verify that $L(M") = \phi$ iff $L(M) = L(\bar{M})$.

References

1. Friedman, E. P., The inclusion problem for simple languages, Theoret. Comput. Sci. 1 (1976) 297-316.

2. Harrison, M. A. and Havel, I. M., Strict deterministic grammars, J. Comput. System. Sci. 7 (1973) 237-277.

3. Jaffe, V. A., Two classes of CF-languages with a solvable equivalence problem, Kibernetika, Kiev, 2 (1974) 89-93.

4. Korenjak, A. J. and Hopcroft, J. E., Simple deterministic languages, IEEE Conf. Record of 7th Annual Symp. on Switching and Automata Theory (1966) 36-46.

5. Kriegel, H. P. and Maurer, H. A., Formal translations and Szilard languages, Information and Control 30 (1976) 187-198.

6. Kriegel, H. P. and Ottmann, Th., Left-fitting translations, manuscript (1976).

7. Moriya, E., The associate language and the derivation properties of formal grammars, Information and Control 22 (1973) 139-162.

8. Penttonen, M., On derivation languages corresponding to context-free grammars, Acta Informatica 3 (1974) 285-291.

9. Rosenkranz, D. J. and Stearns, R. E., Properties of deterministic top-down grammars, Information and Control 17 (1970) 226-255.

10. Taniguchi, K. and Kasami, T., A result on the equivalence problem for deterministic pushdown automata, J. Comput. System. Sci. 13 (1976) 38-50.

11. Valiant, L. G., Decision problems for families of deterministic pushdown automata, Univ. of Warwick Computer Centre, Report No.7, 1973.

12. Valiant, L. G., The equivalence problem for deterministic finite-turn pushdown automata, Information and Control 25 (1974) 123-133.

13. Valiant, L. G. and Paterson, M. S., Deterministic one-counter automata, J. Comput. System. Sci. 10 (1975) 340-350.

ON THE LOGIC OF INCOMPLETE INFORMATION

Witold Lipski, Jr.

Institute of Computer Science

Polish Academy of Sciences

P. O. Box 22

00-901 Warsaw PKiN

Introduction

The problem of incomplete information is undoubtedly inherent in many domains of science, such as Information Retrieval, Pattern Recognition and Artificial Intelligence. In particular -- as the author learnt from Petr Hájek during the previous MFCS'76 Conference -- the problem is vital in the GUHA method of automatic formation of hypotheses (see Hájek et al. [1], Hájek [2]).

In the context of information retrieval, problems related to information incompleteness were studied by Jaegermann [5] and Lipski [8,9]. These papers were an attempt to extend to the case of incomplete information the mathematical model of an information storage and retrieval system proposed by Marek and Pawlak [11] (see also Lipski and Marek [10]).

In the present paper we discuss two approaches to interpreting formulas of the Predicate Calculus in an incompletely specified model. These approaches were formulated in [9] for formulas of a specific language tailored to express queries to an information storage and retrieval system.

1. Two ways of interpreting Predicate Calculus formulas in the case of incomplete information

We shall consider a first-order Predicate Calculus (PC) with predicates $P,Q,R,\ldots$ (each one of arity $n(P)\geq 1$), no function symbols or constants, with individual variables $x,y,z,\ldots$, universal quantifier $\forall$, existential quantifier $\exists$, logical constants $\bigvee$ (truth), $\bigwedge$ (falsity), and logical connectives $\neg, \vee, \wedge, \Rightarrow, \Leftrightarrow$. All elementary notions and definitions concerning PC which we use throughout the paper can be found in any text-book of logic, e.g. Rasiowa and Sikorski [12]. Formulas will be denoted by $\Phi, \Psi, \ldots$ or by $\Phi(x_1,\ldots,x_n)$, $\Psi(x_1,\ldots,x_n)$ where

$\{x_1,\dots,x_n\}$ contains all free variables occurring in Φ,Ψ.

By an <u>incomplete model</u> (or a <u>model</u> for short) of our PC we shall mean any triple $M = \langle X,u,U\rangle$ where X is a nonempty set and u, U are functions which associate some subsets $u(P) \subseteq U(P) \subseteq X^{n(P)}$ with every predicate P. If $u = U$ then we obtain the notion of an ordinary -- or, as we shall call it, <u>complete</u> -- model of PC. Notice that according to these definitions a complete model is a special case of an incomplete model.

Given two models $M_1 = \langle X,u_1,U_1\rangle$, $M_2 = \langle X,u_2,U_2\rangle$ with the same universe X, we say that M_2 is an <u>extension</u> of M_1, and we write $M_1 \preccurlyeq M_2$ or $M_2 \succcurlyeq M_1$, if for every predicate P

$$u_1(P) \subseteq u_2(P) \subseteq U_2(P) \subseteq U_1(P).$$

If we think of M_1, M_2 as representing incomplete information about some complete model $M = \langle X,u,U\rangle$ with

$$u_1(P) \subseteq u(P) = U(P) \subseteq U_1(P)$$
$$u_2(P) \subseteq u(P) = U(P) \subseteq U_2(P)$$

then $M_1 \preccurlyeq M_2$ means that this information is more complete in M_2 than in M_1 (or $M_1 = M_2$). Indeed, if $M_1 \preccurlyeq M_2$ and $M_1 \neq M_2$ then there exist in M_1 some predicates P and some "undecided" tuples $\langle a_1,\dots,a_{n(P)}\rangle \in U_1(P)\setminus u_1(P)$ which in M_2 either "turn out to be in $u(P)$" (and are added to $u_2(P)$), or "turn out not to be in $U(P)$" (and are deleted from $U_2(P)$). Any complete extension of a model M will be called a <u>completion</u> of M. Using the notion of a completion we can give the following interpretation to an arbitrary model M: the model M describes, in an incomplete way, some completion $M' \succcurlyeq M$, we do not know which one Similar approach to incomplete information has been presented, in terms of "earthly" (M) and "heavenly" (M') models, by Hájek et al. [1].

Let $\Phi(x_1,\dots,x_n)$ be a formula, let $M = \langle X,u,U\rangle$ be a complete model and let $a_1,\dots,a_n \in X$. It is then intuitively clear what is the meaning of the following (meta)sentence: "$\Phi(x_1,\dots,x_n)$ is satisfied in M when $x_1,\dots,x_n$ are interpreted as $a_1,\dots,a_n$, respectively", in symbols

(1) $$M \models \Phi(x_1,\dots,x_n)[a_1,\dots,a_n]$$

(The formal Tarski-style definition of satisfiability, by induction on the complexity of Φ, can be found in any text-book of logic.)

It is not quite obvious how to generalize the meaning of (1) to the case of non-complete M. It seems that, basically speaking, two different approaches to the problem are possible. To describe them let us think of M as being an incomplete description of some "right" (or, in terminology of [1], "heavenly") model M'.

The first approach to interpreting formulas in M consists in refering them directly to M'. We call such an interpretation <u>external</u>. The advantage of such an interpretation -- apart from its clear intuitive meaning -- is that, since M'

is complete, we can use the ordinary first-order PC axioms for equivalent transformations of formulas. Let us call two formulas Φ, Ψ externally equivalent (in symbols $\Phi \underset{e}{\approx} \Psi$) if their respective external interpretations (i.e. truth or falsity) coincide for every model and every interpretation of free variables occurring in Φ, Ψ. It is clear that $\Phi \underset{e}{\approx} \Psi$ iff $\Phi \Leftrightarrow \Psi$ can be derived from the axioms of PC (it follows from the Completeness Theorem for PC). The obvious drawback of the external interpretation is that it is, in general, impossible to determine it for a given formula Φ in model M. Since the "right" model -- which can be any completion of M -- is not available, we can only determine the following "lower bound" $\models_*$ and "upper bound" $\models^*$ instead of $\models$:

$M \models_* \Phi(x_1,\dots,x_n)[a_1,\dots,a_n]$ iff for every completion $M' \succcurlyeq M$ $M' \models \Phi(x_1,\dots,x_n)[a_1,\dots,a_n]$

$M \models^* \Phi(x_1,\dots,x_n)[a_1,\dots,a_n]$ iff there is a completion $M' \succcurlyeq M$ with $M' \models \Phi(x_1,\dots,x_n)[a_1,\dots,a_n]$

It is convenient to use the following notation:

$$\|\Phi(x_1,\dots,x_n)\|_{*M} = \{\langle a_1,\dots,a_n\rangle \in X^n:\ M \models_* \Phi(x_1,\dots,x_n)[a_1,\dots,a_n]\},$$

$$\|\Phi(x_1,\dots,x_n)\|^*_M = \{\langle a_1,\dots,a_n\rangle \in X^n:\ M \models^* \Phi(x_1,\dots,x_n)[a_1,\dots,a_n]\},$$

and, if Φ is closed, i.e. if it does not contain any free variables,

$$\|\Phi\|_{*M} = \begin{cases} \bigvee & \text{if } M \models_* \Phi \\ \bigwedge & \text{otherwise} \end{cases} \qquad \|\Phi\|^*_M = \begin{cases} \bigvee & \text{if } M \models^* \Phi \\ \bigwedge & \text{otherwise} \end{cases}$$

We call $\|\cdot\|_{*M}$ and $\|\cdot\|^*_M$ the lower value and the upper value of a formula in M. The following lemma follows easily from the definitions of $\|\cdot\|_{*M}$ and $\|\cdot\|^*_M$.

LEMMA 1.1. For any model $M = \langle X,u,U\rangle$, any $n \geqslant 1$, and any formulas $\Phi(x_1,\dots,x_n)$, $\Psi(x_1,\dots,x_n)$

(i) $\|\bigvee\|_{*M} = \|\bigvee\|^*_M = \bigvee \qquad \|\bigwedge\|_{*M} = \|\bigwedge\|^*_M = \bigwedge$

(ii) $\|P(x_1,\dots,x_n)\|_{*M} = u(P) \qquad (n = n(P))$

(iii) $\|P(x_1,\dots,x_n)\|^*_M = U(P) \qquad (n = n(P))$

(iv) $\|\neg\Phi(x_1,\dots,x_n)\|_{*M} = X^n \setminus \|\Phi(x_1,\dots,x_n)\|^*_M$

(v) $\|\neg\Phi(x_1,\dots,x_n)\|^*_M = X^n \setminus \|\Phi(x_1,\dots,x_n)\|_{*M}$

(vi) $\|(\Phi\vee\Psi)(x_1,\dots,x_n)\|_{*M} \supseteq \|\Phi(x_1,\dots,x_n)\|_{*M} \cup \|\Psi(x_1,\dots,x_n)\|_{*M}$

(vii) $\|(\Phi\vee\Psi)(x_1,\dots,x_n)\|^*_M = \|\Phi(x_1,\dots,x_n)\|^*_M \cup \|\Psi(x_1,\dots,x_n)\|^*_M$

(viii) $\|(\Phi\wedge\Psi)(x_1,\dots,x_n)\|_{*M} = \|\Phi(x_1,\dots,x_n)\|_{*M} \cap \|\Psi(x_1,\dots,x_n)\|_{*M}$

(ix) $\|(\Phi\wedge\Psi)(x_1,\dots,x_n)\|^*_M \subseteq \|\Phi(x_1,\dots,x_n)\|^*_M \cap \|\Psi(x_1,\dots,x_n)\|^*_M$

(x) $\|(\Phi\Rightarrow\Psi)(x_1,\dots,x_n)\|_{*M} \supseteq (X^n \setminus \|\Phi(x_1,\dots,x_n)\|^*_M) \cup \|\Psi(x_1,\dots,x_n)\|_{*M}$

(xi) $\|(\Phi\Rightarrow\Psi)(x_1,\dots,x_n)\|^*_M = (X^n \setminus \|\Phi(x_1,\dots,x_n)\|_{*M}) \cup \|\Psi(x_1,\dots,x_n)\|^*_M$

(xii) $\|(\forall x\Phi)(x_1,\ldots,x_n)\|_{*M}$
$= \{\langle a_1,\ldots,a_n\rangle \in X^n:\ (\forall a\in X)\ \langle a_1,\ldots,a_n,a\rangle \in \|\Phi(x_1,\ldots,x_n,x)\|_{*M}\}$

(xiii) $\|(\forall x\Phi)(x_1,\ldots,x_n)\|^*_M$
$\subseteq \{\langle a_1,\ldots,a_n\rangle \in X^n:\ (\forall a\in X)\ \langle a_1,\ldots,a_n,a\rangle \in \|\Phi(x_1,\ldots,x_n,x)\|^*_M\}$

(xiv) $\|(\exists x\Phi)(x_1,\ldots,x_n)\|_{*M}$
$\supseteq \{\langle a_1,\ldots,a_n\rangle \in X^n:\ (\exists a\in X)\ \langle a_1,\ldots,a_n,a\rangle \in \|\Phi(x_1,\ldots,x_n,x)\|_{*M}\}$

(xv) $\|(\exists x\Phi)(x_1,\ldots,x_n)\|^*_M$
$= \{\langle a_1,\ldots,a_n\rangle \in X^n:\ (\exists a\in X)\ \langle a_1,\ldots,a_n,a\rangle \in \|\Phi(x_1,\ldots,x_n,x)\|^*_M\}$

In (xii)-(xv) we assume that Φ does not contain any free occurrence of x. Parts (iv)-(xi) of the lemma are also true, mutatis mutandis, for $\|\Phi\|_{*M}$, $\|\Psi\|_{*M}$, $\|\Phi\|^*_M$ and $\|\Psi\|^*_M$ where Φ, Ψ are closed.

Of course, if $\Phi \approx_e \Psi$ then $\|\Phi(x_1,\ldots,x_n)\|_{*M} = \|\Psi(x_1,\ldots,x_n)\|_{*M}$ and $\|\Phi(x_1,\ldots,x_n)\|^*_M = \|\Psi(x_1,\ldots,x_n)\|^*_M$ for any model M. The main trouble with $\|\cdot\|_{*M}$ and $\|\cdot\|^*_M$ is that the inclusions in (vi),(ix),(x),(xiii),(xiv) cannot, in general, be replaced by equalities. In fact, it is easy to see that $\|(\Phi\vee\Psi)(x_1,\ldots,x_n)\|_{*M}$ is not determined by the upper and lower values of all subformulas of $\Phi\vee\Psi$ but also depends on the formula $\Phi\vee\Psi$ itself. The situation in the remaining cases is similar. Thus, no inductive definition -- similar to that in the complete case -- of the values $\|\cdot\|_{*M}$, $\|\cdot\|^*_M$ can exist, unless M is complete. But this trouble does not occur in the following special case.

<u>LEMMA</u> 1.2. If no predicate occurs both in Φ and Ψ then the equalities in (vi),(ix),(x) do hold.

This lemma provides the following simple method for evaluating $\|\Phi(x_1,\ldots,x_n)$ when Φ is <u>open</u>, i.e. does not contain quantifiers (see Lipski [8,9]; Theorem 16 of Hájek et al. [1] has a very similar meaning). First we transform Φ to (an externally equivalent) disjunctive normal form (DNF) $\bigvee_i \bigwedge_j P_{ij}^{\varepsilon_{ij}}$ where $\varepsilon_{ij} \in \{0,1\}$ and no predicate occurs more than once in $\bigwedge_j P_{ij}^{\varepsilon_{ij}}$ for any i (P^0 denotes $\neg P$ and P^1 denotes P). Then we can compute $\|\Phi(x_1,\ldots,x_n)\|^*_M$ inductively using Lemma 1.1 with the inclusion in (ix) replaced by equality. Evaluating $\|\Phi(x_1,\ldots,x_n)\|_{*M}$ involves a dual conjunctive normal form (CNF). For formulas containing quantifiers the problem seems to be very difficult, unless all predicates are unary -- the situation which is described in more detail below.

Let $\Phi(x_1,\ldots,x_n)$ be a formula of Monadic Predicate Calculus (MPC), i.e. a PC with only unary predicates. We shall show a method to determine $\|\Phi(x_1,\ldots,x_n)\|^*_M$ for any model M. Using the PC axioms it is not difficult to transform Φ to an (externally equivalent) formula of the form $\bigvee_i \Phi_i$ with every Φ_i of the form

$$\Psi_1(x_1)\wedge\ldots\wedge\Psi_n(x_n)\wedge(\exists x\Psi_{n+1}(x))\wedge\ldots\wedge(\exists x\Psi_{n+p}(x))$$
$$\neg(\exists x\Psi_{i+p+1}(x))\wedge\ldots\wedge\neg(\exists x\Psi_{n+p+q}(x)) \tag{2}$$

Moreover, we may assume that every Ψ_j is a conjunction of some number of predicates, and that for any $j \neq k$, $1 \leqslant j,k \leqslant n+p+q$,

$$\exists x(\Psi_j(x) \wedge \Psi_k(x)) \approx_e \bigwedge,$$

i.e., there is a predicate occurring positively in one of Ψ_j, Ψ_k and negatively in the other. We allow some of $\Psi_1, \ldots, \Psi_n$ to be $\bigvee$, the conjunction of the empty number of predicates.

By Lemma 1.1(vii), $\|\Phi(x_1,\ldots,x_n)\|^*_M = \bigcup_i \|\Phi_i(x_1,\ldots,x_n)\|^*_M$, so it suffices to give a method to evaluate the upper value of (2). The idea of our method of doing this can be explained by using the following simple example. Suppose that three objects a,b,c are classified in respect to colour by means of three unary predicates, Red, Green, Blue. Assume that the colour of no object is known (i.e., u(Red) = u(Green) = u(Blue) = $\emptyset$), and consider the following two situations:

	I	II
U(Red)	$A_1 = \{a\}$	$B_1 = \{a,b\}$
U(Blue)	$A_2 = \{a,b\}$	$B_2 = \{b\}$
U(Green)	$A_3 = \{a,b\}$	$B_3 = \{a,c\}$

Now we ask the following question: "Is it possible for our collection to contain objects of all colours ?", or, more formally, "what is the value

$$\|(\exists x\ \text{Red}(x)) \wedge (\exists x\ \text{Green}(x)) \wedge (\exists x\ \text{Blue}(x))\|^* \text{ ?".}$$

It is evident that this value is $\bigwedge$ in situation I and $\bigvee$ in situation II. The reason for that is clear: the sequence of sets B_1, B_2, B_3 has a system of distinct representatives (SDR), whereas A_1, A_2, A_3 has not. By an SDR of a sequence of sets $S_1, \ldots, S_n$ we mean here a sequence of pairwise distinct elements $r_1, \ldots, r_n$ such that $r_i \in S_i$ for $1 \leqslant i \leqslant n$ (see Hall [3]). In our problem r_i plays the role of an object which "turns out to be of i-th colour". For an efficient method of testing a sequence of sets for the existence of an SDR the reader is referred to Hopcroft and Karp [4].

With this intuition in mind it is not difficult to prove the following general theorem.

THEOREM 1.3. Let $\Psi(x_1,\ldots,x_n)$ denote the formula (2). Then,

$$\langle a_1,\ldots,a_n\rangle \in \|\Psi(x_1,\ldots,x_n)\|^*_M$$

iff the following two conditions are satisfied:

(a) $\|(\Psi_{i+p+1} \vee \ldots \vee \Psi_{i+p+q})(x)\|_{*M} = \emptyset$,

(b) The sequence $a_1,\ldots,a_n$ can be extended to an SDR $a_1,\ldots,a_n,a_{n+1},\ldots,a_{n+p}$ of

$$\|\Psi_1(x)\|^*_M, \ldots, \|\Psi_n(x)\|^*_M, \|\Psi_{n+1}(x)\|^*_M, \ldots, \|\Psi_{n+p}(x)\|^*_M.$$

In other words, $a_1,\ldots,a_n$ is an SDR of $\|\Psi_1(x)\|^*_M, \ldots, \|\Psi_n(x)\|^*_M$ and the sequence

$$\|\Psi_{n+1}(x)\|^*_M \setminus \{a_1,\dots,a_n\}, \dots, \|\Psi_{n+p}(x)\|^*_M \setminus \{a_1,\dots,a_n\}$$

has an SDR.

By our previous remarks, this theorem gives an effective method to evaluate $\|\Phi(x_1,\dots,x_n)\|^*_M$ for an arbitrary formula Φ of MPC and any model M. To evaluate lower values we can make use of the fact that

$$\|\Phi(x_1,\dots,x_n)\|_{*M} = X^n \setminus \|\neg\Phi(x_1,\dots,x_n)\|^*_M.$$

Now we pass to the second way of interpreting formulas of PC in an incomplete model. This second approach consists in assuming that the meaning of $P(x_1,\dots,x_{n(P)})$ is: "it is known that $P(x_1,\dots,x_{n(P)})$ is satisfied in reality". In other words, the interpretation of a formula $\Phi(x_1,\dots,x_n)$ in a model $M = \langle X,u,U\rangle$ coincides with the usual interpretation of $\Phi(x_1,\dots,x_n)$ in the complete model $M' = \langle X,u,u\rangle \succcurlyeq M$. We call this interpretation of Φ in M the <u>internal interpretation</u> and we denote it by $\|\Phi(x_1,\dots,x_n)\|_M$. Of course, the internal interpretation of a formula has all properties of the usual interpretation in a complete model. The situation is no longer trivial when we introduce an additional unary connective $\Box$ to our language, with the following interpretation:

$$\langle a_1,\dots,a_n\rangle \in \|\Box\Phi(x_1,\dots,x_n)\|_M \quad \text{iff for every } M' \succcurlyeq M, \quad \langle a_1,\dots,a_n\rangle \in \|\Phi(x_1,\dots,x_n)\|_{M'}$$

(Note: M′ is <u>not</u> assumed to be complete).

By an <u>extended formula</u> we shall mean any formula which (possibly) contains $\Box$. It is also convenient to abbreviate $\neg\Box\neg$ to $\Diamond$. We have

$$\langle a_1,\dots,a_n\rangle \in \|\Diamond\Phi(x_1,\dots,x_n)\|_M \quad \text{iff there is an } M' \succcurlyeq M \text{ with} \quad \langle a_1,\dots,a_n\rangle \in \|\Phi(x_1,\dots,x_n)\|_{M'}$$

It should be noted that under the external interpretation a formula in M expresses a fact about the "right" completion M′ of M, and so it is "external" with respect to M Contrary to this, under the internal interpretation an (extended) formula expresses a fact about our information about M′ available in M.

Two extended formulas Φ,Ψ are said to be <u>internally equivalent</u> (in symbols $\Phi \approx_i \Psi$) if $\|\Phi(x_1,\dots,x_n)\|_M = \|\Psi(x_1,\dots,x_n)\|_M$ for every model M. The idea of introducing the modal connective $\Box$ to the language was suggested by the Kripke models for the modal logic S4, see Kripke [6]. From the obvious fact that $\preccurlyeq$ is a partial order, it follows easily that in addition to the usual PC axioms we can use the axioms of the modal logic S4 in the process of internally equivalent transformations of formulas. In particular,

(3) $\Box\bigvee \approx_i \bigvee$

(4) $\Box\Box\Phi \approx_i \Box\Phi$

(5) $\Box(\Phi\wedge\Psi) \approx_i \Box\Phi\wedge\Box\Psi$

(6) $\Phi\wedge\Box\Phi \approx_i \Box\Phi$

In addition, we have some other axioms, such as

(7) $\Box P \Leftrightarrow P$

(8) $\Box\Diamond(\Phi\wedge\Psi) \Leftrightarrow \Box\Diamond\Phi\wedge\Box\Diamond\Psi$

(9) $\Diamond\Box(\Phi\vee\Psi) \Leftrightarrow \Diamond\Box\Phi\vee\Diamond\Box\Psi$

(10) $\Box\Diamond\forall x\Phi \Leftrightarrow \forall x\,\Box\Diamond\Phi$

(11) $\Diamond\Box\exists x\Phi \Leftrightarrow \exists x\,\Diamond\Box\Phi$

(12) $\Box(\bigvee_{i=1}^{m} P_i \vee \bigvee_{j=m+1}^{n} \Diamond P_j \vee \bigvee_{k=n+1}^{p} \neg P_k \vee \bigvee_{l=p+1}^{q} \Box\neg P_l)$

$\Leftrightarrow \bigvee_{i=1}^{n} P_i \vee \bigvee_{j=n+1}^{q} \Box\neg P_j$ ($P_s \neq P_r$ unless $1 \leq s \leq m$ and $p+1 \leq r \leq q$)

which are not S4-tautologies. It is not known to the author whether all these axioms completely axiomatize $\approx_i$. Also it is not known whether internal equivalence of extended formulas containing only unary predicates is decidable, though we conjecture that this is the case (notice that, in contrast to the classical case, modal MPC is undecidable, see Kripke [7]).

The following is a theorem which gives a relation between the external and internal interpretations.

THEOREM 1.4. For any formula Φ and any model M

$$\|\Phi(x_1,\ldots,x_n)\|_{*M} = \|\Box\Diamond\Phi(x_1,\ldots,x_n)\|_M$$
$$\|\Phi(x_1,\ldots,x_n)\|^{*}_{M} = \|\Diamond\Box\Phi(x_1,\ldots,x_n)\|_M$$

The proof is omitted.

Now we shall sketch a method for evaluating the internal interpretation of an arbitrary open extended formula. Let us call an occurrence of $\Box$ inessential if it precedes a predicate or a negation of predicate, and essential otherwise.

LEMMA 1.5. For any open extended formula Φ there is an internally equivalent extended formula without essential occurrences of $\Box$.

Proof. If Φ contains an essential occurrence of $\Box$ then it contains a subformula $\Box\Psi$ where all occurrences of $\Box$ in Ψ are inessential. We transform Ψ to a CNF, say $\bigwedge_i \bigvee_j \Psi_{ij}$, where every Ψ_{ij} is of one of the following four forms: P, $\neg P$, $\Box\neg P$, $\Diamond P$. Now, by using (5) and (12), we can decrease by one the number of essential occurrences of $\Box$. Repeating the above procedure we ultimately eliminate all essential occurrences of $\Box$. ∎

The internal interpretation of an open formula without essential occurrences of $\Box$ can easily be determined, if we notice that in any model $M = \langle X,u,U\rangle$

$$\|P(x_1,\ldots,x_n)\|_M = u(P) \qquad (n = n(P))$$
$$\|\neg P(x_1,\ldots,x_n)\|_M = X^n \setminus u(P)$$
$$\|\Box\neg P(x_1,\ldots,x_n)\|_M = X^n \setminus U(P)$$
$$\|\Diamond P(x_1,\ldots,x_n)\|_M = U(P)$$

This brief survey of problems arising when we deal with incompletely specified models of PC shows that there are interesting non-trivial problems in this subject. Moreover, the more general situation when we consider incompletely specified models of a first-order theory seems to be a good research topic.

References

1. Hájek, P., Bendová, K. and Renc, Z., The GUHA method and the three-valued logic. Kybernetika 7(1971)421-435.
2. Hájek, P., Automatic listing of important observational statements III. Kybernetika 10(1974)95-124.
3. Hall, Ph., On representatives of subsets. J. Lond. Math. Soc. 10(1935)26-30.
4. Hopcroft, J. E. and Karp, R. M., An $n^{5/2}$ algorithm for maximum matchings in bipartite graphs. SIAM J. Comp. 2(1973)225-231.
5. Jaegermann, M., Information storage and retrieval systems -- mathematical foundations IV. Systems with incomplete information. Fundamenta Informaticae, to appear (a preliminary version available as CC PAS Report 214, Warsaw 1975).
6. Kripke, S. A., Semantical analysis of modal logic I. Zeitschr. Math. Logik Grund. Math. 9(1963)67-96.
7. Kripke, S. A., The undecidability of monadic modal quantification theory. Zeitschr. Math. Logik Grund. Math. 8(1962)113-116.
8. Lipski, W., Informational systems with incomplete information. In: Proc. Third International Colloquium on Automata, Languages and Programming, Edinburgh 1976 (S. Michaelson and R. Milner, Eds), pp. 120-130, Edinburgh University Press, Edinburgh 1976.
9. Lipski, W., Informational systems: semantic issues related to incomplete information, Part I. CC PAS Report 275, Warsaw 1977.
10. Lipski, W. and Marek, W., On information storage and retrieval systems. In: Proc. Summer School on Mathematical Foundations of Computer Science, Warsaw 1974 (A. Mazurkiewicz, Ed.), Banach Center Publications, vol. 2, Polish Scientific Publishers, to appear. (Also available as CC PAS Report 200, Warsaw 1975.)
11. Marek, W and Pawlak, Z., Information storage and retrieval systems: mathematical foundations. Theoretical Computer Science 1(1976)331-354. (A preliminar version available as CC PAS Report 149, Warsaw 1974.)
12. Rasiowa, H. and Sikorski, R., The mathematics of metamathematics. Polish Scientific Publishers, Warsaw 1963.

MEASURES OF AMBIGUITY IN THE ANALYSIS OF COMPLEX SYSTEMS

Aldo De Luca and Settimo Termini

Laboratorio di Cibernetica del C.N.R., 80072 Arco Felice, Naples, Italy.

1. *Motivations and Introductory Remarks.*

One of the main problems with which one is confronted during the description and modelling of *"complex"* systems, i.e., for instance, those of artificial intelligence or social and economical ones or the study of a natural language, is the impossibility of sharply defining the meaningful parameters of them. This means that a sort of *ambiguity* is present from the beginning and usually every effort of eliminating it induces an oversimplification of the model and so a loss of information on the real systems one wants to describe [1]. One has to observe that the major part of (classical) mathematics has been used for (and also originated from) the modelling of exact systems and then it does not seem to give, immediately, too much space for the formal treatment of ambiguous situations. However, a glimpse to the history of mathematics shows that in its development many things that appeared outside the mathematical domain because too much unprecise, or difficult to define, became progressively fully describable by new developed chapters of it (remember, for instance, the irrational numbers or the theory of probability versus the mathematical thinking of the Greeks). Moreover there presently exists a lot of formal theories that take into account, from different points of view, the previous necessity of a treatment of ambiguity. Among them we can recall *i) many valued logics; ii) probabilistic von Neumann logics; iii) non-deterministic aspects of the theory of automata and formal languages; iv) the use of characteristic membership functions which do not take only the values 0 and 1 but also intermediate ones (partial membership).* Also the theory of probability can be put into this setting even if at its base there is the conviction of the possibility of a crisp description - at least platonically: only the intractability of the corresponding system forces to use probabilistic statements.

Considering, in particular, the numerous researches usually collected under the name of Artificial Intelligence, we want to stress also some other points. One of the main aims of the previous field consists in finding some "euristic procedures" by means of which *to prove,* inside a given formal system, non trivial theorems in such a way that the *"complexity",* does not exceed realistic limitations. The importance of the "complexity" be it *static* (complexity of the description) or *dynamic,* (amount of needed resource) in Artificial Intelligence as well as in many other fields has been stressed by many authors (see for instance, [1,2]). It seems to us that, besides the attempts at formalizing the euristics, another possible approach to the analysis of very complex systems, as the ones with which Artificial Intelligence is concerned, can be obtained by a suitable change in the *descriptions* of the systems by means of a language which, taking into account such elements as *"ambiguity"* or *"unprecision"*, makes *"tractable"* those problems whose solution in the classical description-languages requires tremendous amounts of complexity.

Let us briefly summarize the problem by saying that a developed mathematical calculus which formalizes also the notion of ambiguity can be of great importance mainly for two kind of purposes: i) *to give a formal way of treating problems and systems in which the ambiguity plays an intrinsic role for the same definition of the problem or of the system;* ii) *to provide a formalism adequate for obtaining approximate descriptions of systems or problems exactly definable - in classical unambiguous terms - but, practically, intractable.* As regards point ii) above, one of the main open problems is to find a standard way, or a procedure, (as is the case for probabilistic descriptions) to pass from the classical language of (exact) description to the non-standard (new) language in which the original problem becomes tractable. Once the importance of a formal treatment of ambiguity is acknowledged then it is natural to consider *"measures"* of it. These are obviously strictly related to the particular mathematical context; for instance, in the case of formal systems a measure of ambiguity is given by the number of derivations by which a given "string" can be obtained; in the setting of variable length codes by the number of different factorizations that a message admits; in the case of a probabilistic system by the classical notion of entropy. In these last years also some of the efforts of people working on fuzzy sets theory [3] have been oriented in developing such measures. A superimposition of the *probabilistic notion of entropy* to the formalism of fuzzy sets [4] is very useful for the study of situations in which probabilistic (random) effects are present in ambiguous situations but, as has been observed by Kaufmann [5], it does not furnish real measures of fuzziness. Our proposal [6] is based uniquely on the generalized characteristic functions and on a restricted number of very natural and intuitive assumptions. In the following we want to give a brief critical survey of the work already done in order to indicate some new technical results and discuss some open interpretative questions of these measures with respect to the notion of information.

2. *Entropy Measures in the Theory of Fuzzy Sets.*

We recall that a generalized characteristic function, or *fuzzy set* in the terminology of Zadeh [3] is any map $f : I \to [0,1]$ from a given universe of objects I to the interval $[0,1]$ of the real line.

The class $\mathcal{L}(I)$ of all fuzzy sets defined over I is a (noncomplemented) lattice with respect to the two binary operations $\vee$ and $\wedge$ defined for all f and g of $\mathcal{L}(I)$ point by point as

$$(f \vee g)\ (x) := \max\{f(x), g(x)\}; \quad (f \wedge g)\ (x) := \min\{f(x), g(x)\} .$$

Moreover one can introduce in $\mathcal{L}(I)$ the unary operation $(^{-})$ associating to any f of $\mathcal{L}(I)$ the fuzzy set $\bar{f}$ defined as $\bar{f}(x) = 1-f(x)$ for all x of I. One easily verifies that the *involution law* and the *De Morgan relations* are satisfied:

$$f = \bar{\bar{f}}; \quad \overline{f \vee g} = \bar{f} \wedge \bar{g}; \quad \overline{f \wedge g} = \bar{f} \vee \bar{g} .$$

When the support I is finite, in [6] we have introduced in $\mathcal{L}(I)$ two functionals P and d called respectively *"power"* and (logarithmic) *"entropy"*. The power defined for all f of $\mathcal{L}(I)$ as

$$P(f) := \sum_{x \in I} f(x) \tag{2.1}$$

generalizes the cardinality of a classical set. The entropy d, which vanishes in the classical case, is a measure of the total amount of ambiguity of a fuzzy set and is defined for all f of $\mathcal{L}(I)$ as:

$$d(f) := \sum_{x \in I} S(f(x)), \tag{2.2}$$

where S denotes the Shannon function $S(x) := x \ln 1/x + (1-x) \ln[1/(1-x)]$.

The measure d is only one possible measure of ambiguity; in the general case an entropy measure of a fuzzy set is a functional satisfying a certain number of reasonable axioms. For lists of proposed axioms see [6] and [7].

We stress that the requirements which have to be satisfied by a measure of ambiguity, differently from the probabilistic case, do not uniquely determine the entropy measure (see,for instance, the recent considerations made by Trillas and Riera [8]). This is not a weakness of the theory since the particular form of the functional has to be strictly related to the context and use of the measure. We emphasize that, even in the probabilistic setting, the importance of measures of uncertainty or of information different from the Shannon one have,been stressed by some authors as Vajda [9] for statistical pattern recognition and White [10] for decision theory. Moreover, in pattern recognition a number-valued measure has to be replaced with a vector-valued one, when noncomparable properties are needed for the classification of the objects [11, 12]. A remarkable class of entropy measures u is the one obtained by replacing in (2.2) the function S with a function T defined as $T(x) := \mu(x) + \mu(1-x)$ where μ

is a continuous and concave function such that $\lim_{x\to 0} \mu(x) = \lim_{x\to 1} \mu(x) = 0$ [13, 14] . The function μ can be written for $x \in (0,1)$ as $\mu(x) = xL(1/x)$, where L is a continuous concave function in $[1, +\infty)$ which reduces to the logarithm function in the case of the entropy d(f). We refer the reader to [12, 15] for a detailed examination of some properties of the functional u; here we only remember that a) an interesting relationship subsists between u and P, in fact from the concavity of μ it follows that $u(f) \leq |I| \quad T(P(t)/ |I|)$ where $|I|$ is the cardinality of I ; b) u is a (lattice-theoretic) *valuation* on $\mathcal{L}(I)$, that is

$$u(f \vee g) + u(f \wedge g) = u(f) + u(g), \text{ for all f and g of } \mathcal{L}(I).$$

In the case of an infinite support I a preliminary problem is the one of the existence of the entropy. This problem can be faced with the technique of measure theory, under suitable assumptions on the functions f and the set-theoretic measure of I, as has been made by Knopfmacher [7].

A worth-noting case, that is not included in the previous scheme, is the natural extension of the entropy measures u when the support I is denumerable. In the case of logarithmic entropy d a necessary and sufficient condition for the convergence of d is given by the following:

Theorem [14] . *For any fuzzy set f of $\mathcal{L}(I)$ the logarithmic entropy d(f) is convergent if and only if $P(f \wedge \bar{f}) < +\infty$ and the series $\sum_{n=1}^{\infty} (f \wedge \bar{f})_n^{\circ} \ln n < \infty$ where $(f \wedge \bar{f})_n^{\circ}$ denotes the n-th value of the fuzzy set $(f \wedge \bar{f})^{\circ}$ which is obtained by arranging the values of $f \wedge \bar{f}$ in a nonincreasing order.*

In the general case of measures u an analogous, only necessary, condition has been shown in [15] . We moreover remember that, in any case, the convergence of u implies the convergence of the power $P(f \wedge \bar{f})$ of the fuzzy set $f \wedge \bar{f}$ and that $P(f \wedge \bar{f}) < +\infty$ iff the measure of fuzziness $\sigma(f) := \sum_{x \in I} f(x) [1-f(x)] < +\infty$.

3. *Informational Interpretation of the Notion of Entropy and its Relation to Decision Processes*

In this paragraph we shall briefly outline the way in which it is possible to interpret the entropy measures of a fuzzy set as measures of the information needed in order to take a decision.

The main points of the brief overview are the following:

a) A distinction of two principal decision processes.

b) The individuation of a subclass of the class of all the possible decisions that we shall call class of *coherent* decisions.

c) The interpretation of the degree of fuzziness f(x) as a sort of average obtained by taking into account only the coherent decisions *("frequentistic" interpretation of a fuzzy set - with respect to coherent decisions).*

Let us first of all outline a main difference between two (of all the possible) decision techniques. The first one that we may call of *"fixed paradigms"* consists in considering as *a-priori given* two ideal classes of prototypes possessing two measurable *orthogonal* properties [12] (for instance the class of *white* and *black* objects). The process of decision then consists in assigning each of the elements of our universe to one of the two classes. For those objects which possess with certainty one of the two properties (and then, being the two properties orthogonal, which do not possess with certainty the other one) there is no problem; those objects which possess it with a certain degree are forced by the act of decision in one of the two classes according to some accepted (and reasonable) rules. At the end of this process then we have divided our universe into two parts by transforming our fuzzy set describing the situation into a classical characteristic function. Three features of this kind of decision procedure are worthnoting: a) the process has not changed our prototypes (our conception of "black" and "white", in our simple example); b) a decision generally changes the membership values and then the power of the fuzzy set; c) every decision is not influenced by the previous ones. The second process which can be called of *"changing paradigms"* is based on the assumption that the properties according to which we want to divide our universe into two classes *are not fixed (and existing) a priori* but are changed by the decision process. That is, we start from two initial prototypes, for instance the elements x of I whose value f(x) is respectively 0 and 1 (*kernels* of the properties) if they exist, otherwise the elements of I which assume respectively the maximum and the minimum values on [0,1]. The following steps are to extend these initial kernels by adjoining other elements according to some rules. Moreover the rules have to be such as to consider as prototype of the property, step by step, the new class obtained by adjoining the new elements. Conceptually this corresponds to a conception of the world in which the properties are not platonically existing and given once and for all but are modified (according to the context) on the basis of the new acquired informations. Some implications of this second approach is that a) the membership value f(x) of the element x on which the decision is taken does not change; b) what has changed after the decision process are the properties themselves; c) every decision is strongly influenced by the previous ones; there can be, then, a sort of *"learning process"*.

Formally, a decision D over $\mathcal{L}(I)$ can be defined as any map $D: I \times [0,1] \to \{0,1\}$, where the values 0 and 1 of the range of D refer to one of the two properties which has to be attributed to the elements of I. Furthermore it is natural to add the condition that $D(x,0)=0$ and $D(x,1)=1$ for all x of I.

In [6] we gave an interpretation of the logarithmic entropy d(f) of a fuzzy set f, relative to the first kind of decision process, as a measure (by definition) of the total amount of information missed in a fuzzy pattern and that one needs in order to have no uncertainty in the classification of the objects of I. When anyone of the possible decisions takes place the final entropy vanishes and one receives an amount of information measured just by d(f). This informational interpretation of d(f) (and which can be also extended to measures u(f)) is quite different from that of probabilistic entropy since this latter quantity gives (by definition) a measure of the (average) information needed in order to make a prevision about the result of a random experiment.

More complex appears the interpretation of the entropy of a fuzzy set as a quantity of information in the setting of the second decision process and it will not be considered here. In fact one has to give a more detailed description of the decision process itself. Intuitively there is, step by step, a gain of information related to the underlying "learning process".

We observe that it is possible, however, to give to the entropy of a fuzzy set an interpretation similar to that of probabilistic information by making suitable hypothesis on the decisions.

Let us define, for instance, the subclass of the *coherent* decisions in the following way:

A decision D is coherent iff $D(x, \alpha) = 1 \rightarrow D(x, \beta) = 1$ for all $\beta > \alpha$ and for all x of I.

The following result holds:

For any f of $\mathcal{L}(I)$ the membership value f(x) of x is equal to the average $\langle D(f(x),x) \rangle$ of D(f(x),x) with respect to all the coherent decisions. Moreover, if we associate to a single decision D over f a measure of uncertainty I(D,f) equal to

$$I(D,f) \ : = \sum_{x \in I} \{ D(f(x),x) \ L(1/f(x)) + (1-D(f(x),x)) \ L(1/(1-f(x))) \}$$

then the average of I(D,f) with respect to all the coherent decisions D is just equal to the entropy u(f) : $\langle I(D,f) \rangle = u(f)$.

The proof of the previous property is quite direct but, due to lack of space, will not be given here. We want, instead, to make few comments on the result. If we restrict ourselves to the coherent decisions, I(D,f) can be seen as a measure of the *"unforseeability"* of the decision D itself and the membership value f(x) as the frequency with which a coherent decision will give the answer 1. The interpretation of the entropy measure of a fuzzy set as a measure of (missing) information in order to take a decision is then quite similar to the one of the probabilistic entropy in the case of a probabilistic scheme. Let us stress that nevertheless the strong analogy a main conceptual difference subsists. In the case of the frequentistic conception of probability the occurrence of an event is something independent of the context, while in the previous decision scheme this notion has been substituted with something strictly related to the decision criteria, i.e. to the context.

4. *Some Remarks on the Notion of Information.*

At the end of the previous Section we arrived at the conclusion that passing from the probabilistic setting to a decision-theoretic one, the notion of entropy considered as a measure of information, apart from formal similarities and differences, became relativized to the context in which it is considered. We want to stress that this is the case in general for those notions like *"ambiguity"* and *"information"* that do not admit a unique formalization. However, this is not a defect but corresponds to the present and actual development of these notions and the related quantitative theories. An uncritical use and extension of Shannon entropy outside its original field of definition and also of a probabilistic setting originated many conceptual difficulties [16,17] .

We do not enter here into details for which we refer to our paper [18] but briefly observe that two main conceptions about the notion of information exist: the *entropic* and the *logical-algorithmic* one of Kolmogorov and Chaitin. This latter relates the notion of information to the set of data required *"to produce"* an object of a given class. According to the first conception, information is related to the *"ignorance"* about the particular determination that an object can assume inside a class of possible ones. As regards this last conception we note that the different measures of uncertainty which have been introduced in different contexts and based on the notion of measures of "ignorance" have a substantially similar mathematical structure which can be essentially always reduced to the combinatorial model of information, i.e. to determine an object, even if with different weights (as in the probabilistic case) within a given set. The situation appears to be completely different in the case of fuzzy sets since the membership relation is not $\{0,1\}$ -valued.

The mathematical structure of such an information theory is then outside the standard setting of mathematical theory of probability.

The next step in this direction is to insert the various different results we now possess into a unitary mathematical framework allowing a general treatment of decision processes.

References.

1. A. De Luca, S. Termini - Algorithmic Aspects in Complex System Analysis - *Scientia, 106, 659 (1971)*

2. G. J. Chaitin - Information-Theoretic Computational Complexity- *IEEE Trans. on Information Theory IT 20, 10-15 (1974)*

3. L.A. Zadeh - Fuzzy Sets - *Information and Control 8, 338 (1965)*

4. L.A. Zadeh - Probability Measures of fuzzy events - *J. Math. Anal. Appl. 23, 421 (1968)*

5. A. Kaufmann - *Introduction to the Theory of Fuzzy Subsets, Vol. 1 - Fundamental Theoretical Elements*. Academic Press, New York (1975) (see, in particular, page 27).

6. A. De Luca, S. Termini - A Definition of a Non-probabilistic Entropy in the Setting of Fuzzy Sets Theory - *Information and Control 20, 301 (1972)*

7. J. Knopfmacher - On Measures of Fuzziness - *J. Math. Anal. Appl. 49, 529 (1975)*

8. E. Trillas and T. Riera - Sobre la Entropia de Conjuntos Difusos Finitos - *Preprint E.T.S., Universidad Politecnica de Barcelona (1977)*

9. I. Vajda - A Contribution to the Informational Analysis of Pattern - *"Methodologies of Pattern Recognition"* (S. Watanabe ed.), 509, Academic Press, New York (1969).

10. D. J. White - Entropy and Decision - *Opl. Res. Q., 26, 15 (1975)*

11. J. A. Goguen - L-Fuzzy Sets - *J. Math. Anal. Appl. 18, 145 (1967)*

12. A. De Luca, S. Termini - Entropy of L-Fuzzy Sets - *Information and Control 24, 55 (1974)*

13. R. Capocelli, A. De Luca - Fuzzy Sets and Decision Theory - *Information and Control 23, 446 (1973)*

14. A. De Luca, S. Termini - Una Condizione Necessaria e Sufficiente per la Convergenza dell'Entropia Logaritmica di un "Fuzzy-set". *Proc. IV Congresso di Cibernetica e Biofisica, Siena (Italy), Ottobre 1976.*

15. A. De Luca and S. Termini - On the Convergence of Entropy Measures of a Fuzzy Set - *Kybernetes, July 1977.*

16. R. Arnheim - *Entropy and Art* - University of California Press, Berkeley (1971)

17. S. Termini - Appunti per una Definizione di Cibernetica - *Proc. IV Congresso di Cibernetica e Biofisica - Siena (Italy), Ottobre 1976.*

18. A. De Luca and S. Termini - On some quantitative aspects of the notion of information *(preprint).*

TWO-LEVEL META-CONTROLLED SUBSTITUTION GRAMMARS

R. Meersman and G. Rozenberg
Department of Mathematics
University of Antwerp (U.I.A)
B-2610 Wilrijk, Belgium

ABSTRACT

A new language-generating mechanism, inspired on the two-level Van Wijngaarden syntax for Algol 68, is defined. Its language generating properties are studied and compared to those of well-known classical systems and grammars. The new mechanism is called a 2MSG, for "two-level meta-controlled substitution grammar."

§0. INTRODUCTION AND MOTIVATION

In 1969, Van Wijngaarden [9] introduced the mechanism of two-level grammar into formal language theory. This was intended to describe the syntax and semantics of ALGOL 68. Since then, these grammars have been studied in several ways [1],[4]. When carefully considering the formalism, one observes that a two-level grammar, 1) has a possibly infinite set of variables, 2) has a possibly infinite set of productions, 3) the actual productions and variables can be supplied by an "auxiliary" context-free grammar, the top level, 4) this happens by substituting words from the language of the top level for "placeholders" in a finite set of context-free productions, the "rule schemes" or lower level, and 5) this substitution is done in a particular (synchronized) manner, reminiscent of "indian parallel" [7] since equal placeholders in the rule schemes are to be replaced by equal words supplied by the top level. The whole mechanism is controlled by a meta-alphabet (the placeholders in a way) which triggers the call for substitution from the top level. Thus, it can be argued that a two-level grammar results in fact from the interaction of three (!) grammar mechanisms. In this paper we want to focus on this "hidden third", or delivery grammar and investigate which is its role in the language-generating power of a two-level grammar. A two-level grammar derives this power predominantly from two facts; 1) although the lower level "looks" context-free, it can rewrite whole substrings because the placeholders are allowed to be also the left-hand side of a production, and as a matter of fact a bracketing mechanism [4],[1] is needed to keep this in check; and 2) the synchronization of the substitution in indian-parallel fashion. As expressed before, we shall study the second mechanism more profoundly in this paper and therefore we have considered it not unwise to dispense with the first, i.e. our grammars do not allow rewriting rules for meta symbols on the lower level and hence do not need the bracketing mechanism. This restriction of the original Van Wijngaarden formalism brings us closer to the theory of iteration grammars.

In our present framework, natural questions such as "Can the synchronization mechanism be omitted and replaced by synchronization on lower or upper level?" can be asked and are, in fact, answered. Indeed several rather interesting inclusions and equalities are shown to hold between different types of two-level substitution grammars, as we shall call them. For this we needed a formalism and notation allowing us to view a grammar as a "chip" to be inserted or replaced in the two-level "module", in order to study its effect on the language-generating power; in particular the dependence on the type of derivation used is stressed. Thus we have found it useful to redefine the notion of grammar in such a way that the actual derivation (relation) is part of the "chip". As the last motivation, we can rather dramatically illustrate the importance of the "third" grammar mechanism even with the full bracketing mechanism present, by the following theorem.

0.1. Theorem [for definitions, see [1],[4] or this paper.]
If G is a Van-Wijngaarden two level grammar without the condition that equal meta-variables must be substituted by equal words from the top level, then $L(G) \in \mathcal{L}(CF)$. ■
In short, without indian-parallel synchronization, Van Wijngaarden syntaxes generate nothing more than context-free languages!

§1. PRELIMINARY NOTIONS

Knowledge is assumed of formal language theory as found in [2], [3],[6]. However in this paper we have found it useful to define the grammar concept in a slightly different manner to emphasize its derivation mechanism. This is done since we will compare and use in conjunction grammars of different "types". We introduce some notation and terminology.

N 1.1 Notation
An alphabet is a finite set of letters. If A is an alphabet, $A^\star$ and A^+ are respectively the sets of words and nonempty words over A. The empty word is denoted Λ. If A and B are alphabets, $[A \to B^\star]$ is the set of objects $\{a \to w \mid a \in A,\ w \in B^\star\}$, called productions. The length of a word w is denoted $|w|$. The complement of a set V relative to a universe W is denoted $W \setminus V$, and ${}^cV$ if W is understood. For a production $\pi : a \to w$ we shall denote its right hand side, w, by $RH(\pi)$ and its left hand side, a, by $LH(\pi)$. ■

D 1.2 Definition
A grammar scheme is a construct $G = \langle V, F, \Rightarrow \rangle$ where V is an alphabet, $F \subset V^\star$ called the filter, and $\Rightarrow$ is a binary relation, $\Rightarrow \subset V^+ \times V^\star$, called the derivation relation of G. A grammar is a construct $G = \langle V, F, \Rightarrow, w \rangle$ where $\langle V, F, \Rightarrow \rangle$ is a grammar scheme and $w \in V$, the axiom of G. When $(v,w) \in \Rightarrow$ we shall say that v directly derives w in G and write it $v \underset{G}{\Rightarrow} w$.
Let $\overset{\star}{\Rightarrow}$ be the transitive and reflexive closure of $\Rightarrow$. When $v \overset{\star}{\underset{G}{\Rightarrow}} w$, we say that v derives w in G. Put $\xrightarrow{\Delta(F)} = \overset{\star}{\Rightarrow} \cap (V^+ \times F)$, the F-derivation relation of G; when $(v,w) \in \xrightarrow{\Delta(F)}$ we say that v F-derives w in G and write $v \underset{G}{\xrightarrow{\Delta(F)}} w$.

E 1.3 Examples

Let $G = \langle V,F,\Rightarrow\rangle$ be given. The following special choices for V,F and $\Rightarrow$ give well-known language generating devices.

a) $F = \Sigma^\star$ for some $\Sigma \subset V$, called the terminals, and $\underset{G}{\Rightarrow}$ is defined by a finite production set $R_G \subset [V\setminus\Sigma \to V^\star]$ such that $v \underset{G}{\Rightarrow} w$ iff there exists $A \to \alpha \in R_G$ and $v = \gamma_1 A\gamma_2$, $w = \gamma_1\alpha\gamma_2$ for some $\gamma_1,\gamma_2 \in V^\star$. In this case G is called a context-free grammar scheme. (CF grammar scheme).

b) $F = \Sigma^\star, \Sigma \subset V$, and $\Rightarrow$ is total and defined by a finite production set $R_G \subset [V \to V^\star]$ such that $v \underset{G}{\Rightarrow} w$ iff $v = A_1 \ldots A_k$, $w = \alpha_1 \ldots \alpha_k$ and $A_i \to \alpha_i \in R_G$ for $i = 1,\ldots,k$. The reader should recognize G as an EOL-grammar scheme.

c) F and $\Rightarrow$ are as in example (a), only now $v \underset{G}{\Rightarrow} w$ iff $v = \gamma_1 A\gamma_2 A \ldots \gamma_k A\gamma_{k+1}$, $w = \gamma_1\alpha\gamma_2\alpha \ \ \gamma_k\alpha\gamma_{k+1}$, $A \to \alpha \in R_G$ and $\gamma_i \in (V\setminus\{A\})^\star$ for $i = 1,\ldots,k+1$. Here we have an Indian-Parallel grammar scheme (IP grammar scheme).

D 1.4 Definition

A grammar scheme $G = \langle V,F,\Rightarrow\rangle$ is a production grammar scheme if its derivation relation $\Rightarrow$ is given as a finite set of productions $R \subset [V \to V^\star]$ and an algorithm A (called the extension algorithm of G) extending a relation in $V \times V^\star$ to a relation in $V^\star \times V^\star$ such that $\Rightarrow = A(R)$. In this case we say that $\Rightarrow$ is A-generated from R. If R is allowed to be infinite, we say that G is an unbounded production grammar scheme. These notions carry over to grammars in the obvious manner. ∎

The reader should have no difficulty to determine the extension relations for the grammar mechansims of, say, E 1.3.

R 1.5 Remarks and terminology

a. All grammar schemes form Example 1.3 are production grammar schemes. In this paper we shall only consider these and shall often refer to them just as "grammar schemes" or "grammars".

b. With the relation $\Rightarrow$ of a grammar there is naturally associated its domain, $\mathrm{Dom}(\Rightarrow)$, the projection of $\Rightarrow$ on its first component V^+. Note that for CF grammars and IP grammars, $\mathrm{Dom}(\Rightarrow) = {}^cF$ ("terminals are not rewritten") while for EOL $F \subset \mathrm{Dom}(\Rightarrow) \cup \{\Lambda\}$.

c. For words $v,w \in V^\star$ and a grammar scheme $G = \langle V,F,\Rightarrow\rangle$ we shall denote $v \overset{\vee}{\underset{G}{\Rightarrow}} w$ iff $v \overset{\star}{\underset{G}{\Rightarrow}} w$ and $w \notin \mathrm{Dom}(\Rightarrow)$. In relational notation, $\overset{\vee}{\Rightarrow} = \overset{\star}{\Rightarrow} \cap (V^+ \times {}^c\mathrm{Dom}(\Rightarrow))$. ∎

D 1.6 Definition

Let $G = \langle V,F,\Rightarrow,\omega\rangle$ be a grammar. The language of G, denoted L(G), is the set

$$L(G) = \{w \mid \omega \overset{\Delta(F)}{\underset{G}{\Longrightarrow}} w\}.$$

If $\mathbf{G}$ is a family of grammars, we write $\mathcal{L}(\mathbf{G})$ for the class of languages generated by the grammars in $\mathbf{G}$ (e.g. $\mathcal{L}(\mathrm{IP})$, $\mathcal{L}(\mathrm{CF})$ etc.) ∎

We are now in a position to give the basic definition of this paper, the two level grammar.

D 1.7 Definition

A two-level (meta-controlled) substitution grammar (2MSG) is a construct $K = \langle V, M, F, \underset{\ell}{\Rightarrow}, \underset{d}{\Rightarrow}, \underset{u}{\Rightarrow}, \omega \rangle$ such that V, M are alphabets, $M \subset V$, $\omega \in V \setminus M$ and $F \subset (V \setminus M)^*$; $L = \langle V, F, \underset{\ell}{\Rightarrow}, \omega \rangle$ is a production grammar with production set $R_\ell \subset [V \setminus M \to V^*]$; $U = \langle V, (V \setminus M)^*, \underset{u}{\Rightarrow} \rangle$ is a grammar scheme; $\underset{d}{\Rightarrow}$ is a derivation relation on $V^+ \times V^*$ generated from the (possibly infinite) production set $R_d = \bigcup_{m \in M} [m \to L(\langle U, m \rangle)]$ where $\langle U, m \rangle$ is the grammar obtained from U by adjoining to it the axiom m.

We name M the metaalphabet, $V \setminus M$ the protoalphabet, L the lower level, U the upper level and $\underset{d}{\Rightarrow}$ the delivery mechanism. The unbounded production grammar scheme $D = \langle V, (V \setminus M)^*, \underset{d}{\Rightarrow} \rangle$ will sometimes be called the delivery level. ■

A 2MSG can be used to generate languages in several ways. Two important ones are the local mechanism and the global mechanism, both defined below although this paper deals only with the former while we reserve the latter for a next paper.

Suppose a 2MSG K is given as above. It is useful to consider $\underset{\ell}{\Rightarrow}$ as the disjoint union of relations $\underset{\ell P}{\Longrightarrow}$ and $\underset{\ell M}{\Longrightarrow}$ where $\underset{\ell P}{\Longrightarrow} = \underset{\ell}{\Rightarrow} \cap ((V \setminus M) \times (V \setminus M)^*)$. The corresponding productions $R_{\ell P}$ are called pure protoproductions, we also have $R_\ell = R_{\ell P} \cup R_{\ell M}$ with $R_{\ell P} \cap R_{\ell M} = \phi$. Clearly $\underset{\ell M}{\Longrightarrow}$ is generated from $R_{\ell M}$ in an analogous manner.

From $R_{\ell M}$, construct the set $R^{\#}_{\ell M}$ defined as below :

$$R^{\#}_{\ell M} = \left\{ a \to [\![\alpha]\!] \,\middle|\, (a \to \alpha) \in R_{\ell M} \right\}, \text{ where }]\!] \text{ and } [\![\text{ are new symbols,}$$

and denote the corresponding direct derivation relation by $\overset{\#}{\underset{\ell M}{\Longrightarrow}}$.

Define the (partial) substitution $\delta_d : [\![V^+]\!] \to 2^{V^*}$ by

$$\delta_d([\![\alpha]\!]) = \{ \beta \mid \alpha \overset{\Delta(V \setminus M)^*}{\underset{d}{\Longrightarrow}} \beta \}.$$

We will use $\delta_d(R^{\#}_{\ell M})$ to denote the set $\{ a \to \beta : a \to [\![\alpha]\!] \text{ is in } R^{\#}_{\ell M} \text{ and } \beta \in \delta_d([\![\alpha]\!]) \}$; although this constitutes a slight abuse of notation, no confusion should arise.

Let δ^*_d be the usual (homomorphic) extension of δ_d to words over $[\![V^+]\!] \cup (V \setminus M)$ by setting $\delta^*_d(a) = a$ for all $a \in V \setminus M$. With all this, we can now define the language of a 2MSG.

D 1.8 Definition

1) The local (delivery) language of a 2MSG K, denoted $L_p(K)$, is defined as follows.

Let $v \underset{K}{\Rightarrow} w$ iff $v \underset{\ell P}{\Longrightarrow} w$, or

$$v \overset{\#}{\underset{\ell M}{\Longrightarrow}} w' \text{ and } w \in \delta^*(w').$$

Then $L_p(K) = \{ w \mid \omega \overset{\Delta(F)}{\underset{K}{\Longrightarrow}} w \}$

2) The global (delivery) language of a 2MSG K, denoted $L_g(K)$, is defined as follows.

Let $\underset{Kg}{\Longrightarrow}$ be the relation generated by the extension algorithm of L from

$R_{\ell P} \cup \delta_d(R^{\#}_{\ell M})$. Then $L_g(K) = \{w \mid \omega \xrightarrow[K\ g]{\Delta(F)} w\}$. ■

R 1.9 Remarks

a. The formalism above appears quite involved and possibly requires some explanation and motivation. Essentially a two-level grammar consists of a lower level L which is incomplete in the sense that for some symbols, the metasymbols in M, there are no productions. This in itself is nothing peculiar since in E 1.3 one can see that e.g. for a CF grammar, elements of the terminal alphabet Σ are also not rewritten once they are "produced". However, a 2MSG when producing a metasymbol can "call for help" from the upper level through the delivery level. The grammar scheme U takes a metasymbol as axiom and derives words in $(V \setminus M)^{\star}$ for it. This is done for each metasymbol appearing in the right hand side of the production just applied, and then the delivery mechanism selects a word for each metasymbol in some well-defined way. Now this can be considered from two viewpoints : either we allow the delivery to act only locally, that is, the particular selection of words from the upper level languages only holds within the range of one production, and thus the selection may differ for the possibly several right-hand sides of productions applied at this moment by L; or delivery can act globally in the sense that the selection of a word for every appearing metasymbol is done only once at each step and then applied, again in a well-defined way, to all occurrences of those metasymbols.

Technically, to recognize the right-hand sides of the production(s) applied, we mark them with the double brackets ⟧ and ⟦ , otherwise they would "merge" with the rest of the word making local application impossible. It follows that for the global definition we can do without these brackets, and the reader is invited to check that actually $\underset{K^g}{\Longrightarrow} = \underset{\ell P}{\Longrightarrow} \cup (\underset{\ell M}{\Longrightarrow} \xrightarrow[d]{\Delta(V \setminus M)^{\star}})$. The substitution $\delta^{\star}_d$ finally replaces the words within the brackets by "protowords" in an independent manner while leaving protosymbols untouched. Although a discussion of such matters is scheduled for a next paper, it should already be apparent that for instance $L_p(K) = L_g(K)$ if $\underset{\ell}{\Rightarrow}$ is context-free since only a single production is applied at each ℓ-step.

b. The original notion of a two-level grammar comes from Van Wijngaarden [9]. A concise definition is found in Greibach [4], and called a W-grammar. In a W-grammar, L and U are context-free and $D = \langle V, (V \setminus M), \underset{d}{\Rightarrow} \rangle$ is indian-parallel, but it is also equipped with a bracketing system allowing for a possibly infinite number of variables (A variable is a symbol appearing on the left-hand side of a production). As remarked above, since $\underset{\ell}{\Rightarrow}$ is CF, global and local mechanisms coincide and formally we have that a W-grammar is a construct $K = \langle V, M, \Sigma^{\star}, \underset{\ell}{\Rightarrow}, \underset{d}{\Rightarrow}, \underset{u}{\Rightarrow}, \omega \rangle$ with $\underset{\ell}{\Rightarrow}$ generated in CF-way from $R_\ell \subset [(V \setminus M) \cup \langle V^+ \rangle \to (V \cup \langle V^+ \rangle)^{\star}]$ where > and < are the brackets mentioned above (not to be confused with our ⟧ and ⟦ !), and $v \underset{K}{\Rightarrow} w$ iff, putting $P = (V \setminus M) \cup \langle (V \setminus M)^+ \rangle$, $v \in P^+$, $w \in P^{\star}$, $v \underset{\ell}{\Rightarrow} w$, or there exist v',w' with $v' \underset{\ell}{\Rightarrow} w'$ and $v'w' \xrightarrow[d]{\Delta(P^{\star})} vw$. We leave it to the reader to compare this with the definition in [4] and to see that by dropping the brackets > and < and setting $v = v'$ one is reduced again to our 2MSG. Note however that a W-grammar should be considered also as an interaction between three language-generating systems.

§2. RELATIONS BETWEEN CERTAIN TWO-LEVEL SUBSTITUTION GRAMMARS

In this section we intend to compare the language generating power (with local delivery) several 2MSG's namely those while can be constructed from the CF and IP mechanisms using the local language definition. There are eight such types of 2MSG.

N 2.1 Notation

Let L,D,U be the grammars (-schemes) associated with a 2MSG K. If $L \in G_\ell$, $D \in G_d$, $U \in G_u$, then we say that $K = \langle V,M,F,\underset{\ell}{\Rightarrow},\underset{d}{\Rightarrow},\underset{u}{\Rightarrow},\omega\rangle$ is of type (G_ℓ,G_d,G_u). The local language class generated by 2MSG's of this type is denoted $\mathcal{L}_p(G_\ell,G_d,G_u)$. ∎

The following eight types will be studied in relation to each other in this section and to other well-known classes in the next:

$\mathcal{L}_p(CF,CF,CF)$, $\mathcal{L}_p(CF,CF,IP)$, $\mathcal{L}_p(CF,IP,CF)$, $\mathcal{L}_p(IP,CF,CF)$, $\mathcal{L}_p(CF,IP,IP)$, $\mathcal{L}_p(IP,IP,CF)$, $\mathcal{L}_p(IP,CF,IP)$, $\mathcal{L}_p(IP,IP,IP)$.

T 2.2 Theorem For $G_1,G_3 \in \{CF,IP\}$, $\mathcal{L}_p(G_1,CF,G_3) \subseteq \mathcal{L}_p(G_1,IP,G_3)$.

L 2.3 Lemma $\mathcal{L}_p(CF,IP,IP) \subseteq \mathcal{L}_p(CF,CF,IP)$.

From T 2.2 and L 2.6, one has a.o.

T 2.4 Theorem $\mathcal{L}_p(CF,IP,IP) = \mathcal{L}_p(CF,CF,IP)$.

Comparing a CF lower level with an IP lower level, we found

T 2.5 Theorem For $G_2,G_3 \in \{CF,IP\}$, $\mathcal{L}_p(CF,G_2,G_3) \subseteq \mathcal{L}_p(IP,G_2,G_3)$.

When two 2MSG's of the above types differ in both upper and lower levels, and delivery is CF, one still has

L 2.6 Lemma $\mathcal{L}_p(CF,CF,IP) \subseteq \mathcal{L}_p(IP,CF,CF)$.

Finally,

L 2.7 Lemma $\mathcal{L}_p(IP,IP,IP) \subseteq \mathcal{L}_p(IP,CF,IP)$.

This implies with T 2.2,

T 2.8 Theorem $\mathcal{L}_p(IP,IP,IP) = \mathcal{L}_p(IP,CF,IP)$.

The results of this section can be summarized in the following scheme where as usual "$\mathcal{L}(G')$ connected to and above $\mathcal{L}(G)$" means $\mathcal{L}_p(G) \subseteq \mathcal{L}_p(G')$.

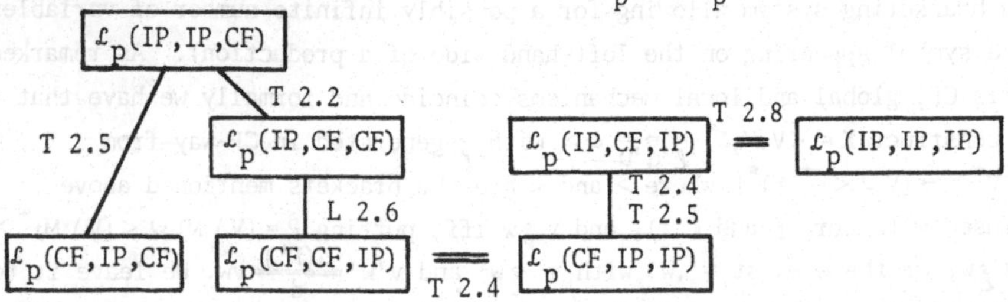

§3. RELATIONS BETWEEN 2MSG GRAMMARS AND OTHER LANGUAGE-GENERATING SYSTEMS

The following trivial result will be used sometimes implicitly.

L 3.1 Lemma $\mathcal{L}(G_\ell) \subseteq \mathcal{L}_p(G_\ell, G_d, G_u)$ for all G_ℓ, G_d, G_u. (Proof : Take $M = \emptyset$).

T 3.2 Theorem $\mathcal{L}_p(\mathrm{CF,CF,CF}) = \mathcal{L}(\mathrm{CF})$.

This result should not be surprising in view of T 0.1; nevertheless it required essentially different proof techniques.

T 3.3 Theorem For $G_1, G_2, G_3 \in \{\mathrm{CF,IP}\}$, $\mathcal{L}(\mathrm{CF}) \subseteq \mathcal{L}_p(G_1, G_2, G_3)$.

As for IP, a similar inclusion does not hold. Indeed, by a simple growth argument one proves

L 3.4 Lemma $\mathcal{L}(\mathrm{IP}) \not\subseteq \mathcal{L}_p(\mathrm{CF,IP,CF})$.

T 3.5 Theorem Let $G_2, G_3 \in \{\mathrm{CF,IP}\}$. Then $\mathcal{L}(\mathrm{IP}) \subseteq \mathcal{L}_p(\mathrm{IP}, G_2, G_3)$ and $\mathcal{L}(\mathrm{IP}) \subseteq \mathcal{L}_p(\mathrm{CF}, G_2, \mathrm{IP})$.

Since $\mathcal{L}(\mathrm{CF})$ and $\mathcal{L}(\mathrm{IP})$ are incomparable [8], we obtain the strict inclusions

C 3.6 Corollary $\mathcal{L}(\mathrm{CF}) \subsetneq \mathcal{L}_p(\mathrm{CF,CF,IP})$.

C 3.7 Corollary $\mathcal{L}(\mathrm{IP}) \subsetneq \mathcal{L}_p(\mathrm{CF,CF,IP})$.

L 3.8 Lemma $\mathcal{L}(\mathrm{CF}) \subsetneq \mathcal{L}_p(\mathrm{CF,IP,CF})$.

The above allows us to derive a strict inclusion between 2MSG's, namely

T 3.9 Theorem $\mathcal{L}_p(\mathrm{CF,IP,CF}) \subsetneq \mathcal{L}_p(\mathrm{IP,IP,CF})$.

The IP mechanism introduced a certain degree of parallelism into our 2MSG. Thus it is now natural to compare them with $\mathcal{L}(\mathrm{ET0L})$ (see e.g. [2]), the central class in L-systems theory.

L 3.10 Lemma $\mathcal{L}_p(\mathrm{CF,IP,CF}) \not\subseteq \mathcal{L}(\mathrm{ET0L})$.

C 3.11 Corollary $\mathcal{L}_p(\mathrm{IP,IP,CF}) \not\subseteq \mathcal{L}(\mathrm{ET0L})$.

L 3.12 Lemma $\mathcal{L}_p(\mathrm{IP,CF},G_3) \subseteq \mathcal{L}(\mathrm{ET0L})$ for $G_3 \in \{\mathrm{CF,IP}\}$.

Again summarizing the result obtained in a diagram, one has

T 3.13 Theorem The following relations hold among the language classes indicated. A directed path denotes a strict inclusion.

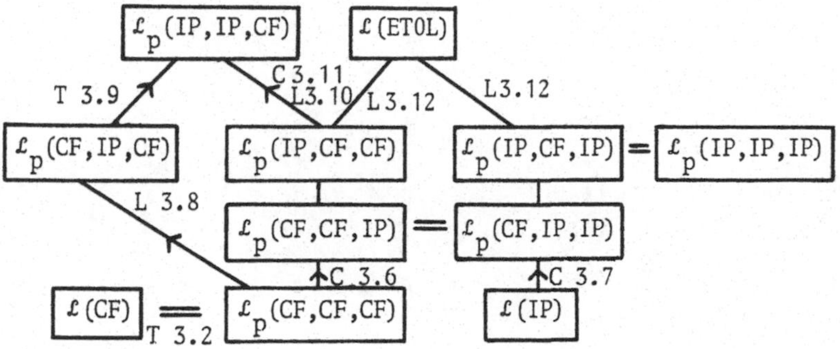

<u>REFERENCES</u>

1. Baker, J.L., Grammars with Structured Vocabulary: a Model for the ALGOL 68 Definition. <u>Information and Control</u>, <u>20</u> (1972), 351-398.
2. Herman, G. and Rozenberg, G., <u>Developmental Systems and Languages.</u> North Holland, 1974.
3. Hopcroft, J. and Ullman, J., <u>Formal Languages and Their Relation to Automata.</u> Addison-Wesley, 1969.
4. Greibach, S., Some Restrictions on W-grammars", <u>Int. J. of Comp. and Inf. Sc.,</u> <u>3</u> (1974), 289-327.
5. Meersman, R. and Rozenberg, G., Two-level Synchronized-Grammars. Report of the Dept. of Math. U.I.A. 76-26, 1976.
6. Salomaa, A., <u>Formal Languages.</u> Academic Press, 1973.
7. Salomaa, A., Parallelism in Rewriting Systems, in "<u>Automata, Languages and Programming</u> (Loeckx J. Ed.). <u>Lecture Notes in Computer Science, Vol.</u> <u>14</u>, Springer Verlag, 1974.
8. Skyum, S., Parallel Context-free Languages. <u>Information and Control</u>, <u>25</u> 1974 , 280-285.
9. Van Wijngaarden, A., Report on the algorithmic language ALGOL 68. <u>Num. Math.</u>, <u>14</u> (1969), 79-218.

A CALCULUS TO BUILD UP CORRECT PROGRAMS

P.A.Miglioli, M. Ornaghi

Istituto di Cibernetica dell'Università di Milano

Via Viotti, 5, 20133 Milano, Italy

Introduction.

In the last years, many authors have investigated the problem of the synthesis of programs according to the following schema:

Problem: given a motivaton defined in some language, build up an algorithm expressed in some formalism, i.e. a procedural definition having the same "meaning" as the non procedural one represented by the motivation.

A precise formulation of the above problem involves the following questions:

A. One has to define the motivation language $\mathcal{L}_m$ and to assign a meaning to motivations

B. One has to choose the formalism $\mathcal{Q}$ to write down the algorithms and has to assign a meaning to the latter

C. One has to investigate the synthesis-maps, intended as computable functions $S : \mathcal{L}_m \to \mathcal{Q}$.

In this introduction, we will briefly review the most significant papers on the subject; we will distinguish two different attitudes:

I. The informal attitude: points A and B are not clearly defined and are analyzed informally, starting from the well known notion of function computed (or defined) by an algorithm and from an intuitive interpretation (a "common sense" interpretation) of the motivations; point C is usually investigated by euristic methods. There are many examples in literature of such an attitude [7, 8].

II. The formal attitude: it requires a well defined (formal) frame in which points A and B can be precisely stated and which allows the developement of some criteria and techniques in order to systematically investigate point C. Here, the formalism adopted to define the motivations and to state the meaning of algorithms is generally inspired by formal logic, while there is a wide range of choises for the algorithmic language $\mathcal{Q}$. In this attitude, we may distinguish two different ways to write down motivations, from which different developements of point C arise:

(a) for the first one, the typical frame is the predicate calculus [2, 3, 11] or any other formalism suitable to specify properties in a context less restrictive than the one of a formal theory describing a specific structure; e.g. the set theoretic formalism used in [5] (see also [1]); here, one defines the problem (or the motivation), to be solved, essentially by means of a description of its properties in the chosen formalism, and a motivation is something as: "build up an algorithm which computes a function satisfying the given properties".

(b) for the second point of view, the frame is defined by a formal theory describing a specific but powerful enough structure (for instance a number theory T_N, which allows induction proofs), where one expresses the function to be computed by a formula of the theory; here a motivation is something as: "construct an algorithm to compute the function expressed by the formula" [4, 6, 10, 13, 14]

The aim of our paper is to describe a synthesis-procedure based on a Gentzen-like calculus, to which special "construction-rules" (synthesis-rules) are added. More precisely, the proposed synthesis-procedure arises from a merging of the synthesis-method in T_{NI} expounded in [6] (T_{NI} is Kleene's intuitionistic number theory) and of the assertion-method to verify the correctness of programs.

The synthesis-method in T_{NI} is outlined in the following schema:

- the synthesis-problem ("motivation") is expressed by a formula of the language of T_{NI}, a formula such as $\exists z\ \psi(x,z)$, which is to be interpreted in the following way: "for every $\hat{x}$ such that $\models \exists z\ \psi(\tilde{x},z)$ holds, find a value $\hat{z}$ such that $\models \psi(\tilde{x},\tilde{z})$" (NOTE 1)
- the synthesis is obtained by applying a standard proof-procedure, in order to verify the i.w.c.-ness property of the formula $\exists z\ \psi(x,z)$ (for the definition of "i.w.c.-ness", we send to [6]); starting from such a verification, one can automatically construct a program to compute, for every $\hat{x}$ such that $\models \exists z\ \psi(\tilde{x},z)$, an appropriate $\hat{z}$ such that $\models \psi(\tilde{x},\tilde{z})$ (there is, indeed, an implementable algorithm to do so, expounded in [6]).

On the other hand the assertion method requires (as it is well known) to associa-

- - - - - - - - - -

NOTE 1. "$\models$" means "validity" on the structure of the natural numbers (according to the definition of validity for the classical theories -i.e., we do not attach any sophisticated meaning to our "motivations", even if our procedure is based on intuitionism-); $\hat{x}$ denotes a natural number and $\tilde{x}$ denotes the corresponding numeral in the language of the theory.

te "assertions" to some points of a program and to verify that such assertions are "invariant" with respect to the various computations; in particular, the output assertion must describe the intended relation between the input and the output values of the program, i.e. it must be a description of the function (of the relation) to be computed (see [12] ; see also [9]).

The unification of the synthesis-procedure in T_{NI} and of the assertion-method is based on the following facts:

1. From Hoare's rules for correctness, it is possible to extract, by analogy, a set of "construction-rules" which enable, given two assertions, to construct a statement (assignment, if-then-else, do-while) having the first one as the input assertion and the second one as the output assertion; these rules can be applied, however, only if the two assertions have a particular and well defined structure (for some examples, see [16]).
2. From the synthesis-procedure in T_{NI} one can obtain a systematical method to transform two given assertions from their initial form into a form which is appropriate in order to apply the construction-rules; this method is based on a top-down procedure to achieve the standardized proof of the i.w.c.-ness property of a formula [6].

Thus the proposed calculus consists in a set of "assertion-modifying" rules, allowing to obtain standard i.w.c.-ness proofs, and in a set of construction-rules (see point 1), allowing to introduce tests and assignments in a "logical proof". In other words, the assertion-modifying rules, the construction-rules and the transformation-rules, allowing top-down-ness, define a "deductive calculus" to systematically derive correct programs equiped by input assertions, intermediate assertions and output assertions: the rules of the calculus work in such a way that a program is built up together with these assertions.

1. The calculus.

As we have said above, our calculus consists of "purely logical rules" (the assertion-modifying rules, which, alone, give rise to a Gentzen-like logical calculus) and of "construction-rules", which allow to introduce program-statements. These two kinds of rules, however, do not work separately, but co-operate in building up structures which, generally, neither are "pure proofs" nor are "pure programs", but are "asserted programs" (even if there are cases where such constructions may be pure proofs, i.e., when only assertion modifying rules are applied; the pure programs are not allowed). In this line, our rules are graph-manipulation rules: we distinguish the zero-premisses rules, allowing the construction of elementary graphs, from the many (one or more) premisses rules, allowing to connect previously constructed graphs into a new graph.

To better understand the explanation of our rules, the following remarks are in order.

= In a graph the nodes are either logical formulas, or assignment-statements, or test-statements.

A formula-node may be:

(1) a node with only input arcs (bottom-formula);

(2) a node with one output arc and no input arcs (top-formula);

(3) a node with input arcs (one or more) and output arcs(intermediate formula).

An assignment-node -a test-node- has always input arcs (coming from formula-nodes) and one output arc -two output arcs- (entering into a formula-node).

= By the above, the entries of our graphs are top-formulas and the exits are bottom-formulas; since they may contain test-nodes, they may have more than one exit (in the particular case where they are pure proof-graphs they have only one exit, the proved formula, and essentially coincide with the usual proof-trees).

= Our graphs may contain assignment-nodes, which are of two kinds:

(1) $w := \tau$ (basic assignment, where τ is a term and w is the assigned variable);

(2) $w \,/\, A(\underline{x},w)$ (high-level assignment, where $A(\underline{x},w)$ is a formula and w is the assigned variable).

= The assigned variables in a graph play a particular role (they have a "contextual meaning"). These variables may appear not bound by quantifiers also in formula-nodes: in this case they are considered as bound variables (contextually bound variables).

= One has to carefully analyze the unquantified variables occurring in the top and in the bottom formulas of a graph: if a top formula -a bottom formula- contains a variable which is not quantified but is contextually bound in the graph, it is said to be a "contextual top-formula" -a "contextual bottom-formula"- .

= To explain the many premisses rules, we need a notation for graph-schemas: a graph-schema will be represented as in fig.1, where some top-formulas (A and B in the figure) may be put into evidence (we will put into evidence only the top-formulas and the bottom-formulas relevant for the explanation of the various rules). In a many premisses rule the premisses (separated by semicolons) will be separated from the conclusion by a slash.

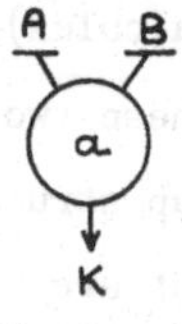

fig.1

1.1 The assertion-modifying rules.

These rules consist of "basic connection rules" (BCR1, BCR2 and BCR3, where BCR1 may be seen as a variant of the usual "cut-rule" for the sequent calculi and the other ones allow suitable manipulations), of a basic introduction rule (BIR, which is a generalization of the usual assumption-introduction rule) and of introduction and elimination rules for the logical constants (which, we recall, may be applied to graphs wich are not necessarily pure proofs). To complete our calculus for a number-theory, we should insert the usual identity-calculus rules, the rules for "successor", "sum" and "product" and a "purely logical induction-rule": these rules are omitted for sake of conciseness, while the "construction-induction-rules" are expounded below.

BASIC RULES

BCR 1.

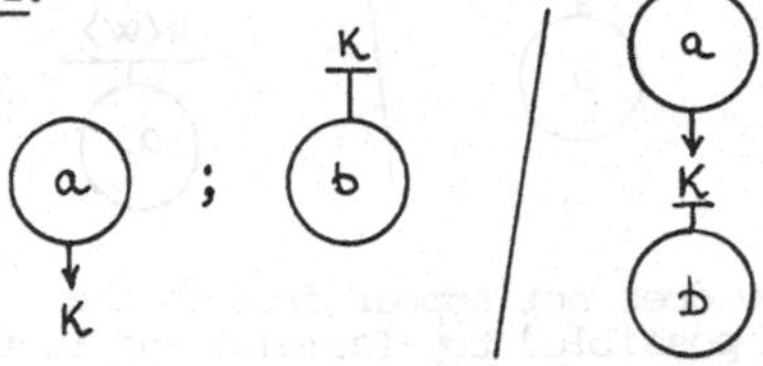

where the contextually bound variables of K in a do not appear unquantified in the top-formulas of D fifferent from K

BCR 2.

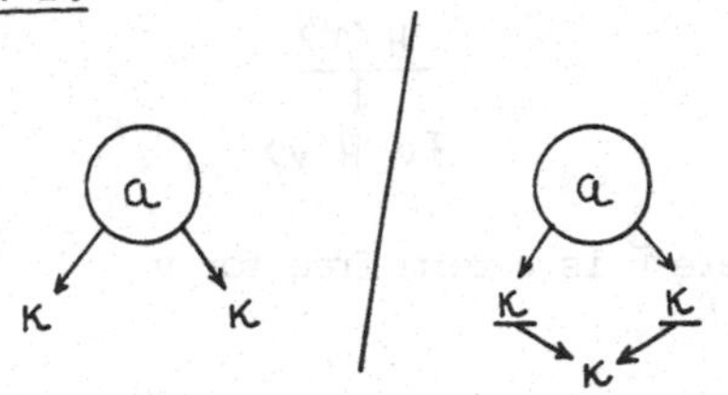

BCR 3.

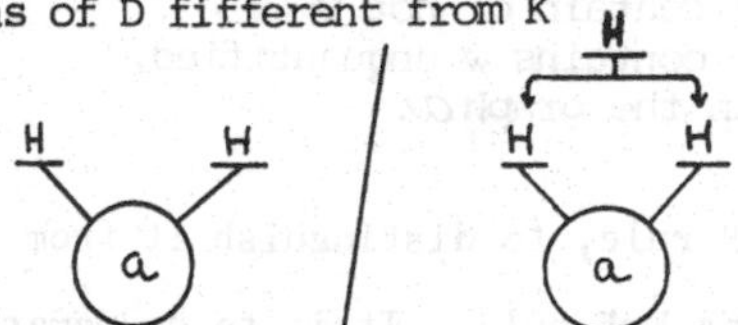

BIR.

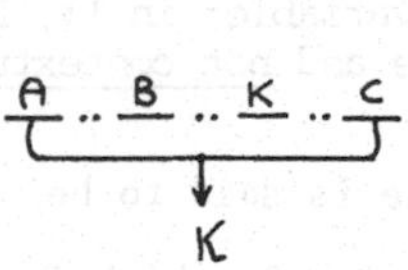

Introduction rules

I¬.

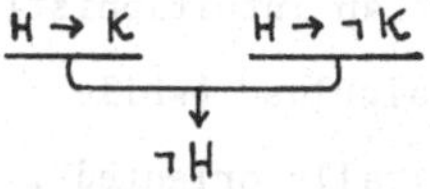

I∧.

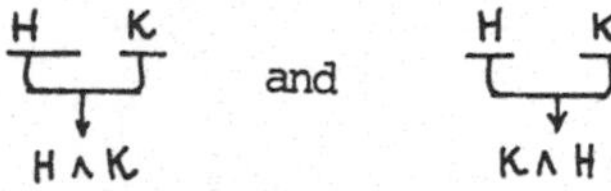

I∨.

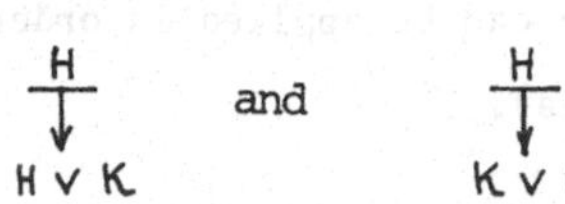

Elimitation rules

W-E¬.

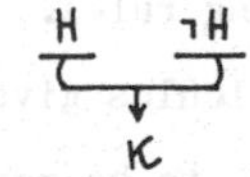

(NOTE 2)

E∧.

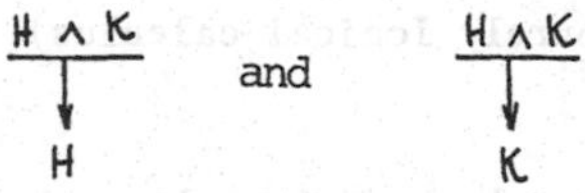

E∨.

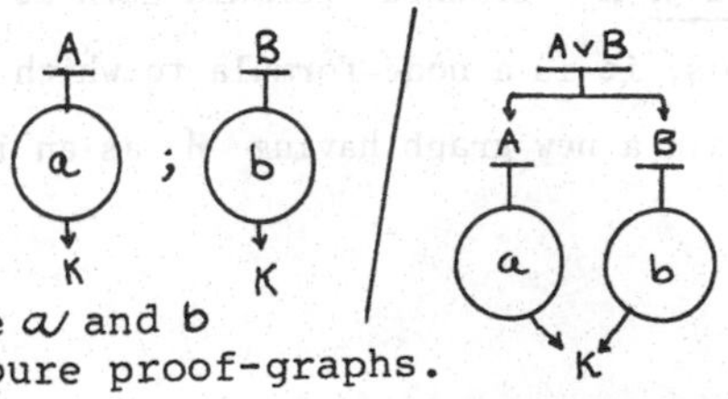

where a and b are pure proof-graphs.

I→.

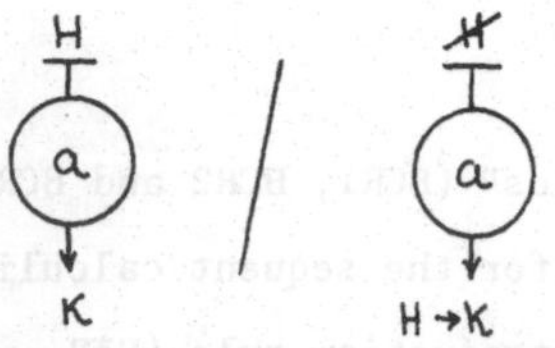

where H is not contextual in a (NOTE 3).

I∀.

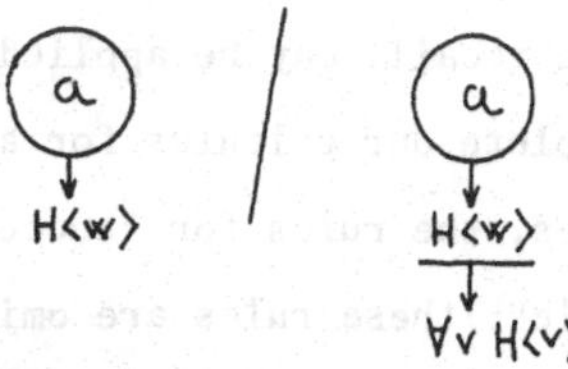

where w does not appear free in the top-formulas of a.

I∃.

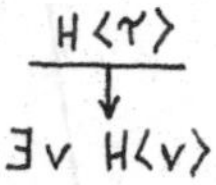

where τ is a term free for v in H.

E→.

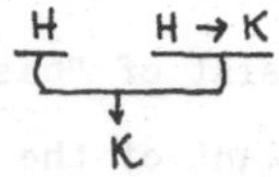

E∀.

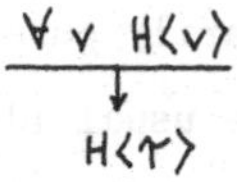

where τ is any term

E∃.

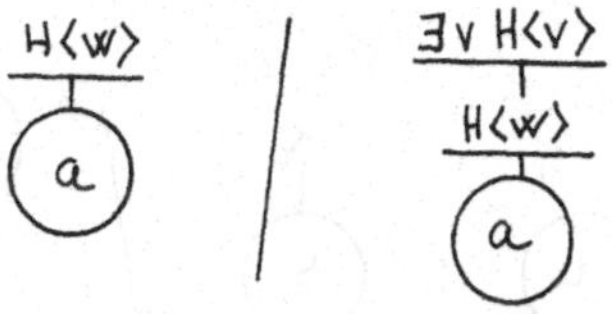

where w does not appear free in the other (possible) top-formulas and in the bottom-formulas of a.

in the rules I∀, E∀, I∃, E∃, H ⟨w⟩ (H ⟨v⟩) may contain or not w (v) as a unquantified variable; in I∀, E∃, if H ⟨w⟩ contains w unquantified, then w must be free and not contextually bound in the graph a.

NOTE 2. The W-E rule is said to be the "Weak E¬" rule, to distinguish it from the rule in fig.2, which is called "Strong E¬" rule. It is to be remarked that the latter rule cannot be deduced (as a derived rule) in our calculus, while, conversely, W-E¬ can be obtained starting from S-E¬ and the other assertion-modifying rules. The strong E¬ has not an intuitionistic meaning: his insertion in our calculus gives rise to a "classical calculus" (while our calculus is "intuitionistic", or, to be more precise, "intuitionistically oriented", since it is not a purely logical calculus).

SE¬.

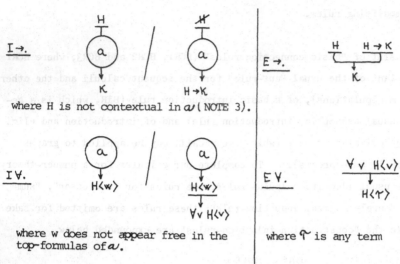

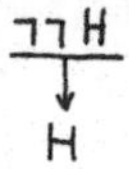

fig.2.

NOTE 3. A "slashed" formula such as H̸ is interpreted as an erased formula (in other words, it is a node-formula to which no connection rule can be applied in order to obtain a new graph having H̸ as an intermediate formula).

1.2 The construction rules.

These are the rules introducing program-statements in our graphs and, as well, contextually bound variables. The special cautions needed in handling such rules are a part of their explanation; their meaning is briefly expounded in footnotes.

High-level Rules:

GTI.

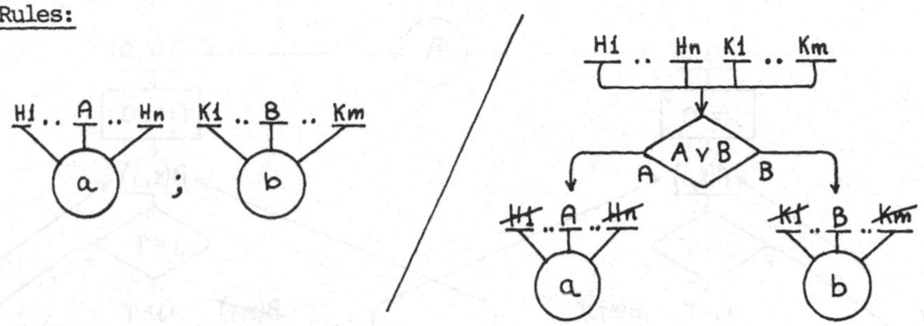

for the "slashed" formulas, see the above NOTE 3; see also NOTE 4. Here (and in GAI) H1,.,Hn,A,K1,.,Km are all the top-formulas of a and b.

GAI.

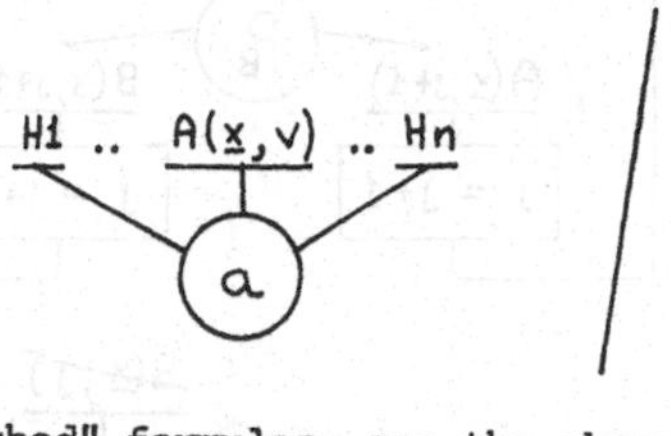

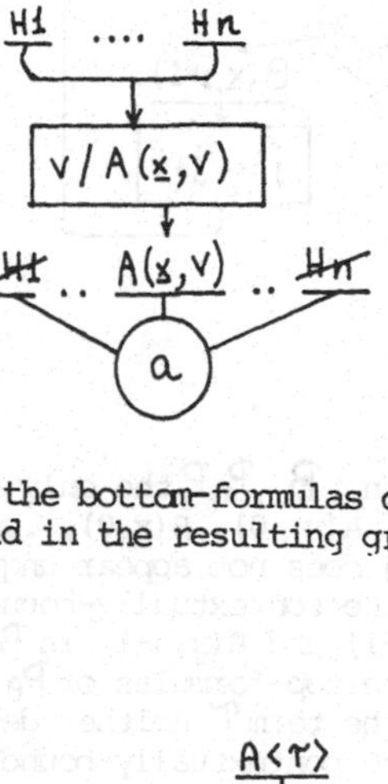

- for the "slashed" formulas, see the above NOTE 3; see also NOTE 5;
- here, H1,.., Hm must not contain unquantified the variable v and v must not appear free in the bottom-formulas of a;
- the variable v is said to be contextually-bound in the resulting graph.

Basic Rules:

BTI.

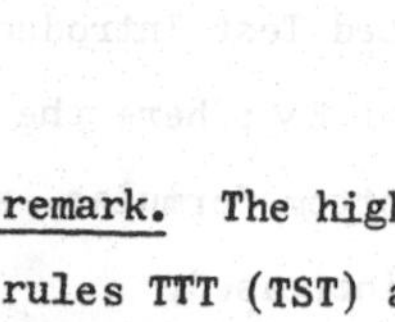

see NOTE 6.

BAI.

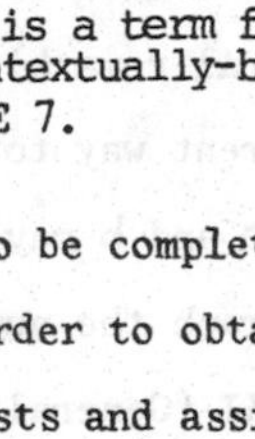

- where τ is a term free for v in A; v is contextually-bound in the graph
- see NOTE 7.

General remark. The high-level rules GTI and GAI are to be completed by the transformation rules TTT (TST) and ATT (AST) respectively, in order to obtain executable asserted programs, i.e. , programs containing only basic tests and assignments: thus, these rules "capture" the top-down-ness involved in our attitude.

Ind-CR2.: given the graphs

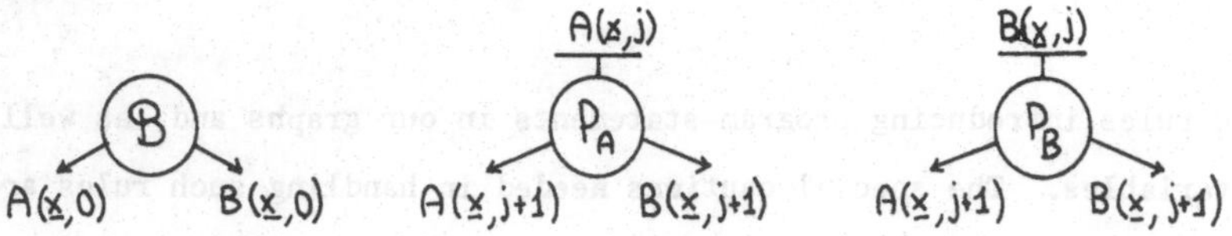

one may construct the following "induction-graph"

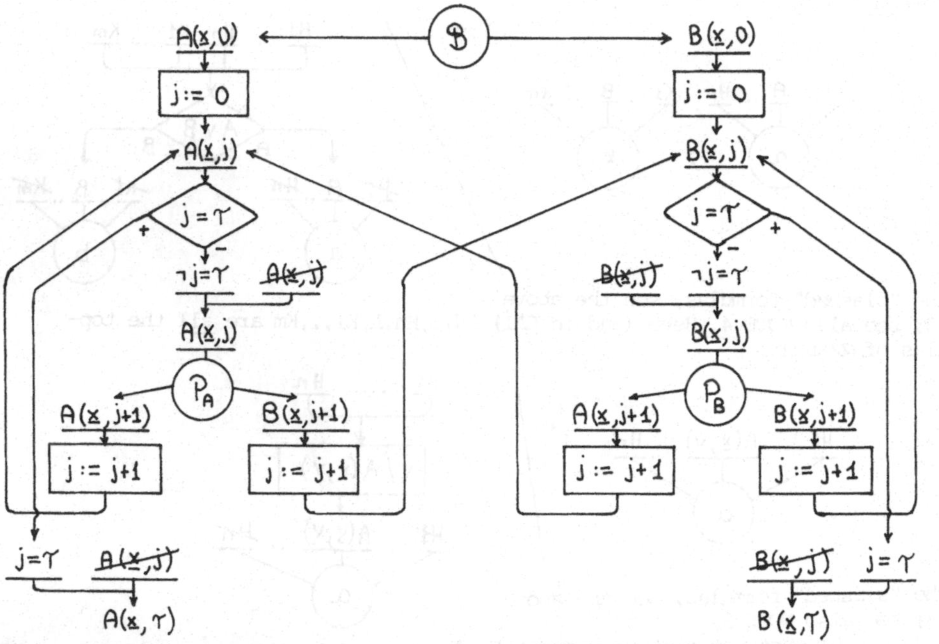

provided that: • in $\mathcal{B}$, P_A, P_B the only bottom formulas are the ones put into evidence A(x, 0), B(x,0), ...)

• j does not appear unquantified in $\mathcal{B}$, P_A, P_B

• the contextually-bound variables of A(x,0) and B(x,0) in and of A(x,j+1) and B(x,j+1) in P_A and P_B (respectively) do not appear unquantified in the top-formulas of P_A and P_B different from A(x,j) and B(x,j).

• the term $\mathcal{T}$ neither depends on j nor depends on variables which are contextually-bound in $\mathcal{B}$, or in P_B, or in P_A.

See NOTE 8.

NOTE 4. If A∨B = A∨¬A and A is atomic, we have a basic test; otherwise, we have to apply (in a second time) the transformation rule TTT or TST, we will expound below (see also the general remark). The rule GTI (Generalized Test Introduction) can be seen as a different way to express the "logical content" of E∨; here the interesting fact is that a and b may have different (one or more) bottom formulas, so that in the resulting graph the number of bottom-formulas may be increased.

NOTE 5. The rule GAI (Generalized Assignment Introduction) may be seen as a kind of variant of E∃, which, instead of introducing a existentially-bound variable, introduces a contextually bound-variable. The intended meaning of $v / A(\underline{x},v)$ is the following: v assumes some value such that $A(\underline{x},v)$ is true. Such a value of v is generally specified (in a second time) by means of some graph having $A(\underline{x},v)$ as a bottom formula, so that one can apply the transformation rule ATT or AST (in this sense GAI is a high-level rule; see also the general remark). Of course, if $A(\underline{x},v) \equiv v=\Upsilon$, then the intended meaning of $v / A(\underline{x},v)$ coincides with the one of $v := \Upsilon$.

NOTE 6. This rule is a different way to express the "logical content" of I$\vee$. Here T means "True", so that in the constructed test the only allowed exit is + (in other words, the relevant information on A is not destroyed; this is not the case in an application of I$\vee$).

NOTE 7. This rule, which introduces basic assignments, is a different way to express the "logical content" of I$\exists$. Here the assignment stores the relevant information contained in $A\langle\Upsilon\rangle$, while such information is destroyed by an application of I$\exists$.

NOTE 8. The rule Ind-CR2 (Induction Connection Rule for 2 exits) we have expounded is a particular instance, for n = 2, of a rule Ind-CRn (with $n \geqslant 1$), we have omitted for sake of conciseness. The rule Ind-CRn can be applied to n+1 graphs $\mathcal{B}, \varphi_{A1}, ..., \varphi_{An}$, where the bottom-formulas of $\mathcal{B}$ are exactly $A1(\underline{x},0),..,An(\underline{x},0)$, and $A1(\underline{x},j),..,An(\underline{x},j)$ are top-formulas of $\varphi_{A1}, .., \varphi_{An}$ respectively, and $A1(\underline{x},j+1),..,An(\underline{x},j+1)$ are exactly the bottom-formulas of every φ_{Ai} $(1 \leqslant i \leqslant n)$; the clauses needed in order to correctly apply Ind-CRn and the connections among the graphs $\mathcal{B}, \varphi_{A1}, .., \varphi_{An}$ in the resulting induction-graph are a natural generalization of the ones related to Ind-CR2.

1.3 The transformation rules.

These rules, completing GTI and GAI , consist of TTT (Test Top Transformation), TST (Test Substitution Transformation), ATT (Assignement Top Transformation) and AST (Assignement Substitution transformation), explained below.

TTT.

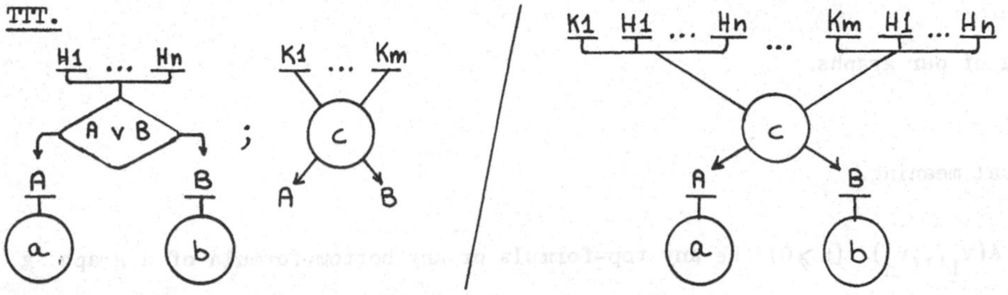

where TTT is applicable provided that the contextually-bound variables of A and B in G do not appear unquantified in the formulas H1,..,Hn.

TST.

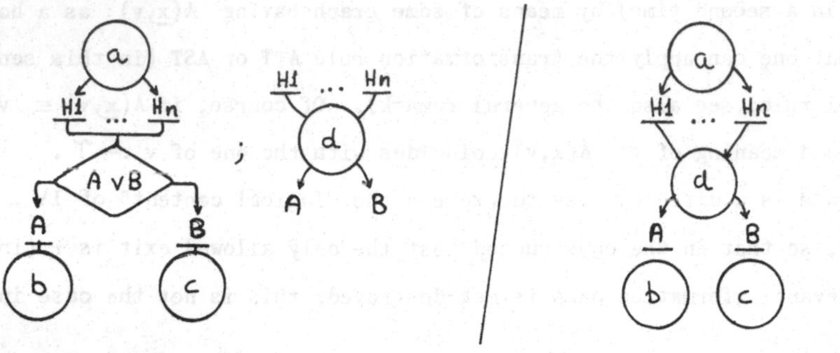

where H1,..,Hn are exactly the top formulas of d.

ATT.

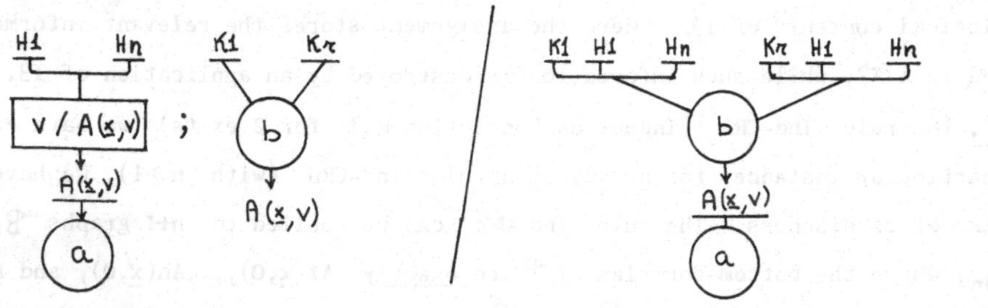

where the contextually-bound variables of A(x,v) in b do not appear unquantified in the formulas H1,..,Hn

AST.

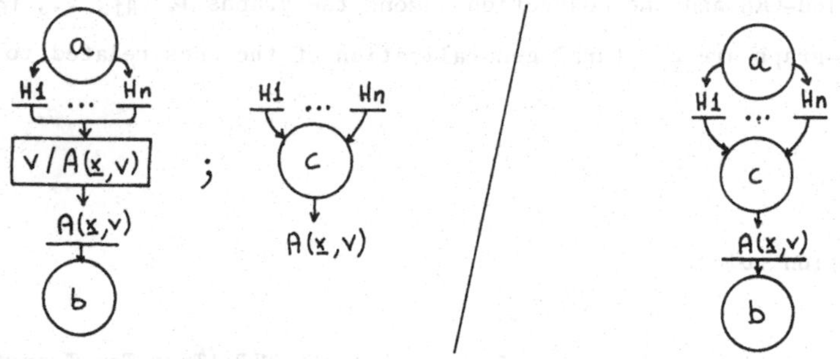

where H1,..,Hn are exactly the top-formulas of c .

2. Meaning of our graphs.

2.1 Logical meaning.

Let $A(v_1,..,v_n)$ $(n \geqslant 0)$ be any top-formula or any bottom-formula of a graph g and let $v_1,..,v_n$ be exactly the variables of A which are contextually-bound in g : then A^* will represent the formula $\exists v_1..\exists v_n\, A(v_1,..,v_n)$.

Theorem 1. Let g be any graph and let $A_1, .., A_n$ and $B_1, .., B_m$ be exactly the top-formulas of g and the bottom-formulas of g respectively: then $A_1^* \wedge ... \wedge A_n^* \rightarrow$ $\rightarrow B_1^* \vee ... \vee B_m^*$ is provable in T_{NI} (also, one can construct a pure proof-graph in our calculus with $A_1^*, .. ,A_n^*$ as the top-formulas and $B_1^* \vee ... \vee B_m^*$ as the bottom formula).

2.2 Programming meaning.

Our graphs are immediately meaningful in terms of the usual operational semantics for flow-charts, when there is only one open entry, i.e. only one "unslashed" top-formula: we say that such graphs are asserted program-graphs.

For the asserted program-graphs we assume the usual definition of correctness (remark that such a correctness is total correctness, i.e., if the input-formula is true at the entry, then the program terminates and reaches a bottom-formula satisfied at the exit). One can prove the following fact:

Theorem 2. Every asserted program-graph is correct.

If a graph has more than one top-formula, then its interpretation as an executable program is not the usual one. A precise and complete interpretation in this sense (which treats the various graphs entering into a given formula as a set of programs to be parallelly computed) would exceed the foreseen size of the present paper.

2.3 Completeness.

Here completeness is intended as the possibility of constructing asserted program-graphs to decide desirable predicates. To be more precise, we equire that every predicate expressed by a formula such as $\exists z\, \psi(\underline{x},z)$ can be decided by our graphs (and a value $\tilde{z}$ satisfying $\models \psi(\tilde{\underline{x}},\tilde{z})$ when $\models \exists z\, \psi(\tilde{\underline{x}},z)$ can be found -see also Introduction-) if $T_{NI} \vdash \exists z\, \psi(\underline{x},z) \vee \neg \exists z\, \psi(\underline{x},z)$: if this can be obtained, then, according to [6] , the possibility of constructing asserted programs to compute all the partial recursive functions immediately follows. Indeed, the following can be proved:

Theorem 3. If $T_{NI} \vdash \exists z\, \psi(\underline{x},z) \vee \neg \exists z\, \psi(\underline{x},z)$, then there is an asserted program-graph without "unslashed"top-formulas and having $\exists z\, \psi(\underline{x},z)$ and $\psi(\underline{x},z)$ as the only bottom-formulas, where $\underline{x} = x_1,.,x_n$ are free in both formulas and z is contextually-bound in $\psi(\underline{x},z)$.

REFERENCES

1. Burstall, R.M. and Darlington, J., Some transformations for developing recursive programs. Proc. of 1975 International Conference on Reliable Software, Los Angeles.

2. Chang, C.L. and Lee, R.C.T., Symbolic logic and mechanical theorem proving, Academic Press Inc., New Jork 1973.

3. Chang, C.L., Lee, R.C.T. and Waldinger, R.J., An improved program-synthesizing algorithm and its correctness. Com. ACM, vol.17; n.4, 1974.

4. Constable, R.L., Constructive mathematics and automatic program writers. IFIP Congress 1971, North Holland, Amsterdam.

5. Darlington, J., Application of program tarnsformation to program synthesis. Proc. of International Symposium on Proving and Improving Programs, Arc et Senans, France.

6. Degli Antoni,G., Miglioli,P.A.,and Ornaghi,M., The synthesis of programs as an approach to the construction of reliable programs. Proc. of International Symposium on Proving and Improving Programs, Arc et Senans, France, 1975.

7. Dershowitz,N. and Manna,Z., On automating structured programming. Proc. of International Symposium on Proving and Improving Programs, Arc et Senans, France,1975.

8. Dijkstra, E.W., Guarded commands, nondeterminacy and formal derivation of programs. Comm. of the ACM, vol 18, n.8.

9. Hoare, C.A.R., An axiomatic basis of computer programming. Com of the ACM, vol.12, n.10, 1969.

10. Kleene, S.C., Introduction to methamatematics, North Holland, Amsterdam 1950.

11. Kowalski, R., Predicate logic as a programming language. Proc. IFIP 1974.

12. Manna, Z., The correctness of programs. J. of Comp. and System Science, 3, 1969.

13. Miglioli,P. and Ornaghi,M., Notes on motivation languages and synthesis maps. Internal report of the Istituto di Cibernetica dell'Università di Milano, Via Viotti, 5 Milano (1976) , available.

14. Miglioli,M. and Ornaghi,M., A purely logical computing model: the open proofs as programs. Internal report of the Istituto di Cibernetica - Università di Milano, Via Viotti, 5 Milano (1977), available (presented at the Workshop on Artificial Intelligence, Bad Honnef 1977, Germany).

15. Prawitz, D., Ideas and results in proof-theory. Proc. of the second scandinavian logic symposium, North Holland, Amsterdam.

16. Degli Antoni,G., Miglioli, P. and Ornaghi,M., Procedure per la sintesi di programmi. To appear in Informatica.

Research sponsered by CNR and HISI (Honeywell Information System Italy).

ANOTHER APPROACH FOR PROVING PROGRAM CORRECTNESS

Peter A. Ng
Department of Computer Science
University of Missouri-Columbia
Columbia, Missouri 65201

and

Sung Y. Bang
Michigan Bell Telephone
Southfield, Michigan 48075

Abstract

In this paper we investigate the strong verification of programs using both inductive assertions which involve probability distributions of program variables [4] and the concept of predicate transformer [2]. This deductive system for proving program correctness and program performance is extended to include Parallelism. Methods for proving the absence of deadlock and for predicting the occurrence of deadlock are also discussed.

I. The Concept of a Predicate Transformer

Let P, Q and R denote predicates defined on the state space of a program. Let T denote the predicate which is satisfied by all states, and F denote the predicate which is satisfied by no state. For each predicate P, we denote by P* the set of states satisfying P.

Let S be a given program. A specification of S is meant here to be a pair of predicates (P, Q) such that P is an input predicate characterizing all legal initial states of S, and Q is an output predicate characterizing all desirable final states of S.

For a given program S, the notation P[S]Q means: if P is true on certain initial state vector and the program S is initiated with this state vector, then S terminates and the assertion Q is true on the final state vector. Predicates P and Q in P[S]Q are referred to as the pre- and post-condition of S.

The analogous notation P{S}Q means: if P is true on certain initial state vector and the program S which initiated with the state vector terminates, then Q is true on the final state vector.

Given a pair of input-output predicates (P, Q) and a program S, S terminates with respect to P if the underlying function $f_S(x)$ that S computes, is defined for all x in P*. S is consistent with respect to (P, Q) if P{S}Q. S is strongly verifiable (or correct) with respect to (P, Q) if P[S]Q. S is incorrect with respect to (P, Q) if for some x in P*, either S does not terminate when input with x, or S terminates but Q is false at output.

Let WP(S, Q) denote the weakest precondition for all the initial states of S such that activation of S is guaranteed to lead to a proper termination with the final state of S satisfying the postcondition Q. The function WP is called a predicate transformer because it transforms a postcondition Q into a precondition WP(S, Q). Then WP(S,Q)* $= \{x | f_S(x) \epsilon Q^*\}$. Clearly, for arbitrary P and Q and a program S, P[S]Q if and only if $[P(x) \rightarrow Q(f_S(x))]$ for all x in P*.

II. A Probabilitistic-Deductive System for Program Proofs

In this paper, analogous to the concept of verifying program performance [4], the semantics definitions of various program constructs are annotated with specifications which include probability distributions of program variables and relations on these variables. Strong verification of a program then consists of a demonstration of consistency between the program and its specifications, and a proof that the program terminates for all input state vectors that satisfy the input predicate. We now proceed to give a probabilistic approach in describing a deductive system for proving properties of sequential programs.

For a program S, let x = <r, n> be the state vector, where r is a vector of those program variables whose values are to be treated as random variables; and n is a vector of program variables whose values are treated in the usual assertion sense.
Let B be a Boolean valued function of the state x. Let Pr{B(x)} be the probability of the new random variable B(x) evaluating to true. Consider a predicate of the form Q(n, Pr{B(x)}), where Q includes conjunctions which relate the probability of B(x) to the current value of the nonrandom portion of the state condition. Some properties of the predicate transformer for a given S and Q(n, Pr{B(x)}) can be derived in the following.

Theorem 1: Let $\overline{P}$ be the negation of P. Then the following identities and implications hold.

(1) $P(n, Pr\{B(x)\})[S]Q(f_S(n), Pr\{B(f_S(x))\})$ if and only if

$[P(n, Pr\{B(x)\}) \rightarrow Q(f_S(n), Pr\{B(f_S(x))\})]$ for all x in P*.

(2) $WP(S,F) \equiv F$.

(3) $[P(n,Pr\{B_1(x)\}) \rightarrow Q(n,Pr\{B_2(x)\})] \rightarrow [WP(S,P(n,Pr\{B_1(x)\})) \rightarrow WP(S,Q(n,Pr\{B_2(x)\}))]$.

(4) $WP(S,P(n, Pr\{B_1(x)\}) \vee Q(n, Pr\{B_2(x)\}))$.

$\equiv WP(S,P(n, Pr\{B_1(x)\})) \vee WP(S,Q(n, Pr\{B_2(x)\}))$.

(5) $WP(S,P(n, Pr\{B_1(x)\}) \,\&\, Q(n, Pr\{B_2(x)\}))$

$\equiv WP(S,P(n, Pr\{B_1(x)\})) \,\&\, WP(S,Q(n, Pr\{B_2(x)\}))$.

(6) $[P(n, Pr\{B_1(x)\}) \equiv Q(n, Pr\{B_2(x)\})] \rightarrow [WP(S,P(n, Pr\{B_1(x)\}))$

$\equiv WP(S,Q(n, Pr\{B_2(x)\}))]$.

(7) $WP(S,\overline{Q}(n, Pr\{B(x)\})) \equiv WP(S,T) \,\&\, \overline{WP(S,Q(n, Pr\{B(x)\}))}$.

(8) $\overline{WP(S,Q(n, Pr\{B(x)\}))} \equiv WP(S,\overline{Q}(n, Pr\{B(x)\})) \vee \overline{WP(S,T)}$.

The proof of the theorem is straightforward and is left to the reader. In fact, the formal definition of program correctness can be stated as in (1).

Using the concept of weakest precondition, we can derive a simple formal characterization of termination without using some weight functions [5]. We can provide convenience and flexibility in carrying out the proof of a program and whether it is strongly verifiable or incorrect.

Theorem 2:

(1) A program S terminates with respect to an input predicate $I(n, Pr\{B(x)\})$ if and only if $I(n, Pr\{B(x)\}) \rightarrow WP(S,T)$.

(2) The following statements are equivalent:

(a) a program S is strongly verifiable with respect to specification $(I(n, Pr\{B_1(x)\}), Q(n, Pr\{B_2(x)\}))$;

(b) $I(n, Pr\{B_1(x)\}) \rightarrow WP(S,Q(n, Pr\{B_2(x)\}))$;

(c) there exists a predicate $P(n, Pr\{B(x)\})$ such that $I(n, Pr\{B_1(x)\}) \rightarrow P(n, Pr\{B(x)\}) \,\&\, P(n, Pr\{B(x)\})[S]Q(n, Pr\{B_2(x)\})$;

(d) there exists a predicate $R(n, Pr\{B(x)\})$ such that $I(n, Pr\{B(x)\})[S]R(n, Pr\{B(x)\}) \,\&\, R(n, Pr\{B(x)\}) \rightarrow Q(n, Pr\{B_2(x)\})$;

(e) there exists predicates $P(n, Pr\{B_1(x)\})$ and $R(n, Pr\{B_2(x)\})$ such that $I(n, Pr\{B_0(x)\}) \rightarrow P(n, Pr\{B_1(x)\}) \,\&\, P(n, Pr\{B_1(x)\})\ [S]R(n, Pr\{B_2(x)\})$ $\&\, R(n, Pr\{B_2(x)\}) \rightarrow Q(n, Pr\{B_3(x)\})$.

(3) A program S is incorrect with respect to a pair of input-output predicates $[I(n, Pr\{B_1(x)\}), Q(n, Pr\{B_2(x)\}))$ if and only if

$I(n, Pr\{B_1(x)\}) \rightarrow WP(S,Q(n, Pr\{B_2(x)\})))]$ is false.

In fact, both theorems 1 and 2 still hold if the predicates P,Q and R are defined without involving any probability distribution [1,2]. If S is nondeterministic [2], then both theorems hold except replacing the equality "≡" by implication "→" in the theorems 1.4 and 1.7.

Let Q(n, Pr{B(x)}) be an arbitrary postcondition. For using the concept of predicate transformer to prove that a program is strongly verifiable, we now proceed to provide axiomatic definitions given in terms of the weakest precondition of the given construct with respect to Q(n, Pr{B(x)}).

1. Primitive statements
   WP(skip,Q(n, Pr{B(x)})) ≡ Q(n, Pr{B(x)}).
   WP(abort,Q(n, Pr{B(x)})) ≡ F&Q(n, Pr{B(x)}).

2. Axiom of assignment
   WP(y := E,Q(n, Pr{B(x)})) ≡ $Q(n, Pr\{B(x)\})^y_E$, where $Q(n, Pr\{B(x)\})^y_E$ is by substituting the expression E for every free occurrence of the variable y.

3. Axiom of alterations
   WP(if D then S_1 else S_2, Q(n, Pr{B(x)})) ≡ [D & WP(S_1,Q(n, Pr{B(x)}))]
   ∨ [$\overline{D}$ & WP(S_2,Q(n, Pr{B(x)}))].

   WP(if D then S_1, Q(n, Pr{B(x)})) ≡ [D & Q(n, Pr{B(x)})]
   ∨ [$\overline{D}$ & WP(S_1, Q(n, Pr{B(x)}))].

4. Axiom of iteration
   WP(while D do S, Q(n, Pr{B(x)})) ≡ [$\overline{D}$ & Q(n, Pr{B(x)})]
   ∨ [D & WP(S, WP(while D do S, Q(n, Pr{B(x)})))].

5. Axiom of composition
   WP(S_1;S_2, Q(n, Pr{B(x)})) ≡ WP(S_1,WP(S_2, Q(n, Pr{B(x)}))).

III. Computing the Weakest Precondition

In computing the weakest precondition of alternative constructs and the weakest precondition of iterative constructs, except for the predicates which include probability distributions, the process is in the usual way [1,2]. If the predicates include probability distributions, then probabilities are conditioned by the partial information added at decisions; that is, substitution due to assignments and conditioning due to decisions must balance [4].

Consider an alternative construct "S: if D(x) then S_1 else S_2." Then the weakest precondition of S with respect to the postcondition Q(n, Pr{B(x)}) is WP(S, Q(n, Pr{B(x)})) ≡ [$\overline{D}$(x)& WP(S_2, Q(n, Pr{B(x)}))] ∨ [D(x) & WP(S_1, Q(n, Pr{B(x)}))]. Assume that the predicate $D(x)$ is without side effect. S_1 and S_2 are assignments which replace x by $f_i(x)$ and, in particular, n by $g_i(n)$. Then $WP(S, Q(n, Pr\{B(x)\})) \equiv [\overline{D}(x) \,\&\, Q(g_2(n), Pr\{B(f_2(x))\})] \vee [D(x) \,\&\, Q(g_1(n), Pr\{B(f_1(x))\})]$. The appearances of the conditions $Q(g_1(n), Pr\{B(f_1(x))\})$ and $Q(g_2(n), Pr\{B(f_2(x))\})$, which are the weakest preconditions of S_1 and S_2, respectively, are just after the "<u>then</u>" and "<u>else</u>", respectively within the program text. Each of these conditions holds just after the test $D(x)$. Now, the algebraic simplication of the nonrandom portion in the right hand side of the equation can be treated in the usual way. Let us examine the verification conditions for predicates involving distributions.

For the condition $[D(x) \,\&\, Q(g_1(n), Pr\{B(f_1(x))\})] \vee [D(x) \,\&\, Q(g_2(n), Pr\{B(f_2(x))\})]$, there exists a probability distribution of intermediary states of the computation just before the "if," $Pr\{B^0(x)\}$ such that $Pr\{B^0(x)|D(x)\} \equiv Pr\{B(f_1(x))\}$ and $Pr\{B^0(x)|\overline{D}(x)\} \equiv Pr\{B(f_2(x))\}$. Using these two equations to determine $Pr\{B^0(x)\}$ is principally an issue of algebraic manipulation. Thus, we have $WP(S,Q(n, Pr\{B(x)\})) \equiv U(n, Pr\{B^0(x)\})$.

Consider an iterative construct of the form "S: <u>while</u> D(x) <u>do</u> S_1." For any postcondition $Q(n, Pr\{B(x)\})$, $WP(S,Q(n, Pr\{B(x)\})) \equiv [\overline{D}(x) \,\&\, Q(n, Pr\{B(x)\})] \vee [D(x) \,\&\, WP(S_1, WP(S,Q(n, Pr\{B(x)\})))]$, which is a recursive equation. The occurrence of $WP(S,Q(n, Pr\{B(x)\}))$ in the right hand of the equation can be replaced repeatedly by the whole expression of the right hand of the equation. Thus, by induction, we have the following result.

<u>Theorem 3:</u>

Let S be the statement "<u>while</u> D(x) <u>do</u> S_1." Then, for any postcondition $Q(n, Pr\{B(x)\})$, $WP(S,Q(n, Pr\{B(x)\})) \equiv (\exists j\geq 0)[A_{Sj}(Q(n, Pr\{B(x)\}))]$, where $A_{S0}(Q(n, Pr\{B(x)\})) \equiv [\overline{D}(x) \,\&\, Q(n, Pr\{B(x)\})]$, and $A_{Sj}(Q(n, Pr\{B(x)\})) \equiv [D(x) \,\&\, WP(S_1, A_{Sj-1}(Q(n, Pr\{B(x)\})))]$, for $j>0$.

Intuitively, $A_{Sj}(Q(n, Pr\{B(x)\}))$ can be interpreted as the weakest precondition which guarantees termination after S iterates exactly j times, and leaves the system in a final state satisfying $Q(n, Pr\{B(x)\})$. The conditions $WP(S_1, A_{Sj-1}(Q(n, Pr\{B(x)\})))$, $j>0$ are just after the test $D(x)$. The predicate involving probability distributions can be treated in the similar way as for the alternative constructs. Thus, this theorem provides a heuristic way of finding $WP(S,Q(n, Pr\{B(x)\}))$. Moreover if Q does not involve distributions, the theorem holds [1].

<u>Example 1:</u> Consider the following program SORT [4], sorting the array B[1:N] by insertion. In the program assertions are enclosed in brace brackets.

```
{P} begin J := 1;
        while J<N
        do  begin
            I := J;
            while I>0 & B[I]>B[I+1]
            do  begin
                exchange (B[I], B[I+1]);
                I := I-1
                end;
            J := J+1
            end;
      J := J-1  end  {Q}.
```

Where P and Q are defined as follows.

Let $\delta_{n,j}$ be the Kronecker delta function defined as "<u>if</u> n=j <u>then</u> 1 <u>else</u> 0." Let $Pr\{S(k)=n\}$ denote the probability that the number $S(k)$ of elements to the left of B[k], which are smaller than or equal to B[k]. If the array B is a randomly arranged sequence of distinct elements, then the input predicate P is $[1 \le N \& Pr\{S(k)=n\} \equiv$ <u>if</u> $0 \le n < k \le N$ <u>then</u> $1/k$ <u>else</u> $0]$. The output predicate Q, which describes the output to our sorting program is $[I=0 \ \& \ J=N-1] \ \& \ [Pr\{S(k)=n\} \equiv \delta_{n,k-1}$, for $1 \le k \le J+1]$. That is, the array B[1:N] is completely rearranged in an ascending order.

It can be shown that $P \rightarrow WP(SORT,Q)$ is a theorem, where $WP(SORT,Q) \equiv (\exists i,j \ge 0)[j-i=0 \ \& \ 1+j=N \ \& \ \neg(j-i>0 \ \& \ B[j-i]>B[j-i+1] \ \& \ (j-i+1>0 \ \& \ B[j-i+1]>B[j-i+2]) \& \ldots \& (j>0 \ \& \ B[j]>B[j+1]) \ \& \ j<N] \ \& \ [1 \le j \le N-1 \ \& \ g_1(k)]$, where $g_1(k)$ is

$$
Pr\{S(k)=n\} \equiv \begin{cases} \delta_{n,k-1} & \text{if } 1 \le k \le 1+j \ \& \ k \ne 1+j, \\ (k-1)^i/k^{i+1} & \text{if } k=1+j \ \& \ 0 \le n < k-1, \\ 1/k & \text{if } k=1+j \ \& \ k-1 \le n < k, \\ 0 & \text{if } k=1+j \ \& \ n \ge k, \\ 1/k & \text{if } k=j+2 \le k \le N \ \& \ 0 \le n < k, \\ 0 & \text{if } j+2 \le k \le N \ \& \ n \ge k \ . \end{cases}
$$

Thus, we have proved that the program SORT is strongly verifiable with respect to (P, Q). "The program SORT terminates" is due to basic properties of integers $P \rightarrow WP(SORT,Q)$, which is inherent in the algorithm realized by the program SORT.

In addition, the novel of this approach, in which the inductive assertions include probability distributions, is that one should be able to use the predicates of branching possibilities, which are obtained in the proof of program consistency and termination by using predicate transformer WP, to determine directly program performance, such as the mean number iterations, the mean execution time, and so forth [4]. Hence, both verifying program correctness and verifying program performance can be handled simultaneously.

IV. Strong Verification of Parallel Programs

We introduce parallelism [3] by extending the set of programsconstructs with two new constructs--one to initiate parallel processing, the other to coordinate processes to be executed in parallel.

Let S1, S2,...,Sn be statements. Then the language notation

cobegin S1//S2//...//Sn **coend**

indicates that the statements Si can be executed concurrently. Execution of the cobegin statement terminates when execution of all the processes Si have terminated.

The second statement has the form

await B **then** S

where B is a Boolean expression and S a statement not containing a cobegin or another await statement.

Suppose that a statement S is being executed. S is *blocked* if it has not terminated, but no progress in its execution is possible because it is delayed at an await. Execution of a program S *ends in deadlock* if it is blocked. Thus, a program S is *free from deadlock* if no execution of S which begins with P true ends in deadlock.

Let Q be an arbitrary postcondition which may include probability distributions. The formal semantic definition for the await statement is defined by

$$WP(\underline{await}\ B\ \underline{then}\ S, Q) \equiv [B \,\&\, WP(S, Q)].$$

Thus, from the definition, in order to show P[await]Q, we need to show P→[B & WP(S,Q)]. Since WP(S,Q) guarantees the termination for the process await, the Boolean expression B must be well-defined with respect to the whole program environment, so that the program is free from deadlock.

Let S' be any statement within S but not within an await. Let Q' be the postcondition of S'. Given a proof P[S]Q and a statement T with postcondition R, we say that T *does not interfere with* P[S]Q if Q & WP(T,R)[T]Q and WP(S',Q') & WP(T,R)[T] WP(S',Q') hold.

Let S1, S2,...,Sn be statements with proofs P1[S1]Q1, P2[S2]Q2,...,Pn[Sn]Qn. Let T be an await or assignment statement (which does not appear in an await) of process Si. If, for all j, j≠i, T does not interfere with Pj[Sj]Qj, then P1[S1]Q1, P2[S2]Q2, ...,Pn[Sn]Qn are said to be *interference-free*.

We now define the axiomatic definition of cobegin statement. If P1[S1]Q1, P2[S2]

Q2,..., Pn[Sn]Qn are interference free, then $\&_{i=1}^{n}$ Pi[<u>cobegin</u> S1//S2//...//Sn <u>coend</u>] $\&_{i=1}^{n}$ Qi. That is, to show the cobegin statement correct with respect to ($\&_{i=1}^{n}$ Pi, $\&_{i=1}^{n}$ Qi), we need to show first for each process S_i, it is strongly verifiable with respect to (Pi,Qi). If awaits are appearing in the process S_i, then S_i must be free from deadlock. Owicki and Gries [3] provides sufficient conditions for freedom from deadlock. Finally, we need to show that they are interference-free.

<u>Example 2</u>: Consider the following producer-consumer program S [3], which copies an array of values A[1:M] into an array B[1:M] with assertions enclosed in brace brackets. Let R ≡ [{buffer[(k-1)<u>mod</u> N] = A[k] & out<k≤in} & 0≤in-out≤N & 1≤i≤M+1 & 1≤j≤M+1].

```
{I≡[M>0 & N>0]}
S: begin
   in := out := 0; i := j := 1;
   cobegin
   {P1≡[R & i=in+1]}
   Producer: while i≤M
             do   begin
                  x:=A[i]
                  await in-out<N then skip;
                  add: buffer[in mod N] := x;
                  markin : in := in+1;
                  i := i+1
                  end;
   {P2≡[R& i=in+1 & i≤M+1 & buffer[in-1 mod N]=A[i-1] & in-1-out≤N]}
   //
   {C1≡[R & j=out+1]}
   Consumer: while j≤M
             do   begin
                    await in-out>0 then skip;
                    remove : y := buffer[out mod N];
                    markout : out := out+1;
                    B[j] := y;
                    j := j+1
                    end
   {C2≡[R& B[k]=A[k]& 1≤k<j}& j=out+1 & j≤M+1]}

   coend
   end  {Q≡[B[k]=A[k& 1≤k≤M]]}.
```

By inspection, if N>0, then the program S is free from deadlock. In order to prove that S is strongly verifiable with respect to (I,Q), we need to establish P1 & C1[<u>cobegin</u> producer:...//consumer:... <u>coend</u>] P2 & C2 by showing that P1[producer]P2, C1[consumer]C2, and they are interference-free. The first two can be shown by P1→WP (producer, P2) and C1→WP(consumer, C2) respectively, where WP(producer, P2) is (∃ ℓ ≤0)[i+ℓ-1≤M<i+ℓ & {buffer[(k-1)mod N] = A[k] & out<k≤in+ℓ} & 0≤in+ℓ-out≤N & 1≤i+ℓ≤M+1 & 1≤j≤M+1 & i+ℓ=in+ℓ+1 & i+ℓ=M+1 & A[i]=A[i] &...& A[i+ℓ-1]=A[i+ℓ-1] & in-out<N &...& in+ℓ-1-out<N], and WP(consumer, C2) is (∃ ℓ'≥0)[j+ℓ'-1≤M<j+ℓ' & in-out>0 &...& in-(out+ℓ'-1)>0 & {buffer[(k-1)mod N] = A[k] & out+ℓ'<k≤in} & 0≤in-(out+ℓ')≤N & 1≤i≤M+1 & 1≤j+ℓ'≤M+1 &{B[k]=A[k] & 1≤k<j} & buffer[out mod N]=A[j]&...& buffer[out+ℓ'-1 mod N]=A[j+ℓ'-1] & j+ℓ' = out+ℓ'+1 & j+ℓ'≤M+1]. The proof of the interference free property is straightforward and is left to the reader.

V. Blocking and Deadlock

The program SORT is free from deadlock, since it has no awaits. For the producer-consumer program S if N>0 then WP(producer, P2) and WP(consumer, C2) are the conditions that S is free from deadlock. Thus, the condition of awaits 0<in-out<N are true.

It is perhaps, reasonable to use probability distributions to determine the necessary and sufficient conditions under which a program is free from deadlock. For example, one may ask the probability that the difference between the random variables "in-out" is ranged between 0 and N, that is, Pr{0<in-out<N}. If the assertions for proving the program include this probability distribution, these may provide a dynamic check for showing freedom from deadlock, or for showing that certain conditions may arise within the program which leads to a deadlock.

Consider the producer-consumer program. Let α be the observed arrival rate at which elements are added to the buffer per time unit. Let β be the observed service rate at which elements are removed from the buffer per time unit. Both α and β can be defined in terms of the program variables "in" and "out" per time unit, respectively. Suppose that the arrival rate α and the service rate β do not noticeably change. After an initialization period the system arrives at an equilibrium (i.e., the steady state). Then the probabilities for finding exactly "in-out" elements in the buffer is constant in time, for $\alpha<\beta$, $P_{in-out}(t) = \rho^i * P_0(t)$ where $\rho = \alpha/\beta$ and $P_0(t) = 1-\rho$. The equation $P_0(t) = 1-\rho$ says that the probability of finding the buffer empty in the steady state is $1-\rho$, so the probability of finding the system not empty is ρ. Furthermore, the expected value for the number $n=E(i)$ elements in the buffer is $\rho/(1-\rho)$. Let T be T be the expected response time, which includes both waiting time in the buffer and the time needed to be served. Thus, when an element leaves the buffer, we expect a number of $n=\alpha T$ elements to be in the buffer. Therefore, the expected response time as function of ρ is $\beta T = 1/(1-\rho)$. If ρ is close to one, the probability of finding the buffer not empty is high, and we have a serious slowdown problem if ρ gets too close to one. Under what environment does this latter fact imply that deadlock may arise? If there is, then how do the Poisson distributions fix in the assertions for proving correctness, program performance and program freedom from deadlock? A paper is in preparation concerning these problems.

References

1. Basu, S. K. and Yeh, R. T., "Strong verification of programs," IEEE Trans. Software Engineering, Vol. SE-1, No. 3, pp. 339-345, Sept. 1975.

2. Dijkstra, E. W., "A discipline of programming," Prentice-Hall, Englewood Cliffs, New Jersey, 1976.

3. Owicki, S. and Gries, D., "An axiomatic proof technique for parallel programs I," Acta Informatia, Vol. 6, pp. 319-340, 1976.

4. Wegbreit, B., "Verifying program performance," JACM, Vol. 23, No. 4, pp. 691-699, Oct. 1976.

5. Manna, Z. and Vuillemin, J., "Fixpoint approach to the theory of computation," CACM, Vol. 15, pp. 528-536, 1972.

COVER RESULTS AND NORMAL FORMS

Anton Nijholt
Vrije Universiteit
Department of Mathematics
P.O.Box 7161, Amsterdam
The Netherlands.

1. INTRODUCTION.

It has been recognized that the idea of *covering* of grammars is very useful. Since the first time definitions of cover appeared in the literature (see Aho & Ullman [1] and Gray & Harrison [4]) several papers have been written in which (variants of) these definitions were used. Consider two context-free grammars. We can talk about a relationship between these grammars. For example, we may conclude that both grammars are LR(k) grammars and therefore their sentences can be parsed with an LR(k) parsing method. Another type of relationship between these two grammars may be that they generate the same language, i.e. they are *equivalent*. A more restrictive type of relationship is that one grammar *covers* the other, which means that not only the grammars are equivalent, but also that their parse trees are close related. Intuitively we say that a context-free grammar (cfg) G' covers a cfg G, when the ability to parse G' allows one to parse G. Hence we can look for grammars which are 'easily parsable' and which cover grammars which are more 'difficult parsable'. In general the cover-relationship between two grammars is expressed by a homomorphism between parses.

In Gray & Harrison [4] results were obtained for the covering of context-free grammars by grammars which are in a certain normal form. The question, which was stated as an open problem in Aho & Ullman [1] and Harrison [7], whether each LR(k) grammar is (right) covered by an LR(1) or LR(0) grammar found its answer in Mickunas [14], Mickunas, Lancaster & Schneider [15] and Nijholt [17]. Some decidability results for covering appeared in Hunt [8] and in Hunt, Rosenkrantz & Szymanski [9], [10]. More results on covering appeared, sometimes informally, in Aho & Ullman [1], Graham [3], Hammer [5], McAfee & Presser [13] and Nijholt [18]. In Nijholt [16] it was proved that every proper cfg can be right covered by a non-left-recursive grammar.

However, a lot of problems have not yet been investigated. In the present paper we try to collect the, in our eyes at this moment, most interesting problems on covering and we give answers to some of them. The most important results in this paper can be obtained in rather simple ways from existing literature. First we show that in spite of some remarks in the literature the possibility to cover context-free grammars by context-free grammars in Greibach normal form is an open question. Another result we present says that each LR(k) grammar is right covered by a non-left-recursive LR(1) grammar or (in case the language is prefix-free) by a strict deterministic grammar (notice that strict deterministic grammars are not left-recursive).

The organization of this paper is as follows. This section concludes with some preliminaries. In the second section we present some results and open problems on the covering of (arbitrary) cfg's by cfg's in GNF (Greibach normal form) and by cfg's in a non-left-recursive form. In the third section we show, and illustrate with examples, some properties of the relationship between *parsability* and *covers*. In the fourth section we have some remarks and results for cover problems for the class of LR(k) grammars and some of its subclasses.

PRELIMINARIES

Definition 1.1 (normal forms)

A *context-free grammar* (cfg) is denoted by the four-tuple $G = (N,T,P,S)$. We make the following conventions. Elements of T are denoted by a,b,c, etc.; u,v,w, etc. denote elements of T^*; A,B,C, etc., denote elements of N; X,Y,Z, etc. denote elements of $V = N \cup T$; and α,β,γ, etc., denote elements of $(N \cup T)^*$. The empty string is denoted by ε. The notation $\alpha \overset{*}{\underset{\ell}{\Longrightarrow}} \beta$ is used for a *leftmost derivation* of β from α; $\alpha \overset{*}{\underset{r}{\Longrightarrow}} \beta$ denotes a *rightmost derivation*.

A cfg G is said to be *unambiguous* if each sentence has exactly one leftmost derivation. Otherwise G is said to be ambiguous. G is said to be *cycle-free* if there is no derivation $A \overset{+}{\Longrightarrow} A$, for any $A \in N$. Cfg G is said to be *ε-free* if there are no productions, except for $S \to \varepsilon$, of the form $A \to \varepsilon$ in P. A nonterminal A is said to be *left-recursive* if $A \overset{+}{\Longrightarrow} A\alpha$ for some $\alpha \in V^*$. A cfg G is said to be left-recursive if there is at least one left-recursive nonterminal. Cfg G is in pseudo- *Greibach normal form* (pseudo-GNF) if every production is of the form $A \to a\alpha$, where $a \in T$ and $\alpha \in V^*$. If $\alpha \in N^*$ then G is said to be in GNF.

Definition 1.2. (homomorphism)

Let T_1 and T_2 be two alphabets. Let f be a function, $f: T_1 \to T_2^*$; f is extended to a homomorphism $f': T_1^+ \to T_2^*$ by letting $f'(a_1a_2\ldots a_n) = f(a_1)f(a_2)\ldots f(a_n)$, for $a_1a_2\ldots a_n \in T_1^+$; f' is said to be *fine* if for each $a \in T_1$, $f'(a) \in T_2 \cup \{\varepsilon\}$.

Definition 1.3. (cover)
Let G' and G be cfg's, G' = (N',T,P',S') and G = (N,T,P,S). We say that G' *right covers* G under cover-homomorphism h: $P'^{+} \to P^{*}$, if for all w in T^{*}

(i) if $S' \overset{\pi'}{\underset{r}{\Longrightarrow}} w$, then $S \overset{h(\pi')}{\underset{r}{\Longrightarrow}} w$, and

(ii) if $S \overset{\pi}{\underset{r}{\Longrightarrow}} w$, then there exist π' such that $S' \overset{\pi'}{\underset{r}{\Longrightarrow}} w$ and $h(\pi') = \pi$.

Analogously the notion of *left cover* is defined. Moreover, if left parses with respect to G' are mapped on right parses (i.e. the concatenation of productions used in a rightmost derivation but in a reversed order) with respect to G, then we say G' *left-to-right* covers G. Analogously the notion of *right-to-left* cover is defined.

Other definitions and notations will be given on the places where they are needed or the reader is referred to literature. All cfg's in this paper are assumed to be *reduced*.

2. TO COVER OR NOT TO COVER.

Before we give in this and in coming sections our, in general rather negative, results on the covering of context-free grammars, we want to start with a more positive result.

Consider the following cfg G_0 with only productions

$$0./1./2./3./\ S \to S0|S1|0|1$$

In Aho & Ullman [1,p.280] it is stated in a problem that G_0 can not be right covered by a cfg in GNF under an arbitrary cover-homomorphism, moreover, according to the following problem given there, even if we replace the homomorphism in the definition of cover by a finite transducer mapping there is no such a cover. Intuitively we agreed with this, but in our paper Nijholt [16] we asked for a proof. There is no such proof. The following cfg G is in GNF and right covers G_0. Below we list the productions of G; the start symbol is S', each production is followed by its image under the cover-homomorphism.

0. $S' \to 0$ *(2)*	10. $S \to 0$ *(0)*	20. $C \to 1$ *(11)*
1. $S' \to 1$ *(3)*	11. $S \to 1$ *(1)*	21. $F \to 1$ *(10)*
2. $S' \to 0D'$ *(ε)*	12. $S \to 0D''$ *(ε)*	22. $C'' \to 0$ *(01)*
3. $S' \to 0F'$ *(ε)*	13. $S \to 1C''$ *(ε)*	23. $C'' \to 1$ *(11)*
4. $S' \to 1E'$ *(ε)*	14. $S \to 0DS$ *(ε)*	24. $D'' \to 0$ *(00)*
5. $S' \to 1C'$ *(ε)*	15. $S \to 0FS$ *(ε)*	25. $D'' \to 1$ *(10)*
6. $S' \to 1E'S$ *(ε)*	16. $S \to 1CS$ *(ε)*	26. $E' \to 0$ *(03)*
7. $S' \to 1C'S$ *(ε)*	17. $S \to 1ES$ *(ε)*	27. $D' \to 0$ *(02)*
8. $S' \to 0D'S$ *(ε)*	18. $E \to 0$ *(01)*	28. $C' \to 1$ *(13)*
9. $S' \to 0F'S$ *(ε)*	19. $D \to 0$ *(00)*	29. $F' \to 1$ *(12)*

Table I. Productions for G'.

The proof that G right covers cfg G_0 is straightforward and is therefore omitted. Although the long list of productions suggests the contrary G can be derived from G_0 in a rather intuitive way. In Gray & Harrison [4] there is a theorem which states that cfg G_0 can not be right covered by a cfg in GNF (pseudo-GNF) under a fine cover-homomorphism. Their proof is not correct since their claim 3 is incorrect. However, to show that there exist cfg's which cannot be right (or left) covered by a cfg in GNF we can look at more simple grammars. For example, the unambiguous cfg G_1 with only productions 0. $S \to A$ and 1.$A \to a$ can not be right (left) covered by a cfg G' = (N',T,P',S') under a fine cover-homomorphism h, since such a cover-homomorphism should map the only production $S' \to a$ on 01, hence h can not be fine.

Corollary 2.1

Not every cfg can be right (left) covered by a cfg in GNF under a fine cover-homomorphism.

Arbitrary cover-homomorphisms (i.e. not necessarily fine) lead to more interesting problems. First we list a few properties of covers.

Notation: Let $\alpha \in V^*$ then α^R is the string α written in reversed order.

Lemma 2.1.

If G' right (left) covers G then the degree of ambiguity of G' (see Aho & Ullman [1]) is greater then or equal to the degree of ambiguity of G.

Proof. Follows directly from the definition of cover.□

Observation 2.1.

Clearly there is a close relation between right covers (which are defined for rightmost derivations) and mappings of right parses. If G' right covers G under h then right parses of G' can be mapped on right parses of G. Define h' as: for each

$i \in P'$, if $h(i) = \rho$ then $h'(i) = \rho^R$. If G' right covers G under h then we have that

(i) if $S' \overset{\pi'}{\underset{r}{\Longrightarrow}} w$ then $S \overset{h(\pi')}{\underset{r}{\Longrightarrow}} w$, which means, if we let $\pi = h(\pi')$, that $h'(\pi'^R) = \pi^R$ and

(ii) if $S \overset{\pi}{\underset{r}{\Longrightarrow}} w$, then there exists π' such that $S' \overset{\pi'}{\underset{r}{\Longrightarrow}} w$, where $h(\pi') = \pi$, i.e. $h'(\pi'^R) = \pi^R$.□

The proof of the following lemma is straightforward and therefore omitted.

Lemma 2.2.
A cfg G is right (left) covered by a cfg in pseudo-GNF iff G is right (left) covered by a cfg in GNF.

Can each cfg be right (left) covered (under an arbitrary cover-homomorphism) by a cfg in GNF? Consider the following cfg G_2 with only productions $S \rightarrow A|a$ and $A \rightarrow S$. Clearly a cfg in GNF which rightcovers G_2 does not exist. The same result holds for the (also ambiguous) cfg G_3 with only productions.

$$S \rightarrow A|B,\ A \rightarrow a \text{ and } B \rightarrow a.$$

Corollary 2.2.
Not every cfg can be right (left) covered by a cfg in GNF.

There remain the following questions. Can each unambiguous cfg be right (left) covered by a cfg in GNF? Can each ε-free unambiguous cfg be right (left) covered by a cfg in GNF? If there are at least two ways to derive ε in a cfg then clearly this cfg can not be right (left) covered by an ε-free grammar.

Corollary 2.3.
Not every cfg can be right (left) covered by an ε-free cfg.

There remains the question: Can each unambifuous cfg be right (left) covered by an ε-free cfg?
Instead of GNF we can consider the less restricted class of cfg's which are not left-recursive. Then we have from Nijholt [16] the following result.

Corollary 2.4.
Each cfg which is ε-free and cycle-free is right covered by a non-left-recursive cfg.

The following lemma can easily be obtained from the usual tranformation of a non-left-recursive cfg to a cfg in GNF (see for example Aho & Ullman [1]), therefore the proof is omitted.

Lemma 2.3.
Each unambiguous and ε-free non-left-recursive grammar is left covered by a cfg in GNF.

Notice that the condition of unambiguity is necessary, see for example the non-left-recursive cfg G_1 mentioned above which cannot be left covered by a cfg in GNF.
In section 4 we return to some of the questions here but then for more restricted classes of cfg's.

3. PARSABILITY AND COVERS.

For the formal definitions of some notions in this section we refer the reader to Aho & Ullman [1] and Nijholt [17]. A *deterministic pushdown transducer* P (dpdt) is said to be a *valid* dpdt for cfg G if P acts as a *parser* for G. P may for example act as a left parser (producing left parses) or as a right parser (producing right parses). If for a cfg G there exists a valid dpdt then G is said to be a *parsable* grammar (*left parsable, right parsable*).

Examples. The cfg G_4 with only productions

$S \to BAb \mid CAc \qquad B \to a$

$A \to BA \mid a \qquad C \to a$

is a left parsable grammar. The cfg G_5 with only productions

$S \to Ab \mid Ac \qquad B \to a$

$A \to AB\ a$

is a right parsable grammar. It is not difficult to prove that G_4 is not right parsable and G_5 is not left parsable.

We can use the idea of parsable grammars to show the impossibility of certain covers.

Lemma 3.1.
(i) Suppose cfg G is not left parsable. Then G cannot be left covered by a left parsable grammar.
(ii) Suppose cfg G is not right parsable. Then G cannot be right covered by a right parsable grammar.

Proof. (sketch) Part(i). Suppose there exists G', G' left covers G under cover-homomorphism h and G' is left parsable. Hence there exists a valid dpdt P' for G' which acts as a left parser. By applying h to the output of P' we obtain a new dpdt P which is, since G' left covers G, a valid dpdt for G, hence G is left parsable. This contradicts the assumption that G is not left parsable.

Therefore we must conclude that G cannot be left covered by a left parsable grammar. Part (ii) goes analogously.□

With two examples we show the use of this lemma.

Example 3.1. In Nijholt [19] the definition of a *simple chain grammar* was introduced. Let $G = (N,T,P,S)$ be an ε-free grammar. Let $X_0 \in V$, then $CH(X_0) = \{<X_0X_1 \ldots X_n> \mid X_0X_1 \ldots X_n \in N^*T \ \& \ X_0 \underset{\ell}{\Longrightarrow} X_1\psi_1 \underset{\ell}{\Longrightarrow} \ldots \underset{\ell}{\Longrightarrow} X_n\psi_n$, where $\psi_i \in V^*$, $1 \leq i \leq n\}$. If $\pi = <X_0X_1 \ldots X_n> \in CH(X_0)$ then $l(\pi) = X_n$. V is said to be chain-independent if for all X in V, if π_1,π_2 in CH(X) and $\pi_1 \neq \pi_2$ then $l(\pi_1) \neq l(\pi_2)$. Let $X,Y \in V$, $X \neq Y$. We write $X \not\equiv Y$ if for each pair $\pi_1 \in CH(X)$ and $\pi_2 \in CH(Y)$ we have that $l(\pi_1) \neq l(\pi_2)$. We use this notation also if V is chain-independent, then if π_1,π_2 in CH(X) we have $l(\pi_1) \neq l(\pi_2)$, hence $X \not\equiv X$. A set of productions P is prefix-free if $A \to \alpha$ and $A \to \alpha\beta$ in P implies $\beta = \varepsilon$. A cfg $G = (N,T,P,S)$ is said to be a *simple chain grammar* if V is chain-independent, P is prefix-free and for each pair productions $A \to \alpha X\phi$ and $A \to \alpha Y\psi$, where $X \neq Y$, we have $X \not\equiv Y$.
In Nijholt [20] it is shown that each simple chain grammar can be transformed to a simple LL(1) grammar (i.e. a cfg which satisfies (i) each production is of the form $A \to a\phi$ and (ii) if $A \to a\phi$ and $A \to b\psi$ then $a \neq b$ or $a\phi = b\psi$).
Now consider the cfg G with only productions

$$S \to aEc \mid aEd \quad \text{and} \quad E \to aEb \mid ab.$$

One can easily verify that G satisfies the conditions of a simple chain grammar and moreover that G is not a left parsable grammar. Therefore, with lemma 3.1. we can immediately conclude that there is no transformation from simple chain grammars to simple LL(1) grammars which yields a left cover.

Example 3.2. In Hammer [5] the class of *k-transformable* grammars is introduced, a subclass of the LR(k) grammars. Moreover, a transformation is presented from k-transformable grammars to (strong) LL(k) grammars. Consider the following k-transformable grammar G from that paper, with only productions

$$S \to bAc \qquad A \to ABx \mid ABy \mid a \qquad B \to Bd \mid d$$

Again, one can easily verify that G is not a left parsable grammar. Therefore, with lemma 3.1, we can conclude immediately that there is no transformation from k-transformable to LL(k) grammars which yields a left cover.

The result of example 3.1. is rather surprising. An extremely simple transformation can yield a simple LL(1) grammar. For example, replace

$$S \to aEc \mid aEd \quad \text{and} \quad E \to aEb \mid ab$$

by

$$S \to aED, \quad E \to aEb \mid ab \quad \text{and} \quad D \to c \mid d.$$

This new grammar does not left cover the original grammar. Moreover, with the same type of argument, there is no LL(k) grammar which left covers the original grammar.

4. COVERS AND DETERMINISTIC GRAMMARS.

In this last section we give some remarks on problems and results for the covering of LR(k) grammars and of grammars belonging to subclasses of the class of LR(k) grammars. In the preceeding section we already saw two (negative) results. From example 3.1. it follows that not every LR(k) grammar which generates an LL(k) language has an left covering LL(k) grammar.
In Lomet [12] and in Geller, Harrison & Havel [2] it is shown that each LR(k) language may be given an LR(1) grammar in GNF. Moreover each SD-grammar (*Strict Deterministic* grammar, see Harrison & Havel [6]) can be transformed to a SD-grammar in GNF. Therefore we ask the same questions as we did in section 2, i.e. can each SD-grammar be right covered by a SD-grammar in GNF?; can each LR(k) grammar be right covered by an LR(1) grammar in GNF? Questions for which we have no answers yet. However, trivially we obtain again (see for example cfg G_1 of section 2) that for a fine cover-homomorphism the answers are no. Consider also the following properties. First recall that SD-grammars are not left-recursive. In Nijholt [17] it is shown that each LR(k) grammar G can be transformed to an LR(1) grammar (or in case L(G) is prefix-free to a SD-grammar) which right covers G. Moreover, although not mentioned there, it can easily be verified that the LR(1) grammar which is obtained is non-left-recursive.

Corollary 4.1.
Each LR(k) grammar G is right covered by a non-left-recursive LR(1) grammar, or in case L(G) is prefix-free by a SD-grammar.

The following result can also be obtained from Nijholt [17]; here we prefer to use some other results. Let G = (N,T,P,S) be an LL(k) grammar. Let p be the total number of productions in P. Then construct a new cfg G' = (N',T,P',S) where
$N' = N \cup \{H_i \mid 1 \leq i \leq p\}$ (the H_i's are newly introduced nonterminals);
$P' = P \cup \{H_i \to \varepsilon \mid 1 \leq i \leq p\}$. In Hunt III & Szymanski [11] it is proved that G' is LL(k) if and only if G is LL(k). One can easily prove that G' right-to-left covers G. Since G' is LL(k) and hence LR(k) we have

Corollary 4.2.
Each LL(k) grammar is right-to-left covered by an LR(k) grammar.
In this corollary we can replace, with the aid of corollary 4.1. LR(k) by LR(1) (or SD). The last result in this section is obtained from Geller, Harrison & Havel [6]. The transformation given there to obtain a SD-grammar in GNF from a SD-grammar yields a left cover.

Corollary 4.3.
Each ε-free SD-grammar is left covered by a SD-grammar in GNF.

5. CONCLUSIONS.

The purpose of this paper was to sketch an area of problems for the concept of cover. We showed that in spite of some remarks in the literature the problem of covering (unambiguous and ε-free) cfg's with cfg's in GNF is open. Moreover we gave some properties of covers and we showed a relation between covers and parsability.

References.

1. Aho A.V. and Ullman J.D., The Theory of Parsing, Translation and Compiling, Vols. I and II, Prentice Hall, Englewood Cliffs, New Jersey, 1972 and 1973.

2. Geller M.M., Harrison M.A. and Havel I.M., Normal forms of deterministic languages, Discrete Mathematics, Vol. 16, pp. 313-322, 1976.

3. Graham S.L., On bounded right context languages and grammars, SIAM Journal on Computing, Vol. 3, pp. 224-254, 1974.

4. Gray J.N. and Harrison M.A., On the covering and reduction problems for context-free grammars, Journal of the Association for Computing Machinery, Vol. 19, pp. 675-698, 1972.

5. Hammer M, A new grammatical transformation into LL(k) form, Conference Record of the 6th annual ACM Symposium on Theory of Computing, pp. 266-275, 1974.

6. Harrison M.A. and Havel I.M., Strict deterministic grammars, Journal of Computer and System Sciences, Vol. 7, pp. 237-277, 1973.

7. Harrison M.A., On covers and precedence analysis, Lecture Notes in Computer Science 1, G.I. 3. Jahrestagung, pp. 2-17, 1973.

8. Hunt III H.B., A complexity theory of grammar problems, Conference Record of the 3rd ACM Symposium on Principles of Programming Languages, pp. 12-18, 1976.

9. Hunt III H.B., Rosenkrantz D.J. and Szymanski T.G., The covering problem for linear context-free grammars, Theoretical Computer Science, Vol. 2, pp. 361-382, 1976.

10.Hunt III H.B., Rosenkrantz D.J. and Szymanski T.G., On the equivalence, containment, and covering problems for the regular and context-free languages, Journal of Computer and System Sciences, Vol. 12, pp. 222-268, 1976.

11.Hunt III H.B., Szymanski T.G., Lower bounds and reductions between grammar problems, Technical Report 216, Princeton University, 1976.

12.Lomet D.B., A formalization of transition diagram systems, Journal of the Association for Computing Machinery, Vol. 20, pp. 235-257, 1973.

13.McAfee J. and Presser L., An algorithm for the design of simple precedence grammars, Journal of the Association for Computing Machinery, Vol. 19, pp. 385-395, 1972.

14.Mickunas M.D., On the complete covering problem for LR(k) grammars, Journal of the Association for Computing Machinery, Vol. 23, pp. 17-30, 1976.

15.Mickunas M.D., Lancaster R.L. and Schneider V.B., Transforming LR(k) grammars to LR(1), SLR(1) and (1,1) Bounded Right Context grammars, Journal of the Association for Computing Machinery, Vol. 23, pp. 511-533, 1976.

16.Nijholt A., On the covering of left-recursive grammars, Conference Record of the 4th ACM Symposium on Principles of Programming Languages, pp. 86-96, 1977.

17.Nijholt A., On the covering of parsable grammars, to appear in Journal of Computer and System Sciences.

18.Nijholt A., On the parsing of LL-Regular grammars, Lecture Notes in Computer Science 45, Proc. 5th Int. Symposium on Mathematical Foundations of Computer Science, pp. 446-452, 1976.

19.Nijholt A., Simple Chain Grammars, Proc. 4th Int. Conference on Automata, Languages and Programming, 1977 (to appear).

20.Nijholt A., Simple Chain Languages, manuscript, march 1977.

ON A DETERMINISTIC SUBCLASS OF CONTEXT-FREE LANGUAGES

Jan Peckel
Charles University, Faculty of Mathematics and Physics
Malostranské nám. 25
118 00 Prague, Czechoslovakia

Introduction

G. Wechsung [1] has introduced a new complexity measure and has proved that the class of all context-free languages turns out to be a complexity class of the mentioned complexity measure for nondeterministic Turing machines.

His results induce several interesting problems :

- whether the class of all deterministic context-free languages is a subclass of the class of all languages recognizable deterministically with the Wechsung's complexity limited by a constant,
- what relations exist between the class of all languages recognizable deterministically with the Wechsung's complexity limited by the constant k and the class of all languages recognizable deterministically with the Wechsung's complexity limited by the constant k+1.

This paper is discussing the above mentioned problems and dealing with the closure properties of the class of all languages recognizable deterministically with the Wechsung's complexity limited by a constant and with the comparability of this class and the class of all linear context-free languages.

Wechsung's complexity measure

By a Turing machine (or simply TM) $M = (Q,X,d,q_0,F)$ we shall mean a deterministic one-tape, one-head model of Turing machine with the state space Q, the alphabet X, the next-state function d, the initial state q_0 and the accepting state space F. The alphabet of every TM will contain the blank symbol b. X_b will denote the set $X-\{b\}$.

By <u>computation of a TM $M = (Q,X,d,q_0,F)$</u> <u>on a word $w \in X^*$</u> we shall mean the computation starting in the initial state q_0 on the leftmost symbol of w.

A <u>TM $M = (Q,X,d,q_0,F)$ accepts a word $w \in X_b^*$</u> iff the computation of M on w halts in an accepting state.

A <u>TM M</u> $= (Q,X,d,q_0,F)$ <u>recognizes a language $L \subseteq X_b^*$</u> iff for every word $w \in X_b^*$ the following condition holds : $w \in L \iff M$ accepts w .

In case that during a computation the content of a tape square is changed, every visit of the head payed to this square after its first **rewriting** shall be called <u>active visit</u>. For every word w accepted by a TM M the maximal number of all active visits on one tape square during the computation of M on w shall be denoted as $g_M(w)$.

Let k be a nonnegative integer.

A <u>TM M</u> $= (Q,X,d,q_0,F)$ <u>recognizes a language $L \subseteq X_b^*$ with the Wechsung's complexity k</u> iff

1/ M recognizes L and

2/ for every word $w \in L$, $g_M(w) \leq k$.

A <u>language L is recognizable with the Wechsung's complexity k</u> iff there is a TM recognizing L with the Wechsung's complexity k.

<u>Notations</u>

For every nonnegative integer k denote by W(k) the class of all languages recognizable with the Wechsung's complexity k. **Denote**

$C =_{df} \bigcup_{k=0}^{\infty} W(k)$,

CFL $=_{df}$ the class of all context-free languages,

DCFL $=_{df}$ the class of all deterministic context-free languages,

LIN $=_{df}$ the class of all linear context-free languages,

$\overleftarrow{w} =_{df}$ the "mirror image" of the word w.

<u>Theorems</u>

<u>Theorem 1</u>. DCFL and C are incomparable, i.e. DCFL $\not\subseteq$ C & C $\not\subseteq$ DCFL.

<u>Theorem 2</u>. For every nonnegative integer k, $W(k) \subsetneqq W(k+1)$ holds.

<u>Theorem 3</u>. LIN and C are incomparable, i.e. LIN $\not\subseteq$ C & C $\not\subseteq$ LIN.

<u>Theorem 4</u>. Let $L \subseteq X^*$, where X is an alphabet not containing the symbol b and let k be a nonnegative integer. Then $L^c \in W(k+1)$ whenever $L \in W(k)$.

Theorem 5. C is not closed under intersection, union, concatenation, iteration and homomorphism.

Proofs

For detailed proofs of the theorems we refer to [2]. We outline only the main ideas here.

Let $L_1 =_{df} \{a^m c^{m+n} a^n \; ; \; m,n=1,2,\ldots\}$,

$L_2 =_{df} \{w \overleftarrow{w} \; ; \; w \in \{a,c\}^+\}$,

$L_3 =_{df} \{a^n c^n a^i \; ; \; i,n=1,2,\ldots\} \cup \{a^i c^n a^n \; ; \; i,n=1,2,\ldots\}$,

$L_4 =_{df} \{a^m c^m \S\, a^n c^n \; ; \; m,n=1,2,\ldots\}$.

Then it can be proved that

$L_1 \in \mathrm{DCFL} - C$,

$L_2 \in W(1) - \mathrm{DCFL}$,

$L_3 \in \mathrm{LIN} - C$,

$L_4 \in W(2) - \mathrm{LIN}$

and this implies Theorem 1 and Theorem 3.

As for Theorem 2, the inclusions $W(k) \subseteq W(k+1)$ are obvious.

Define $\hat{L}_1 =_{df} \{a^n c^n \; ; \; n=1,2,\ldots\}$,

$X_2 =_{df} \{a, c, \boxed{1}\}$,

$\hat{L}_2 =_{df} \{a^m c^m \boxed{1}\, c^n a^n \; ; \; m,n=1,2,\ldots\}$.

For k=2,3,... define $X_{k+1} =_{df} \{a, c, \boxed{1}, \boxed{2}, \ldots \boxed{k}\}$ and

$$\hat{L}_{k+1} =_{df} \{a^n c^n a^i \boxed{k} \; ; \; i,n=1,2,\ldots\} \cdot \hat{L}_k \cdot \{\boxed{k}\, a^i c^n a^n \; ; \; i,n=1,2,\ldots\} \cup$$
$$\cup \{a^i c^n a^n \boxed{k} \; ; \; i,n=1,2,\ldots\} \cdot (X_k^* - \hat{L}_k) \cdot \{\boxed{k}\, a^n c^n a^i \; ; \; i,n=1,2,\ldots\}.$$

It can be proved that for every nonnegative integer k

$\hat{L}_{k+1} \in W(k+1) - W(k)$.

Theorem 4 is proved as follows.

Let the assumption of the Theorem 4 be satisfied and let $M = (Q, X_1, d, q_0, F)$, where $X \subseteq X_1$, be a TM recognizing L with the Wechsung's complexity k. Let l be such a positive integer that during the computation of M on any word $w \in L$ the head will reach maximally l-1 squares from the part of the tape which was initially occupied by the symbols of the input word w (such a number exists). Consider a TM $\hat{M} = (\hat{Q},\hat{X},\hat{d},\hat{q}_0,\hat{F})$ where $X_1 \subseteq \hat{X}$, such that the computation of $\hat{M}$ on any word $w \in \hat{X}_b^*$ halts in an accepting state iff $w \in X^*$ and during the computation of M on w would appear at least one of these possibilities :

- k+1 active visits will appear on a square,
- the head will reach l squares from the part of the tape which was initially occupied by the symbols of the input word w,
- M will enter an infinite cycle in which the head does not perform any active visit,
- the computation will halt in a situation for which the next-state function is not defined.

Such a TM can be defined in such a way that during the computation on an arbitrary word $w \in X^*$ there will not appear more than k+1 active visits on any square.

The nonclosure properties of Theorem 5 can be demonstrated by the languages

$$L_5 = \{a^n c^n d^i \ ; \ i,n=1,2,\dots\},$$

$$L_6 = \{a^i c^n d^n \ ; \ i,n=1,2,\dots\},$$

$$L_7 = \{a^n c^n \ ; \ n=1,2,\dots\},$$

$$L_8 = \{c^n a^n \ ; \ n=1,2,\dots\},$$

$$L_9 = \{a^m c^m d^n a^n \ ; \ m,n=1,2,\dots\}.$$

It can be proved that

$L_5 \in W(1)$ & $L_6 \in W(1)$ & $L_5 \cap L_6 \notin C$ (by Wechsung [1], $C \subseteq CFL$),

$L_7 \in W(1)$ & $L_8 \in W(1)$ & $L_7 \cdot L_8 \notin C$,

$L_7 \cup L_8 \in W(1)$ & $(L_7 \cup L_8)^* \notin C$,

$L_9 \in W(2)$ & $h(L_9) \notin C$, where h is the homomorphism

$h : \{a,c,d\}^* \longrightarrow \{a,c\}^*$ defined by $h(a)=_{df} a$, $h(c)=_{df} c$ and $h(d)=_{df} c$.

Finally, C is not closed under union, because C is closed under complement (by Theorem 4) and is not closed under intersection.

References

1. Wechsung, G., Kompliziertheitstheoretische Charakterisierung der kontextfreien und linearen Sprachen. EIK 12 (1976) 6, 289-300.

2. Peckel, J., A Deterministic Subclass of Context-Free Languages, in preparation.

EXPONENTIAL OPTIMIZATION FOR THE LLP(k) PARSING METHOD

Jan Pittl

Fetrovská 31

160 00 Praha 6

Czechoslovakia

Abstract

LLP(k) parsing was introduced by Lomet [9]. This paper presents an LLP(k) version of the LR(k) characteristic parsing method developed by Geller and Harrison [4]. The new construction allows an essential extension of the class of grammars admitting the optimization of parser size. While the till known application works for the class of strict deterministic grammars (see Harrison and Havel [6,7]) the method presented here covers the whole class of LLP(k) grammars. The improvement in parser size can be even exponential.

Introduction

This paper is meant to be an informal explanation of the ideas involved in Pittl [12]. We shall use familiar terminology of formal languages and parsing without explicit repeating (see Aho and Ullman [1]). Special notational conventions are listed below.

A context-free grammar G is a quadruple $G=(N,T,P,S)$ where N,T are nonterminal and terminal alphabets, respectively, $S \in N$ is the initial symbol, P is a finite set of productions that will be written as $A \to w$ where $A \in N$, $w \in (N \cup T)^*$. Define $V = N \cup T$, denote e the empty word. Let k be a nonnegative integer. For $y,z \in V^*$ write ${}^{(k)}y = z$ iff $\text{length}(z) = \min(\text{length}(y),k)$ & $y = zx$ for some $x \in V^*$. Denote $T^{*k} = \{ x \in T^* \ / \ \text{length}(x) \leq k \}$. For $w \in V^*$ define

$$FIRST_k(w) = \{ x \in T^{*k} \ / \ w \overset{*}{\Rightarrow} y \text{ for some } y \in T^* \ \& \ x = {}^{(k)}y \} .$$

$$FOLLOW_k(w) = \{ x \in T^{*k} \ / \ S \overset{*}{\Rightarrow} vwy \text{ for some } v \in V^* \ \& \ x \in FIRST_k(y) \} .$$

A parse point is an expression $(A \to x.y,u)$ where $A \to xy$ is a production and $u \in FOLLOW_k(A)$. A parse set is any set of parse points.

Let us make a global assumption that every grammar we are talking about is context-free, reduced, and generates a nonempty language.

The parsing method

Our parsing algorithm (see Pittl [12]) represents a slight modification of the original one of Lomet [10]. The actions of the parsing automaton are preserved but the set of states is reconstructed to enable the optimalization in size. Similarly to the well known LR(k) parsers (Aho and Ullman [1], deRemer [2]) it is formed by a collection of parse sets. Lomet [10] first creates such a collection and then applies the optimizations to diminish its size. The characteristic parsing method (see Geller and Harrison [4,5]) uses an opposite approach. Some informations about the possibility of optimization are obtained and then parse sets are computed in accordance with them. The generation of the parse set follows the original method with the modification that some other parse points can be added into the parse set. A characteristic is some strategy for adding parse points into parse sets.

Algorithm 1. Input: A grammar $G=(N,T,P,S)$, $k \geq 0$, a characteristic C.
Output: CPS(C,G,k), the collection of parse sets for G.
Method: The given grammar is extended by an additional production $S' \rightarrow S$, where S' is a new symbol not included in V. Initially let CPS(C,G,k) be empty.

Step 1. Place $R_0 = \{(S' \rightarrow .S, e)\}$ in CPS(C,G,k) as an unmarked set.

Step 2. If a set $R \in CPS(C,G,k)$ is unmarked then

(a) Compute for each $X \in V$ the set

$GOTO(R,X) = \{(A \rightarrow vX.w,u) \ / \ (A \rightarrow v.Xw,u) \in R\}$.

If $GOTO(R,X) \neq \emptyset$ then add GOTO(R,X) to CPS(C,G,k) unmarked.

(b) Compute $CALL(R) = \{(B \rightarrow .w,v) \ / \ (A \rightarrow x.By,u) \in R \ \& \ \& \ B \rightarrow w \in P \ \& \ v \in FIRST_k(yu)\}$.

If $CALL(R) \neq \emptyset$ then using the characteristic C add to CALL(R) some parse points of the form $(D \rightarrow .z,d)$ where $D \rightarrow z \in P$ and $d \in FOLLOW_k(D)$. Denote the obtained set as $CALL^C(R)$ and add it to CPS(C,G,k) unmarked.

(c) Mark R.

Step 3. Repeat step 2 until all sets in CPS(C,G,k) are marked.

Example 1. Consider the grammar G=({S,A,B,D}, {a,b},P,S) where P is formed by productions

$S \to aA \qquad S \to aD \qquad A \to a$

$S \to bB \qquad D \to ab \qquad B \to a$

Let k=1 and C be the characteristic defined as follows: For every parse set R add into $CALL^C(R)$ all parse points $(Y \to .w,y)$ for all $Y \to w \in P$ and $y \in FOLLOW_k(Y)$. The collection CPS(C,G,1) consists of 9 members.

$R_o = \{(S' \to .S,e)\}$ $\qquad R_1 = GOTO(R_o,S) = \{(S' \to S.,e)\}$

$R_2 = CALL^C(R_o) = \{(S \to .aA,e), (S \to .bB,e), (S \to .aD,e), (D \to .ab,e), (A \to .a,e), (B \to .a,e)\}$ $\qquad R_3 = GOTO(R_2,a) = \{(S \to a.A,e), (S \to a.D,e), (D \to a.b,e), (A \to a.,e), (B \to a.,e)\}$

$R_4 = GOTO(R_2,b) = \{(S \to b.B,e)\}$ $\qquad R_5 = GOTO(R_3,A) = \{(S \to aA.,e)\}$

$R_6 = GOTO(R_3,D) = \{(S \to aD.,e)\}$ $\qquad R_7 = GOTO(R_3,b) = \{(D \to ab.,e)\}$

$R_8 = GOTO(R_4,B) = \{(S \to bB.,e)\}$

Since our concern is in parser size we shall omit here the detailed construction of our parser (see Pittl [12]). We shall outline only the main ideas of the LLP(k) parsing algorithm. To determine the parsing actions Lomet [10] introduces so called <u>left local precedence (LLP) relations</u> $⋖, \doteq, ⋗$. Let R be a parse set, $w \in T^{*k}$. Then

$R ⋖ w$, if there is a parse point $(A \to x.y,u) \in R$ so that $w \in FIRST_k(yu)$ & $^{(1)}y \in N$
(Intuitivelly, a phrase is starting.)

$R \doteq w$, if there is $(A \to x.y,u) \in R$ so that $w \in FIRST_k(yu)$ & $^{(1)}y \in T$.
(i.e. a phrase is continuing.)

$R ⋗ w$, if there is $(A \to x.y,u) \in R$ so that $w \in FIRST_k(yu)$ & $^{(1)}y = e$.
(i.e. the end of some phrase has occured.)

As an illustration consider the parse set R_3 from example 1. Since $(S \to a.A,e) \in R_3$ the relation $R_3 ⋖ a$ holds. Similarly $(D \to a.b,e) \in R_3$ implies $R_3 \doteq b$, from $(A \to a.,e) \in R_3$ it follows $R_3 ⋗ e$.

The original Lomet's method assumes that the LLP relations are disjoint for every parse set $R \in CPS$. Moreover, the relation $⋗$ must uniquely determine the end of any production, i.e. for all $R \in CPS$

if $(A \rightarrow v.,u) \in R$ & $(B \rightarrow w.,u) \in R$ then $A \rightarrow v = B \rightarrow w$. The CPS's posessing the property mentioned above are called <u>LLP consistent</u>. This condition insures for the LLP(k) parser to be deterministic.

In the characteristic case a weaker condition can be used. This concerns the uniqueness of the relation $\gg$. If $(A \rightarrow v.,u) \in R$ & $(B \rightarrow w.,u) \in R$ then from algorithm 1 it follows that w=v holds. Hence both productions belong to the same phrase. Now it is sufficient to be able to determine the nonterminal being reduced from the parse set designating the start of this phrase. Formally, no $R' \in$ CPS exists so that $GOTO(R',A) \neq \emptyset$ & $GOTO(R',B) \neq \emptyset$. The CPS's having this modified property are called <u>characteristic LLP consistent</u>. Clearly, LLP consistency implies the characteristic LLP consistency. Note that the converse assertion is invalid (cf. example 1 where $(A \rightarrow a.,e) \in R_3$ & $(B \rightarrow a.,e) \in R_3$).

Consider the characteristic C_o (called canonical) that makes the additional phase of algorithm 1 to be empty, i.e. adds no parse points. We define a grammar G to be an <u>LLP(k) grammar</u> iff the collection $CPS(C_o,G,k)$ is LLP consistent. In Pittl [12] it is shown that this definition agrees with the original one given by Lomet [10]. One can prove following assertions dealing with the notions defined above.

<u>Theorem 1</u>. Let G be a grammar, C a characteristic. If the collection CPS(C,G,k) is characteristic LLP consistent then G is an LLP(k) grammar.

<u>Theorem 2</u>. A grammar G is an LLP(k) grammar iff there exists a characteristic C so that the collection CPS(C,G,k) is characteristic LLP consistent.

We conclude that our method is able to parse exactly the class of LLP(k) grammars.

<u>Weak partitions and characteristics</u>

To obtain characteristics convenient for the optimalization of the LLP(k) parser we shall use the notion of a weak partition.

<u>Definition 1</u>. A set W of some subsets of a given set X is a <u>weak partition</u> of X iff X is the union of all members of W. For $a,b \in X$ write aWb iff there is $Y \in W$ so that $a \in Y$ & $b \in Y$. Denote $\bar{a}^W$ the intersection of all $Y \in W$ so that $a \in Y$ holds for them. A weak partition W is a <u>partition</u> if the members of W are pairwise disjoint.

Let G=(N,T,P,S) be a grammar, k≥0. Consider the set

$M_k(G) = \{ (A,u) \ / \ A \in N \ \& \ u \in FOLLOW_k(A) \}$.

For every weak partition W of $M_k(G)$ we define the characteristic C_W as follows: Let R be a parse set, $(A \rightarrow .y,u) \in CALL(R)$. Add into $CALL^{C_W}(R)$ all the parse points $(B \rightarrow .x,v)$ where $B \rightarrow x \in P$, $(B,v) \in \overline{(A,u)}^W$

Example 2. Consider the grammar G from example 1. with the weak partition W defined $W = \{\{(S,e),(A,e),(B,e),(D,e)\}\}$. Since C_W adds the same parse points as the characteristic C from example 1 the collection $CPS(C_W,G,1)$ is equal to CPS(C,G,1).

Let W be a weak partition of $M_k(G)$, $Y \in W$, $x \in V^*$. Define

$Pr(Y) = \{ x \in V^* \ / \ (A,u) \in Y \ \& \ A \rightarrow xz \in P \text{ for some } z \in V^* \}$.

$NT(x,Y) = \{ (A \rightarrow x.z,u) \ / \ (A,u) \in Y \ \& \ A \rightarrow xz \in P \text{ for some } z \in V^* \}$.

We shall study weak partitions by means of a set of parse sets

$SP(W) = \{ NT(x,Y) \ / \ Y \in W \ \& \ x \in Pr(Y) \}$.

Compared with the collection $CPS(C_W,G,k)$ the set SP(W) is simple and its definition doesn't involve any induction. We shall suggest some conditions on W and SP(W) that will imply convenient properties of the collection $CPS(C_W,G,k)$. To be able to use such a collection in our parser we must insure for it to be characteristic LLP consistent.

Definition 2. Let G be a grammar, W a weak partition of $M_k(G)$. W is called admissible for G iff for every $R \in SP(W)$ holds:
If $(A \rightarrow .x,u) \in CALL(R)$ & $(B \rightarrow .y,v) \in CALL(R)$ then (A,u)W(B,v) .
W is k-admissible for G if moreover SP(W) is characteristic LLP consistent.

Consider the grammar G from example 1 and the partition W of $M_1(G)$ from example 2 W is admissible for G as it consists of an unique member. Since no violation of the characteristic LLP consistency of SP(W) occurs W is 1-admissible for G.

Theorem 3. Let G be a grammar, W a weak partition of $M_k(G)$. If W is k-admissible for G then $CPS(C_W,G,k)$ is characteristic LLP consistent.

The main idea of the optimalization is to find for the given grammar a convenient k-admissible weak partition which minimizes the size of the parser.

Weak partitions and LLP(k) grammars

The notion of the k-admissible weak partition allows us to establish a new grammatical characterization of the class of LLP(k) grammars that was not known till now.

Theorem 4. A grammar G is an LLP(k) grammar iff there exists some k-admissible weak partition for G.

From this point of view the class of LLP(k) grammars seems to be an extension of the class of strict deterministic grammars (see Harrison and Havel [6,7]). In terms of our notations these grammars can be defined as follows. A grammar G is a strict deterministic grammar iff there is a partition W of $M_0(G)$ so that W is admissible for G and SP(W) is LLP consistent. It is interesting that in the above theorem the notion of a weak partition is necessary. There are LLP(k) grammars that no k-admissible partition exists.

Parser size bounds

For optimalization purposes it is necessary to obtain an estimation of cardinality of the collections generated by weak partitions. This problem can be solved under a condition somewhat stronger than admissibility.

Definition 3. Let G be a grammar, W a weak partition of $M_k(G)$. W is called normalized for G iff $\overline{(S,e)}^W \in W$ and for every $R \in SP(W)$ if $CALL(R) \neq \emptyset$ then $\{(A,u) \ / \ (A \rightarrow .x,u) \in CALL^C W(R)\} \in W$.
W is k-normalized for G if moreover SP(W) is characteristic LLP consistent.

It is important that every admissible partition is normalized. Hence the partition W from example 2 is 1-normalized .

Theorem 5. Let G be a grammar, W a normalized weak partition for G. Denote /X/ the cardinality of a set X. Then

$$/CPS(C_W,G,k)/ \leqslant 2 + \sum_{Y \in W} /Pr(Y)/$$

Naturally one can ask whether the generality of the optimalization method won't be lost using normalized weak partitions only.

Theorem 6. Let G be a grammar. If W is an admissible weak partition for G then there exists a normalized weak partition Z for G so that $CPS(C_W,G,k) = CPS(C_Z,G,k)$. If W is k-admissible for G then Z is k-normalized for G.

Theorems 4 and 6 imply that for every LLP(k) grammar G there is a k-normalized weak partition such that the cardinality of the generated CPS is minimal for the class of all k-admissible weak partitions for G. It is open whether such a minimal weak partition can be found by a polynomial algorithm. Unfortunately, this problem seems to rank among the polynomially complete ones. At the conclusion we shall illustrate the power of our method by an example of an exponential improvement in parser size for the LLP(k) parser.

Example 3. Let n be a nonnegative integer, $n \geq 1$. Consider the family of grammars $G_n=(N_n,T_n,P_n,S)$ where $N_n = \{A_1, \dots ,A_n ,S,A,B,C,D\}$, $T_n = \{a_1, \dots ,a_n , b_1, \dots ,b_n ,a,b\}$, P_n consists of productions

$$S \to bA_i \quad , i=1, \dots ,n$$
$$A_i \to a_jA_i \quad , i=1, \dots ,n , j=1, \dots ,n , j \neq i$$
$$A_i \to b_i \quad , i=1, \dots ,n$$

$$S \to aD \qquad D \to aB \qquad D \to bC \qquad A \to ab$$
$$D \to aA \qquad D \to bB \qquad B \to b \qquad C \to aB$$

Let W_n be weak partitions of $M_o(G_n)$ defined

$$W_n = \{ \{(S,e)\},\{(D,e)\},\{(A_1,e), \dots ,(A_n,e)\},\{(A,e),(B,e)\},\{(B,e),(C,e)\}\}$$

W_n are 0-normalized weak partitions for G_n, $\sum_{Y \in W_n} /Pr(Y)/ = n^2+n+19$.

It can be shown that both LLP(0) and LR(0) canonical parsers for G_n have more than 2^n states. So the improvement by our method is exponential. Note that for $n \geq 1$ any G_n is strict deterministic since there is no 0-admissible partition for G_n. It follows that the method of Geller and Harrison [4,5] cannot provide the improvement in parser size for G_n.

References

1. Aho, A.V. and Ullman, J.D., The Theory of Parsing, Translation, and Compiling, Vols. I,II, Prentice Hall, Englewood Cliffs, N.J., 1972-3.

2. deRemer, F.L., Simple LR(k) Grammars, CACM, 14 (1971), 453-460

3. Geller, M.M., Graham, S.L., and Harrison, M.A., Production Prefix Parsing (extended abstract), in Automata, Languages, and Programming, 2nd Colloquium, University of Saarbrücken (J. Loeckx, ed.), 1974, 232-241.

4. Geller, M.M., Harrison, M.A., Strict Deterministic Versus LR(0) Parsing, Conference Record of ACM Symposium on Principles of Programming Languages, 1973, 22-32.

5. Geller, M.M., Harrison, M.A., Characteristic Parsing: A Framework for Producing Compact Deterministic Parsers, Parts I,II, unpublished

6. Harrison, M.A. and Havel, I.M., Strict Deterministic Grammars, Journal of Computer and System Sciences, 7 (1973), 237-277.

7. Harrison, M.A. and Havel, I.M., On the Parsing of Deterministic Languages, JACM, 21 (1974), 525-548.

8. Král, J., Demner, J., Parsing As a Subtask of Compiling, MFCS´75, Lecture Notes in Computer Science 32, Springer-Verlag, Berlin, 1975, 61-73.

9. Lomet, D.B., The Construction of Efficient Deterministic Language Processors, Ph.d. diss., University of Pennsylvania, Philadelphia, 1969, and IBM Research Report RC 2738, 1970.

10. Lomet, D.B., Formal Construction of Multiple Exit Parsing Routines, Report IBM.

11. Lomet, D.B., Automatic Generation of Multiple Exit Parsing Subroutines, in Automata, Languages, and Programming, 2nd Colloquium, University of Saarbrücken (J. Loeckx, ed.), 1974, 214-231.

12. Pittl, J., Characteristic Parsing of LLP(k) Grammars, (in Czech), SVOČ Thesis, Prague, 1977.

THE MEDIAL AXIS OF A SIMPLE POLYGON

F. P. Preparata
Coordinated Science Laboratory
University of Illinois at Urbana

1. Introduction

The medial axis M(G) of an arbitrary simple polygon G is defined as the set of points of the plane internal to G which have more than one closest point on the boundary of G.

The medial axis M(G) is a tree-like planar structure (see figure 1) which partitions the interior of G into regions, each of which is the locus of the points closest either to an edge or to a vertex of G. For this reason, the construction of the medial axis has been appropriately referred to by M. I. Shamos as the solution of the "closest boundary point" problem ([1], Problem POL 9).

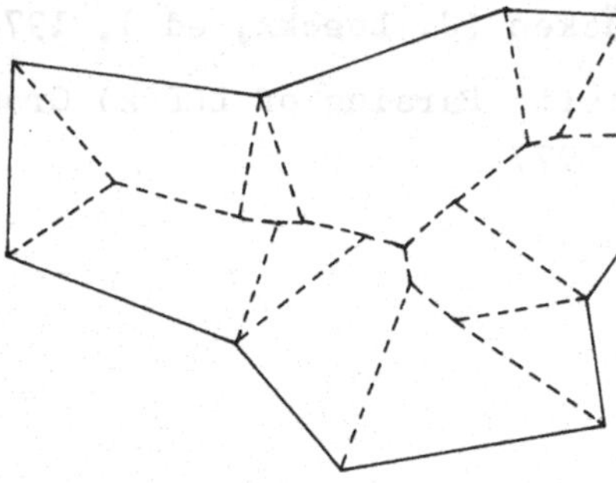

Figure 1 - A polygon G and its medial axis M(G).

The notion of medial axis received considerable attention some years ago from researchers interested in image recognition [2], after H. Blum [3] introduced it as an effective descriptor of shape (and it was referred to as the "skeleton" of a figure). In that context, algorithms [4] were proposed for the construction of the medial axis.

Those algorithms operated on a digitized figure and, in terms of the interpretation of the latter as a polygon, they were quite inefficient.

The definition of medial axis is so simple that one, using a good deal of visual intuition, can draw it with little difficulty, especially for convex polygons. However, as reported by Shamos in his collection of problems in Computational Geometry [1], an actual algorithm has not been developed even for convex polygons.

In this paper we shall describe two algorithms for the construction of the medial axis of a polygon G with n vertices, which respectively apply to convex and arbitrary simple polygons. The running times of these two algorithms are at most O(nlogn) and $O(n^2)$, respectively.

The objective of the algorithms is the construction of M(G) one vertex at a time. Although the ideas are analogous in both instances, there are clear differences between the convex and the nonconvex cases to warrant separate treatments. The convex case will be considered in some detail in Section 2; in Section 3, we shall outline the procedure for the general case.

Incidentally, the construction of M(G) of G also solves, with additional time O(n), the related problem of finding the largest circle contained (incircle of) in G; indeed, it is immediate to realize that the largest incircle of G has center at one of the vertices of M(G).

2. Medial axis of a convex polygon

Let G be a convex polygon with n vertices. If u denotes a vertex of G, we let B(u) denote the bisector of the angle at vertex u. If (u,v) denotes an edge of G, we shall call c(u,v) the intersection of B(u) and B(v), and r(u,v) the distance of c(u,v) from (u,v). Notice that c(u,v) is the center of the circle tangent to (u,v) and to the two straight-lines containing respectively the edges adjacent to (u,v).

The medial axis of a convex polygon is a (binary) tree whose edges are straight-line segments, since they are the loci of points equidistant from pairs of edges. The vertices of M(G) are center of circles tangent to three edges of G. Let r(G) be the minimum of r(u,v) over all edges (u,v) of G. We have the following lemma:

Lemma 1: Let r(u,v) = r(G). The circle $\mathcal{C}$(u,v) with center c(u,v) and radius r(u,v) is tangent to (u,v) and its two adjacent edges.

Proof: By contradiction. Let (w,u) be an edge adjacent to (u,v) and assume that $\mathcal{C}$(u,v) is not tangent to (w,u) (figure 2). This means that point A, intersection of the line containing (w,u) and its normal through c(u,v), is external to (w,u). This and convexity imply that B(w) intersects the segment (u,c(u,v)) between u and B, where B is the intersection of (u,c(u,v)) and the normal to (w,u) in w. Hence r(w,u)<r(u,v)= r(G), a contradiction. □

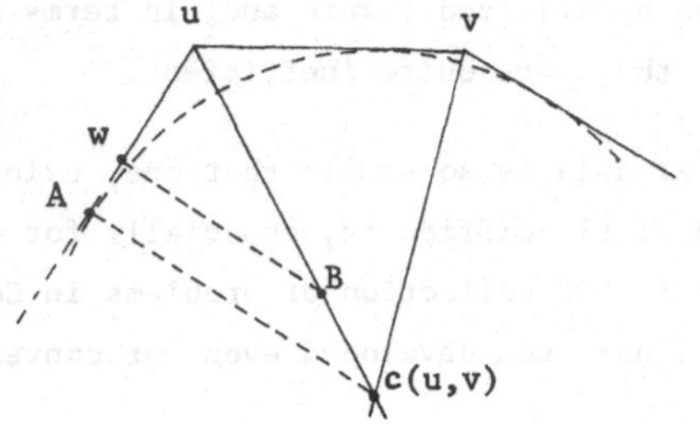

Figure 2. Illustration for the proof of Lemma 1.

Thus, if r(u,v) = r(G), c(u,v) is a vertex of M(G) provided that $\mathcal{C}$(u,v) does not intersect any edge of G. Fortunately, the convexity of G enables us to dispense with this costly check, as we shall now show. Let w,u,v,t be four consecutive vertices of G and let z be the intersection of the prolongations of (w,u) and (v,t) (figure 3). We claim:

Lemma 2: min(r(w,z), r(z,t)) ≥ min(r(w,u), r(u,v), r(v,t)).

Proof: Assume, without loss of generality that r(w,z) ≤ r(z,t). Clearly, c(u,v) belongs to B(z). Let $r \triangleq$ min(r(w,u), r(u,v), r(v,t)) and $r' \triangleq$ min(r(w,z),r(z,t)). We distinguish two cases:

(1) c(u,v)∈[z,c(w,z)]. In this case, r = r(u,v) ≤ r(w,z) = r', trivially (figure 3a).

(2) c(u,v)∈[c(w,z),∞]. In this case, r = r(w,u) ≤ r(w,z) = r' (figure 3b). □

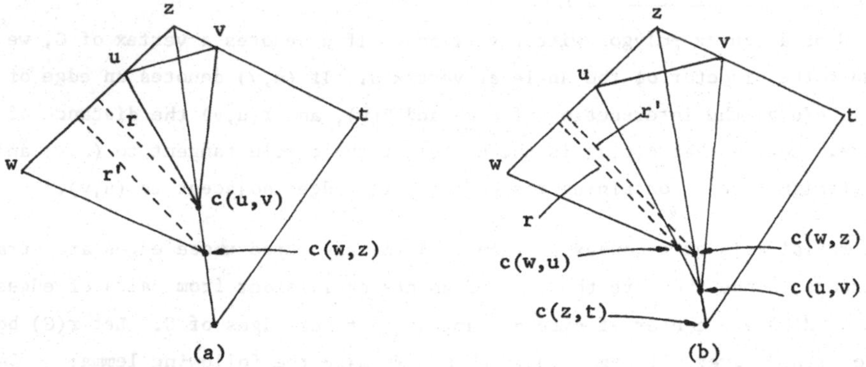

Figure 3. Illustration for the proof of Lemma 2.

We now define as removal of edge (u,v) the operation of replacing the vertex sequence wuvt with the vertex sequence wzt. Let G' be the resulting polygon. The preceding lemma has the obvious consequence:

Corollary: If G' is obtained from G by edge removal, then r(G) ≤ r(G').

The reverse operation of edge removal will be called vertex cutting and obviously, if G' is obtained from G by vertex cutting, then $r(G) \geq r(G')$.

Lemma 3: If $r(u,v) = r(G)$, the circle $\mathcal{C}(u,v)$ does not intersect G.

Proof: By contradiction. Assume $\mathcal{C}(u,v)$ intersects G. Then there is an edge (u',v') closer to c(u,v) than (u,v) (figure 4). We prolong both (u,v) and (u',v') until they meet at a point z. Without loss of generality, assume that z is closer to v than to u and is also closer to v' than to u'. Let G_0 be the polygon obtained from G by replacing the vertex sequence uv...v'u' with the sequence uzu'. The assumption that $\mathcal{C}(u,v)$ intersects G is equivalent to

$$r(u,v) > \text{dist}(c(u,v),(u',v')) = \text{length } (c(u,v),A')$$

whence the bisector B(z) of ∢uzu' intersects segment (u,c(u,v)) in a point F. Obviously

$$\text{length } (u,F) < \text{length } (u,c(u,v)) \Rightarrow r(G_0) \leq r(u,z) < r(u,v) = r(G).$$

We may now think of obtaining G from G_0 through a sequence of polygons $G_0, G_1, \ldots, G_k = G$, where G_i is obtained from G_{i-1} $(1 \leq i \leq k)$ by vertex cutting. Thus, by the previous result: $r(G_0) \geq r(G_1) \geq \ldots \geq r(G_k) = r(G)$, that is, $r(u,v) > r(G_0) \geq \ldots \geq r(G_k) = r(G)$, violating the hypothesis that $r(u,v) = r(G)$. □

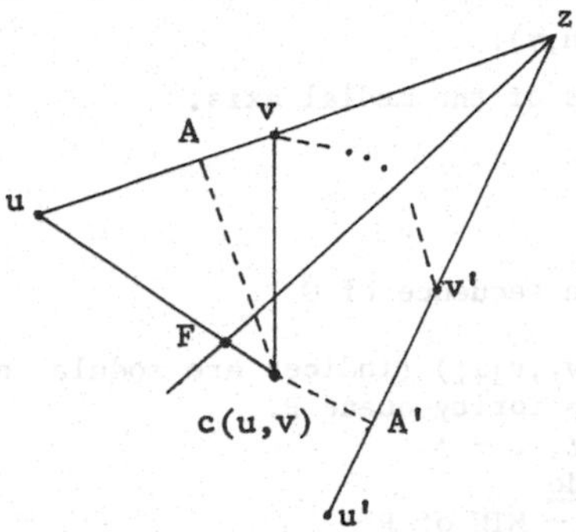

Figure 4. Illustration for the proof of Lemma 3.

Lemmas 1 and 3 yield the following conclusion.

Theorem. If $r(u,v) = r(G)$, then c(u,v) is a vertex of M(G).

The ideas embodied in the proofs of the preceding propositions can be used to develop an algorithm for the construction of M(G). The algorithm consists of two phases. The first is the reduction phase, which constructs a sequence of polygons $G_n, G_{n-1}, \ldots, G_3$, where $G_n = G$ and G_i is obtained from G_{i+1} by edge removal. The edge to be removed from G_{i+1} is some (u,v) for which $r(u,v) = r(G_{i+1})$. By so doing we ensure that c(u,v) can be inserted into $M(G_i)$ with a fixed amount of work. In fact, returning to figure 3a, assume that in G_{i+1} vertices w,u,v,t are consecutive and that $r(u,v) = r(G_{i+1})$. We then obtain G_i by replacing the string wuvt with wzt. Suppose now that we can algorithmically construct $M(G_i)$: then $M(G_{i+1})$ can be obtained from $M(G_i)$ by replacing in the latter the edge (c(w,z),z) with a tree whose edges are (c(w,z),c(u,v)), (c(u,v),u), and (c(u,v),v). Therefore the reduction phase terminates with G_3, a triangle, for which the medial axis is trivially constructed.

At this point the construction phase begins, which generates the sequence of binary trees $M(G_3), M(G_4), \ldots, M(G_n) = M(G)$, where $M(G_{i+1})$ is obtained from $M(G_i)$ as previously illustrated.

Assume that the polygon G is originally given as the clockwise sequence $v_0, v_1, \ldots, v_{n-1}$ of its vertices; during the reduction phase n-3 new vertices $v_n, v_{n+1}, \ldots, v_{2n-4}$ are created by effect of edge removals. From an implementation standpoint the algorithm makes convenient use of several data structures:

(i) An array $A[1:2n-3]$ to store for each of the 2n-3 vertices the following items: PRED(v), the polygon vertex which precedes v clockwise; SUCC(v), the polygon vertex which follows v clockwise; VERTEX(v), the medial axis vertex which gets connected to v in the construction phase.

(ii) A stack S, with operations PUSH and POP, to store the sequence of the removed edges.

(iii) A priority queue P, with operations MIN, DELETE, INSERT, to store the values of the parameters r(u,v).

(iv) A list L of the edges of the medial axis.

Algorithm

```
        Input:  The clockwise sequence of G
        Output: M(G)
   begin     For each edge (v_i,v_{i+1}) (indices are modulo n) compute r(v_i,v_{i+1}) and
             insert it into priority queue P.
             Set j ← 0, S ← ∅, L ← ∅
             While j < n-3 do
               begin r(u,v) ← MIN of P
                     PUSH (u,v) into stack S
                     w ← PRED(u), t ← SUCC(v)
                     construct v_{n+j}, intersection of straight lines containing wu
                     and vt
                     SUCC(w) ← v_{n+j}, PRED(t) ← v_{n+j}, PRED(v_{n+j}) ← w, SUCC(v_{n+j}) ← t
                     DELETE r(w,u), r(u,v), r(v,t) from P
                     INSERT r(w,v_{n+j}), r(v_{n+j},t) into P
                     j ← j+1
               end
             (Let u_1,u_2, and u_3 be the vertices of G_3)
             VERTEX(u_1) = VERTEX(u_2) = VERTEX(u_3) ← c(u_1,u_2)
             While j > 0      do
               begin POP (u,v) from S
                     w ← PRED(u), t ← SUCC(v)
                     z ← SUCC(w)
                     C ← VERTEX(z)
                     Join(c(u,v),C) to L
                     SUCC(w) ← u,PRED(t) ← v
                     VERTEX(z) ← ∅
                     VERTEX(u) = VERTEX(v) ← c(u,v)
                     j ← j-1
               end
             For i=0,...,n-1 do join (v_i,VERTEX(v_i)) to L
   end
```

Step 1 sets up the priority queue, steps 3-11 implement the reduction phase, and steps 13-22 implement the construction phase. Finally, step 23 completes the construction of L. From a performance viewpoint, we note that step 1 takes at most time O(nlogn). Each operation on the priority queue P (steps 4,9, and 10) uses time O(logn), whereas steps 5, 6, 7, and 8 require a fixed amount of work; thus the reduction phase is completed in time O(nlogn). It is also easily realized that each of the steps 14-22 runs in fixed time, whence the construction phase runs in time O(n). Finally, step 23 requires time O(n). We conclude that the described algorithm runs in time O(nlogn).

3. Medial axis of a nonconvex simple polygon

When G is not convex, but simple, M(G) is substantially more complex. In fact M(G) is still a tree-like structure, but its edges are not necessarily line segments. We recall the following simple facts:

F1. The locus of the points equidistant from two half-lines meeting at their common extreme is the bisector of the convex angle formed by the two half-lines;

F2. The locus of the points equidistant from two points is the perpendicular bisector of the segment joining the two points;

F3. The locus of the points equidistant from a line and a point is a parabola, whose focus and directrix are the given point and line, respectively.

Thus, since the boundary of an arbitrary polygon G consists of points and straight line segments, M(G) is a planar graph, whose vertices are connected by generalized edges, which are either straight-line segments or arcs of parabolas.

The boundary of G and the medial axis of G subdivide the interior of G into regions, each of which is associated either with an edge of G or with a nonconvex (reflex) vertex of G. If G has $m > 0$ reflex vertices, then there are $n+m$ such regions.

Let $v_0, v_1, \ldots, v_{n-1}$ be the clockwise sequence of the vertices of G. We shall describe G by a list L(G) of $n+m$ items $a_1, a_2, \ldots, a_{n+m}$, where each a_j is called an element and is either an edge (v_i, v_{i+1}) or a reflex vertex of G. Our objective is again "reduction", that is, the generation of a sequence $G_{n+m}, G_{n+m-1}, \ldots, G_2$ where $G_{n+m} = G$ and G_i is now a sequence of elements obtained from G_{i+1} by removal of an element (either an edge or a reflex vertex). Thus G_i contains exactly i elements and G_2 consists of two elements, for which the construction of the medial axis is trivially solved by rules F1, F2, and F3 above.

For each element a_j in L(G) we define two lines $\lambda(a_j)$ and $\rho(a_j)$ as follows. If a_i is a segment, let a_i' denote the straight line containing a_i; if a_i is a vertex, then $a_i' = a_i$. The lines $\lambda(a_j)$ and $\rho(a_j)$ are respectively the loci of the points equidistant from a_{j-1}' and a_j' and from a_j' and a_{j+1}'. Obviously, $\rho(a_j) = \lambda(a_{j+1})$ for every j. We now define $c(a_j)$ as the intersection of $\lambda(a_j)$ and $\rho(a_j)$ and $r(a_j) \triangleq \mathrm{dist}(c(a_j),a_j)$. Notice that if a_j is a reflex vertex, and a_{j-1} and a_{j+1} are its incident edges, $\lambda(a_j)$ and $\rho(a_j)$ are the normals in a_j to the edges a_{j-1} and a_{j+1}, respectively; in this case we conventionally set $r(a_j) = \infty$. We also let $r(G) = \min\{r(a_j)|a_j \in L(G)\}$.

A reduction consists in deleting an element a_j from L(G). Specifically, the string of elements $a_{j-1}a_ja_{j+1}$ is replaced by $a_{j-1}a_{j+1}$; consequently, $\rho(a_{j-1})$ and $\lambda(a_{j+1})$ are both redefined as the locus of the points equidistant from a'_{j-1} and a'_{j+1}.

Let $\mathcal{C}(a_j)$ be the circle with radius $r(a_j)$ and center $c(a_j)$; $c(a_j)$ is a vertex of the medial axis if the following two conditions hold:

(i) $\mathcal{C}(a_j)$ shares a point with a_{j-1}, a_j, and a_{j+1} (if any of these three elements is a segment, then $\mathcal{C}(a_j)$ is tangent to it);

(ii) $\mathcal{C}(a_j)$ does not share more than one point with any other element of L(G).

We saw in Section 2 that, by the properties of convexity, these two conditions were automatically satisfied by an element with smallest $r(a_j)$; here, however, except in special cases, the tests (i) and (ii) have to be carried out explicitly, using at most O(n) operations.

Thus, the algorithm given in Section 2 may be modified as follows. The set $\{r(a_j)|a_j \in G\}$ is again arranged as a priority queue P. Let a_j be the element called by the MIN operation on P. Tests (i) and (ii) are performed on a_j. If they pass, then $c(a_j)$ belongs to M(G) and a reduction takes place; otherwise, $r(a_j)$ is deleted from P and a new MIN operation must be performed on it.

From the performance standpoint, we recall that (n+m-2) elements are originally in P. Each MIN deletes an element from P, whereas two insertions into P occur when a reduction takes place. Since we globally perform (n+m-2) reductions, 2(n+m-2) elements are inserted into P by the algorithm. Thus, at most 3(n+m-2) MIN operations are performed on P; since for each MIN we have at most O(n) additional operations, and $m \leq n-3$, we conclude that the running time of the algorithm in the general case is at most $O(n^2)$.

Acknowledgement

This work was supported in part by the National Science Foundation under Grant MCS 76-17321.

References

1. Shamos, M. I., "Problems in Computational Geometry," Dept. of Comp. Sci., Yale University, New Haven, Conn., May 1975 (to be published by Springer Verlag).

2. Duda, R. O. and Hart, P. E., Pattern Classification and Scene Analysis, Wiley Interscience, N. Y., 1973.
3. Blum, H., "A transformation for extracting new descriptors of shape," in Symp. Models for Perception of Speech and Visual Forms, pp. 362-380, MIT Press, 1967.
4. Montanari, U., "Continuous skeletons from digitized images," Journal of the ACM, 16, 534-549, October 1969.

SEMANTICS AND PROOF RULES FOR COROUTINE HIERARCHIES IN BLOCK-STRUCTURED PROGRAMMING LANGUAGES

Peter Raulefs
Institut für Informatik I
Universität Karlsruhe
Postfach 6380
D-7500 Karlsruhe 1, Fed. Rep. Germany

1. Introduction

Coroutines constitute a control structure modelling situations where several processes incrementally transform streams of data. In programming languages, coroutine constructs are a way of implementing "call-by-need" or "lazy" evaluation [1,2,3,4] of program modules, where control is transferred from one module to another whenever the next increment of manipulating data one module works on is to be done by another module.

The simplest set-up usually modelled by coroutines is the cooperation of a producer generating a data stream, and a consumer manipulating the data received from the producer. Each time the consumer is done, additional data input is requested from the producer; vice versa, each time the producer has generated a chunk of data, the consumer is requested to fetch the data for further processing. It is the slightly more general situation of several modules (**"coroutines"**, "processes") mutually transferring control among each other which is implemented in several current programming languages [4,5,6].

In SIMULA 67, the coroutine mechanism has been embedded into a block-structured language. However, in all such languages systems of coroutines must work on the *same* hierarchical level of block structure. Structuring a program into textually enclosing blocks corresponds to structuring a task into static subtasks, where subtasks have access to information in enclosing tasks but not vice versa.Similarly, systems of coroutines may be further structured by introducing coroutine systems within coroutines that share information with surrounding blocks, and may transfer control to coroutines declared in textually surrounding blocks. This additional facility allows modelling hierarchies of cooperating systems of tasks into substaks which may activate or deactivate tasks higher up in the hierarchy.

Various approaches to realize the control structure of coroutines operating at the same hierarchical level have been suggested: (1) Explicit sequencing by executing specific instructions causing another coroutine to resume control (e.g. in SIMULA 67 [5,5]); (2) implicit sequencing by call-by-need/lazy evaluation [1,2,3], resp. by making all processes work continuously in parallel and exchange information via buffers whenever needed [4]. Without expressing any preference, we choose the first approach of explicit sequencing in this paper. Following SIMULA, explicit sequencing is done by executing CALL-, RESUME-, and DETACH-instructions. Our extension to coroutine hierarchies allows CALLing, RESUMEing and DETACHing coroutines declared in textually surrounding blocks. As a consequence, our DETACH-instruction includes a coroutine identifier (unlike SIMULA where a "detach"-instruction transfers control back to the calling coroutine resp. block body).

A very intuitive model for coroutine constructs has been developed by Wang and Dahl [7]. However, this model does not suffice for more detailed analyses such as developing proof rules and establishing their validity. Proof rules for special coroutine constructs have been presented by Clint [8], Dahl [9], and Pritchard [10]. One of these rules has turned out to be invalid, and the validity of the other rules has not been shown yet.

Since it exactly captures our intuition, we extend the Wang-Dahl model to coroutine hierarchies. This model is subsequently formalized in a denotational semantics for a block-structured programming language containing coroutine constructs, coroutine sequencing instructions, and an unspecified variety of other constructs. Based on this model, we present a proof rule and indicate the proof of its validity. This proof rule contains all other previously suggested proof rules as special cases.

Our intention is to extract the coroutine control structure from other language mechanisms by considering a programming language that keeps addition of other language facilities orthogonal to our exposition.

The denotational semantics is presented in terms of an *abstraction semantics* [11]. An abstraction semantics specifies the meaning of language constructs with operations that can be performed on the denoted objects being abstracted upon.

2. Intuitive Model

We indicate an extension of the Wang-Dahl model [7] to coroutine hierarchies. We consider syntactically two types of block-constructs:

- *Coroutine blocks* (CB) consisting of declarations for coroutine and other identifiers, and instructions;
- *Coroutines* consisting of a coroutine identifier, declarations of identifiers which are not coroutine identifiers, and instructions.

Both in a CB and a coroutine, particular instructions are "call c", "resume c" and "detach c" where c is a coroutine identifier. In coroutine CBs may again appear as instructions. We do not allow a coroutine to call or resume itself. However, a coroutine detaching itself is just the conventional "detach"-instruction in SIMULA.

A dynamic block instance is visualized as a box associated with a pointer to the next instruction to be executed in its dynamic predecessor. Active dynamic instances of coroutines and CBs form the *operating chain.* We consider two relations $\rightarrow$ and $\Rightarrow$ on block instances x and y:

$x \rightarrow y$ iff x is an immediate dynamic successor to y, i.e. executing an end-of-block instruction in x returns control back to y;

$x \Rightarrow y$ iff x is declared in y. $\overset{*}{\rightarrow}$, $\overset{*}{\Rightarrow}$ denote the reflexive-transitive closure of $\rightarrow$, $\Rightarrow$. D(x) denotes the immediate dynamic predecessor of x, and T(x) the instance of the block carrying the declaration of x.

The activity associated with executing call/detach/resume-instructions is illustrated in the following picture:

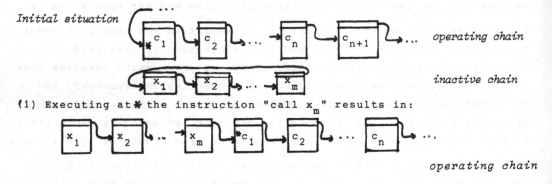

Initial situation

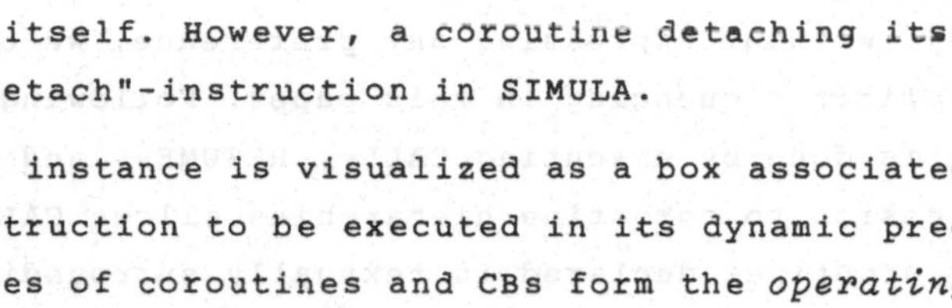

operating chain

inactive chain

(1) Executing at ✱ the instruction "call x_m" results in:

operating chain

(all other inactive chains remain inactive)

(2) Executing at ✱ the instruction "detach c_n" results in:

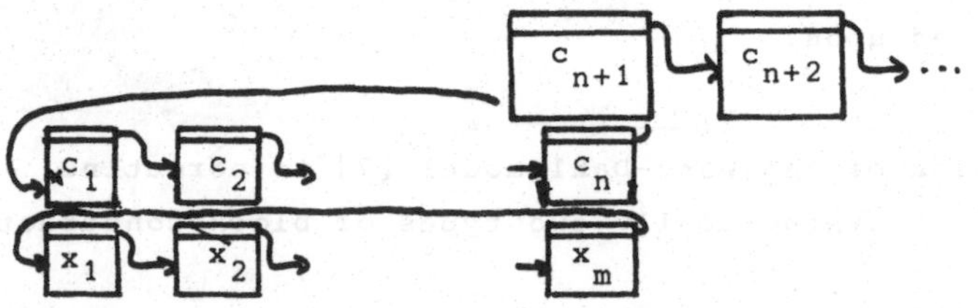

operating chain

new inactive chain

inactive chain

(3) Executing at ✱ the instruction "resume x" results in:

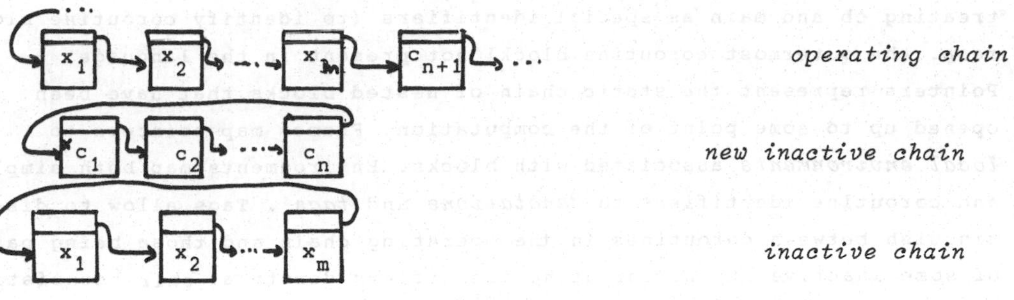

(assuming that (1) $T(x_m) = T(c_n)$ and (2) $\forall(1 \leq i \leq).\ T(c_i) \neq T(x_m)$)

3. Syntax of Coroutine Language

To formalize our intuitive model, we consider a programming language incorporating all features to be studied, but allowing to adjoin an unspecified variety of additional constructs. We specify the syntax of the language in terms of an abstract syntax following the style of VDL [12] . We denote predicates by capitalized, and selectors by lower case strings. Predicates and their extensions are usually confused. For any predicate Any, AnyL denotes the set of all finite lists of objects in Any.

Prog := (<dclsid:DclsidL>, <instr:Instr1L>)
Instr1 := Stmt v Corblock
Corblock := (<dclsid:DclsidL>, <dclcor:DclcorL>, <instr:Instr2L>)
Dclsid := (<id:SId>)
Dclcor := (<corid:CId>, <body:Corbody>)
Corbody := (<dclsid:DclsidL>, <instr:Instr3L)
Instr2 := Instr1 v Call v Detach
Instr3 := Instr2 v Resume
Call := (<corid:CId>)
Resume := (<corid:CId>)
Detach := (<corid:CId>)
Id := Id + SId

CId and SId are disjoint atomic sets of coroutine and simple identifiers.
Constr := Prog+DclsidL+DclcorL+Corblock+Instr3 gathers all *constructs*.
Stmt is an unspecified set of constructs left open for additions.

4. Semantics of Coroutine Language

Following the current style of denotational semantics [13], we describe the semantics of our coroutine language inductively on the structure of language constructs by specifying a function Mp mapping constructs to transformations from states and continuations to states. To capture our notion of coroutine hierarchies, *states* are structured into *pointers* and *frames*. Pointers are strings of coroutine identifiers, treating cb and main as special identifiers (to identify coroutine blocks resp. the outermost coroutine block) not present in the language. Pointers represent the static chain of nested blocks that have been opened up to some point of the computation. Frames map pointers to *local environments* associated with blocks. Environments map both simple and coroutine identifiers to *denotations* and *tags* . Tags allow to distinguish between coroutines in the operating chain and those being part of some inactive chain. Coroutine identifiers denote a **pair** consisting of an *operational abstraction* and *continuation*; the continuation is the state transformation remaining to be done in the dynamic predecessor identified by the coroutine identifier.

Semantic domains:

σ	State	:= Ptr×Frame	states
ϕ	Frame	:= Ptr→Env	frames
ρ	Env	:= Id→Den×Tag	environments
π	Ptr	:= $(\text{CId}+\{\text{cb},\text{main}\})^*$	pointers
	Tag	:= {'active','inactive'}	tags
δ	Den	:= Val+Opab×Cont	denotations
ω	Opab	:= Op→State→Cont→State	operational abstractions
θ	Cont	:= State→State	continuations
	Op	:= {'call','resume','detach'}	

All semantic domains as well as the syntactic domain Constr are taken to be discrete cpo's with bottom element uu.

Mp ∈ Constr→State→Cont→State   meaning function

Notation:

1. For any predicate Pany of the abstract syntax, pany denotes any object in Pany.
2. If pany is a structured object, and subob is a subobject of pany selected by selsubob, then selsubob stands for subob whenever pany and selsubob occur in the same equation.
3. For any tuple pany ∈ Pany1×Pany2×...×Panyk, pany↓panyi ($1 \leq i \leq k$) denotes the i-the component of pany.
4. Juxtaposition stands for functional composition, associating to the left.
5. r→p|q stands for the strict conditional *if* r *then* p *else* q. The conditional is often written as a *case*-clause, omitting the final *else*-alternative tacitly understood to be uu.
6. Syntactic constructs are included in double bars || ||.
7. ι denotes the identity mapping on any domain.

```
Mp||prog||πφθ              := Mp ||dclsid;instr||main uu θ
Mp||corblock||πφθ          := let θ´ := λπ´φ̂. let φ := φ´[(cb.π)←uu] in θπφ̂ in
                                 Mp||dclsid;dclcor;instr||(cb.π)φθ´
Mp||dclsid||πφθ            := let ρ´ := φπ[id←(uu,'active')] in θπφ[π←ρ´ ]
Mp||constr1;constr2 ||πφθ  := Mp||constr1||πφ{λπ´φ´.Mp||constr2||πφ´θ}
Mp||cc x||πφθ              := let πx := getptr xπφ in φ πx'cc' π φ θ
                               where cc ∈ {call, detach, resume}

Mp||dclcor||πφθ :=
 let x := corid in
 let θx := λπ´φ´.Mp||body||(x.π)φι in
 let ωx := fix f.λop1.λπ1φ1θ1.
   case op1='call':
   {fix gλπ2φ2θ2. let θx := λπ´φ´θ2π2φ´ in
   let ω´x := λop3 λπ3φ3θ3.
        case op3='call':uu| case op3='resume':uu|
        case op3='detach': let θ"x := λπ´φ´.θ3π3φ´in
                           let ω"x := λop4 λπ4φ4θ4.
                               case op4='detach':uu| case op4='call':
                                                                gπ4φ4θ4|
                              case op4='resume':f'resume'π4φ4θ4
                           in
                           let φ" := φ3π[x←{↓opab := ω"x, ↓cont := θ"x ,
                                                         ↓tag  := 'inactive'}]
                           in (φ3πx↓cont) uu φ3[π←φ"]
  let φ´:= φ π[x←{↓opab := ω´x, ↓cont := θ´x,↓tag := 'active'}] in
  (φ2 π x ↓cont) uu φ2[π←φ´]}π1φ1θ1|

case op1='resume:
{fix g. λπ2φ2θ2.
 let (z,πz) := getpar cxπ2φ2 in
```

$let\ \theta'_x := (\phi_2\pi_z z{\downarrow}cont),\ \theta'_z := (\phi_2\pi_z x\ {\downarrow}cont)\ in$

$let\ \omega'_x := \lambda op_3.\ \lambda\pi_3\phi_3\theta_3.$

$\quad case\ op_3='call':uu|\ case\ op_3='resume':uu|$

$\quad case\ op_3='detach':\ let\ \theta''_x := \lambda\pi'\phi'\theta_3\pi_3\phi'\ in$

$\qquad let\ \omega''_x := \lambda op_4\ \lambda\pi_4\phi_4\theta_4$

$\qquad\quad case\ op_4='detach':uu|$

$\qquad\quad case\ op_4='resume':g\pi_4\phi_4\theta_4|$

$\qquad\quad case\ op_4='call':f'call'\pi_4\phi_4\theta_4\ in$

$\qquad let\ \rho' := \phi_3\pi_z[x{\leftarrow}\{{\downarrow}opab := \omega''_x,\ {\downarrow}cont := \theta''_x,$

$\qquad\qquad {\downarrow}tag := 'inactive'$

$\qquad in\ (\phi_3\pi_z\ {\downarrow}cont)\ uu\ \phi_3[\pi_z{\leftarrow}\rho'']$

$in\ let\ \omega'_z := \lambda op_3.\lambda\pi_3\phi_3\theta_3.\ case\ op_3='detach':\ uu|$

$\qquad case\ op_3='resume':g\pi_3\phi_3\theta_3|$

$\qquad case\ op_3='call':f'call'\pi_3\phi_3\theta_3\ \ in$

$let\ \rho' := \phi_2\pi_z[x{\leftarrow}\{{\downarrow}opab := \omega'_x,\ {\downarrow}cont := \theta'_x, {\downarrow}tag := 'active'\},$

$\qquad z{\leftarrow}\{{\downarrow}opab := \omega'_z,\ {\downarrow}cont := \theta'_z, {\downarrow}tag := 'inactive'\}]\ in$

$(\phi_2\pi_z z{\downarrow}cont)\ uu\ \phi_2[\pi_z{\leftarrow}\rho']\}\pi_1\phi_1\theta_1$

in

$let\ \rho := \phi\pi[x{\leftarrow}\{{\downarrow}opab := \omega_x,\ {\downarrow}cont := \theta_x,\ {\downarrow}tag := 'inactive'\}]\ in$

$\theta\pi\phi[\pi{\leftarrow}\rho]$

Remarks:
1. Concatenation of strings is denoted by a "."; hd returns the first character of a string.
2. getptr $x\pi\phi$ looks up the frame pointer identifying the chain of local block environments ending with the environment belonging to the innermost (w.r.t. π and ϕ) block x is declared in. getpar $cx\pi\phi$ returns the coroutine identifier z and frame pointer π_z belonging to the first upward coroutine in the operating chain ending with c s.t. T(x)=T(z).
3. End-of-block instructions in coroutines are considered self detaching.

5. Proof Rules

A general proof rule is presented allowing to derive assertions about coroutine blocks with embedded coroutine hierarchies, and entire programs in particular. We assume an assertion language AssL and an interpretation I:AssL→State→Bool evaluating assertions on states to truth values.

<u>Notation:</u> 1. For any assertion $P \in AssL$ and coroutine identifier $x \in (CId+\{main,cb\})$,
$P[x]$ and P^{-} denote assertions to be interpreted as follows:
$I||P[x]||\pi\phi := I||P||(getptr\ x\pi\phi)\phi$
$I||P^{-}||\pi\phi := I||P||(tl\pi)\phi$
where tl chops off the leftmost coroutine identifier of a frame pointer.
2. We adopt the usual Hoare notation[14] P{constr}Q for inductive expressions.

The following rule assumes each coroutine resp. coroutine block x to be associated with an assertion P_x intuitively being an invariant on instruction sequences between successive begin-of-block/call/detach/resume/end-of-block instructions.

For $C \in CId, x,y \in CId+\{cb\}$, let

$HYPD(x,c) := And[P_y[y] | x \neq y,\ (T(y) = T(c)\ or\ y = T(c))]\{detach\ c\}P_c[c]$

$HYPC(x,c) := P_c[c]\{call\ c\}\ let\ y := parob(x,y)\ in\ P_y[y]$

$HYPR(x,c) := P_c[c]\{resume\ c\}\ let\ y := parob(x,y)\ in\ P_y[y]$

$HYPB(x) := P_x[x]\{body\ x\}\ And\ [P_y[y] | x \neq y,\ (T(x) = T(y)\ or\ y = T(x))]$

$HYPCB := S^{-}\{instr\}R^{-}$

where (a) $I||let\ y := parob(x,y)\ in\ P_y[y]||\pi\phi := let\ y := getpar\ (hd\pi)c\pi\phi\ in\ I||P_y[y]||\pi\phi$, and

(b) for $x \in Corbody+Corblock$, body x stands for the instruction part.

Assuming a coroutine block or program $pcb \in Prog+Corblock$ with instruction part instr, we obtain the following general proof rule for deriving an assertion S{pcb}R about pcb:

$$\frac{\begin{array}{l}\forall x \in CId+\{cb\}.\ \{\forall c \in CId.\ HYPD(x,c),\ HYPC(x,c),\ HYPR(x,c)\} \vdash HYPB(x)\\ \{\forall x \in CId+\{cb\}.\ \forall c \in CId.\ HYPD(x,c),\ HYPC(x,c),\ HYPR(x,c)\} \vdash HYPCB\end{array}}{S\ \{pcb\}R}$$

The validity proof of this rule w.r.t . the semantics of Section 4 is quite complex and is contained in the full version of this paper, available from the author. For a given program employing coroutines, this rule allows to generate a system of *local inductive expressions* $P_i\{instr_i\}Q_i$ with $instr_i$ being instruction sequences between successive begin-of-block/call/detach:resume/end-of-block instructions. Then, proving all these inductive expressions establishes overall correctness. Accordingly, the validity of the rule is shown by proving inductively on the structure of computations that the generated system of inductive expression implies overall correctness.

The practical utility of this rule consists in breaking down the correctness problem of a complex coroutine program to a system of much easier subproblems.

Acknowledgment. I am indebted to Mr.J.Bernauer for close cooperation and many revealing discussions.

6. References

1. Wadsworth, C.P. Ph.D. Thesis, Univ. of Oxford, Spt. 1971
2. Morris, J.H., P. Henderson. Proc. 3rd ACM Conf. on Principles of Programming Languages. Atlanta, Jan 1976, 95-103.
3. Friedman, D.P., D.S. Wise. Proc. 3rd Int. Coll. on Automata, Languages and Programming. Edinburgh, July 1976, 257-284.
4. Kahn, G., D. McQueen. Tech.Rept. Nr. 202. IRIA 1976.
5. Dahl, O.-J., K. Nygoard. CACM:10(1966)671-678.
6. Britton, D.E. et al. Proc. 3rd ACM Conf. on Principles of Programming Languages, Atlanta, Jan. 1976, 185-191.
7. Wang, A., O.-I.Dahl. BIT:11(1971)425-449.
8. Clint, M. Acta Informatica:2(1973)50-63.
9. Dahl, O.J. Proc. 3rd Symp. on Math. Foundations of Computer Science. Jadwisin, June 1974, 157-174.
10. Pritchard, P.A. Inf. Proc. Letters:4(1976)141-143.
11. Raulefs ,P. Tech. Rept. (Fall 1977) forthcoming
12. Wegner, P. Computing Surveys:4(1972)5-62.
13. Milne, R., Ch.Strachey. A theory of programming languages semantics. Chapman& Hall, 1976.
14. Hoare, C.A.R. CACM : 12(1969)576-580.

ACCEPTORS FOR ITERATION LANGUAGES

G. Rozenberg
Dept. of Math.
University of Antwerp UIA
2610 Wilrijk, Belgium

D. Vermeir
Dept. T.E.W.
University of Leuven, K.U.L.
3000 Leuven, Belgium

The notion of parallel processing is a central notion in computer science. Within formal language theory there is a big trend now to understand grammars using parallel rewriting (see, e.g. [1],[4] and [6]). Whereas quite a progress has been achieved in this direction, rather little is understood from the dual topic : machines (acceptors) that work in a "parallel fashion". One way of approaching this topic is to construct families of acceptors for various families of languages generated by grammars using parallel rewriting. This has been done for example for various families of L languages (see [2], [3] and [8]). Our work continuous the research on PAC machines started in [3].

First we recall the definition of a PAC machine. (In order to have simple definitions, we state this definition for the Λ-free case.)

Definition 1.

1) A PAC machine is a 6-tuple $M = <\Sigma, V, Q, F, q_0, \delta>$ where Σ, V are alphabets ($\Sigma \subseteq V$), Q is a finite set of states, F is a subset of Q (the set of final states), q_0 is in Q (the central state) and δ is a (partial) function from $Q \times V$ into finite subsets of $Q \times (V \cup \{\Lambda\})$.

2) A configuration of M is a triple (x,y,q) such that $x \in \Sigma^*$, $y \in (V \times \mathbb{N})^*$ and $q \in Q$.

3) A direct transition relation $\underset{M}{\vdash}$ is defined by $(x,y,q) \underset{M}{\vdash} (\bar{x},\bar{y},\bar{q})$ if one of the following conditions holds :

I. (READ INPUT) $x = a\bar{x}$ for some $a \in \Sigma$, $\bar{y} = y<a,0>$ and $\bar{q} = q = q_0$.

II. (OVERWRITE) $y = y'<a,n>$, $(q_0,b) \in \delta(q,a)$, $\bar{y} = y'<b,n+1>$ and $\bar{x} = x$.

III. (POP-UP) $\bar{x} = x$, $y = <a,n>$, $\bar{y} = \Lambda$ and $(\bar{q},\Lambda) \in \delta(q,a)$ where $\bar{q} \neq q_0$.

IV. (POP-UP) $y = y'<a_1,n_1><a_2,n_2>$, $n_2 = n_1$, $\bar{x} = x$, $\bar{y} = y'<a_1,n_1>$ and $(\bar{q},\Lambda) \in \delta(q,a_2)$ where $\bar{q} \neq q_0$.

4) The transition relation in M, denoted as $\overset{*}{\underset{M}{\vdash}}$, is defined as the transitive and reflexive closure of the relation $\underset{M}{\vdash}$.

5) The language of M, denoted as L(M), is defined by $L(M) = \{x \in \Sigma^* : (x,\Lambda,q_0) \overset{*}{\underset{M}{\vdash}} (\Lambda,\Lambda,q), q \in F\}$.

The following diagram illustrates the definitions.

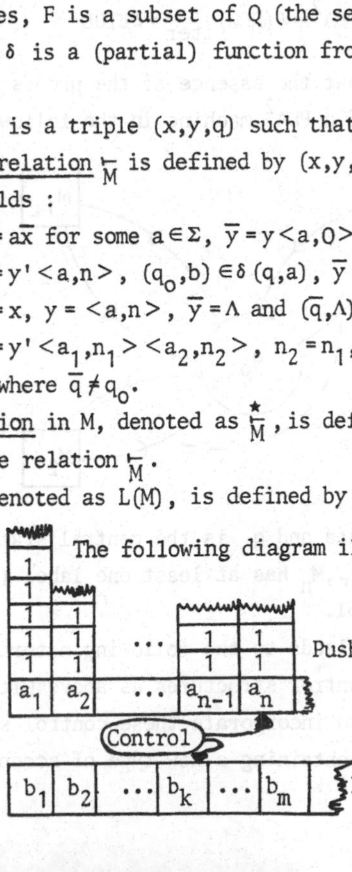

A PAC machine is called restricted if there is a positive integer k such that whenever $s_0 \vdash_M s_1 \vdash_M \cdots \vdash_M s_k$ is a chain of configurations of M, then $s_j = (x,y,q_o)$ for some $1 \leq j \leq k$, $x \in \Sigma^*$ and $y \in (V \times \mathbb{N})^*$.

In [3] it was shown that the class of languages accepted by restricted PAC machines equals the class of E0L-languages. The characterization of the class of languages accepted by unrestricted PAC machines, an open problem from [3], is established in the following theorem.

Theorem 1. $\mathcal{L}PAC = \mathcal{L}(REG)^{(1)}_{iter}$.

Hence, as far as accepting power is concerned, the class of PAC machines is equivalent to the class of pre-set pushdown automata that were introduced in [2].

In [5] the notion of a PAC machine was extended to allow for different kinds of symbols on the pushdown array : thus defining the "pushdown array of (checking pushdowns" automaton, abbreviated PDA^2. With the same restriction as in [3] it was shown in [5] that the class of languages accepted by restricted PDA^2 machines equals the class of ET0L languages. The following theorem solves an open question from [5].

Theorem 2. $\mathcal{L}PDA^2 = \mathcal{L}(REG)_{iter} = \mathcal{L}ET0L$

It turns out that the essence of the proofs of Theorem 1 and Theorem 2 is to represent the control of a PDA^2 machine in the following way :

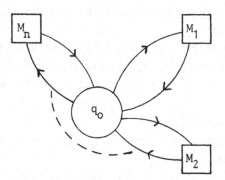

where $M_1, \ldots, M_n$ are finite automata and q_o is the central state of the PDA^2 machine considered. Each automaton $M_1, \ldots, M_n$ has at least one label (A,T) where A is a symbol from V and T is a pushdown-symbol.

This representation immediately leads to the following natural extension of the machine-model. One can allow control structures as above with $M_1, M_2, \ldots, M_n$ being acceptors of arbitrary kind X and incorporate these control structures in PDA^2 machines in the usual way, thus obtaining a new type of acceptor, called XPAC machine.

Before we give a formal definition of an XPAC machine we need some notation. If A,B are alphabets and $x = (a_1,\alpha_1)\dots(a_n,\alpha_n) \in (A,B^{*})^{*}$ then $\underline{\text{inf}}(x) = a_1 \dots a_n$, $\underline{\text{tail}}(x) = \alpha_n$ and we say that x is t-balanced if $\alpha_1 = \alpha_2 = \dots = \alpha_n$. For an alphabet Σ, an acceptor (in Σ) is a function f from Σ^{*} into {o,1}; the language of f, denoted as L(f) is defined by $L(f) = \{x \in \Sigma^{*} : f(x) = 1\}$.

Definition 2.

1) Let X be a family of acceptors. An XPAC machine is a construct $M = (V,\Sigma,P,A,F,L)$ where
V,Σ and P are finite alphabets with $\Sigma \subseteq V$,
A is a finite set of acceptors from X,
F is an acceptor from X, and
L is a function from $V \times P$ onto A.
2) A configuration of M is a pair (w,z) where $w \in \Sigma^{*}$ and $z \in (V,P^{*})^{*}$
3) A direct transition relation in M, denoted $\vdash_{M}$, is defined by $(w,z) \vdash_{M} (\overline{w},\overline{z})$ if one of the following three conditions holds :
I. (READ). $w = a\overline{w}$ with $a \in \Sigma$ and $\overline{z} = z(a,\Lambda)$.
II. (POP-OUT). $w = \overline{w}$, $z = z_1 z_2$ where $z_2 \neq \Lambda$ is t-balanced and there exists an acceptor f in A such that $f(\underline{\text{inf}}(z_2)) = 1$ and $\overline{z} = z_1(a,\underline{\text{tail}}(z_2)c)$ where $L(a,c) = f$.
III. (PUSH-DOWN). $w = \overline{w}$, $\overline{z} = z(A,xc)$ where $x \in P^{*}$ and $A \in V, c \in P$ are such that $L(A,c)(\Lambda) = 1$.
IV. (CLEAR). z is t-balanced, $\overline{z} = \Lambda$, $w = \overline{w} = \Lambda$ and $F(\underline{\text{inf}}(z)) = 1$.

4) The transition relation in M, denoted as $\overset{+}{\vdash}_{M}$, is defined as the transitive and reflexive closure of the relation $\vdash_{M}$.
5) The language of M, denoted as L(M), is defined by $L(M) = \{x \in \Sigma^{*} : (x,\Lambda) \overset{+}{\vdash}_{M} (\Lambda,\Lambda)\}$.

For a family of acceptors X, $\mathcal{L}$X, XPAC and $\mathcal{L}$XPAC denote the family of languages accepted by machines from X, the family of XPAC machines and the family of languages accepted by XPAC machines, respectively.

Clearly, when X = FA is the class of finite automata, then (FA)PAC=PDA[2] and, consequently, $\mathcal{L}$(FA)PAC = $\mathcal{L}(\text{REG})_{\text{iter}}$. As a matter of fact this is a special case of a general result which is stated in the following theorem.

Theorem 3. Let X be a family of acceptors. Then $\mathcal{L}\text{XPAC} = \mathcal{L}(X)_{\text{iter}}$.

Hence we obtain an algorithm which, given a family X of acceptors, constructs a family of acceptors XPAC which accepts precisely the family $\mathcal{L}(X)_{\text{iter}}$.

When we restrict ourselves to unary XPAC machines, that is XPAC machines with #P = 1, then we get the following result. (The letter U denotes the unary restriction.)

Theorem 4. Let X be a family of acceptors. Then $\mathcal{L}XUPAC = \mathcal{L}(X)^{(1)}_{iter}$.

Given an XPAC machine M, we say that a configuration (y,z) is k-limited if $z = (a_1,\alpha_1)(a_2,\alpha_2)\dots(a_n,\alpha_n)$ and $|\alpha_1|,\dots,|\alpha_n| < k$. We say that M is H-limited if there exists a k such that for every word x in L(M), there exists a sequence of configurations leading to acceptance of x such that each configuration appearing in this sequence is k-limited. Then we can show the following.

Theorem 5. Let X be a family of acceptors. If $\mathcal{L}X$ is closed with respect to catenation and substitution (into itself) then for every H-limited XPAC machine M, we have that $L(M) \in \mathcal{L}X$.

The notion of an XPAC machine allows several natural extensions. For instance, although not explicitly mentionned in the definition, XPAC machines have the same control structure as the original PAC machines: the acceptors are 'centered' around a unique "reading-state". A natural question is what happens if we allow several reading states thus obtaining a more complicated control-structure. Such a modified XPAC machine is called a XPACS machine. Hence an XPACS machine operates in the same way as an XPAC machine; only it may alter its state during a POP-OUT or PUSH-DOWN move. There is also an initial state (a set of initial states) where the computation has to start and a set of final states. The following theorem shows that under quite weak conditions on $\mathcal{L}X$, adding more reading states does not alter the accepting power of XPAC machines.

Theorem 6. If $\mathcal{L}X$ is a full trio, then $\mathcal{L}XPACS = \mathcal{L}XPAC$.

Another natural extension can be defined by relaxing the conditions under which a POP-UP or CLEAR move can happen. In the original definition of XPAC (and PAC) it is required that the word to be processed ("popped-up" or "cleared") is t-balanced, that is every letter in it, has the same 'tail'. This requirement can be weakened as follows.

Let $M = (V,\Sigma,P,A,F,L)$ be an XPAC machine and let $R \subseteq P \times P$ be a binary relation in P. Let $z = (a_1,b_{1,1}\dots b_{1,n_1})(a_2,b_{2,1}\dots b_{2,n_2})\dots(a_m,b_{m,1}\dots b_{m,n_m})$ be a word in $(V,P^*)^*$. We call z t_R-balanced if the following conditions are satisfied:

(1) $n_1 = n_2 = \dots = n_m = n$ for some n, and

(2) $(b_{i,j},b_{i+1,j}) \in R$ for all $1 \leq i < m$, $1 \leq j \leq n$.

Clearly, if R is the equality-relation in P, then a word is t_R-balanced if and only if it is t-balanced. This yields the definition of a XPRAC machine as a XPAC machine equipped with a relation R on P. The direct transition relation is defined as for XPAC machines with the exception of the condition that a word can only be popped-up (or cleared) if it is t_R-balanced. The following theorem shows that this modification considerably increases the accepting power of XPAC machines.

Theorem 7. If $\mathcal{L}X$ contains the family $\mathcal{L}FIN$ of finite languages, then $\mathcal{L}XPRAC = \mathcal{RE}$.

Hence XPRAC machines are equivalent to Turing machines if X accepts all finite languages. This increase of accepting power leads to the question what happens if we put various restrictions on the relation R. For example, if we require that R is an equivalence relation then we get the following result.

Theorem 8. If (M,R) is an XPRAC machine where R is an equivalence relation in P, then $L(M) \in \mathcal{L}Y_{iter}$ where $\mathcal{L}Y$ is the closure of $\mathcal{L}X$ under union.

We hope that by now, the reader is convinced of the importance of XPAC machines as a step forward towards our understanding of parallelism in acceptors. At the same time we consider this paper also to be an argument in favor of PAC machines : they are quite flexible constructs because

1) they have been easily modified in [5] to extend their accepting power from $\mathcal{L}E0L$ to $\mathcal{L}ET0L$, and
2) they are easily generalized to extend their accepting power to languages generated by iteration grammars (XPAC) and to the class of recursively enumerable sets (XPRAC).

REFERENCES

1. Herman, G.T. and Rozenberg, G., Developmental systems and languages, North-Holland Publishing Company, Amsterdam, 1975.

2. Leeuwen, J. van, Notes on pre-set pushdown automata, Lecture Notes in Computer Science, No.15:177-188. Springer Verlag, Heidelberg, 1974.

3. Rozenberg, G., On a family of acceptors for some classes of developmental languages, International Journal of Computer Mathematics, 4:199-228, 1974.

4. Rozenberg, G. and Salomaa, A., The mathematical theory of L systems, in J.T. Tou (ed.), Advances in Information Systems Science, 6, 161-206, 1976.

5. Rozenberg, G. and Wood, D., A note on a family of acceptors for some families of developmental languages, Department of Applied Mathematics, Mc Master University, Hamilton, Technical Report, No. 75-CS-7, 1975.

6. Salomaa, A., Parallelism in rewriting systems, Lecture Notes in Computer Science, Springer Verlag, Heidelberg, No. 14, 523-533, 1974.

7. Salomaa, A., Iteration grammars and Lindenmayer AFL´s, Lecture Notes in Computer Science, Springer Verlag, Heidellberg, No. 15,250-253, 1974.

8. Savitch, W.J., Some characterizations of Lindenmayer systems in terms of Chomsky-type grammars and Stack-machines, Information and Control 27, 37-60, 1975.

HOW GOOD IS THE ADVERSARY LOWER BOUND ?

Peter Ružička, Juraj Wiedermann

Computing Research Centre
Dúbravská 3, 885 31 Bratislava

Czechoslovakia

ABSTRACT

In this paper we discuss the strength of the adversary argument in establishing lower bounds on the complexity of certain sorting-type problems. The relationship between adversary argument and so called information theory argument is indicated and the efficiency of adversary argument relative to the type of comparisons involved in the computation of a problem is investigated. The results concern the effect of polynomial comparisons on lower bounds. In certain cases (MIN and MERGE problems) by using polynomial comparisons we are able to obtain assymptotically the same lower bounds as those established when comparisons without arithmetics are used.

INTRODUCTORY FACTS

1.1 (Motivation) Only for relatively few problems there are algorithms known to be optimal in the worst-case. Thus, one of the principal goals in the complexity theory is to determine tight upper and lower bounds for the inherent difficulty of specific problems. Of a special interest there is inherent difficulty of combinatorial calculations which frequently arise in computing.

While the upper bounds on the computational complexity of a problem are relatively easily established by exhibiting an algorithm to solve the task and analyzing its cost, it is usually much more difficult to determine tight lower bounds. The difficulty arises from the fact that only properties common to the whole class of algorithms, which solve the given problem, can be exploited. There are known just few strategies used to determine lower bounds of comparison problems.

1.2 (Problem and computational model) In this paper we shall concentrate on sorting-type decision problems defined in the following way: let X be a set of n elements, S be a subset of all linear orderings of X and P be a partition on S. The decision problem $D(S,P)$ is the problem how to determine for a given ordering $w \in S$ that partition set from P to which w belongs.

For example, if the MAX(n) is considered, then using our notation the problem can be described as $D(S, \{P_1,\ldots, P_n\})$ where

$$P_i = \{ a_{k_1} \ldots a_{k_n} \in S \mid a_{k_i} = \max \{ a_1,\ldots, a_n \} \} ,$$

i.e. P_i is the set of those orderings from S in which the maximal element is in the i-th position. Thus, the problem to find the maximal element of X is identical with the problem to determine for an arbitrary ordering that partition set to which the ordering belongs.

We use a comparison tree as a general model to express decision algorithms. Each interior node of a rooted tree is associated with a comparison operation, and output (result) takes place at the leaves of the tree. Computation proceeds from root, node by node, until a leaf is reached. The path of greatest length indicates a worst-case complexity of a problem.

We shall discuss decision problems not only under the more traditional assumption that only binary comparisons (without arithmetics) are allowed but also under a rarer assumption that more general comparisons (with certain arithmetics) are permitted. Moreover, in comparisons only so called ignorant arithmetics are allowed, i.e. such by means of which the maximum cannot be realized.

1.3 (Information theory argument) One of the most efficient techniques for establishing lower bounds is the one using the information theory argument [2]. The main idea behind is that every algorithm using binary comparisons which is capable of giving r different results must also be capable of distinguishing them by r different computations and thus it must perform at least $\lceil \log_2 r \rceil$ comparisons. A lower bound which is derived using information theory argument will be called information theory bound (ITB).

In the case of binary comparisons Fredman [3] discussed, in a precise manner, the strength of the information theory argument for a class of decision problems. He proved that information theory argument is powerful for the case when P is the partition of S into singleton sets. He showed, however, that in almost all cases the information theory argument is fairly weak by proving that there is a gap of $n.\log_2 n + O(n)$ comparisons between ITB and optimal solution for almost all decision problems $D(S,P)$ where S is the set of all n! orderings and P is a partition of S into two sets.

When certain arithmetics are permitted in computation, the complexity of decision problems can be significantly lowered. For example, to solve the problem due to Chase (see [3, p. 356]) whether an arbitrary ordering of a set of n elements has even or odd parity, only 1 comparison using multiplications and subtractions suffices while $O(n.\log_2 n)$ binary comparisons are necessary. Also using a comparison tree program which allows comparisons between exponential functions over X, the maximum of n integers can be computed with $\lceil \log_2 n \rceil$ comparisons, while n-1 binary comparisons are necessary. In both examples the information theory lower bound has been attained using more general comparisons. However, there still remains a problem if there exists such a decision problem for which ITB would not be attainable by using any allowable comparisons.

The strength of information theory argument in the case of more general comparisons was investigated by author [7] . In this paper the effect of polynomial comparisons on the complexity of certain decision problems is exploited. We show that in the case of minimum problem for n integers the ITB is not attainable by using polynomial comparisons.

1.4 (Adversary argument) Utilization of the adversary argument is another method in obtaining lower bounds. On the contrary to the information theory argument which uses only information about the number of distinguishable results of a problem, the adversary reacts to the computational process of an algorithm. The intuition behind the adversary argument is that the adversary, using certain pattern of input data, forces the algorithm to follow some long path of computation tree. The length of the path constitutes an adversary bound (AB) . This operational strategy of adversary is denoted further as constructive one.

In our opinion the reason for treating adversary argument is that constructive way of determining lower bounds will enable us to penetrate deeper into the problem than a nonconstructive one, and so it would be of a considerable help in understanding the decision problem.

In this paper we characterize adversary argument from three points of view. Firstly, the relationship between ITB and AB is determined by proving that for each decision problem an adversary reaching ITB can be constructed. Secondly, since the essential feature of ITB is that it remains invariant as long as comparisons with ignorant arithmetics are used, the effectiveness of adversary technique relative to the arithmetic operations involved was studied. The case of comparisons using linear functions was investigated by Yao [8], more general case was treated by Dobkin and Lipton [1]. By applying adversary argument we prove for certain problems that assymptotically it is not possible to achieve savings in the number of comparisons by utilizing more general polynomial comparisons. Finally, we prove the existence of a decision problem for which the optimality cannot be proved by using adversary technique.

EFFICIENCY OF ADVERSARY ARGUMENT

2.1 As follows from Fredman´s results the complexity of many nonlinear decision problems can be fairly well lower estimated by using information theory argument. By using this argument a tight lower bound for sorting has also been established which is optimal for small values.

In most cases lower bounds on the complexity of linear decision problems with binary comparisons have been proved using adversary argument. The following theorem claims that using adversary techniques tight lower bounds for nonlinear problems can also be achieved.

Theorem

For each decision problem $D(S,P)$, an adversary determining the lower bound greater than or equal to $\lceil \log_2 |P| \rceil$ can be constructed.

Proof:

Let us consider a decision problem $D(S,P)$ where $P = \{P_1,\dots, P_k\}$ and an arbitrary comparison tree T which solves the problem $D(S,P)$. Denote nodes and leaves of the tree T as $N_1,\dots, N_p$ and $L_1,\dots,L_r$, respectively. With each node N (leaf L) we associate a subset S_N (S_L) of S such that S_N (S_L) will be the set of all such orderings from S which fulfil the sequence of comparisons on the path from the root of T to N (L). To the initial node (root of the tree T) we associate the entire set S. The strategy of adversary will be the following:

Suppose we are in a node N_i, $1 \leqslant i \leqslant p$, with a comparison "f:0". Using the comparison we can split the set S_{N_i} into two parts

$$\{a_{k_1} \dots a_{k_n} \in S_{N_i} \mid f(a_{k_1}, \dots, a_{k_n}) > 0\} \quad \text{and}$$

$$\{a_{k_1} \dots a_{k_n} \in S_{N_i} \mid f(a_{k_1}, \dots, a_{k_n}) \leqslant 0\}.$$

Nodes corresponding to these sets are S_{N_d} and S_{N_e}, respectively.

Thus we have $S_{N_i} = S_{N_d} \cup S_{N_e}$. As the following step in the computation the adversary chooses the node N_d if it holds

$$|\{v \mid S_{N_d} \cap P_v \neq 0, \quad 1 \leqslant v \leqslant k\}| \geqslant |\{v \mid S_{N_e} \cap P_v \neq 0, \quad 1 \leqslant v \leqslant k\}|$$

otherwise it chooses the node N_e.

Informally, the adversary strategy keeps information about a number of partition sets it has to distinguish using bisection.

The theorem follows from the observation that for every accepting leaf L of the tree T it holds $S_L \subseteq P_v$ for some $1 \leqslant v \leqslant k$.

2.2 In general case, the use of more general comparison operations does increase the power of computation. However, Yao conjectured [8] that the complexity of any decision problem $D(S,P)$ where S is the set of all $n!$ orderings of a set with n elements remains unchanged even when linear comparisons are used. But if some restriction is placed on the set S (i.e. not all $n!$ orderings are possible), then decision problems in which linear comparisons speed up the computation are also known.

It is also interesting to investigate the effect of polynomial comparisons on the complexity of certain problems. Firstly, we concentrate on the maximum / minimum problem. Rabin showed [4], that for the number of comparisons necessary to determine maximum of n real numbers, $n-1$ is the lower bound even if we permit the use of analytical functions in comparisons. When considering integers, Rabin´s result cannot be exploited because the proof of it is based on the properties of real numbers. However, Reingold obtained the result [6] that the maximum of n integers can be computed with $\lceil \log_2 n \rceil$ comparisons between exponential functions. If we restrict ourselves to linear comparisons, then $n-1$ comparisons are always necessary to compute the maximum of n integers. Friedman has raised the question whether the minimal integer from the set of n integers can be computed with logarithmic or linear number of polynomial comparisons. The following result claims that polynomial functions in comparisons do not reduce assymptotically the minimum number $MIN_p(n)$ of comparisons necessary for computing the minimum of the set of n integers.

Theorem

$$MIN_p(n) = O(n)$$

We sketch the idea of the proof. Consider an arbitrary set $\mathcal{J}$ of n integers $\{i_1,\ldots,i_n\}$ and an arbitrary comparison tree T which solves the minimum problem for $\mathcal{J}$. During the computation, the algorithm T successively performs comparisons in the form $f(a_1,\ldots,a_n) : 0$ where f is a polynomial of n variables with terms arranged in the usual lexicographical order based on some order of elements in $\mathcal{J}$. The first term with nonzero coefficient is called the leading term. We shall construct a deterministic "responding" strategy which will force the tree algorithm T to make a large number of comparisons. Our responding strategy is the following:

Let R be a partial ordering of $\mathcal{J}$ as established by our strategy in the previous computation and let f:0 be a comparison in consideration. Consider the lexicographical arrangement of terms of f based entirely on the partial ordering R. Two possibilities can occur: either the leading term of f is uniquely determined or it is not. In the latter case, by specifying the order among certain number of elements of $\mathcal{J}$, exactly one term from the set of potential candidates for leading term is choosed (and these binary relations among elements of $\mathcal{J}$ are then added to R). In both cases, the answer to the comparison question will be "$f > 0$" if the leading term is positive, otherwise the answer will be "$f \leqslant 0$".

In order to estimate this responding strategy of adversary, we use the following property:

FACT:

There exists an integer constant $c > 0$ such that for an arbitrary polynomial $f(a_1,\ldots,a_n)$ of n variables with integer coefficients the set

$$\{(i_1,\ldots,i_n) \mid i_1 > i_2 > \ldots > i_c \ , \ i_c > i_k \quad \text{for} \quad c < k \leqslant n$$

and there exists exactly one term g of polynomial f such that

$$f = f' + g \ \text{ and } \ |g(i_1,\ldots,i_n)| > f'(i_1,\ldots,i_n)\} \text{ is nonempty.}$$

Now, the assertion of the theorem follows from the FACT because from one polynomial comparison determined by the previous strategy at most two binary comparisons between two elements in the leading term different from the elements with relations in R can be abstracted.

2.3 Analogously we are able to prove similar result for the $MERGE_P(n)$ problem in which two ordered sequences of n distinct numbers are merged into one ordered sequence of 2n numbers. Let us consider the set $\mathcal{J}$ of 2n integers $\{i_1,\dots,i_{2n}\}$ where it holds $i_{2k} > i_{2k+2}$, $i_{2k-1} > i_{2k+1}$ for $1 \leqslant k \leqslant n-1$.

Again, consider the same lexicographical arrangement and the same responding strategy as in the proof of the previous theorem with the exception that initially the partial ordering R given by the MERGE problem is also considered. Let Q be the sequence of polynomial inequalities generated by a comparison tree program solving the merging problem based on the previously described responding strategy. Suppose that there exists an element, say i_k, such that it does not occur in any inequality in Q as an element with the smallest index in the leading term. Then it must occur in the so called "critical" position (i.e. that position in the term where the decision about the order of this term in the arrangement is made) in the leading term in at least k/2 inequalities of Q. The number of "critical" positions is proportional to n while the number of i_k elements, for which the order using critical positions is determined, is proportional to n^2 by which we conclude

Theorem

$$MERGE_P(n) = 2n - O(\sqrt{n})$$

2.4 Instead of polynomial functions we shall now consider restricted polynomial functions

$$f(a_1,\dots,a_n) = \sum_{i=1}^{n} \sum_{s=1}^{maxexp} c_{i,s} \cdot a_i^s$$

where maxexp denotes maximal exponent. In this case using the idea of previously described adversary strategy we are able to prove that

- for the minimum of n integers it holds $MIN_{RP}(n) = n-1$

- for the merging problem it holds $MERGE_{RP}(n) = 2n-1$

- for the minimum and maximum problem of n integers it holds

$$MINMAX_{RP}(n) \geqslant n - 2 + \lceil \log_2 n \rceil$$

- for the second smallest element of n integers it holds

$$SEC_{RP}(n) = n - 2 + \lceil \log_2 n \rceil$$

LIMITATIONS OF ADVERSARY ARGUMENT

3.1 In the previous section our considerations concerned mostly positive aspects of adversary argument applicability. We already saw that for each sorting-type decision problem ITB can be determined in a constructive way and that for certain decision problems adversary responds sensitevily also to general comparisons of algorithm.

Now we want to point out the fact that for certain problems using adversary argument the complexity of optimal algorithms solving those problems cannot be achieved.

3.2 Let us consider the general selection problem $V(k,n)$ which is the problem to determine the minimum number of binary comparisons that are required to determine the k-th largest of n elements of a linear ordered set X. Consider algorithms which solve the $V(k,n)$ problem for arbitrary n and k, $1 \leqslant k \leqslant n$ and which are of fixed strategy. An algorithm A solving a problem $D(S,P)$ is of a fixed strategy if it holds

1. there exists a comparison tree T for the problem $D(S,P)$ such that for all $w \in S$ the sequence of comparisons performed by T is identical with the sequence of comparisons performed by A

2. for each comparison c from A there exists $w \in S$ such that if w is the input of A, then A must perform c at some step of its computation

Using the notion of fixed strategy we are able to overcome the case in which the process of constructing optimal comparison trees is made using backtracking, and to ensure that even using any kind of coding we still be able to path through all branches of program containing comparison operations (in the case of fixed size of the problem).

3.3 The main result of this section is formulated in the following theorem:

Theorem

There is no algorithm A with fixed strategy for computing $V(k,n)$ which is optimal in the worst-case for all n and k, $1 \leqslant k \leqslant n$.

Proof:

Suppose that A is optimal for $k = 1$ and consider the way in which this algorithm works for an arbitrary k, $1 \leqslant k \leqslant n$. The algorithm compares maxima of partial ordering (so called "local" maxima) until it finds such an element x which is greater than n-k other elements. The algorithm A must proceed in comparing local maxima because in another case, when performing some "nonlocal" comparison, it has to do it in the case of the MAX problem too, as it follows from the fixed strategy. And in this latter case it could not be optimal for $k = 1$.

To find the element x the algorithm A performs at least $\lceil \log_2 (n-k+1) \rceil$ comparisons. Furthermore, the algorithm A knows that x can be among k greatest elements and in the worst-case, if x is not the k-th greatest element (suppose that in determining this fact it does not need any comparison as it is true for the case $k = 1$), then the algorithm must determine the $(k-1)$ -th element of the set $X - \{x\}$, and so at least $V_{k-1}(n-1)$ comparisons are further needed. If A needs $V'_k(n)$ comparisons for computing the k-th largest element, then it holds

$$V'_k(n) \geqslant \lceil \log_2 (n-k+1) \rceil + V_{k-1}(n-1)$$

for $1 \leqslant k \leqslant n$, $V_o(n) = 0$. For $k = 3$ we get

$$V'_3(n) \geqslant n - 3 + \lceil \log_2 (n-1) \rceil + \lceil \log_2 (n-2) \rceil .$$

Following Kirkpatrick [3] it holds

$$V_3(n) \leqslant n - 4 + 2 . \lceil \log_2 (n-1) \rceil$$

for $4.2^s < n-1 \leqslant 5.2^s$ and thus for infinitely many n the algorithm A is not optimal because it holds

$$V'_3(n) > V_3(n)$$

for $n = 4.2^s + 3$, ...

We conclude with remark that for certain problems solved by algorithms with fixed strategy the adversary argument cannot be efficiently exploited because the complexity of these problems can strongly depend on all problem parameters (as there are k and n in the case of the V(k,n) problem).

References

1. Dobkin, D., Lipton, R., On the Complexity of Computations under Varying Sets of Primitives. Automata Theory and Formal Languages 2nd GI Conference, Lecture Notes in Computer Science 33, Springer-Verlag (1975), 110-117.

2. Knuth, D.E., The Art of Computer Programming, Vol. 3, Sorting and Searching, Addison-Wesley, Reading, Mass., 1973.

3. Fredman, M.L., How Good is the Information Theory Bound for Sorting? Theoretical Computer Science 1 (1976), 355-361.

4. Kirkpatrick, D.G., Topics in the Complexity of Combinatorial Algorithms. Department of Computer Science, University of Toronto, Technical Report No. 74, 1974.

5. Rabin, M.O., Proving Simultaneous Positivity of Linear Forms, JCSS 6 (1972), 639-650.

6. Reingold, E.M., Computing the Maxima and the Median, 12th Annual Symposium on Switching and Automata Theory (1971), 216-218.

7. Ružička, P., The Influence of Arithmetics on the Complexity of Comparison Problems, Computing Research Centre, Bratislava, Technical Report (1977), 10-19 (in Slovak).

8. Yao, A. Ch., On the Complexity of Comparison Problems Using Linear Functions, 16th Annual Symposium on Foundations of Computer Science, (1976), 85-89.

TOTAL CORRECTNESS FOR PROCEDURES

Stefan Sokołowski

Institute of Mathematics, University of Gdańsk
ul. Wita Stwosza 57, 80-952 Gdańsk, POLAND

0. Introduction

In [10] an inference system for proving total correctness of programs without procedures is introduced. Since the only construct liable to cause non-termination is while-loop, special care is attached to the handling of loops. This paper deals with another dangerous element from everyday programming - recursive procedure. It turns out that the logical position of rules for procedures is somewhat different to that of simple while-programs. Some of the discussion on inference rules for procedures given in this paper may also concern Hoare's rule for partial correctness as given in [4]. In the last section validity and completeness of the new rule are formally proved.

The notation all over the paper coincides with that of [10]. All procedures are assumed parameter-free and with no local variables. Notation $\{q\}B\{r\}$ is the statement of total correctness of the program B with respect to q and r, x is a constant input vector and y is a variable state vector. All rules except (R4) are classical Hoare's rules from [3]. The troublesome while-rule is the Hoare's one enriched by the loop counter i and its upper bound k. In case of nested loops the predicates depend on a vector of loop counters - one for each depth of nesting. Details are given in [10].

AXIOMS AND RULES:

(A0) axiom of empty program: $\{p\}\ \underline{\text{skip}}\ \{p\}$

(A1) axiom of assignment: $\{p(f(y))\}\ y:=f(y)\ \{p(y)\}$

(A2) axiom of false: $\{\text{false}\}S\{\text{false}\}$

(R1) consequence rule: $$\frac{p\supset q,\ \ \{q\}S\{r\},\ \ r\supset t}{\{p\}S\{t\}}$$

(R2) ; rule: $$\frac{\{p\}R\{q\},\ \ \{q\}S\{t\}}{\{p\}R;S\{t\}}$$

(R3) if-then-else-fi rule: $$\frac{\{p\wedge a\}R\{q\},\ \ \{p\wedge\neg a\}S\{q\}}{\{p\}\ \underline{\text{if}}\ a\ \underline{\text{then}}\ R\ \underline{\text{else}}\ S\ \underline{\text{fi}}\ \{q\}}$$

(R4) <u>while</u>-<u>do</u>-<u>od</u> rule:

$$\frac{\begin{array}{c} p(i)\wedge\neg a \supset q \\ 0\leq i\leq k\wedge p(i)\wedge a \supset i<k \\ \{p(i)\wedge a\}\, S\, \{p(i+1)\} \end{array}}{\{p(0)\}\ \underline{\text{while}}\ a\ \underline{\text{do}}\ S\ \underline{\text{od}}\{q\}}$$

1. In search for a procedure rule

Hoare's rule for partial correctness of procedure calls reads as follows:

$$\text{(H)}\quad \frac{\{q\}\underline{\text{call}}\ p\{r\} \vdash \{q\}B\{r\}}{\{q\}\underline{\text{call}}\ p\{r\}}$$

where the procedure is defined by <u>proc</u> p : B <u>end</u> , p being its name and B being its body.

As the loop counters make the loop rule cover total correctness, it seems that what is needed for procedures is a sort of recursion depth counters. The proposed rule thus takes the form:

$$\text{(M)}\quad \frac{\begin{array}{c}\{q(0)\}B\{r\} \\ \{q(i)\}\underline{\text{call}}\ p\{r\} \vdash \{q(i+1)\}B\{r\}\end{array}}{\{\exists_{i\geq 0}\, q(i)\}\underline{\text{call}}\ p\{r\}}$$

Before discussing details, try the rule on a simple example.

<u>Example 1</u>: factorial.

```
proc factorial:
  if y1=0 then y2:= 1
          else y1:=y1-1; call factorial; y1:=y1+1; y2:=y2×y1
  fi
  end
```

The aim is to prove that

(E1) $\{0\leq y1\wedge r(x,y1,y1!)\}$ <u>call</u> factorial$\{r(x,y1,y2)\}$

is derivable for each predicate r. For simplicity, remaining arguments upon which r might depend, are omitted. By naming any specific r one can get from (E1) anything about the call of factorial. For instance

$\{x\geq 0\}$ y1:=x; <u>call</u> factorial$\{y2=x!\}$

is the case where r(x,y1,y2) is y2=x!.

For the proof of (E1) define the predicates

$q(i) \; : \; 0 \leq y1 \leq i \wedge r(x,y1,y1!)$ and

$r \; : \; r(x,y1,y2)$

and check the assumptions of (M).

(E2) $\{q(0)\} B \{r\}$ (B - body of factorial)

can be derived in usual way making use of

{false} call factorial {false}

that follows from (A2). This is precisely the role of (A2): to serve "dummy" procedure calls when control goes a different way.

From now on use may be made of

(E3) {q(i)} call factorial {r}

until the second assumption of (M) is derived. It is easily done by the usual means and we get

(E4) $\{q(i+1)\} B \{r\}$.

Now (M) applied to (E2) and (E4) yields (E1), and this ends the example.

At a closer inspection several troubles with the rule (M) may occur. In order to cope with them the rule will have to undergo some modifications.

Trouble 1:

No means to deal with mutual recursion.

The external appearance of the modified rule is exactly as in (M) so I do not write it once more. Only everything is understood as vector. Assume $p=(p_1,p_2,\ldots,p_n)$ is a vector of procedures closed upon mutual calls, i.e. these procedures do not call anything not belonging to p. They are defined by

proc p_1 : B_1(call $p_1,\ldots,$call p_n) end

....

proc p_n : B_n(call $p_1,\ldots,$call p_n) end

denoted symbolically by

proc p : B(call p) end.

For vectors $q=(q_1,\ldots,q_n)$, $r=(r_1,\ldots,r_n)$ of formulas and $L=(L_1,\ldots,L_n)$ of programs, $\{q\}L\{r\}$ **means that**

"for each $i=1,\ldots,n$: $\{q_i\}L_i\{r_i\}$ holds".

In this **form** the rule states that the properties of mutually recursive procedures have to be derived simultaneously with the same recursion-depth counter.

2. Remark on predicate transformers

It is desirable to be able to determine properties of a procedure call without any concern about a context of this call. Instead of deriving {q}call p{r} for particular q and r, we would prove a metatheorem of the form

"for each predicate r : {T(r)} call p{r}".

In the above T is a predicate scheme depending on r, or if you prefer, a predicate transformation. As a matter of fact, implicit predicate transformer has been considered in example 1, viz. it has been proved that

"for each predicate r :
$\{0 \leq y1 \wedge r(x,y1,y1!)\}$ call factorial$\{r(x,y1,y2)\}$".

The notion of predicate transformer has been introduced by Dijkstra in [2] and [1], and investigated for procedures by de Roever in [7]. Similar concept has been also investigated by Salwicki in [8].

By Dijkstra's approach semantics of each statement S is completely determined by its predicate transformer wp(S). Given a formula r, wp(S)(r) is the weakest precondition that has to be demanded of input in order that execution of S terminated and output satisfied r.

While wp(S) gives all the truth about S, sometimes it is reasonable to neglect a bit of this truth, as it may be inessential for the cause, or to trade a bit of it for simplicity of preconditions. A predicate transformer T is said to describe S iff {T(r)}S{r} (or, equivalently, $T(r) \supset wp(S)(r)$) holds for each predicate r. This generalisation is justified as long as we do not pretend that T defines the semantics of S. Note that in example 1 it has not been proved that $0 \leq y1 \wedge r(x,y1,y1!)$ is exactly wp(call factorial)(r(x,y1,y2)).

Let us come back to the troubles.

Trouble 2:

While the meaning of {q}K{r} is something like

"if q holds for input then K terminates and r holds for output"

which expresses an essential property of program K, it is not altogether clear what meaning is assigned to $\{p\}K\{r\} \vdash \{s\}L\{t\}$, that appears in (M).

The very first answer that comes to one's mind is

"$\{s\}L\{t\}$ may be derived in the system with the help of $\{p\}K\{r\}$".

This sentence however does not concern programs, but rather the inference system itself.

In view of the fact that without (M) the only means to deal with "call p" is (A2), the first premise of (M) makes it clear that if input satisfies $q(0)$, then no call will be executed while running B. Hence each occurrence of "call p" in B may be replaced by any other statement, which is best denoted by

$$\{q(0)\}\ B(\perp)\ \{r\},$$

with $\perp$ being the nowhere defined statement (abortion of program).

In the situation of $\{q(i)\}$ call $p\{r\} \vdash \{q(i+1)\}\ B($call p$)\{r\}$ each occurrence of "call p" in B has been replaced by a statement about which the only available information is $\{q(i)\}$ call $p\{r\}$. In other words it means that

"$\{q(i+1)\}\ B(X)\{r\}$ holds for each X such that $\{q(i)\}X\{r\}$".

More precisely an infinite sequence $T_0, T_1, T_2, \ldots$ of predicate transformers is constructed and

$$\{T_i(r)\}\text{ call } p\{r\} \vdash \{T_{i+1}(r)\}\ B(\text{call } p)\{r\}$$

means that

"if T_i describes X then T_{i+1} describes B(X)".

So the new shape of (M) is

$$(M') \qquad \frac{T_0 \text{ describes } B(\perp) \qquad \text{if } T_i \text{ describes X then } T_{i+1} \text{ describes } B(X)}{\exists_{i\geq 0}\, T_i \text{ describes call } p}$$

where $\exists_{i\geq 0}\, T_i$ is the transformer defined by $(\exists_{i\geq 0}\, T_i)\, r = \exists_{i\geq 0}(T_i r)$.

Example 2: recursive syntax analyser.

Assume language L is defined by the grammar

<program> ::= <sequence> .

<sequence> ::= <item> {, <item>}* (repetition)

<item> ::= a | (<sequence>)

Assume a word is written in the constant array

t : array [0..+∞] of char

with its first letter in t[0].

The analyser is the program:

```
p:=0; call SEQUENCE; if t[p]≠"." then ⊥ fi
```

together with procedures:

```
proc SEQUENCE: call ITEM; while t[p]="," do p:=p+1; call ITEM od end
```

and

```
proc ITEM:
if t[p]="a" then p:=p+1 else
 if t[p]="(" then p:=p+1; call SEQUENCE; if t[p]=")" then p:=p+1
                                                        else ⊥ fi
          else ⊥ fi
fi end
```

The aim is to derive

(E0) $\{t[0]\ldots t[j]$ is an instance of ⟨program⟩ for some $j\geq 0\}$
PROGRAM
$\{t[0]\ldots t[p]$ is an instance of ⟨program⟩$\}$.

To this aim properties of procedures have to be established:

(E1) $\{p\geq 0$ and for some $j\geq p$: $t[p]\ldots t[j]$ is a maximal instance of ⟨sequence⟩ and $r(j+1)$ holds$\}$
call SEQUENCE
$\{r(p)\}$ for each predicate r.

Maximal means there is no $k>j$ such that $t[p]\ldots t[k]$ is an instance of ⟨sequence⟩.

(E2) $\{p\geq 0$ and for some $j\geq p$: $t[p]\ldots t[j]$ is an instance of ⟨item⟩ and $r(j+1)$ holds$\}$
call ITEM
$\{r(p)\}$ for each predicate r.

In order to prove (E0) from (E1) note that $t[i]\ldots t[j]$ is an instance of ⟨program⟩ iff $t[i]\ldots t[j-1]$ is an instance of ⟨sequence⟩ and $t[j]=$".", and that no instance of ⟨sequence⟩ may contain a dot.

For the proof of (E1) and (E2) introduce predicate vector
$q(p,i)=(q_S(p,i),q_I(p,i))$ (i - the recursion-depth counter):

$q_S(p,i)$: "i is odd and $p\geq 0$ and $t[p]\ldots t[j]$ is a maximal instance of ⟨sequence⟩ for some $j\geq p$ and its depth does not exceed $(i-1)/2$, and $r(j+1)$ holds"

$q_I(p,i)$: "i is even and $p\geq 0$ and $t[p]\ldots t[j]$ is an instance of ⟨item⟩ for some $j\geq p$ and its depth does not exceed $i/2$ and $r(j+1)$ holds".

In the above the depth of a word is its paranthesis depth, i.e. $\mathrm{depth}(w) = \max[j \mid w=uv$ and there are j unpaired "("-s in u$]$.

By (A2) and by definition of q it follows that

(E3) $\{q_S(p,0)\}$ body of SEQUENCE $\{r(p)\}$ and

(E4) $\{q_I(p,0)\}$ body of ITEM $\{r(p)\}$.

The first assumption of (M′) is thus satisfied. From now on we may assume that

(E5) $\{q_S(p,i)\}$ call SEQUENCE $\{r(p)\}$ and

(E6) $\{q_I(p,i)\}$ call ITEM $\{r(p)\}$

hold for each predicate r, and we may use these to prove that

(E7) $\{q_S(p,i+1)\}$ body of SEQUENCE $\{r(p)\}$ and

(E8) $\{q_I(p,i+1)\}$ body of ITEM $\{r(p)\}$

hold for each r.

The proof of (E8) is straightforward. In order to prove (E7) define invariant s(p,i,k) for the while-loop in body of SEQUENCE by:

s(p,i,k) : "i is even and p≥0 and for some j≥p-1: t[p]...t[j] is a maximal sequence of pairs of the form [comma, an instance of ⟨item⟩] and depth of no item exceeds i/2 and there are k commas to the left of t[p] before the first "(" occurs and r(j+1) holds".

The variable k in s is its loop counter. (E7) may be now easily proved making use of (E6) twice for two occurrences of "call ITEM" in body of SEQUENCE: first with s(p,i,0) replaced for r(p), and then with s(p,i,k+1) for r(p).

3. Validity and completeness

Validity and completeness of the inference system without procedures have been proved in [10]. Only rule (M) is lacking.

My favourite way to define semantics of a statement S is by attaching to it its result function f, which is a partial function on input vector x and state vector y, yielding a state vector - such that f(x,y) is defined iff S halts for (x,y) and f(x,y) is then the new state vector after executing S. The x-argument of f will be herefrom omitted for simplicity.

The meaning of procedure definition

proc p : B(call p) end

is given by the functional equation

(3.1) $X = B(X)$

where B(X) is the result function of B(call p) under assumption that X is the result function of call p. The result function X_0 of call p is defined as the least solution of (3.1) (see for instance [9] or [6]). It is given by

(3.2) $X_0 = \bigsqcup_{i=0}^{\infty} B^i(\bot)$.

THEOREM 1: (validity of (M′))

If T_0 describes $B(\bot)$, and T_{i+1} describes $B(X)$ for each X such that T_i describes X

then $\exists_i\, T_i$ describes call p.

Proof:

Let y satisfy $\exists_i\, T_i(r)$. Then there exists such j that y satisfies $T_j(r)$. From the assumption of the theorem it follows by induction that T_j describes $B^{j+1}(\bot)$. So $B^{j+1}(\bot)$ halts on y with the result satisfying r. But by (3.2): $X_0(y)=B^{j+1}(\bot)(y)$. This completes the proof.

THEOREM 2: (completeness of (M′))

For every procedure proc p:B(call p) end, the fact that wp(call p) describes call p may be derived in the inference system.

Because of the very nature of wp, this gives all the truth about call p.

Proof:

Define a sequence of transformers by

$$T_i = wp(B^{i+1}(\bot)) \qquad \text{for } i=0,1,2,\ldots$$

1. It is obvious that T_0 describes $B(\bot)$.

2. The predicate $T_i(r) = wp(B^{i+1}(\bot))(r)$ states that computation of B(call p) terminates with r satisfied and throughout the process the depth of recursion never exceeds i.

For each occurrence of call p in B define the set A of all possible values of state vector y just after execution of this very call p, provided the execution of B started with a state vector satisfying $wp(B^{i+1}(\bot))(r)$. The set A may be identified with its characteristic predicate.

Thus if we start B with $wp(B^{i+1}(\bot))(r)$ satisfied then $wp(B^{i}(\bot))(A)$ is satisfied at the entrance to call p and

3.3 $\{wp(B^{i}(\bot))(A)\}$ call p$\{A\}$

tells everything about call p. In view of the completeness of the system with respect to other programming constructs (see [10]), (3.3) makes it possible to derive $\{wp(B^{i+1}(\bot))(r)\}$ B(call p)$\{r\}$. The proof however remains unchanged if (3.3) is replaced by

$$\{wp(B^{i}(\bot))(A)\}X\{A\}.$$

This proves that if T_{i-1} describes X then T_i describes B(X).

From 1 and 2 by (M′) it may be derived that $\exists_i\, T_i$ describes call p. But

$$\exists_i\, T_i = (\text{by definition}) = \exists_i\, wp(B^{i+1}(\bot)) =$$

$= $ (by continuity of wp - see de Roever [7]) $=$

$= \mathrm{wp}\,(B^{i+1}(\perp)) = $ (by (3.2)) $= \mathrm{wp}($call p$)$.

This ends the proof.

References

1. Dijkstra, E.W. "A Discipline of Programming" Prentice-Hall 1976

2. Dijkstra, E.W. "Guarded Commands, Nondeterminacy and Formal Derivation of Programs" Comm. ACM 18 (1975) 453-457

3. Hoare, C.A.R. "Axiomatic Basis for Computer Programming" Comm. ACM 12 (1969) 576-580

4. Hoare, C.A.R. "Procedures and Parameters: An Axiomatic Approach" Lecture Notes in Mathematics 188 (1971), Symposium on Semantics of Algorithmic Languages (ed. E.Engeler) 62-70

5. Hoare, C.A.R.; Lauer, P. "Consistent and Complementary Formal Theories of the Semantics of Programming Languages" Acta Informatica 3 (1974) 135-153

6. Manna, Z. "Mathematical Theory of Computation" McGraw Hill 1974

7. de Roever, W.P. "Dijkstra's Predicate Transformer, Non-Determinism, Recursion and Termination" Lecture Notes in Computer Science 45 (1976), Mathematical Foundations of Computer Science (ed. A.Mazurkiewicz) 472-481

8. Salwicki, A. "Formalised Algorithmic Languages" Bull.Acad. Polon.Sci., Serie Math.Astr.Phys., 18 (1970) 227-232

9. Scott, D. "Outline of a Mathematical Theory of Computation" Oxford University, Programming Research Group, Technical Monograph PRG-2, 1970

10. Sokołowski, S. "Axioms for Total Correctness" to appear in Acta Informatica

A MODEL FOR RETRIEVAL SYSTEMS AND SOME MATHEMATICAL PROBLEMS BEHIND

Ján Šturc
Computing Research Centre
Dúbravská 3, 885 31 Bratislava
Czechoslovakia

1. Introduction

Although recent trends in data base systems lead to artificial intelligence projects, we prefer systems based on formal languages. The main reason for our approach is that we do not trust in general understanding of a natural language. The model of a retrieval system described in this paper is based on a formal language in the role of a query language and an algebra of data structures. An example of a query language can be the alpha calculus suggested by Codd [1]. This does not mean that we adhere to the alpha calculus as a user query language, we consider it to be a good theoretical model of the latter only. The model of the retrieval system consists of two algorithms. One of them translates the query into an expression of the data structure algebra and the other interpretes this expression to produce a result - - an answer.

In this paper we attempt to treat mathematical problems related to such a system.

2. Basic concepts and denotations

In the following text we employ standard set-theoretic and predicate calculus notations with the exception of the set intersection for which no connective is used, so that AB means $A \cap B$.

Let $t:S \rightarrow U$ be a function from S into U and $P \subset S$, then $t|P$ denotes the restriction of t onto P.

Definition 1: /A record/

Let U be a set of values and S be a finite set of simple attributes, then total function $r:S\to U$ will be called a record with total attribute S.

Note:

In further considerations, especially in paragraph 4, we can imagine U to be a countable set such that for each two its elements a and b it is decidable whether $a=b$.

Definition 2:/A relational data structure /RDS//

A set R of records with the same total attribute S is called a relational data structure and is denoted by $R(S)$.

These definitions are essentially the same as those used in the paper by Hall, Hitchcock and Todd [2].

3. An algebra of RDS

One of the interesting problems related to the modelling of data base systems is construction of a good algebraic model. The model has to be as simple as possible and adequate. On the other hand a rich algebraic structure allows better optimization of expressions. We shall now define the following operations on RDS.

Definition 3: /Algebraic operations/

Let us denote the set of all records with total attribute S by $U(S)$, let $R_1(S_1)$ and $R_2(S_2)$ be RDS with total attributes S_1 and S_2 respectively, then:

the product

$$R_1 \times R_2 = \{t : t \in U(S_1 \cup S_2) \wedge t|S_1 \in R_1 \wedge t|S_2 \in R_2\}$$

the union

$$R_1 + R_2 = \{t : t \in U(S_1 \cup S_2) \wedge (t|S_1 \in R_1 \vee t|S_2 \in R_2)\}$$

the difference

$$R_1 - R_2 = \{t : t \in R_1 \wedge ((\forall t \in R_2)\ t|S_1S_2 \neq t|S_1S_2)\}$$

the sum

$$R_1 \oplus R_2 = \{t : t \in U(S_1 \cup S_2) \wedge (t|S_1 \in R_1 \wedge t|S_2 \notin R_2 \vee t|S_1 \notin R_1 \wedge t|S_2 \in R_2)\}.$$

Let us imagine for a moment that all RDS are defined with the greatest possible attribute S. In this case the records can be considered as partial functions $r : S \rightarrow U$. We denote the domain of the record r by Dom(r). Since RDS is a set of records with the same domain, the concept of the domain can be naturally extended to the RDS, too.

<u>Definition 4:</u> /Mapping Sem/

Let us associate with a record r a set Sem(r) of the total functions $S \rightarrow U$ such that

$$\mathrm{Sem}(r) = \{t : S \rightarrow U \wedge t|\mathrm{Dom}(r) = r\}.$$

We extend the mapping Sem to the RDS so that

$$\mathrm{Sem}(R) = (\bigcup r \in R)\,\mathrm{Sem}(r).$$

<u>Lemma 1:</u>

If the empty RDS and the universal RDS are defined to be equal independently of their different total attribute, then the mapping Sem is an isomorphism.

<u>Proof:</u>

One can easily verify the following identities:

$$\mathrm{Sem}(R_1 * R_2) = \mathrm{Sem}(R_1)\ \mathrm{Sem}(R_2)$$

$$\mathrm{Sem}(R_1 + R_2) = \mathrm{Sem}(R_1) \cup \mathrm{Sem}(R_2)$$

$$\mathrm{Sem}(R_1 - R_2) = \mathrm{Sem}(R_1) - \mathrm{Sem}(R_2).$$

It remains to prove that $R_1 = R_2$ if and only if $\mathrm{Sem}(R_1) = \mathrm{Sem}(R_2)$. Obviously $R_1 = R_2$ implies $\mathrm{Sem}(R_1) = \mathrm{Sem}(R_2)$. Conversely, $R_1 \neq R_2$ implies that $R_1 \oplus R_2 \neq \emptyset$ but in this case symmetric difference $\mathrm{Sem}(R_1)$ and $\mathrm{Sem}(R_2)$ is not empty and that means $\mathrm{Sem}(R_1) \neq \mathrm{Sem}(R_2)$. Thus the proof is completed.

Let us consider a finite set S of the attributes and a set U of the values, let $\mathcal{R}(S)$ be the set of all RDS $R(S')$ such that $S' \subseteq S$. U(S) is the universal RDS and $\emptyset$ is the empty RDS. It is quite natural to define the RDS complementary to R, denoted by $\overline{R} = U(S) - R$. Then the following theorem holds:

Theorem 1:

The structure $\mathcal{A}=(\mathcal{R}(S), *, +, -, U(S), \emptyset)$ is a boolean algebra.

Proof:

The isomorphism Sem maps the structure $\mathcal{A}$ onto the powerset of the set of all total functions $S \to U$. The statement that the powerset of a set with the usual set operation is a boolean algebra completes the proof.

Corollary:

The structure $\mathcal{B}=(\mathcal{R}(S), *, \oplus, U(S), \emptyset)$ is a boolean ring.

Proof:

It is sufficient to note that $Sem(R_1 \oplus R_2)$ is the symmetric difference of the $Sem(R_1)$ and $Sem(R_2)$.

4. Effectiveness

The effectiveness $E(R)$ of a RDS R can be characterised in terms of a set of its total attribute subsets. A subset P of total attribute S belongs to the effectiveness of R if for the given values of attribute P there is an algorithm which produces the set $\{t : t \in R \wedge t|P$ has the given values$\}$. This definition ensures that if P is in $E(R)$, then each superset of P is in $E(R)$, too. So the minimal sets are sufficient for the characterisation of the effectiveness.

The border cases are $\emptyset \in E(R)$, which is synonymous with R is finite, and $E(R)=\{S\}$, which means R works as a recognizer. We do not take $E(R)=\emptyset$ into consideration, since in this case R is an unconstructive object.

Theorem 2: /Hall, Hitchcock, Todd [2]/

The following formulae express the effectiveness of algebraic operations:

$$E(R_1 * R_2) = \{P : PS_1 \in E(R_1) \wedge (P \cup S_1) S_2 \in E(R_2) \vee \vee PS_2 \in E(R_2) \wedge (P \cup S_2) S_1 \in E(R_1)\}$$

$$E(R_1 + R_2) = \{P:\ PS_1 \in E(R_1) \wedge PS_2 \in E(R_2) \wedge\ S_1 \cup S_2 - S_1S_2 \subset P\}$$

$$E(R_1 - R_2) = \underline{\text{if}}\ \ S_1S_2 \in E(R_2)\ \ \underline{\text{then}}\ \ E(R_2)\ \ \underline{\text{else}}\ \ \emptyset$$

$$E(R_1 \oplus R_2) = \underline{\text{if}}\ \ S_1S_2 \in E(R_1)E(R_2)\ \ \underline{\text{then}}\ \ \{P: PS_1 \in E(R_1) \wedge PS_2 \in E(R_2) \wedge \wedge\ S_1 \cup S_2 - S_1S_2 \subset P\}\ \ \underline{\text{else}}\ \ \emptyset.$$

In retrieval systems the key role is played by extremal cases, the finite RDS which represent actual data and the recognizers which are used as selection filters. Most frequently used recognizing RDS are comparison and identity RDS.

5. Equivalence

The equivalence problem of data base can be reduced to one of subalgebras generated by a finite set of RDS. The members of this set are called subalgebra generators.

Definition 5: /A data base/

A data base is a pair $\langle D,D' \rangle$ where D is a finite set of finite RDS and D' is a finite set of recognizers.

Two data bases are considered to behave equivalently if they give the same answers on the equal queries. Despite that we define the equivalence of data bases on the basis of algebras generated by them, so as to avoid difficulties caused by the vague concept of equal query.

Definition 6:

Two data bases are said to be equivalent if they generate the same subalgebra of the algebra $\mathcal{R}$.

Definition 7:

A set of subalgebra generators is called canonical if each element of the subalgebra can be expressed as a union of it generators.

Theorem 3:

If a subalgebra of the RDS algebra has a finite set of finite generators then there is an algorithm which finds the canonical generator set of this subalgebra.

Proof:

Instead of the algebra of RDS we shall consider its image under isomorphism Sem. Further we distribute the elements of $U(S)$ into equivalence classes. Let $R_1, R_2, \ldots, R_n$ be the generators. At first we construct the set U' of all elements occurring in some of the generators. It is always possible because the generators are finite. Then add an element $\perp \notin U - U'$ to U'. This element represents the elements $U - U'$ which are mutually indistinguishable on the basis of the algebra. Further considerations can be conducted in a finite universum $U' \cup \{\perp\}$. At first the desired algorithm constructs a set $Q = (\bigcup\ 1 \leq i \leq n) \mathrm{Sem}(R_i)$, then it associates a binary vector $\bar{q}$ of the length n with each element q of Q in the following way: it sets $\bar{q}[i] = 1$ if and only if $q \in \mathrm{Sem}(R_i)$. In the next step the algorithm forms the equivalence classes T_i so that if there are k distinct values of the vector $\bar{q}$, it creates k classes T_i and to each class it assigns all elements q from Q such that the vectors $\bar{q}$ equals $\bar{q}_i$. So $T_i = \{q : q \in Q \wedge \bar{q} = \bar{q}_i\}$ for $1 \leq i \leq k$. The classes T_i, $1 \leq i \leq k$, are generators of the same subalgebra as the subalgebra generated by R_i, $1 \leq i \leq n$ and they form canonical generator set because the elements of Q belong to the same class if and only if they are mutually indistinguishable on the basis of generators $R_1, R_2, \ldots, R_n$. The algebras are equivalent since we can express

$\mathrm{Sem}(R_j) = \bigcup (1 \leq i \leq k \wedge \bar{q}_i[j] = 1) T_i$ and vice versa

$T_i = \bigcup (1 \leq j \leq n \wedge \bar{q}_i[j] = 1) \mathrm{Sem}(R_i) - \bigcup (1 \leq j \leq n \wedge \bar{q}_i[j] = 0) \mathrm{Sem}(R_j)$.

Since Sem is an isomorphism we can easily return to the original algebra by its inverse. The last statement completes the proof.

Corollary:

The equivalence problem for data bases is decidable.

Proof:

To decide the equivalence of data bases, it suffices to find the canonical generator sets for subalgebras generated by both data bases and then to compare them. Since there is an algorithm which finds the canonical generator set and the generators are finite, this can be done.

6. Projections and renamings

In an actual retrieval system another operation is often needed. Such an operation is defined both in [1] and [2].

Definition 8: /A projection/

Let R be a RDS with total attribute S and $P \subset S$, then the projection R on P is

$$R|P = \{t : t \in U(P) \wedge (\exists r \in R) r|P = t\}.$$

Theorem 4:

The projection cannot be expressed in terms of boolean algebra $\mathcal{A}$.

Proof:

Let $S = \{A, B\}$ and $U = \{1, 2, 3, 4\}$ and let us consider a subalgebra generated by the RDS

$R_1 = \{(\langle A,1\rangle, \langle B,2\rangle), (\langle A,3\rangle, \langle B,4\rangle)\}$ and

$R_2 = \{(\langle A,1\rangle)\}$.

In this algebra the records $(\langle A,2\rangle, \langle B,1\rangle)$ and $(\langle A,3\rangle, \langle B\ 1\rangle)$ are indistinguishable from each other. This can be easily shown finding the canonical generator set of this algebra. On the other hand, using projection, we can obtain from this algebra an algebra with generators R_1, R_2, R_3, R_4 , where

$R_3 = \{(\langle A,1\rangle), (\langle A,3\rangle)\}$ and $R_4 = \{(\langle B,2\rangle, \langle B,4\rangle)\}$.

But in the latter algebra the previously mentioned records are distinguishable, thus using the projection we go beyond the scope of the given algebra. That completes the proof.

According to the Theorem 3, if we want to obtain a realistic model we need to introduce the projection into the algebra. Instead of defining an additional operation and working with some particular case of a universal algebra we prefer another way of introducing this operation. Let F be the set of all functions from S into S. We define the composition of the functions $(f \circ g)(x) = f(g(x))$ and if $g(x)$ is undefined, then so is $(f \circ g)(x)$.

Definition 9:

Let $F = \{f\colon f\colon S \rightarrow S\}$ and R be a RDS with the total attribute $P \subset S$. Let $f \in F$ and $Dom(f) = P$. Then the renaming operation denoted by $R|f$ means

$$R|f = \{t\colon t = r \circ f \wedge r \in R\}.$$

In the particular case that f is an identity function for some simple attributes and that it is undefined for other simple attributes, the renaming operation performs the projection. The advantage of such an approach is that the renamings need not be actually done but they can be read from the original relation through the proper renaming function.

7. The model and its relationship with the relational model

Now we can formally define the model for the retrieval system. Our definition is based on algebraic structures $\mathcal{A}$ resp. $\mathcal{B}$.

Definition 10: /A retrieval system/

A retrieval system is a quintuple $(\mathcal{a}, S, F, D', D)$, where:
$\mathcal{a}$ is an algebraic structure $\mathcal{A}$ or $\mathcal{B}$,
S is a set of simple attributes,
F is a set of renaming functions,
D' is a set of identities and comparisons RDS and
D is a set of finite RDS.

This definition enable us to treat the equivalence of retrieval systems formally on the basis of morphisms of algebraic structures. There are two types of equivalence, the stronger one which does not consider projections and the weaker one which also considers the projections. The equivalence problem for both types of equivalence is decidable. Both equivalences ensure that the systems which are equivalent behave equivalently i.e. that they produce the same answers for the same queries. On the other hand there are retrieval systems which behave equivalently and are not equivalent according to either type of equivalence.

Theorem 5:

For each formula in the relational model / Codd [1]/ there is an equivalent algebraic expression in our model.

Proof:

It suffices to show that the cartesian product and restriction operations of relational algebra may be expressed in terms of the boolean operations and renamings. The product $R_1 * R_2$ performs this job because it is the cartesian product, provided the total attributes S_1 and S_2 are disjoint. This can be achieved using the proper renaming operation. The product $R_1 * E$ performs the restriction for some comparison RDS E in case that the total attribute P of E is a subset of S_1. And by this the proof is completed.

8. Conclusion

We presented here a more formal alternative of the relational model. The advantages of this model as we see them lie in the fact that the more detailed formalization allows formal treatment of the equivalence problem and the rich algebraic structure gives a good possibility to exploit algebraical laws for the expression optimization. Moreover, the existing experience with the minimization of boolean expressions and optimization of arithmetical expressions may be utilized.

References:

1. Codd, E.F.: Relational completeness of data base sublanguages. In Data base systems. / Ed: Rustin R. /, Prentice Hall, Englewood Cliffs, 1972, pp. 65-98
2. Hall, P.; Hitchcock, P.; Todd, S.: An algebra for machine computation. Proceedings of the Second symposium on principles of programming languages, Palo Alto, 1975, pp. 225-232

TIME AND TAPE BOUNDED AUXILIARY PUSHDOWN AUTOMATA*

I. H. Sudborough

Department of Computer Science
The Technological Institute
Northwestern University
Evanston, Illinois 60201
U.S.A.

Abstract

We consider language families defined by nondeterministic and deterministic log(n)-tape bounded auxiliary pushdown automata within polynomial time. It is known that these families are precisely the set of languages which are (many-one) log tape reducible to context-free languages and deterministic context-free languages, respectively. The results described here relate questions concerning these classes to other complexity classes and to questions concerning the tape complexity of context-free languages, resolution based proof procedures, solvable path systems, and deterministic context-free languages.

Introduction

In [1] the author has shown that the family of languages recognized by nondeterministic (deterministic) log(n)-tape bounded auxiliary PDA's in polynomial time is identical to the family of languages which are (many-one) log-tape reducible to context-free (deterministic context-free) languages. The concept of an L(n)-tape bounded auxiliary PDA was introduced in [2]; (many-one) log-tape reducibility is defined and investigated in [3,4]. Although Cook has shown in [2] that nondeterministic and deterministic L(n)-tape bounded auxiliary PDA have the same computing power for all $L(n) \geq \log(n)$, it is as yet unknown whether or not this equiva-

* This work is supported in part by the National Science Foundation under grant GJ - 43228.

lence remains valid when a polynomial time constraint is imposed. That is, it is as yet unknown whether or not LOG(CFL)=LOG(DCFL), where LOG($\mathcal{L}$) denotes the family of all languages (many-one) log-tape reducible to languages in $\mathcal{L}$. Since Greibach's hardest context-free language L_0 [5] is such that for every context-free language L there is a homomorphism h such that $L=h^{-1}(L_0)$, it follows that L_0 is log-tape complete for CFL (and, therefore, also for LOG(CFL)). It follows that LOG(CFL)=LOG (DCFL) iff L_0 can be recognized by a deterministic log(n)-tape bounded auxiliary PDA in polynomial time. Moreover, since L_0 is recognized in real-time by a nondeterministic log(n)-tape bounded auxiliary PDA, LOG(CFL)=LOG(DCFL) iff all nondeterministic real-time AuxPDA(log n) languages can be recognized by a deterministic polynomial time bounded AuxDPDA(log n). Recent results reported in [6] show that all context-free languages can be recognized by a two-way deterministic pushdown automaton with as few as three heads if the polynomial time constraint is not imposed.

In [1] the author has also described a deterministic context-free language L_S which is log-tape complete for the family LOG(DCFL). In other words, the DCFL L_S is a hardest deterministic context-free language with respect to the tape (or workspace) complexity measure. For example, LOG(DCFL)=DSPACE(log n) iff L_S can be recognized by a deterministic log(n)-tape bounded Turing machine. It is shown in [1], moreover, that L_S is a simple LL(1) language and a simple precedence language. (These families are discussed for example in [7]. It is known that the simple LL(1) language family and the simple precedence language family are properly contained in the full family of DCFL's.)

In [8,9] the author has shown that the context-independent extended Lindenmayer (EOL) languages, any homomorphic replication of a context-free language, the restricted derivation state grammar languages of [10], and certain families of vector grammar languages described in [11] are in LOG(CFL). Thus the family LOG(CFL) is large enough to encompass many of the language families described in the literature. Since Cook [2] has shown that AuxPDA(log n)=DTIME(poly), where $\text{DTIME(poly)}=\bigcup_{k\geq 1}\text{DTIME}(n^k)$, it follows that LOG(CFL)$\subseteq$DTIME(poly). Also, since CFL$\subseteq$DSPACE($(\log n)^2$) [12], it follows that LOG(CFL)$\subseteq$DSPACE($(\log n)^2$). Therefore, LOG(CFL)$\subseteq$DTIME(poly) $\cap$ DSPACE($(\log n)^2$). The following definitions and lemmas are from [3,4]:

Definition. Let Σ,Δ be alphabets and $f\colon \Sigma^* \to \Delta^*$ be a function. f is log-tape computable if there is a deterministic Turing machine with a two-way read-only input tape, a one-way output tape, and a two-way read-write worktape, which when started with $x \in \Sigma^*$ on its input tape will halt having written $f(x) \in \Delta^*$ on its output tape and having visited at most $\log(|x|)$ tape squares on its worktape.

Definition. Let $A \subseteq \Sigma^*$ and $B \subseteq \Delta^*$ be arbitrary sets of words. A is (many-one) log-tape reducible to B, denoted $A \leq_{\log} B$, if there is a log-tape computable function f such that $\forall x \in \Sigma^* (x \in A \Leftrightarrow f(x) \in B)$.

Lemma. $\leq_{log}$ is a transitive relation.

Lemma. Let $A \subseteq \Sigma^*$ and $B \subseteq \Delta^*$. If $A \leq_{log} B$ and $B \in$ DSPACE($(\log n)^k$), then $A \in$ DSPACE($(\log n)^k$), for any $k \geq 1$.

It is known that the above lemma remains true if NSPACE($(\log n)^k$) or DTIME (poly) is substituted for each occurrence of DSPACE($(\log n)^k$).

Definition. Let $\mathcal{L}$ be a family of languages. $L \subseteq \Sigma^*$ is log-tape complete for $\mathcal{L}$ if (1) $L \in \mathcal{L}$, and (2) for every L' in $\mathcal{L}$, $L' \leq_{log} L$.

Definition. For any family of languages $\mathcal{L}$, LOG($\mathcal{L}$) = $\{L \mid \exists L' \in \mathcal{L}\ (L \leq_{log} L')\}$

In the following CFL and DCFL will denote the family of context-free languages and the family of deterministic context-free languages, respectively.

For any function T(n) and L(n) from the nonnegative integers to the natural numbers, let T(n)-AuxPDA(L(n)) and T(n)-AuxDPDA(L(n)) denote the set of languages recognized by nondeterministic and deterministic L(n)-tape bounded auxiliary pushdown automata within T(n) steps. Let poly-AuxPDA(L(n)) = $\bigcup_k n^k$ - AuxPDA(L(n)). The relevant theorem from [1] can then be described as follows:

Theorem. poly-AuxPDA(log n) = LOG(CFL)

poly-AuxDPDA(log n) = LOG(DCFL).

By a rather straightforward diagonalization argument one can show that a hierarchy of language families exists within the family of L(n)-tape bounded AuxPDA languages based upon the amount of time and the number of worktape symbols allowed. Hierarchial results defined by the number of worktape symbols or the number of worktape heads with no time constraint are described in [6]. Here we are more interested in relating nondeterministic and deterministic time and tape bounded auxiliary pushdown automata classes and in relating these classes to the nondeterministic and deterministic tape bounded Turing machine classes.

The following relationships can be shown by a suitable modification of a technique described in [21]:

(1) poly-AuxPDA(log n) = poly-AuxDPDA(log n) iff $\bigcup_{c>0} 2^{cL(n)}$-AuxPDA(L(n)) = $\bigcup_{c>0} 2^{cL(n)}$-AuxDPDA(L(n)), for all $L(n) \geq \log n$.

(2) poly-AuxPDA(log n) = DSPACE(log n) iff $\bigcup_{c>0} 2^{cL(n)}$-AuxPDA(L(n)) = DSPACE(L(n)), for all $L(n) \geq \log n$.

Statement (2) above remains valid when every occurrence of DSPACE is replaced by NSPACE and when every occurence of AuxPDA is replaced by AuxDPDA.

Problems which are log-tape complete for LOG(CFL)

As indicated previously the hardest context-free language described in [5] is an example of a language which is log-tape complete for LOG(CFL). Here we are interested in describing complete problems about graphs and propositional formulas, as has been done for many other complexity classes such as, (1) for NTIME(poly) = $\bigcup_{k>0}$ NTIME(n^k) in [13,14], (2) for DTIME(poly) in [15,16], and (3) for NSPACE(log n) in [17,18,19]. It is felt that this may help toward obtaining a better understanding of the family LOG(CFL) = poly-AuxPDA(log n) and its relationship to the more traditional complexity classes. For example, in [15,20] Cook has described the concept of a solvable path system and has shown that the set of codings of solvable path systems is log-tape complete for DTIME(poly). In [21] Savitch describes the set of threadable mazes and shows that this set is log-tape complete for NSPACE(log n). We shall describe a path system problem which is log-tape complete for LOG(CFL).

Definition. A path system is a quadruple $\mathscr{P}$=(X,R,S,T), where X is a finite set (of nodes), R is a three place relation on X (the incidence relation), S $\subseteq$ X (S is the set of source nodes), and T $\subseteq$ X (T is the set of terminal nodes)

The admissible nodes of $\mathscr{P}$ are the least set A such that T $\subseteq$ A and such that if y, z $\in$ A and R(x,y,z) holds, then x $\in$ A. We say $\mathscr{P}$ is solvable if at least one admissible node is a source node (i.e. a member of S).

Let us code a path system $\mathscr{P}$ = (X,R,S,T) as a string E($\mathscr{P}$) over the alphabet {0,1,*} by coding the nodes of X with strings over {0,1}, and then listing the codes for the members of X, followed by the triples in R and members of S and T, using * appropriately as a separator. We shall assume that the coding is efficient in the sense that if there are N nodes, then no node is assigned a string of length exceeding $\log_2 N+1$. Thus the length of the code E($\mathscr{P}$) is $O(N^3 \log N)$.

Let SP be the set of all strings over {0,1,*} which code solvable path systems. Cook in [15] has shown that SP is log-tape complete for DTIME(poly). In [15,20] Cook also defined the class of tree solvable path systems.

Definition. $\mathscr{P}$=(X,R,S,T) is tree solvable if there is a binary rooted tree whose nodes are in X, whose leaves are in T, whose root is in S, and if the node x has son nodes y and z, then R(x,y,z) holds or R(x,z,y) holds.

Let TSPS be the set of all strings which code tree solvable path systems.

Cook shows (implicitly) that every context-free language is log-tape reducible to TSPS. That is, for each context-free grammar G in Chomsky normal form and string of terminals w one can associate the path system $\mathscr{P}=\mathscr{P}$(w,G) such that $\mathscr{P}$ is (tree) solvable iff w is generated by G. The description of $\mathcal{P}(w,G)$ is included here for completeness:

Let $G=(N,\Sigma,P,\sigma)$ be a context-free grammar in Chomsky normal form. For a nonempty string $w \in \Sigma^*$ we construct the path system $\mathcal{P}(w,G)=(X,R,S,T)$, where:

(1) X is the set of triples (A,i,j), where A is a nonterminal in N and i and j are integers satisfying $1 \le i \le j \le |w|$

(2) R(x,y,z) holds iff x,y,z have the form (A,i,k), (B,i,j), (C,j+1,k), respectively, where $A \to BC$ is a production in P.

(3) $S=\{(\sigma,1,|w|)\}$.

(4) T is the set of all nodes of the form (A,i,i), where $A \to a_i$ is a production in P and $w= a_1 a_2 \ldots a_n$ ($a_i \in \Sigma$, for all $1 \le i \le n$).

It is straightforward to verify that $\mathcal{P}(w,G)$ is tree solvable iff w is generated by G. In fact, the node (A,i,j) is admissible iff the nonterminal A generates $a_i a_{i+1} \ldots a_j$. The fact that $\mathcal{P}(w,G)$ is tree solvable when w is generated by G can be seen by observing that the derivation tree of w in G with final branches deleted is isomorphic to a binary rooted tree which demonstrates the solvability of $\mathcal{P}(w,G)$.

We are not able to show that TSPS is in LOG(CFL). In [20] Cook claims that TSPS is in DSPACE($(\log n)^2$). In the following the concept of a p(n)-tree solvable path system is introduced, for any polynomial p(n), and it is shown that the family of p(n)-tree solvable path systems is log-tape complete for LOG(CFL), for all p(n) such that $p(n) \ge 1$ for all $n \ge 1$.

<u>Definition</u>. Let $\mathcal{P}=(X,R,S,T)$ be a path system. A rooted directed acyclic graph $G=(V,E,r)$ is a <u>solution graph</u> for $\mathcal{P}$ if

(a) V is a subset of X.

(b) If (x,y) is in E, then there is a unique vertex z in V such that $(x,z) \in E$ and either R(x,y,z) holds or R(x,z,y) holds.

(c) r is in S (r is a node with no incoming edges).

(d) Every node x is either in T or there are two edges leading out from X.

The <u>binary solution tree</u> corresponding to a solution graph $G=(V,E,r)$ is the graph $G_T=(V',E',r^{(0)})$, where V' and E' are defined inductively as follows:

(1) let $V^{(0)}=\{r^{(0)}\}$ and $E^{(0)}=\emptyset$; $r^{(0)}$ will be called a copy of r.

(2) for each $i \ge 1$ until $V^{(i)}=\emptyset$ do the following, where $V^{(i)}$ is assumed to consist of the nodes $\{x_1^{(i)}, x_2^{(i)}, \ldots, x_k^{(i)}\}$; for each

$1 \le i \le k$, if $x_\ell^{(i)}$ is a copy of x and there are nodes y,z in V such that $(x,y) \in E$ and $(x,z) \in E$, then (a) let $y_\ell^{(i+1)}$ and $z_\ell^{(i+1)}$ be nodes in $V^{(i+1)}$, (b) let $(x_\ell^{(i)}, y_\ell^{(i+1)})$ and $(x_\ell^{(i)}, z_\ell^{(i+1)})$ be nodes in $E^{(i+1)}$. $y_\ell^{(i+1)}$ and $z_\ell^{(i+1)}$ are called copies of y and z, respectively.

When $V^{(k)} = \emptyset$, then define $V' = \bigcup_{0 \le i \le k} V^{(i)}$, and $E' = \bigcup_{0 \le i \le k} E(i)$.

Example. Consider the graph G described in the following:

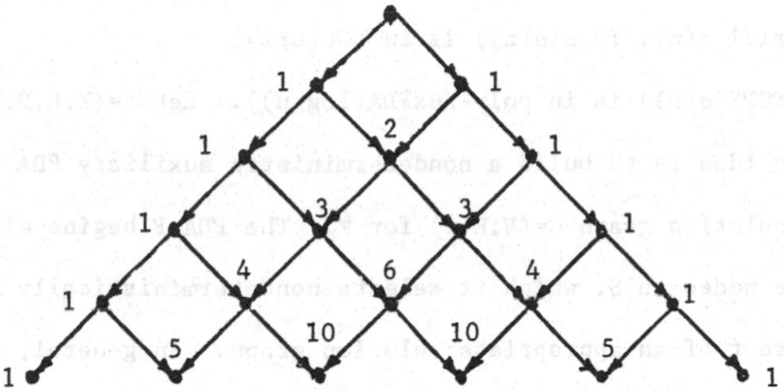

Figure 1.

The binary solution tree G_T corresponding to G(G is here considered as a solution graph for some path system $\mathcal{P}$) has 63 nodes, although G itself has 21 nodes. (The labels on the nodes of G describe how many copies of that node appear in G_T.)

For each m≥1, we shall refer to the graph G_m, which consists of a pyramid of M rows, with the bottom row having m nodes, the next row having m-1 nodes, and so on until the top row has only a single node. The edges of G_m are defined so that the i-th element of the j-th row has the i-th and (i+1)-st element of the (j+1)-st row as sons. The graph G_6 is shown in Figure 1. (These graphs were used in [15] to show that recognition of SP requires more than $(\log n)^k$ space, for any k, using the natural extension of the context-free language recognition algorithm described in [12].) Since the (i+1)-st node in the (j+1)-st row of G_m has C(j,i) copies in the corresponding binary tree (where C(j,i) is the coefficient of the i-th term of $(x+1)^j$), it follows that there are path systems that are not p(n)-tree solvable, for any fixed polynomial p(n), where p(n)-tree solvable is defined as follows:

<u>Definition</u>. Let p(n) be a polynomial. $\mathcal{P}$=(X,R,S,T) is a <u>p(n)-tree solvable path system</u> if there exists a solution graph G=(V,E,r) such that the corresponding binary solution tree has at most p(N) nodes, where N is the number of nodes in $\mathcal{P}$. Let TSPS (p(n)) denote the set of codings of p(n)-tree solvable path system.

We observe that any tree solvable path system is a 1-tree solvable path system, since for a tree solvable path system we may choose a solution graph G whose corresponding binary solution tree is isomorphic to G. It follows that CFL $\leq_{\log}$ TSPS(1), since for each context-free grammar G and string of terminals w we have shown how to construct a tree solvable path system $\mathscr{P}$(w,G) without using more than log(|w|) worktape space and $\mathscr{P}$(w,G) is tree solvable ⇔ $\mathscr{P}$(w,G) is 1-tree solvable ⇔ w is generated by G.

In order to complete the proof that TSPS(p(n)) is log-tape complete for LOG (CFL), for any p(n)≥1, it is sufficient to show that TSPS(p(n)) is in LOG(CFL).

Lemma. For any polynomial q(n), TSPS(q(n)) is in LOG(CFL).

Proof. (We show that TSPS(q(n)) is in poly-AuxPDA(log n)). Let $\mathscr{P}$=(X,R,S,T) be a path system. The basic idea is to build a nondeterministic auxiliary PDA P which attempts to locate a solution graph G=(V,E,r) for $\mathscr{P}$. The PDA P begins with a "visit" to one of the source nodes in S, which it selects nondeterministically and which is guessed to be the root of an appropriate solution graph. In general, if P is visiting a node x, then P determines whether x is a terminal node in T or not and (1) if x is a terminal node, then P visits next the topmost node stored in its pushdown store(if there are no nodes stored in the pushdown store, P halts and accepts) or (2) if x is not a terminal node, then P selects nondeterministically two nodes y,z in X such that R(x,y,z) holds and P next visits node y and puts node z on top of the pushdown store.

It follows that a solution graph G=(V,E,r) exists such that the number of times P visits any of the nodes in G is less than or equal to q(N), where N is the number of nodes in X, iff $\mathscr{P}$ is q(n)-tree solvable. That is, the number of distinct visits to a node x in G is the same as the number of copies of the node x in the corresponding binary solution tree G_T. Thus, if the total number of visits is bounded by q(N) for some solution graph selected, then $\mathscr{P}$ is q(n)-tree solvable.

It follows that P can be constructed to recognize whether or not $\mathscr{P}$ is q(n)-tree solvable by performing the steps indicated above and simply counting the number of visits. If the number of visits ever exceeds the value q(N), then P stops and rejects. Since the length of E($\mathscr{P}$) is $O(N^3 \log N)$, the counter to represent a number in binary no greater than q(N) can be represented in log n space, where n is the length of the input. It is also clear that, since P stops after q(N) steps, P is polynomial time bounded. ∎

In [16] Jones has shown that the problem of deciding whether or not a well-formed formula in the propositional calculus is such that it can be shown to be unsatisfiable by unit resolution is log-tape complete for DTIME(poly). In [19] it was shown that the problem of deciding whether or not a well-formed formula in conjunctive normal form with at most two literals per clause is such that it can be shown to be unsatisfiable by unit resolution is log-tape complete for NSPACE(log n). We define the notion of unit p(n)-tree resolution, for any polynomial p(n), and show that the problem of deciding whether or not a well-formed formula is such that it can be shown unsatisfiable by unit p(n)-tree resolution is log-tape complete for LOG(CFL).

Definition. Let w be a well-formed formula which is the conjunction of clauses in $\{C_1, C_2, \ldots, C_k\}$. Let X be the set of all clauses that can be obtained from C_1, ..., C_k by deleting some or all of the literals in each clause C_i. Let R be the three place relation on X defined by: R(x,y,z) holds iff one of y and z is a unit clause and the resolvent of y and z is x. Let S consist of the empty clause and T be the set of clauses $\{C_1, C_2, \ldots, C_k\}$. For a fixed polynomial p(n), we say that w is refutable by unit p(n)-tree resolution iff the path system $\mathcal{P}(w)=(X,R,S,T)$ is p(n)-tree solvable.

That is, w is refutable by unit p(n)-tree resolution iff the solution graph G for the corresponding path system is such that there is at most a p(n) expansion in the number of nodes when transformed to a binary tree G_T. It is evident that the set of well-formed formulas that are refutable by unit p(n)-tree resolution, for any polynomial p(n), is in LOG(CFL). This follows from the definition, since the transformation from the well-formed formula w into the corresponding path system $\mathcal{P}(w)$ can be accomplished by a log-tape bounded Turing machine and the set of p(n)-tree solvable path systems is in LOG(CFL).

It is also evident that any context-free language is log-tape reducible to a well-formed formula which is refutable by unit p(n)-tree resolution, for any polynomial $p(n) \geq 1$. That is, if $G=(N, \Sigma, P, S)$ is a context-free grammar in Chomsky normal form and $x=a_1 a_2 \ldots a_n$ a string of n terminal symbols over Σ, then we may construct a well-formed formula in conjunctive normal form w(G,x) which consists of the set of clauses $C=\{(A_{ii}) | A \to a_i \text{ is a production in } G\} \cup \{(\sim B_{ij} \vee \sim C_{j+1,k} \vee A_{ik}) | \forall i,j,k\ (1 \leq i \leq j < k \leq n) \text{ and } A \to BC \text{ is a production in } G\} \cup \{\sim S_{1n})\}$. (There are individual variables of the form A_{ij}, where A is a nonterminal in G, for all i,j such that $1 \leq i \leq j \leq n$ in w(G,x).) w(G,x) is inconsistent iff G generates the string x. In fact, the refutation of w(G,x) will yield a tree which is isomorphic to a derivation tree of x with the final branches deleted. Therefore, w(G,x) is refutable by unit p(n)-tree resolution, for any polynomial $p(n) \geq 1$. It is straightforward to verify that the transformation from x to w(G,x) can be accomplished by a Turing machine using at most log(|x|) worktape cells.

Therefore, the set of well-formed formulas that are refutable by unit p(n)-tree resolution, for any fixed polynomial p(n), is log-tape complete for LOG(CFL). It is observed that well-formed formulas exist that are refutable by unit resolution, but not refutable by unit p(n)-tree resolution, for any polynomial p(n).

Let $LOG^{TM}(CFL)$ and $LOG^{TM}(DCFL)$ denote the family of languages recognized by deterministic log-tape bounded oracle machines (see, for example, Ladner and Lynch [22] for a definition of log-tape bounded oracle machine) with oracle sets chosen from CFL and DCFL, respectively. We list the following results without proof (because of restrictions on space):

(1) LOG(CFL)= $LOG^{TM}(CFL)$ iff LOG(CFL) is closed under complementation,

(2) LOG(DCFL) = $LOG^{TM}(DCFL)$

(3) LOG(DCFL) is closed under union, intersection, complementation, concatenation, and inverse homomorphism.

(4) LOG(CFL) is closed under substitution into context-free languages (hence under union, concatenation, and Kleene star), inverse homomorphism, and intersection.

References

1. Sudborough, I.H., On the tape complexity of deterministic context-free languages, to appear in Journal of Assoc. for Comput. Mach.

2. Cook, S.A., Characterizations of pushdown machines in terms of time-bounded computers, Journal of Assoc. for Comput. Mach. 18 (1971), 4-18.

3. Jones, N.D., Space bounded reducibility among combinatorial problems, Journal of Comput. and System Sci. 11 (1975), 62-85.

4. Meyer, A.R. and L.J. Stockmeyer, Word problems requiring exponential time, in Proceedings of Fifth Annual Assoc. for Comput. Mach. Symposium on Theory of Computing (1973), 1-9. Association for Computing Machinery, 1133 Avenue of the Americas, New York.

5. Greibach, S.A., The hardest context-free language, SIAM Journal on Computing 2 (1973), 304-310.

6. Sudborough, I.H., Separating tape bounded auxiliary pushdown automata classes, to appear in Proceedings of Ninth Annual Assoc. for Comput. Mach. Symposium on Theory of Computing (1977). (See reference 4 for address of ACM.)

7. Aho, A.V. and J.D. Ullman, The Theory of Parsing, Translation, and Compiling, Vols. I and II, Prentice-Hall Publishing Co., Englewood Cliffs, New Jersey, U.S.A., 1972 and 1973.

8. Sudborough, I.H., The complexity of the membership problem for some extensions of context-free languages, to appear in International Journal of Computer Math.

9. Sudborough, I.H., The time and tape complexity of developmental languages, to appear in Proceedings of Fourth International Conference on Automata, Languages, and Programming, to be held in Turku, Finland (July 18-22, 1977). (The proceedings will be published in the Lecture Notes in Computer Science Series, Springer-Verlag Publishing Co., New York.)

10. Kasai, T., An hierarchy between context-free and context-sensitive languages, Journal of Computer and System Sci. 4 (1970), 492-508.

11. Cremers, A.B. and O. Mayer, On vector languages, Journal of Computer and System Sci. 8 (1974), 142-157.

12. Lewis, P.M., R.E. Stearns, and J. Hartmanis, Memory bounds for the recognition of context-free and context-sensitive languages, in Proceedings of the Sixth Annual IEEE Symposium on Switching Circuit Theory and Logical Design (1965), 199-212. (copies available from IEEE Computer Society, 5855 Naples Plaza, Suite 301, Long Beach, California , U.S.A.)

13. Cook, S.A., The complexity of theorem proving procedures, in Proceedings of the third Annual Assoc. for Comput. Mach. Symposium on Theory of Computing (1971), 151-158. (See reference 4 for address of ACM.)

14. Karp, R.M., Reducibilities among combinatorial problems, in Complexity of Computer Computation (R. Miller and J. Thatcher, Eds.), Plenum Publishing Company, New York, 1972.

15. Jones, N.D. and W.T. Laaser, Problems complete for deterministic polynomial time, to appear in Theoretical Computer Science. (A preliminary version appears in the Proceedings of the Sixth Annual ACM Symposium on Theory of Computing; see reference 4 for address information)

16. Cook, S.A., On observation on time-storage trade-off, Journal of Computer and System Sci. 9 (1974), 308-316.

17. Sudborough, I.H., On tape bounded complexity classes and multihead finite automata, Journal of Computer and System Sci. 10 (1975), 62-76.

18. Sudborough, I.H., On tape bounded complexity classes and linear context-free languages, Journal of Assoc. for Comput. Mach. 22 (1975), 500-501.

19. Jones, N.D., Y.E. Lien and W.T. Laaser, New problems complete for nondeterministic log space, Mathematical Systems Theory 10 (1976), 1-17.

20. Cook, S.A., Path systems and language recognition, in Proceedings of Second Annual ACM Symposium on Theory of Computing (1970), 70-72. (See reference 4 for address information.)

21. Savitch, W.J., Relationships between nondeterministic and deterministic tape complexities, Journal of Computer and System Sci. 4 (1970), 177-192.

22. Ladner, R.E. and N.A. Lynch, Relativization of questions about log space computability, Mathematical Systems Theory 10 (1976), 19-32.

A FAST NON-COMMUTATIVE ALGORITHM FOR MATRIX MULTIPLICATION

Ondrej Sýkora

Institute of Technical Cybernetics, Slovak Academy of Sciences

Dúbravská cesta 3, 809 31 Bratislava, Czechoslovakia

ABSTRACT

In the paper a non-commutative algorithm for the multiplication of two square matrices of order n is presented. The algorithm requires $n^3 - (n-1)^2$ multiplications and $n^3 - n^2 + 11(n-1)^2$ additions. The recursive application of the algorithm for matrices of order n^k leads to $O\left(n^{k \log_n [n^3 - (n-1)^2]}\right)$ operations to be executed. It is shown that some well-known algorithms are special cases of our algorithm. Finally, an improvement of the algorithm is given for matrices of order 5.

1. INTRODUCTION

In 1969 Strassen [1] described an algorithm for the multiplication of two 2 x 2 matrices whereby the algorithm requires only 7 multiplications and 18 additions. This algorithm does not require commutativity of multiplication and may hence be applied also recursively. Having a product of two square matrices of the order $n = 2^k$, the recursive application of the Strassen algorithm allows to calculate this product by using $n^{\log_2 7}$ multiplications / the standard algorithm for the product of two n x n matrices requires n^3 multiplications /. Hopcroft and Kerr showed in [2] that seven multiplications are required by any non-commutative algorithm and Winograd [3] proved, that seven multiplications are required by any algorithm for the product of two 2 x 2 matrices. The non-commutative algorithm invented by Winograd [4] uses 7 multiplications and only 15 additions. Probert [5] proved that in the case of 7 multiplications the minimal number of additions is 15. These results have caused, that algorithms for fast multiplication of $n \times n$ matrices, $n \geq 3$, are being sought. To bring about an improvement for n=3 it is necessary to find an algorithm requiring only 21 multiplications, because it holds that $\log_3 21 < \log_2 7 < \log_3 22$.

In [6] Gastinel presented a non-commutative algorithm using 25 multiplications. Hopcroft and Kerr [7] described the construction of a non-commutative algorithm using 24 multiplications and Hopcroft with Musinski [8] established explicitly some of such algorithms. The hitherto best result for such a case was established by Laderman [9] whose algorithm requires 23 multiplications only. We are not aware of the way Strassen and Winograd had derived their algorithms. In seeking his algorithm, Laderman was compelled to search for an integer solution of 729 nonlinear equations of 621 unknowns.

In the present paper we are suggesting a general non-commutative algorithm for the product of two square matrices of the order $n \geq 2$ that requires $n^3 - (n-1)^2$ multiplications and $n^3 - n^2 + 11(n-1)^2$ additions. We shall also show that some of the known algorithms are special cases of our algorithm, for example Winograd's / for n = 2 / and Laderman's / for n = 3/ algorithms.

2. THE ALGORITHM

Before presenting the main result let us give the following definition :

Definition : Let $N = \{1, 2, \ldots, n\}$ and let i, j, s be arbitrary but fixed elements from N. A modified latin square L_{nijs} of the order n is defined to be a matrix of the order n such that

a/ in the i-th row and j-th column there is the number s only

b/ every other row and column contains all elements from N.

Let us further denote $S = N - \{i\}$, $T = N - \{j\}$.

Let D be an nxn matrix. Then $D[i_1, \ldots i_u; j_1, \ldots j_v]$ will denote the $u \times v$ submatrix of the matrix D which contains the i_1-th, ...,i_u-th rows and the j_1-th, ..., j_v-th columns of the matrix D.

Agreement : A, B, C, will denote $n \times n$ matrices related by the equality $C = A \times B$.

Theorem : There exists a non- commutative algorithm for calculating C that requires $n^3 - (n-1)^2$ multiplications and $n^3 - n^2 + 11(n-1)^2$ additions.

Proof : Choose arbitrary but fixed indices i, j, $s \in N$. We shall distinguish three types of elements of C.

The first type : c_{ij} only.

The second type : c_{qr}, $q \in S$, $r \in T$ / i.e. all elements of matrix C with the exception of the i-th row and the j-th column /.

The third type : c_{ir} and c_{qj}, $q \in S$, $r \in T$ / i.e. the i-th row and j-th column of matrix C with the exception of element c_{ij} /.

We shall now desribe an algorithm for the computation of C. The algorithm consists of three parts. In each of them the elements of the corresponding type will be computed.

Part I : For $k \in N$ denote $P_k = a_{ik} b_{kj}$. The element c_{ij} will be calculated in the standard way, i.e. $c_{ij} = \sum_{k=1}^{n} P_k$.

Part II : Let us choose an arbitrary but fixed modified latin square L_{nijs}. To each pair $\langle q, r \rangle$, $q \in S$, $r \in T$, let us assign the integer $m_{qr} = L_{nijs}[q; r]$. The elements c_{qr}, $q \in S$, $r \in T$ are now calculated as follows :

Denote
$$M_{qr1} = \left(-a_{i,m_{qr}} + a_{q,m_{qr}} + a_{qs}\right)\left(b_{m_{qr},j} + b_{sr} - b_{m_{qr},r}\right)$$

$$M_{qr2} = \left(a_{q,m_{qr}} + a_{qs}\right)\left(b_{m_{qr},r} - b_{m_{qr},j}\right)$$

$$M_{qr3} = \left(a_{i,m_{qr}} - a_{q,m_{qr}}\right)\left(b_{sr} - b_{m_{qr},r}\right)$$

$$H_{qrp} = a_{qp} b_{pr}, \text{ where } p \in N, p \neq m_{qr}, p \neq s.$$

Then $$c_{qr} = P_{m_{qr}} + \sum_{k=1}^{3} M_{qrk} + \sum_{\substack{p=1 \\ p \neq s, m_{qr}}}^{n} H_{qrp}.$$

Part III : This part is divided into two segments. In the first one, we shall calculate elements c_{ir}, $r \in T$. In the second one elements c_{qj}, $q \in S$ will be calculated.

a/ Let $$R_r = \left[\sum_{k=1}^{n} a_{ik} - \sum_{\substack{q=1 \\ q \neq i}}^{n} \left(a_{qs} + a_{q,m_{qr}} \right) \right] b_{sr}, \ r \in T$$

then $$c_{ir} = R_r + \sum_{\substack{q=1 \\ q \neq i}}^{n} \left(M_{qr1} + M_{qr2} + P_{mqr} \right).$$

b/ Let $$Q_q = a_{qs} \left[b_{sj} - \sum_{\substack{k=1 \\ k \neq s}}^{n} b_{kj} + \sum_{\substack{r=1 \\ r \neq j}}^{n} \left(b_{m_{qr}, r} - b_{sr} \right) \right], \ q \in S$$

then $$c_{qj} = Q_q + \sum_{\substack{r=1 \\ r \neq i}}^{n} \left(M_{qr1} + M_{qr3} + P_{mqr} \right).$$

It will be shown that all the elements of C could be calculated in the described manner. In part I the element c_{ij} is obtained in the standard way.
In part II for $q \in S$, $r \in T$, it holds :

$$c_{qr} = a_{i,m_{qr}} b_{m_{qr},j} + \left(-a_{i,m_{qr}} + a_{q,m_{qr}} + a_{qs} \right)\left(b_{m_{qr},j} + b_{s,r} - b_{m_{qr},r} \right) +$$

$$+\left(a_{q,m_{qr}}+a_{qs}\right)\left(b_{m_{qr},r}-b_{m_{qr},j}\right)+\left(a_{i,m_{qr}}-a_{q,m_{qr}}\right)\left(b_{sr}-b_{m_{qr},r}\right)+\sum_{\substack{p=1\\ p\neq s,m_{qr}}}^{n} a_{qp}\, b_{pr}$$

whence, by arrangement, we get $c_{qr}=\sum_{p=1}^{n} a_{qp} b_{pr}$, i.e. the scalar product required.

In part III a/ for elements of the i-th row c_{ir}, $r\in T$, it holds :

$$c_{ir}=\sum_{k=1}^{n} a_{ik} b_{sr}-\sum_{\substack{q=1\\ q\neq i}}^{n}\left(a_{qs}+a_{q,m_{qr}}\right)b_{sr}+\sum_{\substack{q=1\\ q\neq i}}^{n} a_{i,m_{qr}}\, b_{m_{qr},r}-\sum_{\substack{q=1\\ q\neq i}}^{n} a_{i,m_{qr}}\, b_{sr}+$$

$+\sum_{\substack{q=1\\ q\neq i}}^{n}\left(a_{q,m_{qr}}+a_{qs}\right)b_{sr}$. From this relation, after suitable re-indexing and

arrangement, we get the required scalar product : $c_{ir}=\sum_{k=1}^{n} a_{ik} b_{kr}$.

In part III b/ for elements of the j-th column c_{qj}, $q\in S$, it holds :

$$c_{qj}=a_{qs} b_{sj}-\sum_{\substack{k=1\\ k\neq s}}^{n} a_{qs} b_{kj}+\sum_{\substack{r=1\\ r\neq j}}^{n} a_{qs}\left(b_{m_{qr},r}-b_{sr}\right)+\sum_{\substack{r=1\\ r\neq j}}^{n} a_{q,m_{qr}}\, b_{m_{qr},j}+$$

$$+\sum_{\substack{r=1\\ r\neq j}}^{n} a_{qs}\, b_{m_{qr},j}+\sum_{\substack{r=1\\ r\neq j}}^{n} a_{qs}\left(b_{sr}-b_{m_{qr},r}\right).$$

After suitable re-indexing and arrangement , we get the required relation from the

last expression $c_{qj}=\sum_{r=1}^{n} a_{qr} b_{rj}$.

Thus the non-commutative algorithm for calculating matrix C is composed of the following steps / indices i,j,s,m_{qr} are of the same meaning as previously / :

I. The calculation of c_{ij} : $P_k = a_{ik}\, b_{kj}$, $k \in N$, $c_{ij} = \sum_{k=1}^{n} P_k$.

II. The calculation of c_{qr}, $q \in S$, $r \in T$, :

$$K_{qr1} = a_{q,m_{qr}} + a_{qs}\,; \qquad K_{qr2} = b_{m_{qr},r} - b_{m_{qr},j}\,;$$

$$M_{qr2} = K_{qr1} K_{qr2}\,; \qquad K_{qr3} = K_{qr1} - a_{i,m_{qr}}\,;$$

$$K_{qr4} = b_{sr} - K_{qr2}\,; \qquad M_{qr1} = K_{qr3} K_{qr4}\,;$$

$$M_{qr3} = \left(a_{i,m_{qr}} - a_{q,m_{qr}}\right)\left(b_{sr} - b_{m_{qr},r}\right); \qquad K_{qr5} = M_{qr1} + P_{m_{qr}}\,;$$

$$K_{qr6} = K_{qr5} + M_{qr2}\,; \qquad c_{qr} = K_{qr5} + M_{qr3} + \sum_{\substack{p=1 \\ p \neq s, m_{qr}}}^{n} a_{qp}\, b_{pr}\,.$$

III. a/ The calculation of c_{ir}, $r \in T$, : $R_r = \left(a_{is} - \sum_{\substack{q=1 \\ q \neq i}}^{n} K_{qr3}\right) b_{sr}$;

$$c_{ir} = R_r + \sum_{\substack{q=1 \\ q \neq i}}^{n} K_{qr6}\,.$$

III. b/ The calculation of c_{qj}, $q \in S$, : $Q_q = a_{qs}\left(b_{sj} - \sum_{\substack{r=1 \\ r \neq j}}^{n} K_{qr4}\right)$;

$$c_{qj} = Q_q + \sum_{\substack{r=1 \\ r \neq j}}^{n} \left(K_{qr5} - M_{qr3}\right).$$

The number of arithmetical operations :

parts :	multiplications :	additions :
I.	n	$n-1$
II.	$(n+1)(n-1)^2$	$(n+7)(n-1)^2$
III. a	$n-1$	$2(n-1)^2$
III. b	$n-1$	$3(n-1)^2$

The total number of arithmetical operations of this algorithm is thus $n^3-(n-1)^2$ multiplications and $n^3-n^2+11(n-1)^2$ additions.

The described algorithm is non-commutative i.e. it is recursively applicable in the sense of [1]. If we have a product of square matrices of the order n^k and if the algorithm for the product of n order square matrices is applied recursively to this product, the required number of multiplications is $n^{k\log_n\left[n^3-(n-1)^2\right]}$

and hence the total number of operations is of the order $O\left(n^{k\log_n\left[n^3-(n-1)^2\right]}\right)$

Two well-known algorithms are special cases of the algorithm described here.

For $n=2$, $i=j=1$, $s=2$ and $L_{2,1,1,2}=\begin{bmatrix}2&2\\2&1\end{bmatrix}$ our algorithm coincides with Winograd's.

For $n=3$, $i=j=1$, $s=2$ and $L_{3,1,1,2}=\begin{bmatrix}2&2&2\\2&1&3\\2&3&1\end{bmatrix}$ our algorithm coincides with Laderman's.

It is remarkable that Strassen's algorithm is not a special case of the algorithm described here.

3. The improvement of the algorithm for 5x5 matrices.

In part II, for $n \geq 3$, the expression $\sum_{\substack{p=1 \\ p \neq s, m_{qr}}}^{n} a_{qp} b_{pr}$, $q \in S$, $r \in T$, is to be calculated.

Let us concentrate upon the case n=5. Particularly, for $i = j = 1$, $s = 2$ and

$$L_{5,1,1,2} = \begin{bmatrix} 2 & 2 & 2 & 2 & 2 \\ 2 & 1 & 3 & 4 & 5 \\ 2 & 3 & 1 & 5 & 4 \\ 2 & 4 & 5 & 1 & 3 \\ 2 & 5 & 4 & 3 & 1 \end{bmatrix}$$

the expressions

$$a_{23}b_{32} + a_{24}b_{42} + a_{25}b_{52} \quad \text{for } c_{22}$$
$$a_{21}b_{13} + a_{24}b_{43} + a_{25}b_{53} \quad \text{for } c_{23}$$
$$a_{31}b_{12} + a_{34}b_{42} + a_{35}b_{52} \quad \text{for } c_{32}$$
$$a_{23}b_{33} + a_{34}b_{43} + a_{35}b_{53} \quad \text{for } c_{33}$$

etc.

are to be calculated. It means that, for the submatrix C [2,3; 2,3] , the elements of the matrix

$$\begin{bmatrix} a_{24}, & a_{25} \\ a_{34}, & a_{35} \end{bmatrix} \begin{bmatrix} b_{42}, & b_{43} \\ b_{52}, & b_{53} \end{bmatrix} + \begin{bmatrix} a_{23}b_{32}, & a_{21}b_{13} \\ a_{31}b_{12}, & a_{23}b_{33} \end{bmatrix}$$

are to be calculated. Using our algorithm for this calculation we can decrease the number of multiplications from 12 to 11. The situation is similar for submatrices C [2,3; 4,5], C [4,5; 2,3] and C [4,5; 4,5] . In contrast to the described algorithm, which for n = 5 requires 109 multiplications, we get an algorithm that requires 105 multiplications. Note, a similar improvement could be made for arbitrary i, j, s and $L_{5,i,j,s}$.

Acknowledgment

My thanks are due to J. Mikloško, for his critical comments.

References

1. Strassen,V., Gaussian elimination is not optimal, Numer.Math. 13, 354-356 / 1969/.
2. Hopcroft, J.E. and Kerr, L.R., Some techniques for proving certain simple programs optimal, Proc. Tenth Ann. Symposium on Switching and Automata Theory, pp. 36 - 45, / 1969 /.
3. Winograd, S., On multiplication of 2x2 matrices, Linear Algebra and its Applications 4, 381-388 / 1971 /.
4. Fischer, P.C., Further schemes for combining matrix algorithms, in : Automata, Languages and Programming - 2nd Colloquium / Loeckx, J., Hrsg. / University of Saarbrücken. Lecture Notes in Computer Science / 1974 /.
5. Probert, R.L., On the complexity of matrix multiplication, University of Waterloo, Ontario, Tech. Report CS-73-27 / 1973 /.
6. Gastinel, N., Sur le calcul des produits de matrices, Numer. Math. 17, 222-229 / 1971 /.
7. Hopcroft, J. and Kerr, L., On minimizing the number of multiplications necessary for matrix multiplication, SIAM J. Appl. Math. 20, 30-36 / 1971 /.
8. Hopcroft, J. and Musinski, J., Duality aplied to the complexity of matrix multiplication and other bilinear forms, SIAM J. Comput. 2, 159-173 / 1973 /.
9. Laderman, J. D., A noncommutative algorithm for multiplying 3x3 matrices using 23 multiplications, Bull. of the Amer. Math. Soc. Vol. 82, Num. 1, Jan. / 1976 /.

FIXED-POINTS AND ALGEBRAS WITH INFINITELY LONG EXPRESSIONS, I

J.Tiuryn

Institute of Mathematics

Warsaw University

00-901 Warsaw, PKiN IX p.

Poland

1. Introduction.

It has been shown by many authors that the approach to computer science (especially to the semantics of programming languages) via fixed-points of continuous mappings is very useful and of great expressive power. The main idea of this approach is that one may define complex objects as least fixed-point solutions of certain equations, i.e. complex (infinite) objects can be completely defined by finite descriptions. On the other hand, the fixed-point approach enables us to treat in a unified way regular languages, context-free languages, program schemes, recursive program schemes, and other notions which may be defined in the aforementioned manner.

Thus it would be useful to have a general theory in which it is possible to express all the above notions, One of the possible ways to achieve this is to define syntax in an algebraic manner (as an algebra SYN of formal expressions), and then choose a sufficiently large class J of algebras (which will serve a class of interpretations) containing the algebra SYN and having the property that for every algebra A in J there exists exactly one homomorphism SEM(A) : SYN $\longrightarrow$ A (this means that SYN is an initial algebra in J). Then SEM(A) may be viewed as an interpretation while the class $\{$SEM(A) : A $\in$ J$\}$ may be viewed as semantics. This is the idea of the initial algebra semantics presented in Goguen and Thatcher [3] . Goguen and Thatcher proposed in their paper a model of an algebra SYN — this was the algebra R_Σ of regular Σ - trees (for a given signature Σ). The elements of R_Σ can be treated as uninterpreted program schemes (more exactly, as unfoldments of program schemes). Now the question naturally arises: in which (sufficiently large) class of algebras R_Σ is an initial algebra — this is one of the problems listed in Goguen and Thatcher [3].

The aim of this paper is to present the solution of this problem. We have found a class $\underline{Reg}_\Sigma$ (for a given signature Σ) in which R_Σ is an initial algebra. The elements of $\underline{Reg}_\Sigma$ we have called regular algebras. The investigation of the properties of $\underline{Reg}_\Sigma$ may be of intrinsic interest ; in particular it leads to a very nice generalization of the notion of a polynomial in an algebra (for the notion of a polynomial see for example Grätzer [4]). Such "new" polynomials may be determined by infinitely long expressions ; the results which we obtained show that they play a role in $\underline{Reg}_\Sigma$ analogous to that of ordinary polynomials in universal algebras.

It should be remarked that another approach, using the language of category theory, to solve the abovementioned problem has been presented in ADJ [2].

All the results presented in this note are given without proofs. For a more detailed treatement of this subject the reader is referred to Tiuryn [7] and Tiuryn [8].

2. Preliminary definitions and notations.

By $\omega = \{0,1,\dots\}$ we denote the first infinite ordinal. A finite ordinal $n < \omega$ will be identified with the set $\{0,\dots,n-1\}$. If X and A are sets then the elements of the set A^X will be identified with functions having X as a domain and A as a codomain. If A is a set and $i < n < \omega$, then by $e_i^n : A^n \longrightarrow A$ we denote a projection on the i-th coordinate, i.e. $e_i^n(a) = a(i)$ for all $a \in A^n$.

If $f_i : A \longrightarrow B$ is a function for $i < n$, then $\langle f_0,\dots, f_{n-1}\rangle : A \longrightarrow B^n$ is a function defined as follows : $\langle f_0,\dots, f_{n-1}\rangle (a)(i) = f_i(a)$ for $a \in A$, $i < n$.

Suppose P is a poset (partially ordered set), for a subset $X \subset P$ denote by $\sup_P X$ the least upper bound of X in P (if it exists). If $\sup_P \phi$ exists in P, then it is the least element in P, and will be denoted by $\bot_P$. A poset P is said to be $\underline{\omega\text{-complete}}$ ($\underline{\Delta\text{- complete}}$) iff all denumerable chains (directed sets) in P have least upper bounds. Notice that any ω-complete poset has the least element, and thus any Δ-complete poset has the least element, as well. A mapping $f:P_0 \longrightarrow P_1$ between posets is called <u>ω-continuous</u> (<u>Δ-continuous</u>) iff f preserves the least upper bounds of all nonempty denumerable chains (all nonempty directed sets) that exist in P_0. If P_0 and P_1 are posets with least elements, then a function $f:P_0 \longrightarrow P_1$ is said to be <u>strict</u> whenever $f(\bot_{P_0}) = \bot_{P_1}$. If P is a poset and X in an arbitrary set, then P^X is a poset with ordering defined coordinate - wise.

3. ω-continuous algebras, the algebra of regular trees.

The aim of this section is to present the idea of an algebra of regular trees (the reader seeking a more comprehensive exposition of this subject may want to consult Goguen and Thatcher [3]).

We start with the notion of a partial Σ-tree, where $\Sigma = \langle \Sigma_n \rangle_{n<\omega}$ is a similarity type. The elements of Σ_n are called n-ary operation symbols. A <u>partial Σ-tree</u> is a partial mapping $t:\omega^* \longrightarrow \bigcup_{n<\omega} \Sigma_n$ (ω^* denotes the set of all finite words over the set ω) satisfying the following condition for all $w \in \omega^*$ and $i<\omega$

(3.1) $\quad wi \in \mathrm{Dom}(t) \Rightarrow (w \in \mathrm{Dom}(t) \;\&\; (\exists i < n < \omega) t(w) \in \Sigma_n)$

Informally: if we denote by $\bot$ an undefined value and put $t(w) = \bot$ iff $w \notin \mathrm{Dom}(t)$, then a partial Σ-tree may be viewed as a tree (possibly infinite) such that every node is labelled by some operation symbol from Σ or by $\bot$ and (by treating $\bot$ as a new nullary operation symbol) (3.1) can be reformulated: there are exactly n arrows leaving a node labelled by an n-ary operation symbol. Denote by CT_Σ the set of all partial Σ-trees. This set can be made into a Σ - algebra in the following way.

(3.2) If $\sigma \in \Sigma_0$, then $\sigma_{CT} = \{\langle \varepsilon, \sigma \rangle\}$, where ε denotes the empty word.

(3.3) If $\sigma \in \Sigma_n$, $0<n<\omega$, and $t_0, \dots, t_{n-1} \in CT_\Sigma$, then

$$\sigma_{CT}(t_0, \dots, t_{n-1}) = \{\langle \varepsilon, \sigma \rangle\} \cup \bigcup_{i<n} \{\langle iw, \sigma' \rangle : \langle w, \sigma' \rangle \in t_i\}$$

The set CT_Σ, as a set of partial mappings, is naturally ordered by inclusion, and the empty mapping is the least element in CT_Σ . We will denote this least element by $\perp$ when no confusion will result.

If X is a set disjoint from each $\Sigma_n (n<\omega)$, then one may define the extension $\Sigma(X)$ of Σ by constants from X ; $\Sigma(X)_0 = \Sigma_0 \cup X$, $\Sigma(X)_n = \Sigma_n$ for all $0 < n$. Denote by $CT_\Sigma(X)$ the Σ-algebra of all partial $\Sigma(X)$ - trees. For the rest of this paper: when we write $\Sigma(X)$ or $CT_\Sigma(X)$ it will be assumed always that X is disjoint from each Σ_n for all $n<\omega$.

Denote by ω-alg_Σ the category of all ω-continuous Σ-algebras, with strict ω-continuous Σ-homomorphisms.

The following result shows that CT_Σ plays a very important role in ω-alg_Σ

Theorem 3.1 (Goguen and Thatcher [3])

For an arbitrary similarity type Σ and an arbitrary set the following hold :

(i) $CT_\Sigma(X)$ is an ω-continuous Σ-algebra ;

(ii) $CT_\Sigma(X)$ is freely generated in ω-alg_Σ by the set X .

One may distinguish in $CT_\Sigma(X)$ two important classes of Σ - trees. Denote by $F_\Sigma(X)$ the set of all those $t \in CT_\Sigma(X)$ with Dom(t) finite, while denote by $TF_\Sigma(X)$ the set of all those $t \in F_\Sigma(X)$ satisfying the following condition : if $w \in Dom(t)$ and $t(w) \in \Sigma(X)_n$ (for some $n<\omega$), then $wi \in Dom(t)$ for all $i < n$. The elements of $F_\Sigma(X)$ (resp. of $TF_\Sigma(X)$) may be identified with $\Sigma(\perp)$ polynomial symbols (resp. with Σ -polynomial symbols) with variables in X. Here polynomial symbols are meant in the sence of Gratzer [4] , The following result is well known in universal algebra.

Theorem 3.2.

For an arbitrary similarity type Σ and an arbitrary set X the following hold :

(i) $TF_\Sigma(X)$ is a Σ-algebra freely generated in the category of Σ- algebras, and Σ -homomorphisms, by the set X;

(ii) $F_\Sigma(X)$ is a Σ - algebra with an ordered carrier having a least element ; and this algebra is freely generated by the set X in the category of Σ-algebras with an ordered carrier having a least element, and strict Σ -homomorphisms.

The above results enables us to define derived operations (polynomials) in appropriate algebras. For example, if $n<\omega$, $t \in F_\Sigma(n)$, and A is a Σ-algebra with an ordered carrier having least element, then the tree t defines in A a derived n-ary operation $t_A : A^n \to A$ in the following way: $t_A(a) = \bar{a}(t)$ where $a : n \to A$ is an arbitrary function and $\bar{a} : F_\Sigma(n) \to A$ is the unique extension of a to a strict Σ-homomorphism. If A is a Σ- algebra, then a mapping $f : A^n \to A$ is called an n-ary Σ - algebraic mapping in A provided there exist $k < \omega$, $t \in TF_\Sigma(n+k)$, and $a \in A^k$ such that $f(x) = t_A(x,a)$ for all $x \in A^n$.

By Tarski fixed - point theorem (c.f. Tarski [6]) one may solve (obtaining least solutions) in an arbitrary ω-continuous Σ-algebra systems of fixed - point equations of the following form:

$$(3.4) \qquad \{ x_i = f_i\,(x_0, \ldots, x_{n-1}) : i < n \},$$

where $f_0, \ldots, f_{n-1}$ are n-ary Σ-algebraic mappings and $n < \omega$.

For an arbitrary set X, let $R_\Sigma(X)$ be the set consisting of all components of least solutions in $CT_\Sigma(X)$ of systems (3.4), where $f_0, \ldots, f_{n-1}$ are $\Sigma(\perp)$- polynomials in $CT_\Sigma(X)$. The elements of $R_\Sigma(X)$ are called <u>regular $\Sigma(X)$ - trees.</u>

It is known (c.f. Goguen and Thatcher [3]) that $R_\Sigma(X)$ is a Σ - subalgebra of $CT_\Sigma(X)$, and $R_\Sigma(X)$ as a poset is not ω-complete. On the other hand, elements of $R_\Sigma(X)$ can be viewed as unfoldements of flow - diagrams (c.f. ADJ [1], Scott [5], Wand [9]) with variables in X. Now we may formulate the problem stated in Goguen and Thatcher [3] : find a class of algebras in which the algebra R_Σ ($= R_\Sigma(\emptyset)$) is an initial object. The next section proposes such a class.

4. Regular algebras, regular polynomials.

In this section all algebras have ordered carrier with least element. We start with a new notion of a strict algebra. The class of strict algebras properly contains all algebras with monotonic operations. Our results show that this class is a natural one for treating solutions of fixed - point algebraic equations. On the other hand, when monotonicity of operations is assumed, no essentially stronger results are obtained.

An algebra A is called a strict Σ-algebra iff for every unary Σ-algebraic mapping f in A, $f(\perp_A)$ is the least element in $f(A)$.

Let $f_0,\dots,f_{n-1}$ be n-ary Σ-algebraic mappings in A. Denote by $L_{f_0,\dots,f_{n-1}} = \{ \langle f_0,\dots,f_{n-1}\rangle^k (\bot_{A^n}) : k < \omega \}$. For any $i<n$, the set $e_i^n(L_{f_0,\dots,f_{n-1}})$ will be called an expansion in A. An algebra A is said to be algebraically complete iff every expansion in A has a least upper bound.

Now we may present the main concept of this section. A Σ-algebra A is said to be regular iff it is strict, algebraically complete and if $f_0,\dots,f_{n-1}$ are n-ary Σ-algebraic mappings in A, then

$$\langle f_0,\dots,f_{n-1}\rangle (\sup_A L_{f_0,\dots,f_{n-1}}) = \sup_A L_{f_0,\dots,f_{n-1}}$$

Proposition 4.1

(i) If $f_0,\dots,f_{n-1}$ are n-ary Σ-algebraic functions in a regular Σ-algebra, then $L_{f_0,\dots,f_{n-1}}$ is a chain in A^n and $\sup_A L_{f_0,\dots,f_{n-1}}$ is the least fixed - point of the mapping $\langle f_0,\dots,f_{n-1}\rangle$.

(ii) Every ω-continuous algebra is regular.

(iii) For an arbitrary set X the algebra $R_\Sigma(X)$ is a regular Σ-algebra which is not ω-continuous.

Suppose A and B are two regular algebras (not necessary with the same similarity type). A mapping $f:A\to B$ is said to be algebraically continuous iff for an arbitrary expansion E in A the following two conditions hold

(4.1) There is an expansion E′ in B such that $f(E)\subset E'$.

(4.2) $f(\sup_A E) = \sup_B f(E)$

Notice that by (4.1) the least upper bound on the right - hand side of the equality (4.2) exists. Subsets of expansions in regular algebras play a role analogous to that of denumerable chains in ω-continuous algebras.

Proposition 4.2

Any algebraic function in a regular algebra is algebraically continuous.

Denote by $\underline{\mathrm{Reg}_{\Sigma}}$ the category of regular Σ-algebras with strict algebraically continuous Σ-homomorphisms. The following result answer the problem stated in the previous section.

Theorem 4.3

For an arbitrary signature Σ and an arbitrary set X, the algebra of regular $\Sigma(X)$ - trees $R_{\Sigma}(X)$ is freely generated in $\underline{\mathrm{Reg}_{\Sigma}}$ by the set X.

Having free algebras for $\underline{\mathrm{Reg}_{\Sigma}}$ one may define derived operations in regular Σ-algebras. Let A be a regular Σ - algebra. Call every function of the form $t_A : A^n \longrightarrow A$ for a certain $t \in R_{\Sigma}(n)$, an n-ary regular Σ - polynomial (here $t_A(a)$ is defined as $\overline{a}(t)$, where $a : n \longrightarrow A$ and $\overline{a} : R_{\Sigma}(n) \longrightarrow A$ is the unique extension of a to a strict algebraically continuous Σ-homomorphism). Therefore regular polynomials in regular algebras are determined by infinitely long expressions can be interpreted as flow - diagrams. Thus nullary regular polynomials (regular algebraic constants) in a regular algebra can be viewed as effectively constructed elements of the carrier. This phenomenon will be presented by examples in the next section. The following result strengthens Proposition 4.2.

Theorem 4.4

Let A be a regular Σ-algebra and let f be a function which may be obtained by fixing same variables of a regular Σ-polynomial in A by some elements of the carrier of A (f may be called a regular Σ-algebraic function in A). Then f is algebraically continuous.

Regular polynomials in regular algebras play very similar role to that of ordinary polynomials in universal algebras. Due to space limitations we present only one such result (c.f. also Tiuryn [7] and Tiuryn [8]).

Theorem 4.5

Let A and B be regular Σ-algebras. Then a function $h : A \longrightarrow B$ is a strict algebraically continuous Σ-homomorphism iff for any $n < \omega$ and any $t \in R_{\Sigma}(n)$ $h(t_A(a_o, \ldots, a_{n-1})) = t_B(h(a_o), \ldots, h(a_{n-1}))$ for all $a_o, \ldots, a_{n-1} \in A$.

5. Examples.

If A is a regular Σ-algebra, then by Theorem 4.3 there is a unique strict algebraically continuous Σ-homomorphism $h_A : R_\Sigma \longrightarrow A$ (here R_Σ means $R(\emptyset)$). It can be shown that the image $h_A(R_\Sigma)$ is the least regular Σ-subalgebra in A. In this section we give a few examples of $h_A(R_\Sigma)$ for particular regular Σ-algebras A.

5.1. Regular languages.

Let X be a set. Define a similarity type Σ by : $\Sigma_0 = \{e\}$, $\Sigma_1 = X$, $\Sigma_2 = \{\cup\}$, $\Sigma_n = \emptyset$ for $2 < n$. Let X^* be the set of all finite words over the alphabet X. Define A to be the set all subsets of X^*. This is a complete lattice under a natural ordering. The Σ-operations in A are defined as follows : $e_A = \{\varepsilon\}$ (ε is the empty word over X) ; if $x \in X$, then $x_A(L) = x \cdot L$ (i.e. $x_A(L)$ is concatenation of x and L) for any $L \subset X^*$; $\cup_A(L_1, L_2) = L_1 \cup L_2$ is set - theoretic union.

Obviously A is a regular Σ-algebra (it is even a lattice algebra in the sence of Wand [9]). Using the same argument as in Wand [9] one proves that $h_A(R_\Sigma)$ is the set all regular languages.

5.2. Context - free languages.

Let X be a set. Extend the similarity type in the above example by adding a new binary operation symbol. Denote the signature obtained in this way by Σ'. Let A be as in Example 5.1. Interpret the new operation symbol in A as the operation of concatenation of languages. All Σ-operation symbols have the same interpretation in A as above.

As in the above example, A treated as a Σ'-algebra ordered by set-theoretic inclusion becomes a lattice algebra, hence it is a regular algebra. Again using the argument presented in Wand [9] one easily proves that $h_A(R_{\Sigma'})$ is the set of all context - free languages over X.

5.3. Functions computable by Ianov schemes.

A Ianov scheme is a program scheme which is built up from unary function symbols and unary predicate symbols.

Suppose we are given a language L consisting of unary function symbols $F = \{f_j : j \in J\}$ and unary predicate symbols $P = \{p_k : k \in K\}$.

Associate with L the signature Σ^L, where $\Sigma^L_0 = \{s\}$ $(s \notin P \cup F)$, $\Sigma^L_1 = F$, $\Sigma^L_2 = P$, and $\Sigma^L_n = \emptyset$ for $2 < n$.

Suppose I is an interpretation of L in a set D (i.e. I assigns to each function symbol $f_j \in F$ a function $f^I_j : D \longrightarrow D$, and to each predicate $p_k \in P$ a unary relation $p^I_k \subset D$). Then I induces the structure of an Σ^L- algebra on the poset of all partial mappings $[D \multimap D] = A(I)$ in the following way:

- $s_{A(I)} = 1_D$ - the identity mapping
- If $f_j \in F$, then $f_{jA(I)} : A(I) \longrightarrow A(I)$ is defined by $f_{jA(I)}(g) = g \bullet f^I_j$, for all $g \in A(I)$.
- If $p_k \in P$, then $p_{kA(I)} : A(I)^2 \longrightarrow A(I)$ is defined by

$$p_{kA(I)}(g_1, g_2)(x) = \begin{cases} g_1(x) & \text{if } x \in p^I_k \cap \mathrm{Dom}(g_1) \\ g_2(x) & \text{if } x \in \mathrm{Dom}(g_2) \setminus p^I_k \\ \text{undefined} & \text{otherwise} \end{cases}$$

for all $g_1, g_2 \in A(I)$, and $x \in D$.

It can be proved that A(I) is an ω-continuous algebra, hence it is regular algebra.

It is not hard to prove that $h_{A(I)}(R_{\Sigma^L})$ is the set of all functions computable by Ianov schemes over the language L under the interpretation I (in a Σ^Lflow - diagram the symbol s corresponds to HALT statement, while the symbol $\perp$ corresponds to LOOPS statement).

5.4. Functions computable by monadic recursive program schemes.

Let L be a language consisting of unary function symbols and unary predicate symbols. Extend the signature Σ^L in the above example adding a new binary operation symbol $\circ$. Denote the extended signature by Σ^{Lr}. Given an interpretation I of the language L. Let A(I) be as above. All Σ^L-operation symbols have the same interpretation in A(I) as above. Interpret the new operation symbol as the operation of composition of functions. It can be proved that A(I) is an ω-continuous Σ^{Lr}-algebra, and that $h_{A(I)}(R_{\Sigma^{Lr}})$ is the set of all functions computable by monadic recursive program schemes over the language L under the interpretation I.

References.

1. ADJ (Authors: J.A.Goguen, J.W.Thatcher, E.G.Wagner, J.B. Wright). Rational algebraic theories and fixed-point solutions (Extended abstract). IBM Research Report, RC 6116 , 1976 .

2. ADJ. Some fundamentals of order - algebraic semantics. In: Mathematical Foundations of Computer Science, Lecture Notes in Computer Science, vol. 45, pp.153-168, Springer Verlag Berlin, 1976.

3. Goguen, J.A. and Thatcher , J.W. Initial algebra semantics. IEEE Conf. Rec. SWAT 15(1974), 63-77.

4. Gratzer, G. Universal algebra. D. Van Nostrand Co. 1968.

5. Scott, D. The lattice of flow diagrams. In : Symposium on Semantics of Algorithmic Languages, Lecture Notes in Mathematics, vol. 182, pp. 311-366, Springer Verlag, 1971.

6. Tarski, A. A lattice theoretical fixpoint theorem and its applications, Pacific J. of Math. 5(1955) 285-309.

7. Tiuryn, J. Fixed - points and algebras with infinitely long. expressions. Part I - regular algebras. To appear.

8. Tiuryn, J. Fixed - points and algebras with infinitely long expressions. Part II - μ-clones of regular algebras. To appear.

9. Wand, M. A concrete approach to abstract recursive definitions. In : Automata Languages and Programming, pp.331--341, North - Holland Publishing C , 1973.

ON LANGUAGES, ACCEPTED BY MACHINES IN THE CATEGORY OF SETS

Věra Trnková
Charles University
Sokolovská 83, Praha 8
Czechoslovakia

Jiří Adámek
Technical University
Suchbátarova 2, Praha 6
Czechoslovakia

Introduction. Though various categorial models of automata have been studied intensively in the recent years, one basic problem has remained more or less unattacked: the characterization of behaviors of finite automata. The present paper is devoted to this problem for Arbib-Manes machines in the category of sets. We define concatenation and star—operation and we prove the analysis theorem for a wide class of set-valued input processes. The synthesis fails in general and we put a problem of characterization of functors for which the synthesis theorem holds. We also show how languages of acceptors can be described via grammatical systems, generalizing those of Büchi and Brainerd. The paper is completely self-contained, the necessary notions from the Arbib-Manes theory being recalled in the first part.

I. F-ACCEPTORS AND TREE-ACCEPTORS

I,1 The background for our investigation is the notion of input process of Arbib and Manes [1]. Sequential Σ-machines are based on the endofunctor $F_{(\Sigma)}$ of the category SET (of sets and mappings), defined by

$$F_{(\Sigma)}X = X \times \Sigma \qquad \text{and} \qquad F_{(\Sigma)}f = f \times id_{\Sigma} \ .$$

In general, we shall investigate machines, based on a functor $F:SET \longrightarrow SET$. The "heart" of any F-machine will be a pair (Q,δ), where Q is a set (of states) and $\delta: FQ \rightarrow Q$ is a map (transition-map). These pairs are called F-algebras; and F-homomorphisms from (Q,δ) to (Q_1, δ_1) are such mappings $f:Q \rightarrow Q_1$ for which $f\cdot\delta = \delta_1 \cdot Ff$. The important construct Σ^*(the free monoid of strings) is captured by the definition of free F-algebra. The free F-algebra, generated by a set I, is such an F-algebra $(I^\#, \varphi)$ that 1) $I \subset I^\#$; 2) every mapping $f:I \rightarrow Q$ into an F-algebra (Q,δ) has a unique extension to an F-homomorphism $f^\# : (I^\#, \varphi) \rightarrow (Q,\delta)$. Arbib and Manes call F an input process if $I^\#$ exists for every set I.

Example. Let Σ be a ranked alphabet, i.e. a finite set equipped with an "arity" function $ar : \Sigma \rightarrow \{0,1,2,\dots\}$. Define a functor F_{Σ} : SET $\rightarrow$ SET as the disjoint union of cartesian $ar(\sigma)$-powers :

$$F_\Sigma X = \coprod_{\sigma\in\Sigma} X^{ar(\sigma)} \quad \text{and} \quad F_\Sigma f = \coprod_{\sigma\in\Sigma} f^{ar(\sigma)} ,$$

where $X^n = X \times X \times \ldots \times X$ for $n > 0$, X^0 is a singleton set. Then F_Σ -algebras are pairs (Q, δ) where δ is, essentially, a collection of operations on X: $\delta_\sigma: X^{ar(\sigma)} \to X$. It is well-known that F_Σ is an input process. I^* consists of all Σ-trees over variables I, i.e. labelled trees, where 1) the labels of leaves are symbols from I or such symbols $\sigma\in\Sigma$ for which $ar(\sigma) = 0$; 2) the labels for nodes with n successors are symbols $\sigma\in\Sigma$ with $ar(\sigma) = n$. E.g., if $\Sigma = \{0, +\}$ with $ar(0)=0$, $ar(+)=2$, then typical elements $\alpha - \delta$ of $\{x,y\}^*$ are:

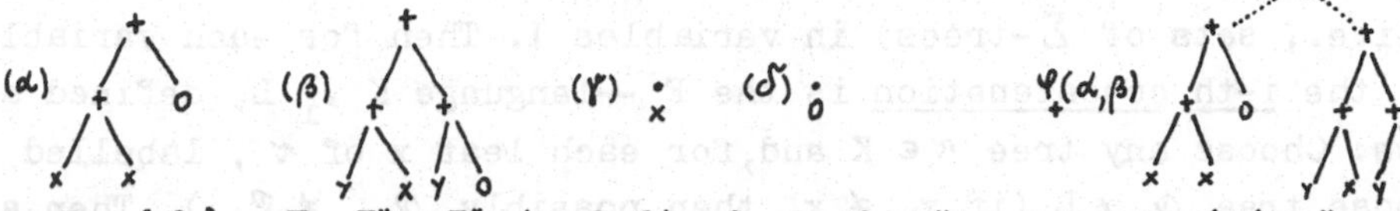

Then $\varphi = \{\varphi_\sigma\} : F_\Sigma I^* \to I^*$ is defined as the "tree composition": φ_σ, with $ar(\sigma) = n$, sends an n-tuple of trees $\tau_1 \ldots \tau_n$ to the tree with root, labelled by σ, and n maximal branches τ_i. The following definition is a small modification of the Arbib-Manes machine [1].

I,2 <u>Definition</u> Let F (:SET $\to$ SET) be an input process. An <u>F-acceptor</u> A = (Q, δ, I, T) consists of a set Q (of states), a map $\delta: FQ \to Q$ (transition map) and of subsets I,T of Q (of initial, respectively terminal, states).

The free extension of the inclusion - map $I \to Q$ (sending $i \in I$ to $i \in Q$) is called the <u>run map</u> $r : (I^*, \varphi) \to (Q, \delta)$ of A.

<u>Example</u> F_Σ -acceptor is just the <u>Σ-tree acceptor</u> of Thatcher and Wright [2], i.e., a set Q, equipped by operations $\delta_\sigma: Q^n \to Q$ ($n = ar(\sigma)$) and by subsets I,T. As sequential machines accept strings from Σ^*, these Σ-tree acceptors accept Σ-trees: given a Σ-tree τ over variables I, τ is "computed" by A in several steps. First step: each leaf, labelled by $\sigma\in\Sigma$ is re-labelled by δ_σ (which is a state, since $ar(\sigma) = 0$). Inductive step: each node, labelled by $\sigma\in\Sigma$, whose all successors have been already re-labelled by $q_1, \ldots, q_n \in Q$, respectively, is re-labelled by $\delta_\sigma(q_1, \ldots, q_n) \in Q$. And τ is <u>accepted</u> by A iff the re-labelling $r(\tau)$ of its root is a terminal state: $r(\tau) \in T$.

Now, it is easy to see that the above function $r: \Sigma\text{-trees} \to Q$ is in fact an F_Σ-homomorphism $r: (I^*, \varphi) \to (Q, \delta)$. Since $r(i) = i$ (the leaves, labelled by $i \in I$, are never re-labelled), r is the extension of the inclusion - map $I \to Q$. Hence, r is the run map of A. We see that the language of a tree acceptor consists of trees $\tau \in I^*$ with $r(\tau) \in T$.

<u>Definition</u> For a fixed input process F and a fixed set I (of variables), subsets of I are called <u>languages.</u> The language <u>L(A)</u> accep-

ted by an acceptor A = (Q, δ, I, T) is defined by

$$L(A) = \{ \tau \in I^* ; r(\tau) \in T \},$$

where $r: I^* \longrightarrow Q$ is the run map of A. A language L is <u>recognizable</u> if there exists a finite acceptor A (i.e., such an acceptor that Q is a finite set) with L=L(A).

I,3 Languages, recognizable by sequential machines, are characterized by Kleene's theorem as the closure of finite languages to the operations +, . and $*$. This result has been very nicely generalized by Thatcher and Wright [2] to Σ-tree acceptors. Let K, L be F-languages (i.e., sets of Σ-trees) in variables I. Then for each variable $i \in I$, the <u>i-th</u> <u>concatenation</u> is the F —language $K \cdot_i L$, defined as follows: Choose any tree $\tau \in K$ and, for each leaf x of τ , labelled by i, choose tree $\varrho_x \in L$ (if $x_1 \neq x_2$ then possibly $\varrho_{x_1} \neq \varrho_{x2}$). Then a typical element of $K \cdot_i L$ is the tree τ , in which leaves x, labelled by i, are substituted by trees ϱ_x. Example: $\Sigma = \{0, +\}$, I = $\{x,y\}$ as above:

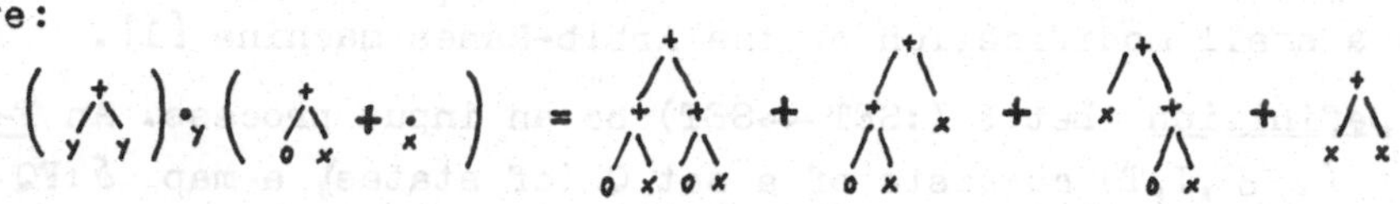

Furthermore, the i-th star operation is defined by $K^{*i} = \{i\} \cup K \cup \cup (K \cdot_i K) \cup \ldots$.

<u>Definition</u> A set of Σ-trees in variables I is <u>regular</u> if it can be obtained from finite sets via operation + (union), $\cdot_i$ and i ($i \in I$) in a finite number of steps.

<u>Note</u> Union is denoted by + only as a "rational" operation, otherwise by $\cup$. Thus $A + B \overset{\text{def}}{=} A \cup B$.

<u>Theorem</u> (Thacher,Wright) A set of Σ-trees is regualr iff it is recognizable.

II. <u>REGULAR</u> <u>SYSTEMS</u>

II,1 Brainerd has defined in [3] tree-generating regular systems as a generalization of regular systems of Büchi. A <u>regular</u> <u>system</u> (without non-terminals) over a ranked alphabeth Σ is a triple of finite sets $\mathcal{S}$ = (I,S,P) where S is a set of Σ-trees over variables I and P is a set of productions $p: \underline{a} \longrightarrow \underline{b}$ where $\underline{a}$, $\underline{b}$ are Σ-trees over I. Using a production p we can derive a tree $\underline{x}$ from a tree $\underline{y}$: choose nodes in $\underline{y}$, the branches of which are trees $\underline{a}$ and change all these branches to the tree $\underline{b}$; if $\underline{x}$ is the result, write $\underline{y} \xrightarrow{p} \underline{x}$. The <u>language</u> <u>L($\mathcal{S}$)</u>, generated by the system $\mathcal{S}$, is defined as the set of all trees, which can be derived from trees in S by a successive use of P-productions.

II,2 Derivations of trees has a simple categorical description. Recall that Σ-trees over variables I are just elements of $I^{\#}$ (for F_{Σ}). Add a new variable, say k, and define morphisms

$$\xi_a, \xi_b : (I \cup \{k\})^{\#} \longrightarrow I^{\#}$$

by extending the following maps: $\xi_a(i) = \xi_b(i) = i$ for $i \in I$; $\xi_a(k)=\underline{a}$ and $\xi_b(k)=\underline{b}$. Then a tree $\underline{w}$ in variables $I \cup \{k\}$ is sent by ξ_a to the tree $\xi_a(\underline{w})$, where each occurence of a k-labelled leaf is substituted by the tree $\underline{a}$; analogously $\xi_b(\underline{w})$. It is clear that $\underline{y} \xrightarrow{p} \underline{x}$ is equivalent to: $\underline{y} = \xi_a(\underline{w})$ and $\underline{x} = \xi_b(\underline{w})$ for some $\underline{w} \in (I \cup \{k\})^{\#}$.

These morphisms ξ_a, ξ_b can be defined for an arbitrary input process F in the same way.

<u>Definition</u> Let F be an input process. Given $a, b \in I^{\#}$ let $p : a \rightarrow b$ be a production (i.e., an element of $I^{\#} \times I^{\#}$). We write $Y \xrightarrow{p} x$ for $x, y \in I^{\#}$ iff there exists $w \in (I \cup \{k\})^{\#}$ with $y = \xi_a(w)$ and $x = \xi_b(w)$. If $P \subset I^{\#} \times I^{\#}$ is a set of productions, we write $y \overset{P}{\Longrightarrow} x$ if there exist $x_o, \dots, x_n \in I^{\#}$ and $p_1, \dots, p_n \in P$ such that

$$y = x_o \xrightarrow{p_1} x_1 \xrightarrow{p_2} \dots \xrightarrow{p_n} x_n = x .$$

<u>Definition</u> Let F be an input process. A <u>regular</u> <u>F-system</u> is a triple $\mathcal{G} = (I,S,P)$ of finite sets such that $S \subset I^{\#}$ and $P \subset I^{\#} \times I^{\#}$. The <u>language</u>, <u>generated</u> <u>by</u> $\underline{\mathcal{G}}$, is defined by

$$L(\mathcal{G}) = \{x \in I^{\#} ;\ y \overset{P}{\Longrightarrow} x \text{ for some } y \in S\} .$$

II,3 The basic result of Brainerd [3] is that an F_{Σ}-language is recognizable iff it is generated by some regular F_{Σ}-system. We shall generalize the necessity and discuss the sufficiency for input processes.

We recall from [4] that an input process F, preserving countable sets (i.e., FX is countable whenever X is) has free algebras over finite sets I constructed in the following way: define sets $W_o^I = I$, $W_{n+1}^I = I \vee FW_n^I$ ($\vee$ denotes disjoint union), then $I^{\#} = \bigcup_{n=o}^{\infty} W_n^I$. Given $i : I \rightarrow Q$ and $\delta : FQ \rightarrow Q$, the extension $i^{\#} : (I^{\#}, \varphi) \longrightarrow (Q, \delta)$ is obtained as $i^{\#} = \bigcup_{n=o}^{\infty} i^n$ where $i^o = i$, $i^{n+1} = i \vee Fi^n$. If F preserves also finite sets, then each W_n is finite, of course.

<u>Theorem</u> Let F be an input process preserving both finite and countable sets. Then every recognizable language can be generated by a regular system.

Proof. Given a finite acceptor $A = (Q,\delta,I,T)$ with q states and a run map $r : I^{*} \longrightarrow Q$, we define a regular system $\mathcal{S} = (I,S,P)$: $S = L(A) \cap W^{I}_{q-1}$ and $P = \{a \rightarrow b;\ a \in W_q,\ b \in W_{q-1}$ and $r(a) = r(b)\}$. We shall prove that $L(A) = L(\mathcal{S})$. The inclusion $L(\mathcal{S}) \subset L(A)$ is rather easy: since $S \subset L(A)$, it suffices to show for each $p : a \rightarrow b$ in P that if $y \xrightarrow{p} x$ and $y \in L(A)$ then $x \in L(A)$: We have $y = \xi_a(w)$ and $x = \xi_b(w)$ (see II,2) and $r(a) = r(b)$. Hence, $r \cdot \xi_a = r \cdot \xi_b$: $(I \cup \{k\})^{*} \rightarrow Q$ (indeed, $r \cdot \xi_a$ and $r \cdot \xi_b$ are F-homomorphisms, equal on $I \cup \{k\}$). Therefore, $r(y) = r(x)$ and $r(y) \in T$ really implies $r(x) \in T$.

To prove $L(A) \subset L(\mathcal{S})$, first put $Q_n = r(W_n) \cap Q$. Since $r = i^{*}$ for the inclusion - map $i : I \rightarrow Q$, $Q_n = i^{n}(W_n)$ and it follows from $i^{n} = i \vee Fi^{n-1}$ that, whenever $Q_{n-1} = Q_n$, also $Q_n = Q_{n+1}$. Since $Q_o \leq Q_1 \leq Q_2 \ldots$ and card $Q = q$, necessarily $Q_{q-1} = Q_q$: For each $z \in W_q$ we can choose $z' \in W_{q-1}$ with $r(z) = r(z')$ (and, moreover, $z=z'$ if $z \in W_{q-1}$).

Put $W_q = \{z_1,\ldots,z_m\}$ and define homomorphisms $\lambda_1,\ldots,\lambda_m$: $((W_q)^{*},\varphi) \longrightarrow ((I\cup\{k\})^{*},\varphi)$ as extensions of the following maps $W_q \rightarrow (I \cup \{k\})^{*}$:

$$\lambda_j(z_i) = z_i \text{ for } i < j;\ = k \text{ for } i = j;\ = z_i' \text{ for } i > j\ .$$

Then 1) $\xi z_m \cdot \lambda_m$ maps $W_n^{W_q}$ onto W^{I}_{n+q} and $\xi_{z_1'} \cdot \lambda_1$ maps $W_n^{W_q}$ onto W^{I}_{n+q-1}; 2) for each j, $\xi_{z_j} \cdot \lambda_j = \xi_{z'_{j+1}} \cdot \lambda_{j+1}$ and $r \cdot \xi_{z_m} \cdot \lambda_m = r \cdot \xi_{z_1'} \cdot \lambda_1$ (the proof of 2) is based on the fact that all these morphisms are homomorphisms, so that we only have to show the equalities on W_q).

Now we prove that $x \in L(A) \cap W^{I}_n$ implies $x \in L(\mathcal{S})$ by induction in n. If $n < q$ then $x \in S \subset L(\mathcal{S})$. Let $n > q$, then there exists $w \in W_{n-q}^{W_q}$ with $\xi_{z_m} \lambda_m(w) = x$. Put $x' = \xi_{z_1'} \cdot \lambda_1(w)$, then $r(x) = r(x')$ so that $x' \in L(A)$; and $x' \in W^{I}_{n-1}$. By induction hypothesis, $x' \in L(\mathcal{S})$. It suffices to verify that $x' \overset{P}{\Longrightarrow} x$. Put $p_j : z_j \rightarrow z_j'$; clearly $p_j \in P$. Let $x_j = \xi_{z_j}(\lambda_j(w)) = \xi_{z'_{j+1}}(\lambda_{j+1}(w))$, $j = 0,\ldots,m$, then $x' = x_o$ and $x = x_m$, while $x_j \xrightarrow{p_{j+1}} x_{j+1}$, because $x_j = \xi_{z'_{j+1}}(\lambda_{j+1}(w))$ while $x_{j+1} = \xi_{z_{j+1}}(\lambda_{j+1}(w))$.

II,4 <u>Example</u> Denote by D the following set functor. $D\emptyset = \emptyset$ while

$$DX = \{(x,y) \in X \times X;\ x \neq y\} \cup \{\Delta\} \quad (\text{for } X \neq \emptyset)$$

$$Df(x,y) = (fx,fy) \text{ if } fx \neq fy;\ = \Delta = Df(\Delta) \text{ if } fx = fy \quad (\text{for } f: X \rightarrow Y).$$

Notice that D-acceptors are Σ-tree acceptors for $\Sigma = \{+\}$, ar(+) = z, with the additional property on $\delta : Q \times Q \longrightarrow Q$ that $\delta(x,x) = \delta(y,y)$ for all $x,y \in Q$. Further, D is an input process such that $I^{\#}$ is the set of binary trees in variables $I \cup \{\Delta\}$, with the property that the two branches of any given node are distinct trees. The operation $\varphi : DI^{\#} \longrightarrow I^{\#}$ is again the tree composition: $\varphi(\tau, \tau')$ is the tree with two maximal branches τ, τ'; $\varphi(\Delta) = \Delta$.

Proposition The D-language $\{\Delta\}$ ($\subset I^{\#}$ for any I) is not recognizable.

Proof. Let $A = (Q, \delta, I, T)$ be a finite D-acceptor with $L(A) = \{\Delta\}$. Finiteness makes the run map $r : I^{\#} \longrightarrow Q$ not one-to-one. Choose distinct trees $\tau, \tau' \in I^{\#}$ with $r(\tau) = r(\tau')$. We shall prove that the tree $\varphi(\tau, \tau')$ is accepted by A - a contradiction.

Since $r \cdot \varphi = \delta \cdot Fr$ and $Dr(\tau, \tau') = \Delta$ (b cause $r(\tau) = r(\tau')$), we have $r(\varphi(\tau, \tau')) = \delta(\Delta) = \delta \cdot Fr(\Delta) = r(\varphi(\Delta)) = r(\Delta)$. Since $r(\Delta) \in T$, also $r(\varphi(\tau, \tau')) \in T$.

Corollary Not every language, generated by a regular D-system, is recognizable. E.g., consider $\mathcal{S} = (I, \{\Delta\}, \emptyset)$.

III. REGULAR LANGUAGES

III,1 To give a categorial model of the i-th concatenation of F-languages $K \cdot_i L$, mentioned in I,3, consider the set

$$L(i) \overset{\text{def}}{=} L \cup I - \{i\}$$

and form the free F_Σ-algebra $L(i)^{\#}$ (of trees in variables L(i)). We have two natural maps $\alpha, \beta : L(i)^{\#} \longrightarrow I^{\#}$: α interprets variables in $L (\subset L(i))$ as the variable i, while β makes a "tree in trees" become a tree. More precisely, define $\alpha_0, \beta_0 : L(i) \longrightarrow I^{\#}$ by $\alpha_0(\tau) = i$, $\beta_0(\tau) = \tau$ if $\tau \in L$; $\alpha_0(j) = \beta_0(j) = j$ if $j \in I - \{i\}$, then $\alpha = \alpha_0^{\#}$ and $\beta = \beta_0^{\#}$. Example: $\Sigma = \{0, +\}$, $I = \{i,j,k\}$ and $L = \{a,b\}$ below; choosing $\tau \in L(j)^{\#} = \{i,k,a,b\}^{\#}$ we show $\alpha(\tau)$, $\beta(\tau)$:

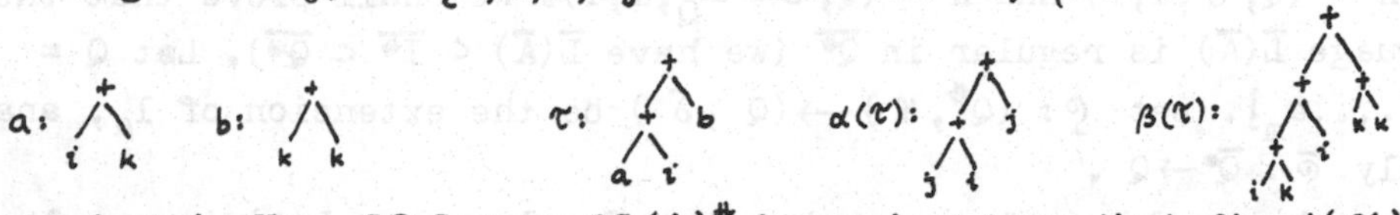

Now, what is $K \cdot_i L$? Let $\tau \in L(i)^{\#}$ be such a tree that $\tau_1 = \alpha(\tau) \in K$; then $\beta(\tau)$ is the tree τ_1, in which every leaf, indexed by i (i.e., every leaf of τ, indexed by some tree in L !) is substituted by a tree from L (namely, its index in τ). We see that $K \cdot_i L = \{\beta(\tau);\ \tau \in L(i)^{\#} \text{ and } \alpha(\tau) \in K\}$. This allows an immediate generalization.

III,2 Given F-languages $K, L \subset I^*$ and $i \in I$ we can define L(i) as above and $\alpha_0, \beta_0 : L(i) \to I^*$ are, again, defined by

$$\alpha_0(\tau) = i; \quad \beta_0(\tau) = \tau \quad \text{for } \tau \in L$$
$$\alpha_0(j) = \beta_0(j) = j \quad \text{for } j \in I - \{i\} .$$

The free extensions are denoted by $\alpha, \beta : (L(i)^{\#}, \varphi) \to (I^{\#}, \varphi)$.

<u>Definition</u> The <u>i-th</u> <u>concatenation</u> $K \cdot_i L$ of F-languages $K, L \subset I^{\#}$ is defined by

$$K \cdot_i L = \{ \beta(\tau);\ \tau \in L(i)^{\#} \text{ and } \alpha(\tau) \in K \}.$$

The <u>i-th</u> <u>star</u> <u>operation</u> <u>$*i$</u> is defined by

$$K^{*i} = \{i\} \cup K \cup (K \cdot_i K) \cup (K \cdot_i K) \cdot_i K \cup \dots \ .$$

Finally, a language is <u>regular</u> if it can be obtained from finite languages via the operations $+$, $\cdot_i$ and $* i$ $(i \in I)$.

III,3 <u>Definition</u> A set functor F is <u>super-finitary</u> if

(i) F preserves finite sets (i.e., for every finite X also FX is finite);

(ii) there is a natural number n such that for every set X: FX = $= \bigcup Ff(FT)$, where the union ranges over all maps $f : T \to X$ with card $T \le n$.

<u>Note</u> It is easy to verify (by Yoneda lemma) that super-finitary functors are exactly the quotient-functors of functors F_Σ .

<u>Analysis</u> <u>theorem</u> Let F be a super-finitary input process. Then every recognizable language is regular.

Proof. We have a ranked alphabet Σ and an epi-transformation $\varepsilon : F_\Sigma \to F$. Given a set Q, we have a free F_Σ-algebra $(Q^{\#}, \varphi)$ and a free F-algebra $(\overline{Q^{\#}}, \overline{\varphi})$ (we use bar to distinbuish F-concepts from F_Σ-ones). A free extension of the inclusion $Q \to \overline{Q^{\#}}$ yields an F_Σ-homomorphism $\hat{\varepsilon}_Q : (Q^{\#}, \varphi) \to (\overline{Q^{\#}}, \overline{\varphi} \cdot \varepsilon_Q)$.

Let $\overline{A}$ be a finite F-acceptor and A the corresponding F_Σ-acceptor. I.e., $\overline{A} = (Q, \overline{\delta}, I, T)$ and $A = (Q, \overline{\delta} \cdot \varepsilon_Q, I, T)$. We shall prove that the F-language $\overline{L}(\overline{A})$ is regular in $\overline{Q^{\#}}$ (we have $\overline{L}(\overline{A}) \subset \overline{I^{\#}} \subset \overline{Q^{\#}}$). Let $Q = \{a_1, \dots, a_m\}$. Let $\rho : (Q^{\#}, \varphi) \to (Q, \delta)$ be the extension of 1_Q, analogously $\overline{\rho} : \overline{Q^{\#}} \to Q$.

Thatcher and Wright prove that the F_Σ-language L(A) is regular in $Q^{\#}$ (theorem 9 in [2]) in a manner which we describe now. First, we can assume that $\overline{A}(A)$ has a single terminal state [and, for general $\overline{A}$, we use the operation union: $\overline{L}(\overline{A}) = \bigcup_{t \in T} \overline{L}(Q, \delta, I, \{t\})$]. Then L(A) is proved to be equal to the following regular language L : first, finite languages U_k, Λ_k (k = 1...m) are defined with the property $\rho(U_k) = \rho(\Lambda_k) = a_k$ and $\Lambda_k = \emptyset$ if $a_k \in Q - I$. Then $T_i^k \subset Q^*(i,k = 1,\dots,m)$ are defined recursively :

(i) $T_1^1 = U_1^{*a_1}$ and $T_i^1 = \{a_i\}, i \neq 1$;

$$T_i^{k+1} = T_i^k \cdot_{a_{k+1}} [(\dots((U_k \cdot_{a_2} T_1^k) \cdot_{a_2} T_2^k)\dots) \cdot_{a_k} T_k^k]^{*a_k}$$

and, finally,

(ii) $L = (\dots(((T^m_{k_o} \cdot_{a_1} \Lambda_1) \cdot_{a_2} \Lambda_2) \cdot \quad \dots) \cdot_{a_k} \Lambda_k$ where $\{a_{k_o}\} = T$ is the terminal set.

Assuming L = L(A), we shall prove that $\overline{L} = \overline{L}(\overline{A})$, where $\overline{L}$ is the following regular language: put $\overline{U}_k = \hat{\varepsilon}_Q(U_k)$ and $\overline{\Lambda}_k = \hat{\varepsilon}_Q(\Lambda_k)$ and define $\overline{T}_i^k$, $\overline{L}$ exactly as in (i), (ii) above, only inserting bar over each capital letter and using F-concatenation $\cdot_{a_k}$ and F-iteration $*_{a_k}$.

A) $\overline{L} \subset \overline{L}(\overline{A})$. First, notice that $\hat{\varepsilon}_Q(I^*) = \overline{I^*}$ and that $\rho = \bar{\rho}\cdot\hat{\varepsilon}$ (since ρ, $\bar{\rho}\cdot\hat{\varepsilon}$ are F_Σ-homomorphisms, equal on Q). Second, the run map of A is a restriction of ρ to I^*, analogously $\bar{\rho}$ to $\overline{I^*}$. Finally, we shall prove that

(*) Given $C,D \subset \overline{Q^*}$ with $\bar{\rho}(D) = \{a_i\}$ then $\bar{\rho}(C \cdot_{a_1} D) = \bar{\rho}(C)$; $\bar{\rho}(D^{*a_i}) = \{a_i\}$.

Indeed, the morphisms $\bar{\alpha}, \bar{\beta} : \overline{D(a_i)^*} \to \overline{Q^*}$ (see III,2) fulfil $\bar{\rho}\cdot\bar{\alpha} = \bar{\rho}\cdot\bar{\beta}$, because $\bar{\rho}\cdot\bar{\alpha}$; $\bar{\rho}\cdot\bar{\beta}$ are homomorphisms, equal on $D(a_i)$. If $z \in C \cdot_{a_1} D$, then $z = \bar{\beta}(z_1)$ where $\bar{\alpha}(z_1) \in C$. Then $\bar{\rho}(z) = \bar{\rho}\cdot\bar{\beta}(z_1) = \bar{\rho}\cdot\bar{\alpha}(z_1) \in \bar{\rho}(C)$; thus $\bar{\rho}(C \cdot_{a_1} D) \subset \bar{\rho}(C)$. By iteration, $\bar{\rho}(D^{*a_i}) \subset \{a_i\}$.

Now, we prove $\overline{L} \subset \overline{L}(\overline{A})$ quite easily. Since $\rho(U_k) = \{a_k\}$, and $\rho = \bar{\rho}\cdot\hat{\varepsilon}$ we have $\bar{\rho}(\overline{U}_k) = \{a_k\}$. Using (*) inductively on (i), we see that $\bar{\rho}(\overline{T}_i^k) = \{a_i\}$. Since $\bar{\rho}(\overline{\Lambda}_k) = \{a_k\}$, another use of (*) on (ii) yields $\bar{\rho}(\overline{L}) = \bar{\rho}(\overline{T}^m_{k_o}) = \{a_{k_o}\}$. Since the run map of $\overline{A}$ is the restriction of $\bar{\rho}$ to $\overline{I^*}$, what remains to be verified is $\overline{L} \subset \overline{I^*}$. This follows easily from (ii) above and from the fact that for $a_k \in Q - I$ we have $\Lambda_k = \emptyset$, hence $\overline{\Lambda}_k = \emptyset$: Clearly, given a language $C \subset \overline{Q^*}$ then $C \cdot_{a_i} \emptyset \subset \overline{(Q - \{a_i\})^*}$ (indeed, $\emptyset(a_i) = Q - \{a_i\}$ and β from III,2 is the inclusion $\overline{(Q - \{a_i\})^*} \hookrightarrow \overline{Q^*}$). Therefore, $\overline{L} \subset \overline{(Q - (Q - I))^*} = \overline{I^*}$ and we see that $\overline{L} \subset \overline{L}(\overline{A})$.

B) $\overline{L}(\overline{A}) \subset \overline{L}$. First, $\overline{L}(\overline{A}) \subset \hat{\varepsilon}(L)$: given $x \in \overline{L}(\overline{A})$ we have $x \in \overline{I^*}$ and so $x = \hat{\varepsilon}(x_1)$, $x_1 \in I^*$. Since $\bar{\rho}(x) = a_{k_o}$ ($\bar{\rho}$ is an extension of the run map), $\rho(x_1) = a_{k_o}$ and so $x_1 \in L(A) = L$. Hence $x \in \hat{\varepsilon}(L)$.

To verify $\hat{\varepsilon}(L) \subset \overline{L}$, it suffices to prove that

(**) given C, $D \subset Q^{*}$ and $a_i \in Q$ then $\hat{\varepsilon}(C \cdot_{a_1} D) \subset \hat{\varepsilon}(C) \cdot_{a_1} \hat{\varepsilon}(D)$; $\hat{\varepsilon}(D^{*a_i}) \subset \hat{\varepsilon}(D)^{*a_i}$. (Since $\overline{U}_k = \hat{\varepsilon}(U_k)$, an inductive use of (**) yields $\hat{\varepsilon}(T_i^k) \subset \overline{T}_i^k$ and, since $\overline{\Lambda}_k = \hat{\varepsilon}(\Lambda_k)$, finally $\hat{\varepsilon}(L) \subset \overline{L}$.)

To prove (**) consider $\alpha, \beta : D(a_i)^{*} \longrightarrow Q^{*}$ and, analogously, $\overline{\alpha}$, $\overline{\beta}$. Define $\sigma_o : D(a_i) \rightarrow \overline{\hat{\varepsilon} D(a_i)^{*}}$ by $\sigma_o(x) = \hat{\varepsilon}(x)$ for $x \in D$; $\sigma_o(j) = j$ for $j \in I - \{i\}$. Extending σ_o to a homomorphism $\sigma : D(a_i)^{*} \longrightarrow \overline{\hat{\varepsilon} D(a_i)^{*}}$, we see that the following diagram (of F_Z -homomorphisms !) commutes :

$$\begin{array}{ccccc} Q & \xleftarrow{\alpha} & D(a_i)^{*} & \xrightarrow{\beta} & Q \\ \hat{\varepsilon}\downarrow & & \sigma\downarrow & & \downarrow\hat{\varepsilon} \\ Q^{*} & \xleftarrow{\overline{\alpha}} & \hat{\varepsilon}D(a_i)^{*} & \xrightarrow{\overline{\beta}} & Q^{*} \end{array}$$

Hence, given $z \in \hat{\varepsilon}(C \cdot_{a_i} D)$, we have $z = \hat{\varepsilon}(x)$ with $x = \beta(x_1)$ such that $\alpha(x_1) \in C$. Then $z = \hat{\varepsilon} \cdot \beta(x_1) = \overline{\beta}(\sigma(x_1))$ where $\overline{\alpha}(\sigma(x_1)) \in \hat{\varepsilon}(C)$. Thus $\hat{\varepsilon}(C \cdot_{a_i} D) \subset \hat{\varepsilon}(C) \cdot_{a_1} \hat{\varepsilon}(D)$. Iteration yields $\hat{\varepsilon}(D^{*a_i}) \subset (D)^{*a_i}$.

III,4 The synthesis theorem causes difficulties of various kinds. One is indicated by Proposition II,4: even finite languages need not be recognizable. Another is the transition between non-deterministic machines, which will be discussed elsewhere by the first author.

Let us finally mention that the properties of concatenation can also be quite dissimilar from those in case of trees:

Example For the functor D of II,4, put $I = \{i,j,k\}$ and let $K = \{\Delta\}$, $L = \{a,b\} \subset I^{*}$ be defined as follows:

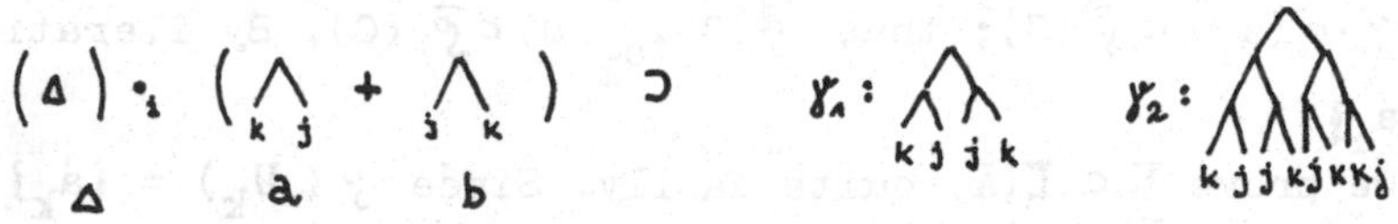

Then $K \cdot_i L$ is an infinite set ! E.g., $\gamma_1, \gamma_2, \ldots \in K \cdot_i L$.

References

1. Arbib M. A., Manes E. G., Machines in a category, an expository introduction. SIAM Review 16(1974), 163-192.
2. Thatcher J.W., Wright J.B., Generalized finite automata theory with an application to a decision problem of second-order logic. Math. Systems Theory 2(1968), 57-81.
3. Brainerd W.S., Tree generating regular systems. Information and Control 14(1969), 217-231.
4. Trnková V., On minimal realizations of behavior maps in categorial automata theory, Comment.Math.Univ.Carolinae 15(1975), 555-566.

REAL TIME COMPUTATIONS WITH RESTRICTIONS ON TAPE ALPHABET

M.K.Valiev
Institute of Mathematics,
Novosibirsk 90, USSR

1. There is a number of papers in which is discussed the part which play restrictions on tape alphabet for tape bounded Turing computations. In particular, in [1] we announced a result which (after some reinterpretation) shows that for the tape bounded Turing machines the increase of tape alphabets from m symbols to $2m^2$ symbols augments the computational power of machines. Some later this result was extended and partially strengthened by Seiferas, Meyer and Fischer [2], Ibarra [3], Ibarra and Sahni [4]. In particular, Ibarra [3] proved that for any integers $m \geq 2$, $r \geq 1$, n^r -tape bounded Turing machines with m tape symbols are more powerful than n^r - tape bounded Turing machines with m-1 tape symbols. In our paper we attempt to clear up the role of restrictions on tape alphabets for time bounded Turing machines and show the existence of the hierarchy for real time computations (see Rabin [5]) similar to that in [3]. We prove in fact a somewhat stronger result which we formulate below including beforehand necessary definitions.

2. Following Freivald [6] we consider Turing machines with the single working tape and with input (MTI) which work in the following way: during first $|w|$ steps ($|w|$ being the length of the input string) the machine proceeds in real time, afterwards it works ignoring its input tape. We permit nondeterministic MTI's as well. We say that a nondeterministic MTI accepts an input word w in time $t_M(w)$ if $t_M(w)$ is equal to the minimum of lengths of resultative paths for w, i.e. of paths which lead to accepting states. By $t_M(n)$ we denote max $t_M(w)$, where maximum is taken over all the words w with the length n

which are accepted by M.

3. The following theorem is true.

<u>Theorem</u>. For any integer $m \geq 2$ there exists a set $A_m \subset \{0,1,2\}^*$ such that

1) A_m can be recognized in real time by a (deterministic) MTI with m+1 working tape symbols,

2) for any nondeterministic MTI M which has m working tape symbols and accepts A_m $t_M(n)$ cannot be of the order less than n^2.

From the assertion 2) of this theorem it follows that A_m cannot be accepted (and thus, recognized) in real time.

In [7] we announced a weaker form of this theorem (assertion 2) for deterministic machines only). We note that the proof of our theorem coincides essentially with the unpublished proof of the result of [7] . The only additional observation used in the proof of the assertion 2) is the possibility of the transfer of the Replacement <u>Lemma</u> (lemma 1 of Freivald [6]) from the deterministic case to the nondeterministic case as indicated by R.V.Freivald (the formulation of this lemma for nondeterministic MTI's is given in the Section 6 below).

4. Let us begin with presenting the set A_3.

$$A_3 = \{x_1x_2\dots x_{2n}2yz : y = x_{2n-1}x_{2n-3} \dots x_1, \\ z = x_2x_4 \dots x_{2n},\ x_i \in \{0,1\}\}.$$

The assertion 1) for A_3 may be verified very easily. Namely, the machine with four tape symbols which recognizes A_3 proceeds as follows: up to the moment when appears the symbol 2 it writes read input symbols onto working tape by pairs (a pair into a square), afterwards passing from the right to the left and backwards it checks whether the word received after the indicated moment has the required form or not.

5. Now we present the sets A_m for all m. Let k and l be numbers such that $m^k < 2^l \leq (m+1)^k$ (such numbers may be found for each m). Then A_m is defined as follows:

$$A_m = \{x_{11}\, x_{12}\ldots x_{1l} x_{21} x_{22}\ldots x_{2l}\ldots x_{n1} x_{n2}\ldots x_{nl} 2yz, \text{where}$$

$$y = x_{n1} x_{n2}\ldots x_{nk} x_{n-1\,1} x_{n-1\,2}\ldots x_{n-1\,k}\ldots x_{11} x_{12}\ldots x_{1k},$$

$$z = x_{1\,k+1} x_{1\,k+2}\ldots x_{1l} x_{2\,k+1} x_{2\,k+2}\ldots x_{2l}\ldots x_{n\,k+1}\ldots x_{nl},$$

$$x_{ij} \in \{0,1\}\ ,\ i = 1,2,\ldots,n,\ j = 1,2\ldots,l, n=1,2,3,\ldots\}$$

The proof of the assertion 1) for A_m is similar to that for A_3 and shall be omitted (we note only that the condition $2^l \leq (m+1)^k$ must be used in the proof).

6. For the sequel, following [6], we introduce some conventions and notations. We assume that the working tapes of MTI's are bounded to the left. The squares of the tape and the border points of squares (which are called further points simply) are numbered from left to right by numerals 0,1,2,.... Let D be a path of processing a word w by a MTI M, P be a point and i_1, i_2, i_3,... be the sequence of moments in which the head of M crosses P. Let q_i be the state of M in the moment i. Further, assume that $i_r < |w| \leq i_{r+1}$. Then the sequence $\langle r, q_{i_1}, q_{i_2}, \ldots \rangle$ is called a crossing sequence of D at P and is denoted by C(w,D,P). The word w may be represented in form

$$w_1 w_2 \ldots\ w_{r+1} \tag{1}$$

where for $j \neq 1, r+1$ w_j is the word read from input between the moments i_{j-1} and i_j. We call the representation (1) for w a division of w induced by D and P . Let v be a word such that C(w,D,P)= = C(v,E,Q) for a path E and a point Q, and $v_1 v_2 \ldots v_{r+1}$ be the division of v induced by E and Q. S(w,v,D,E,P,Q) denotes the word $w_1 v_2 w_3 v_4 \ldots w_r v_{r+1}$, if r is odd, and the word $w_1 v_2 w_3 v_4 \ldots w_{r-1} v_r w_{r+1}$, if r is even . Then the following easily verifiable proposition is true.

<u>Replacement Lemma</u> (R.V.Freivald). If the path D is resultative for w or the path E is resultative for v, then M accepts the word S(w,v,D,E,P,Q).

7. Let us turn to the proof of the assertion 2). Let M be a MTI which accepts A_m and has m tape symbols. For any word w in A_m we fix a resultative path D(w) and mentioning below processing a word w

by M we mean that it is processed relatively to D(w). We fix also a (sufficiently large) number n and denote by B_0 the set of words in A_m which have the length 2nl + 1.

It is easy to see that configurations of M which appear at the moment nl while processing different words in B_0 must be different. Otherwise M would accept a word not in A_m. Hence, we obtain that for $2^{nl} - o(2^{nl})$ words in B_0 during first nl steps the head of M visits at least $nk(1+\varepsilon)$ squares of the tape, where $\varepsilon = 1/k \log_2 m - 1$ (we note that $\varepsilon > 0$ because $m^k < 2^l$).

Let P_1 and P_2 be the points with the numbers $nk\varepsilon/2$ and $nk(1+\varepsilon/2)$ respectively. For each word w of the form x2yz in B_1 one of the following conditions is satisfied (because $|y| = nk$):

(1) while processing the subword y the head of M is to the left of P_2,

(2) while processing y the head is to the right of P_1.

Let $B_{1,i}$, i = 1,2, denote the set of words in B_1 satisfying the condition (i), and B_2 be that of sets $B_{1,i}$ which has more elements. Let us assume that $B_2 = B_{1,1}$ (in the case $B_2 = B_{1,2}$ the proof is similar).

Let P(w) denote the point for which the length of crossing sequence is minimal among the points with the numbers $nk(1+\varepsilon/2)$, $nk(1+\varepsilon/2) + 1$, ..., $nk(1+3\varepsilon/4)$. Let B_3 be the set with maximal number of elements among the sets $B_{2,P}$, where $B_{2,P}$ consists of words w such that P(w) = P.

Any word w in B_3 may be represented in the form

$$u_1 u_2 u_3 2yz, \qquad (2)$$

where $[|u_1|, |u_1 u_2|]$ is the maximal time interval during which the head is to the right of P and which includes the moment of the first visiting of the square with the number $nk(1+\varepsilon)$.

Let $B_{3,\tilde{u}_1,\tilde{u}_3,\tilde{z},q,r}$ consist of words w satisfying the following conditions:

a) the subwords u_1, u_3, z in the representation (2) of w are equal to $\tilde{u}_1$, $\tilde{u}_3$, $\tilde{z}$ respectively (we note that these equalities determine partially the form of the subwords u_2 and y as well),

b) the total number of the symbols of u_3 read from the input while the head is visiting the zone to the right of P is equal to q,

c) the number of crossings of the point P up to moment |w| is equal to r.

Let B_4 be the biggest of the sets $B_{3,u_1,u_3,z,q,r}$. We note that

$|B_4| \geqslant 2^{nk\varepsilon/2 \cdot k/1 - o(n)} = 2^{cn}$ because $|u_2| \geqslant nk\varepsilon/2$.

Let $w_1 w_2 \ldots w_{r+1}$ be the division of a word w in B_4 induced by D(w), P, and $u_1 u_2 u_3 2yz$ be the representation of w in the form (2). Then there exist numbers i, j such that $u_2 = w_{2i}$ and w_{2j+1} contains y. Let $v_1 v_2 \ldots v_{r+1}$ be the division of another word v in B_4 induced by D(v) and P. Let us set for simplicity that $r + 1 = 2s$. Then from the conditions a) and b) we obtain easily that the word

$$S(w,v,D(w),D(v),P,P) = w_1 v_2 w_3 v_4 \ldots w_{2s-1} v_{2s}$$

doesn't belong to A_m. Therefore, from the Replacement Lemma we obtain that the crossing sequences at the point P for different words in B_4 must be different. It follows from this that there exist words in B_4 the lengths of crossing sequences at P for which must be at least c'n, for some c'. Hence, for each such word w the time of processing of this word is at least $c'n \cdot nk\varepsilon/4 = c''|W|^2$. Thus assertion 2) is proved.

References

1. Matveeva, S. G. and Valiev, M. K., Some bounds of computational complexity for Turing machines. Intern. Congr. of Math., Abstracts, Section 13, Moscow, 1966.(Russian).
2. Seiferas, J. I., Fischer, M. J. and Meyer, A. R., Refinements of the hierarchies of time and tape complexities. 14th Annual Symp. on Switch. and Automata Theory, Iowa City, Iowa, 1973.
3. Ibarra, O. H., A hierarchy theorem for polynomial-spase recognition. SIAM J. Comput., 3 (1974) 184-187.
4. Ibarra, O. H. and Sahni, S. K., Hierarchies of Turing machines with restricted tape alphabet size. J. Comp. and Syst. Sci., 11 (1975) 56-67.
5. Rabin, M. O., Real time computation. Israel J. Math., 1 (1963) 203-211.
6. Freivald, R. V., Complexity of palindrome recognition by Turing machines with input. Algebra and Logic, 4 (1965) 47-58 (Russian).
7. Valiev, M. K., On time complexity of Turing machines with restrictions on tape alphabet. V All-Union Symp. on Cybernetics, Tbilisi, 1970 (Russian).

THE BODNARCHUK METRIC SPACE OF LANGUAGES AND THE TOPOLOGY OF THE LEARNING SPACE

Victor Vianu
Faculty of Mathematics, University of Bucharest
Str. Academiei 14, 70109 Bucharest, Romania

1. Introduction

The paper presents some topological properties of the Bodnarchuk metric space of languages [1] and points out a link that exists between this topological space and the learning space [5] . This work was done under the guidance of Prof. Solomon Marcus.

2. Basic concepts and notations.

If A is a set, A^c denotes its complement . Let I be a finite nonvoid set called an alphabet. We denote by I^* the free monoid generated by I. The elements of I^* are called words; a subset of I^* is a language; e is the void word. If $p \in I^*$ we denote by $\lambda(p)$ the length of the word p. In [1], V.Bodnarchuk organizes $\mathcal{P}(I^*)$ as a normed linear space over the field $\{0,1\} = K_2$ as follows: for any $E,F \in \mathcal{P}(I^*)$, $E+F = E \vartriangle F = (E \cup F) - (E \cap F)$; $0 \cdot E = \Phi$, $1 \cdot E = E$. The norm is defined by $\|E\| = 2^{-\lambda(E)}$ where $\lambda(E) = \min\{\lambda(p) \mid p \in E\}$ ($\|\Phi\| = 0$). The Bodnarchuk distance on $\mathcal{P}(I^*)$ is naturaly defined by $\rho(E_1,E_2) = \|E_1 - E_2\|$ for any $E_1,E_2 \in \mathcal{P}(I^*)$. Thus, $\mathcal{P}(I^*)$ is shown to become a complete metric space.

In [5] a theory of learnability is presented. The objects to be learned are assumed to be mappings of N into N. The set of these mappings is denoted by F. The set of datum, D, consists of all finite subsets d of $N \times N$ such that if $(x,x') \in d$ and $(x,x'') \in d$ then $x' = x''$. The set $\{f \mid f \in F, d \subset f\}$ is denoted by $\pi(d)$. F is endowed with the topology which has the base of open sets $\{\pi(d)\}_{d \in D} \cup \{\Phi\}$. This topological space is shown to be metrisable. The subset C of F consisting of all mappings of N into $\{1,2\}$ is compact. It is also shown that for any subspace S of F there exists a homomorphism $\gamma_S : S \longrightarrow \gamma_S(S) \subset C$, i.e. any subspace of F is homomorphic with a subspace of C [6].

3. Some topological properties of the Bodnarchuk metric space.

Lemma 1. $\mathcal{D} \subset \mathcal{P}(I^*)$ is open in the topology induced by the Bodnarchuk distance iff for any $E \in \mathcal{D}$ there exists an $m_E \in N$ such that for all $F \in \mathcal{P}(I^*)$, $\lambda(E \triangle F) \geqslant m_E$ implies that $F \in \mathcal{D}$.

Proof. This is a consequence of the fact that $B(E,\varepsilon) = \{F \mid F \in \mathcal{P}(I^*), \|E - F\| \leqslant 1/2^{m_E}\} = \{F \mid F \in \mathcal{P}(I^*), \lambda(E \triangle F) \geqslant m_E\}$ where $m_E = \min\{n \mid n \in N, 1/2^n < \varepsilon\}$.

We denote by $\mathcal{D}_k$ the set $\{E \mid E \in \mathcal{P}(I^*), \lambda(E) = k\}$, for all $k \in \overline{N}$. ($\mathcal{D}_\infty = \{\Phi\}$).

Proposition 1. $\mathcal{D}_k$ is simultaneously closed and open for all $k \in N$.

Proof. Let us show first that $\mathcal{D}_k$ is open. Consider $E \in \mathcal{D}_k$; then $B(E,1/2^k) \subset \mathcal{D}_k$. Indeed, let $F \in B(E,1/2^k)$, i.e. $\lambda(E \triangle F) > k = \lambda(E)$. Let $p \in E$ such that $\lambda(p) = \lambda(E)$. Clearly $p \notin E \triangle F$ so $p \in E \cap F$ and $\lambda(F) \leqslant \lambda(p) = \lambda(E)$. Let $q \in F$ with $\lambda(q) = \lambda(F)$. If $q \in F - E$ then $\lambda(E \triangle F) \leqslant \lambda(q) \leqslant \lambda(E)$ which is false. It follows that $q \in F \cap E$, $\lambda(q) \geqslant \lambda(E)$ and so $\lambda(F) \geqslant \lambda(E)$. The double inequality implies that $\lambda(F) = \lambda(E) = k$ and $F \in \mathcal{D}_k$. Thus $\mathcal{D}_k$ is open. We will show that $\mathcal{D}_k$ is closed by proving that $\mathcal{D}_k^c$ is open. Let $L \neq \Phi$, $L \in \mathcal{D}_k^c$. Then $B(L,1/2^{\lambda(L)}) \subset \mathcal{D}_{\lambda(L)} \subset \mathcal{D}_k^c$. For the case when $L = \Phi$, $B(\Phi,1/2k) \subset \mathcal{D}_k^c$, since $E \in B(\Phi,1/2^k)$ implies that $\lambda(E) > k$ and so $E \in \mathcal{D}_k^c$.

Remark 1. a) From Proposition 1 it follows that $\mathcal{P}(I^*)$ is nonconnected. b) $\mathcal{D}_\infty$ is closed but not open.

Let $E \in \mathcal{P}(I^*)$. We denote $E_k = \{p \mid p \in E, \lambda(p) \leqslant k\}$.

Theorem 1. For any $E \in \mathcal{P}(I^*)$, $B(E,1/2^k) = \{E_k \cup F \mid F \in \bigcup_{n>k} \mathcal{D}_n\}$.

Proof. Let us denote by $\mathcal{S}$ the set $\{E_k \cup F \mid F \in \bigcup_{n>k} \mathcal{D}_n\}$. Let $H \in B(E,1/2^k)$; $\lambda(E \triangle H) > k$ so clearly $E_k \subset E \cap H$; H may be written as $E_k \cup (H - E_k)$. We will show that $\lambda(H - E_k) > k$, i.e. $H - E_k \in \bigcup_{n>k} \mathcal{D}_n$. Let $p \in H - E_k$; if $p \in E$ then $\lambda(p) > k$; if $p \in H - E$ then $\lambda(p) > k$ for otherwise $\lambda(E \triangle H) \leq \lambda(p) \leq k$ which is false. So for all $p \in H - E_k$, $\lambda(p) > k$ and so $\lambda(H - E_k) > k$. It follows that $H \in \mathcal{S}$. Conversely, let $H \in \mathcal{S}$, $H = E_k \cup F$ with $\lambda(F) > k$. Let $p \in E \triangle H$; if $p \in E - H$ then $p \in E - E_k$ so $\lambda(p) > k$; if $p \in H - E$ then $p \in F$ so $\lambda(p) > k$. Consequently, $\lambda(E \triangle H) > k$ so $H \in B(E, 1/2^k)$. The equality is proved.

Proposition 2. For any $k \in N$, $B(\Phi, 1/2^k)$ is a subgroup of the group $(\mathcal{P}(I^*), +)$ and for any $L \in \mathcal{P}(I^*)$, $B(L, 1/2^k) = \hat{L}$ (the class of L modulo $B(\Phi, 1/2^k)$).

Proof. It is clear that $B(\Phi, 1/2^k)$ is a subgroup of $\mathcal{P}(I^*)$, as $\lambda(E) > k$ and $\lambda(F) > k$ imply that $\lambda(E \triangle F) > k$. The fact that $B(L, 1/2^k)$ coincides with the class of L modulo $B(\Phi, 1/2^k)$ follows from the fact that $B(L, 1/2^k) = L + B(\Phi, 1/2^k)$.

We denote $P(k) = \{ B(L, 1/2^k) \mid L \in \mathcal{P}(I^*) \}$. Let m be the number of elements of I.

Proposition 3. $P(k)$ is a finite partition of $\mathcal{P}(I^*)$ consisting of $2^{(1+m+\ldots+m^k)}$ distinct balls. If $n > k$ then $P(n)$ is finer than $P(k)$.

Proof. $P(k)$ is the partition generated by the following equivalence relation: for all $E, F \in \mathcal{P}(I^*)$, $E \sim F$ iff $E - F \in B(\Phi, 1/2^k)$ which amounts to $\lambda(E \triangle F) > k$ or $E_k = F_k$. Therefore the number of classes in the partition is equal to the cardinality of $\mathcal{P}(I_k^*)$, i.e. $2^{(1+m+\ldots+m^k)}$. The fact that $P(n)$ is finer then $P(k)$ if $n > k$ follows from the fact that $B(\Phi, 1/2^n)$ is a subgroup of $B(\Phi, 1/2^k)$.

Corollary 1. a) Any ball is open and closed simultaneously.

b) Two balls are either disjoint or one of them contains the other.

Remark 2. It follows from Proposition 2 that for any $E, F \in \mathcal{P}(I^*)$ such that $E_k = F_k$, i.e. $\hat{E} = \hat{F}$ modulo $B(\Phi, 1/2^k)$, $B(E, 1/2^k) = B(F, 1/2^k)$. This provides an example of an infinity of balls with the same radius and different centres, which coincide.

Proposition 4. $\mathcal{P}(I^*)$ is compact.

Proof. $(\mathcal{P}(I^*),\rho)$ is a complete metric space, so showing that it is precompact will do. Consider $\varepsilon > 0$, $n = \min\{m \mid m \in N, 1/2^m \leq \varepsilon\}$. The family $\mathcal{P} = \mathcal{P}(\{p \mid p \in I^*, \lambda(p) \leq n\})$ is finite and $\mathcal{P}(I^*) \subset \bigcup_{L\in\mathcal{P}} B(L,1/2^n)$. Indeed, if $L \in \mathcal{P}(I^*)$, maintaining the notations of Theorem 1, $L_n \in \mathcal{P}$ and $L \in B(L_n,1/2^n)$. So

$$\mathcal{P}(I^*) \subset \bigcup_{L\in\mathcal{P}} B(L,1/2^n) \subset \bigcup_{L\in\mathcal{P}} B(L,\varepsilon) \subset \mathcal{P}(I^*)$$

so $\mathcal{P}(I^*) = \bigcup_{L\in\mathcal{P}} B(L,\varepsilon)$.

Proposition 5. The metric space $\mathcal{P}(I^*)$ is separable.

Proof. Let us denote by $\mathcal{A}$ the set $\bigcup_{k\in N} \mathcal{P}(I_k^*)$ where $I_k^* = \{p \mid p \in I^*, \lambda(p) \leq k\}$. $\mathcal{A}$ consists of all finite languages and is clearly numerable. Let $E \in \mathcal{P}(I^*)$; $E_k \in \mathcal{A}$ and $\lambda(E \triangle E_k) > k$ so $\| E - E_k \| < 1/2^k$ for any $k \in N$. It follows easily that $\bar{\mathcal{A}} = \mathcal{P}(I^*)$.

Corollary 2. The topology τ induced by ρ has a numerable base of open sets.

4. The link with the topology of the learning space.

If $L', L'' \in \mathcal{P}(I^*)$ we denote by $D(L',L'')$ the family of languages $\{L \mid L \in \mathcal{P}(I^*), L' \subset L^c, L'' \subset L\}$. Taking into account the fact that I^* is numerable, the function $L \longrightarrow C_L(x) = \begin{cases} 1 & x \notin L \\ 2 & x \in L \end{cases}$ is a homomorphism of the subspace C of F and $\mathcal{P}(I^*)$, provided that $\mathcal{P}(I^*)$ is endowed with the right topology, as shown by Aizawa,..[6]. It is easily seen that this topology, which we denote by τ_1, has the base of open sets $\{D(L',L'') \mid L',L'' \in \mathcal{P}(I^*), L' \text{ and } L'' \text{ finite}\}$. We seek the relationship between the topologies τ_1 and τ on $\mathcal{P}(I^*)$.

Theorem 2. $\tau = \tau_1$.

Proof. We will prove the equality by double inclusion.a) $\tau \subset \tau_1$. It is enough to show that $B(L,\varepsilon) \in \tau_1$ for all $L \in \mathcal{P}(I^*)$ and $\varepsilon > 0$. $B(L,\varepsilon) = B(L,1/2^n)$ where $n = \max\{m \mid m \in N, 1/2^m \geq \varepsilon\}$. According to Theorem 1, $B(L,1/2^n) = \{L_n \cup F \mid F \in \bigcup_{k>n} \mathcal{D}_k\}$. We will show that $\{L_n \cup F \mid F \in \bigcup_{k>n} \mathcal{D}_k\} = D((L^c)_n, L_n)$. Let $E \in B(L,1/2^n)$. $E = L_n \cup F$ with $\lambda(F) > n$. $L_n \subset E$ and $(L^c)_n \cap E = (L^c)_n \cap [L_n \cup F] = [(L^c)_n \cap L_n] \cup [(L^c)_n \cap F] = \Phi \cup \Phi = \Phi$, so

$(L^c)_n \subset E^c$. It follows that $E \in D((L^c)_n, L_n)$. Conversely, let $E \in D((L^c)_n, L_n)$. E may be written as $L_n \cup F$ where $F = E - L_n$. Suppose that $p \in F$ and $\lambda(p) \leq n$. Then $p \in (L^c)_n$ which contradicts the fact that $(L^c)_n \subset E^c$. It follows that $\lambda(F) > n$ and so $E \in B(L, 1/2^n)$.

b) $\tau_1 \subset \tau$. It is sufficient to prove that $D(L', L'') \in \tau$ for all finite languages L' and L''. Let $n = \max\{\lambda(p) | p \in L' \cup L''\}$ and $L \in D(L', L'')$. We will show that $B(L, 1/2^n) \subset D(L', L'')$. Consider $E \in B(L, 1/2^n)$ which means that $E = L_n \cup F$, $\lambda(F) > n$. $L'' \subset L$ and $\lambda(p) \leq n$ for all $p \in L''$ so $L'' \subset L_n \subset E$. $L' \subset L^c$ so $L' \cap E = L' \cap F = \Phi$ since $\lambda(F) > n \geq \max\{\lambda(p) | p \in L'\}$; consequently $E \in D(L', L'')$. This concludes the proof.

<u>Corollary 3</u>. Each of the topological learning space and the Bodnarchuk metric space is homomorphic with a subspace of the other.

<u>Proof</u>. On one hand, Theorem 2 states that the Bodnarchuk space of languages is homomorphic with the subspace C of F. On the other hand F is homomorphic with a subspace of C (see § 2) and consequently with a subspace of the Bodnarchuk metric space.

<u>Remark 3</u>. Theorem 2 and Corollary 3 provide some different proofs for properties of either of the two spaces. For instance the compacity of either C or the Bodnarchuk space follows from the compacity of the other. Also the separability and metrisability of either F or the Bodnarchuk space is a consequence of the separability and metrisability of the other.

5. <u>The Borelian sets in topologies induced by some metrics</u>.

S.Marcus defines in [4] the concepts of context, distribution, classes of distribution, contextual equivalence, the contextual distance d_o. In [2], C.Calude defines the contextual distance $d_{\chi,L}$ and A.Dinca introduces in [3] the contextual distance d_1 between classes of distribution. The Calude and Dinca distances are refinements of the Marcus distance [4]. We have sought to characterize the Borelian sets in topologies generated by these distances and by the Bodnarchuk distance.

<u>Proposition 6</u>. $\tau \subsetneq \mathcal{B}_\tau \subsetneq \mathcal{P}(\mathcal{P}(I^*))$, where τ is the topology induced

by the Bodnarchuk distance and $\mathcal{B}_{\tau}$ the family of Borelian sets.

Proposition 7. The family of Borelian sets in the topologies induced by the Marcus and Calude distances coincide with $\mathcal{P}(I^*)$.

Proposition 8. The family of Borelian sets in the topologies induced by the Dinca metrics [3] coincide with $\mathcal{P}(I^*/\sim_L)$, where $\sim_L$ denotes the equivalence relation generated by the distribution classes.

References

1. Bodnarchuk, V.G., The metrical space of events. Kibernetika Kiev, 1 (1965) , 24 - 27.

2. Calude, C., Asupra distantelor contextuale in lingvistica matematica (On contextual distances in mathematical linguistics). Studii si cercetari matematice, 1 (1976).

3. Dinca, A., Distante contextuale in lingvistica algebrica (Contextual distances in algebraic linguistics). Studii si cercetari matematice, 2 (1973).

4. Marcus, S., Introduction mathématique à la linguistique structurale. Dunod, Paris, 1967.

5. Yoshinori Uesaka, Teruaki Aizawa, Terumasa Ebara, Kazuhiko Ozeki, A theory of learnability. Kibernetik 13 (1973), 123 - 131.

6. Aizawa, T., Ebara, T., Ozeki, K., Uesaka, Y., Sur l'espace topologique lié à une nouvelle théorie de l'apprentissage. Kibernetik 14 (1974), 141 - 149.

COMPLEXITY HIERARCHIES OF ORACLES

Klaus Wagner and Gerd Wechsung

Section of Mathematics, Friedrich Schiller University
Jena, GDR

It is a well known problem in the theory of computational complexity how the gratis knowledge about a given set can reduce the cost of the computation (decision) of another one. In other words (in terms of Turing machine computation with oracles): how can the complexity of a set A be reduced using an oracle B, or: how can A be „helped" by oracles ?

There are results about sets which do not help a given other one or help totally [4], [1] . Stimulated by a result of CHODSHAJEV [2] an infinite hierarchy of „helping" has been established in [5] . However, there are no general hierarchy results.

To fill up this gap we introduce the space complexity classes SPACE (α,A) of oracles for deciding a fixed set A, and we investigate their structure with respect to set inclusion. Our main result is the following: For any two complexity classes SPACE (α,A) and SPACE (β,A) with SPACE $(\alpha,A) \subset$ SPACE (β,A) and appropriately chosen α and β, arbitrary countable partially ordered sets can be imbedded order-isomorphically into the structure of complexity classes between SPACE (α,A) and SPACE (β,A).

For time complexity classes we could not prove such a strong result and therefore we omit all time results herein.

Definitions

Our Turing machines with oracles have a single working tape and a one-way oracle tape. At the beginning of the computation and after any question given to the oracle, the oracle tape is empty.

Let $S^B_{\mathfrak{M}}(w)$ be the maximum of space used on both tapes of the Turing machine $\mathfrak{M}$ with oracle B during its computation on the input string $w \in \Sigma^*$ (where Σ is a finite alphabet), and further $S^B_{\mathfrak{M}}(n) =_{df} \max_{|w|=n} S^B_{\mathfrak{M}}(w)$.

For any functions f,g: $N \longmapsto N$ we define

$$f \leq g \iff_{df} \forall n\,(f(n) \leq g(n))\ ,$$

$$f \stackrel{\leq}{\ast} g \iff_{df} \underline{\lim}_{n\to\infty} \frac{g(n)}{f(n)} > 0\ ,$$

$$f \prec g \iff_{df} f \preccurlyeq g \text{ and not } g \preccurlyeq f\ ,$$

$$f \asymp g \iff_{df} f \preccurlyeq g \text{ and } g \preccurlyeq f\ .$$

Let A,B be subsets of Σ^* and f: $N \longmapsto N$. Then we define

$$\text{comp}^{space,B}(A) \leq f \iff_{df} \exists \mathfrak{M}(\mathfrak{M} \text{ decides A with oracle B and } S^B_{\mathfrak{M}} \leq f),$$

$$\text{comp}^{space,B}(A) \geq f \iff_{df} \forall \mathfrak{M}(\mathfrak{M} \text{ decides A with oracle B} \rightarrow S^B_{\mathfrak{M}} \geq f),$$

$$\text{comp}^{space,B}(A) \preccurlyeq f \iff_{df} \exists \mathfrak{M}(\mathfrak{M} \text{ decides A with oracle B and } S^B_{\mathfrak{M}} \preccurlyeq f),$$

$$\text{comp}^{space,B}(A) \succcurlyeq f \iff_{df} \forall \mathfrak{M}(\mathfrak{M} \text{ decides A with oracle B} \rightarrow S^B_{\mathfrak{M}} \succcurlyeq f),$$

$$\text{comp}^{space,B}(A) \asymp f \iff_{df} \text{comp}^{space,B}(A) \preccurlyeq f \text{ and comp}^{space,B}(A) \succcurlyeq f\ .$$

Instead of $\text{comp}^{space,\emptyset}(A)$ we use $\text{comp}^{space}(A)$.

The oracle complexity class for a fixed set A with the resource function f is defined as follows

$$\text{SPACE}(f,A) =_{df} \{B,\ \text{comp}^{space,B}(A) \leq f\}\ .$$

It is evident that SPACE(id,A) is the smallest and SPACE(f,A) is the largest of these classes for a fixed set A with

$\text{comp}^{space}(A) \asymp f$ (id denotes the identity function).

In this paper the structure of the class

$$H^{space}_A =_{df} \{\text{SPACE}(f,A),\ f: N \longmapsto N\}$$

with respect to set inclusion is of interest.

By b(n) we denote the binary notation of the natural number n .

A function f: $N \longmapsto N$ is said to be space constructable iff the computation $b(n) \longrightarrow b(f(n))$ can be made by an one-tape Turing machine within space f(n) in the case $f \geq id$, and within space n in the case $f \leq id$.

For any increasing function $\alpha : N \longmapsto N$ let $\alpha^{-1} : N \longmapsto N$, $\bar{\alpha} : N \longmapsto N$ and $\alpha : \Sigma^* \longmapsto \Sigma^*$ be functions with

$$\alpha^{-1}(n) =_{df} \curlyvee k\ (\ \alpha(k) \leq n\ )\ ,$$

$$\bar{\alpha}(n) =_{df} \mu k\ (k \cdot \alpha(k) \geq n) \quad \text{and}$$

$$\alpha(w) =_{df} \begin{cases} \text{the initial part of } w \text{ of the length } \alpha(|w|), \text{if } \alpha(|w|) \leq |w| \\ w, \quad \text{otherwise} \end{cases}$$

where $\curlyvee$ means „the greatest" and μ means „the least" .

Note that 1. $\alpha(\alpha^{-1}(n)) \leq n < \alpha(\alpha^{-1}(n) + 1)$,

2. $\alpha^{-1}(\alpha(n)) = n$ for strictly monotonic α and

3. $\bar{\alpha}(n \cdot \alpha(n)) \leq n$.

4. α^{-1} is increasing, if α is increasing and unbounded

In what follows the set $A_\alpha =_{df} \{w\ ,\ \alpha^{-1}(w) \in A\}$ will play an important role.

Results

In order to prove good hierarchy results for a given set A one has to estimate as precisely as possible the complexities $comp^{space,B}(A)$ for a large set of B's. This will be done with the sets A_α defined above.

Lemma 1 Let α, f, h : $N \longmapsto N$ be recursive functions with

a) $f(n) \leq comp^{space}(A) \preccurlyeq h(n)$,

b) $n \preccurlyeq \alpha(n) \leq h(n-1)$

c) h strictly monotonic and α increasing, and

d) α , α^{-1} space constructable.

Then

$$\alpha(h^{-1}(f(n))) \preccurlyeq comp^{space,A_\alpha}(A) \leq \alpha(n)\ .$$

Throughout the rest of this paper we regard only sets A with an „exact tape complexity" , i.e sets A with $comp^{space}(A) \asymp f$ for a suitable function f.

Let F_f be the set of functions $\alpha : N \longmapsto N$ with

a) $n \preccurlyeq \alpha(n) \leq f(n-1)$,

b) α increasing and

c) α , α^{-1} space-constructable.

Then we have as an immediate consequence of lemma 1

Corollary 1 Let A be a recursive set with $comp^{space}(A) \asymp f$ for a recursive strictly monotonic function f.

Then for any functions $\alpha \in F_f$ and β with $n \preccurlyeq \beta(n) \prec \alpha(n)$,

$$SPACE(\beta,A) \subset SPACE(\alpha, A).$$

Now the next lemma is not hard to prove.

Lemma 2 Let A be a recursive set with $comp^{space}(A) \asymp f$ for a recursive strictly monotonic function f.

If the functions $\alpha, \beta \in F_f$ are incomparable with respect to $\preccurlyeq$ then $SPACE(\alpha,A)$ and $SPACE(\beta,A)$ are incomparable with respect to set inclusion.

Corollary 2 Let A be a recursive set with $comp^{space}(A) \asymp f$ for a recursive strictly monotonic function f.
Then the mapping $\alpha \longrightarrow SPACE(\alpha,A)$ is an order-isomorphism from $[F_f, \preccurlyeq]$ into $[H_A^{space}, \subseteq]$.

Originally we are interested in the structure of $[H_A^{space}, \subseteq]$, and by corollary 2 structural properties of $[F_f, \preccurlyeq]$ can be transferred to $[H_A^{space}, \subseteq]$.

As mentioned by H.Enderton [3], arbitrary countable partially ordered sets are order- isomorphically imbeddable in the partially ordered set $[\{N_{k,e}; k,e \in N\}, \subseteq]$ with $N_{k,e} =_{df} k \cdot N+e$.
Using this fact one can prove.

Lemma 3 Let $\alpha, \alpha\cdot\gamma$ be in F_f ($(\alpha\cdot\gamma)(n) = \alpha(n)\cdot\gamma(n)$) with increasing, unbounded and space constructable $\gamma \leq id$. Then arbitrary countable partially ordered sets can be order-isomorphically imbedded between α and $\alpha\cdot\gamma$ in $[F_f, \preccurlyeq]$.

By Lemma 3 and Corollary 2 we get directly

<u>Theorem</u> Let A be a recursive set with $comp^{space}(A) \asymp f$ for a recursive strictly monotonic function f.
Let further α, $\alpha \cdot \gamma$ be in F_f with increasing, unbounded and space constructable $\gamma \leq id$.

Then arbitrary countable partially ordered sets can be order-isomorphically imbedded between SPACE (α,A) and SPACE ($\alpha \cdot \gamma$,A) in $[H_A^{space}, \subseteq]$.

Conclusion

The above result about the structure of space complexity classes of oracles for deciding a given set A can be considered only as a first step in this direction. Further investigations in this structure as well as in the corresponding structures for other complexity measures are desirable. The following questions are of special interest.

1. Can this space hierarchy be refined at least for natural sets A? Note that general linear speed-up for oracle computations is not known.
2. Can similar hierarchy results be proved for other complexity measures ?
3. Are there arbitrarily complex sets in any stage of these hierarchies ? From investigations of LYNCH /MEYER /FISCHER [4] follows that arbitrarily complex sets occur on very high levels of these hierarchies. What can be said especially about the highest stage of these hierarchies ?
4. Can question 3 for natural A's be answered by natural B's ?

References

1. Chodshajev,D. On the complexity of computation on Turing machines with oracle (russian), <u>Voprosij Kibernetiki i vijchislitjelnoi matematiki</u>, <u>12</u> (1967), 69-76 Tashkent.

2. Chodshajev,D. Independent predicates and relative computations of the predicate of symmetry (russian), <u>Voprosij Kibernetiki i vijchislitjelnoi matematiki</u>, <u>33</u> (1969), Tashkent.

3. Enderton,H. Degrees of computational complexity. <u>JCSS 6</u> (1972) 389-396.

4. Lynch,N.A., Meyer,A.R., Fischer,M.J., Relativization of the theory of computational complexity, MIT Project MAC TR - 99, 1972.

5. Mäurer,E., Ein Vergleich zwischen Orakelmengen zur Entscheidung einer festen Menge, Diploma thesis,University of Jena, 1976.

DETERMINING PROCESSES BY VIOLATIONS

Horst Wedde
Gesellschaft fur Mathematik und Datenverarbeitung
Postfach 1240-D-5205 St. Augustin 1 - FRG

Józef Winkowski
Instytut Podstaw Informatyki PAN
00-901 Warszawa, PKiN, P.O.Box 22 - Poland

0. Introduction

In [3] C.A. Petri has introduced the enlogic structure as a very general concept for the specification of system behaviour. Starting with subsets of conditions for a system which may be valid at some time and not valid at some other times he defines a set C of cases (maximal sets of simultaneously holding conditions) and its complement N as the set of non-cases. Given any pair of condition subsets he tests whether or not it is the pair of "differences" of two cases (CC), of a case and non-case (CN) etc., so introducing predicates for transitional forms. It was shown then (see [1]) that one class of transitional forms which are not events (namely facts) have an outstanding importance for the specification of system behaviour. We try to make use here of the class CN, namely of those changes which lead from cases to undesirable situations. These changes which are the basic terms in penal legislation are there called violations. In terms of the enlogic structure they are impure because it depends on some side-conditions whether or not a change is a violation (and so has to be punished).

Although Petri restricts the use of the name to those changes which are violations under any circumstances we feel that it will not lead to a great confusion if we extend it for the purpose of this paper to changes which depend on side-conditions.

In the sequel it will turn out that violations can be understood as a natural basis for the model of Loosely Coupled Systems (LCS) which was introduced in [2] as a convenient tool to describe and to generate control mechanisms by only using mutual exclusion of states. On our way to use it as an independent programming concept we are now closer to the event-oriented character of conventional programming languages. Furthermore we are especially involved in defining an algorithmic method to describe explicitly the processes which can run in an LCS and which are essentially event sequences which "avoid violations". We define these processes in an algebraic way using the general approach in [4] and so succeed to study and handle them in a convenient way.

1. Violations as a Basis for Loosely Coupled Systems

Like in [2] we start to define parts as representations for system components or production units. We are not interested in an independent description of their inner behaviour, and so we identify the parts with the sets of their possible phases (states, sections of activity). (We assume that every part has at least two phases.) So we have the sets B of parts and P of phases such that:

$$\forall_{b \in B}\ b \subseteq P\ ; \quad \forall_{b_1, b_2 \in B}\ (b_1 \neq b_2 \Longrightarrow b_1 \cap b_2 = \emptyset)\ .$$

If k_1 and k_2 are two phase subsets with $|k_i \cap b| \leq 1$ for $b \in B$; $i = 1,2$, the pair (k_1, k_2) is called an elementary change iff $|k_1 \setminus k_2| = |k_2 \setminus k_1| = 1$. The phases from $k_1 \cap k_2$ (which remains constant under this change) are called side-conditions of (k_1, k_2). For the matter of convenience we shall use the following notation:

Let $p_1 := k_1 \setminus k_2$; $p_2 := k_2 \setminus k_1$; $\{q_1, \ldots, q_k\} := k_1 \cap k_2$. Then we shall write:

$$p_1 \longrightarrow p_2\ |\{q_1, \ldots, q_k\}\ .$$

Now look at two parts b_1 and b_2, as given in fig.1.

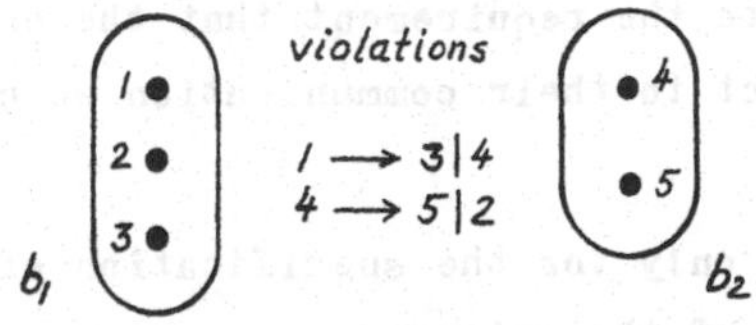

Figure 1

Let us think that two processes pr1 and pr2 in b_1 and b_2, resp. interact such that pr1 must not enter section 3 if it is in section 1 as long as pr2 is in section 4. (So pr1 may enter section 2 meanwhile.) In the same manner pr2 must not enter section 5 as long as pr1 is in section 2.

So we have that $1 \longrightarrow 3|4$ and $4 \longrightarrow 5|2$ are violations. For the following we shall restrict ourselves to this type of elementary violations, namely:

Axiom 1: Violations used for specification of phase transitions are elementary and have exactly one side-condition.

(It can be shown (see [2]) that this restriction is not essential with respect to the formal power of our approach.)

As we understand violations as changes which lead to undesirable situations we are rather interested to avoid consequences of violations than the violations themselves. So we have:

Axiom 2: If $p_1 \longrightarrow p_2 | q$ is a violation; $p_1, p_2 \in b$ and if $p_3 \in b \setminus \{p_1, p_2\}$ then $p_3 \longrightarrow p_2 | q$ is also a violation.

Looking at our example above we have that $2 \longrightarrow 3 | 4$ is an induced violation.*
If the parts b_1 and b_2 are for instance computers in a large network it is not possible for many purposes to govern all processes in b_1 and b_2 by a common supervisor. Indeed, our approach should be general enough also to cover such fields of application, and so we want to understand the interaction between b_1 and b_2 as a kind of formal communication between two partners which are equal in rights. But this gives each of them a certain responsibility for its own activities. When in our example process 2 goes to section 4 it prevents process 1 from going to section 3 as long as it remains in this section. Now it is fair to assume that process 1 is allowed to go to section 3 and to remain there as long as this is not forbidden by actions of process 2. So, if we want that process 1 can rely on this we should say that it is the responsibility of process 2 not to go to section 4 as long as process 1 is in section 3.

More generally spoken, we claim as

Axiom 3: If $p_1, p_2 \in b$; $q \in b'$ and $p_1 \longrightarrow p_2 | q$ is a violation then $q' \longrightarrow q | p_2$ is a violation for every $q' \in b'$.

So, as a formal counterpart to the requirement that the partners b_1 and b_2 have equal rights with respect to their communication we have a "symmetry in violations".

As we want to use violations only for the specification of the behaviour we can easily see, as a consequence of the axioms:

Proposition: Let $b_1, b_2 \in B$. If $p_1, p_2 \in b_1$, $q \in b_2$ then: $p_1 \longrightarrow p_2 | q$ is a violation iff p_2 and q exclude one another.

---

* To emphasize how close the specification above is to the style of program statements we could write for short:

```
pr1: IF phase 4 THEN DO NOT GO TO phase 3 ELSE next step
pr2: IF phase 2 THEN DO NOT GO TO phase 5 ELSE next step
```

So the mutual exclusion relation $K\langle b_1 b_2\rangle \subseteq b_1 \times b_2$ is a shorthand description for the violation structure, it is called a <u>coupling relation</u>, and we have:

$$K\langle b_1 b_2\rangle = K\langle b_2 b_1\rangle^{-1} \quad (K\langle b_1 b_2\rangle \text{ is drawn in fig.2.})$$

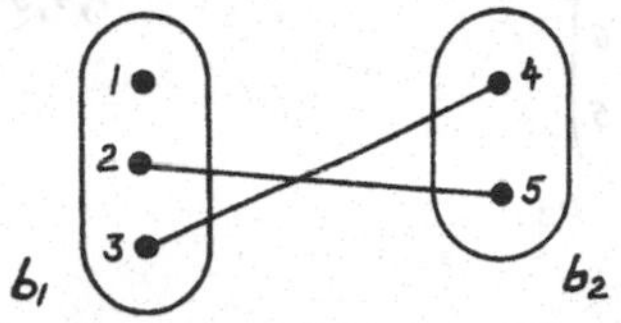

Figure 2

As in [2] we define for the matter of convenience:

$$K\langle bb\rangle := (b \times b) \setminus id\langle b\rangle \;;\quad K := \bigcup_{b_1, b_2 \in B} K\langle b_1 b_2\rangle \;.$$

By means of violations we easily come to a formal concept of undesirable situations, namely:

<u>Definition:</u> $mc \subseteq P$ is a <u>miscase</u> $:\Longleftrightarrow$ 1) $\forall_{b \in B}\ |mc \cap b| = 1$
2) mc is the result of an elementary violation .

We derive at once from our axioms that:

<u>Proposition:</u> $mc \subseteq P$ is a miscase $\Longleftrightarrow$ 1) $\forall_{b \in B}\ |mc \cap b| = 1$
2) $\exists_{p_1, p_2 \in mc}\ (p_1, p_2) \in K$.

<u>Definition:</u> $c \subseteq P$ is a <u>case</u> $:\Longleftrightarrow$ 1) $\forall_{b \in B}\ |c \cap b| = 1$
2) c is not a miscase .

2) means that for any $p_1, p_2 \in c$ we have $(p_1, p_2) \notin K$.

Let C be the set of cases. We shall give the notion of an elementary event as <u>complementary</u> to that of a violation:

<u>Definition:</u> Let $c \in C$; $p_1, p_2 \in b$; $p_1 \in c$. $p_1 \longrightarrow p_2$ is called an <u>elementary event</u> <u>in c</u> $:\Longleftrightarrow \forall_{p_0 \in c \setminus \{p_1\}}$ $p_1 \longrightarrow p_2 | p_0$ is not a violation .

While the violations which we use depend only on one side-condition the elementary events depend on n-1 if n is the number of parts. As a consequence of the definition we have the

<u>Proposition:</u> $p_1 \longrightarrow p_2$ is an elementary event iff $c \setminus \{p_1\} \cup \{p_2\} \in C$.

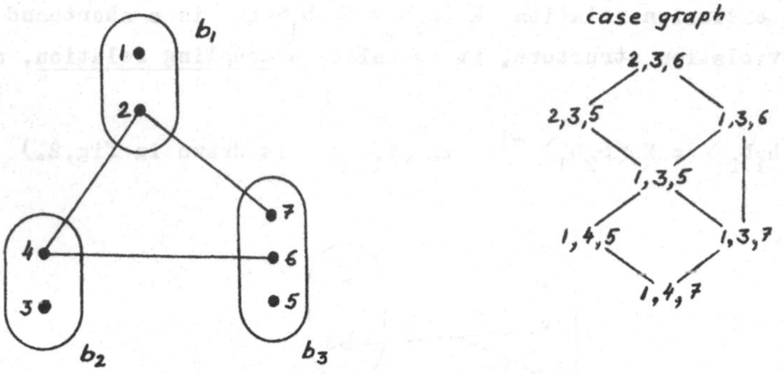

Figure 3

In fig.3 we have drawn the case graph the edges of which represent elementary events.

A loosely coupled system is now a quadruple (P,B,C,K) just as known from [2], but the general system-theoretical approach using violations led to a more natural understanding of coupling edges and especially for elementary events. We mention here that the definition of concurrency (see [2]) is also elementary in terms of violations: Two events $p_1 \longrightarrow q_1$ and $p_2 \longrightarrow q_2$ in c are concurrent iff $(q_1,q_2) \notin K$. At the same time this corresponds to the normal understanding of "commutativity" of $p_1 \longrightarrow q_1$ and $p_2 \longrightarrow q_2$: Look in fig.3 at the events $3 \rightarrow 4$ and $5 \rightarrow 7$ in $\{1,3,5\}$.

Morphisms are often made use of for finding a more "suitable" system where solutions for the adjoint problem can be found easier as in the original system. The preserving properties of the morphism often admit to "lift" the solution up to the original system. As LCS are based on violations we are of course interested in morphisms which may preserve violations (and so considerably change the event structure in general). We have by

Definition: Let (P,B,C,K) and (P′,B′,C′,K′) be LCS; $f : P \longrightarrow P'$.
f is an allomorphism iff it preserves parts, and if mc is a miscase, every feasible extension of f(mc) is a miscase.

So every mapping which preserves coupling edges (and parts) is an allomorphism. If one couples a new part to a given LCS the inclusion map is an allomorphism, and so all generating mechanisms for the restrictions found in [2] are allomorphic extensions of the given system. Merging the phases 6 and 7 in fig.3 leads to the allomorphic image shown in fig.4.

In the second part of the paper we want to show a mechanism by which the processes running in a system are generated in an explicit and computable way. This is of special interest because the description of systems in terms of coupling relations is often very short (see [2]) but the events (and so the processes) are given only in an implicit manner.

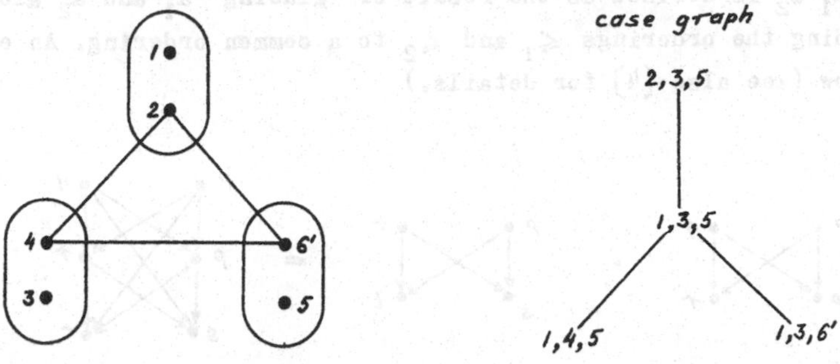

Figure 4

2. Processes in Loosely Coupled Systems

The behaviour of loosely coupled systems can be described by characterizing the classes of processes generated by such systems. For this purpose we first introduce a formal process notion and certain operations on processes. Processes will be represented by labelled partially ordered sets (l.p.o. sets) which are triples $(X, \leqslant, l)$ consisting of a partially ordered set $(X, \leqslant)$ and of a mapping $l : X \longrightarrow L$ (a labelling) such that:

$$l(x) = l(y) \Longleftrightarrow x \leqslant y \text{ or } y \leqslant x .$$

Two l.p.o. sets $s = (X, \leqslant, l)$ and $s' = (X', \leqslant', l')$ are said to be isomorphic iff there is a bijection $f : X \longrightarrow X'$ such that:

$$x \leqslant y \Longleftrightarrow f(x) \leqslant' f(y)$$
$$l(x) = l'(f(x)) .$$

The class of the l.p.o. sets which are isomorphic with an l.p.o. set s is denoted by $[s]$.

Definition: By a process we mean a class of isomorphic labelled partially ordered sets.

Two processes a_1 and a_2 can be composed sequentially into a process $a_1 \cdot a_2$ provided they can be represented as $a_1 = [(X_1, \leqslant_1, l_1)]$ and $a_2 = [(X_2, \leqslant_2, l_2)]$ where:

1) $X_0 = X_1 \cap X_2$ is the set of maximal elements of $(X_1, \leqslant_1)$,
2) X_0 is the set of minimal elements of $(X_2, \leqslant_2)$,

3) every element of X_1 has an upper bound in X_0,
4) every element of X_2 has a lower bound in X_0,
5) $l_1(x) = l_2(x)$ for all $x \in X_0$.

The process $a_1 \cdot a_2$ is defined as the result of "glueing" a_1 and a_2 along X_0, and extending the orderings $\leqslant_1$ and $\leqslant_2$ to a common ordering. An example is given below (see also [4] for details.)

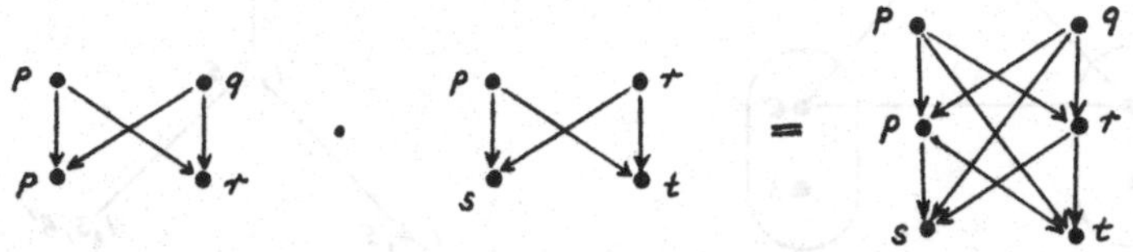

Two processes a_1 and a_2 can be composed <u>in parallel</u> into a process $a_1 \times a_2$ provided the sets of their labels are disjoint. The result $a_1 \times a_2$ is defined as a process composed of two independent parts corresponding to a_1 and a_2. An example is given below.

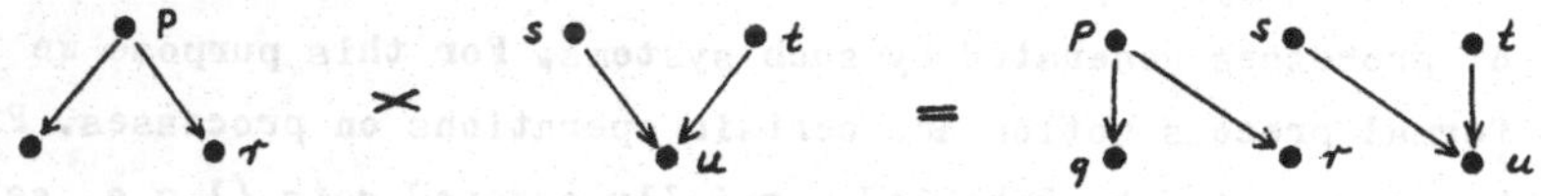

For every loosely coupled system S we shall define a class Beh(S) of processes to be the least class such that:

<u>Axiom 1</u>: The empty process $[(\emptyset,\emptyset,\emptyset)]$ belongs to Beh(S).

<u>Axiom 2</u>: If p is a phase belonging to a case then the one-element process with the label p belongs to Beh(S).

<u>Axiom 3</u>: If an elementary change $p \longrightarrow q \mid \{p_1,\dots,p_n\}$ is an elementary event and the coupling edges from p and q lead exactly to those parts which have phases in $\{p,q,p_1,\dots,p_n\}$ then the following process belongs to Beh(S):

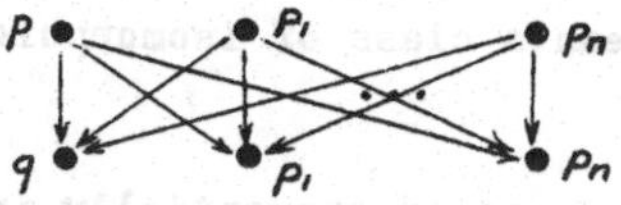

<u>Axiom 4</u>: Every process $[(X,\leqslant,l)]$ which is a parallel or sequential composition of processes from Beh(S) belongs to Beh(S) provided there exists a set r of phases such that $l(Y) \cup r$ is a case for every maximal antichain Y of $(X,\leqslant)$. (By an antichain we mean a set of incomparable elements.)

The processes mentioned in axioms 2 and 3 are said to be <u>elementary</u>. Axiom 4 leads to slight restrictions of the operations of sequential and parallel compositions due to the fact that the conditions in LCS (phases) are not "free" as parts of system situations.

Examples of elementary processes of the system S shown in fig.3 are given in fig.5. Combining these processes according to axiom 4 as follows

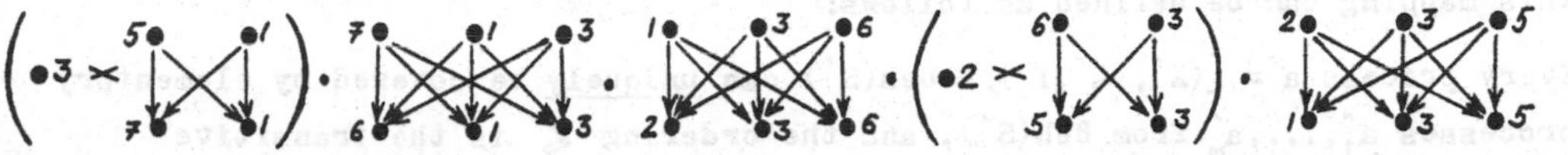

we obtain the process shown in fig.6 which also belongs to Beh(S). This process contains the following transitions of the case graph (see fig.3)

1,3,5——1,3,7——1,3,6——2,3,6——2,3,5——1,3,5

The consecutive cases correspond to the consecutive maximal antichains of the process. For the system S′ shown in fig.4 we have (among others) the elementary processes shown in fig.7 and composing them we get the process shown in fig.8.

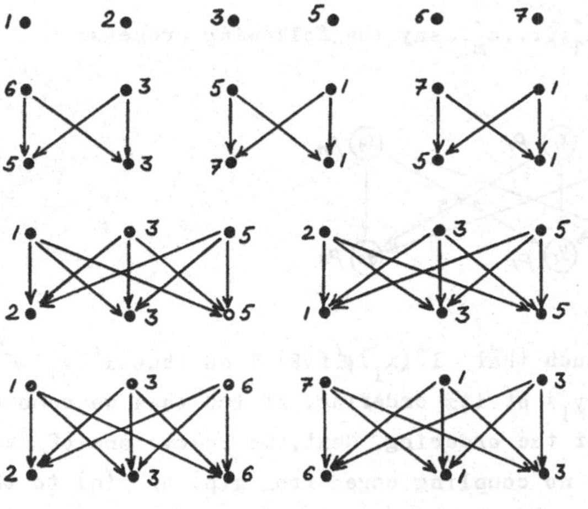

Figure 5

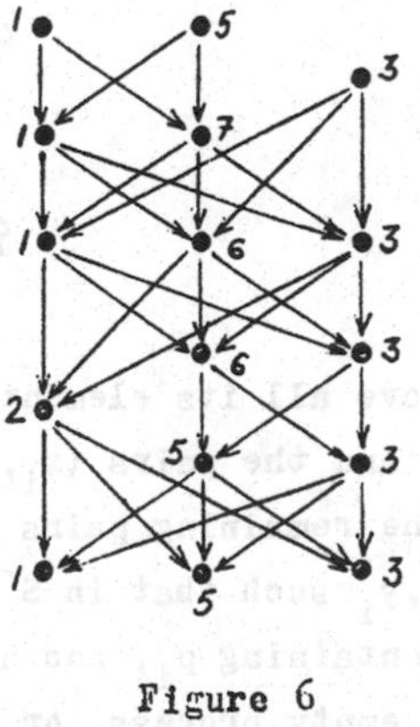

Figure 6

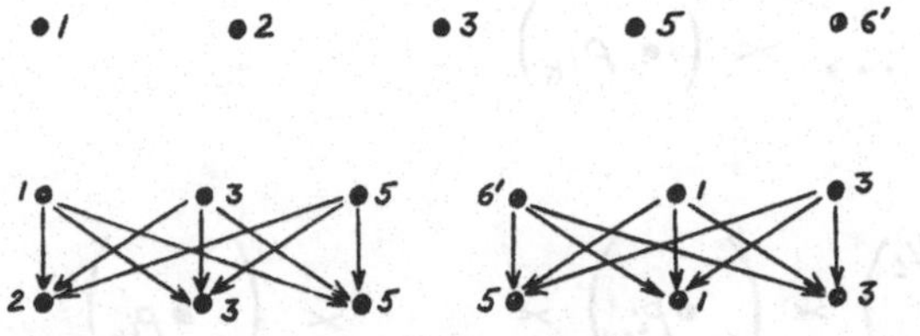

Figure 7

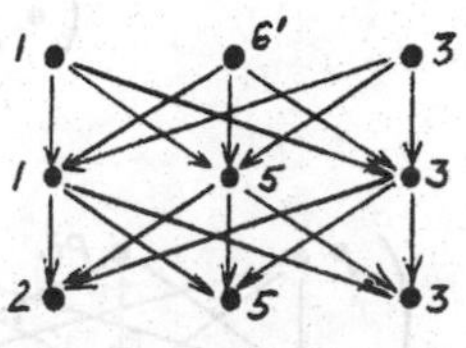

Figure 8

The existence of an allomorphism $f : P \longrightarrow P'$ from an LCS S to another one S' (see 1) gives a relationship between the classes of processes of these systems:

<u>Proposition</u>: To every mapping $g : f(P) \longrightarrow P$ such that $f(g(p')) = p'$ for every $p' \in f(P)$ there corresponds a mapping $\hat{g} : \mathrm{Beh}(S') \longrightarrow \mathrm{Beh}(S)$ satisfying

$$\hat{g}(a' \cdot b') = \hat{g}(a') \cdot \hat{g}(b') \ , \quad \hat{g}(a' \times b') = \hat{g}(a') \times \hat{g}(b') \ .$$

This mapping can be defined as follows:

Every process $a' = [(X', \leqslant', l')] \in \mathrm{Beh}(S')$ can <u>uniquely</u> be covered by elementary processes $a'_1, \dots, a'_m$ from $\mathrm{Beh}(S')$, and the ordering $\leqslant'$ is the transitive closure of the union of the orderings of the processes $a'_1, \dots, a'_m$. So the process from fig.8 can be covered as follows:

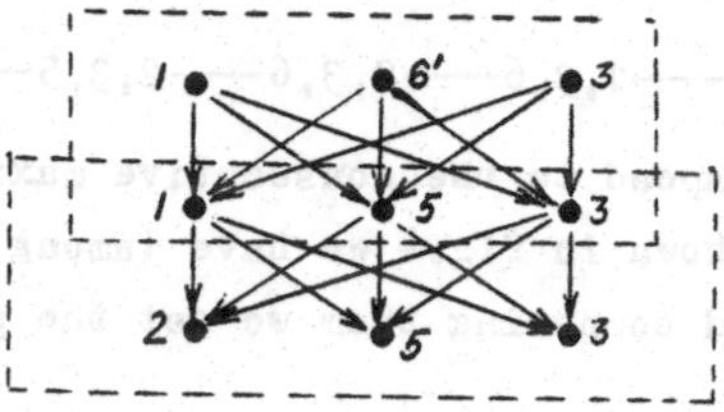

Now, having one of the processes $a'_1, \dots, a'_m$, say the following process:

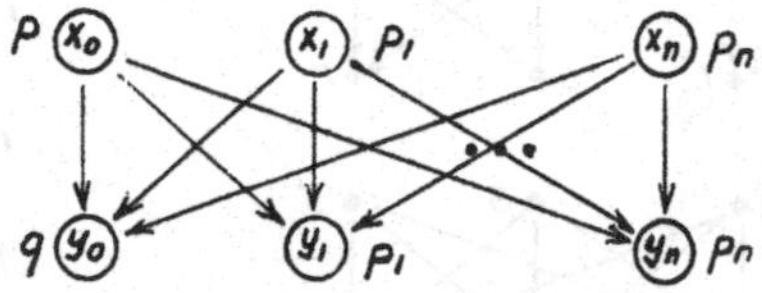

we remove all its elements x_i, y_i such that $l'(x_i) \notin f(P)$ (and thus $l'(y_i) \notin f(P)$), and the pairs (x_i, y_j), (x_k, y_i) of its ordering. If $i=0$ then we remove also the remaining pairs (x_j, y_k) of the ordering. Next, we remove one of every two x_i, y_i such that in S there are no coupling edges from $g(p)$ or $g(q)$ to the part containing p_i, and all the pairs (x_i, y_j), (x_k, y_i). This procedure leads to the empty process, or to a process of the form:

$$(\bullet\, p_{i_1}) \times \dots \times (\bullet\, p_{i_k})$$

or

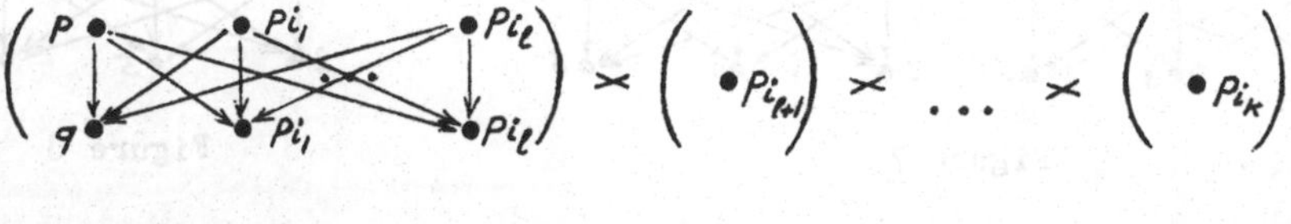

where every of the components belongs to Beh(S). All these processes, when composed as in a' give a process $\hat{g}(a') \in Beh(S)$.

For the allomorphism f from the system S shown in fig.3 into the system S' shown in fig.4 we have the following mappings g_1, g_2:

$$g_1(6') = 6,\ g_2(6') = 7,\ g_1(p) = g_2(p) = p \text{ for } p = 1,2,3,4,5,$$

and $\hat{g}_2$ maps the process from fig.8 into the process in fig.9. As the systems used here as examples are very small we can explain how $\hat{g}_1, \hat{g}_2$ work on the processes in S' by demonstrating the effects in the case graphs (in general there is a need to have a process description which releases us from considering the enormously large number of cases.) Roughly speaking, $\hat{g}_1, \hat{g}_2$ map $Beh(S')$ onto the subsets of Beh(S) which correspond to the parts of the case graph as indicated in fig.10. If we merge the phases 5 and 6 into a phase $6''$ we get another allomorphism F from S to the system S'' in fig.11. For this allomorphism we can choose the following mappings G_1, G_2:

$$G_1(6'') = 5,\ G_2(6'') = 6,\ G_1(p) = G_2(p) = p \text{ for } p = 1,2,3,4,7,$$

and we get two corresponding mappings $\hat{G}_1: Beh(S'') \longrightarrow Beh(S)$ and $\hat{G}_2: Beh(S'') \longrightarrow Beh(S)$ which map the processes of S'' as it is shown in the case graph of S in fig.12.

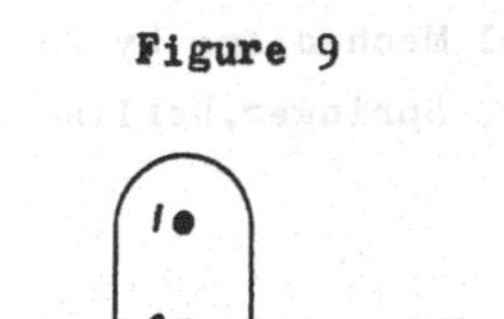

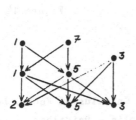

Figure 9

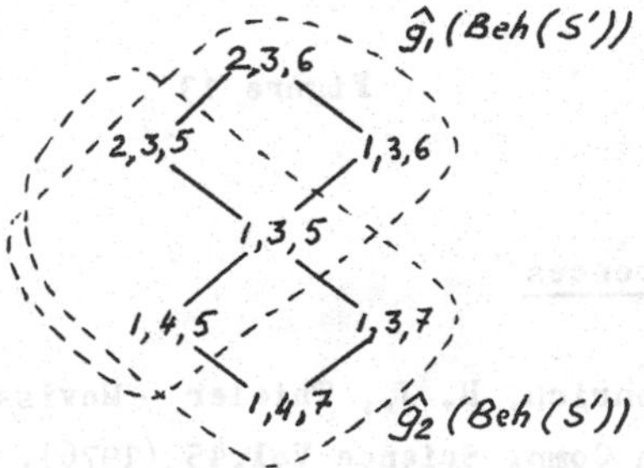

Figure 10

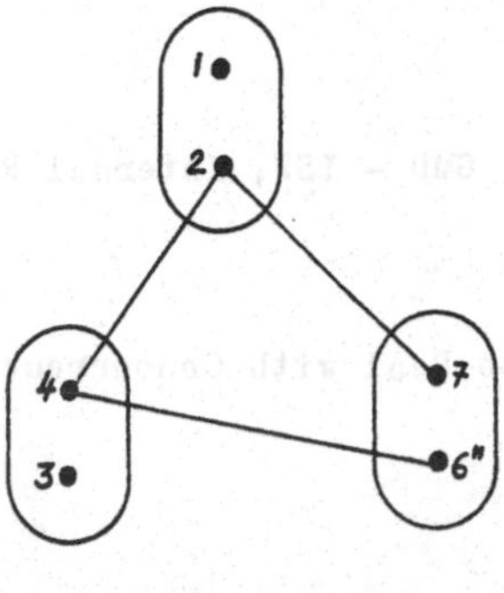

Figure 11

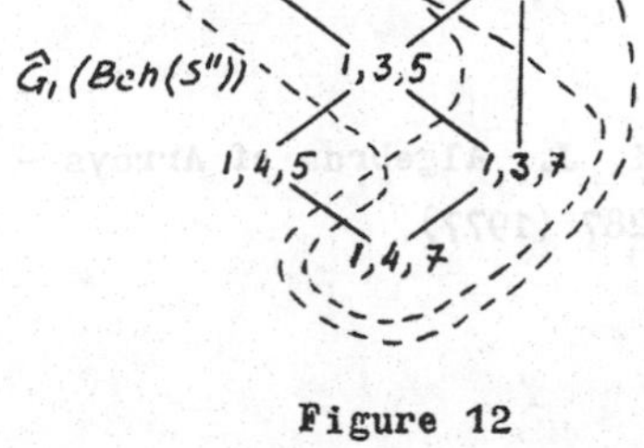

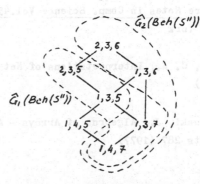

Figure 12

Thus, considering allomorphisms from a system S to other systems and looking at the corresponding mappings of processes we can construct the processes of S, too.

Allomorphisms can also be exploited to modify a system so as to avoid certain undesirable processes. For instance, if we want to avoid in the system S in fig.3 processes with elementary events $6 \longrightarrow 7 \mid \{1,3\}$ and $7 \longrightarrow 6 \mid \{1,3\}$ we extend it allomorphically to the system S_1 in fig.13. Now, for the inclusion map i, which is the allomorphism from S to S_1, we have the converse mapping j and the corresponding mapping $\hat{j} : Beh(S_1) \longrightarrow Beh(S)$. This mapping gives the processes of S found in the case graph of fig.14. This means that the elementary events we wanted to avoid can not occur in S_1.

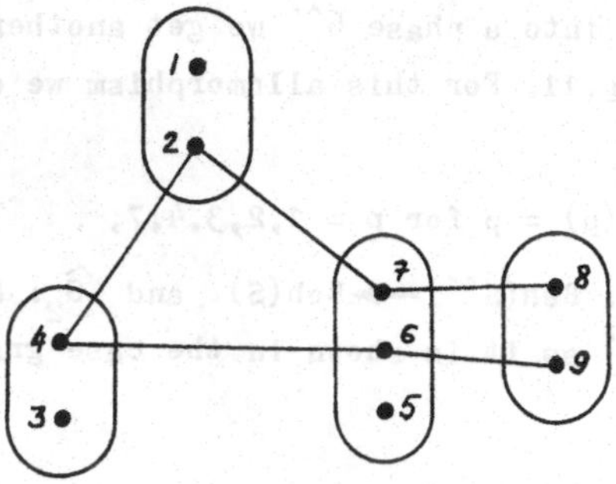

Figure 13

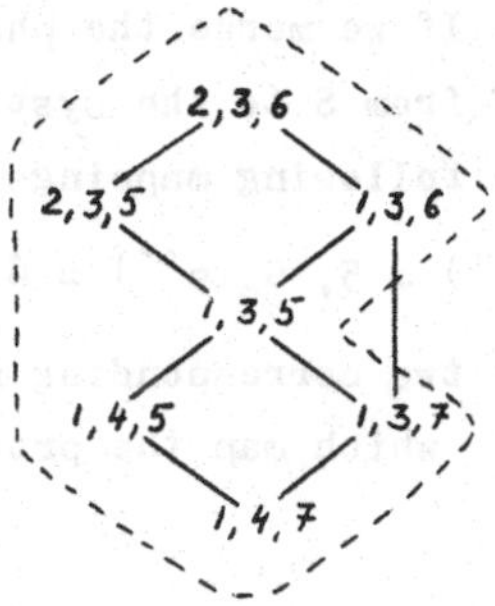

Figure 14

References

1. Genrich, H. J., Thieler - Mevissen, G., The Calculus of Facts. Lecture Notes in Comp. Science Vol.45 (1976), Springer,Berlin - Heidelberg - New York

2. Lautenbach, K., Wedde, H., Generating Control Mechanisms by Restrictions. Lecture Notes in Comp. Science Vol.45 (1976), Springer,Berlin- Heidelberg- - New York

3. Petri, C. A., Interpretations of Net Theory. GMD - ISF, Internal Report 75-07 (1975)

4. Winkowski, J., Algebras of Arrays - A Tool to Deal with Concurrency. CC PAS Reports 287 (1977)

THE INFLUENCE OF THE MACHINE MODEL ON THE TIME COMPLEXITY OF CONTEXT-FREE LANGUAGE RECOGNITION

Reinhold Weicker
Siemens AG, E STE 32
Postfach 3240
D-8520 Erlangen 2
Fed. Rep. of Germany

Abstract: It is shown that the assumption of a RAM model with "unit cost criterion" in the case of context-free language recognition leads to time bounds significantly better than the well-known bounds of $O(n^3)$ or $O(n^{2.81})$. Even a RAM with the usual arithmetic operations $(+, \dot{-})$ only allows some kind of time-saving set manipulations such that general context-free language recognition can be performed in $O(n^2 . \log n)$ steps, provided that a unit cost criterion is assumed.

1. Introduction

When the model of a Random Access Machine (RAM) was formally introduced as a basis of computational complexity considerations [2], two alternative ways for the definition of a basic step were given: The "logarithmic cost criterion" counts an operation involving as operands numbers of size k (length log k) as log k steps, the "unit cost criterion" counts each of the basic machine operations as only one step. Arguments concerning these two alternatives can be found, e.g., in [1].

Later, the results obtained by Pratt / Stockmeyer [9] and Hartmanis / Simon [6] showed that if the use of powerful machine instructions like a variable-length vector shift operation or multiplication is admitted together with Boolean operations, surprising results like P = NP (for these machine models) can be obtained. These models have the ability to generate very large numbers (very long strings of bits) in only a few steps, if a unit cost criterion is assumed. This enables them to use some parallelism and to speed up the computations very much.

In this paper, we shall see that even a much simpler RAM model, for example the "normal" arithmetic RAM model, already has the power to make use of a parallel structure of an algorithm, if a unit cost criterion is used. It is shown that in this case general context-free language recognition can be done in $O(n^2)$ or $O(n^2 . \log n)$ steps, depending on the particular RAM model used.

2. Earley's algorithm for context-free language recognition and its modification

Although for the actual design of programming languages suitable subclasses of context-free grammars are used, the problem of general context-free language recognition still attracts much interest, partly because of its relations to other problems in theoretical computer science, partly because of the large gap between the best lower bound (linear time) and upper bound ($O(n^{2.81})$) known so far for this problem (See [4] for a unified presentation of the various algorithms and for detailed proofs).

The algorithm found by J. Earley [3] assumes that a grammar G is given by a list of productions

$$D_p \rightarrow C_{p1} \dots C_{pn_p} \qquad (1 \leq p \leq d)$$

and that the input string is $X_1 \dots X_n$. The algorithm computes "items" $\langle p,j,f \rangle$ (called "states" in [3]), where $1 \leq p \leq d$, $0 \leq j \leq n_p$, $0 \leq f \leq n$, and collects these items in sets S_i, constructed in a way such that the following condition holds:

$$\langle p,j,f \rangle \in S_i \quad \Longleftrightarrow \quad C_{p1} \dots C_{pj} \xrightarrow{*} X_{f+1} \dots X_i$$
$$\text{and} \quad S \xrightarrow{*} X_1 \dots X_f C_{p1} \dots C_{pj} w \quad \text{for some string } w$$

The algorithm (without the look-ahead feature for LR(k) grammars) can be formulated as follows:

Algorithm 1 (Earley's algorithm):

Initialization:
$S_o := \{\langle p,0,0 \rangle \mid p$ is the number of a production with $D_p =$ root of G$\}$;
for i:=1 **step** 1 **until** n **do** $S_i := \emptyset$;

Main loop:
for i:=0 step 1 until n do
begin process the items of S_i (including those that are added) in some order, performing one of the three following operations for each item $s = \langle p,j,f \rangle$:

(1) Predictor: If s is nonfinal and $C_{p(j+1)}$ is nonterminal, then for each q such that $C_{p(j+1)} = D_q$ add $\langle q,0,i \rangle$ to S_i

(2) Completer: If s is final (i.e. $j = n_p$), then for each $\langle q,k,g \rangle \in S_f$ with $C_{q(k+1)} = D_p$ add $\langle q,k+1,g \rangle$ to S_i

(3) Scanner: If s is nonfinal and $C_{p(j+1)}$ is terminal, then if $C_{p(j+1)} = X_{i+1}$, add $\langle p,j+1,f \rangle$ to S_{i+1}

If after these operations $i < n$ and $S_{i+1} = \emptyset$, reject the input
end;

If $\langle p,n_p,0 \rangle \in S_n$ with D_p = root of G, accept the input string, otherwise reject it.

In the algorithm, an item $\langle p,j,f \rangle$ in a set S_i is characterized mainly by the two indices i,f which grow with n; the other two indices p,j are bounded by fixed constants. It is therefore possible to arrange the item sets S_i as columns of an upper-triangular matrix, with i as column index and f as row index, as shown in the following figure.

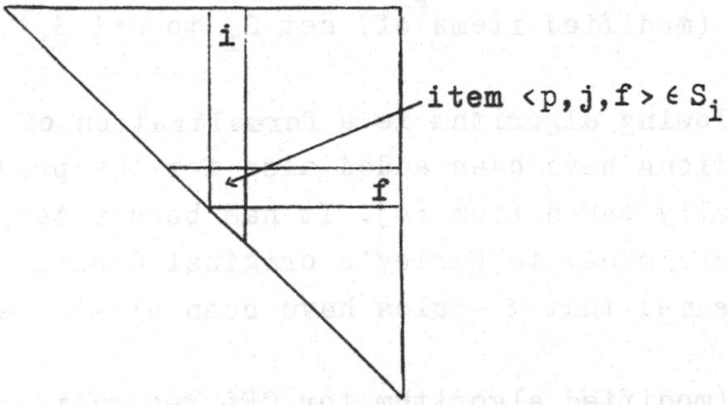

Fig.1: Recognition matrix for Earley's algorithm

This presentation has been used in [4] and [5], it shows the close connection between this algorithm and the Cocke / Kasami / Younger algorithm [11], which is not apparent at the first glance. With this interpretation, an action of the predictor means adding a new element to the bottom of a column, an action of the scanner means adding initial elements to the following column, and an action of the completer means a partial transfer of elements from column f to column i while adding 1 to the index j. Since this part, the completer, dominates the running time of the algorithm, it is to be modified in such a way that the algorithm takes advantage of this matrix structure: The completer transfers a whole column (more precisely: a partial column, i.e. those elements of S_f which have $C_{q(k+1)} = D_p$) in one operation. This implies that, other than in Earley's version, the final items $<p,n_p,f> \in S_i$ are to be processed in a fixed order, namely in decreasing order of f; then after the final items of a column have been processed up to some index f_o, no other final items will be added to the lower part of the column.

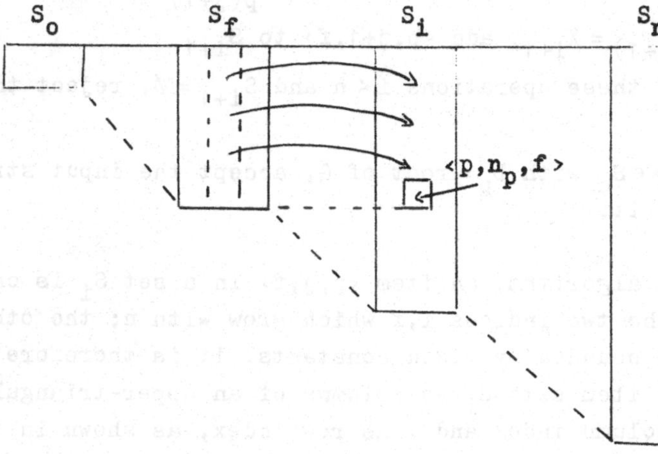

Fig.2: Final item $<p,n_p,f>$ causes partial transfer of (modified items of) set S_f to set S_i

The following algorithm is a formalization of this idea, some minor modifications have been added also for the predictor and scanner parts, partially taken from [4]. It has been attempted to formulate the algorithm closely to Earley's original description. For simplicity, it is assumed that ε-rules have been eliminated from the grammar.

<u>Algorithm 2</u> (modified algorithm for CFL recognition):

Initialization:
NEWS := $\{<p,0,0> \mid D_p = NT_1 = \text{root of } G\}$;
for i:=1 **step** 1 **until** n **do**
for h:=1 **step** 1 **until** r **do**
  PENDINGPROD[i,h] := ∅;
  comment r = number of nonterminals;

```
Main loop (i-loop):
for i:=0 step 1 until n do
begin S := NEWS; NEWS := Ø;
  f-loop 1 (Completer):
  for f:=i step -1 until 0 do
  begin for h:=1 step 1 until r do FLAG[h] := false;
    Process the final items s = <p,n_p,f> ∈ S in some order, performing
    the following operation for each s = <p,n_p,f>:
    if D_p = NT_h and not FLAG[h] then
    begin S := S ∪ PENDINGPROD[f,h];
      FLAG[h] := true
    end
  end f;
  f-loop 2 (Scanner / Predictor, part 1):
  for h:=1 step 1 until r do
  begin WAITING[h] := false;
    SEEN[h] := false
  end;
  for f:=0 step 1 until i do
  begin Process the nonfinal items s = <p,j,f> ∈ S in some order, per-
    forming one of the following two operations for each s = <p,j,f>:
    (1) Scanner, part 1:
    if C_p(j+1) is terminal and C_p(j+1) = X_i+1
    then add <p,j+1,f> to NEWS;
    (2) Predictor, part 1:
    if C_p(j+1) is nonterminal and C_p(j+1) = NT_h then
    begin WAITING[h] := true;
      add <p,j+1,f> to PENDINGPROD[i,h]
    end
  end f;
  Predictor / Scanner, part 2:
  For all h with WAITING[h] = true and SEEN[h] = false do the following:
  begin For all q with D_q = NT_h do the following:
    begin if C_q1 is nonterminal and C_q1 = NT_h'
        then begin add <q,1,i> to PENDINGPROD[i,h'];
                   WAITING[h'] := true
             end
        else if C_q1 is terminal and C_q1 = X_i+1
             then add <q,1,i> to NEWS
    end for all q;
    SEEN[h] := true;
```

<u>end</u> for all h;
<u>if</u> $i < n$ <u>and</u> $NEWS = \emptyset$ <u>then</u> reject
<u>end</u> i;
<u>if</u> some $< p, n_p, 0 > \in S$ with D_p = root of G <u>then</u> accept <u>else</u> reject;

Remarks:

(1) In this algorithm, S contains the same items as S_i (current index i) in Earley's algorithm, NEWS corresponds to S_{i+1}. Since only the items $<p,j,f>$ with $C_{p(j+1)}$ nonterminal will be referred to later by the loops i+1,i+2, ... , it is not necessary to store other items after loop i+1. The items that are possibly referred to later are stored in the sets PENDINGPROD[i,h] (h = 1, ... ,r), the name indicates an unfinished production with NT_h as the next element to come.

(2) Earley's algorithm requires that when the completer finds an item $<q,k,g>$ in S_f (processing $<p,n_p,f> \in S_i$, $D_p = C_{q(k+1)} = NT_h$), $<q,k+1,g>$ is added to S_i. Since this addition of new items is performed here by the set union $S := S \cup$ PENDINGPROD[f,h], the items stored in PENDINGPROD[f,h] must be $<q,k+1,g>$ rather than $<q,k,g>$.

3. <u>Implementation of the algorithm on a unit cost RAM</u>

It can be seen easily from the description of the algorithm that the time bound is $O(n^2 \cdot \max(f(n),g(n)))$, where f(n), g(n) are defined as follows:

(1) f(n) is the time bound for the union of two (possibly non-disjoint) sets of size O(n),

(2) g(n) is the time bound for the look-up of the next item $<p,j,f>$ in the set S (size O(n)) to be processed.

The predictor / scanner part of the algorithm requires, as in Earley's version, only a fixed number of steps for each item (finite table look-up), the completer part has been reduced to one single set-union operation per final item of S.

In order to determine the functions f(n) and g(n) defined above, we first consider a RAM with Boolean operations instead of the usual arithmetic ones. Such a RAM, hereinafter called BOOLRAM, has the following operations:

UNION	operand	bitwise union of accumulator and operand
ISECT	operand	bitwise intersection of accumulator and operand
LSHIFT		shift of the accumulator to the left by one bit, the rightmost bit becomes 0
RSHIFT		shift of the accumulator to the right by one bit, the rightmost bit gets lost

Otherwise, it has the usual RAM operations (Load, Store, Read, Write, Conditional Jump).

With a BOOLRAM, the sets S, NEWS and PENDINGPROD can be represented by the contents of a single register in a straightforward way: Let <p,j> be an encoding of the numbers p and j, bounded above by a fixed constant C_G. Then a set S of items can be represented by the register contents $\overline{S}$ with the $(f.C_G+\langle p,j\rangle)$-th bit of $\overline{S}$ being 1 iff the item <p,j,f> is an element of S.

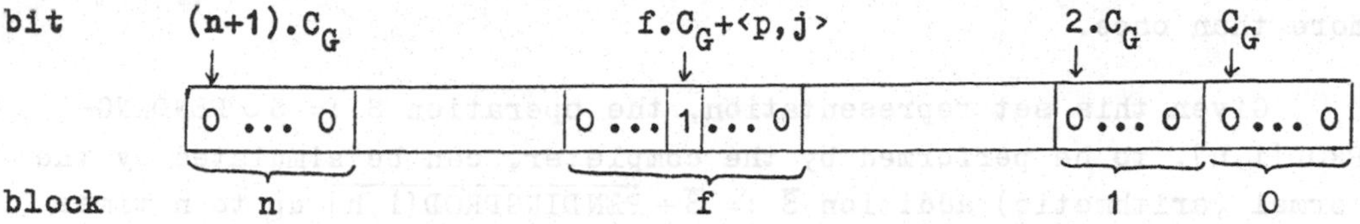

Fig.3: Register contents $\overline{S}$ representing set $S=\{\langle p,j,f\rangle\}$

In a "preprocessing" phase of the algorithm, it is possible to compute representations of single-item sets $S=\{\langle p,j,f\rangle\}$ for all p,j and f in $C_1.n$ steps. It is also possible to organize in $C_2.n$ steps a reference table such that, given p,j and f, the register containing $\overline{\{\langle p,j,f\rangle\}}$ can be found in a fixed number of steps. During the main loop of the algorithm, the union of sets can then be performed in one operation. Similarly, given p,j,f and a set S, it is possible to check whether <p,j,f> is an element of S by intersecting the register contents $\overline{\{\langle p,j,f\rangle\}}$ and $\overline{S}$. Therefore, the functions f(n) and g(n) are constant functions (with a unit cost criterion), and we have the following result:

<u>Theorem 1</u>: Context-free language recognition can be performed by a BOOLRAM (with unit cost criterion) in $O(n^2)$ steps.

For a RAM with the usual arithmetic operations + and $\dot{-}$, hereinafter called PLUSRAM, a similar but slightly more complicated representation of sets can be used. A set of items is again represented by a bit string (interpreted here as a number) consisting of n blocks. Every block contains C_G subblocks of length $\lceil \log n \rceil$ each.

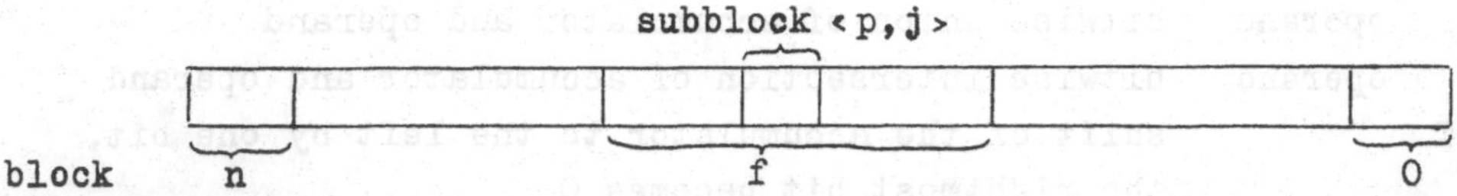

Fig.4: Register contents representing a set S on a PLUSRAM

The sets PENDINGPROD[i,h] are initially empty, the registers initialized with 0. Whenever an item $\langle p,j,f\rangle$ is added to a set PENDINGPROD[i,h], the subblock $\langle p,j\rangle$ of the f-th block is replaced by 0... 01 (length $\lceil \log n\rceil$), this can be done by (arithmetic) addition of the number $2^{f.C_G.\lceil \log n\rceil+(\langle p,j\rangle-1).\lceil \log n\rceil}$ to the previous register contents. Note that in these registers, no subblocks contain other strings than 0 ... 0 or 0 ... 01, because during the i-th main loop a specific item $\langle p,j+1,f\rangle$ is added to PENDINGPROD[i,h] only once, provided that the item $\langle p,j,f\rangle$ will not be extracted from S more than once.

Given this set representation, the operation S := S $\cup$ PENDINGPROD[i,h], to be performed by the completer, can be simulated by the normal (arithmetic) addition $\overline{S} := \overline{S} + \overline{\text{PENDINGPROD[i,h]}}$ up to n times without a subblock in $\overline{S}$ interfering with its neighbour subblock. And during an i-loop, the number 1 (i.e. the string 0 ... 01 of length $\lceil \log n\rceil$) will not be added more than n times to any subblock. In S, an item $\langle p,j,f\rangle$ is then represented by some number a ($1 \leq a \leq n$); a can be regarded as the degree of ambiguity of the substring X_{f+1} .. .. X_1 of the input string. Then, given a number $\overline{S}$ representing the set S, a PLUSRAM can test the presence or absence of an item $\langle p,j,f\rangle$ during an f-loop in the following way: The machine checks for the numbers $a := \overline{S}$, $b := 2^{f.C_G.\lceil \log n\rceil+k}$, where k runs from 0 to $C_G.\lceil \log n\rceil -1$, whether $a \dot{-} b = 0$ and $b \dot{-} a > 0$. In this case the $(f.C_G.\lceil \log n\rceil+k)$-th bit of $\overline{S}$ is 0, otherwise it is 1. So the machine can in O(log n) steps check the presence of an item $\langle p,j,f\rangle$ in S and at the same time remove it from S, so it can continue with the item $\langle p,j,f-1\rangle$ afterwards, as required by the algorithm. For items $\langle p,j,f\rangle$ with f = i in a set PENDINGPROD[i,h], some other representation has to be used in order to avoid backtracking, but this can be organized with a fixed table-lookup and will not be described here in detail.

So we see that in the case of a PLUSRAM, $f(n) \equiv 1$ and $g(n) = \log n$; while n sets of up to n items each can be united with the set S in n operations, it takes not more than n.log n operations to look up every item in S afterwards. We therefore have the result:

Theorem 2: Context-free language recognition can be performed by a PLUSRAM (with unit cost criterion) in $O(n^2 . \log n)$ steps.

4. Relations to other work and conclusion

This paper started with a context-free language recognition algorithm, but it then turned into a paper on set-manipulating operations for different RAM models; these considerations might be of interest in their own right. Both aspects have been studied by other authors as well. The presentation of Earley's algorithm as a matrix algorithm is contained in [4] and [5], our algorithm 2 is similar to algorithms 2 and 4 of Graham / Harrison / Ruzzo [5]. After that step which is similar in both papers they apply a technique known as the "Four Russians' algorithm" to get a time bound of $O(n^3 / \log n)$, also mentioning the $O(n^2)$ or $O(n^2 / \log n)$ time bound for a BOOLRAM, whereas here a specific data representation combined with the unit cost criterion is used in order to achieve the time bound of $O(n^2 . \log n)$ for the PLUSRAM. Also, the same $O(n^2 . \log n)$ result has been found independently by S.R. Kosaraju [8]. He uses the same set representation applied to a modified version of Younger's algorithm [11]. The result for the BOOLRAM, theorem 1, can also be derived from Kosaraju's results on context-free language recognition by iterative arrays [7] and from the fact that a one-dimensional iterative array can be simulated in linear time by a BOOLRAM [10].

As far as the implications of the results are concerned, they can be interpreted in two ways: On the one hand, they show the influence of the unit cost criterion used for the underlying machine model on the performance of an algorithm, this can be considered as an argument against models with unit cost criterion. On the other hand, the argument "We might try to build one" ([9], p. 122) could hold for the models considered here even more than for the Vector Machine, they are simpler and more realistic than the Vector Machine or a Multiplication RAM. In particular, the BOOLRAM seems to be a model equally suitable as the usual arithmetic models, it seems appropriate to give it more attention in computational complexity considerations.

Acknowledgement: This work was done while the author was visiting the Pennsylvania State University, on leave from the University of Hamburg. Discussions with the colleagues at Penn State and with Rao Kosaraju, Michael Harrison and Walter Ruzzo are gratefully acknowledged, as well as the financial support by the German Academic Exchange Service (DAAD, grant no. 430/402/562/6).

References:

1. Aho, A.V., Hopcroft, J.E., and Ullman, J.D., The Design and Analysis of Computer Algorithms. Addison-Wesley Publishing Co., Reading, Mass., 1974
2. Cook, S.A., and Reckhow, R.A., Time-Bounded Random Access Machines. Journal of Computer and System Sciences, 7 (1973), 354 - 375
3. Earley, J., An Efficient Context-Free Parsing Algorithm. Communications of the ACM, 13 (1970), 94 - 102
4. Graham, S.L., and Harrison, M.A., Parsing of General Context-Free Languages. In: Advances in Computers, vol. 14 (Ed.: Rubinoff, M., and Yovits, M.C.), pp. 77 - 185. Academic Press, New York, 1976
5. Graham, S.L., Harrison, M.A., and Ruzzo, W.L., On Line Context Free Language Recognition in Less Than Cubic Time. Eighth Annual ACM Symposium on Theory of Computing (1976), 112 - 120
6. Hartmanis, J., and Simon, J., On the Power of Multiplication in Random Access Machines. 15th Annual Symposium on Switching and Automata Theory (1974), 13 - 23
7. Kosaraju, S.R., Speed of Recognition of Context-Free Languages by Array Automata. SIAM Journal on Computing, 4 (1975), 331 - 340
8. Kosaraju, S.R., Recognition of Context-Free Languages by Random Access Machines. Manuscript, 1976
9. Pratt, V.R., and Stockmeyer, L.J., A Characterization of the Power of Vector Machines. Journal of Computer and System Sciences, 12 (1976), 198 - 221
10. Seiferas, J.I., and Weicker, R., Linear-Time Simulation of an Iterative Array of Finite-State Machines by a RAM with Uniform Cost Criterion. Technical Report No. 201, The Pennsylvania State University, Computer Science Dept., July 1976
11. Younger, D.H., Parsing and Recognition of Context-Free Languages in Time n^3. Information and Control, 10 (1967), 189 - 208

A GENERALIZED COMPUTABILITY THESIS

Klaus Weihrauch

Lehrstuhl für Informatik I

RWTH Aachen

Büchel 29-31, D-5100 Aachen

Abstract: Let $M := [F;G]$, i.e. the smallest set including G which is closed under the functions from F, where F and G are finite. Any numbering ν of M implies ν-computability on M. The effective numberings of M with respect to F are defined in two equivalent ways, firstly as the class of numberings equivalent to the term numbering, and secondly as the minimal numbering (with respect to many-one reducibility) in the class of those numberings for which the functions from F become computable.

By several examples it is shown that the first definition is consistent with earlier ones. The second definition is more elegant from the theoretical point of view. Together they give good reason for the thesis that exactly the "effective" numberings have been defined. (For the full paper see: Proceedings of the FCT'77 conference Poznan / Poland, Springer Lecture Notes.)

IDENTIFICATION OF FORMAL LANGUAGES

Rolf Wiehagen

Sektion Mathematik
der Humboldt-Universität zu Berlin
DDR 1o86 Berlin PSF 1297

0. The standard situation in identification theory is the following : Given a black-box with an unknown object (for instance, a language L) inside. Furthermore, provided that the black-box produces an information sequence describing the object (for instance, a text sequence of L, t(o), t(1), t(2),... such that range t = L). An algorithm is said to identify the object if on the basis of the information sequence it constructs a sequence of hypothesis the limit of which is a correct description of the object (for instance, a sequence of grammars converging to a grammar of L).

Problems like these arise in pattern recognition, automatical programming, learning theory etc. Identification of formal languages has been investigated by Gold [1], Feldman [2], Lindner [3], Thiele [4], Knobe, Knobe [5], and others. What distinguishes this paper from theirs is our purpose to characterize the identifiable language families. A main importance of these characterizations consists in answering the question how algorithms identifying families of languages do work. For characterizing we use terms of complexity theory on the one hand, but on the other hand we state characterizations quite in a recursion (numeration) theoretical way.

In Section 1 we give the basic definitions and some properties of the identifiable language families defined. In Section 2 we characterize these families.

We consider languages as being nonempty subsets of the set N of all natural numbers. Let $\mathcal{L}_o$, $\mathcal{L}_{rec}$, $\mathcal{L}_{prim}$, $\mathcal{L}_{cs}$, $\mathcal{L}_{cf}$, $\mathcal{L}_{reg}$, $\mathcal{L}_{fin}$ denote the families of all recursive enumerable, recursive, primitive recursive, context-sensitive, context-free, regular, finite languages, respectively. Let F, P, R, Pr denote the sets of all the total, partial recursive, total recursive, primitive recursive functions, respectively. Let $\varphi_o, \varphi_1, \ldots$ denote a Gödel numbering of P, and $\Phi_o, \Phi_1, \ldots$ a Blum's complexity measure on the numbering φ. Let R^+ denote the set of all the functions $h \in R$ that enumerates classes of total recursive functions, i.e. $\{\varphi_{h(i)} / i \in N\} \subseteq R$. For $t \in F$, $n \in N$ let $t[n] = (t(o), \ldots, t(n))$. For a partial function f mapping N into N and $n \in N$ let $range_n\ f = \{f(x)/x \leq n$ and $f(x)$ is defined$\}$. We say that $\lim_n a_n$ exists, where $(a_n)_{n \in N}$ is a sequence of natural numbers, if there is a number a such that $a_n = a$ for almost all n. For a set M let pM denote the set of all nonempty subsets of M and card M the cardinality of M.

1. In Definition 1 we formalize how information about the unknown languages is presented and when a family of languages is said to be identifiable. A mapping text is called an admissible method of information presentation if text maps $\mathcal{L}_o$ into pF such that range t=L for all $L \in \mathcal{L}_o$ and all $t \in text(L)$.

Definition 1. Let text be any admissible method of information presentation and $\mathcal{L} \subseteq \mathcal{L}_o$.
$\mathcal{L}$ is said to be text-identifiable iff there is an algorithm $A \in R$ (note that "$A \in P$" is not really more general) such that for all $t \in text(L)$ **it holds** (1) $A(t[n])$ is defined for all n,
(2) (a =) $\lim_n A(t[n])$ exists,
(3) range φ_a = range t (=L). -

The number a can be interpreted as being a grammar (an enumeration procedure) of L. As it follows from the definition for identifying a l a n g u a g e L presented by $t \in text(L)$ it is not necessary in general to identify t itself (provided t recursive), i.e. to generate a number a such that even $\varphi_a = t$, as it is the basic problem in identification theory of f u n c t i o n s (cf., for instance, Gold[6], Barzdin, Ed.[7], Wiehagen[8]). Indeed, it is easy to see that there is a real difference between identification of languages and functions. For instance, the language {o,1} is text-identifiable by text = R_o (the set of all total recursive o-1-valued functions), of course, but R_o is not identifiable in the sense of function identification, as already shown by Gold[6]. Note that the characterization problem in identification theory of functions **has been in detail** investigated in Blum, Blum[9], Wiehagen, Liepe[1o], and Wiehagen, Jung[11].

Now let TEXT denote the class of all text-identifiable language families $\mathcal{L} \subseteq \mathcal{L}_o$. Thus, by varying the admissible method of information presentation text we get new classes of identifiable language families. In this paper we only consider the information presentations arb (arbitrary presentation), incr (increasing presentation), and prim (primitive recursive presentation), where for all $L \in \mathcal{L}_o$ arb(L) denotes the set of all $t \in F$ such that range t = L, incr(L)denotes the set containing the (only) increasing enumeration c_L of L, i.e. $c_L(o) = \min L$, $c_L(n+1) = \min (L - \text{range}_n\, c_L)$, if $L - \text{range}_n\, c_L$ is nonempty, and $c_L(n+1) = c_L(n)$ otherwise, (note that the incr-concept of information presentation is almost equivalent with Gold's so called informant-concept, cf. Gold [1]), prim(L) denotes the set of all $t \in Pr$ such that range t = L.

Then ARB $\subset$ INCR $\subset$ PRIM = $p\mathcal{L}_o$, as shown by Gold [1]. Furthermore, there is shown : If $\mathcal{L}_{fin} \subset \mathcal{L}$, then $\mathcal{L} \notin$ ARB. Hence $\mathcal{L}_{reg}$, $\mathcal{L}_{cf}$, $\mathcal{L}_{cs}$, $\mathcal{L}_o \notin$ ARB. But, as we show in Proposition 1 by an easy application of the recursion theorem, ARB nevertheless "almost" contains $\mathcal{L}_o$. For sets A and B let $A \triangle B = (A \cup B)-(A \cap B)$.

<u>Proposition 1</u>. There is a family $\mathcal{L} \subseteq \mathcal{L}_o$ such that :
(1) $\mathcal{L} \in$ ARB .
(2) For any $L \in \mathcal{L}_o$ there is an $L' \in \mathcal{L}$ such that $L \triangle L'$ is finite.

Proof. Let $L \in \mathcal{L}_o$ and $t \in R$ such that range t = L. Define, using the recursion theorem, $\varphi_a(n) = a$, if n = 0 or $t(n) \leq a$, and $\varphi_a(n) = t(n)$ otherwise. Clearly, $L \triangle \text{range}\, \varphi_a$ is finite and $a = \min \text{range}\, \varphi_a$. Hence $\mathcal{L} = \{ L' / L' \in \mathcal{L}_o \text{ and range } \varphi_{\min L'} = L' \}$ satisfies (2). Furthermore, $\mathcal{L}$ satisfies (1), too; if $L' \in \mathcal{L}$ and $t \in \text{arb}(L')$ then the algorithm A arb-identifies $\mathcal{L}$, where $A(t[n]) = \min \text{range}_n\, t$.

Of course, $\mathcal{L}$ from Proposition 1 does not contain $\mathcal{L}_{fin}$.

In addition, we remark without a formal proof (it is rather technical) the following : Let rec(L), nonrec(L) denote the sets of all $t \in R$, $t \in F-R$, respectively, such that range t = L for any $L \in \mathcal{L}_o$. Then ARB = REC = NONREC.

As for INCR in Gold [1] **there is shown** $\mathcal{L}_{cs} \in$ INCR (**hence** $\mathcal{L}_{reg}$, $\mathcal{L}_{cf} \in$ INCR) and $\mathcal{L}_{prim} \notin$ INCR. In addition, we note the following result : Let $L \in \mathcal{L}_{rec}$, hence $c_L \in R$. **But there is** a family $\mathcal{L} \subseteq \mathcal{L}_{rec}$ such that any algorithm getting the decision procedure $c_L[n]$, n = o,1,..., of $L \in \mathcal{L}$, in general, can only construct a grammar (an enumeration procedure) of L but it cannot reproduce c_L for all $L \in \mathcal{L}$ (i.e. it cannot generate even in the limit for all

$L \in \mathcal{L}$ from the sequence $(c_L[n])_{n \in N}$ a number a such that $\varphi_a = c_L$).

Finally we show by a simple construction that (primitive) recursivness of information presentation is far from necessary to guarantee the identifiability of a l l languages of $\mathcal{L}_0$ by a universal algorithm (as one could think considering Gold's result PRIM = $p\mathcal{L}_0$).

<u>Proposition 2</u>. There is an admissible method of information presentation, text, such that

(1) TEXT = $p\mathcal{L}_0$.

(2) For all $L \in \mathcal{L}_0$, if card $L > 1$, then

(2.1) text(L) does not contain any recursive t.

(2.2) text(L) is not countable.

Proof. Let $L \in \mathcal{L}_0$ such that card L = 1, say L = {y} . Then text(L) only contains the recursive function t, where t(n) = y for all n. Now, let $L \in \mathcal{L}_0$ such that card $L > 1$, say $y, y' \in L$, $y \neq y'$. Then let text(L) contain all nonrecursive functions t such that range t = L and range $\varphi_{\mu n[t(n) = y']}$ = L. Clearly, text is an admissible method of information presentation having the desired properties. -

2. In this section we want to characterize the families of languages in TEXT (where text is any admissible method of information presentation), ARB, and INCR. By proving the sufficiency of the characteristical conditions below we have to construct algorithms that identify the languages of the family presented. Hence, given t[n], these algorithms must answer the question : On what conditions a hypothesis is reasonable for t[n] ? One could think that a hypothesis j is reasonable for t[n] iff there is an x such that range$_x$ φ_j= range$_n$ t. But it can be shown that an algorithm working in such a "consistent" way can identify only small families of languages. In general, an identification algorithm already has to consider an index j as a reasonable one for t[n] if there is an x such that range$_x$ $\varphi_j \supseteq$ range$_n$ t and, moreover, range$_x$ φ_j - range$_n$ t does not contain "too much" elements. More formally, in the general case the identification algorithm has available suitable functions a and b and chooses the hypothesis j for t[n] in such a way that range$_{b(t[n])}$ $\varphi_j \supseteq$ range$_n$ t and, if $y \in$ range$_{b(t[n])}$ φ_j - range$_n$ t and $\varphi_j(x) = y$, then $x > a(t[n])$; equivalently :

(+) $\text{range}_{a(t[n])} \varphi_j \subseteq \text{range}_n t \subseteq \text{range}_{b(t[n])} \varphi_j$.

For checking (+) the identification algorithm has two possibilities, as we show in Theorem 1 : It can check (+) only at such j for which it is already known that $\varphi_j \in R$ (cf. Theorem 1,(2)), or it uses a bound on the computational complexity Φ_j of φ_j (cf. Theorem1,(3)).

Definition 2. Let text be any admissible method of information presentation and $\mathcal{L} \subseteq \mathcal{L}_o$.

- $\mathcal{L}$ is said to be R^+-text-approximable iff there are functions $a \in P$, $b \in P$, and $h \in R^+$ such that for all $L \in \mathcal{L}$ and all $t \in \text{text}(L)$
  (1) $a(t[n])$ and $b(t[n])$ are defined for almost all n.
  (2) $(a(t[n]))_{n \in N}$ is unbounded.
  (3) There is a number j such that
  $\text{range}_{a(t[n])} \varphi_{h(j)} \subseteq \text{range}_n t \subseteq \text{range}_{b(t[n])} \varphi_{h(j)}$ for almost all n.
- $\mathcal{L}$ is said to be Φ-text-approximable iff there are functions $a \in P$, $b \in P$, and $H \in P$ such that for all $L \in \mathcal{L}$ and all $t \in \text{text}(L)$ hold (1), (2), and
  (3') There is a number j such that for almost all n
  (3'.1) $\max\{\Phi_j(x) / x \leq \max(a(t[n]), b(t[n]))\} \leq H(t[n])$ and
  (3'.2) $\text{range}_{a(t[n])} \varphi_j \subseteq \text{range}_n t \subseteq \text{range}_{b(t[n])} \varphi_j$. -

Note that if for j hold (1), (2), (3), then range $\varphi_{h(j)}$ = range t, and if for j hold (1), (2), (3'), then range φ_j = range t.

Theorem 1. Let text be any admissible method of information presentation and $\mathcal{L} \subseteq \mathcal{L}_o$. Then the following conditions are equivalent :

(1) $\mathcal{L}$ is text-identifiable.
(2) $\mathcal{L}$ is R^+-text-approximable.
(3) $\mathcal{L}$ is Φ-text-approximable.

Proof. (1)$\longrightarrow$(2). Let $\mathcal{L}$ be text-identifiable by an algorithm $A' \in R$. Then first we show that there is an algorithm $A \in R$ text-identifying $\mathcal{L}$, too, but with the property that if $j \in$ range A, then $\varphi_j \in R$. Obviously, there is a function $g \in R$ such that range $\varphi_{g(y,j)} = \{y\} \cup \text{range } \varphi_j$ and $\varphi_{g(y,j)} \in R$ for all $y, j \in N$. Define $A(t[n]) = g(t(o), A'(t[n]))$. Clearly, A has the desired properties.

Then let h be any total recursive function such that range h = range A. Clearly, $h \in R^+$. Now, let $t \in F$. Then let $a(t[n])$ be the greatest $x \leq n$ such that $\text{range}_x \varphi_{A(t[n])} \subseteq \text{range}_n t$, if such an x exists, and $a(t[n])$ undefined otherwise. Let $b(t[n])$ be the smallest x such that $\text{range}_n t \subseteq \text{range}_x \varphi_{A(t[n])}$, if such an x exists, and $b(t[n])$ undefined otherwise. Clearly, $a \in P$ and $b \in P$. If $L \in \mathcal{L}$ and

$t \in \text{text}(L)$, then $a(t[n])$, $b(t[n])$ are defined for almost all n (namely, for all n such that range $\varphi_{A(t[n])} = L$) and $(a(t[n]))_{n\in N}$ is unbounded. Furthermore, let $a = \lim_n A(t[n])$ and $h(j) = a$. Then range$_{a(t[n])}\, \varphi_{h(j)} \subseteq \text{range}_n\, t \subseteq \text{range}_{b(t[n])}\, \varphi_{h(j)}$ for almost all n (for all n such that $A(t[n]) = a$). Hence $\mathcal{L}$ is R^+-text-approximable.

(2)$\longrightarrow$(3). Let $\mathcal{L}$ be R^+-text-approximable (by $a \in P$, $b \in P$, and $h \in R^+$). Then the functions a and b remain unchanged. Hence the conditions (1), (2) of the definition of Φ-text-approximability hold. Furthermore, for $t \in F$ let $H(t[n]) = \max\{\Phi_{h(i)}(x)/i \leq n \text{ and } x \leq \max(a(t[n]),b(t[n]))\}$, if both $a(t[n])$ and $b(t[n])$ are defined, and $H(t[n])$ undefined otherwise. If $L \in \mathcal{L}$ and $t \in \text{text}(L)$, then let $i \in N$ be such that range$_{a(t[n])}\, \varphi_{h(i)} \subseteq \text{range}_n t \subseteq \text{range}_{b(t[n])}\, \varphi_{h(i)}$ for almost all n. Then for $j = h(i)$ the condition (3') of the definition of Φ-text-approximability holds, too.

(3)$\longrightarrow$(1). Let $\mathcal{L}$ be Φ-text-approximable. Then for any $L \in \mathcal{L}$ and $t \in \text{text}(L)$ there exists a pair (j,m) of natural numbers such that for all $n \geq m$ $a(t[n])$, $b(t[n])$, and $H(t[n])$ are defined, $\max\{\Phi_j(x)/x \leq \max(a(t[n]),b(t[n]))\} \leq H(t[n])$, and range$_{a(t[n])}\, \varphi_j \subseteq \text{range}_n\, t \subseteq \text{range}_{b(t[n])}\, \varphi_j$. The algorithm A below that text-identifies $\mathcal{L}$ looks for a pair (j,m) described above and converges to j. An auxiliary function z will help the algorithm A to remember the actual pair under consideration.

Let e denote a recursive enumeration of N^2 and $l,r \in R$ such that $e(i) = (le(i),re(i))$ for all i. Furthermore, let $t \in F$.
Then $A(t[o]) = le(o)$ and $z(o) = o$.
Now, let $A(t[x])$ and $z(x)$ be already defined for all $x \leq n-1$. Then
$A(t[n]) =$ " Let $e(z(n-1)) = (j,m)$. Let m' be the greatest number such that $m \leq m' \leq n$ and $a(t[m'])$, $b(t[m'])$, and $H(t[m'])$ are all defined within at most n steps of computation. Then check that $\Phi_j(x) \leq H(t[m'])$ for all $x \leq \max(a(t[m']), b(t[m']))$ and range$_{a(t[m'])}\, \varphi_j \subseteq \text{range}_{m'}\, t \subseteq$ range$_{b(t[m'])}\, \varphi_j$. If this check fails, then $z(n) = z(n-1)+1$ and $A(t[n]) = le(z(n))$. In all the other cases let $z(n) = z(n-1)$ and $A(t[n]) = le(z(n-1))$ $(= A(t[n-1]))$"

Now, let $L \in \mathcal{L}$, $t \in \text{text}(L)$, and i be the least number such that $\max\{\Phi_{le(i)}(x)/x \leq \max(a(t[n]),b(t[n]))\} \leq H(t[n])$, range$_{a(t[n])}\, \varphi_{le(i)} \subseteq$ **range**$_n\, t \subseteq \text{range}_{b(t[n])}\, \varphi_{le(i)}$ for all $n \geq re(i)$, and $(a(t[n]))_{n\in N}$ is unbounded (hence range $\varphi_{le(i)} = L$). Then $z(n) = i$ for almost all n, hence $A(t[n]) = le(i)$ for almost all n, and A text-identifies $\mathcal{L}$. -

Next we state (without proof; roughly speaking, the proof of Theorem 2 is similar to the proof of Theorem 1, though it needs more sophisticated details) that ARB can be characterized in a "stronger" way, namely the order of quantors in comparison with Theorem 1 may be changed ($\exists j \forall t$ instead of $\forall t \exists j$). Furthermore, the families in ARB suffice an honesty-like complexity condition (cf. Theorem 2,(3)).

<u>Definition 3</u>. Let $\mathcal{L} \subseteq \mathcal{L}_o$.

- $\mathcal{L}$ is said to be uniformly R^+-arb-approximable iff there are functions $a \in P$, $b \in P$, $h \in R^+$ such that for all $L \in \mathcal{L}$ there is a number j such that for all $t \in arb(L)$ hold (1), (2) (from Definition 2), and (3) $\text{range}_{a(t[n])} \varphi_{h(j)} \subseteq \text{range}_n\, t \subseteq \text{range}_{b(t[n])} \varphi_{h(j)}$ for almost all n.
- $\mathcal{L}$ is said to be uniformly Φ-arb-approximable iff there are functions $a \in P$, $b \in P$, $H \in P$ such that for all $L \in \mathcal{L}$ there is a number j such that for all $t \in arb(L)$ hold (1), (2), and
  (3') for almost all n
  (3'.1) $\Phi_j(n) \leq H(n, t(n))$,
  (3'.2) $\text{range}_{a(t[n])} \varphi_j \subseteq \text{range}_n\, t \subseteq \text{range}_{b(t[n])} \varphi_j$. -

<u>Theorem 2</u>. Let $\mathcal{L} \subseteq \mathcal{L}_o$. Then the following conditions are equivalent :

(1) $\mathcal{L}$ is arb-identifiable.
(2) $\mathcal{L}$ is uniformly R^+-arb-approximable.
(3) $\mathcal{L}$ is uniformly Φ -arb-approximable. -

For characterizing INCR we need the following abbreviation. For functions $c \in F$, $f \in P$, and $n \in N$ let $f =_n c$ denote the fact that $f(x)$ is defined and $f(x) = c(x)$ for all $x \leq n$.

<u>Theorem 3</u>. Let $\mathcal{L} \subseteq \mathcal{L}_o$. Then the following conditions are equivalent :

(1) $\mathcal{L}$ is incr-identifiable.
(2) There are functions $h \in R^+$, $g \in R$ such that for all $L \in \mathcal{L}$:
  (2.1) The set of all numbers i, such that $\varphi_{h(i)} =_{g(i)} c_L$, is nonempty and finite.
  (2.2) There is a number i such that $\varphi_{h(i)} =_{g(i)} c_L$ and range $\varphi_{h(i)} = L$.
(3) There are functions $b \in P$, $H \in R$ such that for all $L \in \mathcal{L}$:
  (3.1) $b(c_L[n])$ is defined for almost all n.
  (3.2) There is a number j such that range $\varphi_j = L$ and for almost

all n hold $\max\{\Phi_j(x)/x \le b(c_L[n])\} \le H(c_L[n])$ and $\text{range}_n\, c_L \subseteq \text{range}_{b(c_L[n])}\, \varphi_j$.

Proof. We show (1)⟷(2) and (1)⟷(3).

(1)⟶(2). Let L be incr-identifiable by the algorithm $A \in R$ with the property that $\varphi_j \in R$ for all $j \in$ range A (cf. proof of Theorem 1). Furthermore, for a tuple s of natural numbers we get $\bar{s}$ by ordering s in the strictly increasing way (without repetitions); for instance, if s = (6,2,3,3,2,4), then $\bar{s}$ = (2,3,4,6).

Now, let the set $M = \{(j,n)/\ \varphi_j(x)$ is defined for all $x \le n$ and $A(\overline{\varphi_j[n-1]}) = A(\overline{\varphi_j[n]}) = j\}$ be enumerated (without repetitions) by $e \in R$. Let $i \in N$, $e(i) = (j,n)$. Then define g(i) = the length of $\overline{\varphi_j[n]}$, and $\varphi_{h(i)}(x)$ = the x-th component of $\overline{\varphi_j[n]}$, if $x \le g(i)$, and $\varphi_{h(i)}(x) = \varphi_j(x)$, if $x > g(i)$. It is not difficult to show that then the conditions (2.1) and (2.2) hold.

(2)⟶(1). The algorithm that incr-identifies $\mathcal{L}$ works as follows. First it tries to collect the set M of all the numbers i such that $\varphi_{h(i)} =_{g(i)} c_L$, where $L \in \mathcal{L}$. In the limit it will eventually succeed, because there is only a finite number of such numbers i. Then using c_L it cancels all the numbers $i \in M$ with the property that range $\varphi_{h(i)} - L \neq \emptyset$ (to cancel i because of $y \in$ range $\varphi_{h(i)}$ the algorithm has only to wait until $c_L(n) > y$ and $y \notin \text{range}_n\, c_L$ or (if L is finite) c_L will be constant but less than y). Thus, in the limit a set M' remains such that range $\varphi_{h(i)} \subseteq L$ for all $i \in M'$, but because of (2.2) range $\varphi_j = L$ holds for at least one $j \in M'$. Therefore for identifying L it suffices to output a hypothesis a in the limit such that range φ_a is the union of all the ranges φ_i, where $i \in M'$. We omit a formal definition of the algorithm described.

(1)⟶(3). Let $\mathcal{L}$ be incr-identifiable by the algorithm $A \in R$ with the property that $\varphi_j \in R$ for all $j \in$ range A. Then for a language L and $n \in N$ let $b(c_L[n])$ be the least number x such that $\text{range}_n\, c_L \subseteq \text{range}_x\, \varphi_{A(c_L[n])}$, if such an x exists, and $b(c_L[n])$ undefined otherwise. Furthermore, let $H(c_L[n]) = \max\{\Phi_{A(c_L[n])}(x)/x \le b(c_L[n])\}$, if $b(c_L[n])$ is defined, undefined otherwise.

Clearly, if $L \in \mathcal{L}$, then $b(c_L[n])$ is defined for almost all n (for all n such that range $\varphi_j = L$, where $j = \lim_n A(c_L[n])$), and $\max\{\Phi_j(x)/x \le b(c_L[n])\} \le H(c_L[n])$ and $\text{range}_n\, c_L \subseteq \text{range}_{b(c_L[n])}\, \varphi_j$ hold for all n such that $A(c_L[n]) = j$, too.

(3)⟶(1). This proof differs from the proof of (3)⟶(1) of Theorem 1 only in a few details. The function a is not necessary here because c_L is an increasing function. Let $e \in R$ be such that for any $j \in \mathbb{N}$ there are infinitely many x such that $e(x) = j$. Furthermore, let L be a language.

Then $A(c_L[o]) = e(o)$ and $z(o) = o$.

Now, let $A(c_L[x])$ and $z(x)$ be already defined for all $x \leq n-1$. Then $A(c_L[n]) =$ "Let $e(z(n-1)) = j$. Let m be the greatest number such that $m \leq n$ and $b(c_L[m])$, $H(c_L[m])$ are both defined within at most n steps of computation. Then check that (i) $\Phi_j(x) \leq H(c_L[m])$ for all $x \leq b(c_L[m])$, (ii) $\text{range}_m\, c_L \subseteq \text{range}_{b(c_L[m])}\, \varphi_j$, (iii) if $y \in \text{range}_{b(c_L[m])}\, \varphi_j$ and $y \leq \max \text{range}_n\, c_L$, then $y \in \text{range}_n\, c_L$, and (iv) if $c_L(n-1) = c_L(n)$ (i.e. L will be finite), then $\text{range}_n\, c_L = \text{range}_{b(c_L[m])}\, \varphi_j$. If this check fails, then $z(n) = z(n-1)+1$. In all the other cases let $z(n) = z(n-1)$. Define $A(c_L[n]) = e(z(n))$."

Again it is not difficult to show that A incr-identifies $\mathcal{L}$. -

References

1. Gold, E M., Language Identification in the Limit. Information and Control, 1o, 1967, 447-474
2. Feldman, J., Some Decideability Results on Grammatical Inference and Complexity. Information and Control, 2o, 1972,244-262
3. Lindner, R., Algorithmische Erkennung. Diss.B, Jena, 1972
4. Thiele, H., Lernverfahren zur Erkennung formaler Sprachen. In : Kybernetik-Forschung, 3, 1973, 11-93
5. Knobe, B., Knobe, K., A Method of Inferring of Context-free Grammars. Information and Control, 31, 1976, 129-146
6. Gold, E M., Limiting Recursion. Journal of Symbolic Logic, 3o, 1965, 28-48
7. Theory of Algorithms and Programs 1,2,3. (J.M. Barzdin, Ed.), Latvian State University, Riga, 1974,1975,1976. (Russ.)
8. Wiehagen, R., Limes-Erkennung rekursiver Funktionen durch spezielle Strategien. Elektronische Informationsverarbeitung und Kybernetik (EIK), 12, 1976, 93-99
9. Blum, L., Blum, M., Inductive Inference : A Recursion Theoretic Approach. Memorandum No. ERL-M 386, Berkeley, 1973
1o. Wiehagen, R., Liepe, W., Charakteristische Eigenschaften von erkennbaren Klassen rekursiver Funktionen. EIK, 12, 1976, 421-438
11. Wiehagen, R., Jung, H., Rekursionstheoretische Charakterisierung von erkennbaren Klassen rekursiver Funktionen. EIK 13,7/8

CORRECTNESS OF RECURSIVE FLOW DIAGRAM PROGRAMS

J. A. Goguen*
Computer Science Department, UCLA
Los Angeles, California 90024, USA

J. Meseguer†
Departamento de Algebra y Fundamentos, Facultad de Ciencias,
Santiago de Compostela, SPAIN

Abstract

This paper presents a simple algebraic description of the semantics of non-deterministic recursive flow diagram programs with parallel assignment, culminating in a method for proving their partial correctness which generalizes the well-known Floyd-Naur method for ordinary flow diagram programs. Our treatment involves first considering a program scheme, and then interpreting it in an appropriate semantic model. The program schemes are conveniently viewed as diagrams in an algebraic theory, with semantic model a relational algebra. Some examples are given in a simple programming language whose features correspond precisely to our algebraic framework.

1. Introduction

What is most surprising about this paper is that the algebraic and programming concepts correspond so precisely, with simplicity and power on each side; it is almost as if they were designed for each other, even though they developed quite separately. Moreover, it seems to the authors that the modifications of each side from historical development required to bring about this agreement, actually resulted in improvements! We hope the reader enjoys the result as much as we enjoyed the process.

The content is a simple algebraic semantics for non-deterministic recursive flow diagram programs with parallel assignment, culminating in a method for proving their correctness which generalizes the so-called Floyd method for proving ordinary flow diagrams, as reformulated by Burstall (1972) and Goguen (1974), in which a non-deterministic (non-recursive) flow diagram program is a graph, whose nodes are labelled with sets, and whose edges are labelled with relations, such that if $e:n\to n'$ is an edge from n to n', and if the labels of e, n, n' are f, S, S' respectively, then f is a function $\underset{\sim}{P}(S) \to \underset{\sim}{P}(S')$, where $\underset{\sim}{P}(A)$ is the set of all subsets of A, that is, the powerset of A. The nodes correspond to the "states of control" of the program, while an element of the label of a node is an "environment," for the computation (e.g., a memory state). The edges correspond to transitions of control, and are labelled

*supported in part by the U.S. National Science Foundation, Grant No. MCS 72-03633 A04.
†partially supported by a March Foundation Research Fellowship.

by relations which describe the resulting changes of environment.

We give the usual example, a program to compute $X = \Sigma_{I=1}^{N} I$ from $N \geq 0$. Here $S = [\{X,N\} \to \omega]$, the set of possible states of knowing integer values for X, N ,

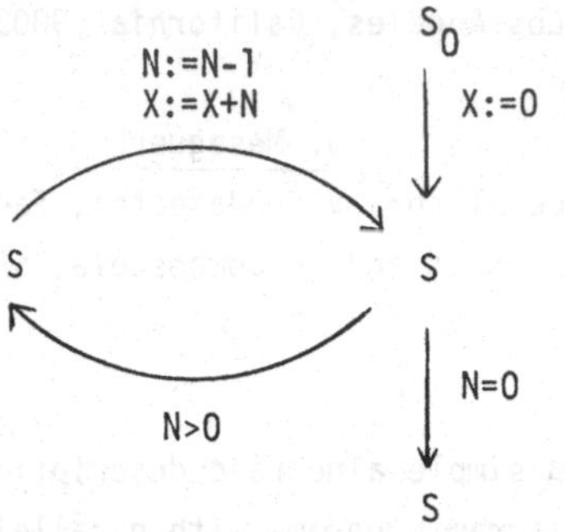

$[A \to B]$ denotes the set of all functions from A to B, ω denotes the set of all non-negative integers, and $S_0 = [\{N\} \to \omega]$. A typical element of S might be $\{\langle X,0\rangle, \langle N,3\rangle\}$.

Non-determinism is taken into account by considering elements of $\underset{\sim}{P}(S)$, sets of possible states of memory. The program above is not properly non-deterministic, so this feature not strictly necessary for its treatment. If $F: S \to S'$ is any relation, it defines a function $\underset{\sim}{P}(f): \underset{\sim}{P}(S) \to \underset{\sim}{P}(S')$ as follows: for $R \subseteq S$, $\underset{\sim}{P}(f)(R) = \cup\{f(s) \mid s \in R\}$, where f(s) is the set of elements in S' which are related under f to $s \in S$. Then "N>0" is $\underset{\sim}{P}(f)$, where $f: S \to S$ is the partial identity function defined for those $s \in S$ with $s(N)>0$, and then with value $f(s) = s$. It has the effect of a conditional branch on N positive. Similarly, "N=0" is $\underset{\sim}{P}(f)$ with $f: S \to S$ the partial identity function defined iff $s(N) = 0$, having the effect of a conditioned branch on zero. Further, "X:=0" is $\underset{\sim}{P}(f)$ with $f: S_0 \to S$ the function sending s to s' with $s'(X) = 0$ and $s'(N) = s(N)$. And "N:=N-1, X:=X+N" is a parallel assignment, $\underset{\sim}{P}(f)$ where $f: S \to S$ sends s to s' defined by $s'(N) = s(N)-1$ and $s'(X) = s(X)+s(N)$; the values of X and N are changed simultaneously, not sequentially. Assuming that "n-1" is a partial function defined iff $n>0$, this function f is defined iff $s(N)>0$; thus the earlier edge "N>0" is actually unnecessary. (We use this observation when we return to this example later.)

One important ingredient of our approach is to pass from such programs to program schemes, in which we no longer know what the states are, but only what variables are involved; and we no longer know the tests and operations, but only their names and how many arguments they went. These names stand for functions, which are given later, in an interpretation. In the scheme, only a name remains, such as "pos(N)" or "dec(N)". A simplified scheme for the program above, is given below.

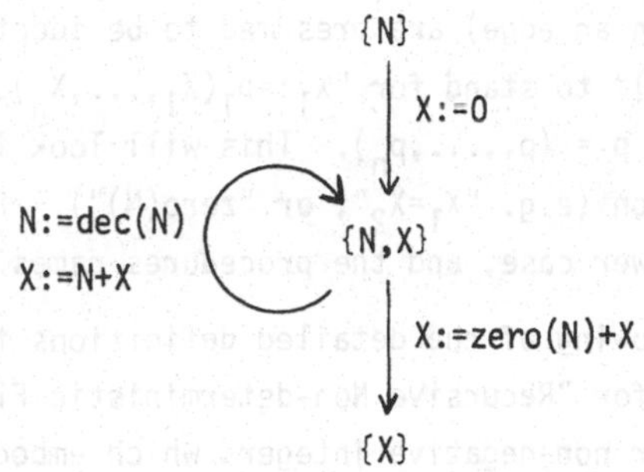

Notice that nodes are now labelled with sets of variables, rather than set of states. (Also notice that we have dropped an irrelevant variable N at the exit node.) If e is an edge from node n to node n', and if n and n' are labelled S and S' respectively, then e is labelled with an S'-tuple of terms in S variables, each component written in the form "$X_i' := t_i(X_1,\ldots, X_n)$" where $S' = \{X_1,\ldots, X_m\}$ and $S = \{X_1,\ldots, X_m\}$ are the sets of variables, and where each t_i is a <u>term</u> in primitive operations.

Looking carefully at the labels of nodes and edges, and the assumptions which must be made about them, leads to the notion of an algebraic theory, orginally formulated by Lawvere (1963), with modifications suggested by ADJ (1973) and John Reynolds. Morever, an interpretation is exactly an algebra for a theory, or more precisely, a relational algebra (see Eilenberg and Wright (1967)).

The major remaining feature is recursion. The idea is to treat a call of a procedure P as a occurrence of an operator defined by a flow diagram of its own. Thus, a recursive flow diagram program with n procedures will consist of n flow diagrams, each labelled with the name of the procedure it defines, and each able to use all procedures within it; the first one is the "main" one, at which execution starts. Below is a recursive version of the sample program we have been discussing, and also a recursive program for factorial:

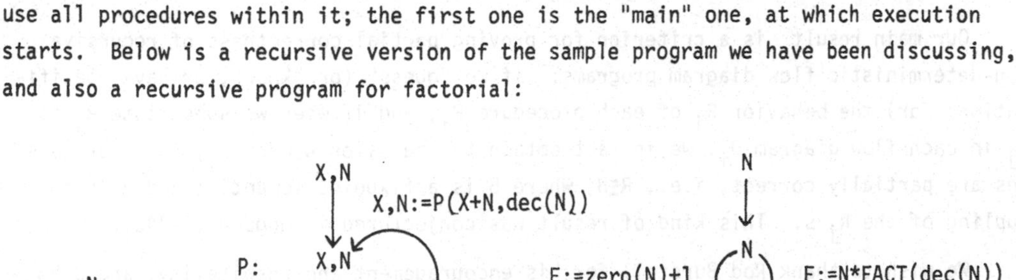

Some further details. First, we no longer bother to put set brackets on node labels. Second, the graphs are <u>protected</u>, meaning that the <u>entrance</u> node has no edges to it, and the <u>exit</u> node has no edges from it. Third, unlabelled edges represent projection functions, or in particular, identity functions (e.g., X,N → X,N);

and unmentioned identifiers (on an edge) are presumed to be identities (e.g., X:=X). Fourth, we permit "$p(X_1,\ldots,X_n)$" to stand for "$X_1:=p_1(X_1,\ldots,X_n)$, $X_2:=p_2(X_1,\ldots,X_n)$, ..., $X_n:=p_n(X_1,\ldots,X_n)$", where $p = (p_1,\ldots,p_n)$. This will look less peculiar when p is a partial identity function (e.g. "$X_1=X_2$", or "zero(N)"). Finally, we write the given operator names in lower case, and the procedures names in upper case.

We conclude this foreshadowing of the detailed definitions to follow by giving the above programs in "RNFD" (for "Recursive Non-deterministic Flow Diagram"), a simple programming language for non-negative integers which embodies the features discussed in this paper; see Appendix 2 for more detail.

```
proc SUM(N)
     source(X,N) assign (X,N):=P(0,N)
     exit(X) corp
proc P(X,N)
     source a(X,N)assign (X,N):=P(N+X,dec(N)),target a
     source a assign zero(N)
     exit (X,N) corp
end

proc FACT(N)
     source a (N) assign F:=inc(zero(N)), target b
     source a assign F:=N*FACT(dec(N))
     exit b (F) corp
end
```

The idea is that a program is a sequence of procedures, where a procedure has both argument and return variable lists, and a body consisting of a sequence of statements, each of the form source ℓ1 assign a1,..., an target ℓ2, where ℓ1 and ℓ2 are labels (corresponding to node names) and a1,..., an are assignments (to be executed in parallel). Note that keywords in RNFD are underlined.

Our main result is a criterion for proving partial correctness of recursive non-deterministic flow diagram programs: if we "guess" (or "know", or have specifications for) the behavior R_j of each procedure P_j, and if when we substitute R_j for P_j in each flow diagram D_i, we in fact obtain the behavior R_i for D_i, then our guesses are partially correct, i.e., $R \subseteq B$, where B is a fixpoint semantics and R is the tupling of the R_j's. This kind of result was conjectured in Goguen (1974a).

We wish to thank Rod Burstall for his encouragement and hospitality, and John Reynolds for the idea of using sets of variables as objects of a theory. We also thank Jesse Wright, Saunders MacLane, Bill Lawvere, Jim Thatcher and Eric Wagner for their inspiration, and our friends Charlotte Linde and Ignacio Sols for help in creating the environment in which the work was done.

2. Notation and Preliminaries

The powerset of X is denoted $\underset{\sim}{P}(X)$; the Cartesian product of a family $(A_i)_{i\in I}$ is denoted $\prod_{i\in I} A_i$. The set of functions from B to A is denoted A^B or [B → A], and the trivial bijection $A^B \cong \prod_{b\in B} A$ is often used implicitly. #A denotes the cardinal of A, and ω denotes the natural numbers. Given a function f:A→B and a set C, let f^C [or C^f] be "left [or right] composition by f", $f^C:A^C \to B^C$ by $g \mapsto f\circ g$ or $C^f:C^B \to C^A$ by $h \mapsto h\circ f$]. The same notation, f:A→B, is used for partial functions and relations However, a relation f:A→B is sometimes viewed as a function $f:A \to \tilde{P}(B)$, and a certain tendency exists to denote relations by capitals, R, F, etc. The tupling $(f_1,\ldots,f_n)$ of functions, [or relations] $f_1:A \to B_1,\ldots, f_n:A \to B_n$ is the function [or relation] $(f_1,\ldots,f_n): A \to B_1\times\ldots\times B_n$ defined by: $a \mapsto (f_1 a,\ldots,f_n a)$ [or $(f_1,\ldots f_n)(a;b_1,\ldots,b_n)$ defined iff each $f_1(a,b_1),\ldots, f_n(a,b_n)$ is defined].

Familiarity with the concepts of category, subcategory, functor, natural transformation and equivalence and isomorphism of categories is assumed. See ADJ (1976), or for more depth MacLane (1971). We double underline categories, as in $\underline{\underline{C}}$, and denote its object class $|\underline{\underline{C}}|$, while $\underline{\underline{C}}(A,B)$ is its set of morphisms (arrows, or maps) from A to B. Given morphisms f: A→B, g:B→C, their composition is denoted g∘f or gf:A→C. The identity map for an object A is denoted 1_A:A→A. $\underline{\underline{Set}}$, $\underline{\underline{Pfn}}$, $\underline{\underline{Rel}}$ denote the categories with objects sets and morpnisms functions, partial functions and relations respectively. Given $B_1,\ldots B_n \in |\underline{\underline{C}}|$, an object $B_1\times\ldots\times B_n$ together with morphisms $\Pi_i:B_1\times\ldots\times B_n \to B_i$, $1\le i\le n$ (called projections) is a direct product of $B_1,\ldots,B_n$ iff for each object A and morphisms f_i:A→B:, $1\le i\le n$, there exists a unique morphism $(f_1,\ldots,f_n):A \to B_1\times\ldots\times B_n$, such that $\Pi_i\circ(f_1,\ldots,f_n) = f$, $1\le i\le n$. Define the direct product, $\prod_{i\in I} A_i$, of an arbitrary family of objects $(A_i)_{i\in I}$ similarly. Cartesian product is a direct product in $\underline{\underline{Set}}$, but not in $\underline{\underline{Pfn}}$ or $\underline{\underline{Rel}}$.

A graph G is a set G of edges, together with a set |G| of nodes and two functions ∂_0,∂_1: G→|G|, called source and target. A graph morphism from $G=(G,|G|,\partial_0,\partial_1)$ to $H=(H,|H|,\partial_0,\partial_1)$ is a pair of functions, F:G→H, |F|:|G|→|H| which "preserve source and target", i.e., $|F|\partial_i=\partial_i F$, for i=0,1. Graphs and graph morphisms form a category $\underline{\underline{Gph}}$. A graph is finite iff both G and |G| are finite. A path p in a graph G is a string $e_0e_1\ldots e_{n-1}$ of edges in G such that $\partial_1 e_{i-1}=\partial_0 e_i$, $0<i<n$; we say that n is the length of p. For n>0, we say $p=e_0\ldots e_{n-1}$ is a path from source $\partial_0 p=\partial_0 e_0$ to target $\partial_1 p=\partial_1 e_{n-1}$. For any v∈|G|, the empty string λ is the length zero path from v to v. Given a graph G, define the path category of G, $\underline{\underline{Pa}}G$ by: $|\underline{\underline{Pa}}G|=|G|$; $\underline{\underline{Pa}}G(u,v)=\{(u,p,v)|p$ is a path from u to v}, for any u,v∈|G|. Composition is path (i.e., string) concatenation, $(w,p',v)\circ(u,p,v) = (u,pp',w)$; and $1_u=(u,\lambda,u)$ for u∈|G|. Any small categoty $\underline{\underline{C}}$ (i.e., $|\underline{\underline{C}}|$ a set) defines a graph $U\underline{\underline{C}}$, with nodes the objects, and edges the morphisms of $\underline{\underline{C}}$. Any functor $F:\underline{\underline{C}}\to\underline{\underline{D}}$ between two small categories induces a graph morphism $UF:U\underline{\underline{C}}\to U\underline{\underline{D}}$, and hence we have a functor $U:\underline{\underline{Cat}}\to\underline{\underline{Gph}}$. There is also a graph morphism $\eta_G:G\to U\underline{\underline{Pa}}G$ which is the identity on nodes, and maps an edge e in G to the path $(\partial_0 e,e,\partial_1 e)$. $\underline{\underline{Pa}}G$ has the following "universal property": Given a small category $\underline{\underline{C}}$ and a graph morphism $F:G\to U\underline{\underline{C}}$, there exists a unique functor $\overline{F}:\underline{\underline{Pa}}G\to\underline{\underline{C}}$ which "extends F", i.e.,

$U\overline{F}\circ\eta_G=F$.

A ranked alphabet is a set Σ, together with a map ar: $\Sigma\to w$, assigning to each $\sigma\in\Sigma$ a natural number called its "arity". The elements of Σ are used as operation symbols: a Σ-algebra is a set A together with for each $\sigma\in\Sigma$ an operation $A\sigma$: $A^n\to A$, for $ar\sigma=n$. A Σ-homomorphism from Σ-algebra A to Σ-algebra B is a map $f:A\to B$, such that for any $\sigma\in\Sigma$, $f\circ A\sigma = B\sigma\circ f^n$, for $ar\sigma=n$, where $f^n(a_1,\ldots,a_n) = (fa_1,\ldots,fa_n)$. Σ-algebras and homomorphism form a category $\underline{\underline{Alg}}_\Sigma$ under function composition, and we have a functor $U:\underline{\underline{Alg}}_\Sigma\to\underline{\underline{Set}}$, sending $f:(A,(A\sigma)_{\sigma\in\Sigma}) \to (B,(B\sigma)_{\sigma\in\Sigma})$ to $f:A\to B$. Given a set X, the free Σ-algebra on X is the smallest set, $T_\Sigma(X)$, of words on the alphabet $\Sigma\cup X\cup\{(,)\}$ such that

i) $X\subset T_\Sigma(X)$, $\Sigma_0\subset T_\Sigma(X)$

ii) if $ar\sigma=n>0$, and $w_1,\ldots w_n\in T_\Sigma(X)$, then $\sigma(w_1\ldots w_n)\in T_\Sigma(X)$.

$T_\Sigma(X)$ is a Σ-algebra with constants Σ_0, and, for $ar\sigma>0$, operations defined by $T_\Sigma(X)\sigma$: $(w_1,\ldots w_n) \mapsto \sigma(w_1\ldots w_n)$. $T_\Sigma(X)$ has the following "universal property": Given a Σ-algebra A, and a map $f:X\to A$, there exists a unique homomorphism $\overline{f}:T_\Sigma(X)\to A$, "extending f" (i.e., $U\overline{f}\circ\eta_X=f$, where η_X is the inclusion map of X in $T_\Sigma(X)$). A partial Σ-algebra [resp. a relational Σ-algebra] is obtained by allowing the operations $A\sigma$: $A^n\to A$ to be partial functions (resp. relations). A homomorphism is than a partial map (resp. relation) f: $A\to B$ such that $f\circ A\sigma = B\sigma\circ f^n$, where $f^n((a_1,\ldots,a_n),(b_1,\ldots,b_n))$ is defined iff $f(a_1,b_1),\ldots,f(a_n,b_n)$ all defined. We then have categories $\underline{\underline{PAlg}}_\Sigma$, $\underline{\underline{RAlg}}_\Sigma$ of partial (resp. relational) Σ-algebras and homomorphisms, and "forgetful" functors $U:\underline{\underline{PAlg}}_\Sigma \to \underline{\underline{Pfn}}$, $U:\underline{\underline{RAlg}}_\Sigma \to \underline{\underline{Rel}}$. Partial algebras are in particular relational algebras, and we shall so view them frequently.

A poset is a set P together with a partial order, denoted $\sqsubseteq$. The least upper bound or supremum of a family $(a_i)_{i\in I}$, if it exists, is denoted $\bigsqcup_{i\in I} a_i$. A poset is complete if every chain has a supremum; in particular the supremum of the empty chain is the minimum element, denoted $\perp$. $\underset{\sim}{P}(A)$, is a complete poset under inclusion. If P and Q are complete posets, $P\times Q$ is also a complete poset with the component-wise ordering. A map $f:P\to Q$ between two posets is continuous if for each nonempty chain $(a_i)_{i\in I}$ with a supremum in P, the image has a supremum, and $f(\bigsqcup_{i\in I} a_i) = \bigsqcup_{i\in I} fa_i$. A theorem of Tarski guarantees a minimal fixpoint for a continuous map $f:P\to P$ of a complete poset into itself, namely the element $\bigsqcup_{m\in\omega} f^m\perp$.

3. The Algebraic Theory of Parallel Assignment

(3.1) Definition. Given a ranked alphabet Σ and a fixed denumerable set $\mathfrak{X}$ of "variables", the algebraic theory of parallel assignment is a category $\underline{\underline{P}}_\Sigma(\mathfrak{X})$ as follows:

objects: finite subsets X,Y,Z,... of $\mathfrak{X}$;

morphisms: $\underline{\underline{P}}_\Sigma(\underline{\underline{X}})(X,Y) = (T_\Sigma(X))^Y$. Thus an arrow $\alpha: X \to Y$ is a map $\alpha: Y \to T_\Sigma(X)$. The composition $\beta \circ \alpha$, for $\alpha: X \to Y$, $\beta: Y \to Z$, is given by

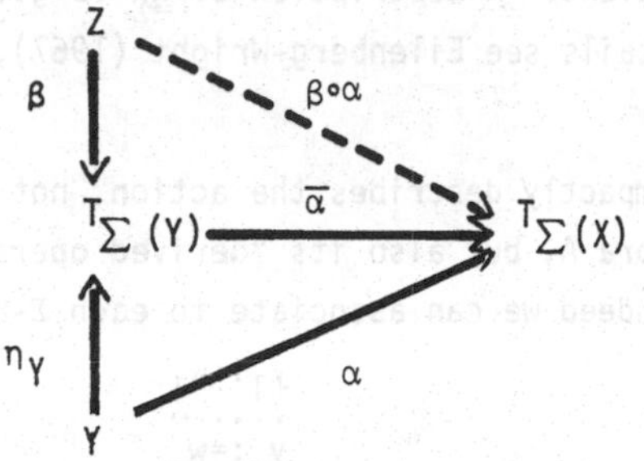

where $\overline{\alpha}$ is the unique homomorphism guaranteed for α by the universal property of $T_\Sigma(Y)$. Finally, the identities $1_X: X \to X$ are the inclusion maps $\eta_X: X \to T_\Sigma(X)$.

(3.2) Notation. Variables in the set X are denoted $x, y, z, x_1, x_2, y_1, y_2$, etc. When reasoning with generic finite subsets X,Y of $\underline{\underline{X}}$ we sometimes find it useful to write $X = \{x_1, \ldots, x_n\}$, $Y = \{y_1, \ldots, y_m\}$, understanding that neither are the variables ordered nor are the subsets disjoint. Words in $T_\Sigma(X)$ are denoted u, v, w, w_1, w_2, etc. We can think of a morphism $\alpha: X \to Y$ in $\underline{\underline{P}}_\Sigma(\underline{\underline{X}})$ as a "Y-indexed list of words," and hence we sometimes use list notation $X \xrightarrow{(w_1,\ldots,w_m)} Y$ to denote the map α sending y_j in Y to $w_j \in T_\Sigma(X)$, $1 \le j \le m$. A variant of this is the assignment notation,

$$X \xrightarrow[\substack{y_1:=w_1 \\ y_2:=w_2 \\ \cdots\cdots \\ y_m:=w_m}]{} Y$$

which makes explicit the variables in the target. Arrows in $\underline{\underline{P}}_\Sigma(\underline{\underline{X}})$ may be referred to as parallel assignments. In fact, composition in $\underline{\underline{P}}_\Sigma(\underline{\underline{X}})$ is word substitution, as the following shows:

(3.3) Example. Let $\Sigma = \{+, \cdot, -, 0, 1\}$ with $+, \cdot, -$ of arity 2 and 0,1 of arity 0. Let $X = \{x,y\}$, $Y = \{x,z,v\}$, $Z = \{x,z\}$. The composition of the parallel assignments

$$X \xrightarrow{\substack{x:=\cdot(+(xx)y) \\ x:=-(x1) \\ v:=+(y1)}} Y \;,\; Y \xrightarrow{\substack{z:=+(+(zv)x) \\ z:=\cdot(xv)}} Z$$

is

$$X \xrightarrow{\substack{x:=+(+(-(x1)+(y1))\cdot(+(xx)y)) \\ z:=\cdot(\cdot(+(xx)y)+(y1))}} Z$$

(3.4) Remark. From the definition of $\underline{\underline{P}}_\Sigma(\underline{\underline{X}})$ it follows that $X = \{x_1, \ldots, x_n\}$ is a direct product of the objects $\{x_1\}, \ldots, \{x_n\}$, with projections $X \xrightarrow{x_i:=x_i} \{x_i\}, 1 \le i \le n$.

Hence $\underline{\underline{P}}_\Sigma(\mathbb{X})$ is a kind of <u>algebraic theory</u>, in fact, the free algebraic theory, $\underline{\underline{N}}_\Sigma$, on Σ, in the Lawvere (1963) sense is a <u>skeletal</u> (cf. Mac Lane (1971)) category of $\underline{\underline{P}}_\Sigma(\mathbb{X})$, hence they are equivalent. A description of $\underline{\underline{N}}_\Sigma$ is given in the proof of theorem (3.5). For more details see Eilenberg-Wright (1967), Pareigis (1970), or ADJ (1975).

An algebraic theory compactly describes the action, not only of the basic operations $\sigma\epsilon\Sigma$ of a given Σ-algebra A, but also its "derived operations," obtained by composition and tupling. Indeed we can associate to each Σ-algebra A, a functor $\underline{A}:\underline{\underline{P}}_\Sigma(\mathbb{X})\to\underline{\text{Set}}$ which maps a parallel assignment $X\xrightarrow{y_1:=w_1 \,\cdots\, y_m:=w_m}Y$ to its interpretation as a function $A^X \xrightarrow{y_1:=w_1 \,\cdots\, y_m:=w_m} A^Y$, mapping an X-indexed list of elements of A to the Y-indexed list of "results after execution of the parallel assignments in the Σ-algebra A."

<u>(3.5) Theorem</u>. The category $\underline{\text{Alg}}_\Sigma$ of Σ-algebras and homomorphisms is isomorphic to the following category, $\underline{\text{Alg}}_{\underline{\underline{P}}_\Sigma(\mathbb{X})}$ having as <u>objects</u>, functors $\underline{A}:\underline{\underline{P}}_\Sigma(\mathbb{X})\to\underline{\text{Set}}$ such that there exists a set A such that

(i) for each object X in $\underline{\underline{P}}_\Sigma(\overline{\mathbb{X}})$, $\underline{A}(X)=A^X$;

(ii) if X is $\{x_1,\ldots,x_n\}$, then for $1\le j\le n$, $\underline{A}(x_j:=x_j):A^X\to A^{\{x_j\}}$ is the "j^{th} projection", mapping each list $a:X\to A$ to the list $x_j\circ a$, i.e., $(a_1,\ldots,a_n)\mapsto a_j$;

<u>morphisms</u> are then all natural transformations between such functors.

Relational algebras also fit into this framework. Relations $f:A\to\underset{\sim}{P}(B)$ correspond bijectively to "additive" maps $f:\underset{\sim}{P}(A)\to\underset{\sim}{P}(B)$; thus a relational Σ-algebra structure on A is the same as an "additive Σ-algebra structure on $\underset{\sim}{P}(A)$." This characterization is used in Eilenberg-Wright (1967), and is expressed by

<u>(3.6) Theorem</u>. The category $\underline{\text{RAlg}}_\Sigma$ of relational Σ-algebras and homomorphisms is isomorphic to the subcategory of $\underline{\text{Alg}}_\Sigma$ with <u>objects</u>: Σ-algebras $\underset{\sim}{P}(A)$, with carrier a powerset, such that for each $n\ge 0$, $\sigma\epsilon\Sigma$ with $\text{ar}\sigma=n$, and $(A_1,\ldots,A_n)\epsilon\underset{\sim}{P}(A)^n$,

(i) $\underset{\sim}{P}(A)\sigma(A_1,\ldots,A_n) = \cup \left\{\underset{\sim}{P}(A)\sigma(\{a_1\},\ldots,\{a_n\}) \,\middle|\, (a_1,\ldots,a_n)\epsilon A_1\text{x}\ldots\text{x}A_n\right\}$

and <u>morphisms</u>: Σ-homomorhpisms $f:\underset{\sim}{P}(A)\to\underset{\sim}{P}(B)$ such that for each $A'\epsilon\underset{\sim}{P}(A)$

(ii) $fA' = \bigcup_{a\epsilon A'} f\{a\}$.

Conditions (i) and (ii) express "additivity". Theorems (3.5) and (3.6) are proved in Appendix 1.

Combining (3.5) and (3.6), we see that to each relational Σ-algebra A corresponds bijectively a functor $\underset{\sim}{P}(A):\underline{\underline{P}}_\Sigma(\mathbb{X})\to\underline{\text{Set}}$. A parallel assignment $\alpha:X\to Y$ corresponds to an (additive) map $\underset{\sim}{P}(A)(\alpha):\underset{\sim}{P}(A)^X\to\underset{\sim}{P}(A)^Y$, called "<u>the relation computed by the parallel</u>

<u>assignment</u> α in the relational Σ-algebra A", denoted $\underline{A}(\alpha)$, and defined to be the composition

$$A^X \xrightarrow{\{-\}^X} \underset{\sim}{P}(A)^X \xrightarrow{\underset{\sim}{P}(A)(\alpha)} \underset{\sim}{P}(A)^Y \xrightarrow{\Pi_Y} \underset{\sim}{P}(A^Y) \qquad (\text{composite: } \underline{A}(\alpha))$$

$$(a_1,\ldots,a_n) \longmapsto (\{a_1\},\ldots,\{a_n\}) \qquad (A_1,\ldots,A_m) \longmapsto A_1 X \ldots X A_m$$

We hope that context will make clear whether $A(\alpha)$ denotes such a relation or a map arising from a $\underline{P}_\Sigma(\overline{X})$-algebra, $\underline{A}:\underline{P}_\Sigma(\overline{X})\to\underline{\text{Set}}$. Contrary to what might be expected, for a given relational Σ-algebra A, the assignment to each $\alpha:X\to Y$ in $\underline{P}_\Sigma(\overline{X})$ of its corresponding relation $\underline{A}(\alpha)$, <u>does not</u> give a functor $\underline{A}:\underline{P}_\Sigma(\overline{X})\to\underline{\text{Rel}}$, but a graph morphism between the corresponding underlying graphs $\underline{A}:\underline{P}_\Sigma(\overline{X})\to\underline{\text{Rel}}$ (we omit the U for convenience; readers who are suspicious about "big graphs" (such as <u>Rel</u>) may take refuge in some Grothendieck universe). If the relational algebra A is actually a partial algebra, then $\underline{A}(\alpha)$ is a partial function, and we get a graph morphism $\underline{A}:\underline{P}_\Sigma(\overline{X})\to\underline{\text{Pfn}}$.

4. <u>Flow Diagram Programs (with parallel assignment)</u>

<u>(4.1) Definition</u>. A <u>flow diagram program schema</u> (FDPS) with parallel assignment and operations Σ, is a graph morphism $S:G\to\underline{P}_\Sigma(\overline{X})$, where $G = (G,v_0,v_1)$ is a fully protected reachable finite graph, i.e., a finite graph with nodes v_0,v_1 such that no edges go out of v_1 (output node) or into v_0 (input node); and every node of G lies on some path from v_0 to v_1.

<u>(4.2) Example</u>. Let $\Sigma = \{+,-,\cdot,\text{zero},\text{pos},0,1\}$ with $+,-,\cdot$, binary, zero and pos unary, and 0,1, constants. Let $S:G\to\underline{P}_\Sigma(\overline{X})$ be the graph morphism with source the graph on the left and image the one on the right:

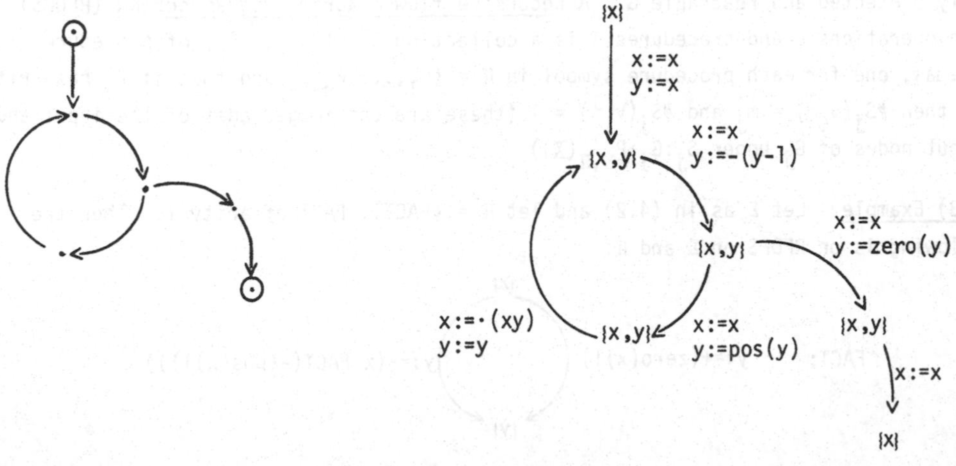

The input and output nodes of G have been circled. We tend to think of S in terms of its image, rather than its underlying graph G.

<u>(4.3) Definition</u>. A <u>flow diagram program</u> (FDP) with parallel assignment and operations Σ, is a pair (S,A) with S a FDPS and A a relational Σ-algebra.

<u>(4.4) Example</u>. Let S be as in (4.2) with A=ω and +,-,$\cdot$, the ordinary addition, subtraction and multiplication; pos(n) defined and equal to n iff n is positive; and zero(n) defined and equal to 0 iff n is 0. With these operations and the constants 0,1, ω is a relational (actually a partial) Σ-algebra.

<u>(4.5) Remark</u>. A FDP (S,A) determines a graph morphism to $\underline{Rel}$, namely the composition $G \overset{S}{\to} \underline{\underline{P}}_\Sigma(\underline{X}) \to \underline{Rel}$. This shows the connection with the more general definition of a flow diagram program as graph morphism P:G$\to\underline{Rel}$ (or P:G$\to\underline{Pfn}$) in Goguen (1974), which also suggests

<u>(4.6) Definition</u>. Given a FDP (S,A), its <u>behavior</u> is the relation $B(S,A): A^{S(v_0)} \to A^{S(v_1)}$ defined to be the union of relations $\bigcup_{f:v_0 \to v_1 \text{ in } \underline{\underline{Pa}}_G} \overline{A\circ S}(f)$, where $\overline{A\circ S}$ is the unique functor $\underline{\underline{Pa}}G\to\underline{Rel}$ extending $\underline{A}\circ S$:G$\to\underline{Rel}$, guaranteed by the universal property of $\underline{\underline{Pa}}_G$.

<u>(4.7) Exercise</u>. Check that for (S,A) as in (4.4), B(S,A) is the factorial function $n \mapsto n!$.

5. <u>The behavior and correctness of Recursive Flow Diagram Programs</u>

<u>(5.1) Definition</u>. Given a ranked alphabet, Σ of "operation symbols", and another, finite, $\Pi = \{P_1,\ldots,P_n\}$, of "procedure symbols", the <u>algebraic theory of parallel assignment with operations Σ and procedures Π</u>, denoted $\underline{\underline{P}}_{\Sigma,\Pi}(\underline{X})$ is simply the algebraic theory $\underline{\underline{P}}_{\Sigma\cup\Pi}(\underline{X})$.

<u>(5.2) Definition</u>. A <u>procedure schema</u> is a graph morphism $G\to\underline{\underline{P}}_{\Sigma,\Pi}(\underline{X})$, from a finite, fully protected and reachable G. A <u>recursive flow diagram program schema</u> (RFDPS) with operations Σ and procedures Π is a collection $S = (S_1,\ldots,S_n)$ of procedure schemas, one for each procedure symbol in $\Pi = \{P_1,\ldots,P_n\}$, such that if P_j has arity m_j, then $\#S_j(v_0^{\,j}) = m_j$ and $\#S_j(v_1^{\,j}) = 1$ (these are the image nodes of the input and output nodes of G_j under $S_j:G_j\to\underline{\underline{P}}_{\Sigma,\Pi}(\underline{X})$).

<u>(5.3) Example</u>. Let Σ as in (4.2) and let Π = {FACT}, FACT of arity 1. Then the following is on RFDPS on Σ and Π:

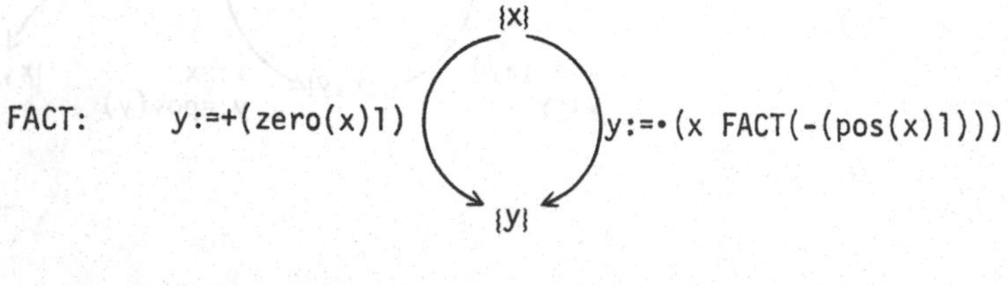

(We shall write the label, P_j: , to the left of S_j).

(5.4) Remark. We only need one procedure symbol, of arity 1, to calculate the factorial, but there is no bound on the number needed in general. This suggests letting $\overline{\Pi} = \{P,Q,R,\ldots,P_1,\ldots,P_n,\ldots\}$ be such that $ar^{-1}(n)\subset\overline{\Pi}$ is denumerable for each n, and then defining $\underline{P}_{\Sigma,\overline{\Pi}}(\underline{X}) = P_{\Sigma\cup\overline{\Pi}}(\underline{X})$. Any finite ranked Π can be seen as contained in $\overline{\Pi}$, so that $\underline{P}_{\Sigma,\Pi}(\underline{X})$ is then a subtheory of $\underline{P}_{\Sigma,\overline{\Pi}}(\underline{X})$. Then a recursive flow diagram program schema with operations Σ is a RFDPS on Σ and Π - in the sense of (5.2) - for some finite $\Pi\subset\overline{\Pi}$.

(5.5) Definition. A recursive flow diagram program (RFDP) on Σ and Π is a pair (S,A), with S a RFDPS on Σ and Π, and A a relational Σ-algebra.

For example, the pair (S,A) with S as in (5.3) and A as in (4.4). Let $R = (R_1,\ldots,R_n)$ be a family of relations, each $R_j:A^{m_j}\to A$, with the same arity, m_j, as P_j; this makes the relational Σ-algebra A into a $\Sigma\cup\Pi$-relational algebra, say A_R, and we can then associate to each S_j in S an ordinary FDP with operations $\Sigma\cup\Pi$, namely (S_j,A_R), and hence a behavior $B(S_j,A_R)$. We call the collection $B(S,A_R) = (B(S_1,A_R),\ldots,B(S_n A_R))$ the behavior of (S,A) relative to $R = (R_1,\ldots,R_n)$. This defines a map

$$B(S,A\_):\underset{\sim}{P}(A^{m_1}xA)x\ldots x\underset{\sim}{P}(A^{m_n}xA)\to\underset{\sim}{P}(A^{m_1}xA)x\ldots x\underset{\sim}{P}(A^{m_n}xA)$$

sending $R = (R_1,\ldots,R_n)$ to $B(S,A_R) = (B(S_1,A_R),\ldots,B(S_n,A_R))$; note that we have identified A^{X_j} with A^{m_j} for $X_j = S_j(v_0^{\,j})$, with $\#X_j = m_j$.

(5.6) Theorem. B(S,A_) is continuous

Proof. For any chain $(R_i = (R_1^{\,i},\ldots,R_n^{\,i}))_{i\in I}$, with I totally ordered and $R_k^{\,i}\subseteq R_k^{\,j}$ if $i\leq j$ and $1\leq k\leq n$, we are to prove that

$$\bigsqcup_{i\in I} B(S,A_{R_i}) = B(S,A_{\bigsqcup_{i\in I} R_i})$$

or more explicitly (cf. (4.6)), that

$$\bigcup_{i\in I}\left(\bigcup\left\{\overline{\underline{A_{R_i}}\circ S_j}(f)\,\middle|\, f:v_0^{\,j}\to v_1^{\,j} \text{ in } \underline{\underline{PaG}}_j\right\}\right) = \bigcup\left\{\overline{\underline{A_{\cup R_i}}\circ S_j}(f)\,\middle|\, f:v_0^{\,j}\to v_1^{\,j} \text{ in } \underline{\underline{PaG}}_j\right\}$$

Now, if we prove that $\bigcup_{i\in I}\overline{A_{R_i}\circ S_j}(f)) = \overline{A_{\cup_i R_i}\circ S_j}(f)$, for each $f:v_0^{\,j}\to v_1^{\,j}$ in $\underline{\underline{PaG}}_j$ and for $1\leq j\leq n$, we are done. But this follows from the universal property of $\underline{\underline{PaG}}_j$ if we prove $\bigcup_{i\in I}(\underline{A_{R_i}}\circ S_j(e)) = \underline{A_{\cup_i R_i}}\circ S_j(e)$, for each edge e in G_j for $1\leq j\leq n$. For this, it suffices to prove

(5.7) Lemma. For any $\alpha:X\to Y$ in $\underline{P}_{\Sigma,\Pi}(\underline{X})$ and chain $(R_i)_{i\in I}$ as above, $\bigcup_{i\in I}\underline{A_{R_i}}(\alpha) = \underline{A_{\cup_i R_i}}(\alpha)$.

The proof is a simple but tedious induction on the depth of (i.e. maximum number of nested parentheses occurring in, or depth of the corresponding tree for) words $w \in T_{\Sigma \cup \Pi}(X)$. □

We are now ready to give the definition of behavior for a RFDP with "call by name" or "copy rule" semantics. If we are only interested in the first "main" procedure, we can select just the first component of the behavior.

<u>(5.8) Definition.</u> The <u>behavior</u> B(S,A) of an RFDP (S,A) is the minimal fixpoint of the continuous function B(S,A_); thus it is given by the formula

$$B(S,A) = \bigsqcup_{k\in\omega} B(S,A\_)^k(\phi,\ldots,\phi)$$

From this definition and the last theorem we get the following reduction of the correctness problem for RFDP's to the previously studied problem of correctness for ordinary FDP's (see Goguen (1974), (1974a)).

<u>(5.9) Theorem.</u> Given an RFDP, (S,A) on Σ and Π and a family $R = (R_1,\ldots,R_n)$ of relations with R_j the same arity as $P_j \in \Pi$, if $B(S,A_R) \sqsubseteq (R_1,\ldots,R_n)$, then (S,A) is partially correct with respect to $R_1,\ldots,R_n$, in the sense that $B(S,A) \sqsubseteq (R_1,\ldots,R_n)$.

<u>Proof.</u> Write $B(S,A_Q)=F(Q)$. Then $F(R) \sqsubseteq R$ and $\bot \sqsubseteq R$ imply by induction $\bot \sqsubseteq F^k(\bot) \sqsubseteq F^k(R) \sqsubseteq R$ for $k\in\omega$. Thus $B(S,A) \sqsubseteq R$. □

<u>Appendix 1</u>

<u>Proof of (3.5).</u> The proof is basically that of Lawvere (1963). First some terminology: $\alpha: X \to Y$ in $\underline{\underline{P}}_\Sigma(\mathbb{X})$ (i.e., a map $Y \xrightarrow{\alpha} T_\Sigma(X)$) is <u>atomic</u> iff it factors through X,

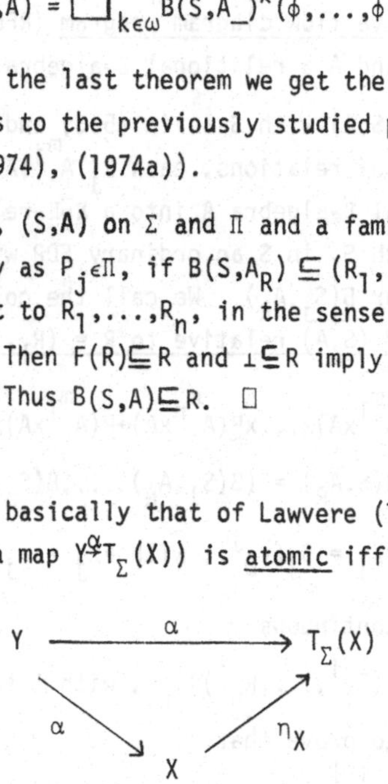

Thus an atomic α is of the form: $(x_{i_1},\ldots,x_{i_m}): X \to Y$, where $x_{i_j} = \alpha(y_j)$; note that some variables in X may be missing or repeated. The condition (3.5)-(ii) and the remark at the beginning of (3.4) give $\underline{A}(\alpha) = A^\alpha: A^X \to A^Y$ for any atomic $\alpha: X \to Y$ in $\underline{\underline{P}}_\Sigma(\mathbb{X})$ (i.e. $\alpha: Y \to X$ a map).

We now prove the isomorphism in the theorem using an intermediate step:

$$\underline{\mathrm{Alg}}_{\underline{\underline{P}}_\Sigma(\mathbb{X})} \simeq \underline{\mathrm{Alg}}_{\underline{\underline{N}}_\Sigma} \simeq \underline{\mathrm{Alg}}_\Sigma$$

where $\underline{\underline{N}}_\Sigma$ is the <u>free Lawvere algebraic theory on operations</u> Σ, defined as follows: fix a bijection $\omega \simeq \mathbb{X}: n \to x_n$, and let $X_n = \{x_1,\ldots,x_n\}$. The $\underline{\underline{N}}_\Sigma$ is the full subcategory of $\underline{\underline{P}}_\Sigma(\mathbb{X})$ with objects X_n for $n\in\omega$; let the inclusion function be $T: \underline{\underline{N}}_\Sigma \to \underline{\underline{P}}_\Sigma(\mathbb{X})$. Then $\underline{\mathrm{Alg}}_{\underline{\underline{N}}_\Sigma}$ has as objects those functors $\underline{A}: \underline{\underline{N}}_\Sigma \to \underline{\mathrm{Set}}$ with $\underline{A}(X_n) = A^{X_n}$ for some set A, and as morphisms, natural transformations between such functors. To pass from $\underline{\mathrm{Alg}}_{\underline{\underline{P}}_\Sigma(\mathbb{X})}$ to

$\underline{\underline{Alg}}_{\underline{\underline{N}}_\Sigma}$, let each $\underline{A}:\underline{\underline{P}}_\Sigma(\mathbb{X})\to\underline{\underline{Set}}$ go to $N\xrightarrow{J}\underline{\underline{P}}_\Sigma(\mathbb{X})\xrightarrow{\underline{A}}\underline{\underline{Set}}$, and each natural transformation $f:\underline{A}\to\underline{B}$ go to $f\circ J:\underline{A}\circ J\to\underline{B}\circ J$.

For the other direction, note that for any $\beta:Y\to Z$ in $\underline{\underline{P}}_\Sigma(\mathbb{X})$, $Y = \{y_1,\ldots,y_n\}$, $Z = \{z_1,\ldots,z_m\}$, there is an $\alpha:X_n\to X_m$, with $\beta = (x_1,\ldots,x_m)\circ\alpha\circ(y_1,\ldots,y_n)$ (namely $\alpha = (z_1,\ldots,z_m)\circ\beta\circ(x_1,\ldots,x_n)$); this uniquely forces the extension of an $\underline{\underline{N}}_\Sigma$-algebra to a $\underline{\underline{P}}_\Sigma(\mathbb{X})$-algebra by

$$\underline{A}(\beta) = A^Y \xrightarrow[\cong]{A^{(y_1,\ldots,y_n)}} A^{X_n} \xrightarrow[\cong]{\underline{A}(\alpha)} A^{X_m} \xrightarrow[\cong]{A^{(z_1,\ldots,z_m)}} A^Z$$

and for a natural transformation,

$$f_Y:A^Y \xrightarrow[\cong]{A^{(y_1,\ldots,y_n)}} A^{X_n} \xrightarrow[\cong]{f_{X_n}} B^{X_n} \xrightarrow[\cong]{B^{(x_1,\ldots,x_n)}} B^Y .$$

For the isomorphism $\underline{\underline{Alg}}_{\underline{\underline{N}}_\Sigma}\cong\underline{\underline{Alg}}_\Sigma$, we associate to an $\underline{\underline{N}}_\Sigma$-algebra $\underline{A}$ the Σ-algebra with operations: $A\sigma = A^n \xrightarrow{\cong} A^{X_n} \xrightarrow{\underline{A}(\sigma(x_1,\ldots,x_n))} A^{X_1} \xrightarrow{\cong} A$, $\sigma\epsilon\Sigma$, $ar\sigma=n$, and to a natural transformation $f:\underline{A}\to\underline{B}$, the homomorphism $f:A\xrightarrow{\cong}A^{X_1}\xrightarrow{f_{X_1}}B^{X_1}\xrightarrow{\cong}B$, using the bijections $A^n\cong A^{X_n}$. For the other direction, note defining "derived operations," e.g., $\underline{A}((x_1+x_2)\cdot x_3):A^{X_3}\longrightarrow A^{X_1}$, gives a $\underline{\underline{N}}_\Sigma$-algebra $\underline{A}$ for a Σ-algebra $\underline{A}$, and condition (3.5)-(ii) then forces f_{X_n} to be $A^{X_n}\xrightarrow{f^{X_n}}B^{X_n}$ for a homomorphism f:A B. For more details see Pareigis (1970), section 3.2, or ADJ (1975), section 3.

Proof of (3.6). Given a relation $f:A\to B$, define $\tilde{f}:A\to\underset{\sim}{P}(B)$ to send a to $\{b\epsilon B|\,f(a,b)\}$; and given a map $\tilde{f}:A\to\underset{\sim}{P}(B)$, define $\hat{f}:\underset{\sim}{P}(A)\to\underset{\sim}{P}(B)$ with the property $\hat{f}(A') = \bigcup_{a\epsilon A'}\hat{f}(\{a\})$, by $\hat{f}(A') = \bigcup_{a\epsilon A'}\tilde{f}(a)$. This defines a bijective correspondence, as does passing from a relation $A\sigma:A^n\to A$ to the map $\widetilde{A\sigma}:A^n\to\underset{\sim}{P}(A)$ as above, and also passing from a map $\widetilde{A\sigma}:A^n\to\underset{\sim}{P}(A)$ to a map $\check{A\sigma}:\underset{\sim}{P}(A)^n\to\underset{\sim}{P}(A)$ with the property $\check{A\sigma}(A_1,\ldots,A_n) = \bigcup_{(a_1,\ldots,a_n)\epsilon A_1\times\ldots\times A_n}\check{A\sigma}(\{a_1\},\ldots,\{a_n\})$, by $\check{A\sigma}(A_1,\ldots,A_n) = \bigcup_{(a_1,\ldots,a_n)\epsilon A_1\times\ldots\times A_n}\widetilde{A\sigma}(a_1,\ldots,a_n)$.

Appendix 2: RNFD

We give loose syntax and semantics, and some further examples, of a programming language RFND embodying the features of this paper; space limitations preclude greater precision or detail.

The syntax definition uses the following conventions: RNFD keywords are underlined; so are "(", ")", and "," when used as terminal symbols in the syntax definition, but not the program text; ":=" is a special terminal used for assignment; nonterminals are enclosed in <>'s; (CR) is "carriage return", which begins a new line (it does not appear in program text, but its effect can ben seen); X* means zero or more instances of X; X^+ means one or more; [X] indicates an optional occurrence of X; "|" means "or"; "::=" is in the metasyntax meaning "is defined as". Now the definition

1) <prog> ::= <proc>$^+$ end

2) <proc> ::= proc <p-name> <var-list> [entry <label>] (CR)
<assign>$^+$ exit[<label>] <var-list> corp (CR)

3) <assign> ::= [source[<label>][<var-list>]]assign[(CR)]
<test>* <op>* [target<label> (CR)]

4) <test> ::= <pred> <term-list> ((CR) |,)

5) <op> ::= <var-list> := <term-list> ((CR) |,)

6) <var-list> ::= ([<var>(,<var>)*])

7) <term-list> ::= ([<term>(,<term>)*])

<label> and <var> will be lower and upper case roman characters, respectively, with primes or subscripts if needed; they denote node and variable names, respectively. <p-name> will be upper case roman strings, for procedure names, in Π. <pred> refers to a special subset, Δ say, of Σ, consisting of predicate symbols. <term> refers to well-formed $(\Sigma\cup\Pi)$-terms, using prefix, infix, or whatever notation is convenient (a precise definition of this would be quite complex).

In rule 2), "[entry<label>]" optionally gives a name to the entry node of the procedure; the first <var-list> gives its parameters; the one or more <assign>s constitute its body; "exit[<label>] <var-list>" [optionally names the exit node and] gives the variables returned; "corp" terminates the procedure definition. Note that <label>s are strictly local to a procedure. In rule 3), names are optionally given to the source and target nodes of an <assign> edge, with its parallel <test>s and <op>s as body; the first time that a source is named, the variables which occur on that node must be given in the <var-list>; the default value for a source is the target (or entry) node above it in the program text; dually the default value of a target node is the source (or exit) node below it. Variables for targets are given at the corresponding source; we require that each target connect to a unique source (or exit) for a RNFD program to be well-formed. The variables used in the <test>s and <op>s of an <assign> have to all be on its source node, and variables assigned to, on its target node. If a target node variable x is not mentioned, default is the identity assignment x: = x. The <pred>s in <test>s (rule 4) must be in Δ, and must be interpreted as partial identity functions.

Basically, the body of this paper gives the semantics of RNFD. One way in which our intention for RNFD differs from this theory is co-arity, that is, operators which return tuples of values. This requires an expanded notion of signature, with a function rank: $\Sigma \to \omega \times \omega$ whose first component gives arity and whose secong gives co-arity (which must be non-zero). It is simplest to let such a signature Σ define another, Σ^1, with trivial coarity, consisting of the untuplings of elements of Σ; thus if $\sigma\epsilon\Sigma$ with rank(σ) = (n,m), m>1, let $\sigma_1,\ldots,\sigma_m \epsilon\Sigma^1$ with each ar(σ_i) = n. Then an instance of σ is regarded as an abbreviation for the tupling $(\sigma_1,\ldots,\sigma_m)$, and we are on familiar ground. But (warning!) if non-determinism is rampant, you may not get the results you expect; this has to do with the difference between sets of tuples and tuples of sets. There is no room here to explain, but things can be patched by giving suitable recursive definitions for tuple-valued relations in an interpretation. Note that we permit non-trivial coarity in the signature Π of procedure names.

A further development of RNFD, which is quite straightforward, provides for many sorts. What we have so far has just one sort, nat, for natural numbers. By using many-sorted signatures and theories, as in ADJ(1975), the present development is easily extended. An example later uses list, for lists of integers, in addition to nat. The syntax definition is changed by replacing rule 6) by

6') <var-list> ::= ([<var>:<sort>(,<var>:<sort>)*])

so that a <sort> is always declared for a <var>; of course, <term>s will have to respect <sort>s in order to be well-formed.

Now examples. First a program which requires a different treatment of co-arity to give the intended result, which is S(N) = {(A,B) | A+B=N}.

```
proc S(N)
     assign A:=0, B:=N
     source (A,B) assign (A,B):= PAIRS(A,B)
     exit (A,B) corp
proc PAIRS(A,B) entry a
     source a target b
     source a assign (A,B):= PAIRS(inc(A), dec (B)), target b
     exit b(A,B) corp
end
```

Here is a more complex program, to sort a list A of numbers.

```
proc SORT(A:list)
     assign N:=length(A)
     source (N:nat,A:list) assign A:=SORTN(N,A)
     exit:(A:list) corp
proc SORTN(N:nat,A:list) entry a
     assign(N,A,T):=EXCH(pos(N),A,0,1), target b
     source b(N:nat,A:list,T:nat) assign one(N),target c
     source b assign zero(T), target c
     source b assign pos(T), A:=SORTN(pos(dec(N)),A), target c
     source a assign zero(N)
     exit c (A:list) corp
```

```
proc EXCH(N:nat, A:list, T:nat, J:nat) entry a
    assign J<N, target b
    source b(N:nat, A:list, T:nat, J:nat) A[J+1]<A[J]
           A[J]:=A[J+1], A[J+1]:=A[J], T:=1, target c
    source b assign A[J+1] ≥ A[j]
    source c (N:nat, A:list, T:nat, J:nat)
           assign (N,A,T):=EXCH(N,A,T,inc(J)), target d
    source a assign J=N
    exit d (N:nat, A:list, T:nat) corp
end
```


References

ADJ (coauthored by J. A. Goguen, J. W. Thatcher, E.C. Wagner and J. B. Wright)

1. (1975) "An introduction to categories, algebraic theories and algebras," IBM Research Report RC 5369.
2. (1976) "A junction between computer science and category thoery: I, Basic definitions and examples," Part 2, IBM Research Report RC 5908.

Burstall, R. M.

3. (1972) "An algebraic description of programs with assertions, verification, and simulation," Proc ACM Confr. Proving Assertions about programs, Las Cruces, New Mexico, 7-14.

Eilenberg, S., and Wright, J. B.

4. (1967) "Automata in general algebras," Inf. Control 11, 452-470.

Goguen, J. A.

5. (1974) "On homomorphisms, correctness termination, unfoldments and equivalence of flow diagram programs," J. Comp. Sys. Sci. 8, 333-365.
6. (1974a) "Set theoretic correctness proofs," Semantics and Theory of Computation Report No. 1, UCLA Computer Science Dept.

Lawvere, F. W.

7. (1963) "Functorial semantics of algebraic theories," thesis, Columbia University; summarized in Proc. Ntl. Acad. Sci. U.S.A. 50, 869-872.

Mac Lane, S.

8. (1971) Category Theory for the Working Mathematician, Springer-Verlag.

Pareigis, B.

9. (1970) Categories and functors, Academic Press, New York.